Who We Are

A Chronicle of the Ideas
That Shaped Our World

Kirk Heriot

LOST
COAST
Fort Bragg
California

Lost Coast Press
155 Cypress Street
Fort Bragg, CA 95437
(707) 964-9520
http://www.cypresshouse.com

Library of Congress Cataloging-in-Publication Data

Heriot, Kirk, 1955–
    Who we are : a chronicle of the ideas that shaped our world / Kirk Heriot.
        p.   cm.
    Includes bibliographical references (p.   ) and index.
    ISBN 1-882897-30-7
    1. Civilization--History.   2. Intellectual life--History.
   3. Thought and thinking--History.   4. Science--History. I. Title.
    CB151.H375 2000   99-35025
909--dc21   CIP

Dedications

I HAVE TWO DEDICATIONS TO MAKE. FIRST, this work is dedicated to my parents, Henry and Mary, who imparted to me a respect for knowledge and scholarship. Second, this work is dedicated to the nameless billions of hardworking, devoted people whose unrecognized sacrifices, dedication, and courage have made us who we are. This work honors the memory of those before, the hope of those now, and the promise of those to come.

Acknowledgments

I AM GRATEFUL TO MANY PEOPLE for their contributions to this work. It would be difficult to enumerate all the individuals who have been of assistance, but I will attempt a partial list.

Donald Johanson, of the Institute of Human Origins, kindly read and commented on my discussion of human evolution. Frank Annunziata, of Rochester Institute of Technology, and Ralph Mathisen, of the University of South Carolina, were very helpful in improving the chapters on the first civilizations. Bruce M.S. Campbell, of Queen's University of Belfast, enhanced the discussion of medieval agriculture.

Michael Dobkowski, of Hobart and William Smith Colleges, read all the sections on the world's religions and kept me on track. Jessica Kross and John Gallant provided additional and much appreciated feedback on Buddhism. I am also indebted to Mohammed Yousufuddin and Asif Sheikh for their helpful discussions on Islam, and to Kaushal Sinha for discussions on Hinduism. A number of people at the Islamic Center of Rochester welcomed me and took the time to improve my knowledge of Islam. Dick McCaughey was very generous and helpful in augmenting my understanding of Christianity.

Ronald Edge, professor emeritus of the University of South Carolina, gave me valuable feedback on the discussion of the history of physics. James Kaler, of the University of Illinois, read and commented on the astronomy section. Adam Frank, of the University of Rochester, took time from a very busy schedule to clarify some issues in cosmology, so that I might write more effectively on the subject, and I am deeply grateful to him for this. I am also indebted to Chris Matzner, of the University of California at Berkeley, for keeping my discussion of astronomy on track. Frank Winter, of the National Air and Space Museum, read the section on rocketry and provided moral support at a time when I thought I may have undertaken too large a project. Robert Friedel, of the University of Maryland, improved my discussion of polymers.

Lucy Durkin, of the University of Rochester Memorial Art Gallery, was kind enough to read my treatment of the history of art. Many of her comments appear in this work virtually verbatim. Pat Rogers, of the University of South Florida, patiently read my necessarily superficial treatment of the history of literature, and kindly restrained himself to constructive comments. I am additionally indebted to my longtime friend and music scholar, Charles Griffith, for his comments on the history of music section.

Morris Pierce, of the University of Rochester, read the sections on the history of technology and provided support and encouragement. Henry King, a longtime scholar of Nazi Germany, and a former Nuremberg prosecutor, gave me the benefit of his years of wisdom and contemplation in the discussion of Fascism.

Michael Hart read the manuscript virtually in its entirety, and provided encouragement and support. His own superb book, *The 100: A Ranking of the Most Influential Persons in History*, was a source for this work.

In addition, I am grateful to two people whose works have set the standard for which I strive. Daniel Boorstin's tremendous trilogy, *The Discoverers*, *The Creators*, and *The Seekers* was very inspirational in the creation of this work. To professor Boorstin, I extend boundless thanks to a boundless mind. The late Kenneth Clark's *Civilization*, originally a television series in the late 1960s, was one of the first works to make me realize how great the capacity of the human mind is. There is more insight into who we are in this relatively small book than in any other I have encountered. It takes a few hours to read and a lifetime to digest.

Contents

A Personal Note to the Reader

THIS WORK IS A VOYAGE OF SELF-DISCOVERY, in which the reader is invited to participate. As Michel de Montaigne says of his famous essays: "This is not my teaching, this is my study; and it is not a lesson for others, it is for me."

I have tried to depart from the traditional Western history and address other cultures, but there are unavoidable limitations of the work. The Western cultural tradition remains my principal focus, and there are cultures (such as those of Africa) that are not addressed because I did not feel I could do justice to them. I hope that readers will understand that a work such as this inevitably reflects the cultural heritage of the chronicler and that no such work can fully record all of the wonderful expressions of the human experience. This is a view from the West, but hopefully a view which is sympathetic to all people from all cultures.

As part of the attempt to recognize non-Western cultures, I have used the terms B.C.E. and C.E. in place of the Western-based terms B.C. and A.D. B.C.E. stands for "before the common era" and refers to periods of time before the birth of Jesus, while C.E. stands for "of the common era" and indicates time periods after the birth of Jesus. Thus, 100 B.C.E. is the same date as 100 B.C., and 100 C.E. is the same date as 100 A.D., but there is no direct reference to the individual perceived in Western culture as the Savior.

This is primarily a history of thinking in the sciences. Every effort is made to introduce readers to the major religions and to the history of common forms of artistic expression, but it would be wrong to think that this work speaks as authoritatively to these areas as it does to the sciences.

In situations where a person changed his or her name to gain greater acceptance, I have generally referred to that person by the name by which he or she would have wanted to be known (for example, George Eliot is referred to as Mary Ann Evans). This may strike some as unusual and awkward, but I believe that calling these people by their actual names—the names they would have liked to use—is a way of belatedly correcting some of the injustice which required them to use a pseudonym.

Many will consider it audacious to offer a work of this scope in a single volume by a single author, and I expect to be criticized for this. But this is only an introduction, intended to acquaint the reader with the basics and stimulate a desire to learn more. I ask readers to accept these limitations and to view this work as a jar half-full rather than half-empty. I also ask specialists and reviewers to understand that because it is better to be partially informed than uninformed, it is a service to leave readers with a partial understanding and an eagerness to improve this knowledge.

No book is ever complete or absolutely accurate. I consider this a work in progress and invite readers to communicate any ideas, thoughts, or corrections. Now, join me in a voyage through time and space, and may you attain a greater sense of who you are.

Rochester, New York, 2000

Prologue:
Lessons from the Past

The past resembles the future more
than one drop of water another.

—Ibn Khaldun, fourteenth-century Arab historian

I HAVE TWO STORIES TO TELL—the story of the progress of people and the story of people themselves. The story of who we are is the story of great ideas and discoveries, which reflect their time, and also the story of the constant nature of humanity. This work is a journey through time that attempts to define ourselves to ourselves. By our very numbers—there are now six billion of us—we have begun to lose our value. This work attempts to partially restore that sense of value by demonstrating that each and every one of us is much more alike than we are different, that we all share a common heritage of heroism and persistence, and that we have progressed because the individual—however many of us there may be—matters.

This work has an unusual focus. Its emphasis is not on specific events or people. I believe history has been shaped more by the gradual flow of ideas than by specific individuals, battles, or coronations. In the end, it is our *ideas* that persist and determine who we are. This work attempts to chronicle the collective thought process of humanity. Specific events are mentioned, but only as building blocks to a larger focus.

There will be names, and some of them will indeed be individuals who have changed the course of history, but I shall repeatedly plead that progress is not the result of giant leaps by qualitatively superior people, but rather the gradual result of many minds in many times. We associate an achievement with a single person because we do not fully understand the development of that idea. When the history and development of a great idea are fully appreciated, it is invariably revealed to be based on the work of innumerable people over a long period of time.

The lessons of history lie not in conquests or landmark dates, but in the common human strengths and frailties shared by each of the billions of us who have lived—repeating generation after generation.

I believe that aspects of our civilization—particularly our treatment of women, children, and minorities—have improved with time, but the basic nature of people does not change from one moment in history to another. We are no better, no worse, no smarter, and not very different from the Mesopotamians, the Greeks, or the Crusaders. Who we are, and how we think and feel, is constant. Given the constancy of human nature, history emerges as a powerful but neglected tool for understanding what our future likely holds. If we listen, we can hear the gentle voices of artists, explorers, and scientists of the past speaking to us today. In those voices, we can see that the past is not a place of ignorance and cruelty, but of wisdom and hope.

The study of history conveys a sense of immortality. The student comes to think of his life as transcending its boundaries, extending back through time, and because of the essentially unchanging nature of people, extending forward through time as well.

This work is an examination of the bygone eternity that is our past which opens us to the unfolding eternity that is our future. It is a view of the past that allows the present to glimpse the future. It champions each of us, allowing all of us to obtain self esteem from our collective achievements while celebrating the community of humanity and the infinite varieties of human experience. It is a search for ourselves.

Chapter 1
Coming To Be

Three million years ago, two or three hominids walked across soft ground, leaving footprints that would one day speak across eons to their distant descendants.

THE STORY OF WHO WE ARE BEGINS in Africa, the place of our evolution. There we developed the traits, predominantly a large brain and an upright posture (bipedalism), that set us apart from other primates. We will see that these attributes did not arise in the order that might be expected.[1] *

The popular opinion of evolution is that we descended *from* apes. Actually, although Darwin himself had little to say about human evolution, the theory of evolution in its present form holds that we descended *with* apes from a common ancestor. Thus, the common objection that if we evolved from apes, there should be no apes today is answered by understanding that contemporary apes are also different from their ancestors, as they too have evolved from this common ancestor.

Fossils are very sparse regarding this common ancestral line of people and apes, but there is another source of information. We carry within each cell genetic material called DNA (deoxyribonucleic acid), and we have learned that this can be as illuminating as any fossil. DNA is the story within us, just as fossils are the story within the earth. From DNA evidence, we can infer that gorillas split from the group that would give rise to humans and chimpanzees around ten million years ago. Five to eight million years ago chimpanzees split from the line that was destined to become human.

Not long after this latter split, the fossil record begins to speak. It has taken some time to arrive at our imperfect understanding of the fossil evidence be-

---

* See Notes starting on page 502.

1

cause the fossils of our ancestors were not discovered in their evolutionary sequence. Neandertal man, a very recent predecessor, was discovered in Germany in 1856. An older relative, *Homo erectus*, was discovered in Asia in 1891 and was called Java Man at the time. (All plants and animals, even those now extinct, are classified into either the plant kingdom or the animal kingdom, and are then successively divided into phylum, class, order, family, genus, and species. The scientific name for a plant or animal is the name of its genus followed by the name of its species. In this case, *Homo* is the name of the genus to which the species *erectus* belongs. Modern people, *Homo sapiens*, are a different species within the *Homo* genus.)

In 1912, a most unfortunate hoax was perpetrated on students of evolution. Remains were found in England suggesting a creature with a large brain but an ape-like jaw. This supposed ancestor was called Piltdown man, and the large brain and primitive jaw fit very well with the common-sense idea that our evolution started with enlarging brain size. The find had its skeptics, but was commonly accepted until 1953, when it was found to be a medieval human skull and a jaw from an orangutan. It is remembered now as an example of the premature acceptance of evidence because it fit a preconceived idea.

Because of Java and Piltdown man, it was commonly believed that our evolution began in Asia, where the oldest fossils had been found, and started with increasing brain size. This was the background facing Raymond Dart (1893–1988). In 1924, Dart found a hominid (a family including humans and their humanoid precursors, but not including any apes) in Africa that appeared very different from those found previously. This creature, a child, was older than *Homo erectus*, and was called *Australopithecus africanus*.

From a brilliant analysis of this skull, Dart argued vigorously against mainstream thinking for two characteristics of human evolution. First, because he found evidence of a human posture and a small brain, he argued that the ascent of man began with skeletal changes rather than increasing brain capacity. Not only is it natural to think that human evolution began with our most distinguishing attribute, but Dart's startling first hypothesis was also contrary to the supposed fossil evidence. Piltdown man had not yet been exposed and was still considered cogent evidence that our evolution had indeed begun with increased brain size.

Second, the age of Dart's fossil convinced him that our evolution had begun in Africa, rather than Asia, as was the prevailing opinion. Again, Dart had to swim against the tide; all other discoveries of hominid fossils had been in Europe or Asia. Dart's point of view was ultimately accepted, and it is largely because of Dart that subsequent excavations were made in Africa, where they would be fruitful and establish that continent as the birthplace of our species. Louis Leakey (1902–1972), his wife Mary (1913–1996), and their children, working predominantly in a place called Olduvai Gorge in Tanzania, established beyond doubt that Africa is our ultimate homeland.

The earliest hominid of which we have knowledge is called *Ardipithecus ramidus*. We know very little about this ancestor, except that it lived almost four and a half million years ago in what is now Ethiopia. It is unknown if this hominid was bipedal. The next member of our family tree is *Australopithecus anamensis*, a bipedal hominid which lived four million years ago in Kenya.

We know more about the next member of our evolutionary family. Fossils remains of a hominid called *Australopithecus afarensis* were discovered by Donald Johanson (1943–) in Ethiopia in 1974. Analysis of these fossils verified both of Dart's hypotheses. Dating to slightly more than three million years ago, these fossils are much older than any hominid found in Asia. *Australopithecus afarensis* clearly walked upright, but had a brain that was roughly 450 cubic centimeters, about the size of a modern chimpanzee, confirming that our ascent began with bipedalism rather than increased brain size. Additional confirmation comes from Mary Leakey's discovery of human-like fossilized footprints, indicative of a hominid that was completely and comfortably bipedal, that are generally believed to be from *Australopithecus afarensis*.

No tools or artifacts have been associated with *Australopithecus afarensis*, indicating that he was not a significant tool maker, and there were no significant increases in brain size for a million years after his appearance. For at least a million years, and probably much longer (depending on when bipedalism first appeared), we were frozen at this first step of evolution and were simply erect apes.

By about two and a half million years ago, *Australopithecus afarensis* had given rise to two daughter species. One of these, *Australopithecus robustus* (also called *Paranthropus robustus*), is thought to have ultimately become extinct. The other daughter species was *Australopithecus africanus*, discovered by Dart.

By about two million years ago, *Homo habilis*, the next member of our family tree and the first known member of the *Homo* genus, had evolved. Some species of *Australopithecus* overlapped chronologically with *Homo habilis*, and it is difficult to determine which species of *Australopithecus*, if any, is the direct ancestor of the *Homo* genus, although it is probable that one of them was. Our evolution is not a simple linear progression from one species to another, but rather forks, has dead ends, and overlapping predecessor species.

Discovered by the Leakeys, *Homo habilis* had a brain size of 650 cubic centimeters, (half again the size of the chimpanzee, and approximately one-half the size of modern man), and not only used stones in their native state as tools, but also modified them. Therefore, the next steps in evolution, tool making and increased brain size, took place more or less concurrently about two to two and a half million years ago. There is much we do not know about *Homo habilis*. Some believe this hominid actually encompasses more than one species, and we do not know whether he was a hunter, a scavenger, or both.

About 1.7 million years ago, *Homo erectus* appeared. At about 1000 cubic centimeters, his brain was two-thirds the size of modern man's. *Homo erectus* may have descended from *Homo habilis*, but some believe the latter hominid was too primitive to be the direct ancestor of *Homo erectus*. Once again, we find ourselves unable to verify direct ancestral relationships.

Homo erectus improved tools and mastered fire (although it is not clear whether he could make fire or simply harnessed naturally occurring fire). There is no doubt that *Homo erectus* was a hunter, and a very effective one. Pursuing prey or familiar ecological niches in changing times, this hominid spread throughout Europe and Asia. A change in climate permitted him to spread even further. A series of ice ages began about the time that *Homo erectus* appeared, resulting in a colder climate and rising polar ice caps. This induced a drop in sea level that permitted *Homo erectus* to walk across newly appearing land bridges to Indonesia. *Homo erectus* became a traveler throughout the Old World. Subtle differences between the skeletons of the *Homo erectus* fossils in Asia and those in Africa have led some to believe the African species was slightly different, calling it *Homo ergaster*.

In 1856, in the Neander Valley in Germany, the remains of what would become known as Neandertal (sometimes spelled Neanderthal) man were uncovered. The immediate impact of this discovery was to fuel the currently raging debate about the newly proposed Darwin-Wallace theory of evolution. The long-term result, once the nature of the fossils was understood, was to introduce one of the most enigmatic of our ancestors. About 230,000 years ago (recent dating indicates that this hominid appeared 100,000 years earlier than had been believed), Neandertals arose in Europe and apparently never migrated to Africa. Degenerative joint disease, which can lead to deformities, was present in some of the first Neandertal skeletons discovered but was not recognized initially, leading to the incorrect and unfortunate stereotype that they were brutish creatures. We now know that although there are significant differences in the skeletons of Neandertal and modern people, they had a brain of the same size as modern humans (roughly 1400 cubic centimeters, on average).

Fossil evidence suggests that about 200,000 years ago, African *Homo erectus* (or *Homo ergaster* to those who have separated these species) gave rise to *Homo sapiens*—truly modern people. The term "Cro-Magnon" refers to the first completely modern *Homo sapiens* in southern Europe. In the colder climate of Europe, *Homo erectus* apparently gave rise to Neandertal (some recognize an intermediate hominid in this progression, called archaic *Homo sapiens* by some and *Homo heidelbergensis* by others), while in Africa, he gave rise to *Homo sapiens* without a Neandertal intermediary. Some 40,000 to 50,000 years ago, *Homo sapiens* migrated to Europe and overlapped Neandertal populations there. Neandertal and *Homo sapiens* shared the same regions in Europe for 15,000 years, but fossils of the two hominids have not been found together at the same site from the same time. By 30,000 years ago, shortly after the appearance of *Homo sapiens* in Europe, Neandertal was gone.

Just as the precise relationship of other hominids is not completely agreed upon, there are also disagreements about the relationship between Neandertal and *Homo sapiens*. Was Neandertal a true *Homo sapiens*, the same species as us? Or was it a related but different species, that like *Australopithecus robustus*, became an evolutionary dead end? On the one hand, Neandertal and *Homo sapiens* had equivalent brain sizes, comparable tool making abilities, and there are few demonstrable cultural differences in the two hominids as long as they coexisted. Cultural differences do not become prominent until 30–35,000 years ago, when Neandertal was gone and *Homo sapiens* entered the artistic phase of our history. It is unclear if Neandertal was as "smart" as *Homo sapiens*, but he may have used markings in a symbolic manner, and perhaps would have been as artistic as *Homo sapiens* had he survived longer. On the other hand, the skeletal differences are striking and cause some to believe they must have been different species. By which criteria does one determine species identity or nonidentity: apparent mental equality or demonstrable skeletal differences?

At this time, it appears that there are two possibilities. Neandertal and *Homo sapiens* may be the same species, in which case Neandertal was our ancestor and became extinct only as a culture, while his genes live on in us. Or *Homo sapiens* may be a separate species that outbred, outcompeted, or destroyed Neandertal, in which case Neandertal was not our ancestor, but a near miss in our history.

The possibility that *Homo sapiens* was an entirely different species has raised a second interesting question. Traditionally, it has been thought that modern man arose in many sites around the Old World, descending from *Homo erectus* in each site. Some (those who believe Neandertal was our direct ancestor and an intermediary between *Homo erectus* and *Homo sapiens*) continue to hold this opinion, called the "multiregional" model. But if *Homo sapiens* is unrelated to Neandertal, and originated in Africa and then migrated around the world, replacing Neandertal, then Africa might be the sole source of modern people, an opinion called the "Out of Africa" model. Stated another way, are contemporary Europeans and Asians descended from the *Homo erectus* and Neandertal populations of those regions, or do they share a single ancestral line of *Homo sapiens* that left Africa about 100,000 years ago?

DNA studies offer intriguing insight into this matter. Nearly all DNA is in the nucleus, the major subdivision of the cell. This DNA is subject to relatively rapid change because it is constantly combined with the nuclear DNA from another individual during sexual reproduction. However, a small part of the cell's DNA is in the mitochondria, the portion of the cell concerned with energy production. Mitochondrial DNA of one individual is not combined with that of another during reproduction. Instead, it is inherited only from the mother; male mitochondrial DNA is not passed to the progeny. Men, like women, get all of their mitochondrial DNA from their mother, but in men, that DNA is never passed on. Because maternal mitochondrial DNA passes intact in the female line from one generation to another (mother to daughter to granddaughter to great granddaughter), it changes at a much more predictable rate than nuclear DNA.

It is this predictable mutation rate which makes mitochondrial DNA valuable. Differences in mitochondrial DNA in different populations yield clues as to when these populations might have diverged. Preliminary studies of mitochondrial DNA have generated two intriguing tentative conclusions. First, mitochondrial DNA is more diverse in Africans than in other populations, suggesting that Africans are the oldest race of modern humans. Second, there really is not much diversity in mitochondrial DNA among any of the world's populations, even Africans, suggesting that all groups of modern man share a much more recent common ancestral stock than once thought: modern humans, or hominids very close to modern humans, living in Africa some 250,000 years ago. Very similar results have been obtained from a study of the male sex chromosome, which is inherited in a father to son fashion without dilution by maternal DNA. In addition, recent work on mitochondrial DNA from a Neandertal skeleton shows that it differs more from contemporary mitochondrial DNA than would be expected if Neandertal were the same species as modern humans. Did Africa, known to be the origin of the hominid line a few million years ago, turn a second miracle and also produce the only source of modern humans, some 250,000 years ago?

This evidence, added to the fact that the oldest *Homo sapiens* fossils are found in Africa, has most scholars moving to the opinion that Africa *was* the sole source of modern humans, who developed from African *Homo erectus* (some would say *Homo ergaster*) without Neandertal. The first steps were taken in Africa, some 250,000 years ago, and *Homo sapiens* physically developed by 100,000 years ago. Like *Homo erectus*, he then migrated around the Old World—this time using boats—replacing his Neandertal cousin and becoming the sole progenitor of modern humans. The development of Neandertal and *Homo sapiens* as different species overlapping in time is another example of the non-linearity of our evolution.

Traditionally, it has been held that *Homo sapiens* experienced a sudden burst of creativity about 35,000 years ago, near the end of Neandertal's time span. While it is true that the oldest painting of which we are aware dates to about this time, tools bearing the same workmanship have been dated to a much earlier period, so we must be careful in concluding that something sudden and unique happened at this point in time. In any event, about 35,000 years ago we began creating lasting reflections of our world, and our distinctive culture began to emerge. Over two hundred caves containing paintings created by early *Homo sapiens* have been found. In addition, there was undoubtedly much outside art destroyed by weathering (although a series of regular depressions dating to 70,000 years ago have survived in exposed rocks in Australia).

We simply do not know the purpose of this art. The meticulous work of Alexander Marshack gives us a picture of early *Homo sapiens* as fully cognitive humans whose mental capacity equals our own. Through microscopic studies of many artifacts, he has shown that different parts of the images were made with different instruments, angles, and pressures, indicating that they were constructed over a protracted period of time, possibly by more than one person. For example, some of the images of animals have wounds and extra body parts, such as multiple heads and tails. The extra body parts, added over time, might have "revitalized" the image and made it available for additional symbolism; one image could be used at different times and perhaps for different reasons.

Marshack provides evidence for the use of symbols among early *Homo sapiens* and indications that they do not reflect a single concept, such as fertility or a successful hunt, but more likely refer to events of daily life, such as the phases of the Moon and the changing of seasons, or to a larger concept of life, death, and renewed life. The wounded animals in some images may not refer to the literal killing of an animal, but instead may be a general artistic statement of life and death.

The recently discovered Chauvet cave in France contains art believed to be over 30,000 years old—the oldest paintings known (the famous cave paintings at Lascaux and Altamira date to 15–20,000 years ago). Music may also date from this era, based on early paintings of bone flutes and percussion instruments, as well as bones apparently carved for use as musical instruments. Jewelry and fired ceramics also date to 25–30,000 years ago. Therefore, we know that art is by no means new to our civilization, and in fact substantially predates what we would call civilization. Whether this leap was driven by biological advances, or cultural, we do not know. It is clear that the human brain, which would become the instrument of genius and hatred, destruction and love, hope and despair—the brain to which we owe our identity and our history—was fully functional by that marvelous period of artistic miracles 35,000 years ago. The long battle to secure a place in the world and survive as a species had been won. From that point on, our greatest enemy would be ourselves.

Virtually the entirety of the human brain developed in the very short period (by evolutionary terms) of two million years. How could the brain evolve so rapidly? To our knowledge, there is no other example in evolution of such an important characteristic, one so greatly changing the nature and competitive position of a species, evolving so rapidly. DNA holds one possible explanation. Genetic research has demonstrated that only a portion of our DNA is actually transcribed into proteins; much of it is dormant. This dormant DNA apparently either is used for regulation, is repressed until needed, or represents obsolete genetic material from our evolutionary past. The rapid evolution of the brain is possible if the genes allowing its development were present all along, but repressed. Evolution would then be the unlocking of genetic material already present, rather than developing it from scratch. Support for this possibility comes from studies of chimpanzee DNA revealing that it is very similar to that of humans. If this is so, then what other giant leaps of evolution may already be present within the DNA of each of our cells?

As Donald Johanson reminds us, we have no assurance that we are the intended final product of evolution. We may ourselves be an evolutionary dead end, equivalent to *Australopithecus robustus*. Perhaps our species, and all of our history, shall give way to some new species of hominid, one whose history will be remembered after everything about who we are is forgotten. If so, let us not mourn *Homo sapiens*, but rather let us hope the new hominid surpasses us and proves worthy of its position.

Our brain has provided us with a second kind of evolution: cultural evolution. Cultural evolution now permits changes that dwarf biological evolution. Indeed, evolution can be defined as changes in DNA, and we will soon acquire the capacity to modify our genetic constitution more rapidly than nature ever could. Our cultural and social evolution, not our biological evolution, will now determine our survival and form. Our fate will be decided long before there are any significant biological changes to *Homo sapiens*. As I hope to show in this work, it is our ability to think long-term that will determine our fate.

Chapter 2
Toward Civilization

*A Phoenician merchant records a transaction by
using the same symbols in different combinations:
the alphabet is born.*

THE WORD "CIVILIZATION" WILL BE USED many times in this work. It is a difficult
concept to define, and we are well served by first considering what civilization is
not and with what it should not be confused. We commonly confuse "civilization" with "culture" or "technology," words with distinctly different meanings.

Civilization is to be distinguished from culture. There is no universal agreement on the characteristics of civilization, but most would include urbanization,
agriculture, division of labor, and writing. Many would also include metalworking for Old World societies, although this is not present to a significant degree in
New World civilizations. Civilization does not mean that a group of people live at
a "higher level." The cave-painters of Lascaux and Altamira and pre-Columbian
North American tribes are examples of highly developed communities that do
not fulfill the technical definition of civilization. The word "uncivilized," with all
of its misleading negative connotations, is a word best left unused.

Culture refers to the behaviors, beliefs, and adaptive mechanisms that a group
of people sharing a common experience have constructed to cope with their
environment. Culture, unlike civilization, is learned and taught and is unique
to a group of people. Agriculture and cities are characteristics of civilization;
religious rituals are examples of culture. A group of people's unique culture is
crucial and irreplaceable for their prosperity. The disruption of a group's culture
impedes the collective accomplishments of the group and prevents the individuals in that group from achieving their potential. It is no coincidence that
very high rates of alcoholism, unemployment, and failure to find a place in
society are found in two groups whose culture was nearly destroyed by Europeans: African-Americans and Native Americans.

10

Technology refers to the mastery of the environment. People often believe that a certain level of technology implies civilization, and assume a society with greater technology must necessarily have a higher civilization. This tragic way of thinking has led to the wholesale destruction of unique civilizations by those with no claim to greater civilization, but who simply possessed better weapons. As civilizations advance, one generally sees a greater technology, but there are exceptions.

As the great art historian Kenneth Clark outlined in *Civilization*, civilization requires a social infrastructure that allows the fulfillment of basic needs, so people have the opportunity to explore and modify their surroundings. A certain amount of material prosperity is necessary, and people must have some degree of confidence both in the current society and their own futures. When prosperity and confidence are lacking, there can be no civilization. Art, science, and other aspects of civilization cannot be advanced, or even preserved, when it is a struggle just to exist. Anyone who doubts this needs only to look at Western Europe in the centuries after the fall of the Roman Empire.

Cities and the Neolithic Revolution

Homo habilis was a scavenger; *Homo erectus* and Neandertal were hunter-gatherers. It was quite late in our evolution, approximately 10,000 years ago, that man learned to farm and domesticate animals, thus allowing much greater production of food. The discovery of agriculture and the domestication of animals ushered in a new era of food production, an era referred to by the noted archeologist Gordon Childe (1892–1957) as the Neolithic Revolution (neolithic, literally meaning "new stone age," refers to the last few millennia of the stone age). Today, we know this "revolution" took several millennia to unfold. We underwent a fundamental change in how we lived and procured food in the latter stone age, and much of how we live today was established before we fulfilled the definition of civilization or could work metal.

Agriculture developed independently in multiple sites. It was initially thought that the introduction of agriculture was the impetus for the formation of villages, but more recent thinking holds that settlements preceded farming. In all probability, settlements and agriculture had a mutually facilitating effect on each other.

To develop agriculture, man had to stay in one place for a period of time. A plausible theory for the sequence of events begins with the postulate that hunt-

11

ers were following herds. Because these herds had predictable migration patterns, it was advantageous for the hunters to establish camps at sites, affording them access to the herds as they pursued their predictable itinerary. These camps led to semi-stable small settlements, which allowed people to be in one place long enough to realize that they could influence their environment, cultivate plants, and domesticate animals.

The greatest mystery in agriculture is why did it develop? Some feel that agriculture developed because of pressure to increase food production. Indeed, in animal populations not subject to extensive predation, population is pressured and limited by a shortage of food. Intuitively, this theory is simple and familiar. The problem is that no one has shown that there was a shortage of food at the time of the development of agriculture. There is even some evidence that in the areas where agriculture originated, food was *not* in short supply. Perhaps agriculture developed as a more dependable food source than the uneven supply of hunting and gathering. Some believe a sudden downturn in average temperature about eleven thousand years ago made hunting and gathering less effective. Another possibility is that agriculture was not an act of desperation, but rather an experiment, a reflection of our desire to explore.

Throughout history, adversity has been humanity's blessing in disguise. Many great advances come when, and only when, adverse circumstances force new ways of thinking. This is true of both civilizations and individuals. In view of this, there was likely some degree of pressure and urgency in the development of agriculture.

The story of agriculture begins with a variety of wild wheat called Einkorn. Einkorn is considered ancestral to contemporary strains because it has only fourteen chromosomes, the fewest in wheat plants. At some time before the advent of agriculture, a natural cross of Einkorn to a goat grass (a genus of grass which is related to wheat, but which does not bear usable grain) resulted in species of wheat with twenty-eight chromosomes. One such species is Emmer, itself a progenitor to other species. Further crosses of Emmer to grasses resulted in species with forty-two chromosomes. These later crosses may have been natural, but it is also possible that they were the result of human intervention, facilitated by the warmer and moister climate at the end of the last ice age, about 12,000 years ago.

These newer wheats, with more chromosomes, are called polyploid wheats (the word "polyploid" refers to a greater than usual content of DNA). Einkorn played some role in agriculture, and is still cultivated to some extent, but Emmer and other polyploid wheats are higher yielding and have been the mainstay of farming. There is also evidence of a mutation in the polyploid wheats that resulted in increased fertility.

These events alone were not sufficient to permit the land to be used for food. There also had to be a water supply. As we shall see, all of the first civilizations arose around rivers—specifically, all began around great rivers between roughly thirty and thirty-five degrees north latitude. Ancient Egypt depended on the Nile; Mesopotamia (a region in present-day Iraq) depended on the Tigris and Euphrates rivers. These rivers periodically flooded their banks. By learning to predict the cycles of flooding, people in those areas obtained a supply of water, which was greatly augmented by the development of irrigation, perhaps around 4,000 B.C.E. (Throughout this work, in an effort to be less focused on Western thinking, the terms B.C.E.—before the common era—and C.E.—of the common era—are used in place of the terms B.C. and A.D.)

By six thousand years ago, the simple plow was in use, as were oxen for pulling it. Coupled with irrigation, these advances enormously enhanced the productivity of the land. Even so, anyone who has ever farmed or gardened can appreciate the enormous difficulty faced by the first farmers.

We tend to think of the Neolithic Revolution as ending many millennia ago. However, a few contemporary societies have yet to experience the agricultural revolution, and it continues even for us, as science becomes increasingly involved in agriculture and food production. This must be so, if we are to feed the teaming billions of an exploding population.

It is well to remember that agriculture alone cannot save us from hunger. At this writing, food production is adequate to feed all people, but many millions are starving because of distribution problems whose origins lie in political turmoil and economic difficulties. In addition, our population grows by almost a quarter of a million every day, and we will soon reach a point where we cannot produce enough food to feed the world, even if we had effective distribution. We will not conquer hunger until we have effective governments in all countries, and until we control our numbers.

Over the course of several thousand years, settlements grew into cities, whose larger populations offered greater security. The definition of a city is debatable, but the basic concept of a city is a large settlement (perhaps 5,000 people or more), characterized by the use of agriculture, the peaceful co-existence of people, and a division of labor which enormously amplifies what can be accomplished.

13

True cities are indicative of civilization and are not found until several thousand years after the first settlements.

Because there is evidence of trading at very early times (certainly by 6,000 B.C.E.), it may also be that semi-permanent settlements were established as a way of facilitating the exchange of goods. This may mean that trade had a major effect on the development of settlements, which as we shall see was the case in the development of mathematics and writing.

Early settlements fulfilling at least part of our definition of a city have been found in many places around the world, and it is no longer believed that all of the first settlements were necessarily in the Middle East. However, the best-characterized early settlements were in this part of the world. Houses at Jericho (in Jordan, now part of the Israeli occupied territory of the West Bank) date to about 8,000 B.C.E. Catal Huyuk (in Turkey) and Ain Ghazal (in Jordan) date to around the same time, and it appears that there were even older communities, presumably with specialization of labor, before this. After these sites, the next settlements of interest to our story are those of early Mesopotamia, a civilization that we will encounter shortly.

Early Religion

All societies independently develop a set of complex religious beliefs, and these beliefs predate civilization. Societies, like individuals, develop along substantially predictable pathways; like individuals, they achieve foreseeable milestones in a predictable order. One such milestone is a belief in a force or forces greater than themselves, both individually and collectively. On one hand, this bestows some sense of equality on the society, since all members must answer to this greater force. It also provides a unifying sense of purpose (this exerted its most pronounced effect in Europe between the years 500 and 1,000). But it may stultify individualism, which is a key ingredient to creativity. Concomitant to facilitating uniformity *within* societies, religion generally accentuates the differences *between* societies; almost all wars have been fought over religion or land or both. It is therefore essential that anyone attempting to understand history understand the religions of humanity. As our history opens before us in these pages, we will examine all of the contemporary religions that have had a significant impact on human history. We begin by exploring the likely steps in the development of religious thought.

To my mind, there are two fundamental reasons for the development of religion. The first is that humans are inherently curious and need to understand the world around them. For most of our history, people lacked the ability to understand or control their environment and had no idea that their progress would eventuate in any understanding of the world, so supernatural deities seemed the only way to explain mysterious events.

The second reason for the development of religion is the search for inner peace. Humans need to believe their lives have meaning and purpose. In a world filled with mysteries and hostile forces, the presence of deities comforted people and gave them a sense of belonging.

Archeological evidence and early writings suggest that all early religions shared certain characteristics: worship of the sun, which all cultures recognized as the ultimate giver of life; as well as belief in, and fascination with, life after death. Many religions had a mother figure, derived from the female's unique role in giving birth and nurturing the infant. Although sun worship has faded, some of these characteristics persist. Most contemporary religions subscribe to an after-life, and the Virgin Mary is the mother figure of Christianity.

Initially, deities took the form of animals, called *theriomorphic* deities. These were superseded by gods with human attributes, in behavior as well as appearance, called *anthropomorphic* deities. Some gods had both animal and human features, such as a human head on an animal body—perhaps a sort of transition form. There are two possible reasons why people began to envision gods in anthropomorphic terms. First, as people gained increasing control over their environment, they became secure and confident enough to conceptualize the processes of the world as being under the control of beings somewhat like themselves. The second reason pertains to the increasing stratification of society that accompanies civilization. It has always been the curse of civilization that it brings with it a greater stratification of society. Tribal societies and pre-civilization cultures generally contained a limited hierarchy, with a small number of priests or chiefs having hegemony over an otherwise substantially equal populace. With the advent of cities and civilization, stratification became more pronounced and more complex. Difficult public works, such as irrigation, required leaders whose power exceeded that of village elders. Now people could see *other people* with vast amounts of power and influence. Still unaware of their own ability to uncover the mysteries of nature and improve their lot (this awareness would not be fully evident until sixth-century B.C.E. Greece), people began to envision deities in human form.

Initially, there was a belief in multiple deities, often with a supreme or chief god. Although the Egyptian Pharaoh Akhenaton (or Akhnaton) is said to have experimented with monotheism, the Western formulation of this concept was essentially the contribution of one people: the Jews. We will continue the story of religion when we discuss that people.

From Ores to Steel: The Working of Metal

Metalworking began approximately 7000 B.C.E., using metals found in their native state, unbound to other elements. Early civilizations were limited to the small amounts of native silver, gold and copper that can be found in nature, and for many centuries quantities of metal were insufficient to materially alter people's lives.

Then, perhaps as early as 5,500 B.C.E., ores were discovered and it was learned that heating certain colored rocks would release metal. This enormously increased the supply of metals, allowing them to be made in sufficient quantities for everyday use. Today, the term "stone age" connotes for many the hunter-gatherer existence of our hominid ancestors. It is worth noting that settlements existed, artistic expression flourished, and agriculture was well underway before metalworking. Indeed, metals were rarely used in the highly developed New World cultures.

The use of heat to release a metal from ore is called smelting, and is distinguished from melting, which refers to the heating of the intact metal until it liquefies. The heat required for smelting is not as intense as that needed to melt, and it was smelting that gave us the use of practical quantities of metal. But how did the people of the sixth millennium B.C.E. discover smelting? At one time, it was thought that smelting was accidentally discovered when a fire was lit over a pile of stones containing copper ore. It is now believed that an ordinary wooden fire cannot achieve the temperature needed to smelt copper ore. Another possibility, since native copper is often found in combination with copper ore, is that people of the sixth millennium B.C.E. placed a piece of metallic copper, attached to a colored, but otherwise ordinary stone, into a kiln, intending to melt and recover the native copper. If this scenario is correct, the surprise would not have come from the base of a campfire, but from greater than expected recovery of copper from the kiln.

Ancient people learned that they could obtain a hotter fire—and thus achieve better smelting—by using charcoal. Charcoal is derived by burning any carbonaceous material without enough air for complete combustion, so that a carbon residue remains after other elements have burned away. This residue, when burned in the presence of adequate oxygen, burns with a higher temperature than the material from which it was derived.

The first metal to be obtained from ore was copper, and some people recognize a copper age, extending from roughly 4,000 B.C.E. to 3,000 B.C.E. in the Middle East. However, metals began to transform history only when it was learned how to make them stronger by mixing them, and the more widely recognized sequence in development is stone age—bronze age—iron age.

Bronze is generally a mixture of copper and tin in a roughly nine-to-one proportion. However, copper-arsenic alloys are also bronzes, and it may be that the first bronzes were arsenic compounds. The precise time period in which bronze was discovered depended on the specific culture and its geographic location. By 3,000 B.C.E., the use of bronze was well underway in Mesopotamia. Because bronze is significantly stronger than copper, civilizations now had access to practical quantities of a metal with genuine strength, and bronze was the first metal that was truly important to civilization. Tin prevents the planes of copper crystals from sliding past each other, a simple fact in crystal science that changed history.

Iron was available in its native form at a very early time, but it was not developed in appreciable quantities until much later because higher tempeatures are required to smelt its ore. Like the bronze age, the precise time for the iron age depends on the specific culture. In the Middle East, the Hittites were working iron by 1,500 B.C.E. By 1,000 B.C.E., other Middle Eastern cultures had entered the iron age. By 600 B.C.E., iron working had come to Europe and China.

Early kilns could only partially smelt iron ore, and the resulting metallic iron contained an appreciable amount of impurities, called slag. The only way to obtain greater purity was to hammer out the slag while the iron was still hot. This process is called forging, and if done well, results in wrought iron, which has an acceptable slag content and very little carbon. Cast iron requires complete smelting of the ore; the necessary blast furnaces were not widely available in Europe until the fourteenth century C.E., though the Chinese could fully smelt and cast iron before the time of Jesus.

Contrary to popular belief, iron's greatest effect on history was not in weaponry. Iron weapons are somewhat more resilient than their bronze counterparts, but iron exerted a greater effect on history by making possible improved tools. The real advantage of iron is that, if the technology to smelt its ore is available, iron can generally be obtained in appreciably greater quantities than bronze.

Steel, a combination of iron and a small amount of carbon, was actually made before the time of Jesus in India, possibly by adding a material containing carbon to wrought iron and heating the mixture, thereby increasing the carbon content of the iron. However, steel had little social impact until the Industrial Revolution.

A word about gold is in order. Gold is very weak and plays no role at all in history from a structural standpoint, but it has two properties which have long fascinated people. First, its rarity, combined with human nature, has given gold a great value despite its structural worthlessness. Second, gold is chemically nonreactive. This fact was made more apparent by alchemy, increasing people's fascination with the metal.

From Pictographs to Alphabets: The Rise of Writing

Writing arose independently in many places; among the first was the ancient Mesopotamian civilization of Sumer (in contemporary Iraq), around 3,000 B.C.E. All of human history prior to that date is unrecorded and therefore considered prehistoric. Agriculture, domestication of animals, the first settlements, and early metalworking all took place in the prehistoric period; so this term, like the term "stone age," does not necessarily indicate primitive societies or a lack of civilization.

The catalyst for writing in the Middle East may have been economics and commerce, as merchants sought to record transactions. The earliest Sumerian writing started as pictographs, crude drawings of the intended object. To be significant, a written language must be able to transcend simple drawings of objects and faithfully transcribe conversation. How was one to depict words for which no obvious picture could be drawn? The earliest Mesopotamian writing could not do this, but over several centuries, two methods were developed. The logogram (also called ideogram), used a picture of an object to convey a related concept. For example, the word "walking" can be portrayed by a picture of a foot. The second method of transcribing a spoken language was to separate the sounds of a word and use a pictograph for each sound. Thus, the word "walking" can be represented by a combination of pictures, none of which has anything to do with walking, but which when sounded in sequence, form an approximation of the spoken word walking. In this type of writing, called syllabic or phonetic, the actual meaning of the image is ignored; only its sound has value. Contemporary shorthand, which consists of otherwise meaningless symbols which carry a sound, is an example of a phonetic writing system. A fully developed ancient writing system used a combination of three elements: an absolute pictorial representation, logograms, and a phonetic combination of signs. Glyphs (the individual elements of the writing) could have an absolute meaning, a conceptual meaning, or a disregarded meaning and be used only for their sounds. Such a writing system, called logo-syllabic, was employed by many ancient civilizations, including Sumer and Egypt.

The Sumerians took some three hundred years to weave these elements into a coherent logo-syllabic writing system, which became widespread about 2,700 B.C.E. While this system was developing, the Sumerians also simplified their images. Using a stick to draw pictures in wet clay was tedious work and resulted in writing that was difficult to read because clay piled up adjacent to the images. To obviate these problems, the Sumerians introduced two modifications. First, they streamlined their images, reducing the curves and relying on a reasonable representation of the object with a set of straight lines. The literal pictograph was succeeded by the approximate pictograph. Second, they replaced the traditional stick with the tip of a reed, which had a triangular cross section. This resulted in the familiar wedge shape of their writing, called cuneiform (Latin for "wedge-shaped"). Impressing the clay with a reed, rather than displacing it with a stick, prevented the build up of clay on the surface.

Mesopotamian logo-syllabic writing was adapted by subsequent Middle Eastern cultures, such as the Akkadians, Hittites, Babylonians, and Assyrians. Writing appears in Egypt at about the same time as in Mesopotamia, and a well-developed logo-syllabic system was widespread in the land of the Pharaohs by about 2,700 B.C.E.

Egypt was blessed with a material the Mesopotamians lacked: papyrus, a reed native to marsh areas in southern Europe and northern Africa. The Egyptians removed the outer skin of the reed and cut the inner pith into strips, which were then laid lengthwise and intertwined with overlapping crosswise strips. The material was then moistened and pressed; as it dried, the overlapping strips adhered to each other, creating a durable medium. The Egyptians could then write on papyrus with ink, obviating the need for the more labor-intensive clay impressions. Although bound books could not be created with papyrus, it was possible to construct long scrolls which could then be unrolled for reading.

Because much less effort was required to produce an image on papyrus than on clay, the Egyptians could utilize curved images, and the pictographs employed in their logo-syllabic writing remained largely literal representations throughout most of their history. But the expedience the Egyptians gained from a more convenient medium, they lost by drawing literal pictures; it takes longer to draw a picture than straight lines. This led to the development of a faster form of hieroglyphics, called hieratic, about 2,000 B.C.E. Hieratic glyphs departed from strict pictorial representation, as the Mesopotamians had done much earlier. By about 800 B.C.E., an even faster cursive form of hieroglyphics, called demotic, had been developed.

Jean-François Champollion (1790–1832), working with Egyptian Hieroglyphics, was the first to realize the logo-syllabic nature of ancient writing. Champollion's deciphering was aided by the Rosetta Stone, which was found by French troops in Egypt in 1799. One of Napoleon's officers rescued it from the wall of a building, after which it was returned to Europe, eventually to reside in the British Museum. The Rosetta Stone contains the same text in three scripts: hieroglyphics, demotic, and ancient Greek (the last of these being easily read). Dating to 195 B.C.E., the text of the Stone turned out to be a tribute to Ptolemy V, who was a Hellenistic (referring to the time just after Alexander the Great) king. The Rosetta Stone was an important aid in the deciphering of hieroglyphics, but not absolutely essential; eventually ancient Egyptian writing would have been deciphered without it.

The deciphering of Mesopotamian cuneiform writing was the work of many people, most notably Henry Rawlinson (1810–1895). In deciphering cuneiform writing, Rawlinson followed the example of Champollion; like the latter, he was aided by a trilingual inscription. Inscribed into a cliff in the Zagros Mountains in Iran was writing in Old Persian, Elamite (an ancient writing of Iran), and Babylonian. Although none of these scripts could be read, it was still an advantage to have the same message presented in three languages. Rawlinson's first task was to copy the inscriptions, which was no mean feat considering their near inaccessibility. Following the lead of Champollion, Rawlinson grasped the logo-syllabic nature of the languages and translated the Old Persian writing, which led to the eventual translations of most of the Mesopotamian scripts.

Egyptian logo-syllabic was based on the same principles as Mesopotamian, but with a difference. In Egyptian, the consonant sounds in a word were invariant, but the vowel sound of a word changed with the context. It was therefore possible to have signs for consonant sounds, and to let the reader furnish the vowel sounds based on the context and his experience. The hieroglyph need only supply the consonant sound, whereas in cuneiform, a sign supplied both a consonant and a vowel sound. Extending this idea to all of the twenty-four consonant sounds in Egyptian, it was theoretically possible, by 2,000 B.C.E., to write any word as a combination of these twenty four invariant consonant signs, with the reader filling in the vowel sounds. For example:

Y cn rd ths

can be read as "You can read this." Does this mean that the Egyptians established the first true alphabet? That is somewhat a matter of opinion, but in any event, it is clear that the Egyptians only very rarely used this method of writing. Formal Hieroglyphics, or one of the two shortened forms, were used in almost all situations. In all probability, the scribes themselves failed to promote a more efficient system that would potentially jeopardize their business. It would be left for the Phoenicians, several centuries later, to develop a true, workable alphabet—one which would change the world.

By 3,000 B.C.E., civilization had come to the Levant (the eastern shore of the Mediterranean), forming the region known in the Bible as Canaan. The Canaanites settled in what is now Israel and Lebanon. Like the Egyptians, their writing system had signs specific for consonants, with the vowels supplied by the reader. It was a short but momentous step when, about 1,700 B.C.E., the Canaanites understood *and implemented* a workable alphabet, called Old Canaanite. Influenced by Egyptian hieroglyphics, Old Canaanite was a pictographic alphabet based on the principle of acrophony, whereby each of the twenty-seven or twenty-eight consonant sounds was represented by a picture of an object whose name began with that sound. For example, the sign for a "b" sound might be a bird, for a "c" sound a cat, and for a "d" sound a dog. Thus, twenty-seven or twenty-eight pictures and the reader's imagination created the world's first workable alphabet.

About 1,200 B.C.E., an enigmatic group of people known simply as the Sea People invaded Egypt and Canaan. The Sea People consisted of a number of groups of people from different homelands. The Philistines, of biblical fame, were one of these groups. Egypt repelled two invasions, but most of Canaan was conquered by the Sea People. A portion of Canaan around the cities of Tyre and Sidon was relatively unscathed by the Sea People. This portion survived as Phoenicia, and it was the Phoenicians who finalized, about 1,100 B.C.E., the alphabet begun by their Canaanite predecessors. The Phoenician alphabet was no longer pictographic—the sign for a sound did not necessarily depict an object whose name began with that sound. Like Old Canaanite, the Phoenician alphabet, which was shortened to twenty-two signs, depicted consonant sounds only—vowels were still supplied by the reader.

Because the Phoenicians were masters of oceanic travel, the Phoenician alphabet spread around the Mediterranean basin and became the forerunner of all other alphabets. Except for Asian civilizations that did not develop alphabets (such as China and Japan), the Phoenician contribution ultimately became a template for all of today's writing systems. One must exercise caution before concluding that a particular invention occurred in only one place, as the independent development of ideas in multiple sites appears now to be the rule, but the alphabet apparently arose only in the Levant, from which it spread around the Old World.

The story of writing now hinges on the differences in two language groups of the Mediterranean world. The Phoenicians wrote and spoke a Semitic language. In the Semitic language group, which includes such present-day languages as Arabic and Hebrew, an alphabet without vowels was workable.

Indo-European is the major language family of today's Western world and includes almost all of the contemporary languages of Russia and Europe, as well as ancient Greek and Latin. Today, approximately 1.6 billion people speak languages derived from the Indo-European stem language (throughout this work, the words billion and trillion refer to their American usage, that is a billion is a thousand millions and a trillion is a million millions), populating a geographically wider area of the world than any other language group. The Indo-European languages are based on a stem language that was spoken by people from a number of poorly understood cultures—possibly located in southern Russia or eastern Europe. Perhaps about 2,000 B.C.E., these people migrated into other areas of the world, imparting aspects of their language to the people with whom they mixed. They arrived in both Mesopotamia and the Indus Valley by 1500 B.C.E. The Indo-European people generally did not conquer the territories to which they migrated, but they influenced the culture and subsequent linguistic development.

Unlike Semitic languages, Indo-European languages needed vowels for their alphabets to achieve any degree of practicality. For example, the above English illustration can be read as "You can read this," "You can rid these," "You can raid those," etc. The Phoenician alphabet was therefore unable to express Indo-European languages. The inclusion of vowels into the alphabet, thus making it practical for Indo-European languages, was the first of the Greek contributions to our heritage. It is widely agreed that the Greeks attained an alphabet from the Phoenicians. Actually, some of the characteristics of the first Greek alphabet are similar to the Old Canaanite alphabet, indicating that the Greeks borrowed before the transition to the Phoenician script was complete. They created five signs for sounds that did not occur in their language and used them for vowels, thereby bringing an alphabet to the Indo-European family of languages (this is the origin of the five vowels in contemporary English). The Greek alphabet was established by 700 B.C.E. and would greatly influence the development of the Etruscan and Latin alphabets, the latter of which became the basis of most of today's Western languages. Other major contemporary alphabets indebted to the Canaanites include Cyrillic, Arabic, Korean, Persian, and Devanagari (which is used in many Indian languages). About this time, two other great events took place in Greek history: the adoption of papyrus as a writing medium from Egypt; and the colonization of Ionia, a region in the western portion of the Aegean Sea, near present-day Turkey.

So it is that the development of writing entails the successive influence of one culture on another, beginning with the Sumerians and Egyptians and continuing with the Greek and Latin alphabets, which remain the basis for contemporary Western writing. The final chapter in our story of writing concerns improvements in writing materials. In time, papyrus gave way to parchment, which was made from animal skin. Parchment was known to the ancient Egyptians, but the ready availability of papyrus made parchment unnecessary in that kingdom. Parchment allowed the first bound books to be constructed and was the principal writing medium in the West until the arrival of paper in the late Middle Ages. Paper, which was exclusively a Chinese invention, was passed through the Muslims to the Western world.

Chapter 3
Lands of the Rivers

For seventy days, the priests worked on the Pharaoh's body. If every detail of the preservation was not perfect, the soul could not return to the body.

The Cradle of Civilization

THE WORD "MESOPOTAMIA" REFERS TO "the land between the rivers" and describes the cultures that flourished between the Tigris and Euphrates rivers in what is now Iraq. In antiquity, the Tigris and Euphrates rivers had separate points of entry into the Persian Gulf, but their deltas were adjacent. It was in or near that common delta that Mesopotamian civilization began. Today, silting has extended the course of the rivers, and they join before entering the gulf.

The pioneering excavations of Leonard Woolley (1888–1960) and those who followed him have taught us much about Mesopotamia, even though wood and textiles are not well preserved in the climate of the Middle East and Mesopotamian sun-dried bricks have not survived burying. Every spring, the Tigris and Euphrates flooded their banks and inundated the land. The early inhabitants of Mesopotamia settled there because these floods held the key to agriculture in the desert. But the large-scale agriculture necessary for a true civilization required irrigation, which began about 4000 B.C.E.

We do not know where the early peoples of Mesopotamia originated. They apparently migrated into the region from an as yet unknown place. Archeologists named early settlements for the sites in which they were found, such as Tell Hassuna, Tell Halaf, and Tell Al Ubaid. (The word "Tell" refers to a mound caused by generations of habitation.) These early settlements are categorized and dated by their pottery—the only consistently surviving aspect of their cultures. Originally designed to hold or carry, pottery is now an invaluable clue to

24

a region's cultural history. Styles of pottery are named for the site in which they were first found, and the study of pottery illuminates the migration and trading patterns of the early cultures of Mesopotamia. Pottery in the Hassuna and Samarra styles was created by 6,000 B.C.E., by which time it was already understood that firing the pottery in a kiln made it more permanent and waterproof. After the Hassuna and Samarra periods came the Halaf period (beginning circa 5500 B.C.E.) and the Ubaid period (lasting from roughly 5000 to 4000 B.C.E.). The Ubaid culture was the first to supplement the annual flooding of the rivers with irrigation.

The first well-defined Mesopotamian culture was Sumer (or Sumeria, known in the *Bible* as Shinar), in contemporary Iraq. The Sumerian civilization began around 4000 B.C.E., when Uruk (known in the *Bible* as Erech), the first true city of history, arose. The Sumerians apparently did not arise from the Ubaid people, but rather entered Mesopotamia in a separate migration. The language of the Sumerians is unrelated to any language group in our knowledge. We thus know nothing about the ultimate origin of either the Sumerians or their predecessor cultures.

The writing of Uruk was not a well-developed logo-syllabic system, but rather was purely pictographic. It cannot be well read, but appears to be an early form of Sumerian, a sort of stepping stone toward a fully developed, practical writing system. In Uruk, the concept of a city-state was born. The city-state is a recurring theme in history and can be defined as an autonomous city within a collection of related and interacting settlements. Shortly after Uruk, other city-states of Sumer appeared, such as Ur, Kish, Larsa, Umma, and Lagash. These are clearly related to Uruk, and leave no doubt that although Mesopotamia was occupied by numerous autonomous city-states, the region was the single culture of Sumer. This area is rightly called the cradle of civilization and was considered the birthplace of civilization even by ancient peoples. Sumerian history figures prominently in the *Bible*, and much of the Old Testament refers to Mesopotamian sites. Indeed, the Sumerian word "Edin," meaning grassland, is likely the origin of Biblical Eden.

It was in Sumer that our contemporary lives took shape. Writing developed, the discovery of bronze ushered in a true age of metals, and the wheel was adapted for general use. The precise origin of the wheel is unclear. At one time, it was thought to have been invented in Sumer and then to have diffused around the Old World. There is now evidence of the separate development of the wheel in multiple sites. In any event, the wheel was in use in Mesopotamia by at least

3,200 B.C.E., and probably earlier. There is some thought that it began as the potter's wheel, and its usefulness to the larger world was grasped subsequently. Pots were often made by coiling a rope of clay, and it was realized, perhaps about 4,000 B.C.E., that this could be done more efficiently if the work were constantly turning. Once the potter's wheel supplied the concept of rotary motion, it could be extended to carry loads.

Some believe that the annual flooding of the Tigris and Euphrates, or perhaps a particularly large such flood, formed the basis for the great Flood in the *Bible*. But the Biblical account is not the only record of a deluge. The Mesopotamian epic *Gilgamesh*—whose hero is part man and part god—records an intrepid flood survivor named Ut-napishtim, who helped Gilgamesh find the secret of immortality. *Gilgamesh* was written about 1,900 B.C.E., but appears to be based on older Sumerian sources (Gilgamesh may have been a real person, possibly a king of Uruk around 2,700 B.C.E.). About the same time, there was another Mesopotamian epic of the flood, the story of Atrahasis. Multiple accounts of an event from independent sources lend credence to its occurrence, so there may truly have been a great flood.

Much of what we know of everyday life in ancient Sumer comes from cylinder seals—small, cylindrical objects containing carved scenes pertaining to everyday life. In general, officials used them to certify the contents of a case of goods. When the case was closed with the required merchandise, it was sealed with clay. An official would verify the contents, then take his seal and roll it across the clay, imprinting its design. This served as that official's verification of the contents of the container. Upon hardening, the clay sealed the contents, and was broken by the consumer to expose the merchandise.

Sumerian culture is considered to be proto-literate (meaning that a mature writing system had not yet developed) until about 3,000 B.C.E. This was followed by an early dynastic period that lasted until about 2,300 B.C.E. During this dynastic period Sumerian culture took full form, and it was in this period that writing became developed enough to leave historically meaningful records.

The Sumerians did not merge into a single culture, as the Egyptians did in the Old Kingdom, but rather existed as autonomous city-states, each ruled by a king, who in contrast to the Egyptian Pharaoh was not considered to be the decisive element in the stability of the society. Also in contrast to the Egyptians, they did not adopt a static view of the world; they attempted to conquer other cultures early in their history. This would ultimately cost them their identity.

About 2,300 B.C.E., the neighboring region of Akkad in northern

Mesopotamia, under king Sargon, conquered the Sumerians and established the world's first empire. The empire of Sargon gives us a look ahead at the good and bad influences that empires throughout history would exert. Prior to Sargon, the Sumerians had a culture of individual, loosely connected city-states. With Sargon, there was one culture. This resulted in substantial standardization of weights and measures throughout Mesopotamia. Safer and more effective trade routes were established; they would become a repeating theme in empires. Although Sargon's empire gave Mesopotamia its first central government, the day-to-day administration of the city-states was left to local officials.

The Akkadians spoke a Semitic language, the first known instance of the Semitic language family in this area. The other major branch of modern languages, the Indo-European branch, arrived in the Mesopotamian basin slightly after the rise of Akkad.

After only some one hundred and fifty years, the Akkadian Empire and much of Sumer fell to the Gutians, a tribal people from the mountains. However, the southern part of Sumer was spared conquest by the Gutians, and here two remarkable events occurred. First, the Sumerians from the south were able to drive the Gutians from Sumer, permitting Sumerian culture, now free from both Akkadian and Gutian domination, to flourish again. Second, there was a particular resurgence of Sumerian civilization in the city of Ur, a period referred to as the third dynasty of Ur, dating to roughly 2,000 B.C.E.

But time was running out on Sumer. A people called the Elamites invaded and conquered the Sumerians, but this invasion masks the more fundamental problem—the lack of cohesion of Sumerian civilization and the failure of its infrastructure. One gets the feeling that Sumer died of old age. History shows us time and again that behind many successful invasions, there is often a failure of basic processes in the conquered nation. After the brief occupation of the Elamites, control of the Mesopotamian region passed to a people called the Amorites, whose presence would mark the end of Sumer and the beginning of Babylon.

Hammurabi was the most celebrated Babylonian ruler. In 1901 and 1902, large fragments of stone were recovered, which when pieced together made a stone column 8.5 feet (2.5 meters) in height. On this stele were written the laws of Hammurabi's famous code. These laws were almost certainly not the actual statutes by which Babylon lived. They were never quoted in any recovered legal writings. Based on the traditions of his Amorite background, Hammurabi's laws were more likely intended as broad guides for his successors, rather than as an integral part of the legal system. Precedent and tradition furnished the actual daily statutes. Now in the Louvre, Hammurabi's code offers the opportunity to step back 4,000 years and see the thought process of a Babylonian mind.

After the Babylonians, control of Mesopotamia passed successively to a number of cultures, the details of which do not concern us. What concerns us now is that in the latter portion of the third millennium B.C.E., people who spoke languages of the Indo-European family migrated into Mesopotamia. So we see that the Indo-European family arrived in Mesopotamia slightly later than the Semitic family.

The Sumerians, and the Babylonians after them, achieved excellence in mathematics. Like writing, it appears that the origin of numbers is in trade. By 5,000 years ago, marks were made to indicate the number of items traded, one mark per item. Subsequently, symbols were used in place of the marks, with the advantage that a one-to-one correspondence of signs and items was no longer needed. The Egyptians more or less stopped at this point, and understood only basic arithmetic operations, but the Sumerians developed an elaborate mathematical system that introduced the idea of place value. This meant that the same sign had a different meaning depending on where it was located in the number. This was a critical advance in mathematics, and the Sumerians became the greatest mathematicians of their time. Although they occasionally employed a decimal system, based on ten, they more often used a sexigesimal system, wherein place value was based on sixty. That is, if a number consisted of three identical numerals, the numeral in the center had sixty times the value of the same numeral to its right and one sixtieth the value of the numeral to its left. The remnants of this sexigesimal system are evident today in timekeeping, latitude, longitude, geometry, and the divisions of a circle.

During the Babylonian period, place value was extended to fractions, enabling people to conveniently work with numbers smaller than one. Skilled in algebra, the Babylonians solved quadratic equations (those based on x^2) and understood the Pythagorean theorem many centuries before Pythagoras.

The Babylonians were one of a number of cultures that understood some, but not all, of the properties of the contemporary zero. They had no symbol for zero until late in their history, and did not understand it as a number with all the properties of any other number and subject to the full range of mathematical operations. Moreover, the symbol was used only between two numbers—it was not used at the end of a number to increase the value of other numerals.

It is already clear that civilization as we know it, with all its foibles and advantages, was firmly established in ancient Mesopotamia. The basic nature of humanity, both good and bad, had developed in Mesopotamia. Who we are was defined in the arid land between the two rivers.

Judaism

The early history of Judaism is the story of a people and a place. The people were the Israelites, and the place was the Levant—a portion of the eastern shore of the Mediterranean encompassing contemporary Israel and Lebanon. Both of these histories are complicated and intricately intertwined, involving a variety of nations and cultures.

We know little about the origin of Judaism. The *Bible* says that the progenitor of the Jews, Abraham, led his people out of the city of Ur in Mesopotamia and into Canaan, probably about 1,800 B.C.E. Famine forced Abraham's decendents to leave Canaan and settle in Egypt. Eventually, under Moses, the Israelites escaped Egyptian oppression and returned to Canaan. Much of this biblical account is unconfirmed and uncertain. Abraham, if he existed at all, may have been attributed to Ur so that the writers of the Old Testament could place their progenitor in a city of great repute and antiquity. Likewise, the date of the Israelite exodus from Egypt—if it occurred—is uncertain. Some favor a date of approximately 1,600 B.C.E., putting Israelites in Canaan before the invasion of the Sea People; but most believe the exodus was on the order of 1,200 B.C.E., implying that the Israelites reached Canaan after the Philistines, the principal tribe of the Sea People, had invaded the Levant. In fact, the Israelites may have made a treaty with Phoenicia, which survived the invasion of the Sea People, in order to subdue the Philistines.

David (fl. c. 1000 B.C.E.) and his son Solomon were noted Israelite kings. After Solomon's death, civil war splintered the Jewish state into two kingdoms, Judah in the south and Israel in the north. The Assyrians destroyed ancient Israel in the eighth century B.C.E., and its population was absorbed into that of Assyria, giving rise to the legend of the ten lost tribes. Judah alone would carry on the Jewish tradition.

Judaism was not originally monotheistic. Polytheism was the general rule in the early history of both Judah and Israel; monotheism, in the form of the worship of Yahweh (sometimes incorrectly called Jehovah) became dominant later. There is some uncertainty as to when this occurred. Traditionally, monotheism was thought to have arisen in the eighth century B.C.E., but many

29

scholars now believe that monotheism developed earlier and was largely in place by 1,200 B.C.E. The prophets known to us as the writers of many of the books of the Old Testament were either champions of monotheism, social reformers in Judah, preservers of Jewish cultural traditions, or heroes of the Jewish state's survival. Jews believed that many of the writings of the prophets foretold a day when God would send a Messiah to Earth to intervene on their behalf. In this respect, Judaism resembles a number of other religions; the idea that a person is the son of a deity, the personal representative of a deity, or is part deity is relatively common in history and can be found in many cultures.

The *nature* of this God is as important a contribution of Judaism as monotheism itself. Judaism broke with other religions of the time by ascribing absolute morality and a genuine interest in humanity to its God. The Jewish God is omnipotent, just, kind, concerned with the welfare of humanity, and willing to intervene on behalf of people—all of which were radical departures from the polytheistic religions of the day. Judaism also confirms the basic goodness of people—anything created by a supremely good God must itself be good. Although people transgress, they are basically good. The world, and everything in it, has a purpose.

A basic tenet in Judaism is the covenant between the Jewish people and their God. After many unsuccessful attempts to reform humanity, God turned to a specific segment of it—the Jews—and formed a special relationship with them. This relationship, called the Covenant, obliges Jews to obey God's commands and set an example for the rest of humanity. Foremost among these commands are the Ten Commandments, which were later adopted by Christianity and Islam and which would become the underpinnings of most of the legal and moral tradition of the Western world. In return, Jews would receive the special protection of God. This is what is meant when the Jews call themselves the chosen people. It does not mean that Jews consider themselves superior, simply that they have been chosen by God to facilitate harmony in the world by acting, in effect, as examples of righteous conduct. A covenant can be thought of as a contract, but with two important differences. First, the covenant encompasses the entire being of the person, not just one aspect of his life. Second, there is no fixed time period for the covenant; it lasts the lifetime of the person. As envisioned by Jews, the covenant binds the whole being of each Jew to God throughout his or her lifetime.

Judaism demanded much from its followers, but it gave something unprecedented in return: the assurance that they possessed value and would receive the personal concern and attention of God. Affirming the goodness and power of God and the basic goodness of people led to another tenet—people, through God, have power over the world. People, like God, can be just and powerful. The idea that people could dominate nature was novel. Christianity and Islam inherited this idea, and it has stayed with Western tradition throughout history.

After the fall of Assyria to the Neo-Babylonians in 612 B.C.E., the Jews were taken captive and held hostage in Babylonia (the Babylonian captivity, 587–537 B.C.E.). After the Persians replaced the Neo-Babylonians as the region's power brokers, the Persian king Cyrus permitted the Jews to return to their homeland. Judah absorbed some critical elements of the Persian religion Zoroastrianism. Zarathustra (c. 628–551 B.C.E., known to us as Zoroaster) was a Persian prophet who opposed the prevailing polytheistic religion of the region. He championed monotheism and, independent of Judaism, arrived at the notion of a personal God who is concerned with the welfare of people. One of the central tenets of this religion is a sharp dichotomy of good and evil. The deity Ahura Mazda represents good, while Ahriman is the God of evil.

In Zoroastrianism, there is a constant struggle between these forces, and humans must take sides and prepare themselves for the final cataclysmic battle between good and evil. Jews under Persian subjugation appropriated this simplistic view of right and wrong (although the concept may not have come solely from Zoroastrianism) and introduced Satan as the source of evil in the world. Thus, the Zoroastrian concept of good and evil was passed through Judaism to the Christians and Muslims. From Zoroastrianism, Judaism also received the idea of a final apocalypse, wherein the battle between good and evil would result in a new world of good. This Zoroastrian influence on Judeo-Christian thought is most clearly seen in the book of *Revelation* in the Christian New Testament. The idea of the resurrection of the dead appeared in Judaism at roughly the same time as Satan and the Apocalypse, and may also reflect Zoroastrian influence.

In this milieu—monotheism, near genocidal oppression of the Jews, the belief that a Messiah was coming, the belief in a final Apocalypse, and the hope for resurrection from death with delivery into Paradise—the background for Jesus would form. As we shall see, the force that Jesus exerted on history was markedly effected by the background circumstances of his world, particularly the Old Testament concept of a Messiah and the concept of the apocalypse, absorbed largely from Persian Zoroastrianism.

Although Judaism recognizes a deity, it is equally concerned with the conduct of people. Judaism was the "parent" religion of Christianity and Islam, and it imparted its legacy of ethical monotheism to these religions. The books of Judaism are contained in the Old Testament, which was originally written mostly in Hebrew (a few passages were written in Aramaic) and consists of thirty nine books (the Old Testament is also acknowledged by Christians, and Catholics recognize an additional seven books). Of prime importance are the first five books of the Old Testament, called the *Torah* or *Pentateuch*. Also of great importance is the *Talmud*, a giant collection of 63 books written from the end of the third to the end of the sixth century C.E. The *Talmud* is an extensive interpretation and commentary of the Torah, and is the written form of an ancient oral tradition.

As is the case for all religions, there is no one version of Judaism. Other than the stipulations regarding conduct, Judaism does not have many official requirements concerning what its followers should believe. Although the belief in life after death is an integral part of Jewish history, and traditional Jews (called Orthodox) embrace this idea completely, less traditional followers (Conservative or Reformed Jews) may or may not believe in an afterlife, and contemporary Judaism affords considerable latitude in this regard. Individual Jews decide this for themselves, just as they do such matters as whether or not a Messiah is coming.

Judaism in the twentieth century has been shaped by two overpowering events: the Nazi Holocaust and Zionism. Six million Jews—one third of the world's total—were killed in concentration camps or ghettos during Hitler's tyranny. Zionism, the movement for the reestablishment of a Jewish homeland, is not new to the twentieth century, but has been more prevalent in this century because of international sympathy engendered by the Holocaust. The establishment of Israel in 1948 gave Jews their first homeland in almost two thousand years.

The history of Judaism, unfortunately, is full of persecution and discrimination. Throughout history, Jews have often been cast as scapegoats. The Nazi Holocaust of the twentieth century is but most the tragic event in a long history of persecution. Jews have been a successful and prosperous people, and therefore a tempting target for those less well off. I submit as history's first lesson that people deprived of basic needs are very likely to behave cruelly and irrationally, and the target of that behavior will be those perceived to be more fortunate.

Jews have contributed to our progress to a degree fantastically out of proportion to their numbers (there are only about seventeen million Jews today, almost half of whom are in the United States). If one postulates, as I believe we must, that people of all nationalities and beliefs are genetically equal, then how can such a small group of people have achieved so much? Perhaps it is their close family structure and reverence for learning, passed down through generations. We are all helpless when we are born and totally dependent on our environment. To my mind, history's second lesson is that if our early environment nurtures us, teaches us, and gives us the self-esteem to believe that we can control our destiny, we will do well. If that environment is hostile, fragmented, unsupportive, and affords minimal opportunities, we will do poorly. Jews have done very well in providing for their young the environment required to control one's destiny and prosper personally and professionally.

The Gift of the Nile

Egypt began as a number of settlements called nomes. These unified over time, eventually coalescing into two distinct regions—Upper and Lower Egypt. Because these names were based on the direction of the flow of the Nile, Upper Egypt was to the south. Lower Egypt was to the north, at the mouth of the Nile.

The Egyptians developed a very different society than their Mesopotamian contemporaries. Although it formed slightly later than Sumer, Egypt united earlier and more completely than its Mesopotamian counterpart and retained its identity for 3,000 years. Much of what we know about ancient Egypt comes from a man named Manetho, who was a Hellenistic (referring to the time just after Alexander the Great) priest who lived about 300 B.C.E. Manetho's original writings are lost, but they were incorporated into later writings. We know that he described 30 dynasties, extending from about 3100 B.C.E. to 332 B.C.E., the date of Alexander the Great's conquest. A king he called Menes united Upper and Lower Egypt to begin the historical period of Egyptian history. A slab dating to about 3,100 B.C.E. found at the ancient city of Hierakonpolis commemorates a victorious king named Narmer, though we do not know if this Narmer is the elusive Menes to whom Manetho alluded, and many now believe that the unification of Egypt preceded this work.

The thirty dynasties (some historians use thirty-one) are roughly, and somewhat arbitrarily, divided into the following periods:

Early Dynastic Period	c. 3100–2613 B.C.E.
The Old Kingdom	c. 2613–2160 B.C.E.
First Intermediate Period	c. 2160–2040 B.C.E.
The Middle Kingdom	c. 2040–1652 B.C.E.
Second Intermediate Period	c. 1652–1567 B.C.E.
The New Kingdom	c. 1567–1069 B.C.E.
Third Intermediate Period	c. 1069–656 B.C.E.
Late Period	c. 656–332 B.C.E.

Egyptian civilization was much more stable than Mesopotamia, for two reasons. First, the geography of Egypt made it very difficult to invade; in the relatively open plains of Mesopotamia all settlements were vulnerable. Second, ancient Egypt had a uniquely static view of the universe. They took great steps to protect and preserve their culture and, until the New Kingdom, waged only infrequent military campaigns against other nations. They conducted isolated raids into Nubia (present day Ethiopia) but made no significant attempts to conquer other people. To conquer is to lose your identity; to force your culture on others is to lose it for yourself. The ancient Egyptians understood this better than their contemporary cultures.

We begin our discussion of Egypt with the Nile River, the lifeblood of Egyptian civilization. The longest river in the world, the Nile is formed from the union of the Blue Nile, whose source is in contemporary Ethiopia, and the White Nile, whose source is in central Africa. In the spring, melting snow in the Ethiopian mountains and the onset of the rainy season in the tropics of Africa distended the Nile. By late July, the added water caused the Nile to flood its banks. These floods brought organic nutrients and moisture to the desert soil and made it easier to till. Too much flooding could wash away whole villages, but too little meant poor crops and certain starvation. Even with the annual flooding, a system of irrigation canals emanating from the Nile was essential to agriculture. Like their Mesopotamian counterparts, the Egyptians introduced an elaborate system of waterways in the desert, and about 1200 B.C.E., they began building a network of canals from the Nile to the Red Sea.

Ancient Egyptian religion was complex, often involving a large number of local gods intertwined with gods of more global significance. The most important gods changed somewhat over the centuries, variously rising to and receding from prominence, but the essence of the religion was remarkably constant for three thousand years, until the advent of Christianity. Although not all Egyptian sources agree on all details, the following outline can be constructed: the Sun, personified as the Sun God Ra (or Re), was the progenitor deity. Two of his grandchildren, the earth (personified as the God Geb) and the Sky (the Goddess Nut), were the parents of Osiris, Isis, and Set (or Seth). Set killed Osiris (very reminiscent of the story of Cain and Able), but Isis was able to reconstruct her brother long enough for them to conceive a child, Horus. Osiris became the God of the Dead, while Horus vied with Set. The rise of additional gods, initially of local significance, was tied to political fortunes.

Egypt's view of the universe as static and benign was unique among early civilizations. All would be right if a stable pattern of behavior were unvaryingly adhered to and the status quo accepted. The ancient Egyptians, especially in the Old Kingdom, believed that the Pharaoh was the guardian and protector of society—the son of Ra (or of Amun in the New Kingdom), through whom the stability of the world could be achieved. In its commitment to stasis, ancient Egypt was very different from Mesopotamia, and was in fact somewhat similar to early China. However, one gets the impression that the Chinese emphasized harmony, while the Egyptians emphasized rigidity.

The great pyramids and the Sphinx were built during the Old Kingdom (2613–2160 B.C.E.). The pyramids were usually not isolated structures, but the largest part of giant complexes (including subsidiary buildings and burial sites) intended to guide the Pharaoh to the afterlife and insure his eternal happiness there. In the minds of the Egyptians, the pyramids preserved more than the existence of the Pharaoh; they preserved the Egyptian way of life. The first of the great pyramids was the step pyramid of Zoser (or Djoser). Constructed about 2,700 B.C.E., it was apparently designed by a man named Imhotep. (The first great thinker of whom we have record, he would later be considered a god.) After Zoser, the pyramids were built with slanted sides and not in a tiered fashion. The Great Pyramid of Khufu (also called Cheops) came perhaps a century later. It was one of the seven wonders of the ancient world and is the only one still in existence. (The other six wonders of the ancient world were the Hanging Gardens of Babylon, the statue of Zeus at Olympia, the Temple of Artemis at Ephesos, the Mausoleum at Helicarnassus, the Colossus of Rhodes, and the Lighthouse at Alexandria.) Constructing these great works was and is a celebration of the human spirit.

The pyramids were not constructed by slaves (there was no significant slavery in Egypt until after the Old Kingdom, and it was relatively uncommon at all times), but by free people in the agricultural off-season. We are not completely certain of the methods used in quarrying, transporting, and assembling the giant stones (some of which weighed more than fifty tons), but the construction of the pyramids certainly required the coordinated efforts of thousands of people over many years. Planning and foresight were essential. The construction of the pyramids is proof of Kenneth Clark's reminder that civilization requires a degree of prosperity and leisure. This is also true for individual works of greatness.

The Old Kingdom collapsed about 2160 B.C.E., beginning the first intermediate period. The reasons are not entirely clear, but there was no invasion. The few records of the time indicate a severe drought, which led to poor flooding and diminished crop yields. Central power weakened, resulting in the relative strengthening of two groups: the local governors and the priests of Ra. The governors apparently increased their authority by making their positions inheritable, thereby keeping power in the family. To us, decentralization of power may not appear to threaten civilization. Indeed, we might view it as a salutary change. But because the Pharaoh was considered the key to stability, decentralization may have struck at the foundation of society. On this point, our knowledge is imperfect.

In approximately 2130 B.C.E., Mentuhotep restored central power and moved the capital from Memphis to Thebes, establishing the Middle Kingdom. To avoid the decentralization of authority that occurred in the Old Kingdom, Middle Kingdom Pharaohs appointed governors and forbade them to make their positions hereditary. Amun, a local god of Thebes, replaced Ra as the supreme deity, partially to appease the local god of the capital city and partially to check the power of the priests of Ra by diminishing the status of their god. To insure that neither Amun nor Ra felt neglected, they were often assimilated into one deity, Amun-Ra. Although no great pyramids were constructed in the Middle Kingdom, there were ambitious building projects, such as the Labyrinth, which was a complex of some 3,500 burial chambers intended to foil grave robbers by confusing them.

In 1786 B.C.E., the Hyksos, a Semitic people who migrated into Egypt from the east, conquered most of Egypt, ending the Middle Kingdom and establishing the second intermediate period. The Hyksos used horse-drawn chariots, but is uncertain whether they conquered by force or by peacefully inserting themselves into the weakened Egyptian power structure. In either case, the Hyksos were expelled about 1570 B.C.E., ushering in the New Kingdom. Ramses and Tutankhamun, two of the most famous Pharaohs, lived during the New

Kingdom, which also saw the exodus of Moses and the Jews. It bears remembering that Egypt had already been a civilization for some 1500 years by the time of its most famous pharaohs and its Biblical infamy. During this time, the Egyptian *Book of the Dead* was written. A series of more than a hundred separate texts, its purpose was to aid the deceased in the journey to the Underworld (mostly through prayers to Amun-Ra and Osiris, as well as through magic spells).

Amenhotep (or Amenophis) IV, in an attempt to appease a new god, Aten (or Atum), changed his name to Akhenaten. There is some disagreement as to whether this was true monotheism, wherein Akhenaten denied the existence of other gods, or whether he believed in other gods and was merely elevating the status of one god. In either case, he was offering Aten special status in the hope of obtaining the god's favor. Like the priests of Ra in the Old Kingdom, the priests of Amun were acquiring formidable power, and it is likely that he sought to lessen their power by curtailing the power of their god. After Akhenaten's more or less catastrophic reign, his successor, Tutankaten, in an appeal to the now-neglected god Amun, changed his name to Tutankhamun (the famous king Tut, whose tomb, excavated in the 1920s, is the only Pharaoh's tomb to be found largely undisturbed).

The art and architecture of ancient Egypt that remain are large-scale public works, commissioned by the state or a Pharaoh, and are generally found in pyramids, temples, or tombs. Reflective of their static view of the universe, their works were intended to champion the status quo rather than individual expression, although some art does both very well. We have very little understanding of their everyday art, if indeed there was any.

In fact, much of what we know about any culture at any time comes largely from official records, state-approved documents, or government-sponsored works. We are woefully lacking in information concerning the everyday lives of common people from all cultures. As the historians Will and Ariel Durant caution: "History as usually written is quite different from history as usually lived." Historians are both aware of and bothered by this deficiency. Efforts such as historical archeology—a branch of archeology which concentrates on common people and attempts to understand the lives of people not usually addressed in the historical record—are underway to study the history of ordinary people. Microhistory is the study of a particular person, place or event. Like historical archeology, microhistory offers a greater understanding of the daily lives of ordinary people of the past. What these new disciplines may find is at present uncertain, but we shall surely find that all people of all times experienced the same joys, sorrows, and frustrations as we do today and our posterity will to-morrow. I submit as history's third lesson that human nature and the human experience do not fundamentally change from one era in history to another. Technology and knowledge advance; political situations change; and many aspects of our civilization improve through our intellectual efforts, but who we are is constant. Ultimately, we do not live very different lives from people in any other time or place.

The Egyptians trailed their Sumerian counterparts in mathematics, employing a decimal system without place value. However, they were the first to establish an accurate 365-day calendar. Just as writing, in most cultures, originates in the practice of commerce, astronomy probably owes its origins to agriculture. People learned that the behavior of heavenly bodies could forecast the flooding of rivers and the coming of the growing season, so they determined to learn more about these bodies. The day, based on the time from the appearance of the sun in the sky to the time it returns to the same location; and the month, based on the interval between two new moons or two full moons, were measured with considerable accuracy by many ancient people. Much more difficult was measuring the length of a year. The Egyptians measured an approximate year as the time between successive floodings of the Nile. Because the flooding of the Nile was more regular than that of the Tigris or Euphrates, the Egyptians could calculate a year with greater accuracy than their Mesopotamian counterparts. But the ultimate origin of the Egyptian year was not a river, but a star. About the time of the Nile flooding, Sirius reappears after an absence, and it was the time between risings of Sirius that became the definitive and accurate Egyptian year. Their year was divided into twelve thirty-day months followed by a five-day period. They had no leap day, which would not come into being until Hellenistic times, and would not be codified until the time of Caesar.

The major achievement of ancient Egypt was the practice of medicine. Egypt's medical reputation during the Old Kingdom lured many there for treatment. Egypt was the first to codify their medical practice. Their physicians were priests—typical of early times, when diseases were thought to be a punishment by the gods. In Egyptian mythology, different gods were responsible for different body parts, so it became customary to go to a priest devoted to the god in charge of the ailing body part. However, to view ancient Egyptian medicine as solely a prayer ritual would be wrong; they had a rich and well-established empirical tradition. The Edwin Smith Papyrus, dating from 1500 B.C.E. but probably a copy of works perhaps a thousand years older, describes the setting of bones, hints at the circulation of blood, and recognizes the pulse as a monitor of heart action. The Ebers Papyrus described 700 medications and discussed massage, diets and even hypnosis.

Egyptian medicine, science, and religion had an unlikely convergence in the embalming process. To fully understand the elaborate Egyptian mummification process, it is necessary to appreciate their concept of immortality. Roughly speaking, the Egyptians believed that the soul had three aspects. The *Ka* was a double of the person and accompanied him during his lifetime. After death, the *Ka* lived in the tomb of the deceased and resided in his body (if the body was damaged, the *Ka* could reside in statues of the deceased, but the body itself was preferable). The *Ba* was the aspect of the soul capable of rejoining and re-animating the body. Unlike the *Ka*, the *Ba* was free to roam outside the tomb during the day, but had to return to the tomb at night. The third aspect of the soul was the *Akh*, which can be roughly thought of as the divine power that made the journey to the afterlife possible. All three of these aspects were equal and essential.

The Egyptians believed there were five requirements for achieving immortality. First, there had to be a tomb, a resting place for the deceased (the pyramids fulfilled this function for the Pharaohs). Second, the name of the deceased had to be inscribed in the tomb, so there would be no doubt as to his or her identity. Third, there had to be food and water for the journey to the afterlife (sometimes, images of these would suffice). Fourth, the descendants of the deceased must perform rituals to insure that the gods remembered him and acted on his behalf. Finally, because the *Ka* and the *Ba* would rejoin the body, the latter must be preserved, if possible, so that it would be recognizable to them. This preservation was achieved through mummification.

In the early part of the Old Kingdom, the body was simply wrapped in linens impregnated with resins. This preserved the outer portion of the body, but did nothing to maintain the internal organs. By the middle of the Old Kingdom, it was realized that the removal and separate treatment of the internal organs would not only facilitate their preservation, but would also allow access to the interior of the body, improving its preservation as well. It was also understood that dehydration was an essential component. (This was learned from the unexpected preservation of bodies that had been buried in the arid desert sand.)

The fully developed process of mummification, as described by Herodotus in the fifth century B.C.E., evolved over many centuries and lasted some seventy days. The abdominal and thoracic organs were removed and separately preserved with desiccating salt compounds, with the exception of the heart, which was thought to be the center of consciousness and was therefore left in the body. The brain was removed (through the nose), but not because its importance was understood. Rather, the embalmers did not want decomposition of the brain to spoil the face and make the body unrecognizable to the *Ba* and the *Ka*.

The body was then desiccated with additional salt compounds, after which linen and resin were placed in the body cavities. The embalming process was completed by wrapping the body in multiple layers of linen. Mummification was originally reserved for people of high status, but it later became possible for common people to conceive of eternal life and participate in the process.

Egyptian and Mesopotamian accomplishments in science and technology introduced the perception of an orderly, structured, and to some extent comprehensible world. Millennia of myths, legends, and incorrect thinking lay in front of humanity, but the first crucial step was taken—the affirmation that people can control their environment and their destiny.

The First City Planners

The civilization of the Indus valley arose in northwest India, along the Indus River at the border of modern India and Pakistan. Its principal cities were Harappa and Mohenjo Daro, but there were hundreds of other sites. The Indus civilization was in bloom by 2,500 B.C.E., but like Egypt and Mesopotamia, some settled communities in the Indus valley were much older than the established civilization with which we are familiar.

Early Indus civilization stretched over a far wider area than Mesopotamia or Egypt, yet this entire area shows considerable cultural uniformity. This culture was remarkably maintained and relatively unaltered until about 1,700 B.C.E. Unlike Mesopotamia or Egypt, there were no kings or centralized authorities, and there is no evidence that force was used to establish or maintain this culture. They traded extensively, and numerous seals from ancient Mesopotamia have been identified in Indus sites.

We know less about ancient Indus civilization than we do about Mesopotamia and Egypt. They spoke a non Indo-European language that appears to be related to Dravidian, a contemporary family of languages encompassing more than twenty languages spoken by two hundred million people, mostly in southern India. We cannot read their writing, in part because only short inscriptions are available for study.

At its height, the Indus civilization provided a remarkably high standard of living. Their principal cities were exceptionally well designed and planned prior to construction. Many houses had bathrooms connecting to a community drain. The larger sites were built with kiln-fired brick (as opposed to the sun-dried brick of Mesopotamia). Unlike Mesopotamia and Egypt, the Indus civilization did not construct great tombs, temples, or palaces. As far as we can determine, their construction was oriented toward daily life, and what remains gives us a glimpse of how ordinary people lived. The absence of great temples and funerary structures deprives us of lasting and imposing structures commemorating the lives of kings and priests. On the other hand, this absence prevents us from being distracted by the lives of the few and forces us to examine the lives of the many.

There is evidence of decline in the Indus civilization around 1,900 B.C.E., perhaps because of drought and diminished trade. By 1,700 B.C.E., the Indus culture had lost much of its identity. About the same time, an Indo-European people came into the Indus Valley. These people were called Aryans, and they spoke Sanskrit, an Indo-European language. The Aryan invaders assimilated many of the indigenous people, but others were driven to the southern part of India, which afforded some degree of protection from the Aryans, and later, from Muslim conquests. Whether the Aryans conquered the Indus civilization in a strict sense or simply filled the void left by their spontaneous decline is not fully clear. Not all Indus sites vanished at the same time, and archeological evidence suggests that the various sites were not all replaced by the same culture, so it is probable that the Indus civilization declined for internal reasons. In either case, we are left with an uncomfortable discontinuity in the historical record. There is a period of perhaps four centuries between the decline of the Indus civilization and the earliest records of the Aryans of which our understanding is woefully lacking. During this time, writing was lost and the archeological record becomes less helpful. We do know that the merging of the Indo-European Aryan culture with the indigenous Indus Valley culture would establish the remainder of Indian history. It was from the merging of these two cultures that Hinduism arose.

Hinduism

Because an understanding of human religions is essential in understanding human history, we will digress a moment and address one of the oldest (with Judaism) human religions still practiced today—Hinduism.

41

Hinduism has evolved from its original conception more than any other religion, and it is still evolving. There is no set of beliefs that describes Hinduism at all times in its history. In addition, there is considerable individual variability in beliefs. Hinduism is a family of related beliefs, with the individual practitioner exercising more discretion than is permitted in Christianity. This evolution and individual variability—along with its ties to Indian culture and its Eastern outlook—makes Hinduism difficult for the Western mind to grasp.

Unlike Christianity, Hinduism is not based on the teachings of any one prophet and has no one text for its sole source. Most important are the four *Vedas*, or sacred books (Veda means knowledge in Sanskrit). The best known of these is the *Rig Veda*, a collection of 1,028 hymns completed about 1000 B.C.E. Many gods are mentioned in the Vedas, and Vishnu and Shiva—who would become principal deities later—are given only minor roles. Several other key works were subsequently added to Hinduism, each of which took centuries to fully form. These were the *Upanishads* (begun about 800 B.C.E.) and the epics *Ramayana* and the *Mahabharata* (both begun about 400 B.C.E.). The latter epic contains the *Bhagavad Gita (Song of God)*, a poem that was precious to Gandhi.

The Upanishads introduced three ideas that became integral to Hinduism. First is the concept of reincarnation, wherein people are reborn until they achieve true realization. Second is the belief that the consequences of one's deeds in this life extend into the next. (These consequences are called Karma.) Third is the possibility of escape from eternal reincarnation by eventually becoming one with the supreme being. This state is called Moksa (also written Mokhsha). The sequential lives of a soul are a series of apprenticeships, if you will, culminating in the achievement of a oneness with God.

Although the Upanishads introduce these ideas, they do so in a somewhat ambiguous manner. Different writers of the Upanishads apparently had different conceptions. This is a source of the variability of beliefs in Hinduism today.

At the time of the Upanishads, Vishnu and Shiva became major deities, and Hinduism began to think of the supreme being as having three aspects. There was Brahma (the Creator), Vishnu (the Preserver), and Shiva (the Destroyer). Shiva is not an evilly destructive aspect of God, but rather destroys so there can be further creation. Together, these aspects form the three-fold manifestation of the divine character, which is called Brahman (spelled deceptively like Brahma, which is one aspect of Brahman).

This stage of Hinduism is often the extent of the Westerner's knowledge of the religion, but in fact, Hinduism continued to evolve. Brahma became less prominent to most Hindus, while Vishnu and Shiva became more prominent. Today, some Hindus believe Vishnu the principal deity, with Shiva a subservient god, while others hold that Shiva is the supreme deity and Vishnu is subordinant. This presents a dilemma to the Western mind: Is Hinduism a polytheistic religion, or is it monotheistic, with multiple aspects of a single god? There is no simple answer to this question. Different Hindus have different conceptions, and Hinduism accepts both single and multiple expressions of the Divine Presence.

Although Vishnu and Shiva are masculine, they both have female consorts who are no less important. Hindu gods are best thought of as gender-balanced, in contrast to the masculine Old Testament God. Additionally, Hindus perceive the Supreme Being differently than Westerners. To the Westerner, God is a discrete being, distinct from the universe He created. The *Bible* even says that God made man in His own image, implying that God looks something like us. But to Hindus, the Supreme Being—whether Brahman, Vishnu, or Shiva—is indescribable and unpersonifiable, permeating and inseparable from the whole of the universe.

Life for Hindus is a process, not an end. Even the universe will be recycled at some point in the distant future. The universe and everything in it is a journey, not a finished product. Hinduism is a religion of eternity. Each individual begins existence as a non-human being and eventually becomes human through successive reincarnations. As a human, the individual has the opportunity to develop full awareness and self-realization, which comes only from the search for truth and the integration of the mind, body, and soul.

The discipline of Yoga is helpful in obtaining this union of the physical, mental, and spiritual portions of the self. It is sad that most Westerners think of Yoga simply as a set of exercises. In fact, there are four Yogas; each is a discipline, a path that seeks to relax and unburden individuals so they can become more aware of their physical existence, more receptive to the truth, and better able to escape the distractions of the world. The four Yogas are the path of devotion, the path of works, the path of meditation, and the path of knowledge. Using the Yogas as a guide, the goal of life is to become aware of the true nature of existence, which extends beyond the ephemeral existence of the body. After achieving full awareness of existence and integration of the body, mind, and soul (this often takes more than one incarnation as a person), the individual is ready for Moksa, the state of perfect existence. Moksa is oneness *with* God;

individualism is surrendered (in contrast to the Christian hope of living forever while maintaining an individual existence distinct from God). At this point, reincarnation ceases. From the *Bhagavad Gita*:

> *Worn out garments are shed by the body:*
> *Worn out bodies are shed by the dweller.*

Not all Hindus agree on the relationship of the caste system and reincarnation. Traditional Hindu thought holds that a person begins human life as a member of the lowest caste, then, if his or her behavior is good, is reincarnated into successively higher castes. However, some Hindus, especially in contemporary times, disavow the caste system, believing it has no relation to reincarnation.

Although the cow occupies a special place in Hindu society, all life is sacred to Hindus. Westerners might believe that Hindus regard cows in particular as sacred, but the Hindu perception of cows is predominantly a reflection of their belief that all living creatures are blessed.

Hinduism is not based so much on *appeasing* God, but on achieving eventual *oneness* with Him through correct behavior. The idea of a religion focusing on personal behavior and attitudes, which we have seen in Judaism and Hinduism, was to be further developed in Confucianism and Buddhism, the other great religion to spring from India. To my mind, the introduction of personal behavior into a religious context was a major advancement in the history of human thought.

The period after the Aryan invasion saw the creation of the works which would lead to Hinduism, but it also saw the loss of many of the hallmarks of civilization in India. The ability to write was remarkably lost, and people ceased to live in large communities. Writing and cities would not return to India until about 600 B.C.E., when a collection of settlements formed around the river Ganges. The principal city in this renaissance was Benares (also called Kasi or Kashi, and now called Varanasi). It was from the area of Benares, a sacred Hindu city, that Buddha began his preaching. With the similarities between Hinduism and Buddhism, it is no mystery that both arose in the same land.

The Wisdom of Ancestors

Like other civilizations of the Old World, the first sites in China arose near a river—the Yellow (or Huang He) river. Ancient Chinese civilization was rediscovered in the 1920s, that marvelous decade when King Tutankhamun's tomb, Ur, and Mohenjo-Daro were also excavated. Excavations at Anyang established the Shang Dynasty (around 1,700 B.C.E. to 1,027 B.C.E.) as the earliest Chinese civilization of which we have certain knowledge. (Chinese tradition speaks of an earlier period called the Hsia, which is now beginning to be archeologically defined, but we currently know almost nothing about this period.)

Ancient Chinese civilization exhibits several major differences from the civilizations discussed previously. In other cultures, cities appear to have arisen for trade or economic reasons. However, in China there is evidence that cities began as ritual centers, where leaders—with the wisdom of ancestors—mediated between Heaven and Earth. The past became crucial to their way of thinking, and the ability to communicate with and influence ancestors held the key to political power. Chinese people believed in a supreme god, called Shang Ti, but ancestor worship was the predominant religion in China throughout its history. The worship of both ancestors and a supreme god was not mutually exclusive. Indeed, the emperor's relationship with Shang Ti was a form of ancestor worship. He was thought to be a direct descendant of Shang Ti, and his authority came directly from his god-ancestor, not from his subjects. The emperor was responsible for worshiping and appeasing his great ancestor, by whose permission he governed. Thus, Chinese emperors were said to rule by the mandate of Heaven.

Oracle bones—usually tortoise shells or ox shoulder blades—were an important part of the rituals involving ancestors. The bone or carapace was indented and then heated. The resulting pattern of cracks was interpreted as revelations of the oracle. Writing adjacent to these cracks preserves the questions asked of the oracle and its responses.

Shang bronzes, among the most beautiful and detailed works of the ancient world, were inscribed with information concerning ancestors and were a crucial tool in rituals to communicate with them. The great Chinese book *I Ching* (also written *Yi-Ching*), which would become a cornerstone of Confucianism, began in Shang times as a compilation of writings used in divination. In Mesopotamian and Egyptian logo-syllabic writing, a sign could be used in three ways: as a literal picture, to convey a concept, or (in combination with other signs) for its phonetic value. Chinese writing was different; it was purely pictographic and had no logo-syllabic component. Although modified significantly over the centuries, contemporary Chinese writing remains somewhat similar to that of the Shang era, making Chinese the world's oldest continuous writing system. (Today, most Chinese signs couple a character conveying an idea with another indicating how the first character should be pronounced. This implies a phonetic element that was only rarely present in ancient writing, but contemporary Chinese is not a logo-syllabic writing.)

Like the Egyptians, the ancient Chinese discouraged change or the pursuit of explanations because it could potentially disturb their harmony with the universe. They did not seek to oppose or conquer nature, or particularly to understand it, but rather endeavored to live in equanimity with it—a key difference from other cultures and one central to understanding the course of Chinese history. Westerners are aware of a tradition of ancestor worship in China, but they fail to understand that it is part of a much larger heritage of living in harmony with the universe. Central to the idea of harmony was the concept that there is a connection between the mind and affairs of people and the workings of the cosmos.

The Shang dynasty was succeeded by the Chou (or Zhou) dynasty (1027 B.C.E. to 256 B.C.E.) During this period, specifically around the fifth century B.C.E., a small handful of thinkers radically and permanently altered Chinese civilization. Foremost among these was Kung Fu Tzu (c. 551–479 B.C.E., known in the West as Confucius). Confucius codified ideas already many centuries old. He was not a particularly original thinker and did not claim to possess special knowledge. He is said to have uttered "I am a transmitter and not a creator." He should not be regarded as the founder of a religion, but as a chronicler and preserver of existing ideas. In fact, China actually practiced Confucianism well before his birth. Confucius is revered, but he has never been deified.

Because the origins of Confucianism date to the beginning of civilization in China, ceremonies and rites are a major part of the religion. Confucianism is based not on any one work, but on five Classics. The first of these is the *I Ching*, the Book of Changes, which dates from Shang times, although it was added to and revised at several points in time. *I Ching* is a book of divination to which commentaries have been added. It is based on sixty-four hexagrams, each accompanied by a philosophical text. The book is consulted by casting lots six times to determine which hexagram is appropriate. The resulting message is expressed in terms of the philosophies of Yin (the force of darkness and secretiveness) and Yang (the force of brightness and effusiveness). Although they are opposites, Yin and Yang are partners in the creative process. They are inseparable, and everything is based on the mixing and alternations of these forces. Indeed, the Chinese concept of unanimity was based on the balance of opposing forces.

The other books pivotal to Confucianism are the *Shu Ching*, or Book of History (the earliest history of China); the *Shi Ching*, or Book of Odes (a collection of ballads and songs); the *Chun Chiu* (a history of the province that Confucius lived in); and the *Li Chi*, or Book of Rites (a collection of ceremonies from the Chou dynasty). In addition, the *Analects* is a compilation of Confucius's sayings written by his followers after his death.

Confucianism accepted and condoned the prevailing feudal order, but advocated more equitable treatment of people within that framework and advancement based on merit, not birth status. Confucius taught that each person has a duty to preserve traditions as a tribute to their sacred ancestors. Ritual, tradition, and personal virtue were the cornerstones of Confucianism. Kindness was important, but not to the extent of embracing the equality of all people. More than equality, Confucius called for concern for the welfare of all people.

Confucianism addresses practical issues of daily life and does not deal at all with deities or life after death. To the Westerner, religion implies a deity, which is not necessarily the case. Indeed, when Confucius was asked about a supreme being or an afterlife, it is said that he replied, "I know nothing of such things." This, of course, is a major difference from Christianity and Hinduism. The emphasis is completely on personal outlook and personal behavior. It is noteworthy that in the history of ancient China, without a supreme being to dogmatically hold as the essential aspect of life, holy wars were rare.

Confucius concluded that humanity, goodness, ritual, and moral virtues are the keys to a stable society and individual happiness. He had no use for progress or change. He recognized that there can be no good civilization without virtuous people, and teaching this simple idea made him one of the most influential people to ever live. His Golden Rule, "Do not do to others what you do not want them to do to you," predated the Christian Golden Rule by five centuries.

Meng-tzu (c. 371–289 B.C.E.; known by his Latinized name of Mencius) was an important follower of Confucius, and second only to the master himself in establishing and promulgating Confucianism. He authored *The Book of Mencius*, a pillar of the religion that insured its dominant position in China.

Taoism arose at roughly the same time as Confucianism. Taoism stresses passive submission to the Tao, the cosmic guiding force which insures the harmony of the universe. The Tao (meaning the Way) is the harmony that flows from the universe and is regarded by Taoists as the compass by which to navigate life.

Taoism is traditionally credited to Lao-Tzu, said to have been born in 604 B.C.E. However, the major book of Taoism, *Tao Te Ching* (*The Way of Virtue*), traditionally credited to Lao-Tzu, appears to have been written in the fourth century B.C.E. In all probability, Lao-Tzu never lived, lived later than is thought, or was not the author of the principal book of Taoism.

There is an aspect of Taoism concerned with deities (this aspect developed later and is not attributed to Lao-Tzu). However, most of Taoism is concerned with achieving the Tao without divine assistance, by means of meditation and the proper perspective on life.

Taoism advocated an outright denunciation of feudalism, believing that people could never reach their potential in a feudal society. Taoism also decreased the Confucian emphasis on family and ancestor worship. The Taoist assumes a non-aggressive posture, preferring to give up control, knowing that to control is often to fail to fully understand and to lose harmony. Taoism encourages relinquishing control of trivial daily events in order to gain control of one's life.

Although Taoism and Confucianism are clearly opposed in some areas, such as feudalism and ancestor worship, they have many similarities. In particular, Taoism and Confucianism both reflect the great Chinese desire for harmony rather than dominance (a great difference from the West). They are therefore best viewed as complementary, and throughout Chinese history there have been many individuals who have tried to be faithful to both doctrines.

The Chou period was followed by the period of the Warring States, which ended with the unification of China in 221 B.C.E. and the establishment of the Ch'in dynasty by an emperor named Shih Huang Ti (also written in English as Ch'in Shih Huang Ti or as Qin Shi Huangdi). Unification resulted in greater standardization of measures, laws, and language, as usually occurs in an empire. There was also some relaxation of feudalism, so common people had more social mobility. Shih Huang Ti is remembered and vilified in history for decreeing that all books, except for a few technical works, were to be burned. The books of Confucianism were a particularly favorite target, and Confucian scholars were killed by the hundreds.

The brief Ch'in dynasty (221–207 B.C.E.) was followed by the Han dynasty (206 B.C.E.–220 C.E.), during which the ideas of Confucius regained favor. After the Han dynasty, China again slipped into civil unrest and disunity. Yang Chien (541–604 C.E., known also as Sui Wen Ti) reunified the country in 589 C.E., establishing the Sui dynasty and instituting one of the most lasting policy changes in any country's history. Sui Wen Ti replaced the existing system of inheritance of government positions with the system of civil service examinations used in Han times but abandoned for centuries. Merit, not heredity, was once again the mechanism by which government posts were acquired. Since Confucianism was the official philosophy of the Han dynasty—the last orderly period in Chinese history—it became the basis for the civil service examinations of the sixth century C.E. and centuries thereafter. For the last two hundred years of the Chou dynasty, four hundred years of the Han dynasty, and from the sixth century C.E. until the advent of communism, the works of Confucius were held in high esteem in China. From the sixth century C.E., until quite recently, Confucianism was the model of the civil servant, and knowledge of Confucianism was required in civil service examinations. This emphasis on Confucianism may have inhibited innovation, but it resulted in many generations of excellent civic leaders.

In the second century B.C.E., Chinese traveled as far west as Persia, where they may have heard of the Greek civilization. By the time of Jesus, China was an empire with a population, size, and power that were comparable to Rome. We now know there was more contact between the East and the West in antiquity than had been thought, and it appears that a few Chinese knew of and had some contact with Rome. But the most significant connection between the great empires was indirect. China repulsed a tribe of nomadic central Asian horsemen called Hsiung Nu, who then migrated westward. Although the identity of this tribe is not completely established, it is probable that they became the tribe known in the West as the Huns, who applied pressure to the barbarians of northern Europe and nearly conquered Rome.

A few words on the scientific achievements of ancient China are in order. A decimal system was adopted in the Shang dynasty. By roughly the second century B.C.E., *Nine Chapters on Mathematical Art*, a treatise on algebra and geometry, was published. Around the same time, numerous treatises on medicine were available. The Chinese adopted a calendar based on a combination of solar and lunar periods with twelve lunar months and a leap month every two to three years.

The Chinese were marvelous observers of the heavens. They made the earliest recorded observation of Halley's comet in the seventh century B.C.E., produced a star map in the fourth century B.C.E., and made detailed observations of solar and lunar eclipses. We are indebted to them for recording a supernova in 1054 C.E., an event no one in Western Europe bothered to chronicle.

The single greatest Chinese invention was paper. The invention of paper is ascribed to Ts'ai Lun about 100 C.E. There is some uncertainty as to whether Ts'ai Lun invented paper or simply made its production more practical. Paper dating to two centuries before Ts'ai Lun has been found, but none has been found bearing writing until the time of Ts'ai Lun. In either case, Ts'ai Lun was responsible for making paper widely available as a writing medium. After a few centuries, knowledge of papermaking spread from China to the Muslims, and from the Muslims to Europe in the twelfth century C.E. Since there is no evidence of the independent invention of paper by either the Muslims or the Europeans, the modern world owes a profound debt to Chinese papermakers.

Chapter 4
Stories of Destruction

*Schliemann's Troy was actually a much older city
than the one of fable. But he had found the site and
fired the public's imagination for more than a
century.*

THE CIVILIZATION OF CRETE, CALLED MINOAN, was the first major civilization of the
Aegean area (the portion of the Mediterranean Sea between Greece and Turkey). The excavations of Arthur Evans (1851–1941) demonstrated that Minoan
culture reached its peak about 2,000 B.C.E., with remarkable achievements in
civil engineering, such as central drainage conduits and planned roads. Their
commerce included trade with the ancient Egyptians.

Minoan writing is a mystery that is still unfolding. They initially used a hieroglyphic script, replacing it later with non-hieroglyphic writing. Evans called the
latter script linear and further divided it into an older Linear A and a more recent
Linear B. Linear A is a truly Minoan script and still cannot be read. In it remain
locked the secrets of the Minoans and their origin. Evans was fascinated with
Linear B and spent his entire life attempting to decipher it. He was not successful,
but fate ironically permitted him, at the age of 85, to unknowingly meet the
person who would make the ancient language speak. In 1936, Evans met a
fourteen-year-old student named Michael Ventris (1922–1956). Ventris became
an architect, but he shared the older man's fascination with Linear B. In 1953,
using statistical techniques developed for code-breaking during World War II,
Ventris deciphered the language and showed that it was an early form of Greek.

About 1,450 B.C.E., Crete suffered a major cataclysm of some sort. A traditional theory is that a volcanic eruption on the adjacent island of Santorini (or
Thera) devastated Minoan culture, but recent evidence suggests that this eruption occurred about 1,650 B.C.E., indicating that the Minoans weathered the
eruption and perished two centuries later. While internal strife and devastation

51

by earthquake have not been completely excluded, most now favor an invasion of Mycenaeans, an ancient people who settled in Greece before what we consider classic Greek civilization. It was the Mycenaeans who left the Linear B writing on Crete for Ventris to decipher.

Mycenaean culture appears to have resulted from a union of indigenous Greek culture and Minoan influence. The Mycenaean civilization began about 1,600 B.C.E., and peaked about 1,300 B.C.E. Around 1,200 B.C.E., fires destroyed many of the Mycenaean centers, forcing a migration from the homeland to other places, including Crete. Whether these fires resulted from war or were the sequelae of an earthquake is not established.

Mycenaean interaction with another ancient culture has spawned centuries of intrigue and speculation. The city of Troy was located in present day Turkey just inland from the coast. Heinrich Schliemann (1822-1890), who also excavated Mycenae, fired the public imagination with his excavations of Troy from 1870-1890. Schliemann found ruins of many different cities on the same site, spanning some 1,500 years. These cities interacted with numerous other cultures, including Mycenae, and it seems certain that one of the cities on this site was the Troy of Homeric legend. Schliemann assumed that Homer's Troy was the oldest, and therefore the deepest of the sites; but in fact, the oldest sites predate the city of Priam and Hector by over a thousand years.

The person known as Homer is something of an historical curiousity. His name may encompass the work of many people, though some believe that all writing under his name shows a consistency of style best explained by a single author. Like Abraham and Hippocrates, Homer is a name given to a person who may not have lived or who may have been more than one person. The style of his work suggests an origin around the eighth century B.C.E. Said to be blind, Homer is credited with the *Iliad*, the story of the Trojan War, and the *Odyssey*, the travails of Odysseus after the war. Whether conceived by Homer or others, these stories were related in oral form before the Greek alphabet existed, and they were not written down until generations later. But, like many oral traditions and apocryphal stories of history, there seems to be considerable truth in Homer's *Iliad*. Although there is no definitive archeological proof that the Mycenaeans conquered Troy, Mycenaean pottery has been found at Troy, and artifacts from Mycenae leave no doubt that it was a militaristic culture. It therefore seems very likely that the Mycenaeans besieged Troy, probably for control of trade routes rather than to reclaim a princess. So the Mycenaeans were probably involved in the destruction of two other cultures, and a blind poet with a phenomenal memory may be one of our greatest historians.

Chapter 5
The White Man Will Never Be Alone

A chief accepts fate, and speaks quietly about the world that will be no more.

IT SEEMS CLEAR THAT ASIANS MIGRATED TO AMERICA thousands of years ago via the then-continuous Bering Strait. (Today, we can show similarity between Native American DNA and that of some Asians.) At one time, this was thought to have been a single migration, occurring at the end of the last ice age, some 12,000 years ago. Now most investigators believe there were multiple migrations, some perhaps as far back as 40,000 years ago. After the last ice age ended, melting ice raised sea level, closing the land bridge and isolating the Americas.

Migrating all the way down to the tip of South America, these native Americans established hundreds of unique cultures, including the well-known Aztec, Maya, and Inca cultures. Unlike the first civilizations of the Old World, civilizations in the New World were not so clearly centered around rivers.

All societies of antiquity had the wheel, with the apparent exception of Native American cultures. Even here, there is some room for debate, since the wheel has been found in toys in Mesoamerica (contemporary Mexico and Central America). Because toys mimic the macroenvironment, it appears likely that the people of the New World understood the principle of the wheel, but chose not to apply it. The wheel assumed its primary importance when attached to a draft animal, and it is possible that the wheel was not utilized in the New World because the lack of a suitable animal diminished its usefulness. In addition, most of the North American cultures did not have a well-developed network of roads, and the effectiveness of the wheel is sharply diminished on rough terrain.

The pre-Columbian Western Hemisphere was a land of astonishing diversity. At least three hundred languages were spoken in the New World. Few

53

realize, or stop to think, that there were many more cultures and greater cul-tural diversity in Pre-Columbian America than in Europe. This may explain why Native Americans were more tolerant and trusting of Europeans than the reverse: they were not shocked by diversity. While each of these cultures had a slightly different view of the world, all shared a harmony with and reverence for nature that still eludes the white man.

The cultures of Mesoamerica are often grouped together because of their geo-graphic proximity and because they shared a similar social structure, with more rigid classes than North American native cultures. The first established culture of the Mesoamerica was the Olmec civilization, on what is now the eastern coast of Mexico, some three hundred miles (five hundred kilometers) from contemporary Mexico City. Flourishing between 1,200 B.C.E. and 400 B.C.E., the Olmecs are regarded as the mother culture of Mesoamerica because their influence is widely evident in the Mesoamerican cultures that followed them. Noted for their out-standing sculpture, particularly of giant heads, the Olmecs devised a calendar and may have begun to develop an incipient hieroglyphic writing.

The Zapotecs flourished from 600 B.C.E. to the mid-eighth century C.E. in what is today southern Mexico. Their principal city and capital for 1,200 years was Monte Alban, built on top of a leveled-off mountain. The Zapotecs were skilled in the working of precious stones and metals, and their hieroglyphics were the first functional writing in the New World.

The city of Teotihuacan was a separate culture, flourishing between 100 B.C.E. and 750 C.E., and located some twenty-five miles (forty kilometers) from con-temporary Mexico City. Its name (meaning "place of the gods") was given to it by awed Aztecs when they came upon its ruins. With a population of greater than 100,000 people, Teotihuacan was the largest city of pre-Columbian America and one of the largest in the world. Although Teotihuacan consisted of only one principal city, settlements surrounded it for some distance, and its geographic area of influence was vast. Teotihuacan came to a mysterious, fiery end about 750 C.E., apparently a victim of war.

The Maya culture peaked from 300–900 C.E. and was centered in the Yucatan peninsula. In 1839, John Lloyd Stephens gave us a nearly poetic description of the Maya ruins at Copan:

> Architecture, sculpture, and painting, all of the arts which embellish life, had flourished in this overgrown forest; orators, warriors, and states-men, beauty, ambition, and glory, had lived and passed away, and none knew that such things had been, or could tell of their past existence.

The Maya had the most scientifically advanced culture of the pre-Columbian New World. Their calendar system had three calendars running concurrently—a 365-day solar calendar, a 260-day calendar used for the observance of certain rituals, and a calendar referred to as the long count. The long count is of most interest to historians because it was the calendar used in Maya writing. The Maya perceived time as occurring in Great Cycles, and the long count recorded the time since the beginning of the last great cycle. Each great cycle lasted for slightly over 5,100 years. The current great cycle began, in our terms, August 13, 3114 B.C.E., and will end December 23, 2012. Our knowledge of Maya timekeeping allows us to precisely correlate dates mentioned in their writing with our calendar.

Maya mathematics was vigesimal (based on twenty), and incorporated a symbol for zero. They probably were the first culture in the world to have a completely developed concept of zero, although the history of zero is difficult to fully understand because many cultures grasped some, but not all, of the advantages that such a symbol offered.[2] The Maya were serious and capable observers of the sky, and they often recorded their observations in writing.

Maya writing can now be partially understood, principally through the work of Yuri Knorosov (1922–). Knorosov, working without the benefit of visiting Maya sites, recognized that some apparently unrelated glyphs shared common elements, indicating that there was a phonetic component to the Maya language. Thus, Maya emerged as a logo-syllabic writing system based on principles similar to those of Mesopotamia and Egypt. However, Maya writing is more complex and is still not completely understood.

Contrary to popular belief, the Maya were actually quite violent and warlike. Mutually destructive struggles between Maya cities were commonplace, beginning as ritual warfare and progressing to outright campaigns of conquest, where leaders of the losing city were sacrificed by the victors.

By 900 C.E., most of the major Maya cities had been abandoned. The cause of the decline of the Maya has never been fully established but almost surely involves internal decay rather than external conquest. There is evidence of overpopulation, excessive destruction of forests with inadequate land for agriculture, and damage to the culture from internal warfare. Some believe a drought exacerbated the other problems. It seems safe to conclude that the Maya's enemy was themselves, and their self-destruction teaches a lesson to all succeeding cultures who will but listen.

It should be noted that although the Maya cities are no more, Maya culture

---

* See Notes starting on page 502.

remains. These are not an extinct people. Their culture has survived continuing European persecution (which continues to this day in Guatemala), but it has not perished.

The Toltec culture flourished from roughly 900 C.E. to 1200 C.E. Teotihuacan declined from the mid-eighth century, and the Maya began to decline shortly thereafter, creating a vacuum in which the Toltecs could assume dominance of Mesoamerica. The Toltecs themselves began to decline about 1200 C.E., for unclear reasons, leaving another vacuum, which the Aztecs would fill.

The Aztecs flourished from about 1300 C.E. until the Spanish conquest (completed in 1520). They occupied what is now the central part of Mexico, and their principal city was Tenochtitlan (not to be confused with Teotihuacan, which was a separate and earlier culture). The relationship between the Aztecs and the Toltecs is unclear. In all probability, the Aztecs did not descend from the Toltecs in the strict sense, but they understood and respected Toltec traditions, and some of their rulers appear to have had Toltec ancestors.

The story of the Spanish conquest of the Aztecs is well known. Sailing from Cuba in 1519, Hernando Cortes (1485–1547; also known as Hernan Cortez) and his men arrived in central Mexico at precisely the time that Aztec legends foretold the return of the god Quetzalcoatl. Aided by the perception of some (but not all) Aztecs that he was a god and by the assistance of other Native American cultures chafing under Aztec domination, Cortes wiped a civilization from the earth in the name of God, gold, and a king.

Contemporary Peru was home to many cultures that predated the Inca. The Chavin culture flourished from 1000 B.C.E. to 200 B.C.E. The Chavin are noted for their stone sculpture, pottery, and the earliest gold working in the New World. The Moche lived on the north coast of Peru from the beginning of the Christian era until about 700 C.E. The Nazca (or Nasca) inhabited the south of Peru from 200 B.C.E. to 600 C.E. and produced the famous Nazca lines, which extend for many miles in the desert and have provoked a variety of contemporary interpretations, the most bizarre of which involve extraterrestrial visitors. The Sican culture was prominent from 700 C.E. to 1400 C.E. The Sican were the greatest metalworkers in the pre-Columbian New World and were even able to make and use a bronze derived from copper and arsenic. The Sican fell to the Chimu people, who flourished from 900 C.E. until they were conquered by the Inca around 1470.

The Inca (or Inka) civilization began in what is now Peru, and for most of their history, their capital remained near the city of Cuzco. In the fifteenth century, a sudden acquisition of new territory extended the empire into what is now Ecuador, Bolivia, Chile, and Argentina. At its height, the Inca empire covered over 2,500 miles (4,000 kilometers)—the largest in pre-Columbian America. The Inca relied on cultural accretion as much as military conquest, and they permitted the people they conquered to hold their existing religious beliefs, knowing that in time they would probably convert to Inca beliefs. The Inca were masters of textile arts and stone working, and they created a network of roads throughout their empire. Encompassing 15,000 miles (24,000 kilometers), Inca roads surpassed anything in Europe at that time. (For comparison, the Roman Empire, which existed for a much longer time and employed metal and the wheel, built roads which were perhaps 50,000 kilometers in length.) Inca stonemasons used no mortar, but their joints were so perfect that one cannot pass a sheet of paper between adjacent stones. The Inca made use of symbols woven into textiles and recorded numbers as knots on strings. Their language, Quechua, is still spoken by several million people. The Inca empire flourished for only about a century, from its full bloom in the early fifteenth century until the Spanish conquest in 1532.

Like Cortes, Francisco Pizarro (c.1471–1541) ran into some good fortune. First, he and his small Spanish garrison arrived in 1532, immediately after the conclusion of a civil war, the result of which was that the Inca king Atahualpa sat on the throne of a significantly weakened empire. Second, Atahualpa failed to strike decisively at the Spanish as they approached the Incan city of Cajamarca, and it was here that the Spanish captured him. In Inca society, all authority and power was in the hands of the king, called the Inca. With the Inca (the man) captured, the Inca (the culture) were not able to respond. Pizarro took full advantage of this by installing a puppet Inca, preserving the fabric of the culture, but under his terms. The Inca passed into history, as the Aztec had done thirteen years before.

The decimation of the North American native cultures is a story of cruelty and ignorance. Some of the natives lost their lives from contact with diseases to which they had no immunity, but many were deliberately killed by the Europeans.

Few people realize that many celebrated heroes in early American history were prominent in the near genocidal treatment of Native Americans. In 1838, the Indian Removal Act resulted in the forcible removal of the Cherokees from their homeland, after which they were made to march 1,200 miles (1,900 kilometers) to Oklahoma—a march called the Trail of Tears. The architect of this tragedy was called Sharp Knife by the Indians. The Americans called him Andrew Jackson. Kit Carson, idolized by many school children, subjected the Navajo to a similar fate in the infamous Long Walk in 1864. Every tribe was massacred, relocated, or both. Native American children were forced into boarding schools, where every effort was made to crush their heritage and "Americanize" them. More than half of the cultures of North America were permanently destroyed, their languages forever lost. It is a tragedy of history—one repeated over and again—that one culture can destroy another if it is more technologically advanced. The Europeans and their American descendants, *who had technology*, destroyed the Aztecs, the Inca, and the native people of North America; they removed fourteen million people from Africa in chains. These societies had as great or greater cultures but less technology. The Nazi decimation of the Jews is another such example. The systematic destruction of the Amazon rain forest and its indigenous peoples is a contemporary example.

The common denominator in all of these situations is the belief in what the mathematician and historian Jacob Bronowski called absolute knowledge—the concept that there can be no other culture and no other viewpoint that is worth preserving. This belief is often associated with a belief in God and the opinion that there is only one set of meritorious religious beliefs. With deference to the benefits of religion, a study of history evokes the conclusion that religion can lead, if it is not practiced carefully and with humanism, to a tragic dogmatism that can result the destruction of whole cultures—and the individualism upon which our progress depends.

If human history is full of holocausts and tragedies, it is also full of courage. In 1854 the Duwamish Chief Sealth, facing the extinction of his people, said:

> Every part of this soil is sacred in the estimation of my people. Every hillside, every valley, every plain, and grove has been hallowed by some sad or happy event in days long vanished. The very dust upon which you now stand responds more lovingly to their footsteps than to yours because it is rich with the blood of our ancestors.
>
> Even the little children who lived here and rejoiced here for a brief season will love these somber solitudes and at eventide they greet shadowy returning spirits and when the last redman shall have perished and the memory of my tribe shall have become a myth among the white men, these shores will swarm with the invisible dead of my tribe. And when your children's children think themselves alone in the field, the store, the shop, upon the highway, or in the silence of the pathless woods, they will

not be alone. At night when the streets of your cities and villages are silent and you think them deserted, they will throng with the returning hosts that once filled and still loves this beautiful land. The white man will never be alone.

In thirty years, the work of the Europeans will be completed. By that time the rainforests will be completely destroyed and all of the traditional people living in them will be dead or assimilated. Within thirty years, we will find out what kind of people we are.

Chapter 6
The Rise of the Individual

A young prince preaches the simplest message ever delivered and becomes the most influential person of his time.

As Kenneth Clark says in *Civilization*, there are certain exciting periods of history when the collective consciousness of humanity seems to leap forward at a much greater rate. One of these was 3,000 B.C.E., when so much of what we consider civilization took form in multiple areas of the world. We were collectively defined at that time; we would be individually defined later. Another noteworthy period was the beginning of the Renaissance, approximately 1100 C.E. With the current explosion in both information and methods of gathering information, we may be at a similar crossroads today.

Such was the period around 500 B.C.E., when three established civilizations simultaneously and independently took giant leaps of thought, and the individual became much more fully defined. The sixth century B.C.E. asked basic questions about three areas central to the human experience: God, understanding the world, and the place of authority. These questions, and their answers, shook the foundations of civilization and established much of who we are. We have seen that around this time both Confucianism and Taoism appeared in China. We will consider the Greek miracle shortly, but we begin in India, already the birthplace of Hinduism.

Four Noble Truths

In the sixth century B.C.E., there was a renaissance in India, centered around the Ganges River area. In the Himalayan foothills, a young prince named Siddhartha Gautama (c. 563–483 B.C.E.) left his family at the age of 29 to become a wondering ascetic. This young prince developed the philosophy of life which earned him the name of Buddha (the enlightened one or awakened one) and his movement the name of Buddhism. Buddhism was the first of the world's religions to be based largely on the thinking of one person (Confucius being largely a codifier and recorder of long-existing religious beliefs in China, and Judaism and Hinduism not being identified with any one individual). Originally, Buddhism was more likely intended to be a re-synthesis of Hinduism than a separate religion, but in the hands of those who followed Buddha, it became a fully formed and well-established new religion. Even today, there is a remarkable similarity between Buddhism and Hinduism.

Buddha felt there had to be a way to escape from the endless cycles of birth, a life of pain and desire, death, and rebirth. Although he did not deny the existence of deities, he believed they could not help a person escape this cycle because they too had to die and be reborn. Because it is the craving for more that leads to perpetual rebirth, one must detach from desire.

The essence of Buddhism begins with the four noble truths, which are simply statements of reality. The first is that unhappiness is a fact of life. The second is that there are identifiable causes of unhappiness—dissatisfaction with reality, the craving for more, and attachment to material possessions. The third is that relief from unhappiness is possible by accepting reality and ceasing to desire more. The fourth noble truth is that the mechanism for this relief is the 8-fold path.

The 8-fold path is generally written in English in the following way, although it must be remembered that some of the specific words may not be a precise translation (specifically, the word "right" is only an English approximation):

Right views: This pertains to the optimal understanding of the above situation, namely that there is unhappiness, that it comes from desire and dissatisfaction with what is, and that there can be relief.

Right intent: This is the determination to pursue that which is important to us, and to continue that pursuit through every storm and distraction.

Right speech: This is not only speaking the truth and speaking charitably, but also examining why we have spoken unkind or false words.

Right conduct: This is behaving with kindness and charity. Specifically, there are five prohibitions: killing, stealing, lying, adultery, and the use of intoxicants or mind altering substances (the point of the fifth prohibition is to keep the mind clear). Notice the substantial similarity of these five prohibitions to some of the Ten Commandments of Christianity.

Right livelihood: This is engaging in an occupation that promotes kindness, charity, and life.

Right effort: This is the understanding that persistence is an important part of life. Happiness comes more quickly to one who paces himself and shows determination.

Right mindfulness: Buddhism deeply believes in the power of the mind. It advocates extensive self-examination to achieve self-awareness. But more than this, right mindfulness is being aware of and attentive to all of reality, just as it is, without craving or aversion.

Right concentration: These are the physical and mental exercises to focus the mind, remove superficialities, and see the truth.

Through the four noble truths and 8-fold path, Buddhism strives for a middle way that rejects both extreme asceticism and worldliness. Buddhism arose in the midst of a powerful and deeply held caste system and took the radical position that people of all castes were equal and were equally capable of enlightenment. This egalitarianism is a major similarity to Christianity and Islam. Through the mechanism of the 8-fold path, Buddhists believe that it is possible to achieve Nirvana, which is not just a state of happiness. Nirvana is more properly defined as the state where individual consciousness becomes inseparable from all consciousness. In Nirvana, there is an absence of desire and longing, and a blending of the self into the universe. Nirvana is somewhat similar to the concept of Moksa in Hinduism, but it is not dependent on a deity.

The single overriding aspect of Buddhism most immediately applicable to our daily lives is the concept that unhappiness generally derives from constant wanting, that there is always something that needs to be fixed. Buddhism asks us not to think in terms of "if only": if only this were true; if only that were not true.

Like Hinduism and Confucianism, there is no one text for Buddhism. Perhaps the greatest collection of Buddhist thinking is the *Dhammapada*, the sayings of Buddha recorded after his death. (Buddha himself never wrote down his ideas.) The 423 verses of the *Dhammapada* are the earliest collections of Buddha's teachings and present life from a tranquil Eastern perspective. I think every

Westerner should read the *Dhammapada*. It is a small work whose pages truly sing of the simple truths that are the basis of happiness. From the first verse:

> *We are what we think*
> *All that we are arises with our thoughts.*
> *With our thoughts we make the world.*
> *Speak or act with an impure mind*
> *And trouble will follow you*
> *As the wheel follows the ox that draws the cart.*

From subsequent verses:

> *Your worst enemy cannot harm you as much as your own thoughts unguarded. But once mastered, no one can help you as much, not even your own mother or father.*
>
> *It is better to conquer yourself than to win a thousand battles.*
>
> *How easy it is to see another's faults, but how hard to face your own. Dwelling on another's faults multiplies your own.*
>
> *Resist the desire to hurt until the sorrows vanish.*
>
> *Hate never dispels hate; only love dispels hate. A Master never returns evil for evil.*
>
> *Speak the truth, give whatever you can, never be angry.*
>
> *The fragrance of virtue travels even against the wind.*

Like Confucianism, Buddhism is not inherently a deity-based religion but focuses on individual thinking and behavior. (It is sometimes said that Buddhism attempts to achieve the absence of Self, while Confucianism attempts to achieve a socially oriented Self.) Individual Buddhists may or may not believe in a supreme being, or in an afterlife, but the emphasis is on the human mind and human behavior in this world. Indeed, Confucianism and Buddhism, roughly contemporary, differ from all of the major currently practiced religions in the world today by not postulating a deity or a belief in an afterlife. Like Confucianism (and unlike Christianity and Islam), Buddhism has not left a history of holy wars and forced conquests in its wake. How different might the course of Western Civilization have been if we had embraced Buddhism or Confucianism rather than the deity-based religions of Judaism, Christianity, and Islam?

Just as the reunification of China in the sixth century caused a resurgence of Confucianism, the conversion to Buddhism of an Indian ruler dramatically transformed its scope and history. Alexander the Great's empire extended into northwestern and central India. After his death in 323 B.C.E., India (like the rest of his kingdom) was without an effective government. In this vacuum, Chandragupta Maurya established hegemony over most of India and founded the Mauryan Empire. Chandragupta's grandson, Ashoka (sometimes written in English as Asoka), ruler of the Mauryan Empire in the third century B.C.E., converted to Buddhism and made it the state religion of India. This transformed Buddhism from a local religion of northwest India to the religion of the entire Mauryan Empire, dramatically increasing its followers. The Mauryan Empire faded soon after Ashoka's death, but his influence on the growth of Buddhism remained. Although there are few Buddhists in India today, many Buddhist beliefs were incorporated into Hinduism, and the influence of Buddhism in contemporary India is much greater than the number of followers might indicate.

Today, there are a number of different expressions of Buddhism. Like all religions, Buddhism is a family of related beliefs, not a single doctrine. The original form of Buddhism is called Theravada and is practiced predominantly in Southeast Asia, Sri Lanka, and Burma. A slightly newer version, called Mahayana, is common in Korea, Japan, and China. Relative to Theravada Buddhism, Mahayana places more emphasis on service to other people, stresses kindness more than wisdom, and stipulates that there are no separate entities—every person and every object is part of the whole. Tibetan Buddhism has a number of unique attributes, such as the way in which its spiritual leader, the Dalai Lama, is chosen. Zen Buddhism de-emphasizes ritual, scripture, and images. It differs from other types of Buddhism by having no particular set of beliefs, attempting instead to examine the inner self through meditation and attention to all aspects of everyday life. The heritage and influence of prince Siddhartha has indeed been great.

The Comprehensibility of the World

The third great development in fifth century B.C.E. was the rise of classical Greek civilization. Much is unclear about the origins of Greece. It is known that there were two centers of Bronze Age civilization in the Aegean—the island of Crete, and Mycenae on the mainland—but Greek civilization had to begin anew after they fell.

Traditional teaching has been that about 1,200 B.C.E., the Dorians invaded Greece, possibly destroying Mycenae (which may have declined from internal reasons or natural disaster) and causing a dark age that persisted until about 800 B.C.E. We no longer have confidence that events were this simple. There was a relative dark age in Greece after the fall of Mycenae (the ability to write was lost and the use of iron appears to be the only advance during this period of Mycenaean culture), but it is not firmly established that it was caused by a military invasion rather than a more peaceful influx of Dorians.

Like other civilizations of antiquity, Greece began as a number of autonomous city-states, which would be self-sufficient, poorly cooperative, and often combative throughout Greek history. The archaic period (circa 800 B.C.E. to 500 B.C.E.) saw the re-establishment of a high culture, which would eventuate in the classic period of Greece, as exemplified by Athens in the fifth century B.C.E.

Traditionally, it is often held that organized science suddenly appeared in Greek colonies in the Eastern Aegean in the sixth century B.C.E. (these colonies are collectively called Ionia.) However, there are many examples of rational thinking in all points in history, back to Chauvet cave. The construction of pyramids and ziggurats as well as the achievements discussed earlier indicate that science did not suddenly materialize in one time and place. In fact, the words "suddenly" and "history" rarely belong together. In preparing this work, I was struck by how often existing literature holds that some development "suddenly" appeared, or "burst" upon the scene. Dissection of these events invariably finds a much longer period of development—most revolutions are evolutions.

However, the old notion that an organized search for general principles of science began in earnest in Ionia around 600 B.C.E. is substantially true. However impressive the achievements and observations before 600 B.C.E. might have been, there was no systematic attempt to explain natural phenomena. It was left to the Greek people to conceive an organized system of scientific principles that could attempt to explain the universe.

The Greeks had little use for practical measurements, and because they were a slave society, they had little use for technological innovations, or for anything which would diminish manual labor. Their progress was in abstract thought.

We do not know the precise causes of the Greek advances, but three separate incidents occurred roughly simultaneously in the Aegean and may have contributed to their quantum leap—the adaptation and modification of the

Phoenician alphabet, extensive colonization, and the acquisition of papyrus as a writing medium.

Although the Phoenicians had invented the alphabet, it was an alphabet of consonants only; it could not be used to write an Indo-European language. By the mid-eighth century B.C.E. the Greeks had added vowels, making possible the transcription of Indo-European languages, of which Greek was one. The ability to write, lost since the fall of Mycenae, was regained.

The Greeks colonized areas both east and west of the mainland, probably because of population pressure at home. It is the colonies in the eastern portion of the Aegean, in and near present day Turkey, which concern us now. In these colonies, called Ionia, the Greeks came into contact with other cultures. Foremost among these were the Lydians, a powerful kingdom in the middle of the first millennium B.C.E., in present-day Turkey. The Lydians conquered the Ionian colonies, with the exception of Miletus, located on what is now the shore of southwest Turkey. The Lydians generally were benevolent rulers, and their occupation seems to have been more a time of cultural exchange than a conqueror-conquered relationship. The Greeks clearly obtained ideas in music, literature, and economics from the Lydians. Moreover, through the Lydians, the Greek Ionian colonies gained knowledge of the Asiatic world. Although a besieged and generally conquered people, the Ionian colonies enjoyed a cross-fertilization of ideas that mainland Greeks did not have; this was a factor in what is called the Ionian miracle. Throughout history, a union of cultures generally provides more fertile soil for ideas, even if the relationship of the cultures involved is not one of equality.

The Greeks acquired papyrus from their colonies' contact with Egypt. By obtaining a much more convenient and practical writing medium, the Greeks were able to take full advantage of their alphabet. The Egyptians, because of their commitment to an unchanging world, presumably were unable to capitalize on the advantage of papyrus.

A convenient method of writing has been a key in many periods of advancement. The invention of writing in the fourth millennia B.C.E., the development of Papyrus, the discovery of paper, the invention of the printing press, and now the advent of computers have all made the dissemination of ideas more practical. It is the single most important factor in the advancement of our species.

But there must also have been something in the air of Greek society that encouraged ideas to develop—a belief that people had control over their lives, a willingness to change the status quo. There had to be the courage to explore the unknown. The ebb and flow of civilization is the fluctuation of comfort and courage. There have been a handful of times in our history when human courage has risen to the fore and made us who we are. One such time was the development of agriculture, another was the ancient Greek belief that the world was comprehensible.

The Greek tradition of scholarship began with three remarkable thinkers from the colonies in Ionia. Thales (c. 640–546 B.C.E.), from the Ionian city of Miletus, is regarded as the beginning of the Ionian miracle. Thales is an historical enigma; there are no surviving writings attributed to him, but is seems clear that his sayings and teachings stimulated people to believe that the processes of the world had rational causes. Anaximander (c. 611–546 B.C.E.) and Anaximenes (c. 585–528 B.C.E.) followed Thales. Like Thales, their original writings have not endured, so their precise contributions are unclear. But history reasonably credits these three Ionian thinkers with initiating the search for unifying scientific principles. All three believed that the world was composed of one principal material (although they differed as to the nature of this material), and that it was the separation of this material into different portions that resulted in the form of the world. Following these three, the Greek miracle seems to have spread from the eastern colonies to the mainland, principally to Athens, in the fifth century B.C.E. Greece produced countless innovative thinkers, a few of which we will consider.

Pythagoras (c. 582 B.C.E.–500 B.C.E.) was born on the island of Samos, in Ionia, where he undoubtedly fell under the influence of the three great Ionian scholars. He traveled widely before settling in a Greek colony in southern Italy. Pythagoras is important not only for the theorem that bears his name (which was already known in the Middle East and was probably given to Pythagoras during his travels there), but also for the society he founded. The Pythagoreans believed the universe and everything in it could be explained through numbers. Their greatest success was geometry, which was the pinnacle of Greek mathematics. Pythagoras originated (or more likely, partially borrowed from the neo-Babylonians in the Middle East) the relationship between mathematics and music that would allow music to develop into the form we know today. (For example, all other factors being equal, a string that is half the length of another will produce a sound one octave higher.)

Hippocrates of Chios (fl. c. 460 B.C.E.; not to be confused with the physician Hippocrates) was the greatest mathematician of his time. He was the first to require that each step in the solution of a problem or theorem be proven. He wrote the first treatise on geometry and influenced Euclid.

Democritus (c. 460–370 B.C.E.) developed the atomic theory (i.e., the belief that all matter is made of atoms), which had been put forth earlier by Leucippus of Miletus. Democritus not only believed in atoms, but believed they were in perpetual motion (they are). The latter idea was a leap of understanding in its own right, and meant that Democritus also perceived the concept of inertia. Democritus's idea that all matter is composed of constantly moving atoms was astonishingly ahead of its time—and very close to the contemporary view. Sadly, the atomic theory of Democritus was not followed up upon by others. Although it would be wrong to believe there was no thinking about atoms after Democritus (there was some feeling that matter might have indivisible building blocks throughout the Greco-Roman world, and again from about 1100 C.E.), the failure to follow Democritus's work in a systematic manner made a workable atomic theory impossible until Dalton in the early nineteenth century. Part of the explanation for this is that Democritus was opposed to religion, thus bringing its wrath not only upon himself, but also upon his ideas. How wonderful it would have been if the work of Democritus could have survived alongside that of Aristotle.

Hippocrates (c. 460–377 B.C.E.) is thought of as the founder of medicine. There is some question as to whether Hippocrates was a real person or a composite figure. In any event, he, or the group of people under his name, freed medicine from religion and superstition. This is the first step to progress in all areas. Hippocrates's most famous doctrine (although probably not original with him) was that of the four humors—blood, phlegm, white bile, and black bile. Excess or deficiency of one or more of these humors was thought to be the cause of disease. This theory was an outgrowth of the general Greek metaphysical view of the world, namely that of four basic elements (earth, air, fire, and water), causing four basic qualities (cold, dry, hot, and moist, respectively). Each person had his or her own particular blend of the four humors, and this blend was susceptible to changes during the seasons. It does not matter that this belief was no more accurate than preceding beliefs. What matters is that the new opinions were based on a rational thought process and therefore much easier to modify. Beliefs based on the will of gods are held indefinitely, or at least until those gods go out of favor. Ideas based on evidence can be changed as soon as there is new evidence. This would be a hallmark of the Greek contribution to science. Their beliefs were not particularly accurate, but by developing a process, they made further progress possible. The *Corpus Hippocraticum* is the collection of his (or their) works, and furnished medicine with a scientific approach. One section of the *Corpus* deals with case studies, in which individual patients are described and followed in a manner very similar to that used today.

Greek medicine had coexisting rational and intuitive approaches (as we do today). Alongside the Hippocratic approach was cult of Asclepios (or Aesculapius). The son of Apollo in Greek mythology, Asclepios was the God of healing. Temples to his honor were common in Greece, and as an alternative to the developing analytical method, some patients went to these temples for elaborate rituals thought to have curative power.

Socrates (470–399 B.C.E.) is an enigmatic figure. He left no writings, so we know nothing of him except what his student Plato disclosed. Socrates taught that people must examine their behavior and he attempted to focus intellectual activity on determining what is ethical behavior. Plato tells us that Socrates taught by asking questions intended to draw out the student and guide him to a conclusion. (The name "Socratic" is given to this form of teaching.)

Plato (c. 427–347 B.C.E.) was actually named Aristocles, but was given his nickname (meaning broad) by a wrestling coach because of his stout build. A student of Socrates, he was influenced by Pythagoras and was the teacher of Aristotle. He founded the Academy in Athens, which can be thought of as the first university, and left numerous writings in the form of dialogues, the best known of which is *The Republic*.

In *The Republic*, Plato discussed government, advocating that leaders be selected from the most talented young people and specially trained for their roles. Although Plato felt that women could make good leaders—an unprecedented opinion for the time—he did not advocate true egalitarianism, nor did he support democracy. He believed leaders should wield absolute power—provided they use it wisely—and insisted that they be well-trained and benevolent scholars. From *The Republic*:

> The state will be ruled well when philosophers become kings and kings become philosophers.

Plato argued that leaders cannot simply be a reflection of their people. Rather, they must transcend the abilities of the people. Although we would certainly modify Plato's ideas to reflect egalitarianism and democracy, *The Republic* does have contemporary application. Our politicians would be much more effective if they sought to more fully understand the nature of the problems they address rather than merely reflecting their constituents' wishes.

Aristotle (384–322 B.C.E.) was one of the most influential thinkers in history and a guiding light for intellectual development for fifteen centuries. Perhaps his greatest work was in biology; many do not realize that this phenomenally influential person was first and foremost a botanist and a zoologist. Aristotle left wonderfully accurate descriptions of innumerable plants and animals. The general Greek approach to obtaining new insight was to speculate and theorize. (This was the first scientific method.) Systematic observation was rare; by employing it, Aristotle attained a scientific method not to be achieved again in the Western world for fifteen hundred years.

He was born in Macedonia and came to Athens to study with Plato at the Academy. After the latter died, Aristotle was unwelcome in Athens because of his Macedonian origins. Returning to his homeland, he became tutor to prince Alexander. When the thirteen-year-old prince inherited his father's kingdom (which already included Athens and which he was to greatly expand), Aristotle returned to Athens and founded his own school, the Lyceum. There, he taught during long walks with his students. (Hence the name peripatetics, meaning to walk around, for the followers of Aristotle.) Aristotle was more interested in science than Plato, and the Lyceum reflected this interest. After the death of Alexander the Great, as his pupil became known, Aristotle was again unwelcome in Athens and forced to flee.

Aristotle believed that the universe consisted of eight concentric spheres revolving around the earth. Like many educated Greeks, he was aware of the sphericity of the earth, and like Plato, he seems to have accepted the atomic theory of matter. He understood that objects at rest will remain so unless a force acts on them—the first steps toward an understanding of what we now call inertia.

Aristotle was a major developer of the reasoning process, and he conceived the science of logic as we know it. He developed the syllogism, an argument consisting of two related statements which force a proposition (i.e., only people can read books; Susan can read a book, so Susan must be a person). More than any other person, Aristotle is to be thanked for the knowledge of how to reason. He understood that the way to know is to understand the causes of processes. His invention of logic, his understanding of causation, his observations, and his stimulation of thought defined the first scientific method.

As we shall see, much of the history of the world is based on erroneous

Aristotelian thought, but this must not be held against him. The culprit was the collective Western mind, which took almost two thousand years to extend his work. He taught us how to think, but for nearly two thousand years, we failed to do so. Near-deification of great thinkers is a disservice to them and to us because it impedes continued investigation.

Theophrastos (372–286 B.C.E.), a pupil of Aristotle, took over the directorship of the Lyceum when the latter fled Athenian hostility. The greatest botanist of antiquity, his books, *History of Plants* and *Causes of Plants,* imparted a knowledge of the classification, reproduction, and medicinal uses of plants that was not surpassed until the Renaissance.

Aristarchus (c. 310–230 B.C.E.) formulated a heliocentric model of the universe (with the sun at the center) 2,000 years before Copernicus. This was displaced by Aristotle's geocentric model, and the earth was thought to be the center of the universe for many centuries.

Superb observers, educated ancient Greeks were well aware of the roundness of the earth. They recognized that different constellations are visible at different latitudes; the mast of an approaching ship is visible before the lower portions; and the earth's shadow is always round during lunar eclipses. (An elliptical shadow would be expected from a disk-shaped Earth.) But it was an extraordinary triumph of observation and reason when Eratosthenes (286–194 B.C.E.) calculated its circumference with exceptional cleverness and accuracy. Unfortunately, these great ideas—the roundness of the earth, atomic theory, and heliocentrism—would be lost to history.

Hipparchus (c. 190–120 B.C.E.) developed the concepts of latitude and longitude, estimated the distance to the moon with 90% accuracy, divided stars into six classes according to their brightness, and developed a catalog of some one thousand stars. The most influential astronomer of his day, he preferred Aristotle's geocentric model of the universe to Aristarchus's heliocentric idea, and thus bore some responsibility for the latter concept's demise. He should not be judged harshly for this, because no one person can appreciate the contributions of every other person. As we shall see, even Copernicus made a less than completely convincing case for heliocentrism.

Greek accomplishment went far beyond science and mathematics to embrace every arena of human thought. Herodotus (c. 480–425 B.C.E.) and Thucydides (c. 470–400 B.C.E.), in the fifth century B.C.E., began the organized study of history. Herodotus was the first well-known historian to write in prose and was therefore influential not only in the study of history, but also in establishing prose as an alternative to poetry. His *History* was among the first works to go beyond merely recording events to offer an examination of the collective human mind. Herodotus attributed much of history to the will of the gods, and much of what he wrote was wrong. But, like the founders of any discipline, Herodotus should be remembered for initiating the study of history as we know it, not for the absolute accuracy of his thinking. His thinking was no less accurate than Aristotle's, and he deserves his appellation of father of history.

Thucydides was the first well-known historian to write a purely rational account of history without attributing events to the will of gods. His work is an account of *people* and an examination of their motives. His unfinished masterpiece, *A History of the Peloponnesian War*, is one of the greatest history books ever written.

We will examine the Greek contribution to the arts in more detail later. Greek poetry reached its peak in the work of Homer, whoever he or they may have been. Also noteworthy is Hesiod, whose eighth century B.C.E. poems are the first to reveal something of the personality of the poet. Sappho (fl. c. 600 B.C.E.) was the first well-remembered female poet in history and was widely acclaimed for her love poetry.

Greek drama was a masterpiece of man's ability to reflect on his situation. There were numerous playwrights, but the three who stand out are Aeschylus, Sophocles, and Euripides. Aeschylus (525–456 B.C.E.) was the first playwright to use a second actor. Sophocles (496–406 B.C.E.) would add a third actor, making possible more intricate plots. Euripides (c. 484–406 B.C.E.) made his heroes more human than his predecessors', making drama a more accurate reflection of the human experience. Thirty-two tragedies by these three giants have survived to the present time.

Greek pottery of this period rivals Shang bronzes for beauty and intricacy. By the late seventh century B.C.E., the black figure technique of vase painting (so named because it resulted in a black image against the red background of the vase) had been devised. By the mid-sixth century B.C.E., the red figure technique (resulting in a red figure on a black background) was introduced.

Very often, one hears that Socrates, Plato, and Aristotle were the greatest of the Greek thinkers. This assertion belies the fact that many people, before and after these three, contributed to the Greek miracle. Democritus was enormously ahead of his time, and it is unfortunate that his ideas were largely ignored during the progression of history. Thales, although a shadowy figure, undoubtedly inspired a generation of thinkers, and Pythagoras stands with Aristotle among the most influential and instrumental thinkers of this period.

To the Greeks, we owe the idea that the world is comprehensible because natural phenomena have precise causes, as well as the first skepticism of prevailing beliefs, the first mathematical description of the universe, and the first view of humanity as a force that is important, improving, and able to shape the world. The unique Greek gift to civilization was not the *body* of knowledge they left, but their *reverence* for knowledge and their *systematic approach* to acquiring it. Why is it that the first civilizations demonstrated brilliant observations, but lacked a systematic method of increasing their understanding of the universe? Egypt and Mesopotamia had powerful priesthoods, and science was largely in their hands. Individual ideas were not encouraged and science was important only insofar as it served religion. However, in Greece, religion was less powerful and did not control science. Individual ideas and expression, the heart and soul of science, were permitted. Therefore, science and the individual arose together, at the expense of organized religion—a repeating theme in history.

Much of what these Greek scholars thought was wrong; what matters is *that they thought*. They largely replaced religion and mysticism and bequeathed to us the spirit of inquiry. Incorrect thinking can be fixed, the dogma of religion cannot. The Greeks introduced a true scientific method. Although they used some experimentation and some observation, their scientific method was largely based on reasoning. Later generations would add observation and experimentation as regular components to the scientific method, but developing any scientific method to replace religion and mysticism was the second giant step in our development—after the understanding that the world can be modified—and qualifies classical Greece as a giant milestone of our civilization.

One of the curses of civilization is that invariably power becomes concentrated in the hands of the few. In ancient societies—heavily reliant on religion, tradition, and conformity—individual people did not have enough standing to have a real voice in their affairs. Herein lies another great contribution of the Golden Age of Greece, for it was in Greece that democracy was born. It was an extremely limited democracy by our standards, with only free adult males participating (about 10% of the Athenian population), but—as in the advances in rational thinking—the point is not the finality of the achievement, but in the decisive movement towards what we would recognize as a democratic form of government.

Wars have always been the tragedy of history. The Golden Age of Greece ended with the Peloponnesian War, which broke out between Athens and Sparta in 431 B.C.E. Athens was initially led very ably by Pericles (c. 495–429 B.C.E.), who was both a military and cultural leader. Pericles died in 429 B.C.E., victim of a plague of unknown nature that swept over Athens and killed more than a quarter of its people. Pericles was succeeded by Cleon (d. 422 B.C.E.), who turned down an offer of peace from Sparta in 425 B.C.E., the first of two colossal mistakes for Athens—and for Greece.

Peace was finally achieved in 421 B.C.E. At this point Athens made its second colossal mistake. During this period of peace a militaristic faction of Athenians, headed by Alcibiades (450–404 B.C.E.), made the ultimately fatal mistake of invading the city of Syracuse on the island of Sicily, thereby renewing the conflict with Sparta. In 404 B.C.E., Sparta won the war. Although Athens successfully revolted a few years later, expelling their Spartan conquerors and restoring democracy, the damage to the Athenian cultural and intellectual heritage was lasting. The Peloponnesian War had destroyed the intellectual infrastructure of Greek civilization. The Greeks had managed to unite long enough to defeat the Persians in the early fifth century B.C.E., but thereafter destroyed themselves. Their tragedy was the inability to remain united after an external threat had passed. The next chapter in Greek culture and intellectual contribution would belong to the Macedonians, but it should be remembered that the cultural atmosphere of the time of Alexander the Great and his successors was different from that of classical Greece.

Alexander the Great of Macedonia (356–323 B.C.E.) was twenty years old when he inherited his father's conquered lands and excellent war machine. Over a thirteen-year period, based largely on his father's achievements, Alexander conquered most of the known world. But he moved too rapidly in building his empire. Empires that are built too rapidly do not have time to consolidate or to assemble the infrastructure necessary to make them stable. Upon his death in 323 B.C.E., from unknown natural causes, his empire shattered and disintegrated. Hellenism (or the Hellenic period, the time of classical Greece) gave way to the Hellenistic Period, the period from Alexander the Great's death in 323 B.C.E. until Roman domination. Upon Alexander's death, his generals carved his kingdom into three distinct regions, all sharing Hellenistic culture. These were Macedonia (ruled by the Antigonid dynasty), Egypt (ruled by the dynasty of Ptolemies), and Asia (ruled by the dynasty of the Seleucids).

Alexander founded a number of cities, of which only one—the Egyptian seaport of Alexandria—would have lasting importance. Under Alexander's successors in the Ptolemaic dynasty, Alexandria became one of the most important cultural centers of the ancient world, and the site of the greatest library of antiquity. Not since ancient Athens had one city been so clearly the intellectual leader of the world. The library and museum at Alexandria rank with the Lyceum and the Academy as great universities of antiquity.

In the third century B.C.E., Alexandria was the home of Euclid (fl. c. 300 B.C.E.), a follower of Pythagoras and the author of *Elements of Geometry*, a standard textbook for 2,000 years. Archimedes (287–212 B.C.E.) was educated in Alexandria before settling in Sicily, which was then a Greek colony. He developed the lever, the screw, and the principle of density, among many other accomplishments. His writings include *On the Sphere and the Cylinder, Sand Reckoner*, and *On Floating Bodies*.

We have seen that the scientific and rational advances of this period were made possible by the worth and the ideas of individuals. As individual worth is the foundation of science, it is also the foundation of equality and democracy. It probably would not have been possible to adopt non deity-based religions in India and China if the individual did not have a similarly high status in those areas. The cause of the first golden age of civilization—the period around 3,000 B.C.E., when large cities began to form—is not precisely known. However, we do know the major impetus behind this second golden age around 500 B.C.E., when three different cultures in Greece, India, and China made decisive advances for which we are greatly indebted today. It was the recognition of the worth of the individual. The concept that a single person has value, and that this value is at least partially independent of his or her status or birth situation, was revolutionary. The displacement of religion and mysticism by the worth of the individual powered the dramatic advances in all three of these cultures.

I submit as history's fourth lesson that single individuals matter, and that when their worth is placed ahead of that of tradition, religion, conformity, and rituals, there will be enormous progress. Today, our very numbers make us feel prosaic and ordinary. When we are confused or feel small, it is best to return to first principles. The first principle of our lives should be that we are all unique individuals, worthy of self- and societal-esteem.

Chapter 7
Law and Order

Here was a material far stronger than any previous mortar; it opened a new world of architectural possibilities.

THE ETRUSCANS FLOURISHED FROM ABOUT 800–300 B.C.E. in what is now Tuscany, in Italy. They are of uncertain origin, as is the case with so many ancient peoples. We have only limited knowledge of their language, in part because their surviving documents are short, such as epitaphs. We do not have the number of long documents necessary to develop facility with the language. (Etruscan joins Indus writing, Minoan Linear A, and Proto-Elamite of ancient Iran as the major undeciphered scripts of history.) It can be said that their alphabet is based on Greek, and therefore on Phoenician origins, and it became the basis for the Roman (Latin) alphabet.

In addition to the three fragments of Alexander's empire, the fourth influential site of Hellenistic times was Rome, and it was the Roman Empire that would replace Alexander's empire. The Romans generally absorbed the Etruscans without confrontation, although a small number of battles did occur. Contact with the Etruscans influenced the Romans in a number of ways, of which three (in addition to the alphabet) stand out: engineering, infantry warfare, and religious development.

The fledgling Roman society was profoundly set back when the Celts destroyed Rome in 386 B.C.E. In the first portion of its history, Rome had what is referred to as a republican form of government, traditionally said to begin in 509 B.C.E. We need not concern ourselves with the details of the republic other than to note that it did make a deliberate attempt to give a voice to the common people. Not at all a foolproof system, the republican government left plenty of room for oppression of the poor.

In the first century B.C.E., Rome was embroiled in civil wars, which termi-

76

nated when Julius Caesar (100–44 B.C.E.) effectively became the sole power broker. Ordered by the Senate to return to Rome alone, Caesar instead brought his army with him (the famous crossing of the Rubicon River, which has since come to mean the point of no return) and seized power. Believing that the republic would return upon the death of Caesar, the Senate assassinated him in 44 B.C.E.

But the republic did not fall neatly into place. After yet another civil war, Caesar's grandnephew, Octavian (63 B.C.E.–14 C.E.), remembered principally by the name of Augustus, became "first citizen"—in effect, Rome's first emperor. A person of unusual political and administrative skill, Augustus did not suddenly and forcefully seize imperial power. Rather, he developed his position with the senate over a period of years. Augustus showed a characteristic rare in political leaders, and rarer still in those with absolute power: patience. During his reign and for some two hundred years thereafter, Rome prospered and enjoyed peace in the Mediterranean (the Pax Romana), giving the illusion the replacement of the republic was a positive development.

But the inherent and inescapable weakness of absolutism became apparent. Benign autocracies never last. The advantages of giving one person absolute power are always outweighed by the potential—indeed, the certainty—of corruption and destruction of civil liberties. The dangers posed by concentrating power in the hands of one person are always greater than the problems such a concentration is supposed to solve. Augustus's stepson and successor, Tiberius (reigned 14–37 C.E.), was initially a capable ruler, but became more despotic in his later years. The poverty of the new form of government, and the loss to the people, became manifest under the rule of the madman Caligula (r. 37–41 C.E.). After a thirteen-year rule by Claudius, Nero became emperor in 54 C.E. Initially an enlightened and benevolent ruler, Nero evidently fell victim to an undefined mental illness and ended his reign as a despot almost as malevolent as Caligula. Although accused of setting the fire that devastated Rome in 64 C.E., he probably had nothing to do with it, and he could not have "fiddled while Rome burned" because the violin had not yet been invented.

However capable Augustus might have been, the lack of ability of his successors and the resultant stifling of individualism under the emperors more than counter-balanced the imperial ability to move swiftly and decisively. Herein lies a paradox and a lesson for humanity. There can be, in the long run, no path to effective government that is not democratic or representative in nature. Even if power did not corrupt, the individual cannot flourish in a monarchy. The progress of humanity is totally dependent on the opportunity of individual people to question a way of thinking and to propose alternatives, which cannot happen if individual thinking is suppressed by a monarchy or fundamentalist religion of any sort.

At its height, the Roman Empire was not the largest the world had seen or would see. The empires of Alexander the Great, the Muslims, and the Mongols were all larger in land area. But the Roman Empire was the most stable empire in history, lasting—counting the eastern portion—for almost two thousand years. It was in its stability, not its extent, that the Roman Empire made its mark. The key to this stability was that the Romans assimilated the people they conquered. In general, they were generous in granting citizenship to their subjects. Conquered peoples came to think of themselves as Roman and became loyal contributors to the empire. Indeed, one reason (in addition to their civil and administrative skills) that a small city was able to conquer and hold so much territory was precisely because they did not move too rapidly, achieving the substantial assimilation of one area before moving to another. Conquest is temporary; assimilation is long-term. The Romans benefited from the loyalty and labor of those they conquered and were wise enough to secure these from one region before attempting to acquire more territory. Because of this assimilation, the Roman Empire achieved the long-term unity that eluded the Greeks.

In the third century, the empire was beginning to see genuine cracks in its social order and institutions. The emperor Diocletian (r. 284–305 C.E.) is remembered for the persecution of Christians. However, this was not widespread or successful, and it should be remembered that Rome was far more tolerant of religious freedom, including Christianity, than is generally believed. Concerned about the problem of succession, Diocletian restructured the administration, installing two emperors, along with two junior emperors to succeed them. In a display of restraint and wisdom remarkable for anyone, particularly an emperor, he abdicated in 301, believing that his reforms would provide for a peaceful transition of power. However, without Diocletian's dominating personality his system failed, and Rome entered another period of governmental chaos, with a number of people claiming the throne, sometimes in groups.

Finally Constantine, who had been a significant presence since 307, seized sole power in 324. In 330 C.E., continuing the administrative restructuring begun by Diocletian, he re-founded the city of Byzantium (contemporary Istanbul, Turkey) and established it as the capital of the eastern portion of the empire. Not lacking in ego, Constantine renamed the city Constantinople after himself. He believed that the Roman Empire needed a second administrative center in its eastern frontier, closer to where many of the troops were recruited. He felt that a common religion could provide a cohesive force, and he admired the Christian sense of unity and higher purpose. Probably more because of the potential beneficial effect on his troops than from a true conversion (it is not clear if he was a truly devoted Christian), he made Christianity a legal and tolerated religion. Contrary to popular belief, he did not actually make it the official state religion (this would not happen until 392, when the emperor Theodosius forbade all other religions). The legalization of Christianity applied to Constantinople also, placing a Christian center adjacent to what would become Islamic civilization.

From the fifth century C.E., severe difficulties continued to emerge in the Roman Empire; one gets the feeling that it was simply "wearing out." In 410, the Visigoths entered Rome and devastated the city in a three-day spree of destruction. In the middle of the fifth century C.E., the Huns posed a severe threat to Rome. Entering Europe (probably after failing to conquer China), the Huns were united under Attila and became ruthless and brutal conquerors, destroying everything in their path. The Huns might well have destroyed Rome had not two events fortuitously taken place in rapid succession: In 451, Flavius Aetius, joined by the Visigoths, defeated the Huns in France. In 453 Attila died, just as he had turned his army south to Rome.

There are three misconceptions about the "fall" of Rome in 476 C.E. First, by this time, the Roman army was largely filled with foreigners, mostly from the barbarians north of the empire (today, the word "barbarian" is a derogatory term that often implies stupidity, but the term as used here simply refers to the people living north of Rome in societies which had not achieved all of the hallmarks of civilization). Second, the fall of Rome was hardly noticed by its denizens or by citizens of the empire. In fact, the father of the last emperor of western Rome, Romulus Augustulus, had been a secretary to Attila the Hun. Rome's fall was simply the last in a long series of events marking the gradual replacement of Roman government by that of the barbarians. Third, it is often forgotten that the eastern portion of the empire continued, in one form or another, for almost a thousand years longer, although it adopted a somewhat different heritage and character from its strictly western Roman origins.

One of the most often asked question in history is "why did the Roman Empire fall?" Entire books have been written on this subject, the most famous of which is *The History of The Decline and Fall of the Roman Empire*, by Edward

Gibbon (1737–1794). In the end, it can be said that Rome fell because it exhausted the internal energy required to keep a civilization running. Perhaps the optimism that Kenneth Clark felt essential to civilization had vanished. Civilizations, like individuals, need a certain vibrancy to survive, and like individuals, they have finite lifetimes. All civilizations, sooner or later, lose control of their institutions and infrastructure. Like people, they grow weak, grow old, and die. In the words of the Aztec king Nezahualcoyotl:

> *For this is the inevitable outcome of*
> *all powers, empires, and domains;*
> *transitory are they and unstable.*
> *The time of life is borrowed,*
> *in an instant it must be left behind*

The loss of the ability to think long-term seems to accompany the fall of civilizations. It leads to the inability to adapt to changing situations and maintain the social structures needed for civilization, because maintaining these structures in the face of changing circumstances requires a long-term approach to problems. We must assume that this will happen to us one day, that we too will pass into history, and that all we know and perceive of the world will one day become a child's history lesson.

The creativity of the Romans was more narrowly expressed than that of the Greeks, but they were more creative than they are generally credited, and their contribution to our literature, engineering, law, government, and language cannot be denied.

Roman writing forms an integral part of world literature. The works of Lucretius (99–55 B.C.E.), Virgil (or Vergil, 70–19 B.C.E., author of the *Aeneid*), Horace (65–8 B.C.E.), Livy (59 B.C.E.–17 C.E.), and Ovid (c. 43 B.C.E.–17 C.E.), are well remembered and treasured by history. The speeches and letters of Marcus Tullius Cicero (106–43 B.C.E.) are eloquent expressions of human thought. The histories of Tacitus (c.55–120 C.E.) give us an autobiography of the Roman empire. The philosopher and writer Lucius Annaeus Seneca (c.4 B.C.E.–65 C.E.) was Nero's teacher and probably largely responsible for the benevolence that characterized that emperor's early years. Pliny the Elder (c.23–79 C.E.) was the leading authority on science in ancient Rome. His encyclopedia, *Historia Naturalis*, was the most comprehensive treatment of science to that time and encompassed thirty-seven volumes. The letters of his adopted son, Pliny the Younger (62–113 C.E.), are a rich time capsule of Roman times.

Roman engineering achievements, the marvel of their day, continue to impress us today. Road-building techniques have permitted some Roman routes to remain in use in modern times. Some 31,000 miles (50,000 kilometers) of Roman roads formed the greatest transportation network in antiquity. Such an extensive network was made possible by several characteristics of Roman roads. First, the Romans recognized that roads are much more durable with a foundation, which they made up to five feet (1.5 meters) deep. Their roads were remarkably straight, especially considering the lack of available instruments, allowing them to reduce unnecessary effort during travel. Finally, the Romans understood the importance of adequate drainage, constructing ditches for that purpose on either side of the road.

Like their roads, Roman bridges and buildings have demonstrated great durability. In large part, such permanence was made possible by a distinctly Roman engineering heritage: concrete. Prior to Roman times, sun-dried mud and kiln-fired bricks were used as building blocks. Mortar was available, but limited in durability and strength because it did not chemically combine with the bricks. Concrete is a Roman invention comprised of three components: an aggregate (of stone or gravel), water, and cement. Cement and concrete are therefore not synonymous. Cement is the hardening agent, and today it usually consists of a powder composed of gypsum (hydrated calcium sulfate), lime (calcium oxide or calcium hydroxide), or chalk (calcium carbonate). When concrete is mixed the water reacts chemically, becoming an integral and permanent part of the structure. It does not simply evaporate, as in sun-dried or kiln-fired bricks. Roman concrete had a slightly different composition. For concrete production, the Romans started with a material that other cultures did not have: silica-rich volcanic ash, called Pozzolana, from Mount Vesuvius. After grinding, lime was added. The combination of Pozzolana and lime filled the role of cement. Added to water and aggregate, it formed chemical bonds, giving humanity a new and durable building material. The integration of water into the molecular structure of Roman concrete allowed it to set under water, impossible with mortars that set by evaporation. A wealth of aquatic engineering achievements became attainable. Like so many ideas of antiquity, the knowledge of concrete was lost after the fall of Rome and not fully rediscovered until the eighteenth century.

One of the few inventions of the Romans directly translated to medieval civilization was the arch, which is a method of spanning a gap in a way that does not place more stress on the center than other parts of the span. The principle of the arch was understood by the Egyptians and Greeks but rarely employed by them. Roman arches were simple and based on the circle. The Gothic arch, which was based on the oval, was not invented until the Middle Ages. The Gothic arch was stronger and allowed the great medieval cathedrals to be built; but the Roman arch was sufficient, especially when combined with concrete, to introduce a new era in construction.

Other legacies of Western Rome were in law and societal organization. The principal legal contribution of Rome is the concept that government should be by laws, not by people. That is, that recorded laws, largely invariant through the ages, form a superior and more equitable government than one that might fluctuate as different people came to power. This idea, never well-developed in many Eastern cultures, became the cornerstone of Anglo-American law and Western legal tradition. In addition, Western Rome left us the Latin language, the spine of Western European tongues.

Thus the old idea that the Romans were codifiers, preservers of Greek thought, and builders rather than innovators and scholars is largely untrue, although it is true that Roman contributions in the sciences were minimal compared to their other contributions.

It was under Julius Caesar (acting on the advise of the astronomer Sosigenes) that the Julian calendar was adopted, recognizing a 365.25-day year based solely on the motion of the sun. Leap years were codified and were to occur every fourth year.[3]

Two exceptional scientists of the Roman Empire come to mind, but it should be noted that both had direct connections to the Greeks. One was from Alexandria, which although under Roman domination, offered Greek knowledge to its citizens, and the second was a Greek, who like all Greeks of his time lived under the government of Rome.

One of the seminal thinkers of history was Claudius Ptolemaeus (90–160 C.E., known as Ptolemy), a Roman from Alexandria (not to be confused with the Hellenistic dynasty of the same name). Ptolemy wrote two of the most influential books in history. One of these is the *Mathematike Syntaxis*, a work on astronomy, known to history by the name given it by the Arabs, the *Almagest* (meaning "the greatest of books"). Like the Aristotelian view, this book put forth a geocentric theory and held that the heavens were unchanging. Nonetheless, it was a masterful work, partly because of its extensive star catalog, but more because of its successful mathematical description of the motion of all heavenly bodies. Not all geocentric systems are equal. Ptolemy's geocentric theory was much more powerful than Aristotle's and was mathematically cogent.

* See Notes starting on page 502.

Whereas Aristotle's universe consisted of eight simple concentric spheres, and therefore incapable of explaining the observation that the planets occasionally appeared to stop and even reverse direction, Ptolemy conceived of a more elaborate series of spheres. Attached to the main spheres were smaller spheres, around which the planets rotated. Although the larger sphere may be rotating in one direction, if the planet were rotating in the opposite direction on an attached smaller sphere, it would appear to be reversing direction. The motion about the smaller sphere was called an epicycle. The complexity of these epicycles was a major reason why Copernicus sought the simplicity of heliocentrism.

Ptolemy's second great work, *Geographica*, put forth an incorrectly low value for the circumference of the earth and took the position that most of its surface was covered by land. It also held that the southern tip of Africa extended to the South Pole and over to Southeast Asia, enclosing the Indian Ocean. Because no body of water south of Africa was recognized, sea passage from Europe to Asia was thought to be impossible.

These mistakes notwithstanding, *Geographica* was an extraordinary work for several reasons. First, building on the ideas of Hipparchus, Ptolemy listed locations by longitude and latitude. Ptolemy chose the Canary Islands as the prime meridian because they were the westernmost portion of the generally known world and named meridians eastward from there. Second, Ptolemy's *Geographica* introduced the subdivisions of degrees into minutes and seconds. *Geographica* would make its third and greatest contribution a thousand years after it was written. Ptolemy's geography was the unbroken gospel until Christian dogma began to suppress it and revive "flat earth" thinking. When the sphericity of the earth was again understood, it was the work of Ptolemy that paved the way. Ptolemy's work was revived before Columbus's voyages, and the latter relied extensively on the *Geographica*. In fact, it was largely Ptolemy's underestimation of the circumference of the earth that convinced Columbus that he could reach the Orient by sailing west. By Columbus' time, educated people again knew that the world was round. Columbus did not prove this at all, and the notion that he did is one of the great historical misconceptions. Just as the *Almagest*, by elaborating a complex view of the heavens, inspired Copernicus to seek a simpler explanation of planetary motion, so the *Geographica* inspired Columbus by underestimating the earth's circumference. It is ironic that two of the most significant books ever written exerted much of their influence because of inaccuracies.

Another seminal thinker of the Roman period was Galen (c.130–200 C.E.), a Greek physician living in Roman times. He, too, was often wrong in what he wrote. But as we have seen, the key to human advancement is thinking, not necessarily correct thinking.

Human dissection was forbidden in Galen's time. (This prohibition would become somewhat easier under Christianity because of its strong belief in the disassociation of the body and soul, but would not be lifted in Islam.) Galen therefore dissected monkeys and pigs, and freely extrapolated his findings to humans. He also learned a great deal by observing the wounds of gladiators. These animal dissections and gladiator wounds, combined with his codification of past work, made Galen the most influential physician of his day. Like Hippocrates, Galen believed in the four humors, excess or deficiency of one or more of which was thought to cause disease. Galen was one source of the idea that congestion of the organs caused disease, a belief that led to the practice of bloodletting, which continued into the nineteenth century.

Galen wrote with dogmatism and absolutism, which made his work popular with church authorities. Because he wrote in Greek, his work was very influential in Alexandria, Constantinople, and later, in the Islamic world. However it did not exert an influence on Europe until it was translated into Latin in the sixth century C.E. By Galen's time, knowledge of Greek was becoming rare in Rome. In fact, by the fifth century C.E., Roman knowledge of Greek had died out, and very few Greek books had been translated into Latin. Greek learning was lost to the stream of Western civilization and had to be recaptured early in second millennium from Islamic or Byzantine sources. However, once translated into Latin, Galen's work became the almost completely unchallenged basis of medicine in the Western world until Vesalius produced his landmark work in the sixteenth century. (Indeed, Galen ranks with Aristotle and Ptolemy as the most influential writers of antiquity.) How tragic it is for mankind that work done on pigs in the second century became the absolute dogma of medicine for almost 1500 years. The same tragedy befell the work of Aristotle, likewise taken as absolute truth for centuries. The fault is not Galen's or Aristotle's; these men were giants. The fault is the failure of an entire civilization to follow up on their work. No one person can stand alone in the advancement of knowledge. For much of our history, faithful transmission of established dogma was the priority, not the discovery of new information. Disciples of a great thinker studied the thinker himself, not his discipline, and defended him, rather than extending him. The near-deification of a scholar paradoxically changed his work from a bridge to a barrier.

Though the Romans ignored Galen's work, they inadvertently made a major contribution to medicine. By achieving a standard of living and a degree of public health not to be equaled in Western Europe until the seventeenth century, they greatly slowed the spread of communicable diseases.

Special mention should now be made of the man known as Saint Augustine (354–430), who became—after Paul himself—the most influential Christian thinker until the Reformation. Born Aurelius Augustinus in North Africa, Augustine had a devoutly Christian mother and was initially a follower of Manichaeism (a religion founded in the third century C.E. by Mani and having no adherents today). After converting to Christianity Augustine accepted, like Luther and Calvin eleven centuries later, the doctrine of Justification by Faith Alone as enumerated by the apostle Paul. (The doctrine of Justification by Faith Alone, which we will consider in detail later, holds that people can obtain forgiveness and salvation only by believing that Jesus was the Son of God and by living according to his teaching.) Augustine's book, *The City of God*, is a defense of Christianity, inspired by those who blamed the Christians for the Visigoth sack of Rome in 410 C.E. *The City of God* is a template of Christian thought, and a "manual" of Christianity used to demonstrate its power and perfection. Augustine's formulation of Christian doctrine passed largely unchanged through the Middle Ages, in part because of the conservatism of the Catholic Church, and in part because of the lack of an inquiring spirit in the first centuries after Rome. *The City of God* influenced one and a half millennia of Christian thought, making it one of the most influential books ever written.

Two other people from this time deserve mention as preservers of knowledge. Anicius Manlius Severinus (c. 480–525 C.E.; remembered by the name of Boethius) was a Roman philosopher in the closing years of the Empire. After the fall of Rome, while imprisoned by the Ostrogoth emperor Theodoric, he wrote *On the Consolation of Philosophy*. His most lasting contribution was his translation of Aristotle's works on logic into Latin. (He was killed by Theodoric before he could translate the rest of Aristotle.) He also wrote a treatise on music that was influential in transmitting Greek knowledge of its mathematical basis.

Martianus Capella, a Roman proconsul in Carthage in the fifth century C.E., foresaw the decline of Roman civilization and prepared a compendium of basic knowledge from the common school curriculum. This compendium, the partial translation of Aristotle by Boethius, and a tiny number of classical works, such as Pliny the Elder's *Historia Naturalis*, were among the pitifully small collection of scholarly writings in Europe during the time from 500–1000 C.E.

Greece taught us how to think, and as we shall see, Eastern Rome and the Muslims, largely using Greek knowledge, re-taught us how to think. It is said, with a measure of truth, that Western Rome is the direct ancestor of Western civilization. However, many of Western Rome's achievements, including most of its knowledge and its standard of living, were lost. After Rome was overrun, Western Europe lost the social infrastructure necessary for significant intellectual progress, and the centers of learning and scholarship shifted to other areas. When learning finally returned to Western Europe, it came from the Muslims and the Eastern Roman Empire and was largely based on the knowledge of Greece. Whereas Greek civilization is irreplaceable in our history from every standpoint, the legacy of Rome, although great, is more subtle and more restricted.

Chapter 8
Giving People Hope

A Jewish reformer forever changes the world, and becomes history's most misunderstood figure.

As I HAVE SAID, ONE MUST UNDERSTAND RELIGIONS to understand history and the human condition. Therefore, it is necessary to consider a monumental development of Roman times—the life and death of Jesus and the inception of Christianity.

History has had a static picture of Jesus for centuries because almost nothing was known of his times and his homeland. Just as scientific discoveries become more comprehensible in their historical context, so also the development of Christianity becomes more understandable when viewed in the context of the world Jesus inhabited. New archeological finds and a re-examination of first-century Judah—the surviving southern portion of the ancient Jewish state—reveal more of Jesus than once thought possible.

Archeological evidence of economic and cultural upheaval in first-century-C.E. Judah has proven invaluable, as has the finding and translation of the Dead Sea Scrolls. First discovered in the 1940s, they now number approximately eight hundred documents ranging from the second century before Jesus to the first century C.E. Initially thought to reflect only a small sect of Judaism, the Dead Sea Scrolls are now thought by many to be a hidden library representing the thinking of a large proportion of Jews during this period. As such, they are a priceless, unedited, pristine time capsule of the world in which Jesus lived and by which he was shaped.

Step back with me two thousand years into the world of Roman occupied Judah, and permit me to present a personal view of what happened. This is not an attempt to diminish Christianity, but rather to explain how it came to be.

Before Jesus, two decisive circumstances in history merged. The first were the long-standing Jewish ideas that the world would end in apocalypse and that

God would personally intervene in the affairs of his chosen people by sending a Messiah. The second was the conquest of Judah by Rome in 63 B.C.E. The captured area became the Roman province of Judea (also spelled Judaea). After the Roman conquest, the region was initially ruled by Jewish kings under a Roman administration. (Herod was an example.) The Romans later ruled directly through their own civil servants, one of whom was Pontius Pilate. There is evidence that many Jews thought that their high religious leaders were corrupt and accrued wealth rightfully belonging to the common citizens of Judah. The Romanization of Judah was seen as a threat to the Jewish way of life and as the devastation of Jewish culture, particularly since many Jews felt their religious leaders were colluding with Roman authorities.

Jesus was one of many Jews to protest this state of affairs. Probably born between eight and four B.C.E., Jesus (almost certainly not the name by which he was known) was a leader in the movement to preserve Judaism against Roman domination and the corruption of religious leaders. Jesus and the other protesters sought the restoration of the Jewish way of life and the mitigation of Roman oppression. Theirs was a political as well as a religious message.

Jesus was the Martin Luther King, Jr. of his time and culture. Like the Maccabees (a family that led a Jewish revolt against the Seleucid dynasty in Syria in the second century B.C.E.—remembered as martyrs by the Jews), Jesus fought for the equality of his people, and for their rights and prosperity. He preached a nonviolent message of cultural restoration, hope, egalitarianism, belonging, and universal love, rather than endorsing violent overthrow.

Although the New Testament quotes Jesus as referring to God as "my Father," he was referring to the personal relationship anybody could have with a caring God (a heritage of Jewish tradition), not a literal familial relationship. He did not claim to be the Son of God or a Messiah and asked to be followed, not worshiped. He was an itinerant Jewish preacher who called for the renewal of Judaism, not for a new religion. Roman authorities killed him because they thought he was fomenting rebellion. How did this protester and spokesperson come to be regarded as the Messiah?

To address that question, we must probe into the period just after Jesus died. In understanding the development of Christianity, it is critical to realize that there were no records of Jesus or his teachings until a generation after his death. At the time of his death some believed he was divine, but this opinion was not widespread.

The Roman annexation of Judah and the suppression of Jewish culture rekindled anticipation of a Messiah. Many Jews felt only the direct intervention of God, in the form of a Messiah, could save Judaism. Desperation and the belief that a Messiah was coming led the Jews of Judah to rebel against Roman rule in 66 C.E. The crushing Roman victory only added to Jewish despair. Another revolt in 132–135 C.E. resulted in the removal of Jews from their Holy Land and their dispersal around the world. (This dispersal is sometimes called the Diaspora, although the word "Diaspora" can also be used to refer to the Babylonian captivity in the sixth century B.C.E. or to the dispersal of Jews following the Roman victory in the first century C.E.; it can also refer to Jewish settlements that are not in the Holy Land).

In the years immediately after the death of Jesus, leaders of the movement for restoring Jewish culture, drawing on the long-established Jewish belief in the Messiah, concluded that this Messiah *had come*. Jesus was a recent, popular, and martyred reformer whose teachings were well remembered and whose message gave people hope and a sense of belonging. He was the obvious candidate—just as Martin Luther King, Jr. would undoubtedly be selected if contemporary African-Americans were to choose a recent Messiah from their ranks. Jesus' successors over the next few generations, struggling to retain Jewish cultural identity in the face of Roman occupation, came to believe and taught that Jesus was the Messiah because only the arrival of a Messiah could correct the corruption and despair brought by the Roman occupation. He became known as the Christ, from the Greek word for The Anointed One, or Messiah. The coming of the Messiah would surely lead to a restoration of Jewish culture.

Like all religions, Christianity was influenced by its time. The belief that Jesus was born of a virgin may have arisen from Greek and Hellenistic tradition, in which some heroes were believed to have been sired by gods. Another factor may have been a mistranslation of the original Biblical text indicating that Jesus' mother was a virgin. "Young girl" appears to be a somewhat more accurate translation, and because any young girl was expected to be a virgin, the translation became "virgin."

How did Jesus' followers convince themselves and others that the Messiah had come? By believing and convincing others that Jesus, the putative Messiah, had worked miracles and was the clear culmination of the Old Testament prophesies. After the death of Jesus, other reformers came to believe the stories of virgin birth, birth in Bethlehem, birth in a stable, the star of Bethlehem, miracles, and the resurrection because these stories fit the idea that Jesus was the expected Messiah. The belief that Jesus was the Messiah came first, followed by the beliefs necessary to support that opinion. It is human nature to construct beliefs based on preconceived ideas. This aspect of our nature, filtered through Jewish tradition and the background of the time, would have given these people every good reason to believe as they did.

Most of the stories were created to be continuous with the *Torah*, the first five books of the Old Testament (and the most important works in Judaism) and make Jesus appear to be the culmination of those prophecies. The miracles are particularly interesting. Almost all were medical in nature and may have had a basis in fact, because the psychological component that accompanies illness would have responded to a compassionate "healer", who unlike others of the time did not shun the sick. Let us examine the environment in which these medical miracles took place. About 100 C.E., the first of several plagues of unknown nature swept the Mediterranean basin. This was followed by The Plague of Galen, which ran from 164–180 C.E. (One of its last victims was the emperor Marcus Aurelius.) In 250 C.E., the plague of Cyprian swept the Mediterranean and moved north as far as Scotland. In a world lacking any understanding of disease, the fear caused by these plagues would have underscored a message of a miracle worker who could heal the sick. The larger idea that this person was a Messiah, whose teachings could allow the Jewish community to resist Rome and whose life had made eternal salvation possible, *would be believed* by many.

Had it not been for the work of his followers, principally Paul (c. 3–62 C.E., also called Saul), we might not know the name Jesus today. It was Paul, not Jesus, who formed the doctrines of the early Christian Church and who wrote a large portion of the New Testament. In particular, it was Paul who established the doctrine of Justification by Faith Alone. In Christian theology, the word "Justification" refers to the way in which man, a sinner, can set right his relationship with God. Paul's most influential teaching was that the life and death of Jesus had justified, or set right, man's relationship with God, but only if man accepted Jesus as the son of God and lived according to his teaching. Paul taught that Jesus had given man a second chance, and only through Jesus could salvation be achieved. Jesus' sacrifice enabled *anyone*, if he were willing, to undergo a transformation of the heart allowing him to receive God's gift of salvation. The doctrine of Justification by Faith Alone meant that converts would not have to be Jews or convert to Judaism before becoming Christian, greatly enhancing the spread of Christianity. By excusing converts from adhering to all Jewish traditions, Justification by Faith Alone made conversion more attractive to Gentiles. Paul was one of the few early

Christians to accept non-Jewish converts and not require circumcision.

It was Paul who made the divinity of Jesus believable, it was Paul who effectively converted people outside of the Jewish community, and it was Paul who played the greatest role in transforming Christianity from a small Jewish sect into a worldwide religion. Although it may seem strange and impossible, a strong argument can be made that Jesus was not the founder of Christianity. Jesus had no desire to be perceived as a Messiah or to found a new religion. The religion was founded by his followers, principally Paul.

In the first generations after the death of Jesus, the time was ripe for the acceptance of a Messiah. Jesus' protest and attempt to restore the identity of his people was transformed into a truly new religion after a subset of Jews, called Christians, saw in Jesus the fulfillment of a centuries-old prophesy and separated themselves from the larger Jewish community. The New Testament was written as the story of the life and teachings of Jesus, but it was intended to convert people and keep them faithful, not as an historically accurate account.

Christianity was more fully defined by councils held in the fourth and fifth centuries, and one is struck by how late so many of the basic doctrines of Christianity were formed. The Council of Nicaea in 325 established the Trinity—the belief that there are three equal aspects to God—the Father, the Son, and the Holy Spirit. Although all Christians, by definition, believed in the divinity and messianic mission of Jesus, there was no consensus about how he came to be divine. Was he made divine by God, or was he made of the same substance as God and therefore divine by nature? Both sides had adherents, and the early Church felt the need to settle the matter and avoid any further division. At the Council of Nicaea, those who believed that Jesus was made of the same substance as God and was inherently divine prevailed, creating the first version of the creed of Christianity, the Nicene Creed. By establishing the three equal aspects of God, the Nicene Creed authenticated that Jesus was of the same substance as God and intrinsically divine. The Nicene Creed was reaffirmed and refined at the Council of Constantinople in 381. The Council of Ephesus in 431 affirmed Mary as the Mother of both Jesus and God. The Council of Chalcedon in 451 defined Jesus as both man and God. Additional major ecumenical councils were held in the years 563, 680, and 787.

A thorough study of the life and times of Jesus suggests that he was the most misunderstood and misrepresented figure in human history. To my mind, although Jesus certainly did exist and was a thoroughly good person, the idea that he was the Messiah came largely from his followers—a generation after his death.

Seeking hope, they came to believe in the divinity of Jesus, and, with the best of intentions, they reached out to a fearful people—desperately grasping for solace against the overwhelming power of the Roman Empire—and guided them to what they believed was a source of peace.

This teaches us something truly pivotal about ourselves. We all need hope, and this is as true about any of us today as it was of anyone in the first century C.E. Christianity gave (and gives) its followers hope; it provided a sense of belonging and community. It increased self-esteem because each participant attained a sense of worth from group acceptance—also true for all people of all times. Christianity was a comforting source of hope and belonging in difficult times. It took hold because of the universal need to believe in better times to come. It would be 1,800 years before Thoreau would write "the mass of men lead lives of quiet desperation," but in the truth of those words lies the origin of Christianity.

There is no better example of the ability of historical examination to explain our heritage, and the vibrancy of history is never more evident than in what it teaches us about the origins of Christianity.

Christianity differs from Judaism, Hinduism, Confucianism, and Buddhism by mandating that there can be only one truth, one right path to happiness and salvation: the acceptance of Jesus as the Son of God, and living by His example. There is only one specific source of wisdom—the Old and New Testaments—not a collection of writings as in Hinduism, Buddhism, or Confucianism. The idea of life after death was not invented by the Christians; it was believed by ancient man and followers of many religions. However, Christians brought the concept of eternal salvation to particular prominence. Through faith in Jesus the Christian can achieve, at the end of *this* lifetime, immortality with *retention of his individual identity*. Cycles and reincarnations are not required. On the other hand, a life of evil or disbelief leads directly to eternal damnation, with no reincarnation to afford a second chance. Christianity is filled with absolutes, and its simplistic view of the world comforted and appealed to the unsophisticated early Christians.

So Western man received hope and belonging from Christianity but gave up individualism, and society largely gave up the questioning outlook fostered in Greece. What could abstract thinking or observation of nature possibly furnish when mankind now had the absolute, divine truth? The rise of Christianity, and of Islam 600 years later, re-established the deity as the absolute force in Western religion. In those religions, although there are codes of ethical conduct, much of the mandated behavior is required for the purpose of satisfying an absolute creator.

The expression of Christianity originally took two forms: Catholicism and Orthodoxy. Catholicism accepts the infallibility and primacy of the Pope (although he is considered to be infallible only in certain situations), whereas Orthodoxy has no single leader. They differ in one other respect. In 796, the Catholic Church altered the Nicene Creed to indicate that the Holy Spirit emanated not only from the Father, but also from the Son, and the Orthodox Church objected to this alteration. Today, Orthodoxy is prevalent in Greece, Russia, and Eastern Europe, while Catholicism is more common in Western Europe and the Western Hemisphere. As we shall see, a third form of Christianity would materialize in the sixteenth century.

Chapter 9
The Fragility of Civilization

A king's military campaigns achieve only temporary success, but his reforms improve the education of his people.

THE EARLY MIDDLE AGES IN EUROPE—the years between 500 and 1000 C.E.—are often called "The Dark Ages." Recent thinking posits a more complex social and economic structure during this period than previously believed, and we now know that much of the reason that people of this period appeared to be less ambitious is that their structures were composed of perishable materials. While the term "Dark Ages" is a misnomer, and the lives of individual people during this time were not necessarily difficult, unhappy, or uncivilized, there was a lack of collective societal progress and intellectual activity relative to Greco-Roman times.

As Kenneth Clark tells us, civilization requires a modicum of leisure time, confidence and prosperity. Where these concepts are missing, civilization will not thrive. The fall of Western Rome meant the degradation of the basic societal institutions necessary for the leisure time to pursue thinking. Specifically, it disrupted trade routes and undermined Europe's economic base.

Immediately after the fall of Rome, Europe fell into the hands of a number of tribal societies, who migrated throughout what had been the Empire. The Vandals occupied north Africa; the Visigoths occupied parts of what is now France and Spain; the Angles, Jutes, and Saxons migrated into Britain; while the Franks controlled much of contemporary France and Germany. The Ostrogoths took over most of Italy. In the sixth century, the eastern portion of the Roman Empire under Justinian (c.482–565 C.E.), defeated the Vandals and Ostrogoths but was unable to reunify the old empire and was forced to withdraw, in part because of the plague of Justinian (probably Bubonic Plague). In fact, Justinian's attempt to recreate the old Roman Empire had just the opposite effect in Italy. Fighting between the Byzantine force and the Ostrogoths destroyed so much of Italy that the loss of Greco-Roman knowledge and the consequent "dark age" was virtually assured. The Lombards filled this vacuum in 568, holding much of Italy until defeated by the Franks. The Moors, a nomadic people from north Africa who were early converts to Islam, took advantage of the fighting between the Vandals and the Eastern Roman Empire to conquer much of Spain and Portugal in the early eighth century. The Moors would remain a fixture in Spain until the late fifteenth century, but the conquest of the Lombards by the Franks brought the latter into ascendancy in the rest of Western Europe.

After Justinian's withdrawal from Europe, the territory he seized fell under the control of European tribes. Justinian achieved more lasting influence with his *Corpus Juris Civilis* (*Body of Civil Laws*), a legal work consisting of four parts. The first, the *Code* (or *Codex*), revised and added to Roman Law. This was accompanied by a massive work called the *Digest*, a fifty-book synopsis of the opinions of celebrated Roman legal scholars. The *Institutes* was a textbook of law. The *Novellae* were the new imperil edicts. These latter works were immediately influential in Byzantium, but both were lost in Europe until the eleventh century, when a copy of the *Digest* was found. This greatly influenced the European legal tradition of the late Middle Ages, during which time it was Europe's principal source of legal knowledge. Justinian's ambitious building program resulted in the construction of the Hagia Sophia (Church of Holy Wisdom). Built from 532–537 in Constantinople, it was the largest Christian Church in the East and was exceeded in brilliance only by Saint Peter's Cathedral. Converted into a mosque after the conquest of Byzantium by the Muslims, it has been a museum since 1933. As we shall see, the Hagia Sophia was brilliantly innovative in architecture.

As Europe lapsed, the centers of learning and preservation of knowledge were India, China, Byzantium and, somewhat later, Islamic culture. Byzantium became a cultural center and preserver of late Greco-Roman learning. Western Rome disintegrated in the fifth century C.E. and lost the ability to read Greek, thus losing Greek learning. Because of its location, the Byzantine Empire did not lose the ability to read the Greek language and became uniquely situated to preserve Greek knowledge.

After Justinian's conquest in the West dissolved, some of the barbarians converted to Christianity, which began to serve as an anchor for society. Christianity served as the glue of civilization, because in the midst of disorganization and a collapsing infrastructure, all people could feel a sense of kinship under God. The chaos and fear caused by the lack of societal order in the early Middle Ages further allowed Christianity to become a permanent part of our heritage because the cohesion of the Catholic Church offered hope in difficult times.

Monasteries arose at this time. Founded partially from the desire of like-minded people to affiliate, and partially from the desire of monks to remove themselves from the temptations of the world, they were one of the few organized institutions of the time. Because they preserved whatever works of learning were available, they afforded a rare opportunity to obtain an education. However, it should be noted that people did not go to monasteries explicitly for an education. In fact, in the West, the concept of education was not based on obtaining general knowledge, but on learning the works of God. Inside monastery walls, monks quietly preserved a small portion of Greco-Roman knowledge (the majority was lost to Europe), while around them the Catholic Church gave people hope and a common purpose, preventing the total disintegration of society.

Because of the Christian tradition of caring for the sick, monasteries also became the preservers of medical knowledge (almost exclusively the knowledge of Galen, who by that time had been translated into Latin). The great plagues of the time stimulated Christianity because its medical mission was the only hope people had against the ravages of disease. Additionally, as we shall see, monasteries and churches were the *de facto* birthplace of contemporary Western drama and music.

The rules of Saint Benedict (480–547) formed the cornerstone of early medieval monasteries. The Benedictine rule stipulated that monks should be literate, reasonably (but not unduly) austere, and should spend a portion of each day in manual labor. More than any other order, Benedictine disciples filled the ranks of the Church hierarchy and disseminated their word throughout Europe. Also very important in disseminating literacy were monasteries founded by monks from Ireland. Irish monks copied and preserved literary works and fostered a spirit of learning and knowledge throughout Europe.

Although monasteries became the bedrock of the cohesive force of Christianity, they also siphoned a great deal of talent from the secular community. Western Europe paid a very high price for the cohesive force of the Catholic Church. Whether the Church was instrumental in bringing about the Renaissance is a matter of opinion, but it must be conceded that, given the educational level and beliefs of the people and the lack of societal infrastructure, the Church was an important force in the early Middle Ages.

After the defeat of the Huns and the withdrawal of Justinian's Byzantine forces, the Franks became the most dominent tribe in Europe. Their leader, Clovis, converted to Christianity in 496 C.E. In 732, Charles Martel's defeat of the Muslims at Tours allowed Western Europe to develop along Christian rather than Islamic lines. Some sixty years earlier, a battle of equal importance took place in the East, when Constantinople, the capital of the Byzantine Empire, held off a Muslim attack. Each end of Europe was able to repel an Islamic assault, preserving Christianity, for better or worse, from contemporary France to contemporary Istanbul. Given the much higher state of Islamic civilization at the time, one wonders whether these Christian victories were good or bad for Western civilization.

Charlemagne (742–814) was the grandson of Charles Martel. He conquered the Saxons and the Lombards and brought temporary unification to much of Europe. A Christian, he helped spread Christianity throughout Europe. He founded the Holy Roman Empire in 800 and was crowned its first Emperor by Pope Leo III. The Holy Roman Empire was a loose association of the papacy and the German King, whereby the state was, in theory, spiritually ruled by the Pope and temporally ruled by the King. From this association, the Pope hoped to gain control over temporal affairs by controlling the Emperor. The Emperor, in turn, hoped to gain legitimacy by having papal sanction. Throughout the Middle Ages, power fluctuated between Popes and kings.

Charlemagne's greatest contribution was in fostering education. His military conquests were ephemeral, and shortly after his death Europe splintered again, but his support of literacy made him extremely influential in the history of Western Europe. Charlemagne established monastic schools throughout present-day France. The monastery libraries furnished the textbooks, including works such as those of Capella and Boethius.

Charlemagne also organized a reform of Latin. Although the Romans made occasional use of lower case Latin letters towards the end of their empire, their writing was almost exclusively in upper case letters. Charlemagne introduced the widespread use of lower case letters and spaces between words. This Carolingian (referring to the dynasty of Franks that ruled France and Germany, the epitome of which was Charlemagne) revision of Latin restored the nearly universal status throughout Europe that it had enjoyed during the Roman Empire. It would remain the language of Europe until the substantial dissolution of Charlemagne's empire upon his death, at which time local vernaculars began to come to the fore. However, because these vernaculars were not yet standardized, it was not until the end of the Middle Ages that the national languages we know today took hold. In the meantime, the Catholic Church and the universities continued to function in Carolingian Latin, into which Charlemagne and his librarian, Alcuin, translated the very few surviving manuscripts from ancient times.

Like the Christian monasteries, the Franks provided a measure of cohesion until the beginning of the Renaissance. The frequently expressed notion that Charlemagne saved Western Civilization is not necessarily true, because the awakening in Europe was largely due to economic considerations and contact with the Muslims. Nevertheless, the work of Charlemagne—reformation of Latin, translation and preservation of ancient texts, and support of education—cannot be ignored. Any who doubt that the influence of education outlasts that of armies need only look at Charlemagne's true contribution.

Agricultural techniques in Europe did not change appreciably from the Bronze Age to the fall of the Western Roman Empire. The basic design of the plow had remained largely unchanged, and the actual tilling of the soil was done by the front of the plow, called the share. But in the early Middle Ages, three advancements in agriculture made it one of the few disciplines to advance beyond Roman levels. The first concerned a new design of the plow. In the fifth century C.E., a metal blade was placed in front of the share to loosen the ground ahead of the plow, permitting the tilling of soil in Northern Europe, where the firmness of the dirt had previously made plowing very difficult. Somewhat later, perhaps around 1,000 C.E., a moldboard was added to the plow. Placed behind the share, it funneled dirt out of the trough and away from the plow. The moldboard plow, which had been in use in China for centuries, permitted the plowing of wet ground, because the dirt would no longer flow back into the trough.

The second set of developments concerned the draft animal. Oxen were the traditional agricultural animals in the early Middle Ages. The horse was more powerful but could not be used, because its different build would cause it to be choked by the restraints used for oxen. By the eighth or ninth century, the horse collar was constructed, enabling the horse to be used in the field. About the same time, the nailed horseshoe was devised, permitting full use of the new draft animal. Even so, oxen remained preferable in many situations because they consumed less food, and it was not until the end of the Middle Ages that horses became predominant in agriculture.

The third agricultural innovation of the Middle Ages was the use of longer and more complex crop-rotation strategies, such as the change from the two-field technique to the three-field method. Because farming a field every year depleted it, a given field was farmed only on alternate years. Animals grazed in the intervening years, fertilizing the field with their droppings. In Northern Europe, heavier rainfall permitted a spring crop that was not possible in the Mediterranean basin, making it feasible to plant a field two years out of three. In the three-field technique, the field was planted (usually with wheat) in late October or early November of the first year. It was harvested the following summer and was called the winter crop. The next spring, a different crop was planted, to be harvested that summer. This was called the spring crop. After a fallow period of about fifteen months, the field was again sowed with a winter crop. This led to a sequence of winter-spring-fallow over a three-year period. The harvest times can be illustrated as follows:

	Year		
	1000	1001	1002
Field 1	Winter crop	Spring crop	Fallow
Field 2	Spring crop	Fallow	Winter crop
Field 3	Fallow	Winter crop	Spring crop

Because any given field was planted twice in a three-year period, instead of every other year, productivity was increased by a third. It should be noted, however, that a number of different planting strategies were used simultaneously in any given time and place, as each farmer adapted new thinking to his individual circumstances and environment. It would be wrong to believe that Northern Europe suddenly and completely changed to a three-field planting strategy. Like everything else in history, this "revolution" was actually an evolution. Likewise, the three-field technique is only one example of many productive planting strategies, and should not be thought of as the only new way of planting. The key innovation was not so much this particular planting strategy as the move toward extended and more intricate strategies.

Gradually, farmers learned that planting legumes (plants that could obtain nitrogen directly from the air and transfer it to the soil) in the fallow period replenished the soil. This made diminished idle time, eventuating in the virtual disappearance of dormant land.

After the collapse of Charlemagne's empire in the ninth century, Europe was left with a vacuum as profound as the century after Rome fell. Feudalism arose to provide stability and defense. Feudalism is often confused with the manorial system. The manorial system, which occurred in some parts of Europe in the early Middle Ages, was a simple economic system characterized by large estates (manors) farmed by serfs (virtual slaves). In contrast, the feudal system arose later and was more a political and social institution than an economic one. Feudalism was an arrangement between freemen (not serfs) of different social stature. Political and military relationships were formed between landowning nobles and vassals, who were soldiers. A nobleman granted fiefs to his barons, who might then grant use of their land to knights. The knight was in charge of the vassals—the soldiers who provided the defense. Feudalism was a significant source of social stability in the tenth through twelfth centuries and resulted in the further concentration of power in the hands of the few landowners, thereby contributing to the polarization that has cursed organized society from its inception. I submit as history's fifth lesson that power inevitably comes to be concentrated in the hands of a few. This pyramid structure has had two great consequences. First, it is a tragedy for most of humanity, who do not have the opportunity to control their fate. Second, we have been deprived of the full contribution of most people, for who can reach his or her potential while living in poverty at the bottom of the social order?

While cultures in other parts of the world reached great heights, Europe languished, using the framework provided by the Church, and later feudalism, to maintain just enough of an identity to continue to exist. The stagnation of Europe in this time was very different from the changelessness of Egypt and China. Egypt and China were satisfied with the status quo and embraced its stability and security. To those civilizations, changelessness meant harmony. They did not *want* or *need* to change. Europe was different. Its stability was never based on changelessness. What happened there from 500–1000 C.E. did not bring harmony, but rather a stagnation inappropriate to their culture. This inability to change threatened to destroy their culture.

Did Western Europe really exist for five hundred years without producing innovative thought? Certainly not. There surely were new ideas, but they were not integrated into the fabric of society because the social conditions were not conducive to creativity and innovation. Progress requires individuals, as we have seen. But it also requires a milieu that permits change, which did not happen in the West for half a millennium.

The early Middle Ages of Western Europe illustrate that the human mind, individually and collectively, is like a muscle. If it is not exercised, it will atrophy; but if stimulated, it will grow stronger. This period also demonstrates the fragility of civilization and sends a message about the world today. All that we call civilization is contingent upon a reasonable degree of prosperity and hangs under a sword of Damocles, the slender supporting thread of which can be cut by any force that disrupts the fabric of our lives. At this writing, civil war, or its tragic aftermath, rages in Rwanda, Burundi, Liberia, and Bosnia-Hercegovina, while Yugoslavia is attempting to ethnically cleanse its population. The current century has been by far the bloodiest in human history, and there has been little surcease in the inhumanity we show to each other and to animals. Cruelty and the willingness of otherwise good people to do nothing in the presence of evil remain a part of who we are.

We will have matured as a species when we understand how fragile all that we have is, and take the necessary steps to safeguard it. What is needed now is kindness. Kindness to other people, kindness to animals, and kindness to our planet. The most powerful civilizing element in our history, simple kindness is what truly distinguishes us from animals, and only that will allow us to finally step back from the precipice over which we and our posterity are precariously balanced. Our job is to learn from the past and look to the future with both a head and a heart.

Chapter 10
Brilliant and Beautiful

An Arab merchant preaches two simple doctrines,
and the world is never again the same.

WHILE THE WEST FLOUNDERED, THE ARABS WERE PULLED TOGETHER by a remarkable person, Mohammed (570–632 C.E.; sometimes spelled in English as Mahomet or Muhammad), who formed the last religion to exert a truly significant force on the present-day world: Islam.

As it is necessary to understand religion to understand history, it is equally necessary to understand the milieu of a religion in its formative period. Arabs of Mohammed's time believed in many gods, and Arabia in the seventh century was isolated from centers of culture and learning. Militarily, the tribes were not united and often fought among themselves. Arabia was beginning to find a degree of prosperity through trading, but poverty remained and material goods were few. The milieu of early Islam and early Christianity were technologically and economically similar, but Christianity arose in a background of monotheism—a Jewish heritage—whereas Islam arose in a background of polytheism.

More is known of the life of Mohammed than of any other major religious figure. Orphaned as a small child, he married a wealthy widow as a young man. (It has consistently been true in history that many people of innovation or influence had a degree of leisure time to accomplish their work, and one wonders if history would have been different if the young man's wife had not been wealthy.) Mohammed absorbed the thinking of the few Jews and Christians in the area and came to believe that Al-Lah, the principal god of the Arab pantheon, was identical to the God of the Jews and Christians, and therefore the only God. This became the first of his two great legacies: promoting and persuading his people to accept monotheism.

Apparently involved in the caravan business, he did not begin teaching until he was about forty. As his followers grew in number, Meccan authorities began to see him as a threat (as authorities always view those with new ideas), and in

622 Mohammed and his followers were forced to flee from Mecca to Medina. This flight, called the Hejra (or Hegira), is the event from which the followers of Islam—called Moslems or Muslims—date their calendar. In 630, Mohammed secured control of Arabia and returned in triumph to Mecca, henceforth regarded as the holiest place in Islam.

Mohammed's second legacy was the unification of the tribes of Arabia, which had been fighting among themselves, into a coherent political and military unit. Ideally suited for desert warfare, the united Arabs quickly amassed an immense empire. Mohammed himself orchestrated the early military campaigns and implemented the initial Arab conquests (although some of his successors, notably Umar Ibn Al-Khattab, were able conquerors in their own right). Within one hundred years of Mohammed's death, Islam stretched from Spain across North Africa, the Middle East, and Northern India to the border of China—a far larger empire than Rome at its height. The Islamic Empire was the largest stable empire in history; only the relatively ephemeral empires of Alexander the Great and the Mongols were larger. Because of its size and stability, because so much of the Roman heritage was lost, and because Western Europe largely relied on Muslim knowledge to recover its questing spirit, it can reasonably be argued that the Islamic empire is the most influential in history. Mohammed was profoundly successful, both as a theologian, where he single-handedly founded Islam (in contrast to Christianity, which was as much the work of Paul and the apostles as of Jesus), and as a conqueror, the only person in history for whom that can be said. Although the *Koran* is conceived to be Allah's work, not Mohammed's, it remains true that this one person—by being the instrument of the creation of this book, by shaping both the theology and the code of conduct of Islam, and by spearheading the initial conquests of what would turn out to be a vast, stable empire more historically influential than the Western Roman empire—exerted an enormous influence on history. Michael Hart regards him as history's most influential person, an assessment with which I agree.

Islam readily acknowledges and accepts Judaism and Christianity, and integrates many principles of the older religions into its beliefs. If Mohammed had known more about Judaism and Christianity, it might be argued that Islam began as an attempt to modify these religions, as Buddhism began as a modification of Hinduism, and Christianity as a subset of Judaism. However, Mohammed knew little about the older religions and essentially formed his thinking from scratch. This is not to say it was his intention to form a new religion. His desire was simpler—to introduce monotheism and unity to his people. None of the great religious figures of history set out to establish a new religion; they set forth ideas, which were crafted into religions by their followers. In the hands of his followers, Mohammed's ideas became a new religion that fit well beside Judaism and Christianity.

After Mohammed, other Muslims shaped Islam into a continuation of Judeo-Christian thought. Islam holds that Mohammed was the last in a long line of prophets beginning with Adam and including Noah, Moses, Abraham, Jesus, and many others. According to Islam, Allah revealed monotheism to Abraham; the *Torah* and the Ten Commandments to Moses; the Psalms to David; and to Jesus, the Golden Rule and a set of teachings that were indirectly preserved as the New Testament. Allah then brought Islam to completion by revealing to Mohammed, the last prophet, the greatest of works: the *Koran*.

The *Koran* (sometimes written as *Qur'an*), the Muslim holy book, is believed to have been directly communicated to Mohammed through the angel Gabriel, and therefore to be the direct word of Allah. Mohammed *transmitted*, rather than *wrote*, the *Koran*. Because he could not read or write, he recited it to those around him (hence the name *Koran*, which is Arabic for recitation). Thus, the *Koran* is even more holy to the Muslims than the *Bible* is to Christians. In fact, the counterpart to the *Koran* in Christianity is not the *Bible*, but Jesus himself; and the Islamic counterpart to Jesus is not Mohammed, but their holy book. Muslims believe the *Koran*, not Mohammed, to be divine. Thus it is wholly incorrect to refer to Muslims as Mohammedans.

At the time of Mohammed's death, the *Koran* existed in fragments, written at a variety of times in a variety of places, but all recorded by people who were personally in his presence. (It may be that the *Koran* was largely transcribed by one individual, Mohammed's secretary Zayd Ibn Thabit.) Some twenty years after the prophet's death, these writings were collected into a single volume. This is in contrast to the New Testament, none of which was written by Jesus, none of which is based on accurate transcriptions of his teachings, and all of which was written for the first time a generation after his death.

The *Koran* is not only a religious work, it is also a beautiful literary work. It is the first great work of Arabic prose, and with it, Mohammed stands as one of history's great literary figures. The *Koran* is a portrait of a people and a time, and a study of the development of a religion. There has always been an intimate association of religion and literature, but here is a religion which largely owes its existence to a literary work. It was this great masterpiece that established and has maintained Islam. Because of the paramount importance that Muslims have always attached to the *Koran*, it is the most influential and most read book in history, more so even than the *Bible*. It is sad that westerners often have difficulty relating to the *Koran*, largely because it loses much in translation. Indeed, the rhythm, the spirit, and the power of parts of it are essentially untranslatable. A translation of the *Koran* is not the true *Koran*.

Muslims also recognize two other works that many believe to have emanated from Mohammed: the *Hadith*, dealing with the personal sayings of Mohammed, and the *Sunnah*, dealing with the personal practices of the prophet. Collected in the eighth and ninth centuries, they are often presumed to explain and elaborate upon aspects of the *Koran*.

Islam is monotheism specifically adapted for Arabs. Before Mohammed, Arab religions afforded no special place to humanity and offered no afterlife. But in the *Koran*, Arabs found a religion tailor-made for them. It used their language, was integrated into their history, and gave hope and identity specifically to them. Mohammed gave to his people what Jesus gave to the early Christians, and what all religions offer—hope, identity, and a sense of belonging.

Muslims have two overriding obligations. The first is gratitude. Indeed, the word "infidel" does not refer to a nonbeliever; it refers to one who lacks gratitude. The second is total submission to Allah. (This second obligation gives the religion its name; one of the meanings of Islam is submission.) These obligations are accompanied by five pillars of behavior: Confession (there is no God but Allah, and Mohammed is his prophet); Canonical Prayer; Charity; Observation of Ramadan (the Islamic holy month, the time in which the *Koran* is thought to have been revealed to Mohammed, and during which devout Muslims may not eat between dawn and dusk); and pilgrimage (to Mecca, at least once in a lifetime, if the Muslim is physically and financially able).

There is no priesthood in Islam. The religion is composed of the individual and his or her interaction with Allah. Like Judaism and Christianity, Islam adopted the Ten Commandments. Like the *Bible*, the *Koran* discusses a day of judgement, after which people will go to eternal salvation or eternal damnation. (However, some Muslims, like some Christians, interpret these passages allegorically rather than literally.)

Although the terms Arab and Muslim are sometimes used interchangeably, they should not be. Islam started in Arabia, but soon spread to encompass many other nations. Throughout most of Islamic history, the majority of Muslims have not been Arabs; this is certainly the case today. Ninety percent of Muslims belong to the mainstream branch, called Sunnites. Most of the remaining Muslims are Shiites, who have essentially the same religious beliefs as the Sunnites, but differ from the majority because they believe that Mohammed's son-in-law Ali should have become Caliph (the successor of Mohammed and the leader of Islam, a position unfilled in modern times) immediately after the death of Mohammed instead of being his fourth successor. In Iran and Iraq, most Muslims are Shiites, although Saddam Hussein's regime is Sunnite.

The Western idea that Islam "spread by the sword" deserves comment. The West perceives Islam to be a religion of force, characterized by brutal conquests and the involuntary conversion of others, but this is misleading and unfair. The military conquests of Islam during and after Mohammed were reflective of the times, not of Islam in particular; many cities were added to the empire peacefully. Contrary to popular belief, Muslims did not attempt to force others to convert to their religion. Indeed, Islam showed tolerance and respect for other religions (certainly much more so than Christianity), and much of the conversion to Islam was the result of trade contact and cultural exchange. The *Koran* shows great respect for Jews and Christians and says they can be saved as they are, without having to convert to Islam.

Westerners often believe that Islam denigrates women. In fact, the status of women was much better under Islam than under earlier pagan religions, where women were considered chattel. Initially, Islam treated women more favorably than either Judaism or Christianity, and a strong egalitarianism was characteristic of Mohammed's teaching (as it was for Jesus' teaching). Subsequently, some Muslims have interpreted the *Koran* differently. In an opinion that is not intrinsic to Islam, some Muslims have not considered women equal to men in terms of social roles. However, the gender gap has never been greater in Islam than in Christianity, and even these Muslims believe women are spiritually equal to men.

Islam is distinct from The Nation of Islam, which is a contemporary movement, many of whose members believe in the genetic inferiority of Caucasians. In Islam, the only differentiation is between believers and nonbelievers, regardless of race.

Do not let the Ayatollah Khomeini, Saddam Hussein, Muammar Qaddafi, and the Afgan Taliban fool you. Practiced as intended—and as it usually is—Islam is a brilliant and beautiful religion, and its gift to the world is incalculable.

The basic theory of Islam is essentially that of Judaism and Christianity, the sister religions which preceded and laid the foundation for Islam. Simplistically speaking, Judaism, Christianity, and Islam all start with the same foundations and proceed along similar lines. Each "stops" at a different point, so to speak. The Jews do not believe that a Messiah has come and are still waiting. Christians accept the *Torah*, the great holy work of Judaism, but believe that a particular Jew, Jesus, was the Messiah of Jewish literature. Islam accepts most of the works of Judaism and acknowledges not only the existence of Jesus, but also affords him a position as a great prophet. Islam feels that the Christian trinity compromises monotheism, and does not consider any person (including Mohammed) to be a Messiah, but believes the *Koran*, written by God through Mohammed, has the same significance as a Messiah. Each of these religions, arising sequentially, accepts most of the tenets of the preceding religions, adding a set of beliefs uniquely its own. These three religions are not qualitatively different, but rather are variations of each other. How different would our history be if the followers of these religions had been more aware of the origins of their beliefs.

All three of these religions believe in an omnipotent deity who offers people immediate hope in the present. Contemporary Jews may or may not believe in life after death, but the hope of salvation in an afterlife is an integral part of historical Jewish belief, and this belief is basic to Christianity and Islam. Although these religions do not maximally honor the creativity of the individual, they seek to give meaning to the lives of individuals, and that individualism is never lost, not even in the afterlife. As we have seen, other religions give less importance to a deity and the concept of individualism, placing instead more emphasis on personal behavior, repeating cycles of history, or the ultimate harmony of creation. Christianity and Islam arose in difficult times; religions based on ethical and moral principles, such as Buddhism and Confucianism, arose in more prosperous times. When times are good, people can afford to ponder life and construct complex pathways to happiness. When times are bad, people want the quick fix of absolutes and omnipotence.

We have now examined all of the major religions that have significantly shaped our history and are still practiced. Three religions have arisen from the teachings or compilations of one person: Buddhism, Confucianism, and Islam. One religion—Christianity—arose from the teachings of a small number of people. Two—Judaism and Hinduism—arose from the works and teachings of many people. Four religions recognize a supreme being: Hinduism, Judaism, Christianity, and Islam, although all of these also have a strict code of conduct. In none of these religions does simple acceptance of a deity permit harmful behavior to others. Two religions—Buddhism and Confucianism—do not inherently require a deity. As Karen Armstrong says in *A History of God*, these religions are "uncontaminated by an inadequate theism."

Only one major contemporary religion—Christianity—believes in the divinity of a corporeal person (although this belief is not rare in history and a number of extinct or "minor" religions have recognized the divinity of a person, such as the Egyptian belief that the Pharaoh was the son of the Sun God, and the deification of the Egyptian scientist and architect Imhotep). Two religions—Buddhism and Christianity—began as modifications of two others: Hinduism and Judaism. Three Eastern religions surrender the self in this world: Hinduism, Confucianism, and Buddhism. In Hinduism, the self is also surrendered in the afterlife. As a corollary of the relinquishment of the self, these religions are not based on the domination of the world and others. The Old Testament religions of Judaism, Christianity, and Islam place more emphasis on the self, holding it inviolate throughout eternity. Historically, these religions believe as much in dominating the world as in living in harmony with it. The concept of a final, definitive truth is more a part of Christianity and Islam than the Eastern religions and mirrors the general Western way of thinking. The curious opinion of absolute rights and wrongs, black and white, truths and falsehoods, sent Western history down a much bloodier path than was necessary. We have much to learn from the East, for we lack the inner peace, harmony, and reverence for life that the East has achieved.

We have seen that all religions are much more similar than dissimilar, and we can discern five central commonalities. First, every religion, deity or no deity, East or West, seeks to make the world more understandable and assist in coping with the complexities, realities, and vicissitudes of life. Second, all religions accept an incomprehensible force (deity or otherwise) that is more powerful than daily human existence. Third, all religions require their practitioners not to covet or seek worldly possessions. Fourth, all religions advocate a time of quiet and the setting aside of worldly concerns to achieve a more complete awareness of nature. Fifth, all require somewhat similar codes of conduct with regard to other people. In the current age of ethnic and religious violence, let us hope that people will look to those similarities.

Religions based principally on a deity have two *potential* drawbacks. First, they may abdicate to the deity responsibilities belonging to people, possibly deflecting attention from the present and making us less eager to improve ourselves and the world. The promise of an afterlife reduces the importance of the here and now. As Karen Armstrong reminds us in *A History of God*, "instead of pulling us beyond our limitations, 'He' can encourage us to remain complacently within them." Second, belief in a deity may stultify the creativity of the individual, which is at the heart of our prosperity and progress. It is generally true that the loss of identity and the acceptance of an absolute finality is the antithesis of individualism, and therefore of science and progress. Although some great thinkers have been very religious, *they first sought a full explanation of the world*, and then prefaced that explanation with a deity. They accepted the existence of God as only the first step in the explanation, in sharp contrast to those who simply substitute religion for a rational solution.

The cornerstone of religions which are based on a deity remains the opinion that people alone cannot fully understand the world or perfect it. Some people believe that the final phase in our religious development may be the understanding that deities of all types are not required, and that our own intelligence and basic goodness will one day be sufficient to give us the power and ability we had thought to exist only in gods. This opinion holds that religion is a consequence of our continually developing cultural evolution and that we are still in the anthropomorphic phase of our religious development today, as the world's major deities are thought of in human terms. I am among these people, and we hold that there is hope and good news for humanity, but it does not have to lie with a savior or a supreme being, but rather lies with us, individually and collectively, and with human ingenuity and strength of spirit. We believe it is possible to find your way in the world, and to find happiness, without a deity, the threat of eternal damnation, or the promise of immortality.

Science and religion do not necessarily have to conflict, nor do humanism and religion. God, if there is one, works through a set of laws and allows these laws to run the universe. We can comprehend these laws, to our great benefit, without infringing on the greatness of their creator. Searching for the laws of the universe, with or without the belief that God created these laws, is logical and the hope for our species. To ascribe the state of humanity solely to the will of God is to abdicate logic, and to lose the one gift that can save us. I submit as history's sixth lesson that the belief in God, the holding of any religion, or the acceptance of the divinity of any person, does not by itself imperil civilization. These beliefs are precious and can be among the best of our thought. What is dangerous are the opinions that too often follow: that one way of thinking is the only correct way; that the use of rational thinking to understand the world or better our lot conflicts with the will of the Creator; or that any one religion has a more noble origin, a superior history, or a greater destiny than another. It is the weakness of our nature—and the tragedy of our history—that we desire our ideas and religions to be universal, rather than becoming universal in our experiences and tolerance.

The study of origins teaches us much about commonality. If ever there is a lesson to be learned from history, it is in the commonalities and similar origins of religions. Preparing this work has enabled me to feel a part of all religions, and I hope that reading it has done the same for you. I am a Jew, and a Hindu, and a Confucianist, and a Buddhist, and a Christian, and a Muslim. So are you.

Chapter 11
Ascendancy of the East

*Europeans little suspected that lands largely
unknown to them were vastly superior in learning.*

WHILE THE WEST STRUGGLED THROUGH THE EARLY MIDDLE AGES, India and China enjoyed a higher degree of learning and culture, and their traditions remained substantially unbroken. In India, the Mauryan Empire—under which Buddhism flourished—declined in the second century B.C.E. In the fourth century C.E., the Gupta dynasty arose, providing India with two centuries of cultural and artistic splendor until its decline in the mid-sixth century C.E. In the eighth century C.E., India experienced the first of the Muslim invasions (in the Punjab). Over the next several centuries, northern India fell under substantial Islamic influence. Southern India, spared the full impact of the armies of the Aryans and Alexander the Great, was also spared the full impact of Islam, allowing it to retain its cultural heritage. A number of dynasties arose, of which the Chola (fl. tenth through thirteenth centuries) was predominant.

In China, the Tang dynasty (618–907 AD) was a period of learning and culture light years ahead of contemporary European civilization. The Chinese discovered printing in this period. Because they had no alphabet, it was not movable (or changeable) type printing, but block printing, where the characters for entire pages were "sculpted" into a block. The block could then be used only to print that particular page.

The major city of Tang China was called Chang'an, now called Xian (sometimes written in English as Sian). To illustrate the relative status of Eastern civilization in this time period, we need only remember that the three great cities of the world in the year 900 C.E. were Baghdad, Constantinople, and Xian. Shortly after the Tang dynasty came the Sung dynasty (960–1279), perhaps the high point of Chinese civilization. The principal city of the Sung dynasty was Kaifeng, which became a commercial and manufacturing city.

By 1279 the Mongols had completed the conquest of China. During the period of Mongol rule—called the Yuan dynasty (1279–1368)—conquerors knowing nothing of Confucius, art, or city life poured into China. It is a testament to the resilience of Chinese culture and the little-remembered tolerance of the Mongols that China remained a great cultural center after the conquest. It was Mongol-controlled China that fascinated and enthralled Marco Polo. (At one time, he worked for Kublai Khan.)

As the Mongol Empire crumbled, enterprising Chinese leaders, beginning in the 1340s, began to rebel against their overlords. By 1368 the Mongols were gone, and China entered the Ming dynasty (1368–1644). To keep out their former oppressors, Ming workmen connected and extended a series of walls into the Great Wall, which extended for 1,500 miles (2,400 kilometers) and remains the largest structure ever created by human beings.

During the Ming dynasty, the Chinese navy became the greatest in the world. In the early fifteenth century, ships sailed as far as the east African coast. The Europeans were just beginning to venture down the west African coast, led by the voyages of Henry the Navigator (1394–1460). The Chinese fleet was much larger and more advanced than its European counterpart. Their missions were peaceful, with no religious agenda, no looting, and no taking of slaves. The Chinese philosophy was based on harmony, not conquest, and on peaceful coexistence with nature, not on its mastery. Although they were ideally suited to explore, it was not part of their cultural milieu.

Like the Chinese, the Muslims were in a position to surpass Europe in the approaching age of exploration. Never having lost Ptolemy, they retained the knowledge of the sphericity of the earth, and thus had a five-hundred-year head start on Europe. For the Muslims, the lack of incentive to take to the sea appears economic rather than cultural. Because their empire stretched from North Africa and Spain to Northern India, they could trade with both Europe and the Orient via established land routes. They had no reason to believe that traveling the ocean would add to the quality of their lives.

The West was not so fortuitously situated. Its inability to wrestle control of land routes to Asia from the Muslims forced it to sea to fulfill what it perceived as its destiny. In Western Europe, a unique combination of circumstances—a cultural heritage of domination and an economic incentive—came together to foster exploration. The future of the sea would lie with the West.

At many points in the study of history, we are left asking "what if?" What if

Western Europe had maintained and extended Greco-Roman knowledge from 500–1000 C.E.? What if the Muslims or the Mongols had conquered Europe, as both nearly did? What if the Muslims had conquered Byzantium before 1453? What if Europe had adopted Eastern religions? To these we must add one more: what if the Orient had possessed the "restless" but cruel spirit of the West?

Chapter 12
Flashes of Light

A man scorned as a "dumb ox" unites new
knowledge with the old.

AROUND THE YEAR 1000, Western Europe began to prosper economically and recover its inquiring spirit. Many think of the Middle Ages as the period of minimal intellectual achievement before the Renaissance. For the first half of the Middle Ages, there is truth in this perception. But for the second half, 1000–1400 C.E., this is not so. What we call the Renaissance was the culmination of a series of changes going back to about 1000 C.E., and it was not a unique occurrence in history. Civilization ebbs and flows. Single moments of drastic change are rare. The latter Middle Ages deserve more credit for shaping our world, because the events making the Renaissance possible can be clearly traced to this period.

Prosperity and Contact

Two crucial events occurred about 1000 C.E., bringing about the reawakening that would fully blossom in the Renaissance. The first was the achievement, after six hundred years, of a degree of prosperity. Finally, the West had the economic base and leisure time to look beyond immediate needs. Civilization and progress demand foresight and planning, and therefore are completely dependent on the ability to look beyond immediate needs.

Second, contact with the Islamic world increased, which was a key catalyst in the reawakening of Europe. Westerners often fail to appreciate the excellence and contribution of Eastern and Near Eastern cultures, but we owe much to them. The Islamic world had preserved (and extended) Greco-Roman learning in a way the West had not been able to do. The Muslims were leaders in the preservation of knowledge because they had contact with more cultures than any other ancient or medieval civilization. The Muslim conquest of all but the most northern part of present-day Spain (beginning in 711) placed their culture very close to Western Europe. The victory of Charles Martel kept the Muslims from penetrating further, but they remained in Spain until the end of the fifteenth century. For centuries, the two cultures existed side by side with little contact.

Two events made contact with Islamic culture possible—the fall of the Muslim strongholds of Toledo (in Spain) in 1085 and Sicily in 1091; and the Crusades, which we will consider momentarily. What concerns us now is the repository of Islamic knowledge the West obtained from Toledo and Sicily, particularly the former because of the greater literary stores there. The Christian Europeans found unparalleled literature and learning in Toledo, and scholars came there from all of the northern countries to partake of the literary riches (written on paper, a medium the West had not yet acquired from the Muslims). The furious translation into Latin of Arabic translations of Greek scientific and philosophical works exposed Europe to the full spectrum of Greco-Roman learning for the first time since the fall of the Roman Empire.

The Muslims not only preserved Greco-Roman knowledge, they added to it, and the West was the beneficiary of this as well. Islamic scientific advances were made possible in large part by the separation of science and religion in their society. Although Islam and Christianity are very similar religions, with substantially similar origins, they had different ideas about the acceptability of scientific investigation. In Islam, science advanced freely, without fear of religious recrimination, which was not the case in the West (an exception was dissection of the body, permitted in Christian societies, but not in Islam). Some of the original Muslim contributions were as follows:

Astronomy: The Muslims improved on the existing knowledge of the positions of the stars and planets. Most of our contemporary names for stars come from Arabic.

Mathematics and Physical Sciences: Because Islamic culture was so geographically extensive, it came into contact with both Greece and India. From India, Muslims obtained the numerals that are still called Arabic, as well as the concept of a decimal system. Arabic numerals were not only much more convenient than Roman numerals, they also permitted arithmetic operations on numbers. XII times XII cannot be elucidated, but a child can easily solve 12 times 12.

The Muslims showed that negative numbers and fractions are subject to the same rules as positive whole numbers and can be treated the same way. They showed that there are many possible number systems, all of which are valid.

(For example, any number can be expressed in the decimal system, which is base ten, or in any other base.) They were scholars of algebra and made advances in optics and instrument design. The Arab scientist Ibn al-Haytham (c. 965–1038, known to us as Alhazen) disagreed with the prevailing view that the eye emits light and illuminates the object that is seen, favoring instead the notion that the object emits or reflects light.

Medicine: Although Islam forbade dissection of the body, thus hampering their knowledge of anatomy, they imparted to the West an organized health-care system. Arab physicians were licensed by the government, and hospitals (including mental institutions) were numerous and generally humane. The most famous Arab physician was Abu Ali Ibn Sina (980–1037, known to us as Avicenna). Avicenna wrote the *Canon of Medicine*, a compendium of medical knowledge of the time. However, he is best remembered for a work of philosophy called the *Kitab ash-Shifa* (remembered simply as the *Shifa*), which argued that religion and philosophy should be given equal weight in understanding nature. The *Shifa* furnished an extensive discussion of Aristotle and played a major role in reintroducing him to the Western world.

Chemistry: The Muslims were master alchemists. The goals of alchemy were to transmute metals into gold and to find the elixir of life, the substance conferring immortality. To achieve the former, alchemists searched for the Philosopher's Stone, a substance thought to permit the transmutation of metals. Alchemy was, in fact, a very successful discipline; it invented the idea of experimentation and created laboratory technique, as well as establishing basic principles of metallurgy. Alchemy was to chemistry what astrology was to astronomy—a place to start. Although most of the specific facts were incorrect, we see again that once a people begin inquiring, they will overcome deficiencies in information. To a great extent, contemporary chemistry is alchemy with the belief in magic replaced by the scientific method. As in other fields, Muslim contributions in alchemy benefited from the geographic extent of their culture, which allowed them to combine Eastern work (from both China and India) with Western.

Foremost among those absorbing this new Islamic knowledge was Pierre (or Peter) Abelard (1079–1142). Applying a new spirit of skepticism to everything, including the *Bible*, Abelard insisted that any and all assertions be fully proven before they are accepted as fact. In his book *Sic et Non* (*Yes and No*), he posed questions and then cited authorities whose answers did not always agree. Only by questioning all authorities can we reconcile them with each other. He pointed

116

out that divergent views can be reconciled, but only if none of them is held to be inviolate. From *Sic et Non:*

> Assiduous and frequent questioning is indeed the first key to wisdom. For by doubting, we come to inquiry; and through inquiring, we perceive the truth.

This reconciliation of ostensibly mutually exclusive viewpoints would become the basis of Scholasticism, an intellectual movement which strove to integrate this new knowledge with religious faith.

Not since fourth-century Rome had there been a significant amount of translation of Greek into Latin, and much of that work was lost. Despite the direct cultural continuity of Greek and Roman civilizations and the physical proximity of Roman and Western European civilizations, many Greek works came to Europe only through the Muslims, since the fall of Rome caused many of its contributions to largely disappear. Contrary to popular belief, medieval monasteries preserved only a small portion of Greco-Roman knowledge.

Most people believe the Renaissance began suddenly in fifteenth century Italy. Both components of that belief are wrong. It did not begin suddenly, but was several centuries in the making, beginning with the achievement of reasonable prosperity in Europe after 1000 C.E. and continuing through contact with the Islamic world in the eleventh century. Because of the Christian conquest of Toledo, that city in the twelfth century was actually more the birthplace of the Renaissance than fifteenth-century Italy.

The Crusades also served to bring Europe and the Muslims together. In 1095, Pope Urban II, responding to the Byzantine emperor's request for assistance against the Muslims, decreed that the Holy Land must be reclaimed for Christianity. In actuality, there were a number of causes for the Crusades, only one of which was to reclaim the Holy Land for Christianity. Fear of westward Muslims expansion, work for unemployed knights, and simple expansionism were also causes. From 1096–1272, there were nine organized crusades (plus a children's crusade and a peasant's crusade, both of which were unmitigated disasters). The first crusade (1096–1099) captured Jerusalem, but it was lost again in 1187. The third crusade did not capture Jerusalem, but it did reclaim some Mediterranean islands. The fourth crusade never reached the Holy Land. Without papal knowledge or consent, it sacked Constantinople in 1204, establishing a Latin rule in Byzantium. The sixth crusade was unique in being largely bloodless. In that crusade, the Holy Roman Emperor Frederick II peacefully captured Jerusalem and is best remembered for negotiating peace with the Muslims for some Christian control of the Holy Land.

It is ironic that Christianity sought to destroy Islamic civilization just as it was beginning to benefit from Islamic knowledge. The Crusades were largely unsuccessful, and from a military viewpoint, the Muslims were the victors. The traditional teaching is that the Crusades markedly increased the diffusion of Islamic knowledge into Europe. But with the floodgate of Muslim learning already opened in Toledo and Sicily, it is doubtful that the Crusades augmented the awakening of learning in Europe. In fact, the fourth crusade's sack of Constantinople, the last bastion of Greco-Roman learning in the West, makes it improbable that the Crusades exerted a beneficial effect on Western knowledge. However, they did have consequences for Europe that indirectly stimulated Western scholarship.

The Crusades stimulated the economy of Western Europe, principally of Italy. Economic stimulation is often a byproduct of war. New markets were discovered and new trading routes developed. This would prove an indirect stimulus of the Renaissance.

A second major effect of the crusades lay in their failure, which forced Western Europe to look to the sea. With the overland route blocked, it would ultimately turn to the sea to reach the East, especially after the fall of Constantinople in 1453 further impeded eastward travel. Unable to defeat or convert the Muslims, the West was forced seaward, becoming the beneficiary of all that sea exploration offered. If the Crusades had succeeded, Europe might not have taken to the sea for many more centuries.

A Questing Mind

As humanity obtained more self-esteem and the desire to improve, it was natural for all fields of endeavor to examine the one available example of excellence: antiquity. Slowly, Europe began to add to ancient and Muslim knowledge, but the West was initially unsure how this new learning fit into the existing Christian dogma. Many religious leaders felt that any human description of natural processes infringed on God's unique ability to create and change the world. Albert the Great (Albertus Magnus or Saint Albert, 1193–1280) was a keen observer of the natural world, especially animals, and was one of the first people in the Middle Ages to recognize that knowledge obtained from science is independent of knowledge obtained by faith.

Saint Thomas Aquinas (1225–1274) was a student of Saint Albert and had been derided as a "dumb ox." Aquinas was a founder of Scholasticism, which held that true knowledge could be obtained from both faith and reason. He maintained that scientific knowledge did not diminish God's power, but only served to increase our understanding of it. Aquinas's masterpiece articulation of this view was the *Summa Theologiae*, in which he successfully wove together the cities of Man and God, in contrast to Augustine's sharp separation. By facilitating the integration of this new knowledge into the existing framework, Aquinas fostered its acceptance. His genius lay in his ability to achieve a reconciliation, based on fresh interpretations of both the new knowledge and the holy scriptures. Naturally, not all Christians saw it that way. Many felt that this knowledge, especially that derived from Aristotle, was blasphemous. In 1277, the Pope banned much of this new learning (including much of Aquinas's writings). Overall, however, the Scholastics' approach was largely successful, and Aquinas was instrumental in gaining Church acceptance of Greek and Islamic knowledge. As we shall see, the Church's vehement opposition to new ideas did not start until it felt the challenge of the Reformation.

After two hundred years of debating these new ideas, Europe began to think for itself in the thirteenth century. Roger Bacon (c. 1214–1294) took the remarkable position that one should not rely on the revered authorities of the past, but should draw his own conclusions from experimentation. In his great work, *Opus Majus,* Bacon not only established the importance of experimentation, but also set forth the four obstacles to knowledge, which continue to stand as warnings to everyone who wishes to understand:

> Now there are four chief obstacles in grasping truth, which hinder every man, however learned, and scarcely allow anyone to win a clear title to learning, namely, submission to faulty and unworthy authority, influence of custom, popular prejudice, and concealment of our own ignorance accompanied by an ostentatious display of our knowledge.

By the beginning of the fourteenth century, Europe had in place two new elements critical to our modern scientific method—observation and experimentation. No longer were the ideas of the past taken as absolute truth. Prior to this time, ancient authorities were unquestioned, but now some wanted to see for themselves. A person's (or a culture's) belief that they have knowledge is comfortable and may inhibit further learning. Progress requires skepticism of the three most comfortable pillars we have—common sense, common thinking, and the authority of prior thinkers. That skepticism, accompanied by observation and experimentation, opened the door for the third great advance in our development, following the understanding that the world could be controlled and the rational approach of the Greeks.

Also pivotal in this period was the rise of universities. As more knowledge came from the East, monasteries no longer held a near monopoly on literacy and education. The need for specialized centers of learning was appreciated. Already, predating the general contact with the Muslims, there was a famous medical school in Salerno, Italy (the principal contributions of which were the training of surgeons and the removal of religion from the curriculum), but it was only after contact with the East that universities came into their own. In the thirteenth century, universities arose at Paris, Oxford, Cambridge, Naples, Bologna, and Montpelier. If the nature of people does not change, what causes people in some periods to inquire, while those in others do not? A major part of the answer lies in the social infrastructure (or lack thereof). Some reinforcement for a questing mind, some ability to share ideas with like-minded people is also necessary. Universities became places where educated people could congregate and exchange ideas. They fostered learning by attracting and retaining a critical mass of people, whose scholarly activities now had enough reinforcement and reinfusion to be self-sustaining.

Although the blind acceptance of old knowledge is an impediment to the acquisition of new knowledge, new knowledge has to be based on old knowledge. Consequently, the dissemination of existing knowledge is always paramount to additional learning. To that end, it is noteworthy that paper came to Europe in the twelfth century. As we have seen, about 100 C.E., Ts'ai Lun improved the process of papermaking in China. By 800 C.E., papermaking was known to the Arabs, but only because they learned it from the Chinese. Europe learned to make paper by the twelfth century, but again, the knowledge was imparted to them by contact with the Arabs. There is no evidence that either the Arabs or the Europeans invented paper independently. By replacing earlier, inferior writing material (bamboo in China, parchment and velum in the West), paper made possible much more rapid and efficient transfer of information, becoming another reason for the flashes of light on the European horizon. Most leaps of progress are preceded by the introduction of practical writing media, a theme we will discuss later.

Misunderstood and Maligned

About 1200, a Mongol chief named Temujin (c.1162–1227, known to us as Genghis Khan) unified the Mongol tribes, which had been involved in internal wars. (In this respect, he was the Mohammed of the Far East.) In 1214, he began conquests that would eventually make the Mongol Empire the largest the world would ever see, stretching from the shores of China to eastern Europe. In 1241, when the Mongols reached eastern Europe and imperiled the entire continent, Genghis Khan's death forced the field commander of the European campaign to break off the attack and return home to defend his bid to for leadership. Europe, with luck, once again held off a powerful invading force, just as it had held off the Muslims. We can only speculate how Western Europe would look today if these few key events had been different.

By 1250, the Mongols had conquered much of China, Russia, and Persia. (They conquered many Islamic lands, but not Arabia itself.) These conquests removed the barriers to the Far East imposed by the Muslims. The removal of these barriers, combined with the efficient administration and road building of the Mongols (little remembered in history), opened travel to the East for the first time, allowing Europe its first contact with the Orient, and particularly with the spices of the Orient.

By the mid-fourteenth century, this land bridge disappeared. The Mongol Empire was dissolving. Despite (more likely because of) the great extent and rapid rise of the Mongol Empire, it barely lasted the lifetimes of Genghis and his immediate descendants. Genghis's grandson Kublai Khan (1216–1294) was the last to rule a united Mongol kingdom. Upon his death, the great empire was split into quarreling hordes, one of which was led by Timur (or Tamerlane), who claimed to be a descendant of Genghis Khan, but was in fact a Turk. Tamerlane's military campaigns sealed off the land route through the Middle East.

Another event helped close the land route—the western Khans of the Mongol Empire had converted to Islam and were no longer willing to be ruled from the East. By converting their Mongol conquerors, the Muslims became the most permanent and influential force in that part of the world, providing another example of the conquered becoming the conquerors. This victory re-instituted the pre-Mongol barrier to land travel to Asia, forcing the West to turn to the sea. If the Mongol conquest had never opened the Orient, Europe may not have known what it was missing. If the Mongol Empire had not collapsed into internal struggles, with the concomitant loss of its western portion to Islam, the West would not have had the incentive for a sea route. Europe has the much maligned and misunderstood Mongol Empire to thank for exposing it to the East and ultimately forcing it to explore the sea route.

The Mongols left another lasting legacy in India. Southern India escaped the Mongol invasion, as it earlier had escaped Alexander and Islam. (In fact, southern India has managed to retain aspects of its heritage and language going all the way back to the Indus civilization even to the present day.) But in the early sixteenth century, Baber (or Babur), a descendant of Tamerlane, conquered northern India and founded the Moghul empire (also spelled Mughal or Mogul). By this time, the Mongols in this area were Muslim, so the Moghul dynasty, although founded by Mongols, was actually Islamic. Until European domination, the Moghul leaders were, generation after generation, among the most thoughtful and enlightened in history. The prosperity of India during this time is evidenced by their extraordinary art and architecture, of which the Taj Mahal is an example.

Affluence and Death

Three inventions revolutionized sea travel. The first was the compass, known in China early in the first millennium, and probably before, but not employed in the West until about 1200 C.E. Combined with the ability to determine latitude (long obtainable from the angle of the North Star with the horizon), the compass revolutionized sea travel. But it was not until John Harrison's 1761 invention of a portable marine clock (based on the use of two interacting springs) that it reached its full potential; only then could sailors determine longitude (by carrying on board a clock which accurately recorded the time at their port of departure and comparing it with local time, sailors could determine longitude— each hour of time difference was about a thousand miles, or sixteen hundred kilometers).

The other two maritime innovations of the late middle ages (and also possibly of Oriental derivation) were the triangular sail and the rudder. The triangular sail, mounted to a moveable boom, permitted a ship to sail against the wind, while the rudder provided a much more accurate means of steering the ship. These developments made sea travel in the unpredictable European winds far more reliable.

122

Gunpowder was a fourth invention to come to the West from probable Eastern origins. The first gunpowder weapons were inaccurate, dangerous to those who used them, and little improvement over existing weapons. But the psychological effects were great, and ultimately gunpowder shifted the advantage from the larger army to the army with better equipment.

The mechanical clock, a marvelous engineering achievement that married so much new knowledge, became known in Europe in the fourteenth century but was known in China several centuries earlier.

Partially because of the advances in trading made possible by the innovations in sea travel, the Western economy became more organized and began to resemble contemporary economies. A general rise in the standard of living led to a market for consumer goods not absolutely essential for living. This in turn led to an interest in manufacturing and the rise of a middle class of merchants and traders (what would later be called the Bourgeois). Excluded under feudalism, this new class now had something new to post-Roman Europe—discretionary income, some of which financed the new interest in the science and technology of manufacturing techniques. Cities grew in both number and size and became centers of activity. Prosperity and increased food production significantly increased population.

Another event of this period which shaped European history was its near devastation from bubonic plague. Bubonic plague is caused by the bacterium (the singular of bacteria) Yersinia Pestis (formerly Pasterella Pestis). Carried in the bloodstream of affected rats, it is transmitted to man through the rat flea, which bites the rat and then bites a human victim. The disease causes swelling of lymph nodes. (These swollen nodes are called buboes, from which the disease derives its name.) A more severe form of the disease occurs if it spreads to the lungs (pneumonic stage, or pneumonic plague). The term "black death" referred to the darkening of the skin that terminal patients had secondary to poor lung function. Although the disease is not significantly contagious during the early, bubonic stages, appreciable person-to-person transmission becomes possible once the lungs are affected. The septic phase (i.e., bacteria in the bloodstream with systemic symptoms) meant certain death. Bubonic plague occurred numerous times, dating back to antiquity, but it was the worldwide pandemic of the fourteenth century that devastated Europe.

The precise history of bubonic plague cannot be clarified until its epidemiology is more completely understood. Some believe that the fourteenth-century outbreak was so much worse than previous experiences because trading routes established by the Mongols permitted easier passage of infected rats. The plague was active in Asia in the early 1340s, and many Europeans were aware of this. Its transmission to Europe can in large part be traced to one specific incident. In 1344, a group of merchants from Italy were traveling the overland route to the East when they were besieged in Caffa (now called Feodosia, in the Crimean peninsula of the Ukraine) by a Tatar horde. (The term "Tatar", or "Tartar", is often used synonymously with Mongol, but it has a somewhat different meaning. Tatar refers to people of Turkish origin, who after being conquered by the Mongols, intermarried with them. The term then was used to refer to the Mongols. By the fifteenth century, many Tatars, like many Mongols, had converted to Islam. Today, the term refers to Muslims of Turkish descent living in the lands of the former Soviet Union.)

The Italians dug in and these two groups were still fighting two years later. In 1346, bubonic plague broke out in Caffa. It is not clear if the two sides contracted the disease independently or if the Tatars got it first and then imparted it to the Italians by heaving corpses over their walls. In either case, the plague was soon carried west by the Italians as they fled from Caffa to Genoa. However, had this event not occurred, the plague would surely have entered Europe by another route; greater travel and the shrinking of the world placed the bacterium on an inevitable collision course with humanity.

The population of Europe, which had increased steadily since 1000, was decimated. Overall, perhaps a third of the population of Europe was killed; in some areas mortality exceeded 70%. Both Petrarch and Boccaccio left clear and terrifying descriptions of the catastrophe, the former saying that future generations will not be able to believe that such an event occurred. Another chronicler tells us, "No one wept for the dead because everyone expected death himself." Asia was equally devastated. The population of China in 1400 was half that of 1200. Three species—a rat, a flea, and a bacterium—combined to bring humanity to its knees.

This particular visitation of the plague was largely over by 1350, but it returned in 1361, 1369, and 1379. It would take two hundred years for Europe to regain the population it had in 1345. The resulting labor shortage weakened feudalism and improved the status of workers, helping to establish a middle class in Europe.

In addition to the four visitations of the plague in the fourteenth century, there would be lesser, but still severe, outbreaks in Europe for another three centuries. (One of these would cause the young Isaac Newton to flee to the countryside to do his great work.) Bubonic plague has a history of very long dormancies between outbreaks. (For example, eight hundred years from the plague of Justinian to the Black Death of 1346.) An outbreak in India in the early twentieth century claimed twelve million lives, and the disease reappeared there in 1994, reminding us that we will not master microbes until we have mastered the social conditions of our fellow man. One theory for plague's lesser influence today is that it was primarily carried by fleas that infested the black rat, now largely replaced in Europe by the brown rat. Although the fleas of the brown rat also can carry the disease, this rat is not found in as close proximity to man as the black rat, and its fleas may not leave the animal as often, so there is less likelihood they will bite a person. No one knows why (or if) the disease is no longer a worldwide threat. Will future historians chronicle yet unknown bubonic plagues epidemics?

Unifying, Not Innovative

I do not believe the Catholic Church was the crucial factor in the Renaissance. While it is true that the Church was a unifying force between 500 and 1000 C.E., there is a difference between a unifying force and an innovative force. The change in thinking in Europe about 1000 C.E. was about innovation, which was not the contribution of the Church. Religion and its rituals provide comfort and structure, but it is precisely this comfort that makes people disinterested in new ideas. An economically depressed culture held together by an institution which only stabilizes cannot progress. By contrast, a prosperous culture exposed to new ideas will assimilate them. It was the new prosperity and contact with Islamic ideas that brought about the Renaissance.

Chapter 13
Seeing For Oneself

A Polish cleric believes in simple explanations and
sees the universe in a new way.

WE CALL THE PERIOD THAT FOLLOWED THE LATTER MIDDLE AGES—dating from around 1400—the Renaissance. The word refers to a reawakening of inquiry and learning. To some extent, there was such a re-awakening, but the process was already underway in the preceding period.

During this period, the focus of innovative thought shifted to Western Europe. The East, which did not experience the cultural decline of the West after the fall of Rome, became complacent with respect to new ideas. What determines which cultures will be creative and which complacent? To a considerable extent, creativity accompanies tumult. Much of our progress has taken place in times of uncertainty, because tumult is fertile ground for inquiring minds. Eastern cultures had achieved a high degree of stability and perhaps felt no need to change. Shaken or unstable societies become more creative because their social structure is less rigid, and social structure is a prime inhibitor of innovation. Strange as it may seem, unless the basic infrastructure of civilization is disrupted (such as in Europe between 500–1000 C.E.), there is virtually an inverse relationship between stability and innovation and a direct relationship between tumult and innovation.

Further, the closing of the land passage to the East forced the West to look outward for commercial goods, while there really was very little in the West that the Middle Eastern countries wanted that could not be obtained from North Africa and Spain. China, too, felt it had what it needed and did not need to seek new lands. Progress is not necessarily made by the more advanced culture, but by that which perceives the biggest gain.

More than any other single characteristic, the change that came over Renaissance Europe was an insistence on *seeing for oneself*. No longer were old authorities, secular or religious, accepted without question. All knowledge, new and old, was met with skepticism and not accepted until shown to be true. Individual opinion, valued in ancient Greece but long buried in the dogma of religion and yesterday's authorities, was rediscovered. This new attitude took great courage, as it is always easier to trust an established viewpoint or a revered sage.

The Renaissance fostered a more secular spirit. While the belief in God and the fundamentals of Christian thought were untouched, there was a greater respect for the individual and collective human mind. The belief that individual people are important, and that the focus of thought should be on people and the worldly affairs of people, is called humanism and was a distinguishing characteristic of the Renaissance. Humanism and a secular spirit resulted in a greater emphasis on the present moment and a belief that not everything that mattered was to be found in the afterlife.

Florence became a leading center for the new attitude about learning and humanism for three reasons. It was geographically more or less in the center of the immediate world of Western Europe (i.e., England to Greece, North Africa to Scandinavia), and therefore in a unique position to benefit from contact with a variety of cultures, just as Alexandria was almost two thousand years earlier and the Muslims more recently. Second, beginning around 1400, increased trade and banking in Florence caused the rise of a middle class, whose prosperity led to the confidence and discretionary income that is the catalyst of change. Economic prosperity was partly due to the rise of double-entry bookkeeping and merchant banking, both of which developed in late medieval Italy and were widespread by the fourteenth century. Double-entry bookkeeping is a method of keeping financial records where each transaction is recorded twice—once in regard to its effect on the organization as a credit, and once in regard to its effect as a debit. This method allows a more complete understanding of the organization's financial status and permits better long-term planning. (Great ideas are indeed found in subtle places.) Prior to merchant bankers, transactions involving another location could only be executed with the physical movement of money. Merchant bankers issued notes of credit to an agent in a distant location. The agent would then honor the note and make payment to a third party, thereby facilitating transactions.

The final reason for the rise of Florence was the enlightened rule (either directly, or indirectly through the leaders of its burgeoning banking system) of the de' Medici family, whose most famous members were Cosimo (1389–1464) and his grandson Lorenzo (1449–1492). As Kenneth Clark points out, Florence was such an exciting and pivotal place partly because most of its leaders were scholars. Fifteenth-century Florence very nearly achieved Plato's ideal of philosopher-rulers. Whatever one's political persuasion, it is simply not possible to compare most contemporary American governmental leaders with their Florentine counterparts. Florence became the focal point of the early Renaissance, and nowhere else was humanism felt more strongly. (Hence the common misconception that the reawakening of learning began there.)

The Dissemination of Knowledge

The dissemination of existing knowledge is always key to the acquisition of new knowledge. This was the case with papyrus in sixth century B.C.E. Greece, although it was certainly not the only reason for the miracle of Greece. Likewise, it would be a mistake to think that the invention of printing "caused" the Renaissance. The Renaissance was well underway before moveable-type printing was known in the West. However, printing increased the dissemination of learning exponentially and deserves to inaugurate our discussion of the advancements in science and technology during this period.

The history of printing is more complicated than many Westerners realize. Decorative printing on cloth has ancient origins. Printing on media for the purpose of reading seems to have begun with block printing in China in or before the ninth century, where it served to reproduce holy treatises. In block printing, each page was individually inscribed on a block of wood. Once inscribed, this block became a template and could not be changed. The finished product was a collection of papers, each derived from one block, which were pasted together in a scroll rather than bound into a volume. The *Diamond Sutra*, a Buddhist manuscript and the first printed book of which we have knowledge, was created in this way in China in the ninth century. Block printing appears to have come to the West from the East in the Middle Ages.

The great advance in printing was the invention of moveable type, which allowed a template to be changed. Moveable type was also a Chinese invention, in the eleventh century. But without an alphabet, moveable type involved only the placing and substituting of *characters*, largely diminishing the advantages of the medium, and the Chinese did not pursue the idea. It was simpler to stay with block printing. But in alphabetical languages, moveable type meant the placement and replacement of *letters* and was vastly more efficient than block printing. A template no longer produced only a fixed, static text, such as a page; it could now be modified, making possible the convenient printing of infinite combinations of text from the grouping of small, changeable letter templates. Johann Gutenberg (c. 1400–1468) would make full use of precisely this Western advantage.

Not only were both block and moveable-type printing known in the East before Gutenberg, but in all probability, he was not the only Westerner to conceive of moveable type. He did, however, conceive of moveable type independently, cementing his reputation in history.

For moveable type to be successful, more was required than just the ability to change the type. The letters must be identical and interchangeable; there must be a suitable ink; there must be an appropriate final medium to absorb the ink; and there must be a means of insuring uniform contact of the inked type and the final medium. Paper, arriving in Europe some three centuries earlier, served as a suitable medium. Gutenberg made pivotal advances in every other aspect of the printing process.

Gutenberg broke down the process of moveable-type printing into its components and made ingenious improvement to each of them. He understood the need for identical letter pieces that could be used repeatedly and interchangeably, so he invented a typecasting device that made letters identical. Block printing used a wooden template, but moveable-type printing required that letters be used many times, so they had to be made of metal. Each letter was manually formed in relief on the end of a rod of hard metal, forming a positive image where the letter projected above the surface. This was then punched into softer metal to create a mold; the outline of the letter was now below the surface. When filled with molten metal, the mold formed identical letters that projected above the surface. The need to cast letters in metal explains why the pioneers in moveable-type printing—including Gutenberg—were trained as metal workers.

Gutenberg took advantage of newly discovered oil pigments to develop ink that would reproducibly adhere to the type. Parchment, expensive and relatively rare, was also not porous enough to absorb this new ink; it would have smeared to the point of illegibility. Hence, the profound importance of paper. Gutenberg used a screw press (already used in winemaking and the extraction of oils from plants) to insure uniform contact between the paper and the inked type. Gutenberg did not just conceive of the *concept* of movable-type printing, but also developed the *processes* needed to make the idea work.

The Gutenberg *Bible*, one of the true masterpieces of our civilization, was printed in 1454—one year after the fall of Constantinople—making the printing press fortuitously available precisely as Greek-speaking scholars were fleeing the Byzantine Empire for the West. The effects of this infusion of scholars and a simultaneous means of disseminating knowledge were synergistic. Printing quickly moved from the commercial and business sector to affect every area of European society.

In addition to facilitating the spread of information, printing had two other noteworthy effects. First, by making reading materials more readily available, the printing press provided a previously unknown incentive for the common people to learn to read. Reading moved from the esoteric privilege of an eclectic few to the expected activity of the many. Over the last several centuries, the ready availability of books has allowed literacy rates in developed countries to rise to levels that would have astonished the leaders of the Renaissance or the founding fathers of the United States—both of whom, contrary to popular belief, had considerable doubts about the abilities of the common people. By stimulating reading and making literature more readily available, the invention of the printing press allowed the literary arts to equal the visual arts in influence for the first time in European history.

Second, printing came into existence at about the same time as vernacular languages came to the fore. Chiefly the product of nationalistic pride, the vernacular, or local, languages became serious rivals to Latin in the fifteenth century. By frequently using vernacular languages, printing facilitated their spread, the result of which we see today: the complete replacement of Latin by national languages. William Caxton (1422–1491), a textile merchant turned printer, used his printing press to print the first books in English. Caxton printed dozens of widely read books using the version of English spoken in London, promulgating that version and helping to standardize the contemporary world's most influential language.

Before leaving the subject of printing, we must mention Aldus Manutius (1450–1515), an Italian printer who did more than anyone besides Gutenberg to bring the printing press to its full potential. Manutius made two important contributions in the early days of printing. He printed inexpensive books that common people could afford, and he personally supervised the translation from Greek of numerous classics (using displaced Greeks from Byzantium).

The first writer of note to take advantage of the printing press was Desiderius Erasmus (c.1466–1536). The illegitimate son of a priest, Erasmus was himself ordained as a priest, but later revolted against the regimentation of religious life and chose a more secular existence. Erasmus traveled widely (England was a particularly favored destination), corresponded with many influential people, and searched for ancient manuscripts. His writings, among the finest examples of scholarship and humanism of his time, brought the Renaissance to Northern Europe.

In an effort to quell controversy about the scriptures, Erasmus produced a new Latin translation of the Greek New Testament. This version largely re-placed Saint Jerome's translation of the late fourth century (called the *Vulgate*), which had been the standard Latin *Bible* for centuries. As a religious writer, Erasmus advocated simple Christian behavior and spoke against the corruption of the Catholic Church. He may have influenced Martin Luther, although the two men would follow separate paths. Erasmus attacked the excesses of the Church from a humanist standpoint, while Luther's attack was religious. Erasmus did not have Luther's fanaticism and contempt for the Church, preferring a moderate and rational approach to the differences between Catholicism and Protestantism. (He remained Catholic while supporting many of the ideas of the Reformation.) The tolerant views of Erasmus were buried in the senseless bitterness that characterized both sides in the Reformation, and the Catholic Church condemned his works.

Erasmus's most famous work is *In Praise of Folly*, a witty and clever satire of superstition and ignorance. He wrote in Latin, fearing that the spread of ver-nacular languages would have a divisive effect on international communica-tion—a fear that was well founded. In any language, the works of Erasmus speak for common decency and reason.

Simple Questions

Just as people wanted to see for themselves in the world of nature, so also they wanted to see for themselves in the realm of religion, a desire which launched the Protestant Reformation. As with any great idea, it had no one starting point and no single responsible individual. Early reformationists expressed opinions that were rather commonly held in the general populace, but held in secrecy. John Wycliffe (1328–1384) and Jan Hus (1372–1415, also spelled John Huss) insisted on the priority of the scriptures over the Pope and the Catholic hierar-chy a century before Luther.

But it was Martin Luther (1483–1546), an Augustinian monk and a professor of theology, who changed the way we see Christianity. When he promulgated his *Ninety-Five Theses* in 1517, he inadvertently began 150 years of war, which would end Catholic domination, provide a new concept of Christianity, and make Luther the most important Christian thinker in history other than Paul.

The central point of Luther's theology was Justification by Faith Alone. As promulgated by Paul, Justification (the way in which sinful and unworthy man can obtain God's forgiveness and re-establish his relationship with Him) can be achieved only by accepting Jesus as God's son and living by his teaching. In Luther's time, Justification was commonly obtained by acts of penitence, such as good deeds and indulgences (money paid to the Church in exchange for forgiveness). Luther wanted a return to the Justification by Faith Alone so integral in Paul's teaching. Only by recognizing the true nature of Jesus and following His example could people be saved. General good works were to be encouraged, but salvation of wicked man came from what he believed about Jesus and how well he followed His teachings. Luther was particularly incensed by indulgences. Because only the grace of God could bring about forgiveness of sins, he felt indulgences usurped God's power and arrogated for the Church what only God could do.

If indulgences were not the path to salvation, what purpose did they serve? For that matter, if it was only the faith of individuals that led to salvation, why have the hierarchy of the Catholic Church as a mediator? Luther's *Theses* attacked the abuses of the Church, specifically the sale of indulgences, which Luther regarded as worthless and fraudulent. But Luther's allegations went far beyond specific issues and attacked the infrastructure of the Church itself. He felt that the clergy and the laity were equal in the eyes of God, and that most of the clergy were therefore unnecessary. He resented the superfluous Catholic hierarchy, which obscured the simple fact that it was the faith of individual people that made salvation possible. He wanted a simpler Church, with simpler ceremonies. His was a much stronger and more fundamental criticism of the Church than those of any of his predecessors, and it was directed at the heart of the Church itself. One can reasonably argue that he set out not to reform the Church, but to destroy it in its existing form.

Integral to Luther's hopes for a simpler Church and the direct experience of religion was a *Bible* readily available to the masses. To this end, he translated the *Bible* into German, taking advantage of the printing press, so that people would not be dependent on the clergy for either the provision or the interpretation of the scriptures.

Luther's challenge would likely have been crushed before it got underway were it not for a fortuitous set of political circumstances. There had long been a struggle for power between the Pope and the Holy Roman Emperor, the secular leader of the German State. Pope Leo X, attempting to weaken secular power community by fomenting internal bickering, supported the weaker candidate for Holy Roman Emperor, who happened to be a supporter of Luther. Because of this mitigating factor, four years passed before official papal condemnation of the *Theses* at the Diet of Worms (the word "diet" refers to a meeting, and

132

Worms is the name of the city) in 1521, by which time the Reformation was unstoppable. Additionally, much of Luther's support stemmed less from a desire for religious freedom than a desire to be free from Papal (Italian) domination. German nationalism and the hope of some German noblemen that a break with the Catholic Church might leave them with some of the church's property also aided his cause.

John Calvin (1509–1564) was second only to Luther as a leader of the Reformation; his 1536 book, *The Institutes of the Christian Religion*, is second only to the *Ninety-Five Theses* as a statement of the tenets of Protestantism. Calvin's brand of Protestantism also believed in Justification by Faith, but additionally came to accept, after Calvin's death, the doctrine of Predestination, wherein God had already decided—at or before the moment of birth—who would be saved and who would be condemned to eternal damnation. Calvinists formed a second branch of Protestantism, of which the Huguenots in France are an example, and influenced many Protestant religions, such as the Puritans in England. The contemporary Presbyterian Church adheres to the doctrine of Predestination.

In response to the Reformation, the Catholic Church chose war, or more precisely, chose to adopt an intransigent position that made war inevitable. The Council of Trent met multiple times between 1545 and 1563, reaffirming the Church's structure and infallibility and initiating the Roman (or Universal) Inquisition.

The word "inquisition" has three historical meanings. All pertain to the Catholic Church's persecution of anyone with a differing opinion, but it should be remembered that the Church, until the Reformation, was generally more tolerant than many believe. The Medieval Inquisition occurred in Europe (except England and Scandinavia) from the twelfth to the fifteenth century. As this was prior to the Reformation, this inquisition punished heretic Catholics, Jews, nonbelievers, etc. The Medieval Inquisition was under the control of the Church, although heretics were turned over to local secular authorities for final disposition. Although tragic, its extent and significance have been exaggerated.

The Spanish Inquisition began in 1478 (predating the reformation) under Ferdinand and Isabella, who would later sponsor Columbus. Although a Catholic inquisition, it was under the control of the Spanish royalty and had a dual purpose: punishing heretics and securing the throne. (In fact, these two Spanish rulers would successfully keep the Spanish Catholic Church under royal control.) Its harshness is legendary, as exemplified by the *auto-da-fe* (a brutal public execution), but emanated more from the Spanish monarchs than the Catholic Church. The blow to innovative thinking delivered by the Spanish Inquisition would help keep Spain, the de facto birthplace of the Renaissance, largely out of the mainstream of European thought until almost the present day.

The Roman Inquisition, a specific reaction to the Reformation, targeted Protestants. The Protestants had criticized Catholics for allowing excessively liberal thinking. The literal and rigorous Protestant interpretation of the *Bible* was winning converts by appearing to be more faithful to the scriptures. To counter this perception, the Catholic Church took a hard line on novel ideas, adopting an intransigent posture on purely religious matters and opposing changes to the status quo in any area of human thought. Since the days of Albertus and Aquinas, the Catholic Church had accepted new ideas with more tolerance than most people realize. But no more. The most famous target of this new intolerance was the heliocentric theory of Copernicus. Initially unopposed by the Church, it now became a target, and its proponents (such as Galileo) were persecuted.

Most of Europe became embroiled in the Thirty Years War (1618–1648). One of the most horrible conflicts in history, it killed a quarter of the population of Germany and ultimately forced the Catholic Church to recognize Protestantism in that country. Eventually, Protestantism would become the rule in Northern Europe, while Catholicism remained predominant in the south.

Not all of the Catholic Church's responses were militaristic. Saint Ignatius of Loyola (1491–1556) founded the Jesuit order in 1534 (confirmed by Pope Paul III in 1540). Originally formed to convert the Muslims, the Jesuits were influential in the Reformation by fostering education and spreading Catholicism through missionary work. The Jesuit order attracted bright people from all over Europe and gave them an excellent liberal education. Saint Ignatius thus emerged as the leading reformer of Catholicism from within. Also as a response to the Reformation, the Catholic Church stressed more realistic and highly dramatic art, thereby becoming an indirect cause of the Baroque movement in the visual arts in the seventeenth century.

It would be wrong to conclude that the Reformation led to significantly greater religious and intellectual freedom. Indeed, as discussed above, a "selling point" for the Protestants was that they were closer to God because they tolerated no dissent from the scriptures and no new ideas. Luther was as fanatically dogmatic in his positions as any Catholic; he opposed the theories of Copernicus and was strongly anti-Semitic. Calvin was for a time the de facto dictator of Geneva, and during his tenure opposing opinions warranted burning at the stake. His most famous such victim was Miguel Serveto (1511–1553, generally remembered as Michael Servetus), a physician and theologian who was among the first to describe the pulmonary circulation. Calvin had him burned because he did not accept the Christian Trinity.

If the Reformation did not bring about more liberal thinking, what were its lasting effects? The effect of the Reformation on areas other than religion is difficult to assess, but it did have secular ramifications. The relatively small degree of religious freedom provided by the Reformation contributed in two ways to intellectual liberty. First, Protestantism attached more significance to the individual. Of all the ancient ideas that resurfaced in Western Europe in 1100–1600, none was more important than the concept of individual importance. In the milieu of rapidly expanding knowledge and a renewed sense of human potential, the growing opinion that the Catholic hierarchy was unnecessary further strengthened the Renaissance idea of individual worth. Second, the Reformation provided an alternative viewpoint. Alternatives always enhance intellectual development.

The Reformation mirrored achievements in the scientific community in one important respect. Just as scientific developments of this period were characterized by seeing for oneself, the Reformation allowed people to experience God for themselves. In both science and religion, the individual mattered and had a right to experience for himself.

Luther's contribution to history illustrates a common characteristic of innovative thinking—simplicity. Great thinkers simplify the questions at hand; much of their success is due to the ability to penetrate layers of established thinking to ask crucial questions, questions simpler and more fundamental than those posed by their contemporaries. Overwhelmingly, great thinkers look for simpler ways to achieve their goals.

Autopsy

What Roger Bacon did for physics, Paracelsus (1493–1541) did for medicine. It is unclear whether Paracelsus had formal medical training, but his treatment of prominent people secured his position as a physician. He discarded traditional sources of information, treating only on the basis of his own experience and observations. In his writings, he invited others to do the same:

Study my books and compare my opinions with the opinions of others; then you may be guided by your own judgement.

The established medical profession never accepted him and prevented some of his works from being published. Nevertheless, he was pivotal in the development of medicine because of his influence on the public and with younger physicians.

Prior to Paracelsus, disease was still thought to be an imbalance of humors, a doctrine some two thousand years old. Paracelsus believed in astrology and thought astral forces caused disease. This may not seem any more advanced than the humoral view, but there was a big difference. Since each person had a unique blend of humors in his or her normal state, different abnormal combinations of humors caused a given disease in each person—a disease could be caused by one combination of humors in one person and a different combination in another. This implies an essentially infinite number of causes for any one disease; each person had his own cause based on his unique normal combination of humors. Paracelsus's view, however incorrect, meant that any given disease had only one cause. This one disease-one cause theory was an enormous step for medicine, regardless of whether or not the cause was correctly identified. As we have seen, incorrect thinking can be fixed; clinging to the dogma of the past or a religion causes cultural paralysis. The first step to progress is replacing dogma; it does not matter if the replacement is inaccurate as long as thinking is stimulated.

We owe another stride in medicine to Paracelsus. A long-standing interest in alchemy led him to believe in the chemical nature of the body, and he turned from prevailing herbal remedies to chemical treatments, foreshadowing the medicine of the following centuries. Although we now know that many herbal remedies are meritorious, chemistry remains the basis of contemporary medicine. By participating in the establishment of this basis, Paracelsus helped make medicine into a science.

Paracelsus' effect on chemistry is not often appreciated. The chemical basis of medicine stimulated interest in chemistry, facilitating its advancement enormously. Paracelsus actually discovered ether, but he did not promulgate his findings, and there is no indication he used it or understood its anesthetic properties.

Although the significance of Paracelsus in the development of Western science is somewhat controversial, he brought new thinking to both medicine and chemistry and can be regarded as a transitional figure from the Middles Ages to modern times.

Already a well-known iconoclast, Paracelsus further showed his contempt for the medical establishment by teaching in vernacular instead of Latin, as scholars in all fields were beginning to do throughout Europe. Although not necessarily readable by scholars in other countries, their work could now be read by lay people, allowing common people greater access to knowledge but sacrificing some degree of international communication among scholars. The problem of international communication was addressed by the founding of professional societies (such as the Royal Society), the advent of professional journals, and the rise of translators. Vernacular languages and the printing press combined to make knowledge far more available to the general public than previously possible.

The skepticism of traditional thinking so characteristic of Paracelsus was a step toward replacing the inaccurate Galenic tradition, a process not to be completed until the autopsies of Vesalius.

Ambroise Pare (1510–1590) was trained as a barber-surgeon. This may seem the oddest of combinations, but for much of medical history surgery was performed by barbers. It was customary to place a duty in the hands of those with the necessary instruments, and barbers were the only people who had the tools required for surgery. Surgeons were distinguished from physicians and not held in particular esteem, so including them with barbers would have seemed reasonable. It would be relatively late in the history of medicine before the physician and the surgeon received the same basic training.

Pare was the most innovative surgeon of the sixteenth century. His numerous contributions include advancements in artificial limbs and surgical instruments. He reintroduced the practice of ligating (tying) vessels to reduce hemorrhage. Understood in antiquity, this practice had been replaced by cauterization. However, perhaps Pare's most important achievement concerns not what he did, but what he did not do.

In Pare's time, gunshot wounds were commonly cauterized with boiling oil. One day in 1536, lack of oil forced Pare to treat wounded soldiers without the traditional means. To his surprise, the untreated wounds healed much better. Pare did not set out to test a hypothesis that cauterizing wounds with hot oil impeded healing. *He simply ran out of oil.* But he was astute enough to realize that the outcome was not a coincidence — hot oil retarded, rather than hastened, healing. He was also able to accept that his training and his beliefs were incorrect.

The experience of Pare illustrates a repeating pattern in our history: a great deal of our progress has come in the form of unexpected observations, which then serve as the nidus for further work. Serendipity is immensely valuable in the acquisition of knowledge, but only if minds are open enough to entertain the possibility that the unexpected may lead to improvement.

It is rare that a single book written by one individual decisively influences a scientific discipline, but in 1543, it happened twice. The first was a treatise on anatomy. Unlike Islam, Christianity did not strictly forbid the dissection of the human body, but throughout the Middle Ages autopsies were uncommon, and when they were done, they lacked a systematic approach. Thus, the two principal means of learning anatomy—the study of Galenic textbooks and the performance of autopsies—were both deficient. In the fifteenth century, autopsies became somewhat more frequent and systematic, but autopsies performed by one person in the sixteenth century would teach us anatomy.

Unlike Paracelsus, Andreas Vesalius (1514–1564) was classically trained in medicine. He studied under a leading disciple of Galen and was appointed professor of anatomy at Padua. He departed from the traditional approach of watching from a distance while students performed dissections and autopsies and became personally involved. More than that, he became skeptically involved. He came to his work without the opinion that Galen was always right, and he learned that much of Galen was wrong. His masterpiece, *De Fabrica Humani Corporis* (*The Structure of the Human Body*, often called the *Fabrica*), was published in 1543. It contained only what Vesalius had personally seen and specifically addressed many of Galen's errors. Nowhere is the great idea of seeing for oneself more evident than in Vesalius's great anatomy book. How fitting that the word "autopsy" means just that—seeing for oneself.

Vesalius recognized the importance of accurate illustrations in anatomy, and his work had many superb illustrations. He encouraged acceptance by placing illustrations of noted civil authorities on the book's frontispiece and dedicating it to the Holy Roman Emperor. The combination of scientific genius, superlative illustrations, and political correctness was successful. Within fifty years, Vesalius's great work would become the standard of anatomy.

Our Place in the Universe

Mikotaj Kopernik (1473–1543, also spelled Niklas Koppernigk, and known to us as Nicolaus Copernicus) was trained in medicine and law, but it was his thinking in astronomy that changed the world. He was not the first to conceive of a heliocentric model of the universe (that honor probably falls to the Greek Aristarchus, of whose work Copernicus appears to have known), but he was the first to present a well-conceived and internally consistent model of a sun-centered solar system.

For most of the Middle Ages, Aristotle's view of concentric spheres was the prevailing conception of the universe. By the Renaissance, Ptolemy's view of the heavens was back in vogue, largely replacing the Aristotelian model. As we have seen, Ptolemy's model involved the use of epicycles — smaller spheres attached and sometimes rotating opposite to major spheres. In the late Middle Ages, additional modifications and complications were added to the Ptolemaic model to fit the more detailed observations of the period. By the time of Copernicus, the Ptolemaic model had become incredibly complicated, with multiple layers of complexity.

The immediate stimulus for Copernicus occurred when, as a young man, he was consulted in the matter of calendar reform. He realized that the underlying problem was a lack of synchrony between time measured by the sun and the moon. A year, reflective of what was thought to be the motion of the sun, was 365.25 days, which was not a multiple of the twenty-eight-day lunar period. Copernicus recognized that the motion of the sun and the moon, as well as their relationship to each other, would have to be clarified before there could be meaningful calendar reform. Unlike his predecessors, Copernicus was not willing to add yet another layer of complexity to the existing system. Instead, he had an uneasy feeling that there was a fundamental flaw in our conception of celestial motion, and that a simpler explanation was likely. Copernicus believed that the universe must be simple. Like all great thinkers, he began with a question: could the complicated Ptolemaic model be made simpler through another viewpoint? Copernicus was aware of ancient thinking and seems to have known about the Pythagorean idea that nature worked through simple and mathematical functions and Aristarchus' belief that the earth moved around the sun. In what may have been history's first significant thought experiment, Copernicus envisioned the planets rotating about the sun, and in doing so, saw that their motions immediately became simpler. It is a repeating theme in the history of thought—a new perspective that simplifies the situation becomes the new hypothesis and the nidus for a great idea.

The theory of Copernicus has five principal components:

1. The sun is at the center of the universe.
2. The stars are at the periphery of the universe.
3. The earth rotates on its axis every 24 hours.
4. The earth and the planets revolve around the sun.
5. The moon revolves around the earth.

Beyond these five specific tenets, the Copernican view implied that the earth was, in all probability, only a small part of the universe—and not its most important part, which would have consequences for how humanity saw its place in the universe. Whereas the Ptolemaic model posited an outermost sphere, making the universe finite, the Copernican model suggested a universe vastly larger than had been thought and perhaps unknowable. Copernicus' landmark book, *De Revolutionibus Orbium Coelestium* (*On the Revolution of the Celestial Spheres*), was published in 1543, the same year as Vesalius' book, although it was completed earlier. (Copernicus believed in heliocentrism as early as 1514.)

Five aspects of Copernicus' theory warrant discussion. First, it was not based on Copernicus's own observations; it was a theoretically ingenious model for already existing observations. Second, his work was not based on previously unknown evidence. No dramatic new information came forward to make his great leap possible. Third, the theory was initially put forward and promulgated without opposition by the Catholic Church; that would come later, when the Church's stance would be very different from its position in 1543. Indeed, Copernicus feared public ridicule, not the Church. It may be that the Church was not threatened by Copernicus's book because it was written in Latin, and thus unreadable by the general public. Fourth, there was imperfect agreement between the theory of Copernicus and actual observation. In fact, Copernicus's model really did not fit observational data any better than the Ptolemaic model. It was just a great deal simpler. The reason for this imperfect fit is that Copernicus retained the Ptolemaic notion that planetary orbits were circular, when in fact they are elliptical (oval). Fifth, no cogent evidence for the model was presented, either in the book or by Copernicus himself. In particular, in addition to the common-sense notion that the earth is stationary, and the religious argument that the earth and man, as God's central creations, had to be at the center of the universe, there were two cogent scientific reasons why the new model was thought to be flawed. First, in a time when inertia was incompletely understood, if the earth is moving through space, falling objects should be left behind. Second, a moving Earth should result in a slightly different view of the heavens on either side of the sun, and no such different views were seen.

Because of these difficulties, many intelligent people did not initially accept the new idea. Indeed, heliocentrism was initially rejected by no less a figure than Galileo. Those who accepted the new idea did so for the same reason it was conceived—a deep belief in a simpler system—and not because the evidence was compelling. Today, we regard the slow acceptance of the heliocentric view as a mistake, but we should remember that it ran counter to both common sense and established learning, was presented without compelling evidence, and did not perfectly describe the observed heavens. An understanding of history requires sympathy with viewpoints that seem quite illogical today, but which are perfectly reasonable when examined in context. We must extend this sympathy to our ancestors, as we must ask it from our descendants. The next generation, through the work of Kepler and Galileo, would provide the evidence for the Copernican view.

Observation had been a part of science for several centuries; it did not suddenly spring into science during the Renaissance. But now it was an essential ingredient. 1543 saw the publication of both *The Structure of the Human Body* and *On the Revolution of the Celestial Spheres*. Behind these two books was enough unbiased observation—in search of truth, not the verification of old authorities—to forever change the way science was done.

Tycho Brahe (1546–1601) believed that, although the other planets revolved around the sun, the combination of the sun and planets revolved around the earth. Although this misconception involved a certain amount of "backsliding" from the Copernican theory, Tycho's thorough collection of observations (the most comprehensive of the time, all collected with the unaided eye) sowed the seeds of confirmation for heliocentric theory and enabled Kepler to deduce his planetary laws. Tycho showed that a new heavenly body (which we now know was a comet) moved in eccentric fashion, cutting across Ptolemy's supposedly incorruptible celestial spheres. A supernova he described in 1572 further damaged the Ptolemaic view by showing that the heavens were clearly not unchanging.

Theology was the first love of Johannes Kepler (1571–1630), but he gave it up to become a mathematics teacher because he needed money. Kepler began his scientific career as Tycho's assistant. The two made odd companions. Tycho was a nobleman; Kepler came from peasant origins, and many of his relatives lived at the fringes of the law. Tycho wanted Kepler to use his data to replace the Copernican viewpoint with his own, but fate took the younger man down a different road. When Tycho died, Kepler inherited his rich collection of observations, to which he added many of his own. Kepler focused on planetary motion and could not make their orbits fit a circular model. He noticed that planets moved faster at some times during their orbits than at other times. Uniform velocity would be expected in circular orbits. In a brilliant marriage of observation and theoretical insight, Kepler realized that planetary orbits must be *ellipses,* not circles. With the addition of elliptical orbits, the Copernican model fit very well with observation, and a major obstacle to its acceptance was removed.

Copernicus and Galileo believed that inertia alone kept the planets in orbit. Kepler realized that since the motion was curvilinear, some force was required to sustain the planetary orbits. He even grasped that the sun was somehow responsible for the motion of the planets, but could not fathom the mechanism because there was as yet no theory of gravitation. His three laws of planetary motion are as follows:

1. Planetary orbits are not circles; they are ellipses. An ellipse can be defined as a two-dimensional figure characterized by two foci and consisting of all points for which the distance to one focus plus the distance to the other focus is constant. (A circle is an ellipse whereby the two foci occupy the same point in space.) Planetary orbits are ellipses, and the sun lies at one of the two foci.

2. A line joining any planet to the sun sweeps out equal areas in equal times. This means that planets do not move at uniform velocity, but speed up when they are close to the sun.

3. The length of time it takes a planet to circle the sun and the size of its orbit are linked in an unusual way: the square (the second power) of the time it takes a planet to complete one orbit around the sun is proportional to the cube (the third power) of its average distance from the sun.

Kepler's laws were a triumph in one other way. His mathematical treatment of planetary motion showed for the first time that the same mathematics that explained natural phenomena on Earth *also explained them in the heavens.*

Chapter 14
A New Way of Learning

*A seeker of truth uses a new instrument to change his
mind, and the mind of the world.*

GALILEO GALILEI (1564–1642) WAS A MEDICAL STUDENT when he discovered the
mathematical expression for pendulum motion. The popular story that he noticed the regularity of a pendulum by comparing it to his pulse is probably
untrue. Galileo noticed that the period of a pendulum (the time it takes to
complete one swing and return to its initial position) depended only on its
length, not its mass or the angle defined by its motion. This would subsequently
permit the creation of pendulum clocks.

The story that Galileo disproved Aristotle's idea that heavy objects fall faster than
lighter objects by dropping two differently weighted objects from the tower of Pisa
is probably not true. (This was likely done before Galileo; and it was not until
effective vacuum pumps, after Galileo's death, that it was finally shown that all
objects fall at the same speed if air friction is removed.) Galileo's contribution to the
study of motion was much deeper. He successfully applied mathematics to moving
bodies, founding the science of mechanics (the study of motion, also called dynam-
ics). He discovered that falling bodies do not fall at a uniform rate, but rather accelerate as they fall. Moreover, there was a precise mathematical relationship between
the time an object had been falling and its speed. If two objects fall from rest, and
one falls for twice as long as another, it moves four times as fast. If it falls for three
times as long, it travels nine times as fast. Because freely falling bodies descend too
rapidly for the eye to detect acceleration, Galileo used inclined boards with grooves.
When a ball was placed on these boards, its descent was sufficiently slowed for
Galileo to accurately measure distances traveled per unit of time—velocity. He also
disproved Aristotle's idea that motion on Earth is linear when he discovered that
objects in flight follow a parabolic path. (A parabola is the curved geometric figure
resulting from the intersection of a plane with the side of a cone.)

Galileo did not invent the telescope. Like the belief that he compared a pendulum to his pulse and dropped bodies from the Tower of Pisa, this is a misconception. There likely was no single person behind the telescope; it is speculated that Roger Bacon had one in the thirteenth century. Some believe that Hans Lippershey (1570–1619) played a large role in its development. In any event, Galileo was the first to make a practical telescope that would enable significant astronomical observations. His telescopic study of the sky verified the heliocentric theory; a view Galileo himself had initially rejected. Galileo's telescopic observations and his mathematical analysis of terrestrial phenomena were roughly contemporary with Kepler's mathematical analysis of celestial motion. The two combined to deliver a devastating blow to geocentrism. Galileo published his new opinion in *Sidereus Nuncius* (*The Starry Messenger*) in 1610.

In 1616, Galileo was ordered to appear at a hearing, where Copernican doctrine was condemned but he himself was not, and his works were not forbidden. In 1632, however, he published *Dialogue on the Two Chief World Systems*. A more comprehensive defense of heliocentrism, it produced a cornucopia of new knowledge of the universe based on twenty-two years of telescopic examination and was particularly damaging to the traditional view that all heavenly bodies orbit the earth. He showed that Jupiter had four moons clearly orbiting *it*, not the earth. Second, he demonstrated phases of Venus, which were much more readily explained by Venus orbiting the sun than the earth. Third, he saw sunspots, which arose, moved, and then disappeared, proving that the sun was not immutable. Fourth, his telescope resolved the Milky Way into a myriad number of individual stars, suggesting a universe of previously unguessed immensity. Such size would explain the lack of different views of the universe from opposite sides of the sun, removing one of the major objections to the Copernican view. Fifth, Galileo's study of motion on Earth allowed him to extend Aristotle's concept of inertia to moving bodies. An object in motion would tend to remain in motion unless acted on by a force opposing the motion. Therefore, objects falling to Earth would share in the earth's motion, even as they fell, and would not be left behind by the moving Earth. This removed another major objection to the Copernican view.

Dialogue laid bare the poverty of the Ptolemaic view and was particularly threatening to the Church because it was written in Italian, and could therefore be read by the laity. (In fact, *Dialogue* had a very wide lay readership, and Galileo was hailed as a great popularizer of science.) As long as the Copernican doctrine was an esoteric, unconfirmed theory that could not be read by lay people, the Church saw little need to react to it. In 1632, the Catholic Church faced a very different situation from that in 1543, when Copernicus's work was published, or even in 1610, when *The Starry Messenger* appeared. Threatened by the Reformation, having made the decision to entrench at the Council of Trent, and on the verge of the Thirty Years War, the Catholic Church was in no mood to have the common people presented with cogent evidence that Copernicus was right or to allow any challenge to its authority or the perceived status quo. Heliocentrism was now a threat to homocentrism, the church's doctrine that man was the principal object of God's creation. (Homocentrism differs from humanism because the former ascribes value to man only insofar as he is God's creation, while the latter sees man as having intrinsic value apart from God.) If the earth were not the center of the universe, then it was only a short step of the imagination to conclude that man was not the principal focus of God.

When it became clear just how much Galileo's work would change the perception of the world, the Church moved quickly to censure his achievement. But Galileo's work was already in print and disseminated; the only way to stem the tide of change was to get a full recantation by Galileo himself. Only a full retraction by the perpetrator could undo the damage.

The Catholic Church's persecution of Galileo through the Roman Inquisition is a fascinating and terrifying story, the details of which need not concern us. Although Galileo was not tortured, it was made abundantly clear that torture was a possibility if he did not fully recant. Galileo did so, thereby avoiding torture and death, although he was still placed under house arrest and forbidden to continue his work. Even lifelong house arrest could not stop Galileo, however. His last book, *Discourses Concerning Two New Sciences*, was smuggled out of Italy and published in the Netherlands in 1638. (The new sciences were mechanics and materials science.) Published when Galileo was seventy-four, it showed that if no force acts on an object, it will continue to move at a uniform speed. Although not as well-remembered as his other works, it was a major blow to traditional thinking and a direct bridge to the studies of Newton. Galileo regarded it as his best work.

The Church's action immediately stifled all innovative work in Italy and Southern Europe. Because of the Reformation, Northern Europe was less affected. Although the Renaissance came later to the north, and although the Reformation was no friend of the spirit of inquiry, the new hard line of the Catholic Church shifted the center of intellectual activity in Europe to the north.

Beyond his specific achievements, Galileo established mathematics as the tool for understanding phenomena. He understood that numerical relationships are the key to understanding natural phenomena, and that these relationships are definitive, unchanging, and expressible. After Galileo, mathematics became the language with which humanity described the universe.

Our manner of obtaining new information—called the scientific method—has gone through several phases: from the mythological theories of ancient civilizations; the purely reasoning manner of the Greeks; the sporadic experiments and observations in the Middle Ages; to the present manner of collecting information, establishing a hypothesis, experimenting, modifying the hypothesis, and drawing a conclusion. It is sometimes said that Galileo invented the scientific method. He had a large role, to be sure, and he was one of the first to demonstrate the sequence of constructing the instrument, conducting organized experiments, drawing a conclusion, and publishing the results. But the way we derive information today is not the heritage of Galileo alone. Others contributed as well, including an English statesman and philosopher who was among the most talented public servants ever.

Francis Bacon (1561–1626) became attorney general in 1613 and was appointed Lord Chancellor five years later. Charges of corruption forced his resignation, but his lasting contribution was outside the public arena. Bacon argued that our senses can be misleading, and that we often reach a conclusion because it fits our expectations or the patterns of our experience. In *Novum Organum* (*The New Instrument*), Bacon asserted that nature could only be understood by organized, systematic experimentation. He specifically presented the analysis of experimentally obtained observations as a replacement for the Aristotelian method, and he outlined the steps in our modern scientific method:

1. Use experiments to collect information.

2. Classify new knowledge into categories, allowing for the systematic addition by multiple workers and comparison of all data on a subject.

3. Derive a law or theorem to provide an explanation (hypothesis).

4. The hypothesis must then be substantiated by leading directly to new, verifiable knowledge.

5. Conclusions are always tentative and must be regarded as new hypotheses, thus allowing for the testing and verification of new knowledge as it is obtained and insuring the continuation of the process.

However, our scientific method, like all great ideas, is the work of many people, and it is a predictable outcome of the seeing-for-oneself attitude of the late Middle Ages.

As the scientific method replaced blind faith and revelation as the means to investigate the world, natural laws began to replace God as the cause of natural phenomena. Because natural laws, unlike God, are discoverable and comprehensible, we acquired the means to understand and improve our world. But all things come at a price. The scientific revolution unlocked vast frontiers, but it also stole the simplicity and security that had comforted people and given a sense of completeness.

Another consequence of the new approach was that only ideas that can be absolutely proven to be true were accepted as knowledge, sharply distinguishing scientific endeavor from philosophy. Notice in the pages ahead how often words like "demonstrated", "proved", and "showed" are used to describe scientific advances.

Unexpectedly disproved hypotheses, if pursued, can lead to wondrous findings. Much of our progress has come from disproved hypotheses that were followed with curiosity rather than despair. To do this requires a shifting of the investigator's entire thought process. One must often "start over" and abandon dearly held postulates and assumptions.

Our method of obtaining knowledge is itself a hypothesis, subject to scrutiny and modification like any other hypothesis. Since Bacon, many have pondered how knowledge is obtained and what we can know, perhaps the most important of which was David Hume (1711–1776), a historian and philosopher of compelling scope. Inspired by the work of Newton, Hume attempted, in *A Treatise of Human Nature*, to find laws describing the process of thinking. We shall discuss his treatment of the idea of cause and effect, because cause and effect is at the heart of our method of learning about nature. Hume argued in a forceful and disquieting manner that we can never be certain that two events are related to each other, because our understanding of cause and effect is based on assumptions and common-sense notions that we do not know are true, and on past experiences that we do not know to be currently valid. Hume concluded that neither reason nor experience lead to infallible knowledge; we must accept that we cannot know the true nature of things. As we shall see, his brilliant analysis was mathematically verified in the twentieth century. Hume also produced a cogent criticism of the belief that God's existence can be proven on rational grounds.

Chapter 15
New Worlds

An experienced navigator makes a series of mistakes
and never realizes his contribution to the world.

THE INCREASING PROSPERITY OF EUROPE and the rise of a distinct merchant class enhanced the importance of trade. While intact, the Mongol Empire had enabled a brief (about one hundred years) glimpse of the Far East. Now the Middle East was in Muslim hands; the land passage was closed; and Europe had a strong incentive to turn to the sea.

By this time, the Ptolemaic view of the world was back in vogue, so the roundness of the world was understood, but its circumference was thought smaller than it actually is. It was also believed that the southern tip of Africa looped around to join Southeast Asia, enclosing the Indian Ocean and making sea passage to the Orient impossible.

It cannot be doubted that the Vikings reached North America about 1000 C.E. However, they did not come as explorers and made no effort to learn anything of the new land. Their few journeys to America were among many examples in history of something being glimpsed but not understood or explored.

The ocean travels of Europe, for our purposes, began with Portuguese explorations down the coast of Africa. Henry the Navigator (1394–1460), a prince, led numerous expeditions down the western coast of Africa, but never rounded the Cape. That was left to Bartholomeu Dias (c.1457–1500; also written Bartholomew Diaz), who rounded Africa in 1488, proving that the Ptolemaic view of that part of the world was wrong. But Dias was forced to turn back by his own men and did not reach India.

This was the background facing Cristoforo Colombo (1451–1506; Cristobal Colon in Spanish, Christopher Columbus in English). We know very little about his life. Born in Italy in 1451, he was a merchant seaman of considerable experience and ability.

Shipwrecked off Portugal in 1476, Columbus lived there for nine years, during which he was influenced by the voyages of Henry the Navigator. Like most Europeans of his day, he subscribed to the Ptolemaic view of the world, which held that the world was round but only had a circumference of about 18,000 miles (29,000 kilometers). To Ptolemy's erroneous circumference, Columbus added a crucial error of his own—an error which would change history. He overestimated the eastward extent of Asia. The twin errors of Ptolemy's circumference and Columbus's perception of Asia's eastward boundary led Columbus to believe that only sixty-eight degrees of longitude separated Spain and Asia, rather than the true number of some two hundred and ten degrees. Thus, Columbus thought that it was only 2,700 miles from the Canary Islands to Asia (actually some 15,000 miles). If Eratosthenes' more accurate estimation had been used instead of Ptolemy's, or even if the Ptolemaic view had been more accurately understood, Columbus may not have attempted sailing west to Asia. As it was, if there had not been an intervening land mass, Columbus and his crew would probably have been lost at sea, and lost to history. Nowhere in history is there a better example of a serendipitous discovery coming from misinformed but courageous people. Mistakes and misconceptions are often our best source of new experiences and fresh ideas.

In 1484, he presented his plan to Portugal. He was turned down by a committee assembled to study the situation, not because they felt the world was flat, but because they *correctly* believed that he had severely underestimated the distance to the Orient. The idea that Columbus proved the world is round is a popular historical misconception. The roundness of the earth was understood in Columbus' time, and his perception of the world was actually less accurate than his critics'.

Columbus suffered another setback in his attempt to get Portuguese backing when Dias showed that Africa could be rounded, demonstrating what, in all likelihood, would be a shorter passage to the East. So Columbus had to seek the sponsorship of a country that had not yet rounded Africa. In 1492, he secured the sponsorship of Ferdinand and Isabella, the monarchs who had instituted the Spanish Inquisition fourteen years earlier, and who were then in the process of forcibly removing the Jews from their country. (Ten years later, they would do the same to Muslims.) Columbus shared the religious intolerance of his sponsors and carried with him the usual Western agenda of wealth, domination, and religious fervor. Columbus believed his expedition to Asia was as much a religious crusade as an economic opportunity and wanted all of the profits of the journey devoted to the re-conquest of Jerusalem. He was also intrigued with the possibility of landing troops in Asia to trap Muslims in a pincher movement.

Sailing first to the Canary Islands, Columbus departed westward from there on September 6, 1492. The voyage that changed the world took thirty-six days; land (a Bahamian island) was sighted on October 12. Returning to Spain the following year, Columbus would make three more trips westward. Although others soon realized that Columbus had not reached the East but a heretofore unknown land mass between Europe and Asia, he died firmly believing he had sailed to the Orient because the distance he sailed to America fit well with where he expected Asia to be.

The voyages of Columbus had multifactorial origins and were a consequence of a specific and unusual sequence of events: The land path to the East was opened, then closed. Ptolemy miscalculated the circumference of the earth. Columbus compounded this problem by misinterpreting Ptolemy's work, so that he thought Asia was much closer. The discovery of the New World was an improbable accident.

Columbus is the most famous of the European explorers, but not necessarily the most important. Of numerous other explorers, three deserve mention. Vasco de Gama (c.1460–1524) accomplished what Dias almost did. In a longer and more difficult voyage than Columbus', he sailed around Africa and reached the Orient, verifying that the sea route to the East was commercially feasible for Europe. Vasco de Gama's voyage also had a significant effect on India, particularly the southern portion, which had been relatively isolated from the West and the general course of history. With his voyage, all of India became commercially and culturally tied to the West.

The Italian Amerigo Vespucci (1451–1512) explored the eastern coast of South America, and helped demonstrate the existence of a giant landmass between Europe and Asia. Fernao de Magalhaes (c.1480–1521, known to us as Ferdinand Magellan) and his crew left Spain in 1519 to sail around the world. After three years, a small number of his crew returned from the appallingly difficult journey, having circumnavigated the world. (Magellan died on the voyage.) Few if any explorers could match the courage and perseverance of Magellan and his crew.

The radical revision of geography that these discoveries required meant that the old authorities could not possibly be completely accurate and all-inclusive. In addition, abundant numbers of previously unknown plants and animals were brought back from the New World, demonstrating the inadequacy of existing knowledge of botany and zoology. The explorers, in effect, struck the final blow to the reliance on ancient knowledge.

Chapter 16
The Living World

*A physician uses the new system of gathering
information to discover something never imagined
by the authorities of the past.*

WHAT VESALIUS WAS TO ANATOMY, William Harvey (1578–1657) was to physiology. Harvey's understanding of the circulation of the blood was not just a giant new discovery; it was a triumph of the new method of learning.

Galen constructed an outline of the circulation of the blood based on the very limited available knowledge of anatomy. It was understood that blood vessels connect the intestines with the liver, and the lungs with the heart, and that both food and air are essential for life. Therefore, Galen (and hence almost the entire Western world from the second to the seventeenth century) believed that the liver took food from the intestine, made it into blood, and charged it with a vital spirit. Blood then passed through the inferior vena cava and entered the right side of the heart, where it was again charged with vital energy. The pulmonary artery carried air from the lungs to the right side of the heart. This combination of events placed vitalized blood and air in the right side of the heart. By passing through perforations in the interventricular septum, blood gained access to the left ventricle, after which it was pumped through the aorta to the rest of the body.

The problem was that no one could find any perforations in the interventricular septum. Also, if the pulmonary artery carried air from the lungs to heart, why was it that when the pulmonary artery or pulmonary veins were cut, only blood exuded? These difficulties troubled people like Ibn an-Nafis (c.1210–1280) in the East; and Michael Servetus (1511–1553), Realdo Colombo (c.1510–1559), and Andrea Cesalpino (1519–1603) in the West enough to suggest that blood may move from one side of the heart to the other through a separate, or "lesser" circulation involving the lungs rather than through perforations in the interventricular septum.

Harvey's work hinged on the dissection of living animals. He was not the first to do such experiments, but others had only worked on mammals, whose heartbeat was so rapid that little could be learned. Harvey did much of his work on snakes, whose cold-blooded hearts beat much slower. He also recognized that his best observations came when the animal was near death, slowing its heartbeat even more. (This was one of the first examples of an investigator cleverly and effectively simplifying his experimental system.) From these dissections, he learned that the two ventricles contracted at the same time, which led him to doubt that blood passed through the interventricular septum. He also learned that blood was ejected from the ventricles during contraction (systole), rather than relaxation (diastole), and that the thump of the heart against the chest wall occurred in systole, not in diastole. All of these observations contrasted with the prevailing (but not universal) opinion of the time.

The aorta, and hence the major peripheral arteries, were known to be connected to the left side of the heart. Harvey noticed that the arteries expanded in systole, indicating that the peripheral pulse was caused by blood flowing into general circulation from the left portion of the heart. Tracing blood from the right side of the heart, he showed that it entered the lungs. He now understood the different destinations of blood exiting the left and right portions of the heart: contraction of the right side of the heart propelled blood into the lungs through the pulmonary artery; contraction of the left side propelled blood into the general circulation through the aorta. Cesalpino had discovered valves in the heart, the function and significance of which were made clear by Harvey's observations. When the left ventricle contracted, the mitral valve, between the left atrium and left ventricle, prevented blood from flowing back into the left atrium, forcing it into the body. Likewise, the tricuspid valve, between the two chambers of the right heart, insured that the contraction of the right ventricle propelled blood into the lungs.

These observations proved that the heart was a pump, the first piece of Harvey's great puzzle. But this was not Harvey's greatest work. Harvey's greater leap was dispelling the widely held belief that the body continuously synthesized blood. Harvey's work demonstrated that the heart pumped blood in a circular fashion *in a closed system*, without the need for new blood to be constantly infused into the loop. From his vivisections, Harvey realized that the quantity of blood pumped by the heart was much too great for continual synthesis; there had to be some sort of recycling process. Harvey showed that the application of a tourniquet causes arteries to swell on the side toward the heart and veins to swell on the side away from the heart. Also, by placing two fingers together on vessels and sliding them apart, he depleted the vessel of blood. When he released his fingers, arteries began refilling from the portion nearest the heart, while veins refilled first from the portion furthest from the heart. Further, ligation of the great vein, the vena cava, led to depletion of blood in the heart, while ligation of the aorta led to distention and engorgement of the heart. He now realized that blood exiting from the left side of the heart enters the arteries and must somehow return to the heart by the veins.

Harvey next turned to the work of a former teacher. Fabricius had described valves in the veins in 1574, and shown that blood in veins travelled in only one direction—toward the heart. Harvey now had the second piece of the puzzle—blood flowed in the body in one direction only. Continual synthesis of blood was impossible for two reasons: the body could not possibly make enough, and unidirectional flow was impossible without circulation. The pumping action of the heart, and the unidirectional flow of blood, combined with Harvey's studies of blood leaving the two portions of the heart, virtually completed the puzzle. Blood exited the left side of the heart through the aorta, traveled through the body in the arteries, gained access to the veins, and returned to the right side of the heart, from which it entered the lungs through the pulmonary artery and returned to the left side by the pulmonary veins.

Only one detail was lacking. If blood exits the left side of the heart in the aorta and travels to the periphery through the arteries, then returns to the heart through the veins, how does it go from the arteries to the veins? Harvey could not conclusively answer this question because he lacked a microscope, and therefore could not see capillaries. But he brilliantly postulated their existence, and their subsequent demonstration, by Marcello Malpighi (1628–1694), confirmed his prodigious theory.

Harvey's 1628 work *Anatomical Dissertation Concerning the Motion of the Heart and Blood in Animals*, written in Latin and consisting of only seventy-eight pages, channeled the history of medicine inexorably to its modern path. A brilliant union of hypothesis and experimentation, it was a vindication of the scientific method.

Because people had long realized that there was some sort of motion of the blood, it may seem strange to us that it was not immediately obvious to ancient physicians that the heart was a pump. This was partly because, until Vesalius, knowledge of anatomy was not sufficient to draw meaningful conclusions in physiology. A second reason was the supremacy of Galenic medicine, which ascribed to the heart the role of charging the blood with vital forces, so people thought they understood the function of the heart. It must also be remembered that until the seventeenth century, the concepts of inertia and force were not understood. Physicians before then had no reason to assume that *any* force was propelling the blood. To their minds, once blood was in motion, it could move indefinitely without power to drive it.

Harvey was also an early and effective observer of the development of embryos, and his work in this area was instrumental in establishing the science of embryology. The prevailing view of the time was preformation, the belief that the adult organism was fully formed in either the egg or the sperm. Harvey's observations showed that the embryo began in a form very different from the adult, and slowly evolved to the final form. This was the beginning of epigenesis, the belief that the fully formed organism derives from tissues that are initially undifferentiated, although it would still be a considerable amount of time before epigenesis was fully accepted.

Another founder of experimental medicine was Santorio (1561–1636, also known as Sanctorius. Because the family name was sometimes used as the given name for the oldest son in the Venice of his time, he is also called Santorio Santorio or Sanctorius Sanctorius). Santorio was concerned with the precise measurement of the processes of life. A follower of Galen, he hoped to give mathematical form to Galenic theories. He invented a device for measuring the pulse and adapted the thermometer to measure the temperature of the body. Santorio began an extraordinary series of experiments with the observation that while the weight of his body remained constant, the weight of the food he ate was greater than the weight of his excretions. What happened to the missing weight?

In an experiment remarkable for its scale even today, Santorio weighed himself before and after all bodily functions, such as eating, excreting, sleeping, exercise, etc. His book, *Ars de Medicina Statica* (*Static Medicine*), was compared to Harvey's *Motion of the Heart and Blood* by scholars of the day. While little useful specific information was obtained by this process, Santorio's work is of interest for two reasons. First, it was the beginning of endocrinology, the science of metabolic processes (although there would be no meaningful anatomic correlates of metabolism until the nineteenth century, and no biochemical correlates until the twentieth). Second, and most important, Santorio's work was the beginning of quantification (the determination of precise amounts) in biology. This disciple of Galen sowed the quantitative seeds of his mentor's destruction. No longer would it be sufficient to describe the function of the body in vague, Galenic terms, or in the terms of the four humors. If a biological function could not be measured (and the functions defined by Galen could not), then it did not belong in science. As we shall see, the seventeenth century was the beginning of quantification and the ascendancy of numbers in the study of natural processes. The work of Santorio allowed medicine and biology to participate in this development.

The microscope, like the telescope, has unclear origins and may have been independently invented on more than one occasion. Some believe Zacharias Janssen (1580–1638) played a large role in the invention of the microscope. We do know that the microscope was first put to constructive use by three people, working independently.

Robert Hooke (1635–1703) was a professional scientist and one of the first to employ contemporary scientific method as developed by Francis Bacon. He discovered many concepts, such as using one spring to regulate the motive force supplied by another spring in clocks, as well as the law which bears his name. (A spring exerts a force to return to its relaxed state that is directly proportional to the extent of its displacement.)

Hooke used compound microscopes, which have two sets of lenses (as do contemporary instruments). In a compound microscope, the image is magnified first by one lens, then magnified again by a second lens. Although theoretically allowing greater magnification than possible with one lens, the use of two lenses created optical aberrations that were not corrected until the nineteenth century.

While examining a small piece of cork, Hooke was struck by how the tissue was divided into discrete repeating units resembling the cells of a building. He coined the term "cell," which we still use for the basic functional unit of all living things above a virus. His 1665 book, *Micrographia*, described his observations and expounded on his theories on a variety of scientific matters.[4]

In contrast, Antoni van Leeuwenhoek (1632–1723) was not a professional scientist, but rather made his living as a cloth merchant. In fact, he had no university education and could not read or write Latin (still an important language for scholars, despite the continuing rise of vernacular languages). A deft lens grinder, he made his own microscopes. They had only one lens but were comparable in quality to those of Hooke because of the aberrations caused by two lenses.

Leeuwenhoek was the first to describe bacteria and spermatozoa. But he went

---

* See Notes starting on page 502.

beyond his technical ability as a lens grinder and observer; he recognized the complexity of the tiny organisms he saw. Moreover, because of their complexity, Leeuwenhoek reasoned that these creatures could arise only from others of their kind. At the time (and for a considerable time thereafter), many believed in spontaneous generation, the doctrine that life arises from nonliving substances, mostly dirt, dust, and decaying flesh. Leeuwenhoek's observations led him to believe that these substances were incapable of giving rise to such intricate organisms.

Leeuwenhoek's discovery of microorganisms was, for our civilization, a stride comparable to a journey to another planet. Not until the work of Louis Pasteur, two centuries later, would the scientific establishment catch up to this Dutch cloth merchant.

Marcello Malpighi (1628–1694) was the founder of microscopic study of tissues, which we now call histology. He used the microscope to unravel many mysteries of tissue composition, but what concerns us now is that he discovered capillaries, completing Harvey's theory of the circulation of the blood. He detected capillaries in lung tissue and correctly postulated that they were important to the normal function of the lungs. This was the first step toward unraveling gas exchange in the lungs, a central tenet of physiology. His microscopic studies of embryos at various stages of development made him a founder of embryology and one of the few biologists to be extraordinarily successful in three areas: anatomy, physiology, and embryology.

John Ray (c.1627–1705) classified plants and animals in more detail than had been done prior to that time. His work would make possible the classification system of Linné (Linneaeus), still used today. Ray's greatest contribution was developing the concept of species, which is to the whole of life what the cell is to an individual: the basic unit of function. Ray defined a species by its ability to breed true—a species consists of individuals that, when they reproduce, give rise to others like themselves. Individuals of different species cannot interbreed, or in those rare occasions when they do (such as the breeding of a horse and a donkey, giving rise to a mule), the offspring are sterile. This concept of species is still used today. (Difficulties in the definition of a species persist even in these days of molecular genetics; for example, a radish and a cabbage can be crossed without producing sterile offspring). Although Ray did not believe that species could change with time, he did recognize that fossils were the remains of creatures that had once been living, and he rejected spontaneous generation.

Chapter 17
The Numbers of Nature

*To escape the plague, a young man goes to the
country, where he begins the work which would
establish much of the foundation of modern science.*

THE IDEAS OF OBSERVATION AND EXPERIMENTATION were now firmly planted, and
with an organized way to study the world, European science of the seventeenth
century became more quantitative. Hard numbers and precise details replaced
vague outlines and rough approximations. The effective use of numbers required the increased use of mathematical tools. In the seventeenth century,
mathematics moved ahead of the relatively simple algebra and geometry that
had held it for two thousand years.

John Napier (1550–1617) prefaced the seventeenth century mathematical
developments with two advances. First, he extended an idea of Simon Stevin
(1548–1620), who in 1585 advocated writing fractions as numbers with marks
above the numerals of the fractional portion to denote tenths, hundredths, etc.
For example, 180 and 251/1000 might be written $180\,2'\,5''\,1'''$. Stevin invented
the decimal system for fractional notation but did not use the decimal point.
Napier made it easier still by substituting a decimal point for the superscript
marks, so that the same number would be written 180.251. This greatly facilitated mathematical work with fractions, because mathematical calculations are
much easier if written as 4.8 / 2.4=2 than as $4^{4/5}$ / $2^{2/5}$=2. Napier's second and
greater contribution began with the realization that any number, even a fraction, could be expressed as another number raised to a power. For example,
$16=2^4$, $100=10^2$, and $27=3^3$. Napier called the exponent the logarithm and the
number raised to a power the base. In the above examples, the logarithm of 16
to the base 2 is 4, the logarithm of 100 to the base 10 is 2, and the logarithm of
27 to the base 3 is 3. Any number could therefore be expressed as a base and a
logarithm.

Napier further showed that if two numbers are expressed in this manner with the same base, then their multiplication and division can be simplified. Retaining the same base, multiplication is achieved by adding the logarithms, while division entails subtracting them. The multiplication of 1000 by 10,000 can be thought of as 10^3 times 10^4; the answer is 10^{3+4}, which is 10^7, or 10,000,000. 10,000 divided by 1000 can be thought of as 10^4 divided by 10^3; 10^{4-3}, which is 10^1, or 10. Expressing 16 as 2^4 and 81 as 3^4 does not help in multiplying or dividing these numbers because the bases are different—one is expressed as a base 2 and the other as a base 3.

Napier went on to construct tables of logarithms, familiar (or distant memories) to most people. Contemporary logarithms are often based on 10, but are also often based on a number called e—the name given to an important constant with a value of roughly 2.72. (Logarithms based on e are called natural logarithms.) Napier's work made arithmetic functions enormously easier, and until affordable electronic calculators displaced slide rules in the 1960s, logarithms were the principal means of accomplishing lengthy multiplications and divisions.[5]

Rene Descartes (1596–1650) is familiar to many as the inventor of the Cartesian coordinates, assigning an "x", a "y", and (in three dimensions), a "z" to a given point to fix its location in space. The ability to assign a location to a fixed (or moving) object was crucial to the advancement of physics. The most lasting contribution of Descartes was the invention of analytic geometry, a union of algebra and geometry. Going beyond Euclidian geometry, analytic geometry is an expression of geometry in algebraic terms. It represents position with a set of coordinates and mathematically defines lines, curves, and surfaces. The mathematical representation of geometric figures gives us access to dimensions far beyond what can be depicted on paper and permits mathematical operations to be performed on geometric figures. By liberating geometry from paper and giving mathematics the ability to manipulate figures, Descartes directly paved the way for calculus. Even today, this historical sequence is recapitulated in every curriculum and textbook of mathematics, where some study of analytic geometry invariably precedes the study of calculus.

One of Descartes's contributions was the mechanical view of the world, whereby phenomena can be explained by fixed laws of nature. Descartes's mechanistic theory, like Galileo's belief in numerical relationships, advocated the use of mathematics in science and implied that the same inviolate laws applied to all objects. An outgrowth of Descartes's mechanistic view was the differentia-

---

* See Notes starting on page 502.

tion of rectilinear motion (in a straight line) from curvilinear motion. Galileo incompletely understood this distinction, and felt that an object moving in either a straight line or a curve would continue on the same course if not acted on by an outside force. Descartes agreed with this view for motion in straight lines, but like Kepler, realized that there had to be a continuous force acting on an object for it to remain in curvilinear motion.

His *Discourse on Method* urged skepticism of all beliefs and prevailing knowledge. Instead of starting with faith, Descartes argued that we should start with precisely the opposite—doubt—accepting as truth only that which can be absolutely proven. In the *Discourse*, Descartes was one of the first to realize that information gathered by the senses was suspect, and must be subordinated to knowledge gathered from reasoning. The *Discourse* also proposed a new method for gathering knowledge. But his method dealt with finding a mathematical solution for all problems (somewhat reminiscent of the Greek Pythagoreans), and did not ascribe a significant role to experimentation. Therefore, the *Discourse* is not currently accepted as a fully developed scientific method.

Blaise Pascal (1623–1662) contributed to many branches of mathematics, especially probability theory. He retired from mathematics in 1655 to devote himself to religion, although to distract himself from a toothache, he briefly returned to mathematics later in life and very nearly discovered calculus.

Pascal introduced the concept of mathematical induction. The word "induction" has two meanings. Before we consider Pascal's induction, let us review the nonmathematical use of the term. Nonmathematical induction refers to the drawing of a conclusion based on many observations. (For example: It has been cloudy every day and it has rained every day. It is cloudy again today. Therefore, it will rain today.) A conclusion drawn in this manner is not necessarily true, because one of the initial statements is based on an association (of cloudiness and rain in this example), not on certainty. Inductive reasoning is different from *deductive* reasoning, where the initial statements are more absolute and conclusions must be true. (An example of this type of reasoning, derived from Aristotle's syllogism, is: It *always* rains when it is cloudy. It is cloudy today. Therefore, it will rain today.)

Pascal's mathematical induction is a different process. It is, so to speak, the scientific method of mathematics—proving a hypothesis absolutely by proceeding from one step to the next by "if-then" statements. If statement "a" is true, then statement "b" must be true. If statement "b" is true, then statement "c" must be true, etc. An example is the process of proving a theorem. Pascal, in conjunction with Pierre de Fermat (1601–1665) also significantly advanced probability theory (which was initiated by Gerolamo Cardano in the sixteenth century).

Christiaan Huygens (1629–1695, sometimes written Huyghens) was a seventeenth century scientist of nearly unlimited range. We begin our consideration of him with an abbreviated history of timekeeping. For centuries, time was kept by the sun or by water clocks. The first mechanical clocks were constructed in China, and they were made in the West (apparently by independent invention) about the fourteenth century C.E. Initially based on the use of a single spring, they were not very accurate. In 1657, Huygens, working from Galileo's observation that the period of a pendulum varied only with its length, constructed pendulum clocks, using a pendulum to regulate the downward force of the weight. (Galileo himself, late in life, designed such clocks, but he did not construct one.) These were more accurate, and for a time, pendulum clocks carried the day. But Huygens and Robert Hooke thereafter independently made the spring clock more accurate by using a second spring (balance spring) to regulate the unwinding of the first spring (mainspring). Accurate and portable, they could be used at sea, thereby permitting sailors to find longitude. (We have already seen how one such clock, designed by John Harrison, was used with great accuracy on the seas.)

Huygens was the first to postulate the wave nature of light (today, we believe light has properties of both waves and particles), and independent of Newton, he understood the inverse square relationship in the mutual attraction of objects. The improvements he made to telescope lenses enabled him to discover a moon of Saturn, and to give the first good description of its rings.

Isaac Newton (1642–1727) is justly remembered as the treasure of the seventeenth century. His illiterate father died before the boy was born, and he was raised for a time by his grandmother. Enrolling in Cambridge at age nineteen, Newton began his studies with traditional readings in Aristotle. His journal entries show that in 1663, he began to read the works of more recent thinkers, such as Galileo, Kepler, and Descartes. Although he finished his degree at Cambridge, Newton was almost completely self taught in the areas pertaining to his scientific contributions. To escape an outbreak of bubonic plague, he went to the countryside in 1665. There, he began the work that would make him the most influential scientist in history. The six high points of his work are as follows:

1. *The proof of the binomial theorem*, which is a method of expanding construc-tions in the form of $(x+y)^n$ into a series. A simple example, for n=2, is $(x+y)^2 = x^2 + 2xy + y^2$.

2. *The invention of calculus.* Calculus is a difficult concept for many people to grasp. The first of its central ideas is the concept of the limit, whereby a quantity approaches but never actually reaches a certain point. Consider the calculation of area for an oddly shaped closed figure, such as a piece of a jigsaw puzzle. There is no formula that applies to this specific figure, as there are for the area of a square or a circle. But what if the figure could be broken up into squares? Summing the areas of the squares would give an approxima-tion of the area of the figure, but a small number of squares would leave parts of the figure not enclosed in a square and part of some of the squares might fall outside the boundaries of the figure. Our approximation becomes more accurate if we use smaller squares and employ more of them. We could mea-sure the area precisely using an infinite number of squares, each so small that it comes close to having no area at all. In this example, the number of squares approaches infinity as a limit, while the area of each square approaches zero as a limit.

The second idea is the rate of change, wherein how fast a quantity changes is more important than its actual value. Consider a straight line inclined at an angle of 45 degrees. If you could walk on this line, your position would change as you ascended the line, but at every point you would be facing the same direction at the same angle. You might get bored with the view. Now consider walking around a circle; not only would your position change, but at each step, you would be facing in a new direction at a new angle. There is no change to the line, but there is change to the circle. Now imagine walking along an oddly shaped figure, such as our handy jigsaw puzzle piece. If you were walking along this figure, at some points it might seem that you were on a line, while at other points, it would appear to be a circle or an ellipse. A sharp turn would give you a very different perspective very quickly. Whereas the line has no change, and the circle has a constant, uniform change, the oddly shaped figure has different degrees of change at different points. Calculus is intimately concerned with changes, and with how much change occurs how rapidly. By giving us the mathematical tools to deal with changing quantities, Newton elevated mathematics to a new level.

Calculus was not an endpoint in mathematics, but a beginning. From calcu-lus sprang a myriad of mathematical disciplines, each of which has added enormously to our ability to describe the world. If mathematics is the language with which we describe the world, then calculus is the alphabet.

3. *The discovery that ordinary (white) light is composed of light of a multitude of colors.* He showed that upon entering a glass prism, white light emerges as a rainbow because each component is refracted (bent) to a different extent. Each color had its own unique angle of refraction. Descartes had previously shone light through a prism and had not observed a splitting of the light into colors. However, he had projected the light to a surface a few inches (perhaps 10–15 centimeters) away. Newton projected light through a prism and onto a surface much further away, permitting the split to become evident. As a confirmatory experiment, Newton used multiple prisms to generate multiple rainbows. He found that white light was reconstituted where the rainbows overlapped.

There were several important consequences of this splitting of light. First, Newton took his findings as evidence that light was composed of particles— one of a series of conflicting pieces of evidence that ultimately led to the contemporary view that light is best thought of as having properties of both waves and particles. Second, Newton's work with prisms and the composition of light would eventuate in the science of spectroscopy, which has innumerable applications in physics and astronomy. Third, this work was the inspiration for the reflecting telescope. Lenses of the time had spherical aberration, which meant that they failed to focus light to a single point. Descartes had mathematically shown that lenses that were hyperbolic or elliptical rather than spherical would not have this defect. It had been Newton's intention to construct such lenses, but his work with prisms showed that even if lenses were free of spherical aberration and focused light perfectly to a single point, the prism effect would still lead to color aberration, wherein the different components of light would be refracted to different extents. Although today we can prevent such color aberrations, Newton thought they were inescapable, so he conceived and constructed a reflecting telescope, which was not based on lenses.

4. *The reflecting telescope.* Trying to circumvent the color aberration of the refracting (based on a lens) telescopes of the day, Newton realized that a parabolically shaped mirror would converge light to a single source. Reflecting telescopes avoided the spherical and color aberration of the refracting telescopes, and a mirror can be easily supported from behind, whereas the lens in a refractor can only be supported around its periphery. Contemporary

lenses are substantially free of both spherical and chromatic aberration, and the refractor continues to enjoy a place among astronomers, but reflecting telescopes can be made much larger than refractors.

5. *The law of gravitation.* Newton showed that any two objects, of masses M_1 and M_2, are attracted to each other by a force (F), which increases with the product of their masses and decreases with the square of the distance (R) between them. That is, the gravitational force, F, is given by the equation:

$$F = \frac{GM_1M_2}{R^2}$$

What this says is that the gravitational force equals G, the gravitational constant, times the mass of the first body times the mass of the second body, all divided by R^2, where R is the distance between the *centers* of the two bodies. By this formula, *increases* in mass increase the gravitational force, but not as much as *decreases* in distance, because the distance affects the force exponentially.

We do not know the sequence of steps by which the law of gravitation was derived. The story that Newton was hit on the head by an apple is almost certainly false. While it is possibly true that Newton was inspired by watching an apple fall to the ground (he makes reference to an apple in his later writings), it is more likely that the true source of his inspiration was the moon. Newton understood, like Kepler and Descartes before him, that there had to be some force acting on an object to keep it circling another object. Newton recognized that, in the absence of an external force, the moon would no longer circle the earth, but rather would fly off into space. Apparently, he then made a pivotal leap of understanding when he postulated that the force keeping the moon in its orbit was gravity, the same force that gives us weight on Earth. The thought process after that is unclear, but Newton apparently then calculated the magnitude of the force required to hold the Moon in its orbit and found that this force was 1/3600 as great as the weight the moon would have if it rested on the earth. Knowing that the distance to the Moon is sixty-times the radius of the earth, and that 3600 was 60 squared, he grasped the crucial truth that the force of gravity is inversely proportional to the *square* of the distance between the centers of the two objects. Double the distance between two objects and the gravitational force they feel for each other is one quarter what it was; triple the distance and the force is one ninth as great.

The law of gravity finally provided the theoretical framework for the heliocentric doctrine of Copernicus and the laws of planetary motion of Kepler. Here was the missing link so desperately sought by Kepler. This one law simultaneously explained motion on Earth and motion in the heavens. Just as Kepler had shown that the same mathematics that described processes on Earth also described them in the heavens, so Newton showed that the same force—gravity—operates on Earth and in the universe. Since the same law explained occurrences throughout the known universe, the earth must be part of the heavens, and not distinct from it. Incidentally, it would be a century before the value of the gravitational constant, G, was measured by Henry Cavendish (1731–1810).

6. *The three laws of motion*, the continuation of Galileo's work on motion, and the foundation of physics. These are as follows:

A. The concept of inertia. Newton formalized the concept of inertia, replacing the older idea of impetus. The force that propelled moving objects had long troubled scientists, and motion was often explained as a body's being set in motion by a force (in the case of heavenly bodies, the force was usually thought to be God) and then remaining in motion because the body retained the impetus bestowed upon it. Newton was the first to show that inertia (unlike impetus) applies to both resting and moving bodies. If a body is at rest, it will remain at rest unless acted on by an outside force. If a body is in motion, it will remain in motion, and at the same speed and direction, until acted on by an outside force.

B. The force acting on a body is equal to its mass times the rate of change in its velocity. Since the rate of change of velocity is acceleration, the force acting on a body is its mass times its acceleration. This is $F=MA$ (force equals mass times the acceleration), the most important equation of physics in this time period, and with $E=MC^2$, the most famous equation in physics.

C. For every action, there is an equal and opposite reaction. This is the principle, for example, behind the jet engine. What this law really says is that forces in nature always occur in pairs, although one of the pair may not be obvious. There is never just one force. Consider the case of Newton's famous (but apocryphal) apple—it feels a force from the earth when it falls to the ground, but the earth also feels a minuscule force from the apple drawing it upward to the smaller body.

One reason for Newton's success was his refusal to integrate metaphysics into his thinking. Metaphysics is a confusing branch of philosophy dealing with the nature of existence. Today, it plays no role in physics, but historically it has been nearly inextricably linked to "hard science." (In fact, its name derives from its position in traditional curriculum—it was studied along with physics.) Throughout history, scientific advances have come as much from what was rejected as from what was accepted.

Newton's great compendium, *Philosophiae Naturalis Principia Mathematica* (called the *Principia*), was to a great extent a compilation of Newton's earlier work. However, it was an original and momentous work in its own right. For a century and a half, physics developed along the lines laid out by Newton. Even today, Newton's work describes nature nearly perfectly, except for the very tiny world of the atom and the very giant world of the cosmos. Newton's work was the supreme example of the effective combination of hypothesis, experimentation, and mathematical analysis. It was the final vindication of the scientific method.

Newton was not known for a sense of humility, but he did acknowledge his debt to those who had gone before:

> If I see further than other men, it is because
> I stand upon the shoulders of giants.

He appropriately thought of his achievements as monumental, but he understood they were only a beginning:

> I seem to have been only like a boy, playing on the seashore and diverting myself in now and then finding a smooth pebble or a prettier shell than ordinary, whilst the great ocean of truth lay all undiscovered before me.

We will always be at the seashore, staring out into a vast ocean of mystery; it is the essence of who we are to explore that ocean.

Gottfried Leibniz (1646–1716) was a versatile philosopher, who for a time made his living as a librarian. In addition to his contributions in philosophy, he independently invented calculus, and in fact, used a better notation than Newton. The notation we use today in calculus is derived from Leibniz, not Newton. Newton claimed that Leibniz had plagiarized calculus from him. It appears that Newton did derive calculus before Leibniz, but the latter published first. Newton had an aversion to publishing his findings. (He felt that publishing his work subjected it to the criticism of people he regarded as intellectually inferior.) A bitter and vindictive man, there is little good that can be said for Newton's personality. Among his numerous character flaws, Newton believed he could still claim priority for his work even if he did not publish it. He used his position as the most influential scholar of his day to persecute Leibniz at every opportunity.

While it is true that Leibniz may not have been the completely innocent victim (there is some feeling that he failed to acknowledge both a correspondence with Newton and his reading of a paper by Newton relating to calculus), there is no doubt that Newton was the more vindictive of the two and that both clearly derived calculus independently. It is unfortunate that this dispute over priority could not have been resolved as amicably as the priority of the theory of evolution would be settled between Darwin and Wallace in 1858.

Chemistry lagged somewhat behind physics, mathematics, and biology. There were some advances in chemical techniques, and a few facts were empirically obtained from the experience of the alchemists, but there was no set of principles upon which to build. Chemical experimentation for its own sake largely began with Jan Baptista van Helmont (1580–1644), a physician who gave up the practice of medicine to study chemistry. When some of his experiments produced gases, Helmont was the first to understand that this state of matter was not limited to air. He used a balance in his experiments, and showed that he could, in some cases, reverse a reaction to reacquire the starting materials in the same quantities with which he began. He thus foreshadowed the law of conservation of mass.

Robert Boyle (1627–1691) furnished chemistry with its first principles. By finally removing the notion, prevalent since ancient times, that all matter consists of combinations of the four basic elements of earth, air, fire, and water, he set chemistry on a course clearly different from alchemy. Extending Descartes' mechanistic view to include chemical phenomena, Boyle subscribed to the atomic theory of matter, although it would be another century before this theory was well formulated. He believed that chemical reactions were caused by the composition and motion of matter. A strong advocate of experimentation, he showed that the pressure of a gas varied inversely with its volume, given a constant temperature. This implied that compressed gases were under pressure, and could therefore do work. (This would later become the basis of engines.) Boyle approached chemistry in a systematic manner and was the first person to conceive of qualitative analysis (the ability to identify and differentiate different materials). He showed that animals required air to survive, and that air was needed for combustion. Only Antoine Lavoisier would prove his equal in the development of chemistry.

The large problem with chemistry in this period (and for some time to come) was the erroneous concept that flammable materials contained a substance called phlogiston, and that the process of combustion involved the release of phlogiston to the environment or to the material with which the flammable substance reacts. Working from the age-old opinion that fire was an element, it was natural to think of combustible materials as containing phlogiston, which was, in effect, fire in an inactive state. Under the right conditions, this inactive fire was released, becoming fire in its active state.

Nicolaus Steno (1638–1686) began the science of geology when he realized that both the biological and the geological history of the earth were recorded in rock strata, and that deeper strata were older than the superficial strata. He recognized fossils as the remains of once-living creatures. Although a number of observers speculated that some fossils may be from animals that had no living counterparts, this could not be proven because the antiquity of the earth was not appreciated, and because the concept of species was just beginning to be defined with the work of John Ray.

The quantification of nature and the study of natural processes in mathematical terms meant that observations were put in numeric form. Thus was born the need to analyze numbers in a rigorous mathematical manner.

John Graunt (1620–1674), a London cloth merchant, brought the study of numbers to new heights. In the middle of the sixteenth century, the Parish clerks of London annually published records of burials. Over the course of time, a few bare details concerning causes of death were also published. Graunt accumulated these reports for the years 1601–1661, and by studying them became the first to notice that there are more boys born than girls, but that women live longer. He constructed the first mortality table. As so often happens, the ultimate effects of an intellectual activity were far removed from and much greater than the original question. Graunt had unknowingly launched the field of statistics, the mathematical analysis of numbers. Today, statistics has become the principal method of interpreting data, and an integral part of the contemporary scientific method.

From statistics arose the discipline of probability, a branch of mathematics concerned with the likelihood of a particular outcome from multiple possibilities. Although some pioneering work was done as early as the seventeenth century (some of it by Pascal), probability theory would not become central to experimental science until the late nineteenth and twentieth centuries.

The seventeenth century also saw the advent of professional publications and the rise of professional societies, groups that facilitated the sharing of information. An Italian group, The Academy of the Secrets of Nature, was founded in 1560, but was disbanded by the Inquisition soon thereafter. The first such group to persist was the Royal Society, founded in 1660. Its publication, the *Philosophical Transactions*, started as personal letters to and from Henry Oldenburg (1617–1677) and began what has now become a deluge of professional and specialty journals.

Shortly after the discovery of our modern scientific method, people asked "How," not "Why." The qualitative world gave way to the quantitative, and ways were devised to share the new information derived from measuring.

Chapter 18
The Perfectibility of Humanity

*Not even in the Renaissance was there so much
confidence in the power and goodness of Man.*

THE EIGHTEENTH CENTURY WAS THE TIME of two great movements of profound historical impact—the Enlightenment and the Industrial Revolution. The Enlightenment was an international movement based on rationalism and humanism. It was not anti-religious, but it did convey the idea that religion, the bedrock of Western civilization for more than a millennium, may not be all there is. The Enlightenment placed less emphasis on the salvation of the soul and more emphasis on the improvement of social conditions. It fostered the opinion that not only was Man the measure of all things, but he was also perfectible. Given the knowledge and the opportunity, people will make intelligent choices. Humanity had the means, without divine intervention, to improve itself and the world. The Enlightenment was therefore the direct continuation and extension of Renaissance humanism.

This concept was held by most of the great thinkers of the time, including Jefferson, Franklin, Hume, Kant, and Voltaire. The Enlightenment reinforced humanism and egalitarianism, and was therefore opposed by the religious hierarchy and the nobility. Under the Enlightenment, the status of the individual would achieve greater heights than ever before. Respect for the individual was the fundamental basis of the American and French revolutions, which were substantially inspired by the Enlightenment. Not surprisingly, this was a period of great scientific, technological, and social progress.

People sometimes question the relevance of historical thought to their everyday affairs. To my mind, the ideas of the Enlightenment illustrate how much thought in all areas of human endeavor is inextricably linked, and how government and society are influenced by the ideas of the sciences and humanities. By giving people a greater sense of importance and elucidating the laws governing natural processes, the Enlightenment led people to believe that they could control their own fate and that their destiny was determined by discoverable laws. Political leaders incorporated these ideas and assigned a greater role to the common people.

If one could identify the dawn of the Enlightenment, it would be John Locke (1632–1704). Like so many other people discussed in this work, Locke was trained as a physician. (Until the nineteenth century, with the rise of the professional in science and social science, most great thinkers were trained in medicine, law, or the priesthood, where an education was most readily accessible.) For most of Locke's life, England was in some form of political turmoil, and we need to briefly examine those times to appreciate Locke's contribution to human thought.

Although not Catholic, King Charles I (1600–1649) was tolerant of Catholicism and had a Catholic wife. He was perceived as sympathetic to Catholicism and antagonistic to Puritanism. This perception, combined with his encroachment of the liberties of citizens, precipitated the English Civil Wars of 1642–1660, in which Oliver Cromwell (1599–1658) defeated the forces of Charles and established a more parliamentary government. Shortly after Cromwell's death, Charles's son resumed the monarchy as Charles II. However, Cromwell's ideas persisted, permanently weakening the monarchy, and making the restoration of the monarchy incomplete. Upon the death of Charles II, his brother James II became king. James II was not as deferential to Parliament as his brother had been, and he was openly Catholic, which was unacceptable to the English. In 1688, Parliament forced him to abdicate in favor of the protestants William and Mary in the Glorious Revolution (so called not so much because Catholicism was removed from the throne as because Parliament had demonstrated final and complete authority over the monarchy). Locke's political and religious opinions twice led him to leave England for continental Europe. He was able to return for good after the Glorious Revolution.

An advocate of religious freedom, Locke also outlined the foundations of democratic constitutional government in *Two Treatises on Civil Government* (1689). *Two Treatises*—particularly the second treatise—explored the foundation, extent, purpose, and limits of government. Locke felt that people entered into a contract with their government, and government's only major responsibility was to protect people and property. If the government infringes on the rights of the people, it has broken its contract, and the people have the right to rebel, by violent means if necessary, and remove that government. Special privileges of leaders were unwarranted; rule by Divine Right was completely unacceptable. This thinking had a direct influence on many people, including Thomas Jefferson (1743–1826). The influence of Locke in Jefferson's American *Declaration of Independence* is clear. It is only a small step from

"No one ought to harm another in life, health, liberty, and his possessions"
(John Locke, *Second Treatise on Civil Government*)

to

"life, liberty, and the pursuit of happiness"
(Thomas Jefferson, *Declaration of Independence*)

Locke was among the first to decisively state a general notion that all people had rights. (Although it is commonly believed that the Magna Carta of the twelfth century was the first statement of human rights, it actually gave rights only to certain noblemen in their struggle with the king. It did little for the common person.) Locke advocated separation of Church and state and believed that governmental power should be divided into the three branches we recognize today: legislative, executive, and judicial, with each branch preventing excessive power in the other two. Although democracy was born in ancient Greece, it had to be re-stated for the modern world. By doing that, Locke became the architect of democracy as we know it.

One of the many people that Locke influenced was Voltaire (1694–1778; the pseudonym of François Marie Arouet). A poet, playwright, and essayist, Voltaire was jailed for an argument with a nobleman. He was released on the condition that he leave France. This he did, with a two and a half year sojourn to England, where he became acquainted with English science, politics, and the works of Locke.

Returning to France, Voltaire published *Lettres Philosophiques* (generally translated as *Letters on the English*) in 1734. For the remainder of his long life, Voltaire published voluminously in every literary medium of the day, but always with common themes: religious toleration, the value of knowledge, humanism, and political rights. The ideas of the Enlightenment could (and can) survive only if clearly stated for all to understand. By doing this, Voltaire was one of the most effective and important proponents of the newfound dignity of people. If one believes in reincarnation, one could postulate a soul of reason, humanity, and tolerance residing successively in Erasmus, Locke, and Voltaire, taking us from medieval times through the Enlightenment and into our modern period.

171

Charles-Louis Montesquieu (1689–1755) was a social philosopher (he would be called a sociologist now) who is best remembered for his work *The Spirit of Laws*, wherein he argued that liberty is the absence of one dominating political power. Therefore, he espoused the separation and balance of power into the legislative, judicial, and executive branches that we have today.

Jean Jacques Rousseau (1712–1778), like Voltaire, was a compelling writer and a powerful spokesperson for the Enlightenment. Among his abundant philosophical and political writings, *Émile* advocated a new theory of education wherein children's emotional development is given equal weight to book learning, and they are permitted to express themselves in a less regimented manner. One section of *Émile* describes the religious education of the book's character and fostered Rousseau's belief that people themselves, not church authorities, should decide which aspects of Christianity are essential to their lives. Because of this portion, *Émile* was banned in many places, and warrants for Rousseau's arrest forced him into a series of migrations.

In *The Social Contract*, Rousseau argued that the requirement for security mandated a state whose leaders achieve and maintain their power from a contract with the people. The power of the leaders is actually the power of the people. From *The Social Contract:*

> Man is born free; and everywhere he is in chains.

Rousseau believed in the inherent goodness of people, but felt that the constraints of society tended to breed inequality, mistrust, and possessiveness. Contrary to popular belief, he did not insist that civilization was inherently bad and necessarily corrupted people, only that it often had this effect. This philosophy has been simplified and corrupted to the "noble savage," an idea that Rousseau neither originated nor completely endorsed.

Although Rousseau had substantial differences with other philosophers of the Enlightenment, he was a vigorous defender of civil liberty and individual freedom. He was also greatly influential in the development of Romanticism in literature.

Adam Smith (1723–1790) was among the first significant students of the economic principles of industry and the Industrial Revolution. His treatise, *An Inquiry into the Nature and Causes of the Wealth of Nations* (generally known by the last four words of the title), was published in 1776, the same year as the American Declaration of Independence. *The Wealth of Nations* became the foundation of economic theory and remains the cornerstone of capitalism.

Prior to Smith, land was thought of as the most important commodity. Smith argued that all desirable goods and services can only be obtained by exchanging the products of one person's labor for those of another's. Therefore, labor is the real measure of the value of all commodities and is more important than land. He saw the potential of the Industrial Revolution and felt it could be maximized by division of labor (now indispensable in industry).

Smith believed in an overall order to human activities, even though there is no coordination between individual people. He felt that people seek their own good and possess little in the way of altruism, but he also believed that in the process of seeking profit for themselves, people inadvertently benefit society. The classic example of this is the person who markets a product that is in demand and heretofore unavailable. Profit, said Smith, would accrue to the enterprising individual, while society simultaneously benefits from the newfound availability of the product. From *The Wealth of Nations* comes a statement that summarizes capitalism: each person is "led by an invisible hand to promote an end which was no part of his intention." Smith strongly felt that this unplanned but essential benefit to society can be stymied by unnecessary laws and regulations. To that end, he felt that government should play no role at all in the economy. His theory is often described as *laissez-faire* (French for "let it be" or "hands off").

At first glance, the eighteenth century may seem like a period of only modest scientific progress. Sandwiched between the colossal strides of the seventeenth and nineteenth centuries, the eighteenth century was a period of observation and experimentation but lacked the fund of knowledge to construct a theoretical framework. This would begin to arrive in the last years of the century and in the nineteenth century. But there certainly was some progress in science in the eighteenth century. Progress in sanitation and living conditions led to substantial improvements in public health. With the scientific method firmly in position, there was much progress in the ability to measure and in the techniques of experimentation, as well as in classifying, systematizing, and disseminating knowledge.

This desire to systematize and disseminate knowledge was the driving force behind the *Encyclopedie*, a twenty-eight volume compendium of all humanity's knowledge and an embodiment of the Enlightenment. Edited by Denis Diderot (1713–1784) and Jean le Rond (1717–1783), it was published between 1751 and 1772. It was not the first encyclopedia, but it was the first to reach a wide audience.

To illustrate how observation ran ahead of a theoretical framework in this period, let us consider what was known about electricity and magnetism. Magnetism, of course, had been known about for many centuries, and it was known that proximity to a magnet would magnetize some previously nonmagnetic metals (a process called magnetic induction). It had also been known for a long time that amber became attractive when rubbed.

In 1600, William Gilbert (1544–1603, Queen Elizabeth's physician) published his landmark work *De Magneta*, the first comprehensive treatise on electricity and magnetism, and the beginning of that branch of science as a separate discipline. In *De Magneta*, Gilbert recognized that magnets have two poles and held that the earth was a giant magnet, its magnetic effect being the force that held everything to its surface (an opinion of great merit in the days before gravity was understood). He showed that other substances besides amber became attractive when rubbed, calling them electrics, after the Greek word for amber (hence our word electricity).

It had also been known for many years that a glass ball, when rubbed, would emit a shock. In 1665, Otto von Guericke (1602–1686), also a physician, showed that a sulfur ball that touched something while rotating not only produced a consistent attractive force, but also became charged and could even emit sparks. (He had created the world's first generator.) Further, a charged sulfur ball could induce another to be charged (electrostatic induction). As the sulfur ball gave him a more potent source of electricity, he was able to demonstrate heretofore-unknown properties of the phenomena, one of which was that it could be passed through a length of thread. These observations led to the theory that electricity was a combination of fluid and energy. The true nature of electricity could not be appreciated because the structure of the atom was not understood (nor was the atomic theory universally held), and therefore, the motion of electrons was not fathomable.

In 1745, the Leyden jar, which could store an electric charge, was created. In the initial version, a glass jar was partially filled with water and stoppered. A metal rod was pushed through the stopper and protruded from the jar, so that one end of it contacted the water, while the other could be connected to an electricity-generating device, such as a glass globe or a sulfur ball which was rubbed while it rotated. It was the world's first capacitor (condenser), and because it could store electric charges, it made experiments with electricity easier. Later versions of the jar used a foil lining.

Benjamin Franklin (1706–1790), America's renaissance man, contributed far more to the science of electricity than the famous kite experiment. Of the many substances that attracted small particles when rubbed, some attracted each other when they were both rubbed, while others repelled each other. The prevailing explanation for this was that there were two kinds of electricity.

Franklin's contribution—the gift of American political leaders to science—was to show that there is only one type of electricity, varying quantities of which caused the strange behavior. In the 1740s, he performed a less-remembered experiment that forced this extraordinary conclusion. Franklin positioned three people so that they were not touching each other, but the first two could each touch a glass ball. The first person rubbed the ball. The second person, without touching the first, received a shock by touching the ball. The third person, without touching the ball, received a shock from touching *either* of the first two. Franklin interpreted this to mean that the first person gave up charge to the ball, thus becoming undercharged, while the second person received a charge from the ball, becoming overcharged. The third person, being normally charged, could replenish the charge to the first person or remove the excess from the second, receiving a shock either way. This meant that electricity was a single substance that could be transferred, and this transfer resulted in charge.

This was the background for the kite experiment. By the early 1750s, a number of investigators suspected that lightning and electricity were related. The traditional story is that Franklin received a severe shock while flying a kite with a key on the end of the string during a thunderstorm. This is probably not true, and Franklin's definitive proof that lightning was a form of electricity came from his ability to use the lightning to charge a Leyden jar. For these two experiments, and for his proposal of the lightning conductor, Franklin occupies a position of true greatness in the history of the science of electricity.

Daniel Bernoulli (1700–1782) and Joseph Priestley (1733–1804) had suspected that the strength of electrical attraction might dissipate with the square of the distance between the affected objects, as was the case for gravity. But the proof lay with Charles Coulomb (1736–1806), who demonstrated that the attractive or repulsive force between two charged objects increases with the product of their charges and decreases with the square of the distance between them. (For example, if the distance between two charged objects is doubled, the force falls to one fourth of its prior value.) This corresponded precisely with the inverse square law of gravitation. In fact, if the magnitude of the charges is substituted for the masses of the objects and a different constant is used, the forms of the equations governing gravitational and electrical attraction are identical. Gravitational force, which acts between any bodies having mass (with or without charge), is given by

$$F = \frac{GM_1M_2}{R^2}$$

where M_1 and M_2 represent the masses, R the distance between the centers of the objects, and G the gravitational constant. Electrical force, which acts only between charged bodies, is given by:

$$F = \frac{KQ_1Q_2}{R^2}$$

where Q_1 and Q_2 are the magnitudes of the charges, R is again the distance between the bodies, and K is a constant (not the same as the gravitational constant). Demonstrating that these two seemingly disparate forces are described by equations of identical structure was a major step in our understanding of the structure of the universe. Coulomb had taken the first step toward a unified theory of the forces of nature, one of science's most elusive goals, and one we will return to later.

In the latter years of the eighteenth century, Luigi Galvani (1737–1798) obtained twitches from frog muscles by touching metals to them, suggesting to him that animals produced electricity. Galvani was right; animals do produce electricity, as twentieth-century electrophysiology would show. But in the interpretation of his results, he was right for the wrong reason. A few years later, Alessandro Volta (1745–1827) showed that Galvani's results were actually caused by the differing metals he had used. Two identical metals would elicit no response. The frog muscles were simply a conductor between two different metals. As always, the critical next step was a question. The most difficult part in the acquisition of knowledge is to ask simple questions, because to do this, one must question and challenge the accepted view of the world. In those simple questions are simple answers which change how we live.

Volta's great question was this: if two different metals, connected by a conducting muscle, could generate electricity, might it be possible to duplicate the results with a solution in place of the muscle? Volta then placed salt water in a number of cups and placed rods of zinc and copper in alternating cups. By connecting the rods with a wire, Volta obtained a current. Expanding this idea, Volta constructed the Voltaic pile, a column consisting of alternating plates of two different kinds of metals. (Various combinations were used.) Between each pair of plates, he placed a pad soaked in salt water. By 1800, the Voltaic pile had become the first battery, vastly improving on the Leyden jar as a source of storable electric charge, because, unlike the latter, the battery could be discharged multiple times without recharging. This meant that the battery was able to markedly facilitate research in electricity. It was soon noticed that the current-carrying wires emanating from the top and bottom of the Voltaic pile became hot and incandescent, setting the stage for electric heating and lighting.

Placed in water, these wires produced gas. Henry Cavendish had already shown that water was composed of hydrogen and oxygen, so it was immediately suspected that electricity caused the breakdown of water into those gases. Humphrey Davy (1778–1829) supplied the final proof for this in 1806. The process of creating a chemical reaction by passing electricity through a conducting liquid became known as electrolysis, since the first such reaction was the electrical lysis (decomposition) of water. In addition to decomposing water, other chemical reactions produced by electricity led to the isolation of numerous elements, and Davy's work was at the forefront. The nineteenth century would see electrolysis extensively employed in the process of electroplating—the deposition of a coat of metal onto the surface of an object.

Sometimes great leaps of thinking come in theories; sometimes they come in tangible form. The battery is an example of the latter. At the end of the eighteenth century, the battery ranked with the telescope, microscope, and steam engine as the greatest applications of what was then known about the structure of the world. As we shall see, miraculous developments in electricity and magnetism would occur in the nineteenth century, culminating in the Maxwell equations, and again in the twentieth century, when the structure of the atom began to be elucidated.

Simultaneous with the birth of electricity and magnetism, William Herschel (1738–1822) constructed larger and better telescopes, with which he and his sister Caroline (1750–1848) made a number of significant contributions to early astronomy. William was the first to resolve the hazy clouds we now call nebulae into individual stars and the first to realize that the Milky Way was a collection of thousands of stars. He believed the Milky Way was disk-shaped, with the sun at the center. He also discovered the planet Uranus.

Chemistry, prior to Lavoisier, also accumulated a wealth of observations without enough of a knowledge base to construct a framework. New elements and compounds were discovered, and the idea of fixed proportions in compounds was appreciated. But it was still believed that flammable materials contained phlogiston, and that this substance was given up in combustion. This was not just a failure to understand a specific process, but a more general failure to understand chemistry's basic mechanisms. The handicap of phlogiston was a great one, and chemistry would be seriously impeded until the nature of combustion was understood.

In the eighteenth century, the botanist Stephen Hales (1677–1761) developed the pneumatic trough, a much-improved method of collecting gases. In this technique, a vessel was filled with water and placed upside down in water, after which gases introduced into it through a tube would displace the water. A great improvement over the previous method of collecting gases in animal bladders, it permitted more precise measurements of the amount of gas produced, thereby permitting quantification in chemical reactions involving gases. Quantification, as we have seen, is an essential stage in the development of all sciences.

Joseph Black (1728–1799), in 1755, showed that the burning of certain substances gave off a gas distinct from ordinary air. He called this gas "fixed air" (it is now called carbon dioxide) and showed that it was also produced by respiration. One of the first chemists to make truly accurate measurements, Black was a founder of quantitative analysis, the determination of precise amounts of reactants and products in chemical reactions. He also contributed to the study of heat.

Joseph Priestley (1733–1804) was a Unitarian minister whose interest in chemistry was stimulated by gases released at a nearby brewery. He was an advocate of the phlogiston theory, but ironically, by heating an oxide of mercury, he independently discovered oxygen—the element truly responsible for combustion—and thus took the first steps toward removing phlogiston from our thinking. In addition, by using mercury instead of water in the pneumatic trough, he discovered a number of gases that were soluble in water and would otherwise have escaped detection. Oxygen was independently discovered by Karl Scheele (1742–1786) about the same time as Priestley, but it was the latter who journeyed to France and personally delivered the news of oxygen to Lavoisier, who then transformed the discovery of oxygen into a completely new way of looking at chemical processes.

Antoine Lavoisier (1743–1794) was the giant of eighteenth-century chemistry and the most important person in the development of that science. His enormous contributions can be summarized as follows:

1. He proved the role of oxygen in combustion, showing that combustion is the combining with oxygen, not the giving up of phlogiston. Although it would be wrong to give Lavoisier complete credit for the demise of phlogiston, it was his careful experimentation and insightful analysis that struck the decisive blow. This understanding was achieved largely by a careful analysis of heated metals. It was known that when metal was placed in a container and

heated, its weight often increased. This had been thought to derive from particles of fire that penetrated the container and combined with the metal, but Lavoisier showed that it was instead due to the metal combining with some portion of air. For example, when he burned mercury, it changed color, and one-fifth of the air was consumed. The remaining air was incapable of supporting combustion or animal life. When the mercury was heated again, it returned to its normal color. The "new air" recovered from it, when combined with the residual air from the first heating, would once again support combustion and respiration. This experiment showed that mercury, when burned, did not release anything. Rather, it removed something from the air, *something that was critical to life.* He had identified a separate gas, occupying about one-fifth of air, uniquely critical to both combustion and respiration. He called this gas oxygen and showed that it was the same gas Priestley had told him about. This destruction of the phlogiston theory was arguably the largest single step in the history of chemistry.

2. The combustion of carbon-containing compounds results in carbon dioxide.

3. Air is not an element, but a mixture of about 80% nitrogen and about 20% oxygen.

4. Respiration, the process by which organisms derive energy from food, is biological combustion. Previously, it was understood that respiration was similar to combustion, but both processes were victims of the phlogiston theory. Respiration was thought to be the slow release of phlogiston. Lavoisier showed that carbon compounds in food are ultimately combined with oxygen, resulting in the release of carbon dioxide and energy. This was the source of heat in animals.

5. He was the first to fully understand the composition of water. In the late eighteenth century, many people investigated the composition of water. Much of their work overlapped, and they often knew of each other's work, so priorities are difficult to assign. In 1766, Cavendish discovered a substance which, when burned in air, formed water. Cavendish was thus the first to show that water was a compound, and not a simple substance, but he was a follower of the phlogiston theory and could not properly interpret the results of his superb experiment. In 1783, Lavoisier repeated Cavendish's experiment. Freed from the handicap of phlogiston, he recognized the presence of a new gas, which he named hydrogen (meaning "to form water").

6. He defined an element as a substance that cannot be broken down further, and a compound as two or more elements combined in definite proportions. Based on these definitions, we now know that atoms are to elements what molecules are to compounds: the smallest subdivision and the basic building block.

7. Lavoisier was the first great quantitative experimental chemist. He was among the first to effectively use the more accurate balances becoming available in the eighteenth century, allowing him to make the first convincing and effective statement of the law of conservation of matter (also called the law of conservation of mass). It states that mass is conserved in chemical reactions (i.e., the sum of the mass of the reactants and products before the reaction equals the sum of the mass of the reactants and products after the reaction). Working with Pierre Laplace, he developed the calorimeter, a device for measuring the heat given off by chemical reactions.

8. Working with Guyton de Morveau, Antoine Fourcroy, and Claude Berthollet, Lavoisier introduced much of the nomenclature (the system for naming chemical compounds) that we still use today. Under Lavoisier's system, the names of compounds are long and difficult to pronounce, but describe the compound—an important step forward from previous nomenclature. As long and awkward as a name like 5-chloro-3-t-butyl-2'-chloro-4'-nitrosalicylanilide may be, it tells a chemist the precise structure of the compound, and therefore eliminates ambiguity and confusion. Lavoisier gave language to the science he so brilliantly shaped.

The above contributions—particularly the nature of combustion, the nature of respiration, and the law of conservation of matter—clearly establish Lavoisier as a scientist of sensational rank. In effect, Lavoisier removed the last traces of alchemy from chemistry and established the quantitative approach. He wrote two books, *Methods of Chemical Nomenclature* (1787, with de Morveau and Berthollet), and *An Elementary Treatise on Chemistry* (1789, a landmark work in chemistry). In the latter book, Lavoisier offered the first table of elements. Largely because of Lavoisier, the eighteenth century was to chemistry what the seventeenth had been to physics.

Lavoisier supported many social causes and was an advocate for the common people. But during the reign of terror that followed the French revolution, that was forgotten. He had been a tax collector in pre-revolutionary France to get the money to finance his research. To make matters worse, he came from a wealthy family considered by the revolutionaries to be aristocratic. Tragically, this scholar was labeled an enemy of the people and was beheaded in 1794. The mathematician Joseph Lagrange said of him:

> It required only a moment to sever that head, and perhaps a century will not be sufficient to produce another like it.

John Dalton (1766–1844), who was the first to describe color blindness (from which he suffered), made several contributions to meteorology when he was young. Perhaps because of his interest in the atmosphere, he was drawn to the study of gases, and it was in chemistry that he secured his position in history. He introduced the idea of partial pressures, where the total pressure of a mixture of gases multiplied by the percentage of a particular gas gives the pressure of that gas. He also showed that increasing temperatures cause expansion of gases (generally known as Charles law, after Jacques Charles, who independently discovered it before Dalton but failed to publish his results).

Dalton's greatest contribution was his workable restatement of the atomic theory. There had been thinking since Leucippus and Democritus that matter was composed of atoms. It was discussed throughout Greco-Roman times, and again after about 1100. By 1700, the majority of investigators held some sort of atomic view of matter. However, there was no uniform opinion of the details of an atomic model. Were all atoms identical, with materials differing from each other in the way that atoms combined, or were atoms of each type of material different?

Dalton originally subscribed to the prevailing view that atoms of different materials were of the same size, but his work with gases convinced him otherwise. The recent observation by Joseph Proust (1754–1826) that elements combine only in fixed, integral ratios (now called the Law of Definite Proportions) further satisfied Dalton that atoms of different materials were inherently different.

Having determined that different materials consist of atoms of different sizes, Dalton turned his attention to unraveling the relative sizes of atoms. Knowing that hydrogen was the lightest known element, he assigned it the atomic weight of one, and calculated the weights of twenty other elements relative to hydrogen. To understand how he did this, one must first realize that Dalton believed two atoms of the same kind repelled each other. Therefore, although he recognized rare exceptions, he believed that most compounds contained only one atom of a given type. (For example, he felt that the formula for water was HO rather than H_2O.) Because he believed that, by weight, there was seven times as much oxygen as hydrogen in water, he considered an atom of oxygen to be seven times as heavy as an atom of hydrogen. He knew that there was approximately five times as much nitrogen as hydrogen in ammonia, and therefore concluded that an atom of nitrogen weighed five times as much as an atom of hydrogen. His technique did not permit him to separate the relative weights of nitrogen and carbon, and he concluded that both of these were five times as heavy as hydrogen.

Dalton did not realize that most compounds have more than one atom of a given type, and this introduced an error. In addition, he did not distinguish between atoms and molecules. (For example, a molecule of oxygen or hydrogen, which is the chemically active unit, contains two atoms.) He was further handicapped by the lack of knowledge of atomic structure and knew nothing of protons (which are currently counted alone in the atomic number) and neutrons (which are counted with protons in the atomic weight). Because of these difficulties, his relative weights of atoms differ slightly from contemporary values, but he correctly assessed the order of ascending weights. (An atom of oxygen is heavier than an atom of nitrogen, which is heavier than an atom of hydrogen.)

Dalton published his ideas in *A New System of Chemical Philosophy* (1808). His seminal contribution was in giving a quantitative basis to the atomic theory. He was able to represent compounds schematically in a manner corresponding to their actual molecular structure. His theory was verifiable and enormously useful. Finally, more than two thousand years after Democritus, a practical atomic theory!

Biology during the eighteenth century was handicapped by the failure to understand the chemical basis of life and by the limit of contemporary microscopes. It also was characterized by observation and systematizing, epitomized by the work of Carl von Linné (1707–1778, known by the Latinized name of Carolus Linnaeus). Prior to Linné, plants and animals were customarily classified by their most readily apparent anatomic characteristics, such as general appearance, shape of leaves, etc. Linné's immense contribution to classification derived from Ray's definition of species: a group of organisms which reproduce to form others like themselves. If species were defined by the outcome of their reproduction, why not classify them by the structures which make reproduction possible? Linné departed from tradition, basing his classification of plants on their reproductive organs, and correctly located them in the pistils and stamens of flowers, rather than the petals. This procedure forms the heart of our contemporary taxonomy (classification system) of both plants and animals, and we know today that species that do not at first glance appear to be related may reside in closely related groups.

The fully developed contemporary taxonomic system, based on Linné's ideas, divides all plants and animals, even those now extinct, into the plant or animal kingdom, with each kingdom separated into phyla, each phylum into classes, each class into orders, each order into families, each family into genera, and each genus into species. Linné also originated our contemporary nomenclature, where each species is given a binomial name consisting of its genus followed by its species. An example is *Homo sapiens*, modern man. Another example is *Homo erectus*, an extinct hominid in the same genus as modern man, but of a different species. Like Ray, Linné believed that species do not change (although he may have reconsidered this opinion late in life).

Georges-Louis Leclerc (1707–1788), generally known by his noble name, Comte de Buffon, possessed an exhaustive knowledge of the natural world, reflected in his huge, forty-four volume *Histoire Naturelle*. Contemporary with Diderot's Encyclopedie, Buffon's *Histoire Naturelle* was comparable in size and scope and was the work of only one person.

At the time, the earth was thought to be very young, on the order of thousands of years. Indeed, the Irish bishop James Ussher decreed in 1650 that the earth was created on October 26, 4004 B.C.E., at nine A.M. The supposed youth of the earth meant that any changes in its terrain must have occurred rapidly. This view of sudden metamorphosis, called catastrophism, held back early geology very much as phlogiston held back early chemistry.

Buffon's contributions to natural history were legion, but only two concern us here. First, based largely on his studies of a cooling sphere, he concluded that the earth must be much older than was believed. He still underestimated the true age considerably, but his increased age of the earth gave time for slower, less catastrophic changes to occur, thereby planting the seeds for the revolution in geology that was to come. Second, again based largely on his increased age of the earth, Buffon felt that it was possible for species to change. In fact, he felt that some species may become extinct and that new species may arise. This was in contrast to both Ray and Linné and was a cornerstone to the theory of evolution.

In medicine, Giovanni Battista Morgagni (1682–1771) discovered the field of pathology, the anatomy of disease. Morgagni's great contribution was to correlate autopsy findings with clinical presentation in life, thereby uniting bedside medicine and the structure of disease. By championing this union of premortem and postmortem studies, Morgagni found that some diseases were localized to certain tissues. Previously, it had been thought that diseases were manifestations of generalized dysfunction of all tissues in the body. By proving the localized nature of certain diseases, Morgagni took the first steps toward establishing pathogenesis, the cause of disease processes. His 1761 book, *De Sedibus et Causis Morborum* (*On the Sites and Causes of Disease*) examined over seven hundred cases, each with correlation of premortem and postmortem findings. Morgagni gave form to the autopsy—until recently, medicine's greatest tool, and still an important source of information. As the first pathologist, Morgagni in effect established a scientific method for medicine, setting it on a course it still follows.

Morgagni's work was limited to gross pathology (abnormalities visible to the unaided eye). Extending the study of disease to the microscopic level began with Marie-François-Xavier Bichat (1771–1802). In his *Treatise on Membranes*, published in 1800, Bichat identified twenty-one different types of tissue, many of which are recognized as distinct types today. (For example: muscle, skin, bone, cartilage, and glandular.) The microscopic studies of his brief lifetime suggested that diseases have abnormalities of *microscopic* structure, as well as gross structure. However, for a number of reasons, Bichat could not actually prove this. First, the microscopes of his day did not have enough resolution to reveal subtle changes in tissues. As we shall see, microscopes were significantly improved in the early nineteenth century. Second, there was an insufficient knowledge base upon which to build an understanding of microscopic pathology. The nucleus of the cell had not yet been visualized, and it was not understood that organisms are composed of separate but interacting cells. Finally, Bichat's death at age thirty (from tuberculosis) denied him the time to extend and complete his work. But he remains the father of microscopic pathology, the field in which this chronicler currently earns his living.

A brief word on Edward Jenner (1749–1823) is in order. It was widely known before him that people who survived smallpox were immune to a second attack, and that the deliberate inoculation of material from a smallpox pustule into healthy people conferred immunity (in fact, this was known in ancient China). But inoculation with smallpox material had two severe drawbacks. First, almost everyone so inoculated became ill, and many got a full case of smallpox—exactly what the procedure was designed to avoid. One in fifty died. Second, inoculating people with smallpox increased the pool of carriers, potentially spreading the disease.

Many people who worked around cattle understood that a case of cowpox, a cattle disease transmissible to people, would protect against smallpox. Jenner's contribution was to *prove* that cowpox was protective, and to inaugurate widespread vaccination with the less virulent virus. (The word "inoculate" referred to the administration of material from a smallpox lesion, while vaccinate came to mean the administration of material from a cowpox lesion; today, the words are essentially interchangeable.) A key observation was that those vaccinated with cowpox did not become ill after subsequently being inoculated with smallpox. Jenner was not the first to realize the protective effects of previous exposure to either virus, and his work did not have application to other diseases. It would be left to Pasteur to make vaccinations to many other diseases possible.

The Industrial Revolution, with its demand for raw materials, greatly increased the importance of geology, setting the stage for James Hutton (1726–1797), generally regarded as the founder of modern geology. From mines, Hutton recognized that the interior of the earth produced heat. He accepted volcanic, sedimentary, and metamorphic origins of rocks (as we do today), in contrast to his contemporaries, who tended to believe that all rocks had one origin (some favored volcanic, others precipitation and sedimentation).

Hutton felt that to understand the earth's history, it was necessary to understand the forces that had acted on the earth, which were similar to the forces currently active. Hutton was responsible for the theory of uniformitarianism, which holds that the current forces at work on the earth are similar to those of the past, and that these forces have brought about gradual change. In Hutton's own words: "the present is the key to the past." This theory is in direct opposition to catastrophism, the doctrine that the earth has been shaped by sudden changes wrought by violent forces that are not generally part of the processes of geology. Hutton's 1795 book, *The Theory of the Earth*, championed uniformitarianism and pointed geology in the direction it follows today.

As Newton was the mathematical treasure of the seventeenth century, Leonhard Euler (1707–1783) was the mathematical treasure of the eighteenth century. Euler was a mathematician of protean range, whose thirty-two books and hundreds of papers laid the foundation for much of our current conception of mathematics. Euler conceived of a more sophisticated coordinate system that addressed objects in motion in three dimensions and did not assume that all of an object's mass was located at its center, as Newtonian mechanics had. He opened new vistas in such areas as topology (the mathematics of surfaces), complex numbers (dealing with the square roots of negative numbers), elasticity, trigonometry, the motion of fluids, and a multitude of other fields. His work was the immediate foundation for Lagrange and Fourier. The status of today's physics and mathematics would be dramatically different if not for Euler. Incidentally, 1809 is often referred to as the year of miracles, and so it was, with the birth of Charles Darwin, Abraham Lincoln, and others. But it is worthwhile to remember that Linné, Buffon, and Euler were all born in 1707. Actually, when the poorly remembered thinkers to whom we owe so much are taken into account, the number of "geniuses" is exponentially greater than generally believed. Every year is a year of miracles.

The Bernoulli family was the grand family of mathematics in the eighteenth century. Johann Bernoulli (1667–1748) was instrumental in the advancement of calculus. His brother Jacques was a founder of statistics. Johann's son Daniel (1700–1782) was a pioneer in fluid behavior. Bernoulli's Principle refers to Daniel's discovery that a fluid (gas or liquid) loses pressure when it flows faster. It is the underlying principle of flight, as the shape of an airplane's wing causes the air coursing over the wing to move faster than the air passing under it, so that the pressure on the bottom of the wing exceeds that on the top.

Joseph Lagrange (1736–1813), a protégé of Euler, made many contributions to mathematics, including the Calculus of Variations, a more general treatment of motion (Lagrange's equations), and the advancement of differential equations. After the French Revolution, France became the first country to use the metric system, making scientific calculations much easier because its units of length and weight are based on multiples of ten. Lagrange chaired the commission that established its use.

Pierre Laplace (1749–1827) used Newton's law of gravitation to account fully for planetary motion, and to show that the solar system was stable, thus founding the science of celestial mechanics. Laplace proposed that the planets were formed by matter thrown off by the rapidly rotating sun. Although a more complicated scenario is envisioned today, the correct implication of Laplace's theory is that the universe evolves. He also founded the calculus of probability.

Jean Baptiste Joseph Fourier (1768–1830) was trained for the priesthood but chose a career in mathematics. He made major contributions to the mathematical theory of heat and heat transfer, and in so doing, he established the branch of mathematics, now known as Fourier analysis, dealing with phenomena that are periodic and repeating. In Fourier analysis, complex periodic occurrences are reduced by means of calculus and trigonometry to a series of simpler repeating events. Not only are many phenomena in the sciences expressible as repeating events, but many occurrences in the social sciences, such as the business cycle, are also periodic events, so Fourier analysis has applications in every area of human thought.

Alexander von Humboldt (1769–1859) was one of the best known scientists of the first half of the nineteenth century. A renaissance man of science, he made contributions in geology, meteorology, and biology. He devised methods to measure barometric pressure and humidity was the first to employ isobars and isotherms (lines on a map connecting regions of the same pressure and temperature, respectively). He was, therefore, one of the first meteorologists (as was John Dalton). Humboldt's exceptional range allowed him to combine disciplines, and he was instrumental in the development of fields such as geophysics and biogeography. His most famous work is *Cosmos* (published from 1845–1862), a comprehensive five-volume synthesis of scientific knowledge to that time.

Chapter 19
Triumph and Tragedy

The productivity of people is enormously magnified,
but at a price.

NOTHING IN MODERN TIMES has changed our world and our lives as much as the Industrial Revolution. It is traditionally regarded as beginning in the eighteenth century, but as I hope this work shows, all great "revolutions" in human thought, like all great ideas, are actually the predictable consequences of our development. Intellectual revolutions in our record, like great ideas, appear at first glance to spring rapidly into history, but in actuality, are a long time in the making and are never completed.

The Industrial Revolution was driven by people with cleverness and drive, but equally by a social structure that permitted and rewarded innovation. Unlike the Enlightenment, it began in one country—England. Let us begin by understanding the milieu of the times. In the latter part of the seventeenth century, wood was becoming scarce as a fuel, increasing the demand for coal. Coal was getting harder to come by, however, because the largest deposits were below the water table; flooding was a major barrier to meeting the energy needs of England. The treatment for this flooding was a pump consisting of a tube that was open at one end and contained a piston. The open end was placed in water and the piston drawn back, whereupon water was drawn into the tube. When the piston completed its ascent, a valve at the bottom closed; another valve higher up opened; and the piston descended, expelling the water. Atmospheric pressure was the driving force, and for reasons that would not become clear until Evangelista Torricelli (1608–1647) elucidated this pressure and invented the barometer, this mechanism would not pump water higher than thirty-two feet (nine and a half meters). The beginnings of the Industrial Revolution relate to the evacuation of water from mines, accomplished by harnessing steam.

It is difficult to know just where to begin the discussion of the steam engine.

Von Guericke, whom we have already met as the creator of the sulfur ball, also made the first effective vacuum pump. Using this pump, he was able to force a piston up a cylinder by pumping out the air above it. He then showed that if there was air above but not below the piston, the piston could not be stopped from descending. These findings demonstrated that, in theory, atmospheric pressure in conjunction with a vacuum could do work. Huygens, the remarkably versatile seventeenth-century physicist, used gunpowder to drive the piston upward. One-way valves in the side of the cylinder allowed the hot gases to leave the cylinder immediately after the explosion, leading to a partial vacuum that caused the piston to descend. The problems with this design were that only a mediocre vacuum could be achieved by the valves, and it was difficult to introduce gunpowder into the cylinder fast enough to keep the piston continuously in motion. Because of these difficulties, Huygens's assistant, Denis Papin (1647–1714) then placed water in a cylinder under a piston. Heating the water created steam, which forced the piston upward. Removing the source of heat resulted in the gradual condensation of the steam, creating a vacuum in the cylinder and slowly returning the piston to its original position. Raised in this manner and held in position until the steam was fully condensed, the piston would descend more forcefully. Thus, Papin had also shown that in theory, steam could be used to do work.

Thomas Savery (1650–1715) abandoned the use of a piston in a cylinder and created a steam-driven device to raise water in 1696. It was not a true steam engine as we think of it today, but a boiler connected to a condenser, which was connected to a pipe leading to the water to be removed. The condenser was filled with steam from the boiler. Cold water was then introduced, condensing the steam and resulting in a vacuum in the pipe that caused the unwanted water to run up the pipe and into the condenser, from which it was expelled by the incoming steam. The Savery pump was slow, expensive, inefficient, and could not lift water more than thirty-two feet (nine and a half meters) because, once a vacuum was created in the condenser, the pressure of the atmosphere propelled the water. Although called the "miner's friend," Savery's device was too impractical for use in mines, but found some use in raising water for use in buildings. Savery's accomplishment was to transcend theory to actually use steam, in combination with atmospheric pressure, to do work.

Thomas Newcomen (1663–1729) had a somewhat unclear relationship with Savery. Newcomen entered into a partnership with Savery in 1698, but appears to have done so because the latter's patent made working without him legally difficult. For his part, Savery viewed a partnership with Newcomen as insurance

that he would not be left out by the younger man's superior design. Their partnership was one of mutual convenience, and Newcomen's work is best regarded as
independent of Savery's. Newcomen returned to Papin's idea of using steam to
move a piston inside of a cylinder. Unlike Papin, Newcomen generated steam in
a separate boiler and then fed it into the cylinder below the piston, where it then
forced the piston upward. Whereas Papin had simply removed the heat source
and waited for condensation to generate a vacuum, Newcomen chanced on a way
to quickly create a vacuum to bring the piston back to its original position. Many
scientific and technological advancements are the result of accidents, and in the
early years of the eighteenth century, an accident changed Newcomen's work, and
our history. Cool water accidentally worked its way through the soldering and
into the cylinder below the piston, rapidly condensing the steam and creating a
vacuum. This caused an enormous downward force on the piston, driving it completely through the bottom of the cylinder. Newcomen redesigned his engine so
that water was introduced into the bottom of the cylinder during every stroke,
and the vacuum so formed became the principal motive force of his engine. In
addition to pumping mines, the Newcomen engine was also effective in pumping
water up a grade for subsequent use in water wheels. The Newcomen engine
could not replace a water wheel because it was incapable of rotary motion, but it
was the first engine to do work in a practical manner.

At the age of twenty-eight, James Watt (1736–1819) was asked to repair a
model of a Newcomen steam engine. He realized that the engine had an inherent inefficiency—the cylinder was alternately heated and cooled. It was heated
when it received steam, but suddenly cooled when water was introduced to
condense the steam. Was there a way to achieve the vacuum without cooling
the cylinder? Watt saw that there was. A separate chamber could be attached to
and continuous with the cylinder. When steam was introduced to the cylinder,
the separate chamber would be filled with steam under the same pressure. When
water was introduced into this separate chamber, it would condense the steam
and create a vacuum that extended to the cylinder *without cooling it*. Since the
cylinder was hot all the time, it functioned more efficiently.

Watt went on to make many other improvements to the steam engine. Working in conjunction with cannon-borer John Wilkinson, he obtained a better
seal between the piston and the cylinder. The use of a separate condenser and
the better seal enabled the Watt engine to immeasurably outperform the
Newcomen engine with less consumption of fuel.

But to replace the water wheel as a source of power, rotary motion was required. With two innovations, Watt made the steam engine capable of rotary motion. In the double acting, or reciprocating, engine, steam was alternately admitted to each side of the piston, allowing it to do work on both strokes of its motion. The other was a system of gears (actually developed by his assistant William Murdock) that converted the back and forth motion of the piston to the rotary motion needed by developing industries. The steam engine was no longer simply a means of pumping water, but a power source for industry.

Watt went on to devise numerous other improvements in the steam engine. The centrifugal governor regulated the speed of the engine based on output and was the first use of a feedback mechanism for regulation. Oil lubrication, the steam indicator (which displayed the pressure of the steam), and insulation of the cylinder all came from James Watt. Thanks to him, the world now had a practical source of power, and the Industrial Revolution would never look back.

Prior to an effective steam engine, industries had to be located near a source of water. Consequently, factories were somewhat spread out, and because the limited transportation required people to live near where they worked, population density was relatively low. Steam engines were portable power, and after their invention, factories could be located anywhere. They were placed in and around cities, near sources of labor, forcing people to live in urban areas and resulting in a great increase in the population density of urban areas. Steam power facilitated the urbanization of society, and for the first time in history, there was general overcrowding in cities. This caused an increased susceptibility to infectious diseases, as evidenced by the cholera epidemic, which struck Europe in 1829 and Britain in 1831. So it was that at precisely the point in history when progress began to be made in living conditions, sanitation, and public health, much of it was undone by the crowded living conditions caused by accessible power. This problem was partially alleviated by the advent of reliable transportation, achieved in the next two centuries, but continues to plague us today.

Because Watt made so many improvements to the steam engine and made it a practical source of power for industry, many believe he invented it. As the previous discussion illustrates, this is not true; the technology existed before he was born. Who, then, did invent the steam engine? Was it Newcomen? If so, what about Savery, whose design was the first to actually use steam to do work? What about Papin, who was the first to use steam to move a piston? What about von Guericke, who preceded Papin and demonstrated the power of atmospheric pressure, the ultimate driving force in all early steam engines? What about Robert Boyle, whose work showed that compressed gases increase in pressure? Where do the assistants and financial backers of people like Newcomen and Watt fit in? What about their teachers and mentors?

The history of the steam engine shows that no one person is solely responsible for its development and illustrates a general principle of history. I submit as history's seventh lesson that great ideas have indistinct beginnings and result from the contributions of many people. We tend to remember only the last step of an achievement without understanding the full development of the idea. It is therefore little wonder that we have concluded that our civilization has been made by a small number of people. Any great idea, design, or invention, if carefully enough examined, will be found to be the work of many people—some remembered, most forgotten.

The stuff of genius is not the instant flash of brilliance by a person of superhuman abilities, but a slow methodical synthesis based on simple assumptions, the ideas of many, and the courage to think anew without the prejudice of prevailing dogma. It is in this process—and in the respect for all of the individuals who make this process possible—that our hope lies.

Progress arises not because of a few inherently superior people, but rather because all of us, being closer in ability than we realize, work together, in a strange and uneven sort of way, to make the prominent last step possible. When we think of progress as made by a few geniuses, we rob ourselves of the credit that we deserve. It is the triumph of our history that we have been able to improve our lot, and every one of us deserves credit for that achievement.

The reciprocating steam engine described above (i.e., one that moves a piston back and forth) is not the form of the contemporary steam engine. Today's steam engines are based on the turbine. A turbine is any device that converts the motion of a fluid (liquid or gas) into mechanical energy by undergoing rotary motion in response to the fluid. A waterwheel can be thought of as a turbine in its simplest form. In 1884, Charles Parsons (1854–1931) patented the first steam turbine, whereby the pressurized steam, instead of moving a piston, simply struck blades on a shaft, causing the shaft to rotate. This eliminated many intermediate parts, such as connecting rods, shafts, etc. Very shortly after Parsons, Carl Gustav de Laval (1845–1913) improved the turbine design by forcing the steam through nozzles (Laval nozzles) that accelerated it and permitted it to exert greater force on the blades of the shaft. We will return to the turbine engine later in a different context—air travel.

The second area to be radically altered in the eighteenth century was in metals, specifically iron working. Iron was extracted from ore long before Jesus, and the Hittite culture is known to have worked iron by 1500 B.C.E. Until the Middle Ages, iron was obtained by heating the ore until it became soft. Repeated hammering at this stage removed enough impurities to give a workable product, which was then further hammered into the final form—wrought iron.

In the Middle Ages, the blast furnace was conceived, but it was not hot enough to smelt the ore, so impurities still had to be hammered out. In the fourteenth century, blast furnaces were higher and hotter, allowing iron ore to be effectively smelted. The liquid iron was then cast into molds called pigs (hence the terms cast iron and pig iron, in contrast to wrought iron). Cast iron is much more quickly made into a commercial product than wrought iron.

The fuel that made the blast furnace work was charcoal. As we have seen, charcoal is derived from burning a carbon-containing material with an amount of oxygen inadequate for complete combustion. This leaves a carbon residue, which burns with a higher temperature, once adequate oxygen is available, than the material from which it was derived. The process of incomplete combustion is called destructive distillation (or carbonization), and the production of charcoal from wood in this manner was known to ancient people. Wood charcoal was used in iron smelting before the eighteenth century.

By 1700, iron was in considerable demand, and wood was becoming scarce. Without wood there could be no charcoal and no means to smelt the iron ore. What to do? Coal was an available fuel, but it had been tried in blast furnaces, and its high sulfur content contaminated the iron and made it brittle.

Abraham Darby (1677–1717), the leader of three generations of Darbys to play major roles in industrial development, was the first to make large-scale use of coke in blast furnaces. Coke is derived from the destructive distillation of coal (it can be thought of as coal charcoal, in contrast to wood charcoal). Sulfur was removed from coal during destructive distillation, making coke pure enough to avoid contaminating the iron. In addition, it burns hotter than coal and has greater mechanical strength than wood charcoal, so it can support a higher column of iron ore. Here was a material that brought the iron age to the form we know today. The use of coke made iron commercially suitable for casting, which previously could only be done with more expensive metals, such as brass.

By the end of the eighteenth century, the use of coke in blast furnaces had led to new pathways of innovation. When coal is destructively distilled, two products are released, in addition to coke. One of these is a flammable gas called coal gas (it is primarily methane), and the other is coal tar.

By the early nineteenth century, coal gas was being made for its own sake and

193

became the basis for the gaslights in large cities, wherein the gas was piped into a grid system to provide municipal lighting. (It was also used to illuminate the interior of large buildings, but the risk of fire limited its indoor use.) By 1820, every major European city was using gaslight, a system that remained in effect for fifty years, until the advent of practical electric lighting. Coal gas has been largely replaced by natural gas, which is a mixture of hydrocarbon gases (again, mostly methane) that occurs freely and separate from coal.

Coal tar is a complex mixture of organic compounds obtained from the destructive distillation of coal. Coal tar would prove fruitful in a variety of industries, ranging from pharmaceuticals to commercial dyes. The utilization of coal tar, in effect, inaugurated the field of industrial chemistry.

The efficient transport of coal, raw materials, and manufactured goods was vital to the rise of industry. Prior to the eighteenth century, European roads were significantly inferior to those of the Roman Empire, and transport was precarious and unreliable. Thereafter, developments in transportation paralleled those of energy and metalworking, and roads became more durable and more even. John Metcalf (1717–1810), blind since early childhood, was one of the first engineers to improve roads. He was able to build a road across marshy ground by laying it on rafts. Pierre Tresaguet (1716–1796) recognized the importance of an adequate foundation, but knew that the deep Roman foundations were too labor intensive. Could a thinner foundation achieve the same results? Tresaguet employed a roadbed only ten inches (twenty-five centimeters) in depth. At the bottom, he placed a layer of uniform, flat stones, which provided strength and were placed on edge to facilitate drainage. Smaller stones were then placed on top, presenting a reasonably uniform surface. Tresaguet thus preserved the Roman advantages of a foundation and adequate drainage, while making roads much easier to construct. John McAdam (1756–1836) constructed roads made of layers of small stones packed together. Over time, travel wore the road into a smooth, watertight surface (the origin of the word macadamize, meaning to crush into small fragments). Thomas Telford (1757–1834) began as a stonemason and established a reputation as a builder and engineer. He combined the approaches of Tresaguet and McAdam, using larger stones at the base of the bed, while relying on the wear of smaller stones at the top to provide an even surface. He thus achieved the foundation and drainage from Tresaguet and an even surface from McAdam.

Roughly simultaneously, numerous canals were being built. Initially, boats were pulled along canals by horses. Steamships were pioneered in the latter part of the eighteenth century. Their development slightly preceded that of the locomotive because ships could carry heavier engines than locomotives, obviating the need for the high-pressure steam engines essential to the locomotive. Another historical misconception concerns the steamship, which was not invented by Robert Fulton. Early developers of steamboats were French, and by 1783, a workable steamboat existed in France. In 1788, William Symington (1763–1831) developed a steamboat in England. In 1807, the American Robert Fulton (1765–1815), an early advocate of canal construction, launched the first commercially successful steamboat, running between New York City and Albany. Fulton is another illustration of our inclination to recognize those who gave an idea final form or had commercial success, to think of them as founding the technology rather than to recall the many people whose sequential progressions made the idea work.

Railways preceded the locomotive; horses could pull cargo more readily over rails than roads because there was less friction. The development of the locomotive required a steam engine that was simultaneously small and powerful, so the heavy condenser had to be discarded. The purpose of the condenser was to create a vacuum, so that there would be a pressure differential between the two sides of the piston. Without a condenser, the pressure difference had to be created without a vacuum. Therefore, one side of the piston had to be exposed to greater-than-atmospheric pressure, which required high-pressure steam. The pioneer of that technology was Richard Trevithick (1771–1833). Trevithick began his professional life as a mine engineer and as a young man became engrossed in the dangerous area of steam engines operating at higher-than-atmospheric pressure. His stationary high-pressure engine surpassed the Watt engine for pumping. In 1801, he constructed a steam-driven carriage, and in 1804, he carried the first commercial load by this method. But Trevithick did not pursue the development of the locomotive; he largely abandoned this aspect of his work, thereby securing for himself a smaller place in history than he might have had.

The appellation of "Father of the Railways" fell to George Stephenson (1781–1848). Stephenson began by designing locomotives for use in coal mines, and in 1821, he took the first steps toward popularizing the locomotive. In that year, the English Parliament authorized a railway from Stockton to Darlington. In accord with the custom of the time, the wagons were to be pulled by horses, but Stephenson stepped in and successfully made his case for locomotives. When the railway opened in 1825, thirty-three wagons were pulled by steam at speeds up to twelve miles (nineteen kilometers) per hour, and hundreds of cheering people hung on as the locomotive moved into history. Eight years later,

Stephenson cemented his reputation by building a locomotive called the Rocket, which captured the public imagination and greatly stimulated the embryonic railroad industry.

The Industrial Revolution profoundly changed the textile industry. In the manufacture of cloth, the raw fiber, such as wool, flax, or cotton, must be made into yarn in a process called spinning. Due to the natural tendency of these fibers to adhere to each other, repeated drawing and twisting will result in a coherent fiber. This was done by hand until the fourteenth century, when the spinning wheel was invented. Once the fiber is spun into yarn, the yarn is woven into cloth with a loom, which has been used for centuries. Weaving entails the interdigitation of fibers running lengthwise (the warp) with those running crosswise (the weft). The loom pulls the warp fibers taut, then separates alternating warp fibers by pulling even-numbered and odd-numbered fibers in opposite directions, creating a space into which the weft fiber can be inserted. The laying-down of the weft threads was intensely time consuming, and often required two operators.

After the spinning wheel and the loom, there was very little progress in textiles until 1733, when John Kay (1704–1764) invented the flying shuttle. A wheeled device, it contained, in a bobbin, the yarn which would become the weft. When the warp threads were separated, a single operator, by means of a lever, could quickly move the shuttle from one side to the other, depositing a weft thread as it went.

In the 1760s, John Hargreaves (1720–1788) invented a mechanism that imitated the action of a person spinning fibers into yarn. Called the spinning jenny (after his wife), Hargreaves's device enormously amplified the productivity of the spinner, but produced a fiber suitable only for the weft, because it was not strong enough for the warp. Richard Arkwright (1732–1792), in 1769, invented a water-powered machine (the first powered textile machine) capable of making yarn suitable for warp or weft. Subsequently, Arkwright switched to steam power, heralding our contemporary textile industry. In the brief span from 1733 to 1769, textile production moved from the Middle Ages to automated spinning of raw fibers into yarn and automated weaving of the yarn.

Agriculture was also dramatically affected by the Industrial Revolution. Jethro Tull (1674–1741) was trained as a lawyer and admitted to the bar in 1699, but he never practiced law. Returning to his family farm, he realized that the land would be more productive if the seed were planted in orderly rows instead of scattered by hand, which invariably resulted in uneven distribution. He invented the first

196

seed drill, a device that sowed seeds in rows at a predetermined depth and spacing. Less seed was needed, and because well-defined rows resulted, weeding was facilitated. With the seed drill, Tull doubled the yield of the land.

Joseph Boyce developed the first automated reaper in 1799, and another was patented by Obed Hussey in 1833. But the reaper of Cyrus McCormick (1809–1884), patented in 1834, would become the forerunner of contemporary agricultural machinery and would change agriculture. A skilled entrepreneur, McCormick permitted purchases on the installment plan and established separate departments in his organization for repairs and spare parts.

Fritz Haber (1868–1934) was to agricultural chemistry what McCormick was to agricultural mechanization. Haber developed a practical chemical process to utilize atmospheric nitrogen in the manufacture of fertilizers, freeing the world from its dependence on scarce natural deposits of nitrogen and making available abundant amounts of fertilizers. Agriculture in the twentieth century has been carried forward by continued advances in mechanization, soil chemistry, pesticides, and genetics.

Today, we are roughly two hundred years into the Industrial Revolution. It has caused unparalleled improvements in our standard of living and given us material goods previously undreamed of. It has indeed been a watershed event in our history. But it has also brought greater separation in social class and exploitation of the environment and workers. Originating in a time and culture that accepted slavery, it is no wonder that industry has long oppressed workers. It has been a triumph and a tragedy.

The Industrial Revolution is not over, and it will never be completed. Like the previous revolutions of tool use, agriculture, and democracy, the Industrial Revolution is ongoing. Indeed, to understand our place in history, we must realize that the Neolithic Revolution, the Renaissance, the Enlightenment, and the Industrial Revolution are as alive and developing as our current technological revolution. Like the evolution of civilization itself, the great revolutions of history have no end. Our challenge now is to modify the Industrial Revolution so that industry adopts a more egalitarian approach to workers, a more farsighted interaction with the environment, and a greater willingness to think of long-term success rather than short-term profits.

Chapter 20
Toward Modernity

Missing from the theory of changeable species was an explanation of how such change comes about. By furnishing this, Darwin makes the mutability of species believable.

FREED FROM THE PHLOGISTON THEORY and armed with better techniques, nineteenth-century chemistry was in a position to make substantial headway. The giant of early nineteenth-century chemistry was Jons Jakob Berzelius (1779–1848). Berzelius determined the atomic weights of many elements and the molecular weights of many compounds. He also discovered thorium, selenium, silicon, titanium, and zirconium.

In 1811, Amedeo Avogadro (1776–1856) suggested the famous law that bears his name: at conditions of equal temperature and equal pressure, equal volumes of gases contain the same number of molecules, even if the gases have very different properties. This observation, not accepted until fifty years later, would prove to be of immense significance in the study of gases. Avogadro's law would later be used by Stanislao Cannizzaro (1826–1910) to differentiate between atomic and molecular weights and to help determine these weights precisely, thereby refining the atomic theory of Dalton. Avogadro was also among the first to suggest that atoms can combine with others of their own type, not just with different kinds of atoms, as Dalton had thought. Thus, the interacting particles of common gases might not be individual atoms, but molecules composed of more than one atom.

Despite the work of Lavoisier, who showed that respiration is a form of combustion, and that carbon compounds in food are combined with oxygen, an artificial barrier remained between organic and inorganic chemistry. The processes of life were considered to be uniquely different from the processes of the inanimate world. In 1828, Friedrich Wohler (1800–1882) broke down that barrier by synthesizing urea—a compound intimately associated with the processes of life—from compounds not at all associated with life. Life now had to be seen in a different light because its basic processes were perhaps not so unique in nature. In the one hundred and seventy years since Wohler's experiment, we have learned over and again that the chemistry of life is subject to the same rules as that of the nonliving world.

In 1857, Friedrich Kekule (1829–1896), who had left architecture for chemistry, deduced that carbon atoms can bind up to four other atoms and can bond to each other. (A year later, Archibald Couper independently reached the same conclusion.) Building on this knowledge, in 1865 Kekule discovered that benzene was a ring; its six carbon atoms were closed into a circle. Moreover, each carbon atom used two of its four bonds to bind *twice* to the same carbon atom. He went on to demonstrate that two arrangements of such a ring were possible, and that benzene must alternate between these forms, meaning that the double bond cannot be fixed, but must oscillate. Kekule later said that the inspiration for this discovery was a dream he had showing a snake biting itself.

In 1869, chemistry took an enormous leap forward with the development of the periodic table by Dimitri Mendeleev (1834–1907). Working with the sixty-three known elements, Mendeleev recognized relationships among them and grouped them by their atomic weights (what we now know to be the number of protons and neutrons in the nucleus) in a manner that permitted him to correlate their properties. At the time of Mendeleev's work, it was not understood that atoms had component parts, so the difference between the atomic number (which we now know to be the number of protons in an atom) and the atomic weight (protons and neutrons) was not appreciated. Because Mendeleev used atomic weights (whereas atomic numbers are currently used), a few elements were slightly out of order in his table, but it was a marvel of observational ability, permitting him to successfully predict several elements yet to be discovered (gallium, scandium, and germanium). Two years later, Julius Lothar Meyer (1830–1895) independently conceived a similar table.

For all of these advances, nineteenth-century chemistry was handicapped because no one understood the nature of the forces that bound atoms and molecules together. Toward the very end of that century, it was beginning to be understood that chemical bonding and chemical reactions were a property of the atom's electrons, but it was not until the twentieth century, with the development of the Rutherford-Bohr atomic model and the addition of physics and mathematics to the arsenal of the chemist, that chemistry could take its next step.

Advances in electricity, magnetism, and biology were the triumphs of the nineteenth century. The discovery of the voltaic cell, or battery, by Volta, is a convenient starting point for the next period of intellectual progression. The battery gave investigators a stable, reliable source of electricity with which to do their work. It also brought about the first great commercial application of physics—electroplating, whereby the object to be coated was attached to the negative pole of a battery and immersed in a solution containing the metal to be deposited. (For example, a solution of silver nitrate might be used to coat an object with silver.) A wire was connected to the positive pole and placed in the solution to complete the circuit. The desired metal would then be deposited on the object. Begun by 1805, the process was commercially widespread by the 1840s. Importantly, the same method used in electroplating was used in electrolysis, the breaking down of compounds by an electric current. Electrolysis allowed the generation and study of many more elements than had previously been the case.

In 1820, Hans Oersted (1777–1851) discovered that electricity and magnetism were linked. He had, in fact, believed the opposite, but while demonstrating to his class that current from a battery produces heat, he noticed, to his surprise, that a compass needle was deflected when placed next to a wire carrying a current. He then showed that a wire carrying a current will move when a magnet is brought near it.

Also in 1820, Andre-Marie Ampere (1775–1836) demonstrated that the direction in which the compass needle deflected depended on the direction of the current in the wire. He also showed that two wires carrying electrical current attracted or repelled each other, again depending on the directions of current flow: if the wires carried current in the same direction, they attracted each other; if they carried currents in opposite directions, they repelled each other. Ampere demonstrated that an iron bar could be magnetized by wrapping a wire around it and sending a current through the wire (this is called an electromagnet). He further showed that a wire carrying a current attracts iron particles, proving that electricity can induce magnetism. This is the basis for the motor; the magnetic field induced by the charged wire interacts with a permanent magnetic field to cause motion.

Very few people have started with less and given us more than Michael Faraday (1791–1867). Born into poverty, Faraday was not able to pursue protracted formal education and was forced to apprentice himself to a tradesman. Luckily, he became the apprentice to a bookbinder, affording him the opportunity to read extensively and educate himself. He attended a number of lectures given by Humphrey Davy, and then transcribed them and sent them to their creator, who was so impressed that he took Faraday on as his apprentice. Shortly after Ampere's work, Faraday did Ampere's experiment in reverse. In 1831, he placed an electrical conductor in a magnetic field. As long as there was no motion of the conductor or the magnet, nothing happened. But by moving the conductor or the magnet relative to each other, Faraday was able to induce an electric current, proving that a changing magnetic field can induce electricity. Called electromagnetic induction, this is the basis for the dynamo (generator), by which electricity is obtained. He demonstrated that magnetism affected polarized light and postulated a connection between electricity, light, and magnetism. One of the seminal scientists in history, Faraday also used these findings to create a primitive motor. He gave us much of our current vocabulary in electricity and magnetism, and even glimpsed (in the days before atomic structure was understood) that electricity must be a flow of particles.

The work of Joseph Henry (1797–1878) paralleled that of Faraday in many ways. He independently discovered electromagnetic induction and built an electric motor. His work was to have immense practical applications, particularly in the area of early telecommunications.

The work of Faraday and Henry showed that electricity could be generated by exposing a conductor to a changing magnetic field, but practical amounts of electricity could not be produced until Werner Siemens (1816–1892) conceived the approach that is still largely used today. Electromagnets are used in place of natural magnets because they are stronger and generate greater current. An electromagnet consists of an iron core wrapped in conducting wires. When current (derived from either a battery or a second generator of the natural magnet type) passes through these wires, the iron core becomes more strongly magnetic than a natural magnet. When placed in relative motion with a conductor, current is generated. The initial source of electricity is removed and a small portion of the output is siphoned off and returned to the electromagnet, thus allowing the process to continue. In practice, there is usually enough residual magnetism in the electromagnet, even without activation by a current, to initiate the process without another source of current.

The use of this new generator permitted the introduction of electric lighting. Electric lighting began as arc lighting, whereby particles of carbon were connected to opposite poles of a battery and brought near each other. The difference in potential caused an electrical discharge across the carbon particles, resulting in light. (We now know that a stream of electrons passed from one carbon particle to another, heating the carbon particles so that they glowed.) Introduced for municipal illumination in Paris in 1877 (and in Cleveland and San Francisco two years later), arc lighting was impractical for indoor use and was quickly replaced by the incandescent bulb, wherein the light arose from an enclosed, heated filament. In 1879, Thomas Edison introduced practical incandescent electrical lighting, and electricity began to move to the position in our lives it now occupies. Contrary to popular belief, Edison was not the first to develop an incandescent electric lighting system, but his bulb and filament were a marked improvement over previous versions, and he developed a more efficient system of power distribution, with which he was able to illuminate a portion of New York City in 1882. These developments eventually brought both the gaslight and the arc light eras to a close.

The first generators provided alternating current (which reverses direction periodically). This was initially undesired, because direct current (which never reverses direction) was required for certain processes, such as electroplating. Gradually, however, it was realized that it was easier to change the voltage of alternating current, so that it could be generated and transmitted in high voltage, but "stepped down" to lower voltage at its destination. Today, alternating current is the predominant form of commercial electricity. Many individuals were involved in the creation of an alternating current distribution system, chief of whom was Nikola Tesla (1856–1943), who in 1888 designed the first practical system for generating and transmitting alternating current.

Faraday was not a mathematician. His superb experimental work needed quantification, which was provided by James Clerk Maxwell (1831–1879). At rare moments in history, a brilliant summary of phenomena, a compendium that verifies the accuracy of our thought process, gives us security and beauty. Maxwell provided such a foundation in a set of four equations bearing his name, published in his book *Treatise on Electricity and Magnetism* (1873). Maxwell drew on the work of Ampere, Faraday, and Karl Gauss (1777–1855), but one contribution was decisively his own: he showed that oscillations of electromagnetic fields lead to self-propagating electromagnetic waves, of which light is only one example. That is, light is only one type of electromagnetic radiation, and all such radiation is characterized by the alternation of electric and magnetic fields. Maxwell believed that this radiation propagated in an invisible medium called ether. The Maxwell equations have a simplicity and beauty that prove the validity of the human thought process. They are the foundation of our electromagnetic theory. Essentially, the four Maxwell equations are as follows:

1. Electric charges give rise to electric fields.

2. Electric current and a changing electric field give rise to a magnetic field.

3. Changing magnetic fields give rise to electric fields.

4. Although there is such a thing as a discrete electric charge, there is no discrete magnetic charge. (That is, all magnets have both a north and a south pole.)

The Maxwell equations unified electricity and magnetism, showing that these apparently disparate forces are actually different manifestations of the same force. Maxwell had thus taken—after Coulomb's illustration that the equations governing gravitation and electrical attraction have similar form—the second step toward the grand unified theory of all forces that has long been the elusive Holy Grail of physics.

The Maxwell equations are a milestone in one other sense. Prior to Maxwell, and the work upon which his equations are based, it was usually possible to visualize the processes described by theories. Maxwell's work began the difficult but necessary era in which we cannot precisely envision the processes described by our equations and theories.

For any law or equation to be proven, it should be able to predict a phenomenon not yet known. Heinrich Hertz (1857–1894) used the Maxwell equations to predict a class of invisible electromagnetic radiation, now called radio waves. He subsequently demonstrated these waves, verifying the foundation. Radio waves, like light, are an electromagnetic radiation; to understand how they differ, it is necessary to briefly review two terms.

Any electromagnetic radiation can be thought of as an undulating wave, with alternating crests and troughs. The distance between successive crests (or successive troughs) is the wavelength. The number of crests (or troughs) that pass a given point in a given time is the frequency. Because the speed of electromagnetic waves in a vacuum is constant, the wavelength and frequency are inversely proportional. The longer the wavelength, the fewer crests or troughs pass a given point in a given time, and the lower the frequency. The shorter the wavelength, the more crests and troughs pass a given point in an allotted time, and the higher the frequency. Radio waves have longer wavelengths, and therefore shorter frequencies than visible light. From the longest to the shortest wavelength, the types of electromagnetic radiation are radio waves, microwaves, infrared light, visible light, ultraviolet light, x-rays, and gamma rays. Visible lights of different colors differ by their wavelength; red light has a longer wavelength than blue light. All of these are types of electromagnetic radiation. They all move at the same velocity—the speed of light—and as Hertz showed, they all obey the same laws of physics. They all consist of photons, which have no mass at rest and can be thought of as having properties of both waves and particles. All electromagnetic radiation propagates by a complicated and incompletely understood interaction of electric and magnetic fields. They differ only by their wavelengths, although differing wavelengths confer a number of different properties to the radiation—such as penetrability, applications, and energy—and necessitate different methods of detection. Electromagnetic radiation of longer wavelength (lower frequency) has lower energy. Although radio waves and gamma waves move at the same speed, the latter have much more energy.

Hertz generated radio waves when a high voltage spark jumped across the gap between two metal spikes. For a detector, the process was reversed—Hertz was able to generate current in a loop of wire that was not completely closed, generating a spark across the gap. Other forms of electromagnetic radiation (such as x-rays and gamma rays) were soon found; the next steps in physics became the removal of ether and the understanding of atomic structure.

Experimental evidence against the ether came in 1887, when Albert Michelson (1852–1931) and Edward Morley (1838–1923) performed an ingeniously simple experiment at what is now Case Western Reserve University in Cleveland. The assumption of the Michelson-Morley experiment was that as the earth moves through the supposed ether, light travelling parallel to the earth's motion intersects the ether at a different angle from light that is perpendicular to the earth's motion. If there were an ether, light passing directly into it should be more retarded than light passing through it at a right angle, just as it takes longer to paddle a given distance against a current than across it. Michelson and Morley showed that light has the same velocity with respect to the observer regardless of its direction of travel. There was no difference in the speed of light whether it passed directly into the supposed ether or perpendicular to it. The Michelson-Morley experiment therefore suggested that there was no ether. Subsequently, Einstein independently abolished the ether when he postulated that light always has the same velocity in a vacuum, regardless of the frame of reference of the observer. Einstein's postulate that the speed of light was invariant meant that there could not be a fixed or absolute frame of reference, which was what the ether was touted to be. The removal of the ether was almost as large a step for physics as the removal of phlogiston was for chemistry. Most of the subsequent development of physics was dependent on the certainty of the absence of the ether. It is unclear if Einstein knew of this experiment when he conceived his theory of relativity, but he certainly knew of it afterward and later said "if Michelson-Morley is wrong, relativity is wrong."

The implication that there was no ether was deeply disquieting to the scientific establishment, and many people sought a way to reconcile the Michelson-Morley findings with the presence of the ether. Shortly after the experiment, George Fitzgerald (1851–1901) showed mathematically that as objects approach the speed of light, they might actually become smaller in the dimension in which they are moving. For example, a rocket, with a given length at rest, traveling close to the speed of light, would be significantly shorter. (The other dimensions of the rocket would not be changed.) Hendrik Lorentz (1853–1928) independently came to the same conclusion and further showed that as an object's velocity approached that of light, its mass significantly increased. Lorentz developed a more general set of equations, called the Lorentz transformations, dealing with the changes that take place in an object as it approaches the speed of light. The Lorentz-Fitzgerald contraction, and the Lorentz transformations, in theory, had the potential to explain how the Michelson-Morley experiment might not have dispelled the ether after all, but they seemed far-fetched and absurd. Even though there really was no ether, the theoretical work of Lorentz and Fitzgerald would turn out to be valid, but it was not until Einstein's theory of relativity that it was shown why this was so.

Electricity and magnetism were not the only advances of the nineteenth century. In the 1840s, James Prescott Joule (1818–1889) found that motion generated heat. This led to understanding the equivalence of heat and mechanical energy, and when combined with the work of Herman Helmholtz (1821–1894), William Thomson (1824–1907, better known as Lord Kelvin), and some dozen others, it became the basis of the first law of thermodynamics. This law states that the amount of work applied to a system, minus the heat given off, equals the increase in the system's internal energy. What Joule, Helmholtz, Kelvin, and the others really accomplished was the formulation of the principle of conservation of energy: energy may flow out of or into a system, but only from another system; it cannot be created or destroyed. The two most important conservation laws in science—mass and energy—were now in place.

205

The concept of conservation is pivotal in the history of science. A great advance occurred when the concept of equivalents was added to the concept of conservation. What is really being conserved is not necessarily the immediately obvious quality. Rather, it is all equivalent forms of this quality that are conserved. As an example, Einstein's $E=MC^2$ would show that energy and mass are, in effect, equivalent, and that it is actually the sum of mass and energy, not mass individually and energy individually, that is conserved. (Einstein's finding plays a very small role in everyday life, so in actuality, the nineteenth century established accurate laws of conservation.)

A shortcoming of the first law of thermodynamics was quickly realized and corrected. The first law alone would lead to the conclusion that any system can do any amount of work as long as there is a corresponding decrease in its internal energy. For example, all the air in a room could spontaneously lift a person out of his chair and still be in perfect compliance with the first law if the energy used in lifting the person equaled the loss of energy of the air. The experiments of Nicolas Leonard Sadi Carnot (1796–1832)—revived and given mathematical form by Rudolf J. E. Clausius (1822 –1888), Ludwig Boltzmann (1844–1906), and Lord Kelvin (1824 –1907)—clarified the situation by establishing the second law of thermodynamics, which states that energy cannot spontaneously flow from an area of lesser concentration to an area of greater concentration. Stated another way, one can conceive of a system as having an inherent amount of order. The second law of thermodynamics states that unless external energy is applied to a system, the orderliness of that system cannot increase; it must stay the same or decrease. Often, scientists speak in terms of the *dis*orderliness, or randomness, of a system, called entropy. Unless an external agent acts on a system, its randomness must increase. The air in a room cannot spontaneously lift a person because to do so would require an orderly cooperation of the molecules in the air, constituting a spontaneous increase in order and a decrease in randomness.

A convenient way of looking at the second law of thermodynamics is that, with time, energy in a closed system becomes less available to do work. (The general truth of the second law of thermodynamics is not contested, but many now believe that it may not completely hold in all situations. Another opinion, called self-organization, holds that under certain circumstances, a system actually can spontaneously increase its orderliness. This is part of a contemporary mathematical discipline called chaos theory.)

Two discoveries revolutionized nineteenth-century astronomy. The first was the discovery that the spectra of hot objects (the electromagnetic radiation given off) are not continuous, but consist of lines. Later work would show that most of these lines are caused by the emission or absorption of electromagnetic radiation of particular wavelengths as electrons move from one energy level to another. The workers of the nineteenth century did not yet know this, again because they did not understand atomic structure. They did understand that each element has a unique pattern of lines in its spectrum, and by matching the spectra of heavenly bodies with those generated from known sources on Earth, they were able to determine something about the chemical composition of the sun and stars. (In fact, the element helium received its name because it was first discovered in the spectrum of the sun.)

The other great discovery for astronomy was the camera, the history of which will be described later. Whereas vision is an instantaneous phenomenon, photons have a cumulative effect on film, making prolonged photographic exposure more sensitive than the eye, and more revealing. Using these discoveries, as well as the better telescopes of the day, astronomers discovered that the stars were much further away than had been believed.

A lingering question in biology concerned the nature of fossils. It had been appreciated since Ray and Steno in the seventeenth century that fossils came from once-living creatures, but recognizing that these fossils were from *species* no longer living was hindered by difficulties in understanding the concept of species and grasping the age of the earth. It was not until the comparative anatomy work of Georges Cuvier (1769–1832), building on the work of Edward Tyson (1651–1708), that it became absolutely established that most fossils were derived from extinct species. Cuvier, for example, upon studying the remains of a Pterodactyl, said, "If restored to life, it would resemble nothing living today." Even after this was established, it was not generally understood that species could evolve and change. Therefore, these extinct species were not seen as related to those currently in existence. Did extinct species mean that God had changed his mind? Worse, did they mean that God had made a mistake?

Charles Lyell (1797–1875), following Steno and Hutton, vigorously championed uniformitarianism, the doctrine of slow geologic change. But Lyell went beyond, to the crucial realization that animals also changed and evolved. Lyell's extension of slow geologic change to animals meant that species could become extinct, and that new species could evolve. Lyell was not the first to grasp the evolution of species (certainly Buffon had preceded him in this), and he was not able to offer an explanation of evolution, but he was one of the most effective advocates of this position. In his *Principles of Geology* (1830–1833; one of two books to greatly influence Charles Darwin), Lyell argued for the slow change of all things natural.

Charles Darwin (1809–1882) was, with Louis Pasteur, one of the two great biologists of the nineteenth century. Dropping out of both medical school and the Seminary, his course in history began in 1831 when he obtained a position as a naturalist on the H.M.S. Beagle, which was to explore and map the Pacific coast of South America. Darwin's great idea began from his extraordinary ability to appreciate minute details in nature. During his journey, he came to the Galapagos islands, off the coast of Ecuador, where he noticed a remarkable diversity of wildlife from island to island, but much less variation on a given island. In addition to this clustering of related species, Darwin also noticed that species seemed to "fit" their environment well. For example, birds that fed on large seeds had large beaks, while those that fed on smaller seeds had smaller beaks. Because each island in the Galapagos was separated from other islands by strong oceanic currents, and there was little wind, Darwin realized it was unlikely that a species well-adapted to one island would migrate to another and then undergo a small change to perfectly adapt it to its new home. It was much more likely that each species achieved its adaptation *de novo* on the island where it was found. What force could make all these species, independently, so perfectly adapted?

Darwin additionally discovered fossils related to, but not identical with, current species. This is difficult to explain if all species were created separately and were immutable. But after his return to England, Darwin began to believe that a gradual changing of species would result in fossils imperfectly resembling contemporary creatures, and species of one area slowly becoming slightly different from their counterparts in other locations.

Darwin was by no means the first to suggest that species change. Although the evolution of species was the minority view in the 1830s, it still had a number of adherents. Lyell and Buffon, for example, both preceded Darwin in accepting the mutability of species. Indeed, during his voyage, Darwin read *Principles of Geology*, the multi-volume work of Lyell that put forth the gradual change of the earth *and its species*, and he was greatly influenced by Lyell's ideas. But what force created this diversity and so perfectly matched each species to its environment? Missing from the theory of changeable species as held by people like Lyell and Buffon, was an *explanation* of how such change comes about. It was this explanation of the mechanism of changing species that was Darwin's lasting legacy to humanity; by furnishing it, Darwin made the mutability of species believable.

Darwin noticed that intentional selection, which often resulted in animals with new characteristics, was the key to man's successful breeding of domestic animals. Could selection be a pathway for change in the wild? If so, by what mechanism? Darwin then read the second book to affect his thinking: *An Essay on the Principle of Population as it Affects the Future Improvements of Society*, by Thomas Robert Malthus (1766–1834). Malthus, an economist, argued that humanity's population would tend to increase geometrically, while the food supply would increase in a linear and much slower manner. Malthus went on to imply that human population would be checked by disasters such as famine, war, and disease, meaning that people with greater resources or better health would enjoy a natural advantage in the inevitable struggle to survive. One effect of Malthus's ominous prediction was to stimulate interest in birth control, but it was his effect on Darwin that concerns us now.

From his observations in the Galapagos, his insight into domestic breeding, and by extrapolating the ideas of Malthus and Lyell to the natural world of plants and animals, Darwin arrived at the missing element of the theory of evolution. Species could and did change because changing environmental conditions selected those individuals possessing characteristics that facilitated survival and reproduction in the new environment. The preferential survival and reproduction of these individuals perpetuated those characteristics at the expense of attributes that did not confer a competitive advantage. Others had conceived the possibility of evolving species, including Darwin's own grandfather, but Darwin's great contribution was to provide a mechanism—natural selection.

Darwin realized that a genetic advantage was useful only if it facilitated reproduction. Nature is not concerned with the individual, but with the preservation of the species. Therefore, it was the individual's ability to reproduce that mattered. Survival of the fittest (an appropriate term, but one not used by Darwin) actually meant reproduction of the fittest.

Darwin had the basic concepts of his theory worked out in the 1830s but did not publish his work at that time. In 1858, he learned that Alfred Wallace (1823–1913) had independently come to a similar theory (and through a remarkably parallel thought process, even including being influenced by Malthus). To his credit, Darwin made no attempt to claim priority, but rather arranged to jointly present papers on the evolution of species with Wallace. Darwin is more remembered than Wallace because, after their joint presentation in 1858, he wrote much more prolifically on the subject. His most famous work was the

1859 book *On the Origin of Species by Natural Selection*, usually referred to as *The Origin of Species*.

It should be remembered that the theory of evolution, like all great theories, was incomplete as it was originally proposed and did not answer all legitimate criticisms. Great ideas are rarely fully formed at their inception. In particular, both Darwin and Wallace reached their conclusions without a knowledge of genetics. Gregor Mendel (1822–1884) performed remarkable experiments with peas, and his work would become the basis for the science of genetics. In studying height, for example, Mendel showed that tall plants crossed with dwarf plants always yielded tall progeny, not the fifty-fifty split that had been thought. However, when these progeny were crossed with each other, one-fourth of the second-generation progeny were dwarf. So the factor(s) leading to dwarfness had not disappeared, even though they were completely inoperative in the first generation of progeny. Moreover, when the responsible factor(s) reappeared, most of the plants were still tall. Mendel understood that there must be hereditary units that govern the inheritance of traits. He postulated that there were two such factors for each trait and showed that these factors could be dominant, recessive, or neither. He then derived three laws of inheritance. His first law, the law of segregation, states that there are two factors for each trait, one from each parent. Each gamete (reproductive cell) carries only one of the two possible factors, and it is purely a matter of chance as to which of the two it is. Whichever characteristic that gamete carries is transmitted in an all-or-none fashion. His second law, sometimes called the law of the purity of the gametes, held that these factors retain their character and ability to cause a specific trait, even if temporarily "masked" by association with a dominant factor. Finally, Mendel hypothesized that plants inherit each of their characteristics independently of all other characteristics, known as the law of independent assortment. We now know that if the genes governing two traits are on the same chromosome, they do not sort independently, but rather tend to be inherited as a group.

Mendel's work was among the first in science to employ the statistical analysis of data. In addition, he was fortunate to choose characteristics, such as height, determined by a single set of genes, making their inheritance amenable to the statistical methods at Mendel's disposal. We now know that many traits are governed by multiple sets of genes. If Mendel had worked with one of these traits, he may not have reached his landmark conclusions.

Mendel published his work in 1866 but received little attention. He also sent his results to numerous noted authorities, none of who were interested. Mendel's *ideas* would change history after their rediscovery, but the man himself actually had little impact on the course of events. Darwin, Wallace, and almost all of the remainder of the scientific community were unaware of his work (although Mendel knew of and admired Darwin's work). In studying the history of knowledge, we repeatedly see that much of what we know was learned by amateurs. Mendel's experience illustrates that this learning can be ignored and buried by professionals.

Even after Mendel's work was rediscovered in 1900, it was not until the understanding of the structure of DNA and the advent of population genetics that the genetics of evolution began to be fully elucidated. It is now possible to define the evolution of species as changes in the frequency of genes in a population. Nature constantly introduces new genetic material in offspring, predominantly through sexual reproduction. By requiring that two individuals participate in the creation of new life, it assures that the genetic composition of the offspring will be different from that of either parent. (Indeed, the sole purpose of the male sex in some species is to furnish variations in genetic material.) Mutations, whereby DNA is altered by the environment, are a secondary mechanism for introduction of novel characteristics. These variations in DNA, some of which are favorable to the species, drive the process of natural selection. A stable environment tends to favor the existing genetic pool, whereas changing environments tend to give new DNA an opportunity to confer an advantage upon the organism.

So the fully developed theory of evolution involves a great deal of work by many people, both before and after Darwin. A coherent theory of evolution would have been impossible without the work of Ray and Linné, because Darwin and Wallace could not have understood change if they did not have a framework to understand the present. It was Ray's definition of species and Linné's classification of them that allowed Darwin and Wallace to explain how they came to be as they are. The theory was also dependent on numerous other realizations by many people: that species were not immutable; that the earth is of great age; that the geology of the earth is shaped by gradual processes; and that fossils are the remains of living creatures, some representing species no longer extant.

It is also interesting to note that several people who made major contributions to the theory of evolution did not believe in the mutability of species. The works of John Ray, Carl von Linné, and Georges Cuvier were all essential to the understanding of evolution, yet none of these people believed that species

211

changed with time. History has many examples of people inadvertently proving, or helping to prove, a theory they themselves though to be untrue. Likewise, very often evidence of the untruth of a commonly held belief has come from those seeking to remove all doubt of its verity.

The theory of evolution surely has an indistinct beginning, and the end is not yet visible. At the present time, the combination of fossil and DNA evidence suggests that, some three and a half billion years ago, life arose in the oceans of the earth in the form of simple, unicellular bacteria-like organisms which would become the progenitors of all subsequent life. Perhaps one and a half billion years ago, more complicated unicellular organisms (called eukaryotic) arose, and multicellular creatures emerged slightly less than a billion years ago. Sometime between one billion years ago and 500 million years ago, the oxygen content of the earth dramatically increased from two percent to twenty percent, making possible the emergence of organisms that consume oxygen rather than create it—animals appeared. Some 500 million years ago, two remarkable events are thought to have occurred. Animals with backbones developed, and the first life on land appeared.

Evolution is the disappearance of species as much as the emergence of new species and the changing of existing ones. In an extraordinary and poorly understood event, some 250 million years ago nearly eighty percent of all species became extinct in a phenomenon which dwarfs the extinction of the dinosaurs. From this destruction, however, arose life more like that we know today. Some 65 million years ago, the dinosaurs and about half of other species became extinct in a smaller but better-known mass extinction. Some associate the latter mass extinction with the impact of a large meteorite or an asteroid.

Overlapping the end of the age of dinosaurs, mammals appeared about one hundred million years ago, and the first primate-like creatures sixty million years ago. The whole of human evolution is contained within the last four million years, about one-tenth of one percent of the time that life has been on Earth.

What has been the impact of the Darwin-Wallace theory of evolution? In biology, it has been huge. It was a giant catalyst for additional biological research, and now forms the basis for ecology, the discipline that will in large part determine the natural history of our species. It has also had great implications and applications in agriculture. Darwin himself noticed that mating related strains of corn produced weak progeny, while mating unrelated strains produced larger and more resilient progeny. George Shull formalized this observation by generating highly inbred strains with the specific characteristics needed. Crossing these inbred strains with each other, he obtained hybrids of unusual vigor that retained the desired characteristics of both parents. This was an advance over the prevailing system of open pollination, because it allowed for both the introduction of new genetic material and the targeting of specific attributes.

Outside of biology, the impact of the theory of evolution has been large, but subtler. In *The Origin of Species*, Darwin actually said very little about human evolution. He simply said "much light will be thrown on the origin of man and his history." Nonetheless, it was believed that the theory of evolution implied that "humans descended from apes", a misconception which continues to this day. The theory of evolution caused a furor among fundamentalist Christians, who felt the work jeopardized the uniqueness of man in the eyes of God, and therefore should be discarded. In economics and business, the effects of the theory of evolution stretched from Karl Marx (who thought the theory fit well with his idea of class struggle) to capitalists (who took the work as justification to crush competitors).

An Economic Idea Gone Awry

Karl Marx (1818–1883) is a misunderstood figure. His love of philosophy overcame his desire to study law, and he received a doctorate in philosophy in 1841. For a time, he made his living as a journalist. As a young man, Marx was struck with the disproportionate distribution of wealth and the resulting polarization of society into the rich and the poor. The young Industrial Revolution seemed to Marx to make this polarization worse. Industrial workers were exploited and impoverished as they performed tedious, repetitive tasks.

Like all influential people, Marx built on the ideas of others. He was influenced by the philosopher Georg Wilhelm Friedrich Hegel (1770–1831), who felt that history was moving in a predictable, predetermined manner toward a predictable endpoint, a concept which became central to Marx's thinking. In 1843, Marx went to Paris, then the center of socialist thinking. There, he converted to communism and met Friedrich Engels (1820–1895) in one of the most fortuitous meetings in history. Although Marx by no means founded communism (communist thinking dates to antiquity), he became an eloquent spokesperson for the communist movement at a very critical time in its evolution.

There are, to my mind, four principal characteristics of Marx's thought. First, he interpreted history in economic terms, as a struggle between people of different economic classes. Second, he strongly opposed any such class divisions and subscribed to an egalitarian view of society. Third, he believed that the wealthy class (the bourgeois) would never accept equality with the oppressed worker class (the proletariat), and that short term violent struggles between the classes may be necessary before equality could be achieved. It should be noted that Marx did not advocate violence; he simply felt that it might be a brief, necessary evil in the evolution of social structure. It is also noteworthy that Marx formed this opinion at a time when suffrage was not universal and the voice of the worker was nearly completely muted. The unqualified statement which one often hears that communism advocated violence is misleading. Fourth, he perceived that the best way to address the problem of disproportionate distribution of wealth was through government ownership of the means of production. Again, the common conception that Marx supported an authoritarian central government is far from the truth. Indeed, he felt that the government would essentially atrophy after the victory of the workers. The association of communist states with oppressive central authorities was neither advocated nor foreseen by Marx.

None of these ideas were completely original with Marx, but by developing them more fully, he supplied the formal theoretical basis for communism. In 1848, he and Engels published *The Communist Manifesto*, the first comprehensive treatment of the modern concept of communism. *The Communist Manifesto* held that the economic system of a state is of paramount importance in determining its social organization, political structure, and subsequent history. The *Manifesto* also elaborated Marx's view of class struggle and the belief that the increasing prosperity of the bourgeois at the expense of the proletariat would force the latter to overthrow their economic overlords, thus establishing a classless society.

Shortly after the publication of *The Communist Manifesto*, revolutions occurred in France, Italy, and the nations of central Europe. The book was not responsible for the revolutions; the causes were multifactorial. Crop failures in the preceding years resulted in widespread hunger, always a catalyst for revolution. An international credit collapse had caused the Industrial Revolution's first worldwide depression. The effect of the Industrial Revolution on social classes was now apparent, and a growing class of increasingly sullen workers was, in fact, increasingly dominated by an economic upper class. As if anything more were needed, a cholera epidemic fueled the fear that foments revolutions. Because there was no overall coordination of the separate revolutions in the different countries, and because the revolutionists began to fight each other, the revolutions all failed. Immediately after the revolutions, France, Belgium, and Germany, all fearful that Marx's ideas may cause an insurgence of revolutionary thought, banished him. He went to England, and it was in the reading room of the British Museum that he would complete the majority of his work.

His masterpiece, *Das Kapital*, was published in three volumes. The first of these appeared in 1867. The last two volumes were completed and published by Engels after Marx's death (largely based on the latter's notes). An encyclopedic analysis of the economy of capitalist countries, it elaborated on the social stratification alluded to in the *Manifesto* and held that the bourgeois exploited the proletariat by making use of the surplus value created by the workers.

The increasing disparity of resources between the bourgeois and the proletariat and the inevitability of proletarian revolt were Marx's most lasting and influential legacies. He formed the basis of communist thinking, but his work was purely theoretical. It would be a mistake to blame him for the horrors that have taken place in communist countries or at the hand of communist governments. It was his—and the world's—misfortune that the implementation of his ideas concerning economics, production, and the distribution of resources resulted in the oppression of hundreds of millions of people and the deaths of tens of millions. Communism in the theoretical form as elaborated by Marx is reasonable; it is the expression of it that has been tragic. Marx's intentions were more honorable than he is generally given credit for, and he deserves a better place in our history.

With the recent collapse of communism in every powerful nation except China, capitalism has re-emerged as the world's dominant economic system. (Even China is moving toward a free market, and almost half of its output is in capitalist form.) To my mind, this is a salutary change, because the political oppressiveness that has almost always accompanied communism makes it too risky as an economic system at this time. (For example, Lenin and Stalin in Russia, and Mao Zedong in China all killed millions of their own people.) However, it is unfortunate that Marx's ideal of a classless society could not be achieved, and he appears to have made a valid point when he held that in capitalism, the disparity between the rich and the poor will inevitably widen. This is happening in the United States now, and we must act to stem that tide, or else our future will see either a proletarian revolt and the rejection of capitalism, or the institution of a police state, as the shrinking and fearful upper class acts to protect itself.

We are subject to the same laws of natural selection as any other species, and capitalism is social survival of the fittest. But unlike the natural selection of wildlife, it is our responsibility to insure that those among us unable to meet the challenges of capitalism have a reasonable quality of life. A free market economy has historically oppressed a segment of the population, and we are left with the challenge of insuring that there is not a permanent underclass of people locked out of economic opportunity. The arrogance and insensitivity with which managers routinely lay off thousands of dedicated workers makes one wonder if class warfare may in fact be inevitable in capitalist societies.

Capitalism can never claim final victory while there are millions of homeless people in the United States and many of our hardest working citizens earn barely enough to survive. As Kahlil Gibran says in *The Prophet* "The master spirit of the earth shall not sleep peacefully upon the wind till the needs of the least of you are satisfied."

Chapter 21
The Relief of Suffering

The long journey of medicine to improve the
quantity and quality of people's lives begins.

It is a testament to the greatness of the nineteenth century that it abolished slavery and gave us six great medical advances: the germ theory, the stethoscope, the cell theory, anesthesia, antisepsis, and x-rays.

In 1816, Rene Theophile Hyacinthe Laennec (1781–1826) obtained improved hearing of internal sounds by rolling a stiff paper into a cylinder. He had invented the stethoscope. Following the lead of Morgagni and Bichat, Laennec correlated postmortem pathology with the living patient. With his new instrument, Laennec could take this association a step further by correlating internal sounds in the living patient with his autopsy findings.

Darwin was one giant of nineteenth-century biology; Louis Pasteur (1822–1895) was another. As Darwin was primarily responsible for the theory of evolution, Pasteur was a driving force behind another great idea of nineteenth-century biology: the germ theory of disease.

Although remembered as a biologist, Pasteur first worked in chemistry. It was known that the elemental composition of a compound was sometimes not sufficient to predict its properties, since these also depended on how an element was bound to other elements in the molecule. For example, both butane and isobutane have four carbon atoms and ten hydrogen atoms in each molecule (molecular formula C_4H_{10}), but they have different properties because the atoms in their molecules are linked in different ways. Such compounds are now called isomers. In 1848, Pasteur isolated two types of tartaric acid crystals. He showed that they were identical in their elemental composition and even in the order that the atoms were linked to each other (such that traditional two-dimensional renditions of their structures would be identical) but differed in their properties because they had different *three-dimensional* arrangements. In doing this, Pasteur founded the science of stereochemistry, and introduced the idea of a special kind of isomer called a stereoisomer. To illustrate the concept of stereoisomers, think of left and right hands. Identical in components and basic construction, the hands cannot be superimposed, but rather are mirror images of each other.

Shortly thereafter, he was asked by a local brewer to investigate the process of fermentation. At the time, yeast was thought to be an inanimate chemical catalyst that converted sugar into alcohol, but Pasteur showed that yeast produced other chemicals besides alcohol, and that it multiplied and was motile in media. Therefore, it was a living microorganism.

He next proved that some bacteria required oxygen, while others did not, and that heat could retard the spoilage of wine by killing microorganisms. (The same process is now used for milk; Pasteurization is named for him, although he did not work with milk.)

He was next asked to investigate chicken cholera, which was causing severe losses in the poultry industry. He learned that older cultures of the cholera organism had lost their virulence when injected into chickens, and that those chickens did not develop the disease even when injected with fresh cultures. Pasteur followed this work with similar work on the anthrax bacillus in cattle (a bacillus is a type of bacteria). After a number of empiric treatments of these cultures, he learned that he could weaken them, so that cattle injected with them suffered a much reduced form of anthrax. When subsequently injected with fully virulent anthrax bacilli, these cattle did not become sick.

In 1882, he showed that rabies was caused by an agent that was too small to be seen with a microscope and could not be cultured. Deprived of his usual methods, he developed a means of growing the agent in animals, and then showed that an extract of dried spinal cord from these animals protected other animals. Recognizing that the symptoms of rabies did not appear until some time after exposure, Pasteur delayed giving his extract for several days after an infected bite and found that it was still protective.

In 1885, a boy bitten by a rabid dog was brought to him. Since the alternative was certain death, Pasteur began a series of inoculations of the boy, starting with avirulent, fully attenuated rabies, and gradually increasing the virulence. When the child failed to develop the disease, Pasteur had developed an effective inoculation against rabies, suggesting that vaccination against a wide range of diseases was possible.

But he had shown more than that. It had been suspected that microorganisms were the cause of many diseases. For example, Agostino Bassi (1773–1856) had shown that the Muscardine disease of silkworms was caused by a particular protozoan—the first demonstration that a specific organism causes a specific disease in another organism. The cholera epidemic in Europe in the mid-nineteenth century produced several interesting observations and epidemiological theories. Many of these implicated water, known to contain microorganisms. It was found, for example, that the incidence of cholera dropped dramatically in London when the drainage of sewage was redirected to a site on the Thames away from population centers and near the ocean. But these were only tantalizing hints; the proof that microorganisms cause many diseases began with Pasteur. As we shall see, Koch's extension of Pasteur's work became the germ theory of disease, one of history's greatest ideas.

Even this does not fully encapsulate Pasteur's work. In ancient times, all kinds of living creatures were thought to arise from the environment in which they were usually found (maggots from carrion, insects from garbage, etc.), rather than from other creatures like themselves. By Pasteur's time, this theory, called spontaneous generation, had been abandoned for macroscopic creatures (those that can be seen with the naked eye), but great debate remained over the origin of microorganisms. The tiny size and ubiquitous nature of microorganisms made them unknowingly present in all experimental systems designed to test the theory of spontaneous generation, leading many to conclude that these tiny creatures did arise by this method.

It was known that nothing would grow in jars containing nutrient solutions if they were sealed and then boiled, but there was some feeling that spontaneous generation required contact with air and that this was not a fair test. In the 1860s, Pasteur showed that bacteria would not grow in a nutrient broth if it was sterilized and the neck of the flask was curved. (This shape allowed air to reach the broth, but bacteria from the air would settle in the neck and could not reach the solution.) In this area, Pasteur was largely repeating the work of Lazaro Spallanzani (1729–1799), who had earlier used similar experimental techniques to come to the same conclusion. But the weight of Pasteur's reputation and his public demonstrations ended the debate on spontaneous generation. Pasteur convincingly showed that no life arises from spontaneous generation and provided the evidence that microorganisms *cause*, but do not originate in putrefaction.

The doctrine of spontaneous generation stands with other erroneous theories of the past, such as the phlogiston theory of fire; geocentrism; the belief that the earth is only a few thousand years old; and the belief, from about 500 to 1100 C.E., that the earth is flat. Each of these misconceptions occurred because common sense was allowed to prevail over reason. At first glance, the earth looks flat, it appears that a burning material is releasing something, insects seem to crawl out of garbage, etc. As we gravitate to familiar trails in the woods, so we are drawn to ways of thinking that appeal to our first impressions and are commonly held. It was a profound triumph of science when it was realized that the situation is not always as it appears. There will always be a place for observation, but when it is sifted with deductive logic and experimentation, a far more accurate view of the world emerges. Progress requires skepticism—skepticism of common sense, skepticism of previous great minds, and skepticism of accepted doctrine. Such skepticism requires courage and an ability to look at the world in a new way.

Louis Pasteur would be remembered as a great scientist just for discovering the field of stereochemistry. With his achievements in biology, Pasteur takes his place as one of the pivotal scientific minds of our history, and arguably the most important person in the history of medicine. Pasteur's work, like that of so many other great contributors, began with a focused problem, and ended with sweeping findings in areas that would not have been thought, at the outset of the work, related to the problem at hand. The work of Pasteur illustrates how important it is for a researcher to permit himself to get somewhat off track. If Pasteur had not followed through on nature's tips and hints, his great work might not have been done. This is often true for any leap of understanding. The unexpected opens new doors only if we are curious and brave enough to try something new. As Pasteur said, "fortune favors the prepared mind."

The scientific method must be thought of as a general guide to procedure, not as an absolute, exclusionary code of conduct. Herein lies a challenge to our society. Given that so much of our progress has come through serendipity, we must have a social structure that permits a considerable degree of experimentation not directly related to a specific, immediate problem. I am concerned, in this era of profits, patents, and government cutbacks, that basic research, which has always been the backbone of our progress, and which is always dependent on a degree of "freedom to pursue", may become seriously jeopardized.

We are evolving culturally and intellectually, as well as biologically. Just as a changing environment gives new genetic material a chance to confer a survival and reproductive advantage, the frequent introduction of new perspectives leads to cultural evolution and intellectual progress. We cannot foresee, or create in

220

our laboratories, all the new circumstances and possible permutations that can guide us to new knowledge. Some of these new circumstances and novel perspectives will come to us uninvited and unexpected. We must be ready to take advantage of them.

Robert Koch (1843–1910), was a country physician with boundless interests. To relieve the boredom of his rural medical practice, Koch's wife gave him a microscope, never suspecting the uses to which her husband would put it. Koch extended Pasteur's work, and in doing so, completed the germ theory of disease and founded the science of bacteriology. His first contribution was changing from broth to a gelatin medium for culture. This allowed isolation of individual bacterial species, because streaking with a needle on a solid medium meant that individual bacilli would fall off the needle and then proliferate into pure colonies. In 1876, his studies of anthrax in animals convinced him that the disease was caused by bacteria that form spores, and that these spores maintained their virulence even when they had been in the soil for protracted periods of time. Using his new culture medium, Koch isolated the responsible bacillus from soil and proved that it caused anthrax when injected into mice. This was the first time that an individual bacterium (the singular of bacteria) was shown to cause a particular disease, and to Koch we owe the idea that specific bacteria cause specific diseases.

In 1882, Koch isolated the tubercle bacillus from patients with tuberculosis, and shortly thereafter, isolated the bacteria that cause cholera. His work led to the famous "Koch's postulates" for proving that an organism causes (rather than is incidentally associated with) a disease. First, the candidate organism must be found in all individuals afflicted with the disease. Second, the organism must be isolated in pure form. Third, this isolate must be shown to be capable of causing the disease in healthy animals.

While Koch's postulates effectively distinguish many situations where an organism causes a disease from those where the organism is purely incidental, we now acknowledge a third category, where an organism partially contributes to a disease process, and this circumstance can be very difficult to sort out. Examples of this third category include the role of viruses in certain neoplasms. In any event, Koch's work, in conjunction with that of Pasteur, confirmed that many diseases are caused by microorganisms, and Koch's extension of Pasteur's work brought the germ theory firmly into clinical medicine.

Joining the germ theory of disease was the cell theory. Cells had been known since Robert Hooke, but their true nature and significance were unappreciated.

Robert Brown (1773–1858) was the first to distinguish the nucleus of cells (previously visualized simply as an apparent hole in the cell). Matthias Schleiden (1804–1881) was among the first to understand that every plant was a community of interacting cells, with each cell simultaneously maintaining an independent existence. Theodore Schwann (1810–1882) showed that this was also true of animal life. Schleiden and Schwann are generally credited with the first complete statement that all living things are composed of the subunits Hooke first observed and called cells, and Schwann was the first to use the term "cell theory" to describe this belief. (In 1824, Henri Dutrochet published his opinion that all life is composed of cells, and some afford him priority in this area, but most believe that the work of Schleiden and Schwann was more complete.)

The work of Schleiden and Schwann was made possible by improvements in the microscope, specifically the invention of the achromatic microscope lens. We have seen that ordinary (white) light is a combination of light of different colors. In previous microscopes, different colored components of white light were refracted to differing extents, so not all light was brought to a focus at exactly the same point. (This problem in refracting telescopes led Newton to build a reflecting telescope.) About 1830, several independent workers improved the grinding and coating of lenses and arranged them in pairs, resulting in achromatic (without color) lenses. Today, improvements in the design and construction of lenses and the union of computers and microscopes permit not only higher magnifications, but also three-dimensional reconstructions and the ability to resolve objects less than one wavelength of light in size (previously thought impossible with microscopes based on light).

Rudolph Virchow (1821–1902), the preeminent pathologist of the nineteenth century, made the cell theory an integral part of medicine. He realized that cells derive from other cells, and that abnormal tissue is derived from normal tissue rather than being created *de novo* by the disease. Moreover, disease relates to the cell, and therefore the cell should be the focus of research and treatment. Virchow strove not just to integrate autopsy pathology with clinical medicine, as others before him had done, but also to integrate these two activities with experimental work in the laboratory. Virchow was the launch pad from which the rocket of twentieth-century medicine would depart.

The germ theory and the cell theory complemented each other. By the end of the nineteenth century, it was understood that disease was caused either by the action of microorganisms, or by derangements at the cellular level.

Investigations into the composition of air led to the accidental discovery of nitrous oxide (laughing gas) in the late eighteenth century. Sadly, this gas was used only for amusement for a half century before its anesthetic effects were understood. The precise history of early anesthesia is somewhat unclear. It is said that Horace Wells, a dentist, used nitrous oxide effectively in 1844, and that Crawford Long, a physician in Georgia, used ether as early as 1842. Be this as it may, a public demonstration of nitrous oxide by Wells was unsuccessful, and Long did not publish his results until 1849. By this time, William Morton (1819–1868), a dentist who actually practiced with Wells for a time, had already achieved fame and success as the first person to successfully employ anesthesia in medical practice. Morton used ether, and he arranged for a demonstration at Massachusetts General Hospital in 1846. It was a success, and anesthesia was born, with Morton given principal credit. Chloroform would be added in 1847 by James Simpson (1811–1870). Today, over two dozen agents are employed in operative anesthesia, and the patient may either be placed in the miraculous sleep of general anesthesia, or be awake with the pertinent nerves rendered temporarily inactive.

The reduction in pain brought about by anesthetic agents is a landmark achievement of our civilization. Less appreciated is that anesthesia has also permitted great advances in surgery, by giving surgeons something precious that they previously did not have—time. Many of today's surgical procedures would be wholly inconceivable if surgeons had to rush them, as in the terrible days before anesthesia.

Although the work of Pasteur and Koch came before the full use of antiseptic surgical procedures, several physicians, without knowledge of the germ theory of disease, used experience and observation to grasp the value of cleanliness in medical procedures. In the eighteenth century, Charles White, Joseph Clarke, and Robert Collins all independently reduced postpartum infection through simple cleanliness. Unfortunately, their work was largely ignored, probably because no theoretical context existed within which to interpret their findings.

Ignaz Semmelweis (1818–1865) made a landmark observation in the obstetrical wards of Vienna. He saw that the incidence of postpartum infections were always significantly higher in wards where the physicians had the responsibility of teaching medical students than where deliveries were performed by midwives (who did not teach), despite identical procedures. What was different about the physician-student combination? Semmelweis realized that the difference was in their routines. Physicians generally took their students to the autopsy room before going to visit their patients. Suspecting a transmissible agent originating in the morgue, Semmelweis instructed his students and staff to wash their hands rigorously after an autopsy, a mandate resulting in a dramatic reduction in infections. Sadly, Semmelweis's ideas were so resented by his colleagues that he was fired from his position in the teaching hospital, and it would be left for Joseph Lister to implement a permanent aseptic approach. Bruised egos have always been the enemy of progress.

Empirical experience of this nature can be wondrously effective, but truly crucial advances generally require a theoretical framework. Therefore, Joseph Lister (1827–1912), building directly and intentionally on the work of Pasteur, is rightly credited with antiseptic techniques. In 1865, he read a paper by Pasteur espousing the germ theory of disease. If microorganisms caused disease, might they also be responsible for surgical infections, the symptoms of which were similar to many diseases? If so, how to kill them pre-operatively, before they could contaminate the wound? Pasteur had also suggested that microorganisms cause decay. Lister became intrigued with phenol (also called carbolic acid), a chemical added to sewers to reduce odors and known to retard the decay of cadavers. If microorganisms caused decay, and phenol inhibited the decay of bodies, then perhaps phenol killed microorganisms. He proved that cleansing an area with phenol prior to the surgical incision sharply reduced the incidence of post-operative infections. Lister was not the only person of his time to try phenol, but he had the greatest personal success and the greatest influence on others because he understood Pasteur's germ theory, and developed a complete antiseptic surgical procedure within that context. For others, the use of phenol was mere trial and error, but for Lister, it was a specific, rigorous procedure that was an outgrowth and culmination of the germ theory. Like anesthesia, antisepsis not only decreased suffering, but also increased the number of operations that could be safely performed.

The last of the giant medical advances of the nineteenth century was made by Wilhelm Conrad Roentgen (1845–1923, from the German Röntgen). In the middle of the nineteenth century, it became technically possible to evacuate a glass tube and to place within it two electrodes, each connected to the terminal of a battery. (The electrode connected to the positive terminal was called the anode, while the electrode connected to the negative terminal was the cathode.) A glow, found to emanate from the cathode, was produced in the tube. This emission came to be known as cathode rays, and the evacuated tube in which they arose was called a cathode ray tube (a term still used occasionally today). But the first triumph of the new tube was not in the cathode rays themselves (we will consider them shortly), but rather in a strange radiation originating in the tube, but not confined to it.

Roentgen, a physicist, was working in the area of cathode rays, which we now know to be a stream of electrons. In 1895, he was surprised to see that, even when the tube was covered with black paper, a nearby fluorescent screen glowed. Roentgen dropped his initial research plans and followed up on these observations, going on to show that the cathode ray tube emitted a radiation very different from and much more penetrating than the actual cathode rays themselves. He called this radiation x-rays (because of the mathematical convention of naming an unknown "x") and demonstrated that they penetrated many materials opaque to light, including the soft tissues of the body.

More recent modifications of x-rays include the CT scanner, which takes cross-sectional x-rays of the body. It should be noted that x-rays, which we now know to be electromagnetic radiation very much like visible light but with a shorter wavelength, have many applications beyond medical diagnosis. Three of the most important are: x-ray astronomy (many stellar objects emit most of their electromagnetic radiation in wavelengths shorter than those of visible light); x-ray diffraction (whereby information can be obtained from how crystals scatter x-rays); and x-ray therapy (which uses higher doses of x-rays to attack tumors).

Chapter 22
The Applications of Theory

Centuries of intellectual progress begin to translate
into the technology of the contemporary world.

THERE IS NO SHARP DIVIDING LINE between science and technology. Technology is the application of science and is inextricably interwoven with it. They are mirror images of each other. We have already seen some of the technological advances made possible by scientific theories. Here, we consider other applications of science that have shaped our world.

Writing With Light

The word "photography" means "to write with light" and the word "camera" comes from the Latin *camera obscura*, meaning dark room, as photography got its start when a small hole was made in the wall of a darkened room. An image of the scene outside the room was projected onto the wall opposite the hole. A lens was soon placed in the hole to improve the projection. What was missing was a way of preserving the image.

The key, and often forgotten, basis of photography was the work of Johann Heinrich Schulze, who in 1727 showed that silver halides (silver chloride, silver iodide, and silver bromide) darkened when exposed to light. Thomas Wedgewood (1771–1805) and Humphrey Davy (1778–1829), working independently, cast the image of the *camera obscura* onto paper coated with silver chloride. The image was preserved, but they had no way of stopping the process, so the continued action of light darkened the entire paper and concealed the image.

The history of photography from this time is the story of parallel developments in England and France. Three people should be given credit for independently developing photography. In 1822, Joseph Nicephore Niepce (1765–1833), took the first permanent photograph, letting sunlight fall on a pewter plate coated with a light-sensitive asphalt. Light hardened the asphalt, after which the application of solvents dissolved the asphalt that had not been exposed and hardened. A crude image was formed, but it was indistinct and exposure times of seven to eight hours were required. Because the sun shifted position over this time, areas that should have been unexposed became intermittently exposed, and areas intended to be exposed were periodically shielded from the sun, resulting in poor delineation of light and dark areas. An 1826 image created by this method is the oldest surviving photograph.

In 1829, Niepce and Louis Daguerre (1787–1851) began collaborating, and Daguerre continued the work after the older man's death. The Daguerrotype process abandoned asphalt and returned to silver halides. The process began by treating a silver-coated copper plate with iodine vapors so that the coating became silver iodide instead of native, uncombined silver. This silver iodide coated plate had a brown color; exposure to light changed the silver iodide back to native silver, forming a weak image. Further exposure to sodium thiosulfate fixed the image (i.e., rendered the plate no longer sensitive to light, so that further exposure would not obliterate the image). But the image was faint, and exposure times were long. Was there any way to improve the quality of the image? Daguerre experimented in this area and may eventually have tried mercury vapors, but he was hastened to his answer by a happy serendipity. One day in 1835, a frustrated Daguerre placed exposed plates, bearing a faint image, in his drawer. To his surprise, he found that these plates, after being in his drawer, contained an excellent image. Removing the possibilities one by one, Daguerre correctly concluded that mercury vapors, emanating from a pool of mercury in a dish, had improved his images. The mercury combined with the native silver—produced from the silver iodide by the action of light—to produce a precipitated amalgam, but it did not combine with the silver iodide. The mercury-silver amalgam was white and formed a clearer image than that of silver alone. A positive image was formed; areas exposed to light became white, while areas in the shadows remained dark, provided the Daguerrotype was viewed in subdued light. Exposure times in the Daguerrotype were markedly shortened, to about twenty minutes, and the image was much sharper. Daguerre sold his invention to the French government, which made it public in 1839.

William Henry Fox Talbot (1800–1877), independent of Niepce and Daguerre, mastered photography shortly after Niepce's first pictures, several years before the Daguerrotype. He would likely be remembered as the sole inventor of photography if he had published his early work. In 1840, Talbot introduced the calotype (developed earlier), a photographic process whereby paper was soaked in salt water (sodium chloride) and then painted with silver nitrate. The paper became impregnated with silver chloride, which darkened upon exposure to light. Where there were no objects between the light and the paper, the paper would be exposed, and would darken. Where objects prevented light from striking the paper, no darkening occurred. A negative image was formed, wherein light areas became dark and dark objects showed as light zones. Talbot brilliantly went on to photograph the photograph. When the negative image was photographed, a second reversal of light and dark areas converted it into a realistic image of the scene. Moreover, unlike the Daguerreotype, multiple copies could be made from this negative image. Talbot thus simultaneously provided both paper photographs and the negative-positive process. He, more than Daguerre, is the father of contemporary photography. Like Daguerre, Talbot learned that treatment with sodium thiosulfate after exposure would prevent any further light sensitivity.

George Eastman (1854–1932) mounted emulsion on celluloid (a plastic-like material commercially available after 1869). This flexible film permitted greater convenience in photography and became the basis for the box camera, which Eastman introduced in 1888. In this camera, which he named Kodak (for no particular reason, except that it was easy to pronounce and remember), the film was rolled onto a spool, simplifying photography and film developing. In 1947, Edwin Land (1909–1991) introduced a photographic system that developed pictures inside the camera (the Polaroid process).

The myriad developments in photography since then have culminated in the digital camera, wherein the image is formed digitally, obviating the need for film or chemical developing. As their cost continues to come down, the time-honored traditions of darkroom development or taking film to be developed will draw to a close.

Communication at a Distance

Like all great ideas, telecommunications has indistinct origins. In 1764, George Lesages achieved communication at a distance using static electricity. He used a separate wire for each letter. A charge coming over the wire caused two pith balls to move apart. In 1816, a single-wire telegraph was achieved by Francis Ronalds (1788–1873). In his invention, the sender and the receiver had disks with letters printed on their periphery. These disks rotated and were synchronized between sender and receiver. When the rotating disk displayed a letter the sender wanted to send, he sent an electrical impulse, detected by the receiver very much as in Lesages's device. Since the two disks were synchronized, the receiver's disk displayed the same letter as the sender's.

In 1826, Harrison Gray Dyer added the battery to the telegraph. Shortly thereafter, Joseph Henry added several improvements. First, he placed a sounder on the receiving end, so that the incoming current would make a noise. He also introduced the electrical relay, permitting rejuvenation of the electrical signal, thereby allowing transmission over much longer distances. (This work would lead to the transformer.) He created a code of signals to correspond to letters, doing away with awkward devices such as rotating disks.

Based largely on Henry's improvements, William Cooke (1806–1879) and Charles Wheatstone (1802–1875) devised the first commercial telegraph system in 1837. Two years later, Samuel F.B. Morse (1791–1872), again using Henry's ideas, constructed a telegraph. (The idea that Morse invented the telegraph is another oversimplification.) Morse added his famous code, the first universal transmission code for telegraph use, and successfully transmitted from Washington to Baltimore in 1844. Telegraph cable was laid across the English Channel in 1850, and across the Atlantic Ocean in 1858. From the telegraph would come the idea of voice transmission.

In 1854, Charles Bourseul (1829–1912) suggested that a diaphragm could vibrate in response to a voice, thereby alternately connecting and disconnecting an electric circuit. At the other end, as another diaphragm vibrated in response to the alternating currents, the original sound would be reproduced. In 1861, Philipp Reis created a device, which he termed a telephone, based on this premise, but fidelity was poor because all transmission was caused by a simple on-off mechanism. The current could not be varied, and therefore, was not reflective of the myriad gradations of the human voice.

Alexander Graham Bell (1847–1922) would recognize and correct this defect. Bell had little formal training in the sciences, and the inspiration for his idea was a device he encountered in his capacity as a teacher of the deaf—the phonautograph, which consisted of a membrane attached by a thin stick to a bristle touching a plate of glass. Speaking into a cone in front of the membrane caused the membrane, stick, and bristle to vibrate, drawing a line on the glass plate. Each spoken sound generated a different and unique tracing. In 1876, Bell patented a telephone with a more complex microphone than Reis's simple on or off mechanism.

Bell's microphone used the same structure for both sending and receiving. Attaching a wire to a battery, he wound it around an iron bar at the sending end. He continued the wire to the receiving end, where it was wound around another iron bar. A diaphragm was attached to both bars. When the battery sent current through the wire, both bars became electromagnets, and a magnetic field was created around them. At the sending end, the diaphragm moved in response to a voice. This caused the bar to move, resulting in fluctuations in the magnetic field of that bar, which caused variations in the electrical current carried by the wire. At the receiving end, the process was reversed; the fluctuating currents caused the bar inside the wire to move, which then moved the diaphragm and produced sound. The voice was transmitted as *fluctuations* in current, and this variable current more closely reproduced the human voice than a simple on-off mechanism.

Contrary to popular belief, Bell did not invent the telephone. He made it more practical by bringing together ideas from many people. Like all great ideas, Bell's invention simultaneously built on other ideas and served as the nidus for further work.

Bell's microphone was limited in range. The following year, both Thomas Edison and David Hughes introduced the carbon microphone, in which a current passed through carbon granules covered by a diaphragm. At the speaking end, the vibrations of the diaphragm alternately compressed and uncompressed carbon granules, causing variations in the current. At the receiving end, the process was again reversed; a variable current through the granules caused the overlying diaphragm to move. The carbon microphone could transmit over a much greater distance. We associate the telephone with Bell, but it was not fully practical until the carbon microphone was employed.

It is often said that necessity is the mother of invention. This is illustrated by the case of Almon Strowger, a Kansas City mortician. At the time, calls could be directed from the caller to the intended receiver only by the intervention of a human operator. The wife of one of Strowger's business rivals was an operator. Strowger suspected that she was routing calls intended for him to her husband, so he invented the first automatic switching system, in which the operator plays no role in the destination of the call.

Recent developments in telephone systems involve satellite communications (whereby the telephone signal is piggybacked onto a microwave radio wave and directed to a satellite for redistribution to a distant point), and fiber-optic communications (whereby the signal is sent in a light beam inside tiny glass fibers).

230

Oliver Lodge (1851–1940) gave a public demonstration of radio waves in 1894, using them to send a Morse code message from one building to another. For a receiver, Lodge needed more than Hertz's simple discontinuous wire loop, because his system had to convey information, not just detect the presence of radio waves. Lodge perfected the coherer, originally invented by Edouard Branly (1844–1940), and used it as the first practical radio receiver. The coherer consisted of a glass tube, within which were tiny fragments of iron between two metal plates. Normally, the iron filings did not form a continuity between the plates, but the presence of a radio wave caused them to adhere to each other, filling in the gap between the plates and allowing current to pass. Because the coherer would not support voice communication, Morse code was initially used in the radio, with the transmission of a dot causing the iron filings to adhere for a short time and the transmission of a dash causing them to adhere for a longer time.

Like Bell, Guglielmo Marconi (1874–1937) had little conventional training in the field he would revolutionize. Beginning his work in his parents' attic, Marconi sent a radio message sixty miles in 1899, and in 1901, he astonished the world by sending a message across the Atlantic Ocean. It is commonly thought that Marconi contributed the scientific ideas behind the radio and therefore invented it. In actuality, his contributions to radio were significant, but more to do with making radio transmission commercially viable than contributing the basic ideas. We see yet again that a person commonly believed to have invented something actually built on an already well-developed idea. Marconi did for radio what Henry Ford did for the automobile.

Voice transmission required vacuum tubes (called valves in the United Kingdom), which takes us back to Edison. The most productive inventor in history, Thomas Edison (1847–1931) is remembered for improving on Bell's telephone with a carbon transmitter, improving on incandescent lighting (he did not invent it), and developing the first phonograph, copying machine, and fluoroscope, as well as over a thousand other inventions. His sole contribution to basic physics was the discovery of what is called the Edison effect. He found that heating a metal caused the flow of electricity in the adjacent space. When two wires were placed in a partial vacuum (a minor modification of his light bulb), heating one wire resulted in current flow between the two wires, even though they were not touching each other. Edison, interested in practical applications, failed to follow up on this observation. J.J. Thomson, in the closing years of the nineteenth century, would explain it with the discovery of the electron (discussed subsequently), which was then seen to be the cause of electricity. Heating caused electrons to leave the surface of the metal in the Edison effect. In 1904, John Ambrose Fleming (1849–1945) observed that the electrons leaving the heated metal would flow toward a positively charged anode, so he placed an anode near the metal plate to be heated. Because electrons flow much more efficiently in a vacuum, he evacuated the chamber. When electrons flowed from the heated plate to the anode, Fleming had invented the diode, the first and simplest of the vacuum tubes. The invention of the vacuum tube, which would ultimately make possible an age of electronic devices, found its first application as an improved detector of radio waves. With the diode, voice radio transmission was achieved in 1906.

Also in 1906, Lee de Forest (1873–1961), following on the work of Fleming, found that a grid placed between the plate and the anode, if a small potential was applied to it, could accelerate the electrons and amplify the current. The amplification of a single such triode was very weak, but when de Forest attached several triodes together in series, appreciable amplification was obtained. De Forest's ability to amplify current made practical electronic devices, including radio and the first computers, possible. A scant thirty years after the publication of the Maxwell equations, Hertz had predicted and found radio waves, Lodge and Marconi had harnessed them to give us communication, and Fleming and de Forest had ushered in the age of electronics. The first radio station was established in 1920, and by 1924, there were five hundred in the United States. Unlike the telephone, radio offered humanity the first oral mass communication.

Radio transmission involves the modification, or modulation, of a radio wave. The idea of transmitting images followed almost immediately after successful radio broadcasting. Modifying an electromagnetic wave to carry an image was not the obstacle. Nor was detection of the wave a fundamental problem. The cathode ray tube, developed at the end of the nineteenth century, was quickly seen as suitable for transforming the current caused by the carrier wave into an image; the output could simply be directed at a screen coated with a material that glowed when struck by electrons.

The difficulty was that no camera could faithfully capture an image for transmission. Many materials were known that would emit electrons when exposed to light, and a number of these were tried early on. John Logie Baird (1886–1946) produced the first television image in 1925. He scanned a scene (i.e., converted it into a stream of electrons) by using a spinning disk with holes in it. Light from the scene went through the holes to illuminate a photosensitive material that emitted electrons when exposed to light. The image was generated by the direct liberation of electrons from the photosensitive material in response to light. This mechanical method of converting a scene into electricity was inherently poor. The future of television lay in electronic scanning.

Today, one form of scanning a scene is to focus light through a lens onto the front of a photosensitive material. Simultaneously, electrons from a cathode ray tube strike the back of this material. Scanning is achieved when the light from the scene causes variations in the current caused by the cathode ray tube, a method more sensitive than the use of a photosensitive material alone. In 1911, A. Campbell Swinton (1863–1930) described an electronic camera based on principles very similar to those of today's equipment. This camera was never built, and attention shifted to scanning a scene by Baird's mechanical means.

In 1923, Vladimir Zworykin (1889–1982) resurrected the idea of electronic scanning and patented an electronic television camera. Modifying Campbell Swinton's idea, Zworykin's design placed a thin sheet of mica inside a cathode ray tube. The surface of the mica that received the image was covered with tiny particles of silver coated with cesium oxide; these were the light-sensitive electron emitters. The back of the mica was covered with aluminum and received the output of the cathode ray tube. Light from the scene modified the current caused by the cathode ray tube. A prototype television, based on Zworykin's camera, successfully transmitted an image four miles (six kilometers) in 1933. Working independently, Philo Farnsworth (1906-1971) transmitted an electronic image a much shorter distance in 1927. By 1938, the technology of television was well in hand, but governmental approval did not come until 1941, by which time the war held up production. In 1946, years after the last significant technological obstacle was overcome, television finally went into full production.

The current frontier in television is high-definition television, which uses digital transmission and a higher number of lines on the screen to furnish a picture of greater fidelity. It will require the replacement of existing television sets with sets of greater cost.

Building With Steel

Construction materials were greatly improved in the nineteenth century. Steel, composed of iron with a small amount of carbon (and today, generally other deliberately introduced elements) was known in antiquity, but could not be reliably and economically made until the mid-nineteenth century because of excessive impurities. In particular, structurally superior steel usually contains between 0.7% and 1.7% carbon. Higher carbon contents result in inferior steel, and the carbon content of early nineteenth century steel exceeded that amount. The problem facing early steel makers was not how to get carbon into the iron, but how to get it out.

In 1856 Henry Bessemer (1813–1898), building on an idea of a Kentucky steel maker named William Kelley, created a steel making process that blew air into the blast furnace, so that oxygen would combine with excess carbon and blow off as carbon dioxide. The Bessemer process allowed industrial grade steel to be economically made in great quantities, but by the end of the century, the open-hearth process had largely replaced the Bessemer method. In the open-hearth technique, developed by William Siemens (1823–1883), iron ore is used as a source of oxygen to remove excess carbon, and the exhaust gases are used to preheat the incoming air, providing for greater efficiency and the higher temperatures needed to manufacture steel. Other refinements in steel making would come along, but the Bessemer and open-hearth methods gave human history a new age—the steel age.

Temperature Control

By the early 1800s, it was clear that evaporating liquids and expanding gases were cooler than their surroundings and would therefore absorb heat from the environment. Many people, aware of this observation, would try to harness this property to develop air conditioning and refrigeration.

In 1834, Jacob Perkins (1766–1849) patented a system that produced cold through the evaporation of a volatile liquid. (The word "volatile" refers to a tendency to evaporate readily.) Fifteen years later, John Gorrie (1803–1855), a physician, sought a way to make the wards of his Florida hospital more comfortable for his patients. He developed the first large-scale air conditioning system based on the alternate compression and expansion of air. In 1859, Ferdinand Carre (1824–1900) introduced the use of ammonia, which would be used for many years as a refrigerant (and remains in occasional use today). The design of the air conditioner was improved by Willis Carrier (1876–1950), considered the father of contemporary air conditioning. The first completely air-conditioned commercial building was in San Antonio, Texas, in the 1920s. Because of World War II, air conditioning would not become widespread until the 1950s.

The contemporary air-conditioning or refrigeration system operates on essentially the same mechanism as the prototype models of a hundred and fifty years ago. A refrigerant material, which is a volatile liquid or a gas, passes through coils. As it does so, the liquid evaporates or the gas expands, absorbing heat from the air on the outside of the coils. At the same time, water in the air condenses on the external surface of the coils, so that the air is both cool and dry after it passes across the coils. The difficulty now is to get the warmed refrigerant material to release its heat and return to its initial state so the cycle can repeat. The refrigerant material is passed outside the building, where it is compressed back into a liquid or a denser gas in a process that generates heat. The compressed fluid (liquid or gas) percolates through a condenser, where it gives up heat to the outside air, and where, in liquid systems, the vapor condenses back into liquid. The refrigerant is then returned to the building, where it again evaporates or expands, and absorbs heat. Until recently, the most common refrigerant was Freon, the trade name for a variety of gases related to methane or ethane, in which some of the hydrogen atoms have been replaced by chlorine and fluorine atoms. As a halogenated hydrocarbon, Freon damages the ozone layer, and there is some thinking that it may be contributing to global warming caused by the greenhouse effect (discussed subsequently). Therefore, there is currently a move toward refrigerants based on other materials.

The economic effects of refrigeration have been enormous. By permitting longer transit times of food and other perishable materials, refrigeration greatly increased their availability, permitting industries to exist which would otherwise be impossible.

Air conditioning has made indoor environments much more comfortable. Less often appreciated is the effect it has had on productivity, particularly in the southern states, where summertime indoor temperatures would otherwise compromise the ability to work efficiently. To my mind, it is not a coincidence that the southern part of the United States did not begin to rival the northern portion in industrial capacity and economic influence until air conditioning was widely available.

A Mixed Blessing

The first self-propelled road vehicles ran on steam. Nicolas Joseph Cugnot (1728–1804) built such a vehicle in 1770, and William Murdock and James Watt built a steam-powered automobile in 1781. But steam engines did not have the power-to-weight ratio to permit their practical use in small vehicles. With the use of high-pressure steam, engines could be made small enough for a locomotive, but not for a practical automobile. The story of the automobile is the story of the internal combustion engine.

As steam gave power to the eighteenth century, so the internal combustion engine gave power to the latter part of the nineteenth century. The name of this engine derives from the fact that the combustion takes place in the cylinder, immediately adjacent to the piston, rather than in a separate compartment, as in the steam engine. Few innovations have changed our history as much as relocating the site of combustion in engines.

In 1860, Etienne Lenoir (1822–1900) developed the first internal combustion engine, a two stroke engine that ran on coal gas. In the Lenoir engine, the fuel was not compressed before ignition. When Nikolaus August Otto (1832–1891) heard of Lenoir's accomplishment, he realized that the new engine would be more efficient if the inflammable gas was compressed before ignition. After years of turning the problem over in his head, Otto grasped the solution. In 1876 (the same year that Alexander Bell patented his telephone), Otto introduced his famous four-stroke internal combustion engine. The basic concepts of this engine persist to the present day and can be found in most automobile engines. During the first stroke, the piston moves downward and away from the closed portion of the cylinder. As it does so, a fuel-air mixture is sucked into the cylinder. During the second stroke, the cylinder moves upward, compressing the fuel-air mixture. At peak compression (and only after compression), a spark plug discharges a spark which ignites the fuel-air mixture. The mixture burns so quickly that its rapid expansion is virtually an explosion, driving the piston downward in the third stroke—the power stroke. During the fourth stroke, the exhaust valve opens, and the rising piston drives the spent gases out of the cylinder. Many thought this an inherently inefficient design because only one of the four strokes did any work, but it was Otto's insight that grasped the importance of using the other strokes to maximize the productivity of the power stroke.

The problem with the Otto engine, and the reason it could not directly lead to the automobile, is that is ran on coal gas, and thus had to be connected to a supply. For the new engine to reach its potential and provide transportation, it would have to be adapted to run on liquid fuel, so that it could carry its supply with it. The discovery of petroleum in Pennsylvania in 1859 provided the necessary fuel. The distillation of this crude oil produced a superb replacement for whale oil in lighting. However, the first products to be released during the distillation process were lighter and highly inflammable, not suitable for use in lamps. This light distillate, initially regarded as a nuisance, would become the product we now call gasoline (petrol in the U.K.).

But the Otto engine required that the fuel be in gaseous form. How to convert the newly discovered petroleum products into a form suitable for the new engine? In 1882, one of Otto's employees, Gottlieb Daimler (1834–1900), had a falling out with his boss and left the firm. Daimler worked with Wilhelm Maybach (1847–1929) to develop a way to vaporize these previously unwanted light distillates of petroleum before they were injected into the cylinder. Daimler and Maybach perfected the carburetor, which caused air to move in such a way that its pressure fell. Liquid gasoline adjacent to the airstream vaporized as the low-pressure air rushed by, and the mixture of air and vaporized gasoline was sucked into the cylinder, where it was compressed and burned in the Otto engine. The carburetor permitted Daimler to produce an automobile in 1886. A few months earlier, Karl Benz (1844–1929), who had no connection with Otto, used a carburetor of his own design, and independently produced an automobile. Benz also introduced electric ignition and water-cooling. Eventually, Benz and Daimler merged their companies into Mercedes-Benz (Mercedes was the daughter of a business associate of Daimler).

Rudolph Christian Karl Diesel (1858–1913) took a slightly different approach to the problem of using liquid fuel in the Otto engine. In 1892, he patented the engine bearing his name. Also a four-stroke engine, unlike the gasoline engine, it had no carburetor to vaporize the fuel or spark plug to ignite the compressed gases. Only air was drawn into the cylinder during the intake stroke, and therefore, only air was compressed in the second stroke. At the end of the compression stroke, oil was injected into the cylinder through tiny nozzles that vaporized it without a carburetor. In the pressure and heat of the compressed air, the oil ignited spontaneously without the deliberate ignition of a spark plug. Contemporary Diesel engines do not use oil, but rather a petroleum distillate similar but not identical to gasoline. Diesel engines tend to be more efficient, but slower than their gasoline counterparts.

Henry Ford (1863–1947) played no significant role in the development of the automobile. His lasting contribution was conceiving a practical mass-production process. Ford's system of mass production had three components. The first was standardized, interchangeable parts, also not original with Ford. Indeed, one of the reasons for Gutenberg's success in printing is the use of interchangeable letters. Others had approached manufacturing from the standpoint of standardized parts, including Eli Whitney (1765–1825), of cotton gin fame. But it was Ford who fully implemented the concept in industry. The second component in Ford's mass production process was the division of labor, whereby workers were more productive if they performed only one task. This too, was not original with Ford, and had been a leading idea in the writings of Adam Smith. But again, Ford put the theory into practice, and he did so with the third critical component of mass production—the assembly line. Wouldn't people work more efficiently if their work came to them, rather than their having to go to it? In Ford's assembly line, each worker was stationary, and his work was delivered to him at waist height, ready for his specific modification. Afterward, when the automobile was ready for the next stage, it was moved down the line to the worker responsible for the next step in the production process.

Ford brought mass production to a nearly contemporary form and greatly influenced the means of production. His production process was not significantly changed until after World War II, with the ideas of Edwards Deming. (In fact, many companies still employ the Ford process essentially without modification.) Ford's impact on society extended well beyond manufacturing; his process allowed the worker to be more productive, and thus to enjoy a higher wage.

Almost immediately, the downside of mass production became evident. Workers, restricted to one task, became bored. Resentful of increasing expectations without concomitant rewards, they began to feel that they were making possible the success of Ford and a handful of others while they themselves were being exploited. The higher wages obtained by workers since mass production have generally come only after they have insisted on fair treatment from management.

One final comment about the automobile is appropriate. Modern times have seen the growth of cities to sizes unimagined by earlier periods. To my mind, there are two reasons for this, beyond the improvements in sanitation conditions and building materials. The first was the steam engine, which drew industries and people away from sources of waterpower toward urban centers. I regard the automobile as the second reason for such large metropolitan areas because it permits people to work in and contribute to the size and impact of a city without actually living there. For example, the permanent population of Manhattan Island is some 1.5 million people, but the population swells to approximately twice that during working hours, making it one of the leading commercial and economic centers in the world. It is difficult to imagine how this thirty-one square mile (eighty square kilometer) island could maintain this position if it had to support three million permanent inhabitants.

Today, the automobile has simultaneously made our lives easier and sadder. What we have gained in ease of transportation, we have largely lost in pollution and the toll of highway accidents. It has indeed been a mixed blessing.

A Wilderness of Materials

By the end of the nineteenth century, the endless possibilities of carbon compounds were understood. Organic chemistry, the branch of chemistry dealing with these compounds, became the basis for industrial chemistry. The starting point for these new compounds was coal tar, but in the twentieth century, petroleum would become the originating material. By the latter half of the nineteenth century, empiricism had shown that combinations of phenol (a carbon compound related to benzene, also called carbolic acid) and aldehydes (another class of organic compounds, of which formaldehyde is an example) yielded either resins or hard materials, but little had been done to follow up on this observation.

Leo Baekeland (1863–1944) secured his fortune by developing a new kind of photographic paper, and therefore had the opportunity to experiment and take empiricism in organic chemistry to new heights. At the beginning of the twentieth century, three substances were used for applications now served by plastics. The first was celluloid, created in 1856 by Alexander Parkes (1813–1890) from cellulose nitrate and a solution of camphor in alcohol. Developed commercially and patented by John Hyatt (1837–1920), celluloid was the first plastic and was used in many areas, predominantly as a medium in photography and motion pictures. Its high inflammability made it dangerous, and it is no longer used. The second was rubber, made from the sap of the rubber tree, which could be processed to different degrees of hardness. In 1839, Charles Goodyear (1800–1860) found that adding a small amount of sulfur to rubber improved its strength and elasticity, a process later termed vulcanization. (Sulfur restricts the ability of chains of the subunits of rubber to slide past each other.) The hardest such rubber was firm enough to serve in some capacities now occupied by plastic. The third substance, shellac, was made from the lac insect, native to southern Asia. Primarily used as a varnish or finish, shellac was also available in a solid form for specialized applications. The difficulty with shellac was that demand exceeded supply in the time of Baekeland.

Beginning with the phenol-aldehyde combinations and modifying them, Baekeland created the first practical plastic, which he called Bakelite, in 1909. Bakelite had a property not previously observed in the infant plastics industry. A little heating made it malleable, after which further heating would permanently set it in a desired shape. Because Bakelite was essentially noncombustible, it generally replaced celluloid. In addition, it was water-resistant, an excellent insulator, and easy to cut.

Bakelite did more than begin the age of plastics; it inaugurated the age of polymers. Polymers are giant molecules, constructed from repeating numbers of smaller molecules, and possessing unique properties different from those of the component molecules. The underlying requirement is that the smaller molecule, the subunit, must have two reactive sites, so it can simultaneously bind to a forming polymer and receive another subunit.

Baekeland initially did not appreciate that his creation was a polymer because the size of the resultant molecules could not be measured. Only after Hermann Staudinger (1881–1965) developed a method to measure the size of polymers, proving that they were giant molecules, and Wallace Carothers (1896–1937) created neoprene and nylon, did polymers become fixtures in our lives.

Contemporary polymer chemistry has given us a wilderness of materials previously undreamed of. Examples of polymers are nylon, polyester, synthetic rubber, and plastic. Many polymers are based on carbon, usually obtained from petroleum products. (Hence the dependence of industrialized society on petroleum goes far beyond the need for gasoline.)

Chapter 23
Beyond Our Immediate Experience

The willingness of an amateur to think beyond his immediate experience is as important as all of the world's laboratories.

THE TWENTIETH CENTURY HAS SEEN SUCH DIZZYING PROGRESS in so many areas that it is a daunting task to chronicle it. Never before in history, not even in the Enlightenment, has the potential of humanity been so clearly demonstrated. Concurrent with this, however, humanity has laid bare its nakedness when it comes to the fundamental property of kindness.

As we have seen, since the seventeenth century, data have been expressed numerically, and statistics and probability have been indispensable tools in the interpretation of results. The twentieth century has seen an ever-increasing reliance on the mathematical analysis of data. In fact, the results of an experiment are not the raw numbers generated, but numbers that have been mathematically analyzed according to current concepts in statistics and probability. Karl Gauss (1777–1855) developed the now-familiar bell-shaped curve to describe a population, with the degree of spread above and below an average value being an indication of the variability of the characteristic. Karl Pearson (1857–1936) elaborated on the Gaussian distribution to develop such pivotal statistical methods as the standard deviation (a precise measure of variability of the data) and the Chi Square test (which determines the probability that a given set of results is due to chance versus the probability that it is due to the verity of a theoretical model).

We can begin the history of the twentieth century with physics, because that science was racing toward a crescendo in the year 1900. Indeed, physics of the twentieth century has been given the special designation of modern physics, to indicate that it has taken paths and reached heights never imagined by physicists of the past. To my mind, of the multitude of developments in physics in the first half of the century, three are central: the elucidation of the structure of the atom, relativity, and quantum theory.

In 1896, the year after the discovery of x-rays, Joseph John Thomson (1856–1940) made the second remarkable discovery to emerge from the cathode ray tube. It had been known that these tubes emitted a visible glow, called cathode rays, from the area around the cathode (not to be confused with Roentgen's x-rays, which are also emitted by cathode ray tubes, but cannot be seen). Thomson learned that both electric fields and magnetic fields would deflect cathode rays. Positive and negative particles are deflected in opposite directions in an electric or magnetic field, and the direction of the deflections identified these emissions as negatively charged. Thomson was not able to calculate the actual mass of the particles, but he did determine the ratio of the charge to the mass (charge/mass). It was 2000 times that of the hydrogen ion (what we now call a proton), suggesting that Thomson's particles either had a massive negative charge or a very small mass. Thomson correctly assumed that the charge, although negative, was of the same magnitude as the hydrogen ion. Thus, the particles responsible for cathode rays must have a mass much less than that of an atom. Cathode rays were negatively charged *subatomic* particles. He had discovered the electron, the first of the subatomic particles, and by doing so, he helped us begin to understand that the atom is not indivisible. After the elucidation of the nature of cathode rays, it was only a short step to show that electricity was the flow of electrons. Thomson's work was a bridge from the nineteenth-century work of Faraday and Maxwell to the twentieth-century understanding of the structure of the atom.

Antoine Henri Becquerel (1852–1908), was interested in fluorescence (the process where a substance, if exposed to light, emits light of a different wavelength as long as it continues to be exposed to the original light) and phosphorescence (the same as fluorescence except that the emission continues after the original light has been removed). Could these phenomena be due to the newly discovered x-rays? If so, that would not only give Becquerel the explanation for the interesting phenomena, it would also mean that x-rays could be produced without the cumbersome and expensive cathode ray tube.

Becquerel, using phosphorescent uranium salts, hoped to capture the process on a photographic plate and provide evidence that it was caused by x-rays. Because phosphorescence requires initial exposure to light, he exposed the uranium compounds to sunlight, and then, in darkness, exposed them to a photographic plate. The exposure of the film initially made him believe that x-rays were responsible for the phenomenon, but this interpretation soon ran into a problem. During a series of cloudy days, Becquerel continued his experiments, expecting little or no exposure of the plate since the uranium compounds had not first been exposed to light. To his surprise, the plates were as developed as when the uranium was exposed to sunlight. The ability of the uranium that had not been exposed to light to expose a photographic plate meant that phosphorescence was not the explanation. He had found something new. Here was a process that did not require "priming" with light (as did fluorescence and phosphorescence) or the use of an electric current (as did the x-rays that emanated from the cathode ray tube). This was the spontaneous emission of energy from matter, a process never before identified. It was his failure to achieve his objective, and his realization of that failure, that allowed Becquerel to recognize in 1896 that the uranium salts must be emitting a new type of radiation. The Curies called this new radiation radioactivity.

Perhaps no two people in science have overcome adversity more than Marie (1867–1934) and Pierre (1859–1906) Curie. Pierre, with his brother Jacques, discovered piezoelectricity, wherein pressure causes some crystals to attain an electric potential. Marie found that an ore of uranium called pitchblende was actually more radioactive than the uranium isolated from it. She and Pierre suspected a new element. In 1898, after two years of heroically difficult work under extremely arduous conditions, they discovered two new radioactive elements: polonium and radium, the latter a million times more radioactive than uranium.

Marie died of complications sustained from years of work with radioactivity. Albert Einstein said of her in a memorial statement:

> Her strength, her purity of will, her austerity toward herself, her objectivity, her incorruptible judgment—all these were of a kind seldom found joined in a single individual.

Within two years, x-rays, the electron (representing the divisible atom), and radioactivity were discovered. Twentieth-century physics was on its way.

Ernest Rutherford (1871–1937), a student of J.J. Thomson and the finest experimental physicist of the twentieth century, showed that a million times more energy was obtained from radium by radioactivity than by combustion. No known chemical process could release this much energy. What could be its source? In 1899, Rutherford recognized the existence of at least two different types of radioactivity, based on the penetrating ability of the emitted particles.

Using the first two letters of the Greek alphabet, he called the less-penetrating emissions alpha particles, and the more-penetrating emissions beta.

In 1900, Paul Villard (1860–1934) demonstrated a third type of radioactivity. This type had enormous penetrating power and was not deflected by a magnetic field, indicating that it was uncharged and had little if any mass. Rutherford called them gamma rays (continuing with the Greek alphabet), and showed that they were electromagnetic radiation. Like all electromagnetic radiation, gamma rays consist of photons moving at the speed of light. Only the wavelength differentiates them from visible light or x-rays.

Beta rays were also elucidated quickly. It was shown that they are deflected by a magnetic field in a manner characteristic of negatively charged particles. It was later shown that their mass and charge were those of an electron, recently discovered by Thomson, and we now know that beta radiation is a stream of electrons emanating from the nucleus of certain radioactive particles.

It took a little longer to figure out the nature of alpha rays. In 1903, Rutherford demonstrated that alpha particles, when placed in a magnetic field, were deflected in the direction opposite to that of the beta particles. This indicated a positive charge. Because the magnitude of the deflection was very slight, and because they have little penetrating ability, they had to be massive, positively charged particles. Rutherford guessed that alpha emissions were the nuclei of helium atoms. In 1909, he placed an alpha-emitting material next to a thin-walled, evacuated, closed-glass vessel, which the alpha particles had sufficient energy to enter, but not to exit. By spectroscopically demonstrating helium in the vessel, Rutherford proved that alpha emissions were helium atoms (i.e., what we now know to consist of two protons and two neutrons).

These discoveries provided additional evidence that the atom was not indivisible, since it was clear that the emissions were subatomic, and not caused by chemical reactions between atoms. Likewise, the source of the enormous amount of energy released by radioactivity was intrinsic to the radioactive atom. Here was a completely different source of energy, more powerful than any chemical reaction. Totally unknown to the past, it would be fateful to the future.

After Thomson discovered the electron, he formulated what was called the "plum pudding" model of the atom, based on the knowledge that the electron was negatively charged, but the atom as a whole electrically neutral. In Thomson's model, electrons were discrete units of negatively charged matter dispersed in a homogeneous, positively charged matrix—like plums in pudding. This model accounted for the properties of the electron, the neutrality of the atom, and the

common-sense opinion that atoms should be solid. Rutherford initially subscribed to this view, but in 1911, he found evidence of its incorrectness. In
passing alpha particles through very thin gold foil, he noticed that most passed
straight through, as expected. But some were deflected, passing through at an
angle. A few alpha particles even deflected straight back, failing to penetrate the
foil at all. The complete repulsion of some particles was very surprising, and
Rutherford likened it to a piece of tissue paper repelling an artillery shell. Rutherford hypothesized that the atoms in the foil were not uniform balls, as had
been thought, but inhomogeneous. He proved this hypothesis through an el-
egant set of mathematical and statistical equations, which forced the conclusion that the gold atoms in the foil were mostly empty, with the great majority
of their mass disproportionately concentrated in the center of the atom. Moreover, he showed that the center of the atom was positively charged, and that
Thomson's electrons must orbit around the nucleus. When Rutherford published this work, it not only provided verification of subatomic particles and
subatomic structure, but also caused a complete re-appraisal of a basic tenet of
common sense by showing that solid objects were not so solid. Thomson's plum
pudding model was replaced with Rutherford's model, wherein the atom could
be likened to a miniature solar system, with the nucleus analogous to the sun,
the electrons analogous to the planets, and the electrical attraction between
them replacing the gravitational attraction that holds the solar system together.

If the electron was the ultimate unit of negative charge, was there a corresponding particle with an equal positive charge? Rutherford knew that such a particle
must lie in the nucleus, so he examined nuclei and the particles resulting from
their radioactive decay. He could not find a positively charged particle smaller
than the nucleus of a hydrogen atom, and he correctly took this to be the fundamental positively charged particle—comparable to the electron, although almost
two thousand times as massive. In 1919, Rutherford proposed that this particle
be called the proton (Greek for first). Since the mass of the nucleus was (for all
elements except hydrogen) greater than could be accounted for by the mass of
protons, he hypothesized additional, uncharged particles in the nucleus. (James
Chadwick would discover the neutron in 1932.) Also in 1919, Rutherford allowed alpha particles (what we now know to be two protons and two neutrons) to
collide with nitrogen gas and obtained protons and atoms of oxygen, showing
that radioactivity can change one element into another. Slightly earlier, Bertram
Boltwood had also demonstrated that elements can transmute during radioactivity.
This showed that nature, in fact, does provide for the alchemists' dream of the

transmutation of elements. The emission of protons in Rutherford's work is taken by some as the first example of artificial radioactivity (making a normally nonradioactive element radioactive), although most believe it was not until 1934, with the work of Irene Curie and Frederic Joliot (discussed subsequently), that true artificial radioactivity was achieved. Rutherford's work established the field of atomic physics, but it did more than that. His work showed that to make lasting progress in physics, it would be necessary to discard our common-sense view of the world and accept ideas if and only if they could be confirmed by mathematical or experimental analysis.

Niels Bohr (1885–1962), building on Rutherford's work, introduced his model of the atom in 1913. To Bohr's mind, the Rutherford atomic model had a flaw when examined in conjunction with the Maxwell equations. Maxwell had shown that accelerating charged particles would invariably radiate electromagnetic waves. The word "accelerating" does not necessarily mean an increase in velocity, but can also refer to a change in direction at the same or lower velocity. (A motorist accelerates going around a curve even though he slows down.) To orbit is to constantly change direction, so orbiting electrons are accelerating. Bohr saw that this meant that electrons would radiate, and therefore lose, energy, eventuating in their falling into the nucleus. This meant that the atom was unstable.

To get around this difficulty, Bohr reformulated the atomic model. In Bohr's model, an atom's electrons cannot be just anywhere, but rather are arranged in specific orbits around the nucleus. (These orbits are called shells.) Usually, electrons are found in what is called the ground state, the state of lowest energy. Bohr modified the physical and mathematical treatment of electrons to show that they did not necessarily emit and lose energy in the lowest energy level; these shells are stable. Above the ground state, electrons can exist at higher, unstable energy states, which result in the radiation of energy. However, they are constrained to specific shells at all times. The shells that an electron is permitted to occupy in this model constitute, in effect, a staircase, replacing the ramp of Rutherford's model. As energy is applied to the atom, electrons are moved in specific increments from the ground state into successively higher shells, placing the atom in an excited state. When energy is no longer applied, electrons emit the energy that had been applied to them, dropping back in stepwise fashion to the ground state, from which no further energy is emitted.

Electrons can absorb a photon only if the photon has exactly the same amount of energy that the electron needs to move to a higher shell. If the photon has either more or less energy than the electron needs to move to a higher shell, the electron cannot absorb it. Therefore, electrons absorb and emit energy only in specific amounts. Because the energy of electromagnetic radiation depends on its wavelength, electrons can absorb and emit radiation only if the radiation is of specific wavelengths. The acceptable wavelengths depend on the type of atom, and between which shells the electron is moving. If the wavelength is too short (radiation is too energetic) or too long (radiation is not energetic enough), there is not a match between the energy of the photon and the energy difference between the two shells of the electron, and nothing happens. If the wavelength is such that the energy of the photon precisely matches the difference in energy between the two shells, the electron may absorb energy and move to the higher shell.

When the electron absorbs energy, the spectra of the light passing through the material will contain an absorption line, representing an absence of the wavelength of the photon absorbed by the electron. Likewise, when an excited electron drops back to a lower shell, it emits electromagnetic radiation of a wavelength whose energy matches the energy released by the electron as it falls back to a lower shell. The new wavelength appears as an emission line in the spectra. Most electromagnetic radiation is generated by electrons moving from a higher energy level to a lower level or suddenly decelerating. (However, gamma rays, the highest energy electromagnetic radiation, come from processes in the atomic nucleus.) This explains the earlier finding that the spectra of hot objects contain absorption and emission lines. Bohr showed that electron locations are restricted, and the energy it can emit or absorb is quantized. By restricting the energy an electron can absorb or emit to fixed values, Bohr showed that its gradual loss of energy and subsequent descent into the nucleus are prevented. In 1914, it was experimentally shown that electrons do indeed "jump", in quantized leaps, between distinct shells.

Since chemical reactions result from the interactions of electrons in the outermost shells, the Bohr model predicted that elements with similar chemical properties, although they may have very different numbers of electrons, have similarities in their electron shells, and this too has been experimentally verified. For example, hydrogen and sodium have very different numbers of electrons but behave similarly in chemical reactions because both have a single electron in an unfilled outermost shell. On the other hand, helium and neon atoms, again very different in size, have all of their shells filled, and are thus largely inert.

Bohr's modification of Rutherford's solar system model is the familiar model of the atom that most of us encounter in school, and the concept most of us retain. However, quantum mechanics, that confusing triumph of twentieth-century science about which we will learn momentarily, would teach that the Bohr model is oversimplified, and that electrons cannot be thought of as discrete particles whose location can be determined in the same way that we determine the location of larger objects. Bohr himself acknowledged this a few years after his model was published. However, his model remains a convenient and comfortable way of thinking about the atom.

Henry Moseley (1887–1915) realized that the wavelength of x-rays changed when scattered by elements, and that each element produced a different wavelength when it scattered x-rays of a given initial wavelength. Recognizing that the positive charge in an element's nucleus controlled the wavelength of the scattered x-rays, Moseley determined the amount of positive charge in the nucleus of elements by how much that element changed the wavelength of x-rays. He then modified Mendeleev's periodic table, ordering elements by the charge of their nucleus. Mendeleev based his table on atomic weight (what we now know to be the total number of protons and neutrons in the nucleus), but some elements were slightly out of order to keep them with their families. Moseley showed that if the atomic number (as we now call the charge of an atom's nucleus) were used, elements could be kept with their families while maintaining perfect order.

When Rutherford discovered and clarified the proton shortly after Moseley's work, the latter's contribution became clear; the identity of an element depended on the number of protons in the nucleus. The number of neutrons in the nucleus of a given element may vary, but the number of protons does not. (Forms of the same element with different numbers of neutrons are called isotopes.) Likewise, electrons generally equal protons in number, but may not if the atom is ionized. The number of neutrons may vary with the isotope, and the number of electrons may vary with the state of ionization, but Moseley taught us that the number of protons in the nucleus—the atomic number—determines what an element is. Moseley also used the Bohr model to successfully predict the existence and properties of then-unknown elements.

Moseley was killed in the first World War, several months short of his twenty-eighth birthday. With some creative people who died young, one somehow has the feeling that he or she made their contribution, and that their early death perhaps did not impoverish us significantly. But with Moseley, there is no turning back from the deep conviction that humanity lost a seminal mind for no reason in a war without a cause.

In 1900, Max Planck (1858–1947) found that hot bodies do not radiate heat continuously, but in discrete units. A greater release of energy took the form of greater multiples of a basic unit, which he called a quantum. Planck did not realize (nor did anyone else in 1900) that the concept of a quantum was the beginning of quantum mechanics, which would stand with relativity as one of the landmark events in twentieth-century physics.

In 1905, Albert Einstein (1879–1955) published a number of landmark papers. The first extended Planck's quantum theory and explained a finding by J.J. Thomson. Thomson showed that the application of ultraviolet light to metal caused the emission of electrons, and that the greater the intensity of light, the greater the number of electrons given off. This is called the photoelectric effect. Einstein showed that electromagnetic radiation (in this case, ultraviolet light) must be emitted in discrete packets, called quanta (the plural of quantum), and that these quanta maintain their integrity throughout the journey of the radiation. The ultraviolet light shone on Thomson's metal consisted of tiny discrete bundles of energy, which is why Thomson observed that electrons were emitted by the metal—they were dislodged from the metal by the energy of the light quanta. Several observations guided Einstein to this conclusion. First, every material was associated with a minimum frequency of light required to achieve any emission of electrons. Light of lower frequency (lower energy and longer wavelength) would not cause any emission, regardless of its intensity. Second, once this minimum frequency was achieved, increasing the intensity of the light without changing the frequency would increase the number of electrons emitted but had no effect on the energy of the emitted electrons. The number of emitted electrons was proportional to the intensity (provided the minimum frequency was achieved), but the energy of the electrons was proportional to the frequency. Third, if conditions were right, the release of electrons was essentially instantaneous. If light were a pure wave, a time lag would be expected, because it would take time for the electrons to absorb energy from the wave. The instantaneous release was more consistent with bundles of light energy that exerted their effect at once. Planck had created the idea of the quantum, but only in regard to radiation from hot bodies, and he was not convinced that the concept applied to light. By showing that it did, Einstein's more general conclusion was that energy is quantized, and this idea moved Planck's quantum from an abstract concept to the forefront of physics.

To put Einstein's theory of light into perspective, let us digress a moment and review the history of light. The true nature of light has always been a mystery, and competing wave and particle theories have alternated throughout history. Newton preferred a particle theory, while his contemporary Huygens thought of light as a wave. In the early nineteenth century, Thomas Young (1773–1829) found that light projected through a series of closely spaced slits to a screen did not simply recapitulate the pattern of the slits when it illuminated the screen, as particles would be expected to do. Rather, the light formed a complicated series of light and dark bands on the screen. Waves were known to spread out as they traverse a very narrow opening (a phenomenon called diffraction), and then to strengthen or cancel waves from adjacent openings, depending on whether the crest from one wave coincided with the crest or the trough of an adjacent wave (a phenomenon called interference). Young's results argued for a wave theory of light. Now Einstein argued for discrete packets, bringing the particle theory to the fore again. It is now believed that light has properties of both waves and particles, and should not be regarded as one or the other. Einstein himself always took the position that light must be thought of in terms of a wave-particle duality.

Two of Einstein's 1905 papers introduced the concept of relativity, completely transforming physics. More than any other scientific achievement, relativity has captured the public's attention and imagination. It is the most talked about and most misunderstood scientific theory of our history.

Relativity has both an indistinct, historical beginning and a modern beginning. Galileo knew that two systems that might appear very different to us, such as one in motion, and one stationary, would have the same observable phenomena to people within them. As an example, Galileo contrasted a ship sailing on the sea with a fixed point on the shore. These would look very different to an observer at a third vantagepoint, but experiments performed within either system would be equally valid. Thereafter, this concept was debated for centuries, with most scientists believing that there was no absolute, fixed frame of reference. (Newton was a major exception.)

Progress comes more from providing the right questions than the right answers, and the important questions come from viewpoints and ideas that most people find incongruous. The modern beginning of relativity is a question Einstein asked himself while still a teenager: what would you see if you could ride on a beam of light, or travel along side it at the same speed? From this question, Einstein launched a thought process that paralleled in time and greatness the extraordinary experimental work of Rutherford.

There is only one theory of relativity. It is often divided into the special and general forms, but this is because there are different parts of the theory, published at different times. The first portion, published in 1905, is called special relativity because its conclusions are valid only for the special case of systems in uniform linear motion relative to each other.

Einstein began his deliberations by starting with two postulates, from which all of relativity arose. First, he postulated that the laws of physics did not change from one reference frame to another, provided the two frames are in uniform linear motion with respect to each other. This postulate arose because Einstein had a deep-seated belief in the harmony of nature and felt that the universe responds to only one set of principles. Therefore, he felt that there could be only one set of natural laws. Einstein referred to his first postulate as the principle of relativity, from which the theory as a whole received its name.

The second postulate is that the observed speed of light is not influenced by the motion of the source of the light or the observer. To understand why Einstein postulated the constancy of the speed of light, think back to the question he posed as a teenager: What would you see if you could travel on or alongside a beam of light? How could you do that? One way is by running in the same direction as the beam, then jumping onto another reference frame moving in the same direction, but faster. By running on this faster frame of reference, you could go fast enough to jump onto a still faster frame. By repeating this process, it would appear that you could eventually jump onto a reference frame moving at nearly the speed of light. By running in that frame, you could apparently catch up to the light beam.

The foregoing reasoning makes sense for most objects in our everyday lives. We could, in fact, jump onto successively faster frames of reference and catch up to automobiles or airplanes. But with light, the situation is different in one crucial way. Light, like all electromagnetic radiation, consists of moving and oscillating electric and magnetic fields. In fact, Maxwell's equations quite clearly show that all electromagnetic radiation must be in constant motion. If you could, by jumping to successively faster frames of reference, catch up to light, these fields would then appear to be stationary, meaning there would be no light.

From this thought experiment, Einstein concluded that a person could not catch up to light, and therefore, even if one jumps to ever-faster frames of reference, the speed of light must always appear constant to any observer. Unlike the much slower-moving objects of everyday life, the speed of light cannot be added to or subtracted from by the motion of the source or the observer.

From these two postulates, by mathematics less difficult than you might think, it was possible for Einstein to show, beginning with the first relativity paper of 1905, the following consequences of his theory:

1. As a body reaches speeds approaching that of light, its mass increases, so that at the speed of light, it has infinite mass, which means that the speed of light is not attainable by any technology of which we are currently aware.

2. As a body reaches speeds approaching that of light, time, relative to that body and any passengers traveling in it, slows down. Called time dilation, this means, for example, that if one twin embarks on a space journey at nearly the speed of light, when he returns, he will have aged less than the earth-bound twin. It is also true that the traveling twin will not be aware of any slowdown in time, and will be as surprised to see how much his twin has aged as the earth-bound twin will be at the youth of the traveler. At the end of the trip, even if it took thousands of years relative to observers on the earth, the journey would not appear to the traveling twin to exceed a normal human lifetime, and he would end his journey with no greater productivity than one lifetime on Earth. Relative to an observer on Earth, it would take the traveler a nearly infinite amount of time to complete any task. Although we could outlive everyone on Earth by traveling at speeds approaching light, we cannot lengthen what we would perceive as our lifetimes.

3. As objects approach the speed of light, they actually become smaller in the dimension in which they are moving. For example, a rocket with a given length at rest, traveling at a speed close to the speed of light, would truly be significantly shorter. (The other dimensions of the rocket would not change.)

The effect of travel at speeds close to that of light had been mathematically studied by Hendrik Lorentz (1853–1928) and George Fitzgerald (1851–1901) in their attempt to save the ether after the Michelson-Morley experiment. Their work was brilliant, but isolated and motivated by the desire to protect the familiar. Einstein now independently demonstrated these effects within a much more complete theory and from a different viewpoint, with no "agenda" except where his two postulates led him. In Einstein's work, the elucidation of the effects of high-velocity travel do not argue for an ether. The work of Fitzgerald and Lorentz was verified and given a sense of completeness and a much more important place in science as a result of relativity. It is ironic that these transformations, developed to save the ether, received new significance and meaning from relativity, which proved that the ether is not required.

The origin of relativity reflects the simplicity with which all great ideas must begin. Another characteristic of great advances is that they are unifying. Special relativity was a brilliant union of classical physics and the electrodynamics of Maxwell. It should be noted that none of these results play a role in our everyday life. Einstein's findings are only operative when velocities very close to that of light are reached. Not even the fastest rocket goes anywhere near fast enough to experience the effects on space and time described by relativity (although particle accelerators can accelerate atoms and subatomic particles to speeds that are a significant fraction of the speed of light).

Why should we believe any of special relativity? Two reasons. First, since its publication, special relativity has been confirmed by a variety of experiments on several different levels. For example, experiments with accelerated subatomic particles have indeed verified that their mass and lifetimes measurably increase. Second, the variance of space and time makes possible the invariance of the laws of physics, and the accuracy of our view of the world.

What special relativity really achieved was the understanding that space and time are altered in ways that permit the laws of physics to be the same in all frames of reference in uniform motion relative to one another and the speed of light to be invariant. Time and space may seem sacrosanct in our everyday lives, but their absoluteness and constancy must yield to the greater absoluteness of the laws of physics and the speed of light. It may disturb us to realize that what we believe to be firm is not so firm, but it would be a great deal more disturbing if our entire view of the universe varied from one place of observation to another. Far from showing humanity to be puny in a universe of changing space and time, special relativity is a crowning triumph for us because it proves that we can conceive laws and principles that are accurate, absolute, and enduring.

The second relativity paper of 1905 dealt with the equivalence of mass and energy and introduced the most famous equation in physics: $E=MC^2$. This idea arose from sophisticated mathematics and has been experimentally verified. (Objects that emit energy, such as those which are radioactive, lose mass.)

Since C (the speed of light) is so large, and C^2 so astronomically giant, a very small amount of mass is equivalent to a very large amount of energy. For example, each of the atomic explosions over Hiroshima and Nagasaki converted about as much mass as is in a dime into energy. This equation modifies the law of conservation of mass (derived largely from Lavoisier's work) and the law of conservation of energy (derived largely from Joule's work) into a single law of conservation of mass-energy. Outside of nuclear reactions, this equation has no effect on our everyday lives, but it is a fascinating illustration of the concept of equivalence, alluded to earlier, whereby what is really being conserved is not necessarily the immediately apparent quantity, but all equivalent forms of the immediately apparent quantity. The concept of equivalent forms of a quantity should not be confused with the principle of equivalence, which has a specific meaning in general relativity, to be discussed subsequently. The equivalence of mass and energy joins the wave-particle duality of light and the equivalence of heat and mechanical work as apparently unrelated quantities that are actually different manifestations of the same quantity. We need to think in terms of equivalence and dual appearances, rather than in opposites. It may be that opposites are an artifact of our perception, and do not exist in nature. This concept would serve us well in the political arena also, where we need to subordinate the perception of absolute truths to the understanding that not everything is as simple as it seems.

In 1907, in what he called "the happiest moment of my life", Einstein realized that a frame of reference that is uniformly accelerating is equivalent to a stationary reference frame in a gravitational field. For example, a person in a ship in space accelerating at thirty-two feet (9.8 meters) per second for every second that it moves (the same rate at which objects fall in a gravitational field) experiences a force identical to being accelerated downward by the earth's gravity. Termed the principle of equivalence, this was the beginning of the part of relativity called general relativity, because with the requirement of uniform motion removed, the theory can now be generalized to accelerating frames of reference. By 1915, Einstein had published the remainder of the relativity theory. General relativity is very difficult to understand, and here, the mathematics *are* every bit as difficult as is generally believed.

Since the time of Euclid, people have thought of space as consisting of three dimensions. Georg Friedrich Bernhard Riemann (1826–1866) pioneered the conception of space in non-Euclidean terms, where there may be more than three dimensions and where our usual conceptions may not hold true. Hermann Minkowski (1864–1909) realized that special relativity required that space be thought of in four-dimensional terms, with time being the fourth dimension.

Einstein adopted this idea, incorporating it into his general theory of relativity. If we wish to know the location of an object, we must specify a time. Therefore, time is as important in understanding location as any of the three physical axes. Space and time cannot be considered separately from each other, but must be taken together as space-time. General relativity therefore views space not in the traditional three-dimensional manner, but in four dimensions, with time being the fourth dimension. This is the origin of the expression four-dimensional space-time. What general relativity really does is put forth a more accurate conception of the universe, because it adds a dimension, in the same way that a three-dimensional globe is more accurate than a two-dimensional map. Einstein was by no means the first person to conceive of non-Euclidean geometry, but he was the first to successfully use it to create a fuller description of the universe.

In general relativity, mass is considered to distort the space surrounding it. A large mass results in a large distortion and creates a "valley" in four-dimensional space-time. Smaller masses in the vicinity of a large mass flow down this "valley" toward the larger mass, resulting in the force we perceive as gravity. Hence, general relativity is a theory of gravity and remains our best description of this force.

General relativity deals with the larger arena of the universe and cosmology (the study of the structure and origin of the entire universe, as opposed to the study of parts of it). General relativity improves on Newtonian gravitation theory only in situations of extremely strong gravitational fields. Because we have little experience with such fields, general relativity is not as firmly established as the special theory. However, the general theory has been partially verified by two experiments. First, Einstein felt that light always traversed the shortest distance between any two points in space-time. Since mass distorts space-time, the general theory predicts that mass, in the form of a strong gravitational field, must also distort the path of light, even though the photons which compose light have no mass at rest. In 1919, Arthur Eddington obtained experimental evidence that light from stars was, in fact, bent by the mass of the sun. More recently, the phenomenon of gravitational lensing, wherein massive structures such as clusters of galaxies bend the light from very distant objects, has been documented. Second, some previously unexplained perturbations in the orbit of Mercury are explained by general relativity.

Although the final theory of relativity appears initially to be the work of only one person, Einstein actually drew on the work of many to formulate this theory.

Galileo, Newton, Maxwell, Lorentz, Fitzgerald, Riemann, Minkowski, Michelson, and Morley have been mentioned. Einstein acknowledged his debt to many physicists and mathematicians:

> In science, the work of the individual is so bound up with that of his scientific predecessors and contemporaries, that it appears almost as an impersonal product of his generation.

What makes relativity a truly giant contribution is that it is more than the description of a single phenomenon. It is a set of principles which unifies much of our thinking about the world. What Einstein really gave us was a new way of seeing the world. He described the need to reach "beyond our immediate experience" in attempting to elucidate the processes of nature. Many others, including Francis Bacon and Rene Descartes, had seen that the normal senses may bring incomplete or misleading information, but not until Einstein did we learn just how far beyond our common senses we can go. At the same time that the Cubist movement of Picasso and Braque was finding new ways to portray the world on canvas, Einstein found a new way of portraying the world in the mind. As we shall see, artists, writers, and musicians of the twentieth century have gone beyond our immediate experience to visualize the world in new ways, based as much on reason as on what we can directly perceive with our senses.

When Einstein began this momentous achievement, he was working as a clerk in a Swiss patent office, a post he left in 1907. This means that the entirety of special relativity, his work on the photoelectric effect, and his work on the motion of particles suspended in a fluid (the third subject considered in his 1905 papers) were created when Einstein was, in effect, an amateur physicist. In fact, throughout history until this century, most of our progress has come from people not engaged full time in the field to which they so greatly contributed. Today, the situation is different. Much of science today hinges on the acquisition of funding through research grants, and rigorous credentials are required before a person has access to the facilities needed for many types of research. The amateur scientist is an endangered species. I am particularly concerned about this, because our ascent has historically been kindled by individuals of imagination, often without formal training, working alone in their spare time. The history of progress is the history of the individual, and we must never impose conditions on imaginative individuals that will prevent them from being productive. Because creative people are often iconoclasts, I fear that we are now moving toward a structure of society that will impede these people from reaching their potential.

Ranking with relativity as a giant leap of twentieth-century physics is quantum mechanics, a statistical and mathematical treatment of the structure and behavior of atoms and subatomic particles. Quantum mechanics arose from the work of many people in the first thirty years of the twentieth century, and some of its predictions have now been experimentally verified. The derivation of the term goes back to the word "quantum", referring to the discrete unit of energy discovered by Planck in 1900. Quantum theory was the conceptualization of the world based on this quantization of energy. Quantum mechanics is an extension of quantum theory.

After Planck's quantum theory and Einstein's explanation of the photoelectric effect suggested that electromagnetic radiation had properties of particles, Louis de Broglie (1892–1987) suggested in 1923 that the reverse may be true: particles may have wave properties. This theory was subsequently verified when electrons were passed through a crystal. (A crystal is a solid that has a homogeneous structure with an orderly arrangement of atoms in a repetitive pattern.) We have seen that when waves pass through a series of slits, they show a complicated pattern based on the reinforcement or interference of adjacent waves, called a diffraction pattern. When waves pass through a crystal, the structure of the crystal simulates tiny slits, and a diffraction pattern can be seen. When electrons were passed through a crystal, they exhibited a diffraction pattern characteristic of waves, confirming de Broglie's theory.

The wave properties of particles led Erwin Schrodinger (1887–1961) in 1926 to develop a wave equation of particles, specifically of electrons. The Schrodinger equation, which inaugurated the field of wave mechanics, implied that we cannot precisely know the location of an electron, but can know only the probability of its being in a given location. This equation has been experimentally verified. Werner Heisenberg (1901–1976) worked along similar lines, and is remembered as the driving force behind the early development of quantum mechanics. Heisenberg, one of many people who gave us quantum mechanics, made quantum mechanics conceptually complete and internally consistent by taking incomplete ideas and making them into a rigorous theory that was practical and useful.

Quantum mechanics replaced the absolutes of classical physics with probabilities and incomplete knowledge. Indeed, quantum mechanics has forced us to abandon our view of the atom as a discrete particle composed of smaller, discrete, theoretically visualizable, particles. We can no longer think of these particles as miniature versions of the objects we experience in our daily lives;

rather, we must think of them as bundles of energy, existing as both a wave and a particle, which defy precise description and location. Quantum mechanics replaces the world of the certain with the world of the probable.

One of the initial effects of quantum mechanics was a modification of the Bohr view of the atom. The discrete shells (orbits) proposed by Bohr were replaced by electron waves, which meant it was possible only to give probabilities of the location of electrons in orbit, although the original Bohr model remains a very useful framework for many applications in physics and chemistry.

The inability to know precisely where an electron was led Heisenberg to propose his famous uncertainty principle, which states that we cannot precisely know everything about a particle. The more we know about some of its characteristics, the less we will know about others. Heisenberg's work goes beyond particles and places limits on what we can absolutely know in every area of endeavor. We must now speak of probabilities, not absolute knowledge. Everything we think we know is actually only a probability. Probability theory, which began in the seventeenth century, has now become the basis for our conception of the universe. Heisenberg went on to show that the very act of observing a system or an object changes it because such observation involves an interaction with the object. This finding dealt humanity an even more severe blow because it meant we can never know the true native state of anything. Quantum mechanics in general, and the uncertainty principle in particular, places a limit on what we can know and forces us to come to terms with our fallibility.

The scientific revolution of the sixteenth and seventeenth centuries gave us certainty of knowledge, and we are all more comfortable and secure with certainty. Now, scientific advances were removing that certainty. David Hume, the eighteenth-century philosopher who concluded that we cannot have absolute knowledge, has been validated. Just as science had shown that religion was not an infallible source of knowledge, so science now showed itself to be fallible. While this may appear at first to indicate a lessened significance of humanity, it is more properly thought of as a change in our way of thinking. Specifically, quantum mechanics, like relativity, is not a diminution of humanity, but an extension of it because it provides a new way of seeing and a way to reach beyond our immediate experience. Understanding and accepting limitations expands, rather than diminishes, the collective and individual human mind.

Robert Oppenheimer (1904–1967), describing his recollections of the development of quantum mechanics, expressed the nature of inquiry and provided a view of who we are:

258

It was a heroic time. It was not the doing of any one man. It involved the collaboration of scores of scientists from many different lands... It was a period of patient work in the laboratory, of experiments and daring action, of many false starts and many untenable conjectures, of debate, criticism, and brilliant mathematical improvisation. For those who participated, it was a time of creation. There was terror, as well as exaltation in their new insight.

We would do well to remember that each of those scores of people to whom Oppenheimer referred lived life very much like any of us.

Quantum mechanics, and especially the uncertainty principle, were never fully accepted by Einstein, despite overwhelming evidence, both theoretical and experimental. The creator of relativity was troubled by the uncertainties that quantum mechanics requires us to accept. He wrote to physicist Max Born, "He (God) does not play at dice." Einstein and Niels Bohr constantly debated quantum mechanics, the latter attempting to persuade Einstein of its correctness. Bohr was able to get Einstein to believe that quantum mechanics was internally consistent, but not to embrace it as a truly giant step forward for physics. We now know that in this matter, Einstein was simply wrong. It was an ironic mistake for two reasons. First, quantum mechanics stands with relativity as the great advances of twentieth-century physics. Relativity is concerned with cosmology and the giant structures of the universe, while quantum mechanics is concerned with the world of the subatomic. It is odd that the principal creator of one of these profound advances failed to completely accept the other. Second, Einstein's explanation of the photoelectric effect, published in the same year as his first papers on relativity, was instrumental in launching quantum mechanics. It is interesting to note that every person who has contributed to our civilization—without exception—carried with him serious misconceptions, not just by our standards, but even by the standards of his day. Every great contributor to our knowledge, from Aristotle to Einstein, held incorrect beliefs from which a number of his peers were free. Mistakes and humanity are evident in the examined life of any thinker, making him closer to the rest of us than we had imagined. Great minds extend the thinking of their time, but no one—in the sciences, the arts, or in social change—truly leaps beyond all of his contemporaries.

The unification of relativity and quantum mechanics has proven difficult. In 1928, Paul A.M. Dirac (1902–1984) began the difficult process by deriving a mathematical description of the electron consistent with both of the great advances of twentieth-century physics. The Dirac equation predicted that there should be a particle of the same size as the electron, but with a positive charge. This particle, found in the 1930s, is called the positron. We now know that most (probably all) of the charged particles in nature have a corresponding antiparticle with an opposite charge. This is what is meant by the term "antimatter." Dirac was the first to predict antimatter.

Just as the predictions of relativity match those of Newton in the normal conditions of our lives, so quantum theory matches classical physics in the macroscopic world of our common experience. The probabilities, discontinuous nature of energy levels, and partial knowledge are unnoticed in our daily lives.

For more than its specific achievements, twentieth-century physics is remarkable because it pioneered a new way of approaching the unknown. It defied common sense to define knowledge, not as what we perceive with our immediate senses, but more broadly as what we can know from analysis. If there is one characteristic of science in this time, it is a willingness to go beyond immediate experience and allow our imaginations to bring us truths that are counterintuitive and not evident in the normal course of our lives.

Continued progress will depend on our ability to follow Einstein and the founders of quantum mechanics in reaching beyond our immediate experience. This is equally true in the political and social arena. And it is also true for each of us as individuals, as shown by a remarkable physician from Austria.

The Pioneer of the Mind

As a young man, Sigmund Freud (1856–1939) was deeply influenced by the writings of Goethe. An initial desire to study law gave way to medicine, and Freud graduated from medical school, beginning his career as a researcher in the field of neuroscience. In 1886, he shifted from research to the practice of neurology, probably for financial reasons, since he had just married. As a young practicing physician, he was influenced by Jean Charcot (1825–1893), a famous French neurologist, and spent a few months with him in Paris. Freud was particularly impressed by Charcot's use of hypnosis on some of his patients with mental disorders. Returning to Austria, he began an association with Josef Breuer (1842–1925), a physician who also used hypnosis in certain mental patients, especially those with hysteria. (The term "hysteria", now out of favor, has been misunderstood to mean a patient who is out of control and acting in a frenzied manner—hence, our unfortunately persistent term hysterical. The term actually referred to a patient who manifested bodily difficulties for which there appeared to be a psychological explanation. Hysterical patients were actually quite calm and reasonable and made good subjects for Breuer's hypnosis.)

At one time, Freud felt it probable that hysteria was caused by an abnormal anatomy somewhere in the brain, but he abandoned this view when no such abnormality could be demonstrated. Freud was moved by one of Breuer's hysterical patients, who not only improved after hypnosis, but also recalled forgotten emotional traumas while under hypnosis. Incidents like these convinced Freud that repressed sexual feelings caused the hysteria. Breuer would subsequently lose interest in his association with Freud because the younger man considered sexuality to be the root cause of neurosis.

Proceeding alone, Freud modified traditional techniques in hypnosis to introduce free association. In the state of deep relaxation prerequisite to hypnosis, Freud asked patients to make an association with a word or idea that he supplied. He found that hypnosis, combined with free association, enabled him to detect the resistance that patients unknowingly expressed when called upon to reveal or deal with certain memories, particularly those concerning sex or sexuality.

Freud soon added the interpretation of dreams to free association and found it to be of equal value in drawing out hidden emotions and thoughts. In 1900, he published his landmark work *The Interpretation of Dreams*, marking the founding of psychoanalysis. Freud believed that repressed sexual feelings, often going back to infancy, were highly significant and often the cause of behavioral problems and mental illness. In effect, Freud argued that the sequelae of our repressed sexual feelings is the price we pay for our civilization.

Freud's work unsettled many people because they believed it diminished humanity. Just as people did not want to acknowledge that their ancestors were primates who were not cast in the image of God, many did not want to accept that beneath their newly found and greatly cherished rationalism lay forces beyond reason. Apart from this consideration, however, Freud's work has always been and continues to be controversial because many remain unconvinced that repressed sexual feelings from infancy and early childhood are our prime motivators. However, three contributions to human thought are undeniably his. First, he demonstrated the influence of the unconscious part of our minds. (Sometimes referred to as the subconscious; the proper term is unconscious.) Second, he proved that early experiences, although ostensibly completely forgotten, play significant roles in our lives. Third, by exposing us to unseen aspects of our nature, he gave us a fuller view of ourselves, a view that influenced not only our self-concept, but many works of art as well. His work provided the opportunity to know ourselves better by being aware of parts of ourselves that are "beyond our immediate experience."

As is often the case with those who follow trailblazers, many of Freud's disciples accepted his work as a fully developed theory, rather than extending and improving his ideas. Even today, Freudian psychoanalysis is often performed in the same manner, and with the same poor results, as in Freud's day. Some of Freud's followers even took us backwards in dealing with homosexuality. Freud's theory of the cause of homosexuality was surely wrong, but he did believe it was a not a sickness and was not changeable, whereas some of those who followed him felt that homosexuality was a sickness and should be treated. We need look no further than our own century to understand how the writings of Galen could be taken as absolute truth for fifteen centuries.

Of Freud's many students, Alfred Adler (1870–1937) and Carl Jung (1875–1961) stand out and would go on to found major movements of their own. Adler worked with Freud from 1902–1911, but broke with his teacher when he came to believe that the primary motivation for human behavior was the desire for success and power, not the sex drive or repressed sexual feelings. Adler believed that feelings of inferiority sometimes caused aberrant behavior, and he first used the term "inferiority complex" in describing a reaction to self-perceived inadequacy. Jung worked with Freud from 1906–1914 and came to believe that personal changes and deliberate attempts to discover ourselves can lead to positive changes in personality. It was Jung who developed the now well-known concepts of introvert and extrovert.

Chapter 24
Tragedies of Our Time

The backbone of humanity is almost broken, but in
our resilience, civilization gets another chance.

WORLD WAR I WAS FOUGHT OVER A VARIETY OF REASONS, largely stemming from generations of nationalism and ethnic conflict. Called the war to end all wars, it was followed by an even more destructive war, which was but one of three calamities that accompanied or followed the first World War. World War II is considered by most historians to be the most important event of the twentieth century. But to my mind, the first World War was the century's most influential event; it was the catalyst for many of the great events of the century, including the second world conflict. Indeed, one can reasonably argue that there was only one great World War of the twentieth century, spanning 1914–1945, with a respite in the middle of the conflict. Japan invaded Manchuria, launching the Pacific theater of World War II, only one year after the final Allied withdrawal from Europe. Here we examine three tragedies following from and substantially secondary to the first World War.

The Tragedy of Russia

War is a catalyst for change—sometimes good, sometimes bad. An example of the latter was the changes in Russia during and after the first World War.

Vladimir Ilyich Lenin (1870–1924) was born into the reasonably prosperous home of a government official. When he was seventeen, an older brother was hanged for plotting to overthrow the Czar. Shortly thereafter, Lenin developed an acquaintance with the works of Marx and became an attorney. (For a time, he did pro bono work for the indigent.) Active in Marxist organizations in Saint Petersburg, he was imprisoned for fifteen months for subversive activities. Thereafter, he rose rapidly in the ranks of Russian communism. In 1903, the communist party split into two factions, nearly equally divided in number of members. Because one faction, that headed by Lenin, initially obtained a slight majority, the parties are known in history as the Bolsheviks (from the Russian for majority) and the Mensheviks (Russian for minority).

An attempted revolution in 1905 failed (an uneasy coalition of liberals and radicals won some concessions from the czarist government, but many of these were later retracted), and Lenin went into exile two years later. In March of 1917, amidst a war that Russia was badly losing (at Lenin's urging, the Bolsheviks refused to support the government's war effort), a second revolution was successful in removing the czar. Lenin actually had little to do with this revolution. It happened while he was in exile in Switzerland, and he had not expected it. The overthrow of the czar created a vacuum in Russia, as the upper and lower social classes had very different expectations of what was to follow. The former, Marx's bourgeois, expected a full effort against Germany in the war, followed by democracy and the Westernization of Russia. The latter, Marx's proletariats, were more focused on economic change and an egalitarian social structure. They saw the war as remote and irrelevant.

At this time, Russia was fighting a war with Germany and had just deposed its government, with the victors splitting into two factions based on their socio-economic class. Into this turbulent Russia, Lenin returned in April, 1917. (Germany, seeking to make the situation in Russia even more unstable, cleverly permitted Lenin passage.) The March revolution deposed the czar but did not put the Bolsheviks in power. It was Lenin's political genius to seize on the instability of the moment and guide the Bolsheviks—a radical wing of the communist party and certainly a decisive minority overall—into power in November, 1917. The majority of Russians in the time just after the overthrow of the czar wanted democracy, but Lenin's brand of communism carried the day. Lenin promptly sued for peace with Germany and began the complete transformation of Russian society. Two often forgotten and highly relevant realities of history emerge at this time. First, although the allies won the first World War, Russia was defeated by Germany. Second, in an unsuccessful attempt to prevent the communist seizure of power and force Russia to stay in the war, Russia's Western allies invaded Russia. (This invasion included American forces.) No defense of the cruel, militaristic posture of the Soviet Union from 1917 to 1985 is offered, but Western observers would do well to remember that Russia has an unparalleled history of attacks from other countries, including many that could very reasonably have been considered friendly at the time. Throughout their history, Russians have been surrounded by hostile nations and often have not been the military equal of their potential adversaries. It is very helpful in international relations, as in daily life, to place oneself in the environment and history of a possible antagonist.

Lenin's translation of Marxist ideas was filled with a cruelty unanticipated by the German philosopher. Lenin used violence on his opponents (or supposed opponents) without hesitation. What propaganda could not solve, prison camps could. Millions died at his hands. His successor was worse.

Iosif Vassarionovich Dzhugashvili (1879–1953) won the power struggle after Lenin's death, then continued and accelerated the repression begun by his predecessor. Taking the name Stalin (Russian for man of steel), he killed at least twenty million people in prison camps (the Gulag archipelago described by Aleksandr Solzhenitsyn). Thirty million is perhaps a better approximation. Particularly persecuted were Russia's intellectuals.

Between Stalin and Hitler, Russia lost fifty million people. No nation in recorded history has suffered such losses. It is a credit to the resilience and vitality of the Russian people that they were able to continue as a national entity. It is ironic that Stalin and Hitler, bitter enemies during World War II, should end in the history books as similarities. Both were paranoid, totally without tenderness or kindness, and both supported any degree of violence as an expected and appropriate means to a single, absolute end. The ends that they perceived were not really very different. The theoretical communism of Marx differs completely from Fascism, but the communism practiced by Lenin and Stalin was in many ways similar to it.

Capitalism on the Brink

John Maynard Keynes (1883–1946) began his career, for our purposes, as a British financial representative to the peace conference after World War I. There, he advocated that all international debts be dropped, as any such payments would siphon money away from the long-term growth and prosperity essential for continued peace. He particularly opposed the harsh reparations required of Germany, and when it became clear that such reparations would materialize, he resigned from the conference in protest. In his 1919 book, *The Economic Consequences of the Peace*, he correctly predicted that the stringent punitive measures would result in economic ruin, not just in Germany, but because European economies were inextricably linked, throughout Europe. He also predicted that these measures would result in an increased nationalism and militarism in Germany and would guarantee a continuation of hostilities at some point in the future. This book became one of the most prescient of history, but it was Keynes's thinking about another twentieth-century crisis for which he is most remembered.

It would be wrong to believe that the great depression was specifically caused by the October, 1929 stock market crash. We should always use great caution before concluding that one historical event "caused" another. Any given event is associated with multiple causative factors, and we often oversimplify history by believing that one event directly caused another. During the 1920s, many factors came together to make the economy of the industrialized world precarious and vulnerable. Europe was rebuilding from World War I, and was heavily reliant on American loans to do so. Consumer demand did not keep up with increasing industrial production, and production without demand does not stimulate or maintain real economic growth. Easy credit and widespread speculation in stocks combined to artificially inflate stock prices. Americans appeared prosperous, but their wealth was a pseudo wealth that came from owning stocks whose true value was much less than their price. Signs of economic problems in the United States were becoming apparent throughout the 1920s. (For example, banks failed at an alarming rate throughout the decade.) The stock market crash was simply a massive correction (an adjustment in stock prices so that they more accurately reflect general economic conditions) resulting from the real causes of the depression. The American crash was the proverbial straw that broke the camel's back, and its shockwaves were felt throughout the world. European recovery came to a standstill. Consumer confidence, essential to a capitalist economy, evaporated.

By the early 1930s, stocks had lost 80% of their value, almost half of all banks had failed, the gross national product was falling 10% per year, unemployment was 25%, and many of those employed were receiving much less than their normal salary. The depression rocked the industrialized countries, with similar statistics of misery around the world. Capitalism was on the brink of destruction. In Germany, the despair was a major cause of the rise of fascism, and the situation was not necessarily much better in the United States. Desperate times are always fertile ground for every aspect of our character of which we are not proud, and a more prolonged depression would undoubtedly have caused Americans to turn to radical measures.

Throughout the 1920s, Keynes disagreed with the traditional view that savings were the key to wealth, arguing that it was better to apply that money to activities that would stimulate the economy. *Activity*, not accumulated money, was the key to economic strength. The key to generating this activity was to increase demand, because demand would lead to greater productivity and employment. Keynes further argued that if the private sector was unable to supply this demand, then the government must fill this role, even if doing so required deficit spending. Lowering taxes, in theory, would have a similar effect by giving people more discretionary income, but increased government spending was more immediate and direct. As early as 1924, Keynes called for increased public works as a means to decrease unemployment.

In 1936, his masterpiece, *The General Theory of Employment, Interest, and Money*, was published. Many of the ideas in *The General Theory* had been published in earlier works, but others were new. Ranking with *The Wealth of Nations* as a great work of economics, *The General Theory* revolutionized how we think about the economy. Some of its major tenets include the following:

1. Contrary to prevailing opinion, supply does not always create a corresponding demand. Therefore, there will inevitably be times when the demand for products falls short of the supply and producers will be forced to cut their workforces. This is the major cause of recession.

2. There is no mechanism for self-correction of a recession. Classically, it was thought that the economy is self-correcting in difficult times because an accumulation of savings would result in decreased interest rates, thus stimulating the expansion of business. Keynes showed that this was not true, and in fact, accumulated savings actually prolonged the depression because that money was not doing anything to stimulate the economy. Moreover, Keynes recognized that this self-correction was unreliable because in difficult times people become frightened or discouraged and do not behave as they normally would.

3. Business cannot pull an economy out of recession because it must have new markets in order to expand. Therefore, the government must step in and spend money in times of depression, even if this results in deficit spending. Only government, in the form of public works programs, can create the new markets and new incentives necessary for business to expand. (Keynes later correctly predicted that the second World War would stimulate the economy out of the depression.)

If Keynes's ideas had been put into play earlier (and many were available in the 1920s), could the depression have been prevented? This is a matter of opinion, with some Keynesian economists answering in the affirmative, while others are not so sure. But it cannot be doubted that many of the public works projects of Roosevelt's New Deal, so instrumental in bringing about recovery, were based on Keynes's ideas.

As the author of the theoretical framework of necessary governmental intervention in a capitalist economy, Keynes introduced socialist measures to save capitalism. He was the most influential capitalist economist after Adam Smith, and today, virtually all economists accept Keynes's theory that some form of governmental modification of the economy is occasionally necessary. His ideas illustrate the value of finding a synthesis between two extremes. Almost any concept in its extreme can be improved by an infusion of ideas from the opposite extreme.

A Thousand Years

Although associated with Germany, Adolph Hitler (1889–1945) was actually born and raised in Austria. A full discourse of his rise to power can be found in the works of William L. Shirer (1904–1993), whom history will remember as one of its great chroniclers, but a brief synopsis is given here. At the age of eighteen, he went to Vienna, where for a time he made some money painting postcards. (He was rejected from an art academy.) He did not integrate into Viennese society, and his experiences there amplified his feelings of rejection and paranoia.

In 1913, he left Austria for Germany. After serving in World War I, he returned to a Germany that was defeated, humiliated, and in economic chaos. The treaty ending World War I assigned blame for the war to Germany and required harsh reparations. The treaty had initially been forced on the German people, but the government subsequently supported it, giving its people a deep sense of betrayal and strengthening already powerful nationalist feelings. Germans felt deeply mistreated by the treaty, and to some extent, they had a point. World War I was fought for a multiplicity of vaguely related reasons, and no one country should have been forced to bear the blame. Indeed, a strong argument can be made that the "peace" between the two World Wars was merely a temporary lull in hostilities, because nothing was done to address the causes of the conflict. (In fact, the reparations made the smoldering resentments worse.)

Hitler matured during the brief respite between the World Wars. He joined the new National Socialist German Workers party, the German abbreviation for which is Nazi. In 1923, the German economy had deteriorated to the point that it took four billion marks to equal one dollar, a disintegration which destroyed the savings and financial security of the middle class. In that year, Hitler attempted to seize power in an unsuccessful coup, for which he was imprisoned (an interesting parallel with Lenin). While incarcerated, he wrote *Mein Kampf* (*My Struggle*), where he laid out in plain language his fascist and anti-Semitic views. Paroled after serving one year of a five-year sentence, Hitler was largely forgotten by the general public. But prison had taught him an important lesson. He now knew that it was unlikely he and his small band of associates could prevail by the use of force. It was at this time that Hitler showed one of his two talents—organizational ability. Concentrating on the more impressionable ranks of the young and less educated, Hitler and the Nazis built a well organized, opportunistic party.

The fortunes of the Nazi party declined somewhat during the mid-and late-1920s because of the increasing economic prosperity in Germany. But the organization of the Nazi party remained intact, and Hitler became a credible spokesman. With the worldwide depression of 1929, the Nazis gained strength. By 1931, Hitler was in complete control of the Nazi party, and there were six million unemployed people in Germany, providing the Nazis with their chance. At this time, Hitler's second talent became operative—he was a powerful, charismatic, and effective orator with a superb understanding of the masses. Hitler virtually mesmerized some of the people with promises of prosperity and a great Germany. The Nazi party effectively reached out to the unemployed, the frightened, and the despondent. By promising an orderly society, a sense of belonging, a sense of self-worth, better times to come, and a new Germany, Hitler was able to make an impression on a significant minority of the German people. Hitler studied his audiences and learned what did and did not move them. He cleverly adopted military gestures and mannerisms, correctly assuming that these would impress where the substance of his words could not. He even worked with a photographer to develop more effective gestures. His speeches were a combination of manic power and semi-rational arguments, and with them, he caused his audiences to think on an emotive level. From *Mein Kampf*:

> I must not measure the speech of a statesman to his people by the impression which it leaves in a university professor, but by the effect it exerts on the people. And this alone gives the standard for the speaker's genius.

269

The mass meeting is also necessary for the reason that in it the individual, who at first . . . feels lonely and easily succumbs to the fear of being alone, for the first time gets the picture of a larger community, which in most people has a strengthening, encouraging effect.

. . . when the visible success and agreement of thousands confirm to him the rightness of the new doctrine and for the first time arouse doubt in the truth of his previous conviction—then he himself has succumbed to the magic influence of what we designate as 'mass suggestion'.

Beyond a smattering of artistic ability, Hitler's only aptitude was to arouse people, fill them with his paranoia, and bring out their worst qualities.

In the two elections of 1932, the Nazis received more votes than any of the other numerous parties, although they failed to gain a majority. (To the credit of the German people, they never gave Hitler or the Nazis a clear majority in any election.) The communists finished second, and the two parties together did have a majority. Although there was essentially no cooperation between the Nazis and the communists, many prominent people were terrified of the possibility.

The point of no return occurred in January, 1933, when president Paul von Hindenburg (1847–1934), attempting to form a coalition government, named Hitler chancellor. Today, we might think this appointment is unbelievable, but all events in history must be interpreted in context. Hindenburg was pressured to appoint Hitler chancellor by prominent citizens who were afraid of a communist majority or a coalition between the Nazis and the communists. They felt the Nazis were the lesser of the two evils because they at least had nationalist leanings, were perceived as more orderly than the communists, and would be easier to control. The idea was to pacify the Nazis while containing them by outnumbering them in the cabinet, and holding the communists in check in the process. Ironically, the people wishing to control Hitler in this way may have moved too soon and inadvertently accomplished precisely what they sought to prevent. The Nazis received significantly fewer votes in the second 1932 election, and the party was near bankruptcy. It may be that the Nazis had peaked, and if the prominent citizens who hatched this containment scheme had only waited, fascism might have faded away. This is another of history's giant unanswered "what if" questions. The colossal miscalculation of these people is an example of the tragic consequences that can result when we fight the wrong enemy.

The social infrastructure and societal institutions were not strong enough in Germany to permit this plan to work. Before and during the 1933 elections, the Stormtroopers, the Nazi's bullies, forced radio stations to air Hitler's speeches and intimidated people at the polls. Even so, the Nazis still failed to win a majority, although they shared a majority coalition with conservatives. But ultimately, majorities did not matter. As social order spiraled downward, the people's fear increased, and the vague promises of the Nazis took on more appeal.

As chancellor, Hitler took advantage of the lack of checks and balances in the government and the despair of the people. One step at a time, he seized power from the senile, impotent Hindenburg and the disorganized and ineffective Parliament, and Nazified Germany. By the middle of 1933, banned books were burned, and the first concentration camps were established. With Hindenburg's death in 1934, no systems were in place to prevent Hitler from assuming full control. He proclaimed himself head of state, rearmed Germany, and unleashed the greatest force of evil the world has ever seen. The parallels with the rise of communism in Russia are striking. In both cases, within one generation, a radical minority seized power from a larger, but poorly organized and despairing majority. Hitler placed himself and his nation on a collision course with history, with the very concept of civilization, and with a bewildered and outraged international community. Hitler said that the Nazi Empire would last for a thousand years. But after the loss of fifty million lives, including six million Jews killed in concentration camps, and a nearly fatal disruption of the fabric of our civilization, Nazi Germany was gone after twelve years.

Fascism, unlike other forms of government, never had a written ideology; *Mein Kampf* came the closest. Anti-Semitism, strong nationalism, rigid class structures to the point of racism, and blind obedience to the state with rejection of individual liberties were all present in Hitler's book. No one could reasonably claim to be surprised at how he thought or what he did. How then, was it that a modern, industrialized nation, the home of Beethoven and Einstein, within living memory, embraced this agenda of hate and became the embodiment of evil?

From one viewpoint, there were multiple causes of the rise of fascism. The sense of betrayal from the German government's support of the treaty ending World War I, the political and economic chaos that resulted from the depression, the opposition's bickering and failure to unite, Hitler's organizational skills and oratory ability, overly harsh reparations required after the first World War, the senility and ineffectiveness of Hindenburg, and the lack of restraining checks and balances were all decisive factors.

From another viewpoint, the root cause of fascism comes down to the human weakness that frightened people do not think clearly. Fear breeds hostility. The economic depression removed the hope and optimism that Kenneth Clark reminds us is essential for civilization. Nazi Germany, arising from the economic ashes of World War I and the depression, illustrates how correct Clark was in asserting that civilization requires a modicum of prosperity.

In my view, the rise of Fascism is really about the abdication of our ability to think. When we delegate our cognitive powers to an external authority, be it good or evil, deity or human, we strip ourselves of the only tool we have to protect and preserve our civilization—the worth of the individual. Whenever we believe that "they alone" or "He alone" will take care of us, trouble will surely result. If the abdication is to an overtly evil power like fascism, the result will be immediately catastrophic, but ultimately, any power we trust that is not our own will causes us to be less than we can be. The abdication of reason is a common accompaniment of fear, confusion, and despondency. It is easy to allow another entity to control our destiny, particularly when the world appears hostile and forbidding and that entity appears enticing and charismatic. In times of scarcity, people will follow a charismatic person they would normally reject. Frightened people and a charismatic person make a dangerous combination. It takes courage to trust in ourselves; that pathway often appears more difficult. But in that trust, and in the acceptance of responsibility for our fate, comes the essence and the hope of civilization.

I will restate what I believe to be history's first lesson: people deprived of basic needs are very likely to behave cruelly and irrationally, and the target of that behavior will be those perceived as more fortunate. People who are angry or frightened do not think clearly, but look for a quick and simple solution, abdicating reason in the process. They will be attracted to anything that presents "magical simplifications." This is why it is so essential to provide a reasonable standard of living for all people and enough prosperity to prevent our crueler sides from becoming manifest. To my mind, we must assist the economic stability and standard of living of every country whose economy is in significant distress, to insure that reason always has a chance to prevail around the world.

We must never make the mistake of believing that there was something unique about the German people, some pathology to which the rest of us are immune.

What happened in Nazi Germany was a common human frailty that transcends all cultures and endangers all people. Holocausts have not been rare in human history. In addition to the Nazi catastrophe, there have been at least eight holocausts in the twentieth century: the massacres of Lenin, Stalin, and Mao, the Turkish massacre of a million Armenians in 1915, Idi Amin's reign of terror in Uganda in the 1970s, Pol Pot's killing fields in Cambodia, the 1994 Rwandan civil war, and the recent ethnic cleansings in Bosnia and Yugoslavia. For all of our accumulated wisdom and courage, there is something terrible within us; it is as much a part of who we are as our virtues. Only by accepting this aspect of our nature and preventing the conditions that permit this part of us to become manifest can we be sure it will not happen again. It is my sad task to predict that there will be more holocausts in our future because we have not addressed the conditions that make them possible. Ours is a fragile civilization, capable of being destroyed at any time by hate, ignorance, or fear. Each of these great enemies of civilization must be vigorously and constantly opposed by far-sighted people who understand history and the role of knowledge and security in preventing cruelty. We are never far from fascism.

Chapter 25
The Way We Think

A terrible weapon has minimal impact on a war, but
brings humanity close to extinction.

THE HISTORY OF THE SPLITTING OF THE ATOM BEGINS with studies of radioactivity. Rutherford, during the first World War, bombarded nitrogen with alpha particles, producing oxygen and dislodging positively charged particles (which he named protons in 1919) from nuclei. True artificial radioactivity began in 1934, when Irene Curie (1897–1956, Marie Curie's daughter) and her husband Frederic Joliot (1900–1958) discovered that nonradioactive elements could be made radioactive by bombarding them with alpha particles (helium nuclei). Enrico Fermi (1901–1954), one of the very few physicists in history to be truly superlative in both theoretical and experimental work, then had the idea that neutrons might be even more effective than alpha particles because the latter's positive charge would impede their approach to the positively charged nucleus (like charges repel), whereas neutrons had no charge. It was expected that the atoms formed from bombarding uranium with neutrons would be approximately the same size as uranium.

But in 1938, Otto Hahn (1879–1968) and Fritz Strassmann (1902–1980) bombarded uranium nuclei with neutrons and found that barium, a much smaller atom that had not been present in the beginning, was detectable. Where did the barium come from? In 1939, Lise Meitner (1878–1968) supplied the answer. She and her nephew Otto Frisch (1904–1979), following a 1936 suggestion by Niels Bohr, realized that the force binding the protons and neutrons together in the nucleus (now called the strong force) acts over an extremely short distance. Any deformation of the nucleus that increased the distance between the nuclear particles, even by a tiny amount, could weaken the nuclear attractive force and permit the repulsive force of positively charged protons to overcome it. Meitner and Frisch then supported this theory with a mathematical analysis showing that the uranium nucleus, in part because of its great size, was somewhat precarious to begin with and needed little deformation to lose its cohesion. A high-speed neutron could cause sufficient deformation. *The bombardment of uranium nuclei caused them to split in two, and barium was one of the products.* Frisch coined the term "fission", in analogy with cell division.

Lise Meitner presents a study in quiet courage. Already fighting discrimination because of her sex, she had the additional handicap of being a Jew in Nazi Germany. She worked with Hahn for many years before being forced to flee to Sweden, and it is probable that she was part of the discovery of barium before she emigrated, and that history has not properly credited her for this. Curiously, Meitner was never awarded a Nobel Prize, despite her clearly pivotal work. Demonstrating a foresight rare among her colleagues, she refused to work on the atomic bomb project.

Also in 1939, Leo Szilard (1898–1964) and Walter Zinn (1906–) showed that fission of a uranium nucleus liberates large numbers of neutrons, the particle used to initiate the process. This meant that fission was theoretically self-sustaining, so a chain reaction was possible. Because the fission of a single nucleus involved a very slight loss of mass—with a consequent liberation of energy according to Einstein's $E=MC^2$—a self-sustaining chain reaction meant that a great deal of energy could be obtained from fission. Bohr then showed that although neutrons were liberated from the fission of any uranium nucleus, only a relatively rare isotope, uranium 235 (accounting for no more than one percent of all uranium), had the capacity to undergo a self-sustaining fission process. The separation of uranium 235, followed by its controlled bombardment with neutrons, could produce a new kind of bomb.

In 1939, Szilard persuaded Einstein to write a letter to Franklin Roosevelt saying that a weapon based on uranium fission was possible. It was a difficult letter for Einstein to write, as his deep pacifist beliefs made the use of science for making weapons an anathema to him. It was the menace of Adolph Hitler and Nazi Germany that finally convinced Einstein that force of arms may be acceptable and that American development of an atomic weapon may be the least evil outcome. It should be noted, however, that even without Einstein's letter, the Americans would have undoubtedly developed an atomic bomb. Einstein did not participate in this development, and cannot be thought of as a creator of nuclear weapons.

The American bomb effort, called the Manhattan project, was, with the Apollo moon mission, one of the largest scientific endeavors in history. In 1942, a team headed by Fermi created the first controlled chain reaction at the University of Chicago. The first nuclear bomb was detonated at Los Alamos, New Mexico in July, 1945. A month later, there were two nuclear strikes against Japan. It is debatable whether or not these attacks were really necessary to end the war or prevent an invasion of Japan. It may be that an American acceptance of a conditional Japanese surrender would have ended the war without either an atomic bombing or an invasion.

As it turned out, Germany never got close to developing a nuclear weapon. After the German surrender, when victory against Japan was assured, Einstein wrote a second letter to Roosevelt, one less remembered by history. This letter warned of the catastrophic consequences of atomic attack and pleaded for such a weapon not to be used. Roosevelt died with this second letter unopened, and the first of the bombs exploded over Hiroshima on August 6, 1945. Einstein would later say that he could burn his fingers for writing the first letter to Roosevelt.

Within the span of a decade, humanity was confronted by a force of a completely new and different nature. Whereas chemical reactions, known for millennia, derive energy from electrons, nuclear reactions derive energy from the much more massive interior of the atom, and are therefore far more powerful. In the history of war, nuclear weapons deserve a fundamental position, beside bronze weapons, iron weapons, the medieval English longbow, and gunpowder.

Nuclear weaponry makes this time unique in our history—we now have the capacity to destroy ourselves. Through nuclear war or overpopulation, we can cause our world to cease to exist as we know it. The upward sloping trend of peaks and valleys that have so characterized our ascent is no longer acceptable, because we now have the ability to destroy ourselves while in the valleys. William Shirer reminds us that World War II was the last world conflict we can hope to survive. But has any lesson been learned? Our history since World War II has been one of almost continuous conflicts somewhere in the world, with the superpowers, until recently, poised at an abyss. Albert Einstein, in addition to his greatness as a scientist, perceived the character and nature of humanity as clearly as any figure in history. How sadly accurate were his words: "the splitting of the atom changes everything, except the way we think."

Chapter 26
The Acceleration of Knowledge

The universe is seen to be of unimagined size and complexity.

THE TWENTIETH CENTURY HAS BEEN A TIME of the dramatic acceleration of knowledge. Never before has our fund of knowledge increased so rapidly. The benefits of this exponential increase in abilities are dramatic, but so are the perils. Chemistry benefited from advances in physics, because it was now possible to gain some understanding of the forces involved in chemical reactions. Linus Pauling (1901–1994), who did not receive his high school diploma until after he was awarded a Nobel Prize, was a pioneer in this area. His landmark book, *The Nature of the Chemical Bond*, was a synthesis of chemistry, mathematics, and physics. This synthesis made possible advances in all fields of chemistry, with applications from biochemistry to polymer chemistry.

Astronomy was another beneficiary of the advances in physics. In 1917, Willem de Sitter (1872–1934) showed that general relativity implied that the universe is expanding. In 1922, Alexander Friedmann (1888–1925) elaborated on de Sitter's idea and demonstrated that a static universe was out of the question. At nearly the same time, experimental evidence of an expanding universe was forthcoming. Vesto Slipher (1875–1969), director of the Lowell observatory in Flagstaff, Arizona, discovered that the spectra of stellar objects were shifted to the red. To understand the meaning of this, consider the change in pitch of an automobile as it passes a listener. As the car approaches a listener, sound waves are compressed, because the motion of the source means that each succeeding sound wave is closer to the previous wave than it otherwise would be. As the source moves away from the listener, the waves are stretched out because now the motion of the source means that the sound waves are further apart than they otherwise would be. This compression and stretching of the waves changes their frequency, and thus their pitch. This is called the Doppler shift, after Christian Doppler (1803–1853). The red shift of stellar objects is not exactly the same process, but it is analogous. If the source of the light is receding, the light waves can be thought of as "stretched", and the wavelength is lengthened, making the light appear redder, since red light has a longer wavelength than other light. If the source is approaching, the light waves can be thought of as "compressed", shortening the wavelength and making the light appear bluer, because blue light has a shorter wavelength. The difference between the automobile and the stellar source is that, since the velocity of light is so great, only very rapid motion of the source can cause spectral shifts. Slipher's observations indicated that stellar objects were moving away from the earth at very high speeds. He had discovered the expanding universe, although it was not until the work of Hubble that the full significance of Slipher's finding was appreciated.

Henrietta Leavitt (1868–1921) studied a type of star called a Cepheid, whose brightness periodically changes, and showed that the period of a star (the time between two consecutive moments of maximal brightness) was proportional to its intrinsic brightness. The longer the period, the brighter the star. Cepheids with longer periods are intrinsically brighter than those with shorter periods, and importantly, all Cepheids with the same period are of the same intrinsic brightness. For two cepheids of the same period, any differences in observed brightness can be due only to the distance from Earth.

Against this background came the pioneer astronomer of the early twentieth century—Edwin Hubble (1889–1953). A former high school teacher, he left a law practice to become an astronomer. In 1923, Hubble observed Cepheids in the Andromeda cloud, which was thought by some at the time to be contained within our galaxy. Using the period-intrinsic brightness relationship of the Cepheids, Hubble showed that this cloud must be very far away, well outside of our own galaxy. Beginning in the late nineteenth century, astronomers suspected that some of the fuzzy clouds in the sky were separate galaxies, but by proving it, Hubble greatly expanded the astronomical playing field. The spectra of these new galaxies were also red-shifted. By studying these spectra, Hubble confirmed suspicions that the further away they were, the faster they were receding. Hubble thus built on the work of Leavitt and Slipher to give us the expanding universe that is so much a part of our conception of the cosmos. Because of Hubble, the universe is often thought of as an expanding balloon covered with dots, each dot representing a galaxy moving away from all other galaxies. As we shall see, this analogy required some modification.

If the universe was expanding, might there have been a point in time when all matter was condensed into infinite density? In 1927, Georges Lemaitre (1894–1966) proposed what is now called the "Big Bang" theory, whereby the universe originated as an unimaginably dense cloud of matter, the "explosion" of which created the expansion still evident. (Actually, this was not an explosion in the sense that we know it, rather a very rapid spreading-apart of matter, energy, and space itself.) The objects of the universe as we know them were formed as matter flew apart after the Big Bang. Subsequent mathematical work by George Gamow (1904-1968), Robert Herman (1914-), and Ralph Alpher (1921-) showed that such an event would cause a uniform background radiation throughout the universe. In 1965, Arno Penzias (1933–) and Robert Wilson (1936–) found this radiation, providing experimental evidence for the Big Bang. (It now appears that this radiation is from about 300,000 years after the Big Bang rather than the actual event itself.) The expansion of the universe and the presence of background radiation are two compelling pieces of evidence that strongly support the Big Bang model. A third piece of evidence indicates that there really was a Big Bang. Theoretical studies predicted that a singular event such as a Bang would require matter in the universe to be overwhelmingly in the form of hydrogen and helium. This was verified by experimental studies, as we shall see when we revisit the Big Bang model later.

One question about the universe concerns us now. Will the universe continue to expand indefinitely (called the *open universe* theory), or will the mutual gravitation of the universe's mass eventually cause the expansion to stop, and all matter to contract back into the incomprehensibly dense mass from which it began (the *closed universe* theory)? At this time, it is believed that the average density of the universe is between one atom per twenty cubic meters, and one atom per two cubic meters. A better vacuum than has ever been created on Earth, this density is insufficient for the mutual gravitation of the universe's mass to overpower the inertia of the Big Bang, suggesting that the universe might be open, expanding forever. Indeed, at this writing, there is recent evidence that the universe is expanding at an ever-increasing velocity, with no intent to even slow down, let alone stop and begin to contract; but we await confirmation of this finding.

However, if enough unaccounted-for mass were discovered, we might find that the universe generates enough gravity to contract in on itself. Such unaccounted-for matter has been called "dark," meaning that it has eluded our detection.

One method of detecting the presence of matter that cannot be seen is to observe its gravitational effects. A clue to the possibility of unaccounted-for matter came when clusters of galaxies were found. The distribution of galaxies in the universe is not entirely uniform. Thousands of clusters of galaxies, each consisting of from tens to thousands of galaxies, have been identified. These groups of galaxies often stay together, rather than moving away from each other as would be expected from an unmodified Big Bang model. This means that, instead of an expanding balloon covered with dots, the universe is better thought of as an expanding balloon covered with both dots and non-expanding balls, with each ball covered with multiple dots. With expansion, the single dots do indeed move away from all else, but the dots on the balls stay together as the entire ball moves away from other balls and dots.

In an expanding universe, where everything is moving away from everything else, how can galaxies remain in clusters over the billions of years the universe has existed and been expanding? The visible mass of the galaxies in the clusters is insufficient for their mutual gravitation to permit them to overcome the momentum of expansion and stay together. Is there undetected matter between galaxies in these clusters, adding additional gravitational force and permitting the clusters to stay together? By the same process of reasoning, certain galaxies have a rotational speed that should overcome the gravitational force generated by the amount of matter that we can see in them, resulting in the dispersal of the matter in the galaxy. Does unseen matter in these galaxies provide the additional gravitational force to allow them to remain coherent? Attempts thus far have found a considerable amount of matter that had not been obvious to us. There is, in fact, more dark matter than matter we can see, but still not enough to prove the universe is closed, or to overturn the preliminary evidence that it is open.

Dark matter is of a completely unknown nature. There are a number of theories about it, but at this time, we really know nothing about the nature of the majority of matter in the universe. Is it similar to the matter with which we are familiar, or is it of a totally new nature?

If there is not enough dark matter to close the universe, then the Big Bang was indeed a single and unique event. The universe will expand forever, and what happened before the Big Bang is simply not knowable. On the other hand, what if there is enough dark matter to close the universe? Not only would this mean that the universe will contract in upon itself, back to the fantastically dense mass from which it arose, but it would also mean that the cycle of contraction and expansion has likely been repeated many times. If the universe cycles between expansion and contraction, then there have been innumerable Big Bangs, no one of which is a clear beginning of the universe. In fact, there would be no distinct beginning or ending of the universe. It would have always been, and it will always be. This is a difficult concept for us to grasp. Everything in our lives has a beginning and an end; it is natural for us to believe that the universe also has a beginning and an end. We are prisoners of our everyday experience. But we must realize that we have now entered the stage in our development when the events of our daily lives can no longer govern how we see the universe. The beginning, lifespan, and end of the universe is no exception.

Three advances in geology in the twentieth century should be illustrated. In 1904, Bertram Boltwood (1870–1927) showed that elements can transmute during radioactivity. Concentrating on the transmutation (called decay) of uranium to lead, he studied the ratio of uranium to lead in rocks. He noticed that the older the rock, the less uranium and more lead it contained. In 1907, he learned how to use the half-life of radioactive uranium (the time required for one-half of the uranium to decay to lead) to calculate the age of rocks. After a rock is formed, it no longer exchanges any uranium or lead with the environment. Other than the amount of lead in the rock at its formation, any lead in it must be derived from the decay of uranium. By knowing the amounts of uranium and lead in a rock, the half-life of uranium, and having an idea of how much lead there was in the rock at its formation, Boltwood could calculate the age of a rock. The oldest rocks he could find were about a half billion ($500,000,000$ or 5×10^8) years old, which forced a modification of the prevailing view that the earth was about 100 million ($100,000,000$ or 10^8) years old. The oldest rocks thus far identified are about 4.2 billion ($4,200,000,000$ or 4.2×10^9) years old.

The same principle is applied to the dating of archeological ruins, except that radioactive carbon 14 (carbon atoms with two extra neutrons in the nucleus) is used, because carbon is associated with human activities and remains, and the half-life of uranium is too long, relative to the age of human artifacts. The principle of carbon dating, pioneered by Willard Frank Libby (1908–1980), is that the vast majority of carbon is carbon 12, but there is a small amount of carbon 14 in the environment. Carbon 14 decays to nitrogen 14, with a half-life of 5,730 years. All organisms have a little carbon 14, and while the organism is alive, the amount of this isotope remains constant. Decaying carbon 14 is replaced from the environment. After death, there is no further replacement from the environment, so the amount of carbon 14 in the sample diminishes. The quantity of carbon 14 remaining is, therefore, a reflection of how long the organic material has been dead. The lower the quantity, the longer is the time since death.

The second geological advance of the twentieth century was a greatly improved understanding of the nature of the earth's interior. In large part, this was made possible by a greater understanding of earthquakes. Shortly after the invention of the seismograph, it was realized that earthquakes produce two kinds of waves: P waves, which travel by compression of material along the line of propagation; and S waves, which travel by causing material to oscillate up and down aroud the line of propagation. Think of P waves as a compressed spring expanding and S waves as the motion of a rope tied at one end and shaken up and down at the other. Based on his analysis of seismograph recordings of earthquakes, Andrija Mohorovicic (1857–1936) recognized that there must be a boundary of some sort approximately thirty miles (forty-eight km) below the earth's surface. Later, others showed that S waves will not penetrate liquid, whereas P waves, although attenuated, will. It was observed that S waves appeared to penetrate deeply into the earth, but did not enter an area about 1,800 miles (2,900 km) below the surface. P waves did penetrate this area, and then increased in velocity in the center of the earth, suggesting the following model for the earth's interior: there is a crust that is extremely thin relative to the earth's diameter, varying in thickness from thirty miles (forty-eight km) on land, to six miles (ten km) under the sea floor. Beneath the crust, the mantle is some 1,800 miles (2,900 km) thick. Beneath this is a liquid outer core and a small, solid inner core.

A third advance in geology was primarily the contribution of the most influential geologist of the twentieth century, Alfred Wegener (1880–1930). Like others of his time, Wegener noticed an appreciable similarity in the contours of Africa and South America. He also identified similarities in the coastlines of other continents. Wegener was not the first to suggest that the continents may once have been joined, but he gave the idea life with a thorough study and convincing arguments. For example, it was known that fossils on different continents resembled each other, even if their existing animal life was quite different. The prevailing explanation was that there had been land bridges between the continents, which had eroded or sunk. Wegener used geophysical evidence to show that the land bridge theory was unlikely; it was much more probable that the continents were once joined. In addition, Wegener studied rocks from the eastern coast of Brazil and from the western coast of Africa, showing that they resembled each other in type, structure, and age.

In 1912, he proposed that all landmasses had once been connected in a giant continent he called Pangea (or Pangaea). Wegener believed that this giant continent had broken up, and the resulting landmasses drifted away. Wegener's 1915 book *The Origins of the Continents and Oceans* received a hostile reception, partly because of the conservatism of the scientific establishment, and partly for the more legitimate reason that a mechanism for continental drift had not been proposed. His theory would be largely forgotten until 1962, when Harry Hess (1906–1969) proposed the theory of sea floor spreading. Hess took advantage of recent data indicating that the crust of the ocean's floor was younger than that of the continents, and that there was a series of ridges in the center of the ocean. Hess proposed that material from beneath the surface was emerging onto the surface at the ridges, adding to the crust. This new material pushed the crust of the ocean's floor sideways, towards the continents, resulting in the sliding of oceanic crust under continental crust at shorelines.

Important experimental verification of the sea floor spreading hypothesis was obtained the year after Hess's proposal. To understand it, we need to pause and review the earth's magnetic field. It is currently held that the crust and mantle rotate faster than the liquid outer core. This means that electrons in the outer core move relative to the crust-mantle. The rotation of the earth, according to Ampere's work and Maxwell's equations, then forms a magnetic field from the relative motion of electrons in the earth's interior. The north and south poles of the earth's magnetic field are not in the same location as the geographic north and south poles. Rather, a line drawn between the magnetic poles inclines about eleven degrees from the plane of the earth's rotation, placing the north magnetic pole off the coast of Bathurst Island, in the Canadian Northwest Territories, and the south magnetic pole on the edge, not the center, of Antarctica. Moreover, the earth's magnetic field is not constant. It is subject to minor changes in position, drifting perhaps twelve to fifteen miles (nineteen to twenty-four km) per year, additional confirmation that the earth's magnetic field is not caused by a giant iron magnet in the center, for such a magnetic field would not drift (besides, the heat of the earth's interior would cause iron to lose its magnetism).

Not only is the earth's magnetic field slowly drifting, but for unknown reasons, it completely reverses itself periodically. Today, magnetic north is in the direction of geographic north, but periodically in the past, a compass would have pointed south. Rocks pick up a permanent magnetic tracing when they are formed, or when they are heated and cooled, which matches the earth's magnetic field at the time of their formation or metamorphosis.

In 1963, Frederick Vine (1939–) and Drummond Mathews (1931–), by measuring geomagnetic intensity and orientation, showed that rocks on either side of certain mid-ocean ridges and immediately adjacent to the ridges had the same magnetic orientation. Rocks slightly further from the ridge had a different magnetic orientation, but this orientation matched that of rocks in a corresponding position on the other side of the ridge. Taking N and S as the two orientations of the magnetic field, rocks on either side of a mid-ocean ridge (represented below by —) had the following magnetic tracings:

NSNSNS—SNSNSN

In addition, dating of rocks beside these ridges showed that the youngest rocks were those closest to the ridge, while rocks furthest from the ridge, while still young, were older. Moreover, rocks closest to the ridge lacked the accumulation of millions of years of sea life. So the picture emerged that on either side of the ridge, rocks were continuously formed, displacing older rocks, then displaced from the ridge by still younger rocks. This meant that new crust *was being formed* in the ocean. Since the surface area of the earth is not increasing, crust must be disappearing somewhere.

Here was the missing piece of Wegener's theory. In the late 1960s, Wegener's continental drift theory and Hess's sea floor spreading theory were brilliantly united into the theory of plate tectonics, which was to become the third major advance of twentieth-century geology. Plate tectonics holds that some seven major plates cover the surface of the earth. (Some consider the number to be larger, depending on where one draws the line between major and minor plates.) Each plate consists of the earth's crust and the top forty or so miles (sixty-four km) of the mantle. (Some believe the plates include a thicker portion of mantle.) This combination of the crust and the upper portion of the mantle is called the lithosphere and sits on the lower portion of the mantle, called the asthenosphere.

As material from the earth's interior rises to the surface in the mid-ocean ridges, new crust is formed and the plates move away from each other. The moving apart of oceanic plates forces a collision of these plates with continental plates. The oceanic plate is then forced below the continental plate, in a process called subduction. In subduction, the oceanic plate, as it is pushed below the continental plate, is heated to the point where it is eventually melted and recycled. Because of this process, no part of the crust of the ocean floor is older than about two hundred million (2×10^8) years.

When two continental plates collide, a mountain range may result. Where two plates push against each other, a sudden slippage and release of pressure causes most earthquakes. The heat and pressure occurring at plate junctions are the cause of many volcanoes. Most of the remainder occur in the middle of the ocean, where molten rock forces its way to the surface, pushing apart plates, creating new crust, and sometimes forming islands. Most of the earth's volcanic and earthquake activity arises at the junctions of plates, the hot spots of the earth. An example is the San Andreas Fault, at the junction of the Pacific and North American plates.

Chapter 27
Magic Bullets

Serendipity and trial and error make us the masters of some of the world's tiniest creatures, but the battle is a stalemate, not a victory.

TWENTIETH-CENTURY ADVANCES IN BIOLOGY AND MEDICINE have occurred at a dizzying pace, rivaling those in physics. We shall discuss a few of the most crucial advances in biology and medicine, the first of which was the development of antibiotics.

Like all great ideas, antibiotics have indistinct origins. The occasional effectiveness of fermented or moldy substances to treat wounds was known in antiquity but results were inconsistent, and there was no accompanying knowledge base. In 1874, William Roberts (1830–1899) noticed that fungi and bacteria are antagonistic toward each other. He further noticed that the mold Penicillium was immune to attack by bacteria. Louis Pasteur (1822–1895) and Jules Joubert (1834–1910) both found that anthrax will not grow in cultures contaminated by molds, and both recognized the possible therapeutic implications.

But the history of antibiotics really begins with Paul Ehrlich (1854–1915). Ehrlich had long been fascinated with the idea of a "magic bullet"—a substance that would kill an offending organism without harming a patient's cells. Like so many other ideas in history, the pivotal observation involved an unexpected and frustrating find in another field. Experimenting with industrial dyes in an attempt to stain tissue for microscopic study, Ehrlich noted that some dyes stained certain tissues and not others. After this observation, the crucial next step was to ask a question, as is so often the case. If dyes can be tissue-specific in their staining, is it possible that they may also be selective in their toxicity? He achieved some success with the dye trypan blue in the treatment of African sleeping sickness (caused by a trypanosome, which is a protozoan), but he had no luck in finding a dye that would selectively kill bacteria. But when Ehrlich combined dyes with arsenic, he rewrote history. In 1910 he found that compound 606—so named because it was the six hundred and sixth variation of a central chemical structure based on this combination—was effective against syphilis. This drug came to be called Salvarsan and was the first specific antibacterial agent to come into existence as a result of the actions of people. Ehrlich's discovery of compound 606 not only provided the first effective antibiotic, but it also established the principle of variation, whereby effective drugs are derived from a series of variations on a basic chemical structure. This principle is at the heart of our contemporary pharmaceutical industry.

Nowhere in history is the serendipitous nature of our progress more evident than in the discovery of penicillin. In 1928, Alexander Fleming (1881–1955) found that Penicillium mold had accidentally contaminated a staphylococcal culture. Whereas most people, feeling particularly unfortunate, would simply have discarded the contaminated cultures, Fleming realized that something exciting was afoot. He then did what a great researcher must—he permitted himself to get off track. Putting aside his original research, he found that a bactericidal substance diffused from the mold. He isolated this material and named it penicillin, after the mold that produced it. Fleming published his findings in 1929, but because he could isolate only small and impure quantities of the new antibiotic, he was unable to do critical testing in mice, and his work was largely ignored for a number of years.

A few years later, Gerhard Domagk (1895–1964), inspired by Ehrlich's work with dyes, showed that a synthetic dye called Prontosil was effective against certain bacteria. It was this antibiotic, not penicillin, that was widely used during World War II. Prontosil was the first man-made substance to selectively interfere with the growth of many species of bacteria and the first member of a class of antibiotics called sulfa drugs, or sulfonamides. But the side effects and relatively limited effectiveness of Prontosil elicited an urgent search for another antibiotic, and attention returned to penicillin.

In wartime England, Ernst Chain (1906–1979) and Howard Florey (1898–1968) demonstrated that penicillin had significant clinical effectiveness and began the process of development. The first successful use of penicillin, in 1941, was only a partial success because of limited quantities. World War II interrupted large-scale production in England, but Chain hand-carried a vial of the mold to the United States. The American wartime penicillin effort was huge, second only to the atomic bomb project, and the first military use was in 1943.

In 1944 Selman Waksman (1888–1973) isolated Streptomycin from a soil microbe. (It was Waksman who coined the term "antibiotic.") In 1957, penicillin was synthesized in the laboratory. The manufacture of synthetic and semisynthetic penicillins and related antibiotics followed. Today, antibiotics act through a variety of mechanisms. For example, some, such as penicillin, disrupt the cell wall of the bacterium (upon which the organism is usually dependent for survival). Others target the protein synthetic pathway or DNA replicative ability.

It was once thought certain that the permutations made possible by laboratory research would keep us safe from bacterial infections for the remainder of our history. Today, that is less certain. At this writing, antibiotic resistance is becoming a significant problem in medical treatment and it is no longer assured that we will continue to enjoy the protection from bacteria that we have come to expect. Darwinian evolution also applies to bacteria, and like any species, they can adapt to hostile surroundings by the preferential reproduction of the rare individuals able to cope with the environment. Because the reproduction time for bacteria is so short (on the order of fifteen minutes for some species), evolutionary adaptation is rapid, and resistant organisms quickly become the rule rather than the exception.

In addition to growing bacterial resistance, there is another problem with antibiotics: they do not work against viruses. Viruses attack a human cell by a totally different mechanism than that of bacteria. Bacteria are very small cells, but they are whole cells and are capable of living independently. Viruses, on the other hand, are not even complete cells, are too small to be seen with an ordinary microscope, and can only survive inside a cell. They often integrate their DNA into a human cell's DNA, making them extraordinarily difficult to kill without hurting the host cell. The molecular mechanism of antibiotics is targeted at bacterial metabolism, making them ineffective against viruses. Killing bacteria is like finding a needle in a haystack; killing a virus is like finding a needle that has gone inside the individual straws of hay.

We are just now achieving limited success with drugs specifically targeted at viruses. Antiviral drugs are currently at the level of antibacterial agents in the days of Salvarsan. Our success with vaccines against viral agents has been much greater, but even in this area, we have sustained setbacks, (For example, there is not yet a vaccine against AIDS.) The smallest form of life we know of is our most formidable enemy. As Joshua Lederberg says, "The single biggest threat to man's continued dominance on the planet is the virus."

Chapter 28

The Molecular Basis
of Who We Are

*Tiny molecules determine much—or everything—
about us. Do we have free will?*

WE ARE ALL DROPPED BRIEFLY into a wondrous world of miracles we call life. This chapter is concerned with the exploration of those miracles.

From a purely scientific viewpoint, nothing so clearly tells the story of who we are as the history of our knowledge of genetics and DNA. The story starts with the rediscovery of Gregor Mendel's work in 1900. Mendel's work, as illustrative of the creativity and potential of humanity as any of our endeavors, was tragically ignored, and it had to be rediscovered by three independent investigators: Hugo de Vries, Karl Correns, and Erich Tschermak von Seysenegg. Their work indicated that heredity was controlled by physical units (the term "gene" was first used by Wilhelm Johannsen in 1909), and the detective story of the twentieth century has been the continuing elucidation of the nature and function of these units.

Thomas Hunt Morgan (1866–1945), working with fruit flies, showed that these units of heredity were arranged linearly on the chromosomes. (Walter Sutton appears to have independently reached the conclusion that genes were on chromosomes.) This localization of the genetic material would prove pivotal in further work, because it showed where in the cell to look for the molecular basis of genetics. Morgan's 1915 book *The Mechanism of Mendelian Heredity* was influential in the development of genetics and was followed by *The Theory of the Gene* in 1926. In the latter work, Morgan introduced the idea that genes are not absolutely fixed in position, but can move from one chromosome to another.

In 1941, George Beadle (1903–1989) and Edward Tatum (1909–1975) used x-rays and ultraviolet light to induce mutations in bread mold. From this, they showed that the genes controlled biochemical reactions, providing an important link between genetics and biochemistry. Mendel's gene for height in peas and a person's gene for eye color bring about their effects by controlling the biochemical apparatus in cells. Beadle and Tatum derived the "one gene-one enzyme" hypothesis, whereby each gene was thought to control the synthesis and/or activity of one enzyme. (Enzymes are proteins, sometimes accompanied by non-protein cofactors, which permit most of the biochemical reactions in cells to take place.) Today, this hypothesis has been modified somewhat, because many proteins (of which enzymes are a type) consist of several polypeptides, each of which appears to be coded by one gene.

The work discussed above taught us something about where genes are and how they might operate, but we still knew nothing of their nature or the details of their action. DNA (deoxyribonucleic acid) was known in the nineteenth century, and by the early twentieth century, it was understood that chromosomes contained DNA. But chromosomes also contain protein, and genes were thought to be composed of the protein portion of the chromosome, not DNA. In 1944, Oswald Avery (1877–1955), Colin Macleod (1909–1972), and Maclyn McCarty (1911–) showed that hereditary traits could be passed between bacteria by purified DNA in the absence of protein. Moreover, enzymes that destroyed protein did not inhibit the transfer of genetic information, while enzymes that destroyed DNA did. This finding moved genetic research to a higher plane by demonstrating that DNA, not proteins, was the genetic material.

Twentieth-century science has had two great detective stories, each involving an elucidation of a structure followed by the development of techniques permitting unprecedented applications. Progress in atomic structure, and the applications following therefrom, is the first story. The study of DNA is the second.

The first steps in the elucidation of the structure of DNA were taken through a technique called x-ray crystallography. In 1912, Max von Laue (1879–1960) discovered that crystals diffract x-rays in very much the same way that a series of thin slits diffract light. The crystalline structure of many solids is such that the atoms form planes very close together, approximating the fine spacing of slits. On passing through crystals, x-ray waves spread out and either reinforce or cancel each other depending on whether the peak of one wave is superimposed on the trough (leading to cancellation) or the peak (leading to reinforcement) of another wave. Laue's discovery was brought to fruition by the father-son team of William H. Bragg (1862–1942) and William L. Bragg (1890–1971), who worked out the theory of x-ray diffraction in solids and showed that the interaction of substances with x rays tells us something about their structure. The stage was now set for the discovery that everyone remembers.

X-ray diffraction studies of DNA were begun in the early 1950s by Maurice Wilkins (1916–) and Rosalind Franklin (1920–1958). About this time, Erwin Chargraff (1905–) worked with four small molecules (called bases) known to be constituents of DNA: adenine, thymine, guanine, and cytosine. Chargraff showed that the quantity of adenine in DNA equaled the quantity of thymine, while guanine was present in the same amount as cytosine. This work allowed Francis Crick (1916–) and James Watson (1928–) to deduce the structure of DNA.

Deoxyribonucleic acid, the genetic material of life, consists of two chains twisted into the form of a helix. Each chain is composed of alternating sugar molecules and phosphate groups. Attached to and projecting inward from the chains, each of the four bases projects from one chain halfway to the other chain, to be met in the center by a base attached to the other chain. The base adenine pairs with thymine, and the base guanine pairs with cytosine (hence Chargraff's observation). It was immediately grasped that the four bases in DNA must control protein synthesis by coding for amino acids, the building blocks of proteins. Because there are four bases and twenty amino acids, the coding must involve more than one base. In fact, combinations of two bases can code for only sixteen amino acids, still not enough. Combinations of three bases allow for sixty-four different codes, and it is now known that bases work in groups of three to determine that a particular amino acid will be used in the synthesis of a protein, very much as letters work in groups to generate words.

Shortly after the structure of DNA was elucidated, it was established that protein was not made directly from DNA, but that there was an intermediate molecule called Ribonucleic acid (RNA). RNA is almost always formed from DNA when the latter separates into single strands; using the pairing rules discussed above, one or both of these single strands synthesizes a mirror-image single-stranded molecule of RNA in a process called transcription. For example, a single DNA strand containing the bases adenine, thymine, guanine, and cytosine would generate an RNA molecule with the base sequence thymine, adenine, cytosine, and guanine. (Sometimes the base uracil substitutes for thymine in RNA.) RNA, like DNA, is a nucleic acid, and it is structurally very similar to its parent molecule. Proteins are then made from the RNA in a process called translation. Translation began to be understood when it was realized that amino acids do not bind directly to the RNA, but are brought to it by transport molecules. This led to the conception that the RNA molecule, after its synthesis from a DNA molecule, stretched out and received the amino acids from the transport molecules. The amino acids then bound to each other to make the completed protein. We now know that the situation is a little more complicated, and that tiny structures called ribosomes mediate the interaction of the RNA and the transport molecules.

A team headed by Marshall Nirenberg (1927–) began the work which culminated in the actual breaking of the genetic code, that is, the deciphering of the meaning of each of the sixty-four combinations of three bases. Working in an artificial system without cells, Nirenberg showed that a strand of RNA that contained only the base uracil, coded for a protein containing only the amino acid phenylalanine. Three consecutive uracils in RNA (derived from three consecutive adenine bases in DNA) coded for the amino acid phenylalanine. We now know that there is more than one combination for each amino acid, and some combinations indicate that protein synthesis should stop. Proteins are not only the major structural molecules of the cell, but also the principal components of enzymes, which determine what chemical reactions will take place in the cell. (We will discuss enzymes subsequently.) By controlling both the structures of cells and the chemical reactions that take place in them, the four small molecules that are the bases in DNA determine who we are. It is remarkable that only a little more than a half-century separated the re-discovery of Mendel's work from the elucidation of the structure of DNA and the mechanism of protein synthesis. This extraordinarily rapid progress rivals the lightning pace of twentieth-century physics.

The next great step forward in the study of DNA was some understanding of its regulation. Every cell contains the full complement of DNA, but different types of cells express different portions of DNA. There is a gene for eye color in the cells of your foot, but it lies dormant. Jacques Monod (1910–1976) and François Jacob (1920–) proposed that some substances from the environment can bind to DNA, controlling which portions of it are transcribed to RNA and translated to proteins. It is now believed that no more than ten percent of DNA is directly responsible for coding for proteins. The remaining ninety percent is concerned with regulating the expression of the active ten percent. The regulation of gene expression is an exciting area in molecular biology, and our current conception involves intervening segments of DNA, called introns, which serve a regulatory function and are not translated into proteins. Traits can be expressed much more rapidly if the responsible DNA is physically present and simply must be "unmasked", rather than synthesized de novo. To my mind, it is this "unmasking" of DNA that may be responsible for the extraordinarily rapid increase in the size of the human brain in such a comparatively brief time.

The twentieth century saw marvelous advances in neuroscience as well. By 1865, it was understood that the nervous system consisted of cells, as Schwann had proposed for the body in general, but an understanding of the microscopic structure of the nervous system had been impeded by the lack of a good stain. Processes were known to emanate in both directions from the cell body (we now call these processes axons and dendrites), but there was debate as to whether the processes of one nerve cell fused with processes from another. The key unanswered question was this: are the units of the nervous system autonomous and interacting, or are they joined into one large structure? Camillo Golgi (1843–1926) developed a stain that stained only some of the nerve cells, but those stained were shown in detail never before seen. We now know that the strength of the Golgi stain is also its weakness. By staining only a small percentage of cells, it left unstained (and therefore unapproachable) the vast majority of nerve cells. However, staining of all the cells would have obscured the fine details of the individual cells. It was precisely because so few nerve cells were stained, that those that were could be seen in their rich and elaborate entirety. With his stain, Golgi took the position that the axons of nerve cells connected to each other, thereby linking nerve cells into a giant network.

Santiago Ramon y Cajal (1852–1934) refined the Golgi stain to show that the nervous system was composed of autonomous nerve cells, which we now call neurons, and that these neurons did not directly connect to each other. Cajal recognized that the function of the nervous system must entail the cooperative interaction of these myriad neurons. It is on the shoulders of Cajal that we stand as we begin to understand and treat neurological disorders.

Charles Scott Sherrington (1857–1952), a student of both Virchow and Koch, recognized that such a cooperative interaction must involve very special events at the junction of two neurons. He called this junction the synapse, and because neurons did not actually touch at the synapse, he postulated that a release of some substance at the end of one neuron must activate the adjacent neuron. In 1920, Otto Loewi (1873–1961) proved that nerves supplying the heart release a chemical (now called acetylcholine) onto the heart muscle fibers to cause them to contract.

Something of the basic anatomy of the nervous system was now understood. Millions of neurons connect to each other at synapses through the release of chemicals at the end of one neuron, causing the adjacent neuron to carry an electrical impulse. Alan Hodgkin (1914–1998) and Andrew Huxley (1917–) determined how impulses are transmitted along the fibers of neurons. During rest, the neuron pumps positively charged sodium ions (the sodium atom without the electron in the outermost shell) out of the cell, negatively charging the interior of the cell. During the conduction of an impulse, special channels for sodium in the cell membrane open, and the positively charged sodium ions rush in, changing the electrical potential of the cell's interior. This change in potential causes the adjacent sodium channel to open, continuing the process until the end of the fiber is reached, at which point the influx of sodium leads to the release of a chemical (now called a neurotransmitter) that diffuses across the synaptic gap, opening sodium channels in the next neuron. The studies of Bernard Katz (1911–), on the mechanism of action of acetylcholine, the principal neurotransmitter associated with the junction of neurons and muscle cells, contributed greatly to our understanding of the function of the nervous system. Incidentally, muscle cells, including the cells of the heart muscle, carry an electrical impulse—just as neurons do—and the electrical properties of the heart were brilliantly exploited by Willem Einthoven (1860–1927). Taking advantage of the finding that the electrical impulses of damaged heart muscle cells are altered or absent, Einthoven developed the electrocardiogram (the EKG), one of the great advances in medicine.

We now divide the nervous system into three parts: the central nervous system (the brain and spinal cord), the peripheral nervous system (the nerves of the trunk and extremities), and the autonomic nervous system (nerves of the interior concerned with the regulation of bodily functions). Of these, the central nervous system is by far the most complicated, and we are just beginning to understand its function. In the central nervous system, there is bewildering complexity and an enormous array of neurotransmitters, some of which hinder, rather than excite, the post-synaptic neuron. A great deal of who we are derives from these neurotransmitters, none of which are well understood, and many of which have likely not been discovered.

Now the difficult question arises: are our behaviors our choice, or are they predetermined by the "wiring" of our brains and neurotransmitters? There is no more sobering lesson regarding who we are than the realization that the ultimate philosophical question of free will comes down, at a molecular level, to the anatomy, physiology, and biochemistry of the central nervous system, all of which appear to be at least partially beyond our control. It is disquieting to ponder that we may not control our own fate, but if this is so, we must recognize and accept this.

The molecular biology of the brain, and our lack of understanding of it, has implications in the legal arena. History is full of examples of people who were persecuted because they were perceived as evil or possessed, only to have science later show that they had definable medical conditions. Almost every illness at some time in all cultures was once regarded as an indication of the person's unworthiness. We may find that people we now regard as evil have a medical illness of the brain we do not yet comprehend. Our law attempts to take mental illness into account, but if the functions of our brains are biochemically controlled, and if we are only beginning to understand that control, can we be confident that we can separate those who have control over their actions from those who do not? It is crucial, absolutely decisive, in the survival of our species that we become and remain aware of what we do not know and may never know. Most errors of judgement, and most tragedies of history, are caused by people who believe they have what Jacob Bronowski called absolute knowledge, but in fact have what historian Daniel Boorstin calls the illusion of knowledge. To fulfill the requirement that we learn from the past and look to the future, we should allow for the possibility that there are no evil people, only people who are ill. The desire to punish, although natural, must be subjugated to the ability to consider all aspects of a situation. The construction of a society that acknowledges and allows for imperfect knowledge requires political leaders with a rare degree of insight and wisdom, and an uncommon ability to look beyond the expedient solution. I predict the day will come when we will understand that criminal behavior is a mental illness, caused either by unfortunate circumstances in people's lives or by a molecular defect in the brain. Someday we might be able to identify susceptible individuals and prevent their violent behavior.

To survive in a world full of hostile microorganisms, we must have natural immunity. The work of Jenner and Pasteur showed that we were capable of achieving immunity to organisms, but nothing was known of the mechanism. The first hint came in 1884, when Ilya Mechnikov (1845–1916, sometimes spelled Elie Metchnikoff) discovered phagocytosis, in which certain white blood cells engulf and destroy foreign material.

Ehrlich had postulated that there must be substances produced by cells and released into the blood to confer immunity. In 1890, Emil Behring (1854–1917) and Shibasaburo Kitasato (1852–1931) independently demonstrated that the body develops specific proteins against the tetanus toxin. They had discovered the first antibodies. In 1891, Behring successfully treated a patient with diphtheria using antibodies directed against the toxin. (These were obtained from the blood of a sensitized animal and are now called antitoxins.) By 1894, diphtheria antitoxin therapy was widely used.

Today, we know that immunity has two arms: a cellular portion, as discovered by Mechnikov; and a humoral portion, involving circulating antibodies, as per Ehrlich's postulate and the discoveries of Behring and Kitasato. The cellular and humoral portions of the immune system are interrelated; antibodies bind to a foreign molecule (called an antigen), resulting in an antigen-antibody complex, which signals phagocytic white blood cells to absorb and destroy that antigen.

About the year 1900, Jules Bordet (1870–1961) discovered complement, a series of blood proteins that bind to the antigen-antibody complex. Further work would show that the complement proteins are important in facilitating phagocytosis and causing a complete reaction to foreign material.

In the 1960s, Gerald Edelman (1929–) and Rodney Porter (1917–1985) determined the structure of antibodies. About the same time, William Dreyer and J. Claude Bennet realized that if each of our myriad antibodies required a dedicated portion of DNA for its synthesis, the majority of DNA would be required just for the production of these proteins. They therefore proposed that a lesser amount of DNA would be required to make antibodies if, instead of having a specific sequence of DNA set aside for every antibody, the DNA involved in antibody production were somehow broken, rearranged, and spliced back together. In this way, a given portion of DNA could participate in the coding of more than one antibody, very much as a myriad number of words can be created from an alphabet. We now know that the synthesis of antibodies from DNA involves a fascinating and complicated series of steps whereby the DNA is actually cut, and then reunited in different combinations. (This had been thought impossible and is currently believed to happen only for DNA coding for proteins involved in immune reactions.)

Our current understanding of the immune system involves a set of primarily phagocytic white blood cells, another set responsible for antibody production, and another set which secrete factors to enable the normal functioning of the first two sets. All of these work in conjunction with complement, and all are subject to an array of molecules (called interleukins) that control the immune response.

Like many other areas of endeavor, endocrinology began with a postulate and a series of initially unconnected observations. The history of hormones begins with Claude Bernard (1813–1878), the greatest experimental physiologist of the nineteenth century. Among many other contributions, Bernard introduced the idea of homeostasis, the concept that organisms can and will maintain a constant internal environment. Charles Edouard Brown-Sequard (1817–1894) followed Bernard's idea with a pivotal postulate: that certain organs secrete substances that bring about homeostasis.

By 1891, it was realized that thyroid extract helped some patients with fatigue and obesity. This was followed in the early 1900s with the connection of iodine deficiency and goiter (thyroid enlargement). About 1900, it was understood that some cases of hypertension were secondary to a tumor of the inner part of the adrenal gland. In 1902, Ernest Starling (1866–1927) and William Bayliss (1860–1924) isolated a substance called secretin from the duodenum and showed that it caused the pancreas to discharge its products, which facilitated digestion, into the gastrointestinal tract. In 1904, Starling used the word "hormone" to refer to substances that bring about homeostasis.

Thomas Addison (1783–1860), by recognizing the devastating consequences of diminished function of the outer part of the adrenal gland (now called the cortex), described the disease named for him. In the 1920s, the function of the adrenal cortex began to be understood, permitting some explanation of the symptoms of Addison's disease. Also in the 1920s, the central role of the pituitary gland was elucidated. It was realized that the pituitary exerted a stimulatory effect on the sex organs, and Philip Smith (1884–1970) showed that removing this gland caused a number of other organs to cease to function. The understanding of the pituitary as the "master gland" placed endocrinology on the road it follows today.

Today, we conceive of the endocrine system as a series of glands that discharge their products directly into the bloodstream without ducts (as opposed to exocrine glands, which discharge their products into a duct, which then leads to a specific destination). Most endocrine glands are under the control of the pituitary, a tiny gland at the base of the brain, itself under the control of the hypothalamus, a part of the brain. The products of the endocrine glands, called hormones, act as chemical messengers. In general, they bind to specific sites on the target cells (called receptors), directly or indirectly causing a series of reactions to occur. If their action is indirect through another agent, that agent is called a second messenger, since the hormone is considered to be the first messenger.

Hormones are not to be confused with enzymes. Hormones are released into the blood to act at a distance; enzymes act locally, either inside the cell in which they were made or in a nearby part of the body. Rather than bringing about a series of reactions, as do hormones, each enzyme makes possible one biochemical reaction by acting as a catalyst (a substance that enables chemical reactions that could not otherwise occur). The thousands of chemical reactions in each cell that allow us to exist are made possible by enzymes. The idea of enzymes got its start in 1897, when Eduard Buchner (1860–1917) showed that an extract of yeast would ferment sugar to alcohol just as well as the intact yeast. This was contrary to the opinion of Pasteur, who believed the whole yeast organism was required. In 1926, James Sumner (1887–1955) showed that the enzyme urease is a protein. We now know that although they often work in conjunction with non-protein co-factors, most enzymes are proteins, and as such, structurally determined by the base sequence of DNA.

The great achievement of early endocrinology, and a crowning accomplishment of medicine, was the 1921 discovery of insulin. Much can be learned from an in-depth examination of this event. Diabetes mellitus is a disease characterized essentially by the inability to properly metabolize food. Specifically, the ability to build larger molecules from smaller molecules sharply diminishes, so that the smaller molecules build up. The hallmark of the disease is very high levels of glucose (a small sugar molecule, most of which is normally used to build larger molecules of carbohydrates) in the blood and urine. Acute complications of diabetes include malnutrition, infection, and life-threatening acidosis, where the blood becomes acidic. Chronic complications include obstruction of blood vessels, nerve dysfunction, and visual impairment. The connection between diabetes and the pancreas was appreciated before the isolation of insulin, because it had been shown that removal of the pancreas induced diabetes in experimental animals.

It was also understood that within the pancreas were tiny microscopic collections of cells called Islets of Langerhans. (Today, we know that the pancreas is really two organs—an exocrine portion and an endocrine portion. The exocrine portion forms the vast majority of the gland and secretes enzymes, which are conveyed by way of a duct to the small intestine, where they are important in breaking down food. The Islets, the endocrine portion, secrete a number of hormones, of which insulin is one).

It was also known that ligating (tying closed) the duct that carried pancreatic secretions into the small intestine could result in degeneration of the exocrine pancreas, but would not cause diabetes, indicating that the Islets—the portion not destroyed by ligation of the duct—were likely responsible for the magical anti-diabetic substance. In addition, microscopic abnormalities of the Islets were reported in diabetic patients, further suggesting that these tiny collections of cells were responsible for the substance that prevented the terrible disease.

Pancreatic extracts had been tried, but were ineffectual. (Indeed, some patients were harmed by them.) We now know that these extracts were ineffective because insulin constitutes only a very tiny percentage of the proteins in the pancreas, and there was not enough of it in the extracts. But at the time, there was speculation that the digestive enzymes in the extract were breaking down the unknown anti-diabetic factor.

Frederick Banting (1891–1941) was aware that obstruction of the pancreatic duct—which carries exocrine secretions from the pancreas to the small intestine—sometimes caused the pancreas to degenerate, becoming unable to make digestive enzymes. He had the idea that extracts made from a degenerated pancreas might be spared the effects of the digestive enzymes and thus more beneficial than those made from the whole pancreas. Banting speculated that tying the pancreatic duct shut might cause the majority of the pancreas to degenerate, while leaving the Islets intact. Extracts made from this pancreas would be free of the enzymes thought to damage the anti-diabetic substance. Actually, this idea had already been tried and had failed because the anticipated degeneration could not be consistently produced, but Banting apparently did not know this. He asked John Macleod (1876–1935) for permission to use his laboratory at the University of Toronto while the latter was away. Macleod gave permission, supplied Banting with an assistant named Charles Best (1899–1978), and gave initial guidance before leaving town.

Banting's idea, it turned out, was not productive. Sometimes the expected degeneration of the pancreas did not occur, and even when it did, very often only minimal effect was obtained from the extract. Banting's idea is important only because it served to initiate the research that, by a different mechanism, bore fruit. Banting, Best, and Macleod all realized that extracts prepared from ligated pancreases, even if they could be made effective, were too labor-intensive to have clinical merit. A more effective extraction procedure was needed—

one that could be applied to normal pancreases, and that was enriched in the target substance. Macleod brought in biochemist James Bertram Collip (1892–1965), forming a contentious foursome with Banting and Best on one hand and Macleod and Collip on the other. Collip modified Banting and Best's extraction method, obtaining an extract pure enough to be clinically useful. Although the hormone, called insulin, would not be isolated in completely pure form for some years (by other investigators), Collip's extract, and subsequent modifications of it, gave life to millions of diabetics. Today, insulin is not prepared by extraction from animal pancreases but is the product of recombinant DNA technology (about which we shall learn subsequently). Now human, not animal, insulin is given.

The discovery of insulin gives us an opportunity to examine the Nobel Prize awards. The 1923 prize was awarded to Banting and Macleod. Banting shared his award with Best, while Macleod shared his prize with Collip, but the Nobel committee did not honor these investigators, or the many other people whose work was used by the famous foursome.

There has been much debate over this award, with some believing that Banting and Best should have been the recipients because they did the initial work, without which Macleod and Collip would not have been involved. Others take the opposite opinion—that Macleod and Collip should have been the recipients because it was the former's guidance that kept Banting and Best on the right track, and the latter's effective extract which was clinically useful. Some feel that Banting and Macleod were a reasonable choice, given that the rules of the Nobel prize do not permit more than three recipients in the same category per year, making it inevitable that at least one of the foursome would be left out.

To my mind, the recognition of specific individuals in the Nobel awards in the sciences does not place the credit where it is due—to the innumerable people behind the scenes. The Nobel science awards are not reflective of the true manner in which discoveries come about. Human development does not occur because a small number of qualitatively superior people perform miraculous acts of genius. Rather, we grow because of our collective perseverance and dedication. We move together, *en masse*, toward improved knowledge. Some of us achieve more than others, but it is simply not possible to reliably select one, two, or three people who have made possible a striking innovation, and attempts to do so are unfair to the many unsung heroes who make our progress possible. Ernest Rutherford succinctly summarized how knowledge is obtained:

It is not in the nature of things for any one man to make a sudden, violent discovery. Science goes step by step and every man depends on the work of his predecessors. Scientists are not dependent on the ideas of a single man, but on the combined wisdom of thousands of men.

In addition, the Nobel Prizes in the sciences foster extreme competitiveness among investigators, so they are not inclined to share their data or cooperate. Many workers have a Nobel Prize as their only goal. The net effect of these awards, therefore, is to decrease productivity by diminishing the free interchange of information. Anything that impedes cooperation and fosters competition should be discouraged. One of our bad attributes is that we are competitive and wish to excel over each other, even to the detriment of the final goal. We must not encourage this characteristic, but rather should work to minimize its effect.

The Nobel Peace Prize is perhaps a somewhat different consideration. The Peace Prize does not so overtly foster competition, and it provides valuable reinforcement of gains made in obtaining harmonious relations. It also serves to protect people who could otherwise be crushed by the oppressive forces they courageously battle. The same argument can be made for the literature prize, and indeed, the literature prize partially shielded recipients such as Aleksandr Solzhenitsyn (1918–) from political oppresion. In fact, a Nobel Prize in art or music may have benefited such giants as Dmitry Shostakovich (1906–1975), who lived much of his life under constant threat in the Stalinist Soviet Union. But in the sciences, where a cooperative effort and the sharing of information is essential to our progress, it is with regret that I strongly recommend that Nobel Prizes be abolished.

It had long been known that certain foods were required for health. The most famous example is the inclusion of citrus fruits on long navel voyages to prevent the disease we now call scurvy. In 1906, Frederick Hopkins (1861–1947) suggested that food contained substances required for health that were not in a known food group. He called these substances "accessory food factors." They are now called vitamins. The next twenty years confirmed this hypothesis and saw the characterization of many of these substances, a number of which are associated with a particular disease, if present in insufficient quantities (for example, vitamin C with scurvy, vitamin D with rickets, niacin with pellagra). Later work showed that vitamins have diverse functions in the body, but many of them are necessary for enzymes to work properly.

Karl Landsteiner (1868–1943), trained as a physician, began his research on proteins with the established technique of breaking them down into subunits, but soon became intrigued with the possibility of learning about intact protein molecules. Was there a way to do that? Landsteiner concluded that there was. Intact proteins could be studied by their interaction with cells and tissues. To that end, in 1900, he combined red blood cells from one person with the serum of another. (Serum is the liquid portion of blood obtained after the blood is allowed to clot; plasma is the unclotted liquid portion, and is very similar but not identical to serum.) He observed that sometimes there was no reaction, while on other occasions, the blood cells clumped together. By meticulous study, he concluded that two proteins may be on the surface of blood cells. The cells of a person may have one, both, or neither of these proteins, but all the cells from one person are the same. He called these proteins A and B, so that possible blood types are: A, B, AB, and O (meaning that neither protein is present). Landsteiner also found that a patient's serum contained antibodies to protein or proteins he did not possess. (For example, a person with type A blood has antibodies to the B protein, and a person with type O has antibodies to both the A and B proteins.)

Forty years later, Landsteiner, working with Alexander Wiener, found that a rabbit, after being injected with blood from a Rhesus monkey, developed antibodies not only to the monkey's red blood cells, but also to blood cells from 85% of humans. This was the Rh factor, named for the Rhesus monkey. Landsteiner demonstrated, at a remarkable forty-year interval, the two major red blood cell protein complexes. With this knowledge, blood transfusion went from a nearly uniform disaster to a life-saving procedure performed millions of times a year in the United States.

Some twenty years after the discovery of the Rh factor, it began to be understood that all cells, not just red blood cells, contain proteins important to the recognition of self and non-self. This work led to the elucidation of the major histocompatibility complex, a complicated series of proteins expressed by virtually all cells in the body, and which are critical in organ transplantations. Landsteiner's work not only made blood transfusions possible, but also laid the foundation for organ transplantation and much of our current knowledge of immunology.

A greater understanding of female sex hormones, and how they rise and fall with the menstrual cycle, led to the development of oral contraceptives. The story of hormonal contraception begins in 1937, when it was shown that injections of progesterone inhibited ovulation in laboratory animals. In 1950, Margaret Sanger (1883–1966), a leading proponent of birth control, persuaded Gregory Pincus (1903–1967) to investigate the possibility of oral contraceptives in the 1950s.

With Pincus playing a leading role, additional work showed that *oral* progesterone was also effective in suppressing ovulation in animals. Testing in humans revealed that oral progesterone was effective in inhibiting ovulation, but only in high doses, and with a 10–15% failure rate, making it impractical as a birth control measure. Pincus then recognized the potential of semi-synthetic steroid compounds structurally similar to progesterone. He found that a mixture of two such compounds, norethynodrel and mestranol, held great promise. This combination of hormones, marketed as Enovid, was tested in 1956 and released for general use in 1960.

Pincus further learned that the addition of a small amount of estrogen decreased side effects. The specific compounds used in oral contraceptive agents have changed over the years, and the drugs are now much safer, but the mechanism of oral contraception remains as pioneered by Pincus: high blood levels of progesterone-like hormones "fool" the body into believing it is pregnant, and nature does not permit what it believes to be a second pregnancy.

With our population increasing faster than our resources, overpopulation looms as a greater threat to humanity than even nuclear war, and birth control appears to be the single most important achievement to translate into worldwide reality. But will the potential of birth control be fully realized? Has it come too late in our history?

The use of better microscopes in the early twentieth century made it possible to discern individual parts of cells. The invention of the electron microscope markedly increased our knowledge of the interior of cells. The magnification that a microscope can achieve is inversely proportional to the wavelength of the radiation passing through the object to be examined. With illumination of very short wavelength (and high frequency), higher magnification is possible. With ordinary microscopes, using visible light, focusing is achieved by glass lenses and is easily accomplished, but the wavelength of the light places a magnification limit of about one thousand times. Higher magnification can be obtained with a source that has a wavelength shorter than that of light. X-rays and gamma rays have a shorter wavelength and would work very well, except that they cannot be focused by glass lenses. Ernst Ruska (1906–1988) and Max Knoll were aware of the wave properties of electrons as shown by de Broglie, and realized that an electron beam had a shorter wavelength than light. Although electrons cannot be focused by glass lenses, which they do not penetrate, it was shown in 1926 that they could be focused by a magnetic field. In 1932, Ruska and Knoll built the first electron microscope. Rheinhold Rudenburg had previously filed for a patent, but because he played the major role in the construction of the first electron microscope, Ruska is given principal credit. In 1986, more than fifty years after his achievement, Ruska was finally awarded the Nobel Prize. Today, electron microscopes achieve practical magnifications of some 500,000 times. Because the eye cannot see electrons, a visible image is obtained indirectly through either a photographic plate or a fluorescent screen that emits light when struck by electrons.

Better microscopes, and especially the electron microscope, made possible the visualization of tiny structures within cells. Because these structures were to the whole cell what organs were to the complete organism, they were called organelles. The nucleus, long known to microscopists, was seen to be only one of many organelles. The understanding of organelles and enzymes allowed the elucidation of some of the major biochemical pathways of the cell, among the most important of which are the chemical reactions that lead to energy production.

Biochemistry, the chemistry of biological compounds, benefited greatly from increased understanding of the nature of chemical reactions and became a triumph of science in the twentieth century. By the 1950s, advances in biochemistry demonstrated that cells derive energy from sugar through a sequence of chemical reactions, divided into three phases. The first phase, glycolysis, liberates only a small amount of energy, but can proceed in the absence of oxygen. The second and third phases require oxygen (which is not always available in conditions of extreme fatigue), but generate much more energy than glycolysis.

The second phase, elucidated by Hans Krebs (1900–1981), involves a series of reactions bearing his name. The third phase, called electron transport, involves the removal of electrons from compounds and the passage of these electrons to a number of intermediate compounds in a series of reactions that generate a substantial amount of energy. Much of our understanding of this portion of energy generation comes from the work of Peter Mitchell (1920–1992). The second and third phases take place in the mitochondria, the organelles that are the power stations of the cell. (There is substantial feeling that mitochondria were once free-living bacteria that became incorporated into the larger cells of more advanced organisms.)

One other advance in the biochemistry of life must be mentioned. All animal life, including humans, ultimately depends on plants for food, and plants derive their sugars, the final food of life, from sunlight and atmospheric carbon dioxide in the process of photosynthesis. Photosynthesis also generates oxygen, which all animals require to break down food. Melvin Calvin (1911–1997), using radioactive carbon (which could be traced as it moved through sequential chemical reactions), elucidated the biochemical pathway from carbon dioxide and water to oxygen and carbohydrates.

The indomitable spirit of humanity marches on in the battle to conquer disease and understand who we are at the molecular level. There has been much progress, but it has been patchy, and even the most brilliant innovations, when seen in a broader perspective, have been incomplete. Of all the diseases that afflict humanity, only one has been completely defeated and permanently eradicated: smallpox. To my mind, the challenge of medicine at this time, and the challenge of scientific endeavors in general, is to continue the wonderful tradition of analytic thinking while being more open to new viewpoints and avoiding the Western trap of thinking in absolutes.

Chapter 29
The Wings of Humanity

*Two brothers, neither of whom finished high school,
achieve a dream that had eluded the finest minds for
centuries.*

PROBABLY NOTHING IN HISTORY has so consistently captured our imaginations as
flight. Among the centuries of speculation and fantasy, perhaps the drawings of
da Vinci are best known. One of his drawings involved an ornithopter design
(where wings are flapped in imitation of a bird). Despite da Vinci's wonderful
knowledge of anatomy, he had no way of knowing that the human musculature
could never fly such a device. Da Vinci had more interesting designs involving
fixed winged gliders and power derived from a tightly wound string. In all probability, none would have flown, but his designs are the equal of those several
centuries later.

The story of flight involves two sets of brothers, and begins in 1783. In
that year, Joseph and Etienne Montgolfier made the first human flight in a
hot air balloon, just ten days before the physicist Jacques Charles ascended in
a hydrogen balloon.

Dirigible is a general word referring to power-driven, steerable balloons. Initially, dirigibles were constructed around nonrigid balloons, but the work of
Ferdinand von Zeppelin (1838–1917) led to the perfection of dirigibles based
on rigid design, which were much more steerable. These were called Zeppelins.
Today, dirigibles based on nonrigid designs are colloquially called blimps. (These
are inflated with helium to a pressure slightly exceeding atmospheric pressure
so as to provide for a degree of rigidity.)

George Cayley (1773–1857) was one of the first to realize that practical air
transportation was possible, and that it would require craft heavier than air.
Cayley was the first to think of flight in a scientifically rigorous manner, and
among the first to make a serious study of the wings and flight of birds. He was

306

the first to conduct meaningful experiments with gliders. A model glider he constructed in 1804 was a landmark achievement in heavier-than-air craft. Nearly half a century later, in 1849, he built the first glider to carry a person. Astonishingly prescient in his predictions, he conceived of an airplane in nearly its contemporary form, with a fuselage, fixed wings, and a tail. Cayley was the first to realize that separate systems would be needed for lift, propulsion, and steering. His influence on a generation of imaginative and daring experimenters was incalculable. Wilbur Wright said of Cayley in 1909:

> He carried the science of flying to a point which it had never reached before and which it scarcely reached again during the last century.

Unfortunately, after Cayley's pioneering work, the study of flight lacked the rigorous, methodical approach so characteristic of his work. Some investigators worked with gliders, while others constructed miniature aircraft, hoping to extrapolate the design to full-sized vessels. Still others went immediately to large, powered vehicles, but gave insufficient thought to design and control considerations.

Three of these early, full-sized, powered craft deserve mention. In 1890, Clement Ader (1841–1925) flew a 600-pound (270 kg) steam-powered craft some eight inches (twenty centimeters) off the ground. Ader never established control of his craft and never claimed to have made the first heavier-than-air flight. It does appear, however, that his craft, the *Eole*, was indeed the first large, heavier-than-air craft to defeat gravity, however slightly. In 1894, Hiram Stevens Maxim (1840–1916) placed a steam-powered biplane, weighing no less than three and a half tons (3,180 kg), on guardrails (necessary because there was no other means of controlling the craft). The giant biplane lifted slightly, broke the guardrails, and crashed. As for the *Eole*, it had only minimal lift and no control. In 1896, Samuel Pierpont Langley (1834–1906), the secretary of the Smithsonian Institute, successfully flew steam-powered, unmanned, miniature airplanes up to 4,200 feet (1,280 meters). Encouraged by his success and funded by the United States government, Langley became the first to try a gasoline engine in an aircraft. A test flight with a miniature model was successful, but in October, 1903, a flight with a full-sized, manned version failed, and Langley's pilot had to be fished out of the Potomac River. It would be gliders that would light the pathway to success.

Otto Lilienthal (1848–1896) began his experiments in gliding with an ornithopter design. However, Lilienthal shortly realized that the differences between the musculature of a bird's wing and a person's arm made a strict ornithopter design unworkable. His observation of birds confirmed what others (including Cayley) had suspected: a wing should be arched upward. In his own words:

> Recapitulating, we must, in the first instance, consider the proper wing curvature as the means of making sailing flight possible. Only those wings, the cross-section of which shows a suitable camber (curvature), produce such a favorable direction of the air pressure as to avoid any appreciable restraining component.

Lilienthal contributed the most complete body of data on aerodynamics to that time. Although this data was not perfect, it was a starting point for all aeronautical researchers, including the Wright brothers. Like so many early investigators, Lilienthal had difficulty in controlling his craft. His sole method of control was through shifting his weight. The inadequacy of the method was made horribly clear in August of 1896, when he was killed in a crash. On his tombstone is his prophetic statement: "Sacrifices must be made."

Others continued Lilienthal's work, most notably Octave Chanute (1832–1910). Chanute built gliders of increasing sophistication and took photographs of his gliders in the air, so that he could objectively assess any modifications. He corresponded with virtually everyone involved in aviation, including the second set of brothers in our story of flight—two of the five children of Milton Wright, Bishop of the Church of the United Brethren of Christ.

Wilbur (1867–1912) and Orville (1871–1948) Wright were most influenced by Cayley, Lilienthal, and Chanute. The success of the Wright brothers did not come from a single, breakthrough idea. Rather, they had to work through difficulties at every step. From the beginning, they saw that flight entailed three different but interrelated problems: lift, propulsion, and control. They further understood that control had to be achieved in three dimensions. By breaking the problem down into component parts, and not progressing to the next stage until they were thoroughly satisfied with the previous stage, the Wright brothers present a study in how to address a difficult problem. As the longest journey must be undertaken one step at a time, so the most difficult problem must be broken into smaller problems. To my mind, this is the essence of the creative process, and it is illustrated to perfection in the work of the Wrights. Their skillful breaking-down of the problem into component parts and their methodical, step-by-step approach, with constant re-examination of what was already known, allowed these two people—neither of whom finished high school—to change the world after only a few years of effort.

They began with biplaned kites and progressed to biplaned gliders, using Lilienthal's data and designs. But their glider experience convinced them that they needed to make a fresh start, with their own designs. The first indication of the genius of the brothers from Dayton was their quick understanding that they had to rely on their own data and designs.

They made numerous modifications in kite and glider construction. In 1899, they devised a mechanism whereby a portion of the wings could be twisted slightly, creating unequal lift on one side of the craft. Because the resulting roll results in a small net force pushing to the side in the direction of the lower wing, this wing warping permitted turning, allowing a method of control *that did not depend on shifting of the pilot's weight.*

In line with the general thinking of the time, the Wrights employed wings with a curved upper surface, but they moved the thickest portion of the curve from the center of the wing to the front. They added a horizontal rudder in front of the wings to keep the wings at a constant angle relative to the air coursing over them. In 1902, they began using miniature models of their gliders in a wind tunnel of their own construction. (The Wrights were not the first to build a wind tunnel, but they were the first to use such a tunnel to constructively answer specific questions.) From the data obtained from their wind tunnel experiments, they tested a variety of wing shapes and verified the wisdom of placing the thickest part of the curve forward of center. While they did not change the basic equations of flight, they were able to use their wind tunnel data to improve on a constant found in flight equations, thus permitting them to obtain better lift. Also in 1902, they added a vertical rudder, which provided additional steering assistance, to the rear of the craft.

With the improvement in their 1902 glider, the brothers had largely solved the problem of control. Indeed, the 1902 glider was the first craft to be essentially fully controllable in the air. We think of December, 1903 as the turning point in the history of flight, but, as for all leaps of progress, the "turning point" was actually a series of small steps. None of these steps was larger than the achievement of control in 1902.

The brothers next turned their attention to propulsion. In typical Wright fashion, they immediately saw that the problem of propulsion was not a single problem, but three related problems: there would have to be an engine, a propeller, and a linkage to convey power from the engine to the propeller. Unable to procure a commercial gasoline engine to give them the power-to-weight ratio they needed, they (and their mechanic, Charlie Taylor) built their own. Although this engine should not be regarded as inherently superior to other internal combustion engines of the time, its construction testifies to the Wrights' ingenuity and perseverance.

Using their experience in bicycle repair, they learned how to use a chain to carry power from the engine to the propeller. In the design of the propeller the brothers' cleverness again became manifest, and it—not the engine—was the crux of their propulsion system. At the time, there was little usable literature on propeller design. The marine propeller was the widely held model, but Wilbur and Orville devised another, more appropriate model. Like a wing, a propeller is a curved surface in relative motion with regard to ambient air. Why not treat the propeller as a rotating wing? Using this model, and the data from their wind tunnel, they designed a propeller unlike any before. It is testament to the brothers' thoroughness that the basic ideas behind their designs of the wings, the rudder, and the propeller are not much different from those today.

On December 14, 1903, Wilbur Wright won a coin toss with his brother and became the first person to unequivocally fly a heavier-than-air craft. However, the flight was for only sixty feet (eighteen meters) and control was poor. It actually crashed, and three days were required to effect minor repairs. So history remembers December 17, 1903, when Orville made the world's first sustained and controlled heavier-than-air flight. By the end of the day, both brothers had made sustained and controlled flights, and humanity turned a new page in the book of our history.

The Wright brothers arrived at the shape of their wing empirically, based largely on Lilienthal's experience and their own data. Until the scientific theory of wing design was worked out, there was little chance for significant improvement in performance. Even a perfectly flat wing will generate some lift if attached to the airplane at such an angle that the air strikes it obliquely. Needed was a wing that maximizes lift by having an optimally curved upper surface, so that the pressure of the air on the upper surface is less than the air on the lower surface.

A number of physicists and mathematicians contributed to the new science of airplane design, chief of whom was Ludwig Prandtl (1875–1953), thought of as the father of fluid mechanics. Among many contributions, Prandtl conceived the concept of a boundary layer, wherein the fluid immediately adjacent to a moving body is essentially attached to the body and serves to retard the motion of the rest of the fluid. With Frederick Lanchester (1868–1946), Prandtl developed the first accurate theory of lift in 1908, when their analysis showed a vortex of air at the leading edge of the inclined, curved surface of the wing. This vortex pushed the air on the top of the wing over the surface at a greater speed than that passing under the wing. By Daniel Bernoulli's equations of fluid motion, this caused the air on the upper surface of the wing to have a lower pressure than that on the bottom, creating lift. One of Prandtl's students, Theodore von Karman (1881–1963) extended this work and would go on to lay much of the theoretical groundwork for supersonic flight.

It was not until 1906 that anyone other than the Wright brothers flew, but after that, aviation quickly became a commercial and international venture. The two major improvements in design were the introduction of the pulling propeller in the front of the plane (the Wrights used a pushing propeller at the back of the wing), and the monoplane, which employed only one set of wings. A number of people, including Prandtl, had recognized that biplanes and triplanes had an inherent problem: the upper surface of one wing was also the lower surface of the higher wing, creating competing air currents between the wings. One of the first to successfully employ these new designs was Louis Bleriot (1872–1936), who made the first flight across the English Channel in 1909.

The airplane would receive its next great transformation from the application of the turbine engine. A turbine converts the motion of a fluid (liquid or gas) into mechanical energy by undergoing rotary motion. In the steam turbine, pressurized steam strikes blades on a shaft, causing the shaft to rotate. In the early 1930s, Frank Whittle (1907–1996) and Hans von Ohain (1911–1998) independently developed a jet engine for aircraft by using a gas turbine engine. This was the turbojet engine, which follows the principle of the steam turbine but is somewhat more complex. Air entering the engine is compressed by a compressor, after which it enters the combustion chamber, where it is mixed with fuel and burned. The exhaust gas, still compressed, does two things. First, it powers the turbine, which runs the compressor. Second, as the burned gas is exhausted through special nozzles, the sudden decompression provides forward thrust, in accordance with Newton's third law of motion. (For every action, there is an equal and opposite reaction.) In this type of engine, all of the thrust is provided by the escaping exhaust gas. Both the British and the Germans flew military jets in World War II, but they came late in the conflict and did not affect its outcome.

In the turboprop engine, developed after the turbojet, the design is basically similar, except that the compressed exhaust gases drive additional stages of the turbine or a second turbine, which drives a propeller. Propulsion is provided predominantly by the propeller, but also somewhat by the decompressing gases, as in the turbojet.

The turbofan engine was developed in the early 1950s, principally by Rolls-Royce. The turbofan engine, like the turboprop, is also a hybrid of propeller and true jet (i.e., turbojet) technology. In the turbofan engine, a fan consisting of dozens of blades and powered by a turbine, covers the air intake area. A minority of the air taken in actually enters the engine, where it is compressed, burned, and exhausted, as in the turbojet. This minority, called the primary (or core) stream, provides much of the thrust and drives the turbine powering the fan and the compressor. This primary stream resembles a turbojet engine. Most of the air taken in by a turbofan engine is compressed by the fans (to a lesser extent than the air in the primary stream) and then passes around, not through, the engine. The air compressed by the fans cools the engine as it passes over it, then provides additional thrust as it decompresses and exits at the rear of the engine. This secondary (or fan) stream may provide more thrust than the primary stream.

Today, the turbojet is used primarily for high-speed military craft. Most commercial airliners use the turbofan engine, while the turboprop is used for smaller commercial and some military planes. The piston-driven propeller plane is still used for some small, private airplanes.

So it is that the imagination of da Vinci, the prescience of Cayley, the courage of Lilienthal, the persistence of the Wrights, and the labors of the unknown combined to give wings to humanity.

Chapter 30
A New Way of Writing

*New ways of storing and disseminating information
may bring us another Renaissance.*

A FEW ACHIEVEMENTS IN OUR HISTORY so clearly demonstrate the progression of our civilization that a study of them is a study of who we are. Some examples of these seminal advances include writing, the clock, paper and printing, the steam engine, nuclear power, radio, the airplane, and antibiotics.

Another such example is the computer. The computer is analogous to the clock in that it is pivotal to our development and involves many different technologies from divergent areas of science and technology. As Western civilization in the fourteenth century saw the advent of mechanical clocks, so the twentieth century has seen the rise of the computer.

The history of the computer really starts with the abacus, an ingenious instrument known to many ancient civilizations but not introduced to Europe until about the year 1000. In one of its forms, the abacus consisted of parallel rows of wires. The beads on the lowest wire all had a value of one, with beads on each successive wire having a value ten times that of the beads on the lower wire. A number was denoted by moving beads from one side to the other. Using this system of place value, all arithmetic operations could be carried out. Other forms were slightly more complex, starting with beads on both the left and right sides rather than just one side. In this abacus, numbers were denoted by moving beads to the center of the wire. The value of a given bead depended on which wire it was on as well as from which side it was moved.

The next step takes us to the year 1642, when Blaise Pascal (1623–1662) developed a machine based on a series of wheels, each of which had ten teeth, to represent the ten digits. This machine could add and subtract. Gottfried Leibniz (1646–1716) used a similar design to construct a machine that would conduct all four arithmetic operations. Like Pascal's machine, it saw little practical use because the operator still had to perform all of the steps of the calculation.

Charles Babbage (1792–1871) designed two extraordinary mechanical calculators. The first of these, called the difference engine, was designed in 1812. It differed from the machines of Pascal and Leibniz in being automatic, so an operator was not required to personally perform every step. A prototype of a difference engine was constructed in 1823, but Babbage lost interest in the project because he had conceived its successor, the analytical engine. Fully automatic, the analytical engine was steam-powered and could print its results. The design called for a mill, where arithmetic calculations would be carried out, and a store, where intermediate numbers would be kept until processed further. These foreshadowed our contemporary central processing unit and random access memory. Babbage conceived the idea of storing instructions to the machine in the form of perforated cards, analogous to our contemporary operating system (the portion of the programming that tells the computer what to do). His design even allowed for a changeable sequence of instruction execution, presaging the programming statements that would follow more than a century later.

The analytical engine was one of the most ingenious designs ever, but it was never built, in part because the technology of the time could not machine the parts accurately enough, and perhaps in part because Babbage was more skilled in theorizing than in following his designs through to completion. Although his work did not lead to any significant practical application in his lifetime, his conception of how a computer should be designed would prove to be profoundly prescient.

The development of the computer would have to wait until the development of electronics, which was the product of many disciplines. Indeed, it has always been true that after a great idea—itself the work of many and of indistinct origins—is promulgated, further development depends on interlocking technologies of many fields. If even the greatest ideas had not been subsequently enlarged and extended, by many people, using the tools of many disciplines, they would rarely have proven useful.

The history of the electronic computer does not actually begin with electronics, but with a form of algebraic logic from the nineteenth century. George Boole (1815–1864) was born poor in early nineteenth-century England. Customarily, his education would have been limited to a few years at a "charity school." Although his talent permitted him access to more formal education, he remained largely self-taught, never forgot his roots, and was active in movements to better the lot of the poor.

Boole made many mathematical contributions; the one that concerns us now is the full elaboration and development of the idea that mathematics is a form of thought dealing with the relationships between objects or groups of objects. Called mathematical logic, it made the concepts and objects of everyday life accessible to mathematical treatment. Boole was able to take the definitions of ideas such as wealth and pleasure and express them mathematically. He found a mathematical expression for such statements as "All good people read books, and all bad people do not" and "I will go to the store if it does not rain." In the algebraic system based on Boole's mathematical logic, called Boolean algebra, any logical proposition, even if it is not numeric, is reduced to symbols and made amenable to mathematical manipulation.

This forms the heart of the logical system of computers, and it is the mechanism by which the electronic computer can work with non-numeric statements. Boolean algebra is a bridge from the ideas of our conversational and written language to the electronic circuits and binary operation of the computer. By the late 1930s, the applicability of Boole's works to electric circuits was realized, and the computer could begin to develop.

About 1940, Howard Aiken (1900–1973) developed the first fully automatic computer, the Harvard Mark I. The Mark I, originally named the Automatic Sequence Controlled Calculator, was an electromechanical computer, which relied partially on moving parts. In addition, it did not use vacuum tubes, but rather employed relays, wherein current flowing in one circuit opened or closed switches to other circuits. The instruction sequence was provided by punched paper, thereby preventing any variation. About the same time, Konrad Zuse (1910–1995) also constructed computers based on a combination of electrical and mechanical parts.

The physical aspects of the electronic computer began with vacuum tubes (called valves in the U.K.), developed by John Fleming and Lee de Forest, and first used as radio detectors. In 1942, John Atanasoff (1903–1997) and his student and assistant, Clifford Berry, built the Atanasoff-Berry Computer (called the ABC). The major advance of this instrument was that it was fully electronic, using vacuum tubes and no mechanical parts. It also stored data in a new way. Every number can be written in binary form, using only zeros and ones (simply expressing a number in a base two). Because a capacitor can exist

315

in two states, charged and uncharged, it was an ideal component to store binary information. This system of storing data as binary numbers in charged or uncharged capacitors is still used today. The ABC is generally regarded as the first true electronic computer, functioning slightly before the British Colossus (see below). Like the Harvard Mark I, the ABC was not programmable. It should be noted that, in a supreme example of shortsightedness, the United States government drafted both Atanasoff and Berry for the war, cutting short the development of their electronic computer. Despite the fate of Atanasoff and Berry, the second World War had a strong stimulatory effect on computer development, and it was in that war that the computer would have its first impact on human events.

Germany encrypted its military messages during the war in a code called Enigma, and later in another code which the British called Fish. The British cracked both codes, but it took them so long to decipher a German message that it was often too late to act on the information. An automated approach was essential if the message was to be decoded in time. In 1936, Alan Turing (1912-1954) wrote a paper entitled *On Computable Numbers*, which foresaw the principles of operation of the contemporary computer. World War II gave Turing an opportunity to put his theories to work. He developed a simple machine to decipher the Enigma code, and his ideas later became the basis for Colossus, a computer with 1500 vacuum tubes that began functioning in late 1943, slightly after the ABC. By permitting the Allies to have practical access to German communications, Colossus critically shortened the war and became the first computer to significantly affect human events. It was more influential in the war than the development of the atomic bomb. It was Turing's theoretical work which proved that digital computers could be made practical and effective.

The United States also recognized the utility of computers in warfare. In 1942, it commissioned the University of Pennsylvania to create a computer to calculate trajectory tables for weapons, so soldiers could aim effectively. J. Presper Eckert (1919–1995) and John Mauchly (1907–1980) began to design an electronic computer that would be called ENIAC, for Electronic Numerical Integrator and Calculator. When completed in 1945 (too late to help the war effort), ENIAC was larger, more powerful, and more versatile than Colossus. It was composed of 18,000 vacuum tubes, consumed almost two thousand square feet (almost 170 square meters) of floor space, and used tens of thousands of watts of power. Although data were inputted with punched cards, the instructions for what to do with that data were in the form of a fixed, hard wire arrangement, which meant that ENIAC could be re-programmed only with great difficulty, since it involved actual rewiring. ENIAC stored numbers in a decimal notation, unlike the more efficient binary notation of the ABC.

Then, onto the computer scene came the towering figure of the mathematician John von Neumann (1903–1957). In 1945, von Neumann introduced a new design for computers, a few key aspects of which will be mentioned. Today, we use the word "hardware" to refer to the electronics and electrical circuits of the computer, and the word "software" to designate the programming, of which the operating system (the instructions to the computer) is a part. Von Neumann's design represented significant improvements in the software. First, his design stored all instructions in random access memory (the same place data is stored), rather than as fixed wiring. Thus, instructions could be modified (i.e., the programming changed) while still in memory, without re-wiring the computer. This is the stored program design, which remains basic for contemporary computers. Second, von Neumann believed that the sequence of instructions to the computer should be interruptible at any point, and that it should be possible to return to the sequence precisely at the point of interruption. This introduced a greater degree of flexibility than had been possible and allowed the computer to execute different sets of instructions depending on interim results of its calculations, and then to return to the main instruction set. Think of a book in which the reader can skip to another section and then return to the original place, versus having to read the text in sequence. Third, von Neumann recognized that most programs contain discrete, repeating sets of instructions. He reasoned that it should be possible to separate these sets of instructions in the computer's memory, permitting them to be loaded faster when needed. This is the concept of subroutines, which remains a central feature of today's programming.

In 1947, the first computer to take advantage of the von Neumann design was constructed—the EDVAC, for Electronic Discrete Variable Computer. As powerful as ENIAC, EDVAC had only 2,500 vacuum tubes and was much smaller. Computers based on the von Neumann design are considered the first-generation computers. In 1951, the von Neumann design became available commercially as Univac, the Universal Automatic Computer.

Magnetic core memory, which replaced previous methods based on mercury, cathode ray tubes, or magnetic tape, was perfected by Jay Forrester (1918–) about the same time as the von Neumann design. In magnetic core memory, drums or disks are coated with minute particles of a material that becomes magnetic if exposed to magnetism (such as iron). A head, consisting of a coil of wires wrapped around an iron core, is placed adjacent to the magnetic material, and electricity is passed through the coils, causing the iron core of the head to become an electromagnet. The magnetic field of the head makes the particles on the disk magnetic and aligns them in an orientation corresponding to the current that passed through the coil. The stored data is read by placing the head next to the particles without passing a current through the coil. The particles on the disk, now magnetized, form a magnetic field. As the disk rotates under the head, the head experiences a changing magnetic field. As Faraday and Henry showed, a changing magnetic field will induce a current. The disk and head become a minute generator, and an electrical current reflective of the orientation of the particles on the disk is generated in the wires of the coil on the head.

The stored program design of von Neumann and magnetic core memory brought computers to new heights, but because these instruments were based on vacuum tubes, reliability was a problem. Readers old enough to remember vacuum tubes in electronic devices can readily understand the difficulty in keeping thousands of vacuum tubes simultaneously functional.

As the vacuum tube made possible electronic computers, so the transistor made possible computers as we now know them. Vacuum tubes had replaced crystals as electronic components, but in the 1940s, Bell Laboratories returned to crystals to study the flow of electricity through them. William Shockley (1910–1989), John Bardeen (1908–1991) and Walter Brattain (1902–1987) found that impure crystals were better conductors of electricity. Following this idea, they developed the transistor. In a transistor, minute amounts of an impurity are introduced into a base material that is a pure element (usually silicon, sometimes germanium). The impurity has either one more or one less electron than the base material. Therefore, there is an excess or surplus of electrons relative to the silicon or germanium. An impurity that has one more electron is called a donor, and the bonding of it and the base material leaves one electron free to move in the crystalline lattice. This junction is called an "n" junction—the "n" denoting the negativity that results from a free electron. An impurity with one fewer electron than the base material is called an acceptor, and the bonding of it and the base material results in an electron-deficient area called a "hole." This hole causes the flow of current, because the electrons move toward the hole; as they do so, other holes occur where the moving electrons used to be, creating a continuous electron motion as they react to a localized relative deficiency of charge. This hole, in effect, is a relative positive charge, so these junctions are called "p" type. "N" and "p" junctions are usually combined on the same crystal, so that the excess electrons at the "n" junction move toward the electron deficient area at the "p" junction. This gives the transistor the capacity to carry electricity and amplify a current.

Transistors were more efficient, smaller, emitted less heat, and were much more reliable than vacuum tubes. They completely replaced vacuum tubes and revolutionized all of electronics, not just the computer. The introduction of transistors in computer design inaugurated the so-called second generation of computers.

The next stage of computer development, sometimes called the third generation, began in the mid-1960s with the conception of the integrated circuit. Commonly called a chip, the integrated circuit technology followed directly from the transistor. An integrated circuit is a collection of electronic components on a small wafer of silicon (usually a single crystal) to which impurities have been added. The construction of an integrated circuit may take some two hundred steps and require upwards of sixty days under exquisitely controlled conditions. The precise process of fabricating integrated circuits varies with the purpose for which they will be used, and there is no single method of constructing them. To illustrate: a silicon wafer is made by dipping a small silicon particle into molten silicon to which impurities have been added. When the particle—now coated with molten silicon—dries, it forms a single large crystal, from which many crystals are cut. Initially, the circuit design is drawn on a series of transparencies, which are then photographically reduced to actual size. The silicon crystal is then coated with a photographic emulsion, covered with the transparency of the circuit, and exposed to ultraviolet light. The emulsion not covered by the lines of the circuit drawing is exposed to the light, polymerizes, and becomes hard. The portion of the emulsion directly underneath a part of the circuit drawing is not exposed to the light and does not polymerize. Subsequently, acid is applied. This acid will not etch the polymerized emulsion, but in the areas where the emulsion has not polymerized (i.e., in areas where the lines of the drawing of the circuit protected the emulsion from the light), the acid will etch away the emulsion and into the silicon crystal. In this manner, the design of the circuit on the photoreduced transparency is etched into the silicon crystal. Usually, only a portion of the design can be transferred at one time, so the complete circuit is built a layer at a time on the silicon substrate, by a sequential process of coatings, exposure to light, and etching. It is possible to construct a circuit of a million or more transistors, along with all accompanying resistors, inductors, etc. on an integrated circuit about the size of the palm of a hand.

Advances in integrated circuit design led to what is often called the fourth generation of computers, beginning about 1970. These improved integrated circuits have made possible the dramatic miniaturization of computers so familiar to us as desktop and laptop microcomputers. Because of the integrated circuit, a four pound (two kg) laptop computer is more powerful than ENIAC, which used 18,000 vacuum tubes and required almost 170 square meters of floor space. The microcomputer revolution has placed undreamed of computing power into the hands of the masses and transformed not just industry, but also our personal lives.

Many types of computer programs are useful in the personal lives of individuals. One of the more common types are word processors, where letters, words, sentences, paragraphs, and pages can be deleted, inserted, or moved, making the construction of a document immeasurably easier. Databases allow data previously entered to be recalled by any portion. For example, in a database of names, addresses, and phone numbers, a complete entry can be recalled even if only the first name or the phone number is remembered. Spreadsheets are programs used in financial planning. As an example, assets are listed in one column and liabilities in another. The program automatically calculates profit or loss, and will automatically recalculate profits if any of the component entries changes. Spreadsheets offer the financial planner the opportunity to try different scenarios, to ask a number of "what if" questions.

Another exciting area in contemporary computers is multimedia, the storage of words, numbers, sounds, and pictures (often animated) in a manner permitting all cognitive and sensual experiences of a subject to be brought together. An example would be a biography of a composer where the text is supplemented with the presentation of his music through the computer's speakers and animated pictures of the composer on the monitor. In addition to the usual hardware and software, special software is needed to coordinate the different forms of data, and an optical storage device (CD-ROM) is required because traditional magnetic storage mechanisms (e.g., a hard drive) do not contain sufficient memory.

We must ponder again, as we did for the steam engine, who is responsible for the wonderful achievement of the computer? Charles Babbage, who designed the analytical engine? John Fleming, who made the first vacuum tube? Howard Aiken, who made the first reliable instrument we would recognize as a computer? John Atanasoff, the driving force behind the first electronic computer? Alan Turing, who headed the team that made the first electronic computer to impact human events? John von Neumann, whose design we still use? Shockley, Bardeen, and Brattain, the discoverers of the transistor, the basis for the integrated circuitry underlying all of our electronics? What about the team members of these well-known scientists, whose names and contributions we will never know? Nowhere are the indistinct beginnings of great ideas more evident than in the development of the computer. In the history of the computer, we see again that behind every great idea lie innumerable anonymous people, both in the inception of the idea, and in its subsequent elaboration and development. Every achievement of our history is more the collective work of all of us than the work of a small number of inherently superior people. Civilization and history are bigger than individuals.

Great ideas arise from the simplest of concepts. These concepts, and their elaboration, are the collective possessions of humanity. The computer was a coming together of many people from many disciplines over multiple generations. Its development provides an encapsulated view of the collective human mind at work. Computers, as much as any other accomplishment, illustrate how we progress, and how we think. And therefore, who we are.

Continued improvements in electronics and software have placed us in the fifth generation of computers, now ongoing. Current frontiers in computing include networking, online access of libraries, and artificial intelligence. Networking is the pooling of multiple computers, making the resources of any of the component computers available to all computers on the network, and it has the effect of creating a single giant computer. These networks can then be connected, the theoretical result being the consolidation of all computers in the world into one enormous information system. The Internet, a loose association of networks, is a significant and exciting first step to just such a worldwide system. Still in its infancy, the Internet holds the potential of connecting every computer in the world to every other. It is this type of networking that would form the basis for the national information superhighway.

Networking, combined with the writing of all books in electronic format and the transformation of existing books into that format, would make it possible to access libraries from computers, so that we could sit at home and retrieve the complete contents of any book in any library in the world. All of the world's libraries would become available to anyone with a computer.

Books are the bricks of our civilization. The re-awakening of Western Europe after exposure to the writings of antiquity attests to the ability of books to advance our culture centuries after they are written. Once the contents of a book are digitized into electronic format, it need never go out of print or be lost. The cumulative wisdom of every culture and every age will be as close as a computer. The educational advantages to the populace would be beyond imagination.

Artificial intelligence refers to a combination of hardware and software that allows a computer to function more like the human brain. The essence of artificial intelligence is the creation of software that can learn from experience. Advances in software of this type are integral to the ongoing fifth generation of computers. Several avenues of artificial intelligence are being explored. First, progress is being made in permitting a computer to respond directly to the human voice, without requiring input from a keyboard or mouse. Second, configurations called expert systems allow complicated collections of interim results to cause changes in a computer's actions. Some degree of flexibility has been possible since the von Neumann design, but expert systems allow more sophisticated versions of this. For example, if both conditions x and y are true, and neither a nor b is true, then instruction set z is performed. This more advanced "if-then" programming more closely approximates the decision-making process of the human brain. A third area of artificial intelligence is a neural network, in which there are multiple inputs to a portion of a computer network, but only one output. This simulates the human brain cell, which receives synaptic input from hundreds or thousands of other neurons, the cumulative effect of which has only two possible outcomes: the cell does or does not become activated. Neural networks have the potential to modify their output based on experience, and therefore are capable of rudimentary learning.

Longer-term frontiers in computing include the fabrication of chips from materials others than silicon (possible examples include diamonds and gallium arsenide), molecular electronic devices (where shape changes in individual molecules might be used to store data), nanotechnology (the creation of computerized instruments whose size approaches that of molecules), optical computing (where pulses of light, rather than moving electrons, carry information), and superconductivity (whereby the electrons moving in a computer would face no resistance).

Another interesting application of the computer would be to provide a pure, or direct, democracy. Since the invention of democracy in ancient Greece, the size of populations has made it impractical for all citizens to vote on every issue. Hence, most democratic nations have a representational democracy, whereby elected representatives vote on the issues. With the exception of occasional referendums, the only time the entire populace votes is in the election of these representatives. An inevitable degree of distortion and corruption is inherent in a representational system, as the representatives understandably modify their votes to enhance their chances for re-election. Moreover, as inertia and apathy provide representatives with essential tenure, a representational democracy is likely to become an oligarchy in disguise. Once all people have ready access to a computer, it will become eminently practical for all people to vote on all major issues, with immediate tabulation of the results. It will be possible for us to use the computer to gather information on issues, and then use it to cast a vote in our homes. We will then have direct government by the people themselves. One of the central tenets of this work is that we are all substantially equal. By decreasing decisions made by representatives and increasing those made directly by the people, computers can move our government closer to an accurate reflection of our equality.

The computer provides us with the potential to unlock our creativity by providing freedom from the daily tasks of drudgery that are so much a part of our lives. At the present time, only a small fraction of people reach their full potential; the vast majority spend most of their time in repetitive tasks, both at home and at work. The more of these prosaic tasks in our lives and in the workplace that are automated, the freer we will all be to use our minds to their fullest extent. The full harnessing of the creativity inherent and hidden in each of us is contingent upon release from the menial travails of our world. As Isaac Asimov and Frank White state in *The March of the Millennia*: "What we call creativity today may turn out to be the common property of humanity once the conditions of life are suitably changed."

The computer is the focal point of a technological revolution that we are currently undergoing, and which history will associate with our times. The computer's ultimate contribution to our civilization is providing us with a new way of writing. To a great extent, the computer and electronic storage media replace paper—our intellectual fuel in the West for a thousand years, and in the East, for almost two thousand. What effect will this have on us? It bears noting that periods of intellectual progress have often been preceded by or associated with the development or improvement of writing. Civilization in the Old World occurred concurrently with the development of writing in the late fourth millennium B.C.E. The Greeks received papyrus from the Ionian colonies shortly before the sixth-century-B.C.E. miracle. The invention of paper in the second century C.E. was associated with a rapid advance in Chinese culture, and its spread to the West in the late Middle Ages facilitated learning there. The printing press greatly enhanced the spread of knowledge in the Renaissance. In each of these cases, the new method of writing did not by itself cause the explosion of knowledge. But in all five cases, a new method of storing and conveying information took already favorable social conditions and greatly facilitated their effect on learning. We may have, in the computer, a method of disseminating knowledge that perhaps will have an effect on our history matching that of early writing, the media of papyrus and paper, and the printing press. And the rapid progress of recent years certainly leaves no doubt that the present culture of industrialized countries permits new learning. For all of the troubles of our times, these are years of great and exciting change. To my mind, we now live in a time that has as much potential and excitement as the Renaissance. Perhaps history will show that the computer magnified and extended the promise of our time, and that the Silicon Revolution matched the importance of the Industrial Revolution.

Chapter 31
One Giant Leap for Mankind

*Humanity, whose ancestors made the footprints three
million years ago, reaches into the cosmos.*

A ROCKET IS DEFINED AS A SELF-PROPELLED VEHICLE USING AN ENGINE similar to a jet
engine, but carrying its own fuel and oxidant (the material that combines with
the fuel to enable combustion). This is in contrast to a jet, which carries its own
fuel, but relies on atmospheric oxygen to burn the fuel. A rocket engine works
in a vacuum, while a jet engine does not.

The earliest known rockets are those of thirteenth-century China, which
used gunpowder. The history of the rocket was technologically "frozen" at this
early stage for some five hundred years. William Congreve (1772–1828) made
the first significant improvements in rocket design in half a millennium, in part
by improving gunpowder composition and standardizing construction.
Congreve's rockets were used against Napoleon at Waterloo, and rockets of his
design besieged Fort McHenry in the war of 1812, memorialized in the American national anthem as "the rockets' red glare." In 1844, William Hale added
spin stabilization to Congreve's design. By the second half of the nineteenth
century, the increasing accuracy of artillery led to a reduction in the use of
rockets in warfare.

The early twentieth century saw three great rocket pioneers, people of out-
standing insight and prescience. The first of these, Konstantin Tsiolkovsky (1857–
1935), was a high school mathematics teacher in a small town in Czarist Russia.
Deaf from the age of nine (supposedly from scarlet fever), Tsiolkovsky became
an enthusiastic reader of Jules Verne. His imagination picked up where the
French writer's left off, and Tsiolkovsky was the first person to scientifically
study the problems of rocket travel in space. Financing his own work, he conceived two great advances in rocket design: liquid-fuel propulsion and multistage rockets. Today, liquid fuels, relative to solid fuels, have greater power and

better control of the amount of fuel going into the engine. Fuel and oxidant are stored separately, so it is easy to terminate combustion by stopping the mixing of the two components. In solid fuels, the propellant and oxidizer are mixed together, and once the combustion process starts, it is very difficult to stop. On the other hand, liquid fuels have traditionally been more expensive, and more difficult to handle and store. With advances in the technology of both fuel types, however, there is room in contemporary rocketry for both solid and liquid fuels, and they should be thought of as complementary. Indeed, the most famous contemporary rocket, the Space Shuttle, uses both solid and liquid fueled engines, and some rockets use a solid fuel and a liquid oxidizer.

Tsiolkovsky was a brilliant theorist, but the personal and financial circumstances of his life made it difficult for him to actually conduct experiments. However, this did not matter, as his writing inspired others, and the deaf teacher thereby performed experiments vicariously. His 1903 book, generally translated from the Russian as *Exploration of Space by Means of Rockets* was a thorough treatment of rocketry, including fuel and navigational concerns. There is no better example of the human imagination soaring above the constraints of our lives than when this deaf, unfunded, self-taught school teacher wrote "earth is the cradle of the mind, but one cannot live in the cradle forever."

Robert Goddard (1882–1945) was exhilarated by the works of H.G. Wells, specifically *The War of the Worlds*. Although Goddard was a physics professor and had a small amount funding for a time, his work was primarily that of an amateur. Some of his work was done in his university laboratory or in a testing area in New Mexico, but his early launches were done on his aunt's farm. Throughout his career, he worked alone or with a small team, isolated from others who worked in rocketry.

Goddard showed that rocket propulsion works in a vacuum; it does not need atmospheric air either to push against or to oxidize fuel. He introduced a better solid fuel, and conceived (independently of Tsiolkovsky) both liquid fuel and multistage rockets. He mathematically calculated the ratios of thrust per unit weight for different fuels, including liquid oxygen and liquid hydrogen. In 1919, he published *A Method for Reaching Extreme Altitudes*. He constructed a solid-fuel rocket during the first World War and built and flew the first liquid-fuel rocket in 1926. Goddard went on to make major advances in gyroscopic steering mechanisms, fuel pumps, and engine cooling. One of his most significant contributions was the convergent-divergent nozzle design for the exhaust gases. This design was crucial to the successful rocket because it allowed the gases to escape in such a way as to efficiently provide thrust.

The movement of a rocket is explained by Newton's third law of motion, the forward motion of the rocket being an inevitable reaction to the backward motion of the exhaust gases. To think of it another way, in the combustion chamber, there is enormous pressure, but it is evenly distributed, so there is no net force in any direction. By establishing an exit, there is no longer even distribution of the force, and the backward motion of the gases is balanced by the forward movement of the rocket. Goddard's design allowed the gases to escape in such a way as to translate Newtonian physics into reality, and in 1935, one of his rockets exceeded the speed of sound. Goddard, in effect, was the James Watt of the rocket, making improvements to every part of rocketry, and leaving the world with the first practical rockets. Wernher Von Braun said of him: "until 1936, Goddard was ahead of us all." During World War II, Goddard offered his services to the United States military. Its disinterest was unfortunate, one reason that the Germans assumed the lead in rocketry. As we shall see, it would be Von Braun's V-2 rocket that would become the basis of contemporary rocket science.

Hermann Oberth (1894–1989) was the third member of the rocket trailblazing trio. Like Tsiolkovsky and Goddard, Oberth was an avid reader of science fiction, especially Jules Verne's *From the Earth to the Moon*. Like Tsiolkovsky and Goddard, and independent of them, Oberth proposed the liquid-propelled rocket in 1917. His 1923 book, *The Rocket into Planetary Space*, and its 1929 sequel, *The Road to Space Travel*, were enormously influential in Germany.

The three rocket pioneers had much in common. Fired by science fiction, they all represented the priceless amateur, whom we must always have, and for whom I greatly fear. I submit as history's eighth lesson that amateurs have contributed enormously to our progress, and that we must create and maintain conditions that will permit them to continue to contribute. The best of our thought appears in the living room of the amateur as much as in the laboratory of the professional. As progress has been made possible by the value of the individual, we must make it possible for all individuals to contribute as much as they are able.

Wernher Von Braun (1912–1977) takes an interesting place in history. In 1925, he read Oberth's *The Rocket Into Planetary Space* and became the latter's student. When Von Braun was a young man in Hitler's Germany, all rocket research and testing was forbidden except by the military. Von Braun became the technical director of the German military aeronautics facility at Peenemünde, the principal goal of which was the development of liquid-fueled rockets for military purposes.

It is ironic that our most horrific behavior, war, focuses our imagination. Throughout history, war has always facilitated innovation, and no war has ever amplified our creativity as much as World War II. Like atomic energy, penicillin, radar, the computer, the turbojet engine, and numerous other advances, rocketry developed more quickly as a result of World War II.

Von Braun was the driving force behind the German V-2 rocket, which was largely based on Goddard's ideas. Standing for Vengeance Weapon Two, the V-2 was a liquid-propelled rocket that carried almost 2,000 pounds (900 kg) of explosives at a speed five times that of sound. Von Braun was briefly imprisoned by the Nazis because it was suspected that his goal was space flight, not weapons development. After the war, German rocket scientists surrendered to either the United States or Russia. Von Braun and the larger contingent of German workers came to the United States. Captured V-2 rockets were studied and duplicated, and became the foundation of American rocketry and space exploration.

Having failed to follow up on the studies of their own pioneers—Tsiolkovsky and Goddard—the United States and the Soviet Union were forced to use captured German material and personnel to start their own missile programs. (A missile is a rocket used for warfare.) Von Braun spearheaded American rocket development, while the Soviet program was guided by Sergei Korolev (1907–1966), whose identity was hidden until his death. These two countries then engaged in a senseless "space race" that enormously held back the progress that could have been achieved. The sad history of rocketry is that its early pioneers were largely ignored, and that its progress came from either World War or subsequent Cold War competition.

Immediately after the war, both the United States and the Soviet Union made the development of a more powerful rocket than the V-2 their top priority. This was important for two reasons. First, the V-2 was not capable of intercontinental travel, and therefore could not deliver nuclear weapons from one of the superpowers to the other. Second, the V-2 was incapable of space flight because it could not travel fast enough to achieve orbital velocity (see below).

To understand the development of space flight, a few concepts should be reviewed. Because the atmosphere thins gradually, there is no sharp line of demarcation between atmosphere and space. One hundred miles (160 km) is a convenient and often used number for the beginning of space.

There is a general misconception that craft in orbit are free from gravity because they are too far from the earth to experience the planet's gravity. Actually, the earth's gravity is not much weaker a hundred or a thousand kilometers in space because all of the earth's mass can be thought of as being in the center of the earth. On the surface, we are actually some 4,000 miles (6,400 kilometers) from the earth's center of gravity; an orbit of a few hundred kilometers does not significantly change that effective distance. Orbiting spacecraft continue to feel gravity, and in fact, depend on this gravitational pull, because orbit is achieved by balancing the gravitational pull of the earth with the tendency of moving craft to fly off into space. Satellites stay in orbit not because they do not experience gravity, but because their motion exactly offsets gravity. If the craft moves too fast, it is hurled into space. If it moves too slow, it is pulled to earth. Orbital velocity is the speed that a craft must attain to balance the force of gravity and circle the earth. Since gravity gets slightly weaker with increasing distances from the earth's surface, orbital velocity is greatest for low orbits. To achieve orbit, a craft is sent to the desired altitude, and then tilted so its path is parallel to the earth. It is then made to travel at a speed that balances the earth's gravity at that altitude. Should the altitude change, the velocity must also be changed to maintain the balance. Once equilibrium is achieved, continued thrust is not required, because the inertia of the satellite balances gravity.

An interesting situation occurs at an altitude of 35,700 kilometers (22,300 miles). At this altitude, the gravitational pull of the earth is such that a craft needs to move parallel to the earth at a speed of 7,060 miles (11,300 km) per hour to counter gravity and stay in orbit. At that speed, with an orbit of that diameter (84,200 kilometers counting the diameter of the earth), it takes the satellite twenty-four hours to orbit the earth. Therefore, its orbital motion matches the earth's rotation, and it is always over the same point on the earth's surface. This is called a geosynchronous, or geostationary, orbit and is desirable in certain communications and weather satellites.

The term "escape velocity" refers to the speed required to completely escape the earth's gravitational field. At 25,000 miles (40,000 km) per hour, it is higher than orbital velocity at any altitude.

In 1955, in anticipation of the International Geophysical Year of 1957–1958, both the United States and the Soviet Union announced plans to orbit a satellite. On October 4, 1957, the Soviet Union stunned the world by orbiting

Sputnik (the Russian word for traveler). Coming on the heels of the Soviet Union's detonation of a hydrogen bomb in 1953 (a few months after the first hydrogen bomb test of the United States), Sputnik cast real doubt in the eyes of the world as to which country was the scientific leader. In the aftermath of the Korean War and McCarthyism, Sputnik terrified Americans that communism might prevail through technology, and for the next twelve years, this belief motivated America's efforts in space.

In November, 1957, the Soviet Union launched Sputnik II, which carried a live dog. In December, 1957, the U.S. failed in an attempt to launch its first satellite, but successfully launched Explorer I in January, 1958. The satellite program paid immediate dividends, as Explorer 1 helped to discover the Van Allen radiation belts, regions of charged particles that encircle the earth. The National Aeronautics and Space Administration (NASA) was formed in 1958 for the express purpose of catching up to the Soviet space effort.

After these early launches, space exploration for both the United States and the Soviet Union proceeded along three parallel and overlapping courses. In the foreground were manned expeditions, the goal of which was to land a person on the moon. In the background were two unmanned programs: one launched satellites into earth orbit; the other sent probes to other bodies in the solar system. From a scientific viewpoint, the unmanned expeditions far exceeded the manned flights in importance, but it is the latter, specifically the struggle to reach the moon, that captures who we are.

The first step in manned space flight was to establish that people could function in space and that the problems of weightlessness and re-entry into the atmosphere could be overcome. Once again, the Soviets stunned the world. On April 12, 1961, Yuri Gagarin entered space and made one orbit around the earth. Three weeks later, Alan Shepard became the first American in space, but he did not go into orbit. It was not until February of 1962, with the flight of John Glenn, that an American orbited the earth. Thereafter, both countries launched multiple single-person missions to master the basic skills of astronaut support. The American program, called Mercury, and the Soviet program, named Vostok, both definitively demonstrated that people could live and work in space.

The mastery of such skills as rendezvous, docking, and extravehicular activity, which would be crucial to a moon mission, required practice with more sophisticated craft than were used in the Mercury and Vostok missions, and they would require crews of more than a single person. The United States developed the Gemini program to address these concerns, while the counterpart

Soviet program was called Voskhod. These programs were followed by the Apollo and Soyuz series, which aimed to further develop the skills needed to journey to the moon.

Through the work of countless thousands of people whose names were never known to the public, these programs obtained all of the necessary spacecraft manipulation skills. We now had the rockets, the spacecraft, the training, the experience, and the will to make history stand still. And stand still it did on July 20, 1969, when Neil Armstrong became the first person in human history to walk on the surface of an extraterrestrial body. Never in our history has the potential of humanity been as clear as it was on that day. Television became a time capsule, as millions watched live the equivalent of Columbus discovering the New World. Only sixty-six years, less than one human lifetime, after the Wright brothers' first flight, Neil Armstrong stood on the moon and said, "That's one small step for a man, one giant leap for mankind." But that triumph would turn out to be the smallest of the pathways of the space program. Unmanned planetary expeditions and unmanned satellites in earth orbit would have a greater effect on the long-term course of history.

The second major avenue of the space program has been unmanned satellites orbiting the earth. Communications satellites, originally conceived by Arthur Clarke (1917–), have totally revolutionized telephone and television science. Beginning with Echo I, a simple reflector, communications satellites are now responsible for the connections of our world. They are, with integrated circuits, the laser, and fiberoptics, one of the four immense communications break-throughs of the twentieth century.

Like communications satellites, weather satellites have humble beginnings. The first use of rocketry to collect weather data was in the single-stage rockets of the mid-1940s, which did not achieve orbit but were able to collect data on the upper atmosphere. They also served as the first solar probes, since they could receive radiation in wavelengths that did not penetrate the atmosphere. The first orbiting weather satellites began with the simple photography of the atmosphere, assisting in day-to-day forecasting, and have progressed to important instruments in long-range forecasting and climatology. Today, weather satellites are part of a global atmospheric research program.

The Landsat series of satellites (originally called earth resources technology satellites) are perhaps the least known of the truly important satellites currently in earth orbit. They have proven invaluable in mapping and understanding the surface of the earth. The Landsat series has located oil and mineral deposits, monitored agricultural conditions, and charted difficult to navigate terrain. One of Landsat's most lasting contributions has been detecting and monitoring pollution of the atmosphere, water, and land. As such, it has been central to ecological studies and conservation efforts. Landsat has also made significant contributions to oceanography and food production. It is already helpful in forecasting areas of potential flooding, and earthquake predictions may be forthcoming.

The Global Positioning System, also called Navstar, is a navigation system of twenty-four satellites, each of which emits an identifying signal. To locate position, a user needs a receiver, with which he receives signals from four satellites. The receiver calculates position from the time difference between the signals from the different satellites. Used to its full potential, position can be calculated to within thirty-three feet (ten meters).

No discussion of orbiting satellites would be complete without a mention of their use in defense. Reconnaissance satellites serve a valuable role in treaty verification, and therefore in making treaties possible. On the other hand, to my mind, there is no better example of wasted effort and squandered resources than the folly of the Strategic Defense Initiative (the so-called Star Wars defense). Intended to destroy incoming ballistic missiles with lasers, particle beams, or simple collision, this system is easily defeated by "dummy" or decoy missiles. It was recognized as impractical and unworkable from the start by the majority of the scientific community, and is currently being modified by those in the political arena. The Strategic Defense Initiative is reminiscent of the proliferation of fallout shelters in the 1960s. It was later shown that a nuclear war is fundamentally not survivable, even in a shelter. By the same process of reasoning, the Strategic Defense Initiative cannot protect us against a nuclear holocaust. No technology available to humanity will permit us to survive an exchange of nuclear warheads. The only defense against such a catastrophe is prevention. Parenthetically, it bears noting that more money has been wasted on this inherently unworkable system than is being requested for planetary exploration.

Looking at the heavens through the earth's atmosphere is like looking through thirty-five feet (10.5 m) of water. With pollution, it is often like trying to see through thirty-five feet of muddy water. Add to this dismal situation the fact that certain forms of electromagnetic radiation, which may carry information every bit as important as visible light, do not penetrate the atmosphere at all. As previously mentioned (and it will be mentioned again), we must get beyond the confines of everyday experience to more fully understand the universe. Visible light is a major part of our everyday lives, and we tend to gravitate to it for information, but it is only one of many types of electromagnetic radiation. Some of our most effective probes of the universe have come from other areas of the spectrum. What follows is an abbreviated history of unmanned probes launched to learn more about the universe.

The first spacecraft to teach us about another body were the Soviet Union's extremely successful Luna series. In January, 1959, Luna 1 became the first object to escape the earth's gravitational field completely when it flew past the moon. In September, 1959, Luna 2 became the first man-made object to impact on another celestial body when it was deliberately crashed into the moon. A month later, Luna 3 sent back photographs of the dark side of the moon, never before seen by human eyes. In 1966, Luna 9 made a soft landing on the moon before any American craft. Important moon probes for the United States were as follows:

The Ranger series (1961–1965): These probes gave us our first high-quality look at the lunar surface before being intentionally crashed into the moon.

The Surveyor series (1966–1967): Surveyors 3 and 5 made soft landings on the lunar surface, sent back pictures, and made analyses of lunar soil.

The Lunar Orbiter series: In 1966 and 1967, five lunar orbiters sent more photographs of the lunar surface and were instrumental in selecting Apollo landing sites.

The Orbiting Solar Observatory series was begun in 1962. Freed from atmospheric interference, they were able to collect data from the sun in the ultraviolet, x-ray, and gamma ray portions of the electromagnetic spectrum.

In the arena of planetary studies, our probes have been extraordinarily successful. Venus is covered by a cloud layer so thick that, prior to probes, we knew almost nothing of its surface. The Soviet Venera series was perhaps the finest of the Venetian explorers. Some of the Venera soft-landed and transmitted data from the surface for a short while, before the intense heat and pressure destroyed them. Much was added by the American explorers Pioneer Venus 1 and Pioneer Venus 2, and by the Magellan probe, launched in 1989.

Except for the moon and sun, no object in the sky has fascinated people as much as Mars. With the advent of space exploration, humanity achieved a large part of its dream of understanding the red planet. The Soviet Union's Mars series contained a number of probes that successfully transmitted pictures of the Martian surface prior to crashing. Mariner 9 from the United States orbited Mars, sending back enough pictures to render a reasonable map of the surface. Viking 1 and Viking 2 soft-landed on Mars in 1976 and greatly advanced our knowledge of the planet. Both were equipped with mechanisms to detect indications of life. (There was some uncertainty about the results, but they have generally been regarded as negative.) The 1997 Mars probe Pathfinder has been wildly successful, both in obtaining new information and in animating the public. Pathfinder released Sojourner, a small, wheeled vehicle that explored the area around the spacecraft and amplified the knowledge we were able to obtain.

Mercury, the innermost planet, was substantially elucidated by Mariner 10, which approached the planet three times in 1974. One of these approaches was within 320 kilometers (200 miles). Mariner 10 showed that Mercury has a crater-riddled surface and a magnetic field.

The two giant planets, Jupiter and Saturn, have been made somewhat accessible by probes. In 1973 and 1974, Pioneer 10 and Pioneer 11 (not to be confused with the Pioneer Venus series) passed close to Jupiter, providing the first close-up pictures of the largest planet in our solar system. Pioneer 11 went on to travel past Saturn, while Pioneer 10 became the first object made on earth to pass out of the solar system. Pioneer 10 is now more than six billion miles (almost ten billion kilometers) from the earth and has ended its mission. Its final message to earth indicated that the influence of the sun extends further than had been thought, making the effective size of the solar system larger than had been realized. In 30,000 years, it could encounter a star.

Voyager 1 and Voyager 2 were launched in 1977, the year after the Viking Mars craft. They flew past Jupiter in 1979, then past Saturn in 1980 and 1981. Both Voyagers were fantastically successful, transmitting more data on the two giants than thought possible. Voyager 2 made close approaches to both Uranus and Neptune, before leaving the solar system for a date with infinity. It has just one last mission—if it can remain functional long enough—to duplicate Pioneer 10's journey into the depths of space and transmit information from a part of space beyond the influence of the sun. Perhaps some day, eons hence, another species will find Pioneer 10 or Voyager 2, and learn a little of who we were.

Perhaps the most famous single unmanned exploratory object is the Hubble space telescope. Deployed in 1990, repaired in 1993, and upgraded in 1997, the Hubble telescope functions in the ultraviolet, visible, and infrared portions of the electromagnetic spectrum. It can function over such a broad range because, although ordinary telescope mirrors will not reflect radiation from either end of the electromagnetic spectrum, they reflect all wavelengths in and around visible light. It is therefore the detector that determines what range of wavelengths is studied. Taking into account the markedly superior observing conditions of space, the Hubble is the most powerful optical telescope ever built. It has illuminated almost every area of astronomy.

Because many astronomic processes emit electromagnetic radiation at wavelengths other than visible light, some of the most informative and productive orbiting observatories are dedicated to the infrared, ultraviolet, x-ray, or gamma regions. Infrared light is of lower energy than visible light and is emitted by relatively low energy processes, while ultraviolet light is of higher energy than visible light. X-rays have higher energy than ultraviolet, gamma rays still higher. For example, orbiting infrared observatories have given us a great deal of information about this portion of the spectrum, which is now supplemented by the installation of an infrared camera on the Hubble telescope in 1997. At the high-energy end of the electromagnetic spectrum, gamma ray collectors have introduced us to previously unknown gamma-emitting objects in the sky. At this writing, one of the most interesting mysteries in astronomy concerns the enigmatic nature of enormously powerful bursts of gamma rays—more powerful than supernovas—arising in unknown, very distant sites.

The planetary exploration probes, one of the most fruitful scientific ventures of our civilization, have now been severely cut back because of budgetary constraints and because the manned Shuttle program has siphoned much of the resources of the space program. At the conclusion of this section, we will consider the wisdom of that choice.

A permanent space station has long been a goal of the space program. In 1971, the Soviet Union launched the Salyut space station. The United States placed its permanent station, Skylab, in orbit two years later. Both of these stations subsequently fell out of orbit, and for many years, the only functioning space station was Mir (Russian for peace). There have been cooperative Russian-American missions involving Mir and the American Shuttle. At this writing, the first stage of construction of the International Space Station has begun, but many feel it is more a political than a scientific triumph and would rather see the large amount of funds expended in the construction of the station channeled to unmanned probes.

The space transportation system (known as the Shuttle) is a series of reusable vehicles first launched in April, 1981. The Orbiters each have three main engines powered by liquid fuel stored in a large external fuel tank. On each side of the tank, there are two booster rockets powered by solid fuel. During ascent, the solid rockets are exhausted first, drop off, and are retrieved and reused. The main engines, powered by liquid fuel from the external tank, then achieve the final orbital velocity, after which the external tank drops off. (It burns on reentry and is not reused.) The two solid-fuel rockets are made of multiple modules joined together. The Challenger tragedy of 1986 was caused by a defective O-ring in a solid-fuel rocket booster. This permitted burning fuel to escape, intensely heating the adjacent external fuel tank and igniting the huge amount of fuel therein. Aside from this tragedy, the Shuttle has otherwise proven itself a reliable satellite launcher and a useful craft for effecting repairs. But it is extremely expensive. Each launch costs a half-billion (500 million) dollars.

Almost forty years after achieving the ability to orbit the earth, what can be said about our efforts in space? Has it been worth the effort, the expenditure, and the risks? Multiple questions come to mind: Should we engage in a space program at all? What place do manned missions have in a space program? Is there a way to conduct manned missions at less expense? What is the place of unmanned exploratory probes?

The orbiting unmanned satellites are immediately identifiable as an excellent expenditure of resources. Much of the world as we know it is made possible by these satellites. They furnish crucial information not obtainable by any other mechanism. To them we owe the ability to communicate, as well as invaluable information on topics ranging from weather and earth resources to navigation.

What about the other two branches of the space program: manned flights and unmanned planetary probes? Have these avenues really produced tangible results in our lives? The planetary probes merit a thorough discussion. They are responsible for an explosion of knowledge in physics and astronomy. Our place in the universe is made more clear by what we have learned from these craft. It is said that this program has not produced tangible results, and likely will not. However, every great intellectual advance of history has always been followed by practical consequences. The apparently purely intellectual pursuit of knowledge for its own sake has always been simply the necessary theoretical framework from which later applications arise. I submit as history's ninth lesson that the pursuit of knowledge always leads to practical applications undreamed of at the time of the endeavor. Knowledge for its own sake has given us our civilization and made us who we are. It must be encouraged at all times and at any cost. Our species and the quest for knowledge are inextricably linked and will survive or perish together. Government and industry alike must realize that there is greater long-term success and profit in seeking basic knowledge and extending the freedom to pursue ideas to its people, even for projects that will not bear fruit for years. Thought of with farsightedness, planetary probes are a feature of our culture that we should preserve.

What then, about manned flights? Manned flights are riskier and more costly than unmanned missions. However, they are more versatile because their agenda can be changed. Certain missions, such as the repair of the Hubble telescope, can only be accomplished by manned spacecraft. So manned missions, in some form, appear essential to all components of the space program. But is the Shuttle the best vehicle to launch people and satellites into space? In the early 1980s, no one would have hesitated to answer this question in the affirmative. It is not so clear today. The expense of Shuttle flights has become almost prohibitive, and less expensive alternatives may be available. To my mind, although occasional manned flights in some form will remain essential, we may do well to have fewer of them, launched by less expensive, possibly expendable vehicles in concert with more unmanned missions.

In evaluating the future of the space program, a few comments on motivations of the past are in order. The conquest of space can only be successful if a long-term, farsighted, internationally cooperative approach is taken. And we can succeed only if the motivation is to uncover knowledge—not the case thus far. The whole purpose of the Apollo program was not the gathering of knowledge, but the defeat of the Soviet Union. The Apollo program was as much a part of the Cold War as nuclear ballistic missiles. Therefore, what was achieved was a short-term victory that made Americans feel good, but which did little for the long-term advancement of space exploration. Our priority must be the generation of a knowledge base, upon which we can build future applications. I hope this work has conveyed that throughout history, the lack of a basic knowledge base has retarded our progress, and that the acquisition of basic knowledge has always ultimately led to greater applications than overly targeted research. In retrospect, as wonderful as the moon landings were, they may not ultimately have been the best use of resources, because they were undertaken for the wrong reasons. Likewise, in retrospect, the Shuttle program, with its staggering price tag, may not turn out to be the best choice for getting people into space. If the money spent on the moon landings and the Shuttle had instead been allocated to more probes and more traditional methods of placing people in space, I believe we would have not only enlarged our knowledge base, but we would also be on our way to an organized, long-term, enormously productive program of space exploration. Sending people to the moon and then backing off from further exploration places the United States in a position similar to that of Portugal in the seventeenth century—the role of the former champion, no longer a leader. Adopting a noncompetitive stance, even if it means other countries "beat" us to some particular goal, and carefully creating a long-range plan emphasizing knowledge, not flashiness, places us in the position of England in the seventeenth century—that of the long-term winner. The best approach to the unfamiliar is to develop a coherent, long-term plan to gather as much basic information as possible.

Planetary probes, and the technology behind them, give us something unique in our history: the opportunity to gather knowledge without people. In the time of Columbus, knowledge could only be gained by intrepid people physically exploring the unknown. The same was true for much of this century, as evidenced by the polar explorers. But we now have a way to explore places people cannot go and ways of gathering information people cannot directly garner. While there will always be a place for manned flights, to my mind, we should allow the unique and extraordinary opportunity of unmanned expeditions to play the central role in our space program.

Chapter 32
Every Aspect of Our Lives

Light, the ubiquitous enigma, is harnessed in a new form.

AT THE END OF WORLD WAR II, it was possible to generate radio waves with a frequency of about one centimeter (0.4 inches). The generation of electromagnetic radiation with a shorter wavelength was desired for two reasons. First, the military wanted such radiation for communications, guidance systems, and short-range radar. Second, scientists wanted such radiation so that they could perform spectral analysis in the microwave region (the region of electromagnetic radiation with wavelengths just shorter than radio waves). They wanted to subject molecules to microwaves to study the emission and absorption lines so obtained, as had been done for electromagnetic radiation in the visible region.

Radio waves were generated by vacuum tubes, which were very limited in their ability to generate microwaves. It was the great idea of Charles H. Townes (1915–) to use molecular sources to generate microwaves. As electrons in certain molecules absorbed, then released energy, the radiation emitted might be in the microwave range. Townes realized that ammonia gas would emit microwaves if properly stimulated and then allowed to drop back to a lower energy level. Instead of simply following this particular problem to completion, Townes continued developing his ammonia system. As we have seen, when electrons are exposed to energy from external radiation, they can absorb some of the energy and move to a higher orbital level. They can then spontaneously emit the absorbed radiation and move back to a lower level. In 1917, Einstein showed that there was another alternative, stimulated emission. In stimulated emission, an electron that is already in an excited state, if struck by a photon, may actually drop to a *lower* level, simultaneously emitting a photon of the same wavelength as the original photon. The original photon is not lost (as it is in the usual case), so the number of photons is doubled. Moreover, the peaks and troughs of the electromagnetic radiation formed by the new photons will precisely match the peaks and troughs of the electromagnetic radiation formed by the original photons. In normal electromagnetic radiation, even if it is of a single wavelength, the peaks and troughs of the individual waves overlap each other, partially canceling each other out. In stimulated emission, not only is the wavelength the same, but the peaks and troughs coincide, so the waves reinforce, rather than cancel each other. This property is called coherence.

In stimulated emission, as in usual emission, the energy of the photon must match the energy difference between the electron's initial orbit and the orbit to which it travels. But in the usual case, the original photon is lost as it imparts more energy to the electron, after which the electron goes to a *more* energetic orbit. A photon identical to the original photon is then created when the electron loses this extra energy and returns to its original orbit. Just as the energy gained by the electron precisely matches the energy of the first photon, the energy subsequently lost by the electron as it drops back precisely matches the energy of the new photon. The number of photons does not increase.

In stimulated emission, the original photon is retained, and the electron goes to a *less* energetic orbit. The loss of energy of the electron as it drops down produces a new photon, which has the same energy as the original photon. Hence, stimulated emission differs from ordinary emission because it is caused by incoming electromagnetic radiation (it is not spontaneous), and results in an increase in the number of photons. The resulting emission exactly matches and is in phase with this stimulating electromagnetic radiation. This is called coherent radiation.

The problem with stimulated emission is that it can happen only to electrons that have already been placed in an excited state. When electrons are in an excited state, they tend to rapidly and spontaneously drop back to their lowest energy level, making them ineligible for stimulated emission. How could one keep the electrons excited long enough to allow stimulated emission to occur? At this point, Townes had his second great idea. Once the electrons were brought into excited orbits, if electromagnetic radiation of the desired wavelength was spontaneously emitted, and then reflected continuously back and forth through the system, many of the excited electrons would be exposed to this radiation before they could revert to a lower orbit, and would thus emit radiation perfectly matching the spontaneous radiation. In fact, a chain reaction would occur, since the new radiation would also cause stimulated emission. The effect would be a very great increase in the magnitude of the spontaneous radiation. In 1953, Townes constructed a device that used an electric field to isolate ammonia gas molecules whose electrons were in an excited state. As some of the electrons spontaneously dropped back to lower energy levels, the radiation they emitted was made to oscillate back and forth by a device called a resonator. As the radiation oscillated, it would occasionally strike an ammonia atom in an excited state, causing it to undergo stimulated emission. This stimulated emission precisely matched the radiation that caused it, and itself stimulated other excited ammonia atoms to undergo stimulated emission. The result was a chain reaction amplification of the original spontaneous radiation. Townes chose ammonia because it spontaneously emits in the microwave region, the region of interest at the time. Townes had not just shown that excited ammonia molecules can emit microwaves, he had shown that it was possible to create stimulated emission. Since the stimulated radiation was in the microwave range, Townes's device was called a maser, for microwave amplification by stimulated emission of radiation.

In the late 1950s, the Cold War was in full force, and the Soviet Union had launched Sputnik in 1957. Government and industry were spending large sums of money on scientific research. The natural extension of the maser was to still shorter wavelengths, into the visible region, and a number of university and industrial laboratories were vitally pursuing the laser, a term coined by Gordon Gould, standing for light amplification by stimulated emission of radiation. The laser is based on the same principle as the maser, but the wavelength of the emitted radiation is in the visible range.

Townes and others (such as Gould and Arthur Schawlow) realized that light amplification would require three components: first, a suitable lasing material, whose electrons, when excited, would be capable of spontaneously emitting radiation in the visible range; second, a means of bringing the electrons into the excited state (called pumping the laser); third, a method of causing the spontaneous radiation to be propagated back and forth through the medium. Theodore Maiman (1927–), using the principles of the maser, constructed the first laser in 1960. Maiman took a cylindrical crystal of ruby, coated the ends with a thin layer of silver (the coating on one end was only partially reflective), and surrounded it with flash lamps. The pulsing of the lamps moved electrons of the ruby into an excited state, whereupon spontaneous radiation resulted in stimulated emission. As this radiation was reflected from the silvered ends, it bounced back and forth in the crystal, causing more stimulated emission. The result was coherent visible light emerging from the partially silvered end. Slightly later, a number of other workers independently constructed lasers, based on similar, but not identical, methods.

Today, there are a large variety of lasers, differing in the lasing material, the method of pumping, and the method of causing the radiation to oscillate back and forth across the lasing material. The common property is that a material is chosen such that, when its electrons are excited, some of them will spontaneously drop back to a lower energy level and emit light of the desired wavelength, catalyzing the stimulated emission from other atoms still in an excited state. The lasing material is chosen on the basis of the wavelength of the spontaneous radiation, because this is what will be amplified.

The applications of the laser are legion, and it will transform every aspect of our lives. Perhaps the application that has most profoundly changed the world is in the area of communications, where the laser has teamed brilliantly with fiber optics. In fiber optics, a thin glass fiber of high index of refraction (a measure of how strongly light is bent when it passes from one medium to another) is surrounded by glass of lower index of refraction. When light traveling in the central fiber encounters the border of the encasing glass, it is reflected back into the central fiber in a process called total internal reflection. While light may appear to travel in a curved path, it is actually traveling in a multitude of straight lines, each of which, depending on the sharpness of the turn, is perhaps only a few micrometers long. When laser light is used, there is very little loss over distance. Fiber optics are replacing traditional copper cable in communications systems all over the world.

Lasers are frequently used in the science of materials, where they can weld, cut, or drill with great precision and minimal distortion of the surface. Lasers can also make precise grooves in a surface, and may be used in the manufacture of integrated circuits. Medical applications include the cutting of tissue, the sealing of blood vessels (such as removing undesired new capillaries in the retina of diabetic patients), cauterizing, and vaporizing undesired tissue (such as in an artery blocked by cholesterol deposits). Defense applications in the form of laser-guided bombs became well known during the Persian Gulf war. Since laser light moves at a constant speed in a completely straight line, it has proven valuable in surveying and measuring.

Four fascinating applications of lasers will hopefully occur in the future. The first is laser-induced nuclear fusion, which could potentially provide a method of obtaining a small, controlled fusion reaction without having to generate the extremes of heat currently required. This will be discussed more fully when we consider the question of energy sources for the future.

A second possible application would be the study of events of extremely short duration. Lasers may be continuous or pulsed. If pulsed, the duration of the pulse can be as small as one picosecond (one trillionth of a second). At the speed of light, such a brief pulse has a very finite length, less than a millimeter. By shining such a short light on an object, it may be possible to study phenomena of extremely short duration, very much as one might now use a stroboscope to examine events of short duration.

Optical computers are a third future application of lasers. Fiber optic communications have demonstrated that lasers can carry information. In principle, it should be possible to construct a computer that uses laser light to perform the calculations and to allow communication among the different components. Such a computer would be vastly faster than anything available now and would open a new era for computing.

Finally, lasers may one day be used to transmit energy from one site to another, replacing the electrical wires currently used by power companies. This would provide much more efficient and less-expensive energy transfer, with less loss over distance.

So it is that lasers—born of the desire to generate microwaves—have come to affect every aspect of our lives, illustrating how knowledge obtained for any reason always has undreamed of applications.

Chapter 33
Childhood's End

*As our ideas about the universe take shape, we struggle
to reclaim our bodies from diseases, old and new.*

WE ARE NOW, AS ARTHUR CLARKE HAS SAID, AT CHILDHOOD'S END in our history. The decisions we make now are critical to our survival and development as a species. In this section, some of the challenges of the present are discussed, because how we meet them is a reflection of who we are.

The Standard Model of Matter

In 1934, Hideki Yukawa (1907–1981) showed that two protons, although repelled by mutual positive charges, could be attracted to each other if a particle of certain properties were exchanged between them. The particle that would have to be exchanged between the two protons to achieve this attractive force was unknown at the time, but Yukawa successfully predicted it and described the properties it would have when it was found. Discovered in 1947, the particle is now called the pi-meson, or pion.

Yukawa formed the groundwork for our current conception of the forces of the universe, because he showed that an exchange of particles can create forces on a subatomic level, very much as an exchange of electrons creates the atomic forces of a chemical bond. We will return to this concept when we describe the four forces of nature.

After Yukawa, the next step in achieving our current view of the structure of matter was the identification of some of the many hundreds of existing particles. There are far more particles in nature than the electron, proton, and neutron, but most are unstable and cannot be detected in ordinary circumstances. Their detection requires two conditions: a means to accelerate atoms and common particles, because new particles form at high energies; and a means of detecting particles so created. It had long been known

344

that an electric field would accelerate charged particles, but their velocities were limited, since the particles would travel for only a short distance before impacting on one of the charged plates used to generate the electric field. Linear accelerators continue to have a definite place in physics, as evidenced by the Linear Accelerator Center at Stanford University. But in 1930, Ernest Lawrence (1901–1958) realized that if particles could be made to travel in a circular path, they could travel for a much longer distance and achieve higher velocities than in a straight line. Lawrence developed a circular accelerator, called a cyclotron, in which a magnetic field kept electrons moving in a circular orbit as they were accelerated. However, as the electrons accelerated, the magnetic field was less able to contain them, and the radii of their orbits increased, making detection more difficult. This difficulty is avoided by increasing the strength of the magnetic field as the particles travel faster. The synchronization of the strength of the magnetic field with the velocity of the particles holds the particles in an orbit of constant radius and gives these instruments their name: synchrocyclotrons (or synchrotrons). Two of the most famous are those at the European Center for Nuclear Research (CERN) in Geneva, and at Fermilab, near Chicago. Both of these accelerators have modified their original design to permit two particle beams, each of the maximal energy the accelerator can generate, to travel in opposite directions and collide with each other, thereby generating energies unforeseen by designers. A prototype accelerator called the superconducting supercollider, which would have been five to ten times as powerful as those at Fermilab and CERN, was to have been built in Dallas, but was canceled for political and economic reasons. (We will take another look at the superconducting supercollider later.)

The first practical device to detect particles was the cloud chamber, invented by Charles Wilson (1869–1959). The cloud chamber consisted of a chamber filled with air and alcohol vapor. Charged particles passing through gave rise to ions, atoms that have gained or lost electrons. These ions served as foci for the condensation of the alcohol. New particles could be detected by the tracks of condensed alcohol they left. The cloud chamber was succeeded by the bubble chamber, developed by Donald Glaser (1926–) in the 1950s. To a large extent, the principle of the bubble chamber is the reverse of the cloud chamber. In the bubble chamber, liquid is held under pressure at just below its boiling point. Particles passing through create ions, but now the ions serve as foci for the boiling of the liquid, which causes bubbles to form. The bubbles delineate the path of the particle. Current detectors are very large and expensive, and are designed and built by large teams. They tend to use a mixture of detection methodologies.

Various classification systems arose attempting to make sense of the hundreds of seemingly unrelated particles discovered. One of the most useful classifications is by the forces acting on the particle. Currently, four basic forces are recognized in nature: the strong nuclear force, the electromagnetic force, the weak nuclear force, and gravity. We will consider each, beginning with the strong force, so named because it is the most powerful of all the forces. As we shall see, the strong force, working through Yukawa's pion, overcomes the electrostatic repulsion of like-charged particles to hold protons and neutrons together in the nucleus.

The strong force affects some, but not all, particles. Particles that experience the strong force are called hadrons (after the Greek word for strong). Hadrons are divided into baryons (such as the proton and neutron) and mesons (such as the pion). Particles that do not experience the strong force are called leptons, the most famous of which is the electron.

In 1963, Murray Gell-Mann (1929–) and George Zweig (1937–) independently proposed the quark model of particles. In this model, hadrons are composed of quarks. Quarks, the smallest units of matter of which we know, have fractional charges, as opposed to the +1 and -1 charge of the proton and electron. Quarks combine with each other or an antiquark. A baryon is composed of three quarks, while mesons are composed of a quark and an antiquark. This means that more or less all of the matter in nature is composed of either quarks or leptons.

Although no one has been able to isolate an individual quark, six quarks have been experimentally demonstrated by indirect means, the last of these in 1995 at Fermilab. For each of these, there is an antiquark (with a negative fractional charge), and for each of these twelve, there are three slightly different varieties (called colors), for a probable total of thirty-six quarks. Combined with the leptons, which are not composed of quarks, that is still a lot of particles, but it is a much more manageable number than before the quark model.

The strong force alluded to above is now seen to be the force that affects quarks and subatomic particles that are composed of quarks (hadrons). It does not affect leptons because they are not composed of quarks. The strong force is thought to be mediated by an exchange of massless particles between quarks, appropriately and whimsically called gluons. Gluons, like individual quarks, have not yet been isolated. An exchange of gluons between quarks, analogous to Yukawa's exchange of pions between protons, binds them into hadrons. Baryons, which are composed of three quarks, are the particles of the nucleus and are held together by pions, which are composed of a quark and an antiquark. The strong force thus "assembles" both protons and neutrons and the particles that are exchanged to hold them together in the nucleus.

The strong force has a very short range, on the order of the diameter of a proton. This is the basis for nuclear fission. The slight deformation of the uranium or plutonium nucleus caused by the absorption of a high-energy neutron results in increased distance between the protons and neutrons; the strong force is decreased, while the electrostatic repulsion between protons is hardly affected by such tiny deformations. Atomic fission is possible because the electrostatic force between protons has a longer range than the strong force.

Quantum chromodynamics is the term used for the theory of quarks and their interactions through the strong force. The word "quantum", originally used to refer to the discrete unit of energy discovered by Planck in 1900, more generally refers to the subatomic world. The "chromo" is used because color (used figuratively) is a term applied to one of the properties of quarks. The basic concepts of quantum chromodynamics are as discussed above. Quantum chromodynamics is an example of a theory that is gaining acceptance because it is simple, internally consistent, and consistent with information derived from other sources. The history of science shouts that theories that provide a simpler, unifying view of the world are usually correct.

The second major force is the electromagnetic force. Electricity and magnetism were considered separate forces until nineteenth-century work, culminating in the Maxwell equations, unified them. The electromagnetic force affects charged particles, and unlike other forces, can be attractive or repulsive. This force causes two particles to repel each other if they have the same charge (both positive or both negative) and to attract if they have opposite charges. For example, the electromagnetic force holds the negatively charged electron in the vicinity of the positively charged nucleus. This force is less than 1% as strong as the strong force. Much progress was made in understanding the electromagnetic force through a theory, now accepted as fact, called quantum electrodynamics. Begun by Dirac with his equation of the electron, quantum electrodynamics was published in a more complete form in 1948 by Richard Feynman (1918–1988), Julian Schwinger (1918–1994), and Sin-Itiro Tomonaga (1906–1979). The theory is so named because it is a quantum mechanical treatment of charged particles and the electromagnetic force. Quantum electrodynamics describes the electromagnetic force as caused by an exchange of photons, the same particles that compose electromagnetic radiation such as light, radio waves, x-rays, etc.

The electromagnetic force is inversely proportional to the square of the distance between the affected masses. (For example, at twice the distance, the force is one-fourth as great, while at three times the distance, the force is one-ninth as great.) This has two implications. First, the force weakens quickly, since the distance squared is much greater than the distance. On the other hand, the force is a measurable and potentially significant quantity for an appreciable distance. Therefore, although it falls off rapidly, the electromagnetic force actually has some strength at any distance, almost to infinity. This is in contrast to the strong force, which, within its range, is much stronger than the electromagnetic force, but has a very limited range and drops to zero exceedingly quickly. Beyond the distance of the diameter of a nucleus, the electromagnetic force rapidly overtakes the strong force.

The third force is gravity. Although the force most familiar to us, it is by far the weakest of the forces. Like the electromagnetic force, gravity is inversely proportional to the distance squared, and therefore also has a much longer range than the strong force. Gravity affects all matter (anything which has mass), and therefore affects more of the material in the universe than the strong or electromagnetic forces. This combination of properties gives gravity an importance and familiarity out of proportion to its strength, making it the major force of the large structures of the cosmos, and the force that will determine the evolution and fate of the universe. In accordance with the hypothesis that all forces involve an exchange of particles, gravity is thought to be mediated by an exchange of massless particles called gravitons.

The fourth force is called the weak force. Although very weak compared to the strong, or even the electromagnetic force, it is still many billions of times stronger than gravity. Our understanding of the weak force begins with beta radioactivity, which is the decay of a neutron into a proton and an electron, with the latter particle becoming evident as an emission. Shortly after the nature of beta radioactivity was realized, it became evident that the total energy of a neutron before beta decay was slightly greater than the total energy of the electron and proton after the process, which would violate the law of conservation of energy. To avoid this difficulty, Wolfgang Pauli (1900–1958) hypothesized in 1929 that a tiny, uncharged particle was also produced in the process. Enrico Fermi (1901–1954), who would later change the world by supervising the construction of the first nuclear reactor in 1942, furnished a quantitative mathematical basis for this undiscovered particle and for the force (now called the weak force) responsible for beta decay. Fermi suggested that the elusive particle be called the neutrino (for little neutral one). Finally detected in 1956, the neutrino has no charge and little if any mass. (At this writing, recent experiments suggest that it does have a minute mass, and the world of physics eagerly awaits confirmation of this intriguing finding.)

The weak force is difficult to conceptualize because it does not cause attraction between particles in the simple sense that the other three forces do, but it has been shown to be responsible for beta radioactivity. Theoretical work suggested that there should be two particles that are intermediate in the decay of the neutron. In the 1980s, a team headed by Carlo Rubbia (1934–) and Simon van der Meer (1925–) found these particles, demonstrating that the process of beta decay also proceeds via intermediate particles, and therefore that the weak force is mediated by intermediary particles like the other forces.

Of the four forces in nature, two—the strong and the weak forces—have infinitesimal ranges, on the order of the diameter of a nucleus. The other two—gravity and the electromagnetic force—although diminishing rapidly, have infinite range.

Physicists have long suspected that these four forces are actually different manifestations of a single force. Albert Einstein spent the last twenty years of his life in a valiant but vain search for a theory to unify all of the forces in nature. Today, theories attempting to unify the strong, electromagnetic, and weak forces are called Grand Unified Theories (GUT). A step toward success was achieved when Steven Weinberg (1933–), Abdus Salam (1926–), and Sheldon Glashow (1932–) presented a convincing argument that the electromagnetic and weak forces are different manifestations of the same force. This force, the electroweak, governs the behavior of leptons, while the strong force governs the behavior of the other major class of particles, the hadrons. The strong force awaits inclusion into Grand Unified Theories. Gravity is so different from the other three forces that its inclusion will take longer and will require a theory even more novel than the GUT. Indeed, there are two different conceptions of gravity. One is the quantum mechanical view, where gravity is thought to be caused by an exchange of massless particles, analogous to photons and gluons; the other is the general relativistic view, where gravity is not caused by an exchange of particles, but rather results from the distortion of space by matter. These two views appear completely incompatible, leaving us as confused as if we were sent to the airport to pick up a person for whom we had two entirely different descriptions. But the reconciliation of opposites underlies much of our progress. Theories that incorporate gravity and attempt to explain all four forces as different manifestations of the same force are referred to as a theory of everything (TOE). A TOE will require a final union of quantum mechanics and relativity, the two uneasy bedfellows of modern physics. A TOE might even require an entirely different way of conceptualizing subatomic particles.

The standard model of matter encompasses the ideas in the preceding discussion and recognizes three forces: strong, electroweak, and gravity. In this quantum mechanical view, all of these forces result from the exchange of particles between the involved matter. All matter is fundamentally composed of either quarks (bound by the strong force into hadrons such as protons and neutrons) or leptons (particles such as the electron, which do not experience the strong force).

How We See the Universe

We now revisit the Big Bang model of the universe in light of the standard model of matter, because some of the most exciting ideas in physics result from the union of these two models. The Big Bang model holds that, just before the event, all of the matter *and all of the energy, space, and time* the universe now contains was concentrated into a volume *smaller than an atom.* As difficult as it is to visualize, there was no space or time before the Big Bang. Therefore the event cannot be said to have occurred at any particular place, and it would not have been possible to see the event from some vantage point away from the "explosion." Perhaps there was initially no matter, and all matter formed immediately after the "explosion" from energy. We do not yet know the conditions prior to the Bang because our laws of physics do not apply to such extraordinary situations.

Immediately after the Bang, energies were great enough to generate the elementary particles of matter. There was so much energy that separate types of forces could not have been recognized. Rapid cooling of the universe over very tiny increments of time shaped it into its present form. The first infinitesimal fractions of a second after the Bang were critical. These fractions are so tiny that they cannot be easily written in standard form, so a notation called inverse exponential is used. In inverse exponential notation, 10^{-x} equals one divided by 10^x. Therefore, the larger the exponent, the smaller the number. For example, 10^{-2} equals one divided by 10^2, or one hundredth (.01), while 10^{-3} equals one divided by 10^3, or one thousandth (.001).

Before 10^{-43} seconds (the tiny number created by dividing one by the giant number of one followed by 43 zeros, or one tenth of a billion billion billion billion millionth of a second) after the Bang, all four forces were merged into one force. Until we develop a conception unifying all four forces, events before this time are not approachable. We cannot describe a universe governed by a single unified force until we understand that force. After 10^{-43} seconds after the Bang, the universe, although still unimaginably hot, had cooled to the point that gravity likely disengaged from the other forces and would have been recognizably separate.

At about 10^{-34} seconds (a billionth of a second later than 10^{-43} seconds), the additional cooling of the universe would have allowed the strong force to separate from the electroweak force. At 10^{-30} seconds, the two fundamental groups of particles, leptons and quarks, began to form, but there was still too much energy for quarks to combine into hadrons, such as the proton and neutron. At 10^{-12} seconds, the particles mediating the weak force became separable from photons, which mediate the electromagnetic force. Therefore, at this time, the electroweak force separated into the weak and the electromagnetic forces. Today's particle accelerators cannot achieve the vast energies of the very earliest moments of the universe, but they can achieve energies comparable to that of the universe at 10^{-12} seconds after the Bang. We can use particle accelerators to journey, in effect, back in time to a point when the weak and electromagnetic forces were still unified, but we cannot re-create the very early conditions when all four forces were joined. Thus, it was possible to show the basic unity of the electromagnetic and weak forces, but inclusion of the strong and gravitational forces has thus far eluded us.

At 10^{-6} second (one millionth of a second), the universe had cooled enough to permit quarks to combine into hadrons such as protons and neutrons, but it would not be until one full second after the Bang, and for several minutes thereafter, that energies were low enough to permit the union of these particles into nuclei.

Now our story jumps to large expanses of time. Perhaps after about 300,000 years (although some believe earlier), energies became low enough for electrons and nuclei to combine to form hydrogen and helium atoms. Photons, which had been bound up in the very dense primordial matter, were liberated, which is why the background radiation discovered by Penzias and Wilson dates from slightly after the actual event. Getting information about the actual Bang itself is very difficult because the photons we would need to detect were trapped by the dense matter.

A large team working, with the same cosmic background radiation, has uncovered evidence for very tiny variations in the temperature of this radiation. These temperature variations imply random minuscule fluctuations in the density of matter just after the Big Bang. It is thought that, over eons of time and the fantastic distances of cosmic expansion, gravity magnified these tiny density fluctuations, and they became the giant structures of the universe, such as galaxies and clusters of galaxies. At this writing, several satellites, which will measure the cosmic background radiation in even greater detail, are being planned. Once these tiny variations in the background radiation are known in more detail, we will have a better idea of how the giant structures of today's universe developed.

A modified form of the Big Bang theory, called the inflationary model, was originally put forward independently by Alexei Starobinsky and Alan Guth and subsequently modified by others—most notably Andrei Linde. The inflationary model postulates that for a tiny period of time in the very early moments after the Big Bang, the universe expanded at an enormous velocity—even faster than light. Although this may appear to violate relativity's prohibition against moving faster than the speed of light, that law applies only to objects moving through an *already established* space, whereas this model refers to the establishment and expansion of space itself. (Remember, not only all matter and energy, but also all space and time were formed in the Big Bang.) The expansion of space itself at a speed faster than light is not prohibited. After this infinitesimal period of unimaginably rapid, exponential expansion, the universe settled down into the linear, much slower-than-light expansion it has shown for billions of years and we still see today. The inflationary model accounts for some of the properties of the universe left unexplained by the unmodified Big Bang model. An interesting prediction of this model is that the universe will neither fly apart forever in an open fashion, nor condense back into subatomic size in a closed fashion, but rather that the amount of matter (visible and dark) exactly matches what is required to balance the force of the Big Bang. The universe will expand forever, but at an ever-decreasing rate. If preliminary evidence that the universe is open (that is, will expand at a rapid rate forever) is confirmed, then the inflationary model will need to be modified.

Although a small amount of lithium may have been formed in the Big Bang, conditions in the event itself were never right for the formation of elements heavier than helium, not even after vast amounts of time. To understand the formation of heavier elements, we need to understand the formation of their source—stars.

At one time, it was believed that stars formed from the simple gravitational collapse of large, spherical clouds of dust and gas. Today, we know the story is more complicated. It may be that because the conditions of the early universe were different from later conditions, the first stars formed by a slightly different mechanism than later stars, but for our purposes, star formation began with a giant cloud of dust and gas. Within this cloud, smaller pockets began to collapse. As these pockets collapsed, their spin caused them to flatten; as gravity concentrated matter in the center, the rest of the cloud became a disk. Further contraction of the center generated sufficient heat to start a nuclear fusion reaction, converting hydrogen into helium (as occurs in the hydrogen bomb), and the energy of this process counterbalanced gravity and prevented further contraction as long as there was hydrogen to fuse. The center and the periphery of the smaller cloud evolved together, but towards different ends: the center became a star, and the remainder of the cloud became a disk orbiting the star.

The result was a number of stars, most with disks around them, within a giant cloud of dust and gas. The giant cloud that remains after star formation is called a diffuse nebula (an example of which is the Orion nebula). The first stars consisted only of hydrogen and helium, because these two elements comprised essentially all of the matter in the early universe. Later stars may have a slightly different composition because they formed from a universe that had small amounts of heavier elements.

The remnants of the disk may become a solar system and planets. Because all stars appear to form from a disk, and a residual disk-shaped mass is likely, it may be that a planetary system is the rule rather then the exception. As of January, 2000, most astronomers accept the presence of thirty three planets outside our solar system—almost four times the number within it. This lends credence to the above outline and carries many philosophical and religious implications about our place in the universe.

If all stars have similar origins, they have very different lives and deaths. To understand the evolution of stars, we need to realize that their ultimate fate depends greatly on their size, and we also need to remember that the core and the outer layers will evolve separately and have very different destinies.

Paradoxically, stars with lower masses live longer because their nuclear furnaces burn more slowly, while massive stars burn so quickly that their source of nuclear fuel is, in relative terms, quickly exhausted. Very small stars—those with a mass appreciably less than our sun—burn so slowly that they will not exhaust their supply of hydrogen within the anticipated lifetime of the universe, and they will never experience a change in their status unless the universe is open and expands indefinitely.

Slightly larger stars—those with a mass just less than our sun to a mass approximately ten times greater—will eventually exhaust their supply of hydrogen. When this happens, the nuclear furnace is temporarily impeded, so gravity begins to collapse the star, making it hotter. This additional heat is sufficient to trigger the fusion of three helium atoms into a carbon atom. Carbon is a new element in the life history of the star. The Big Bang created hydrogen and helium, the two lightest elements, but no heavier elements. Helium fusion not only brings forth carbon, but also produces enough energy to stave off further gravitational contraction.

The greater heat in the core causes the gases in the outer part of the star to expand, so that the diameter of the star markedly increases. This is the red giant stage of a star's lifetime, thought to occur for stars of all sizes, except the very small ones discussed above. In the red giant, other nuclear reactions besides the fusion of helium atoms generate showers of neutrons, which may be captured by atoms in the outer portion of the star. Sometimes, the captured neutron breaks down into an electron and a proton, and the electron is ejected from the atom, leaving the atom with one additional proton. Because the number of protons determines the identity of an atom, this process results in the formation of elements heavier than carbon. In stepwise fashion, elements up to atomic number eighty-three (bismuth) can be produced. It is believed that elements heavier than hydrogen and helium formed not in the moments after the Big Bang, but in aging stars. Some of these heavier atoms are released into the universe if they have sufficient energy to escape the star's gravitational field. (This is called the stellar wind.) Thus, the red giant loses appreciable mass, and in doing so, gives the universe something new: elements heavier than helium. Mass loss from these stars accounts for most of the carbon and nitrogen in the universe, as well as some heavier elements. First-generation stars seeded the universe with heavier elements in just this way as they played out their life cycles. But a cataclysmic event was required to release many of the heavy elements into the universe.

When the helium has all been fused into carbon, the gravitational collapse begins again. Stars in this mass-range, up to about ten times the mass of our sun, do not have sufficient mass to cause a second increase in the temperature of the interior. They simply collapse and cool off. These small stars, called white dwarfs, consist mostly of carbon and some oxygen. They are essentially dead, and whatever heat and luminosity they have is left over from their youth. As this residual heat and luminosity fade, a white dwarf may eventually become a black dwarf—a dead ball—although there are no black dwarfs now because the universe is not old enough for the complete cooling of a white dwarf to have occurred. In a white dwarf, all of the star's mass is concentrated in a volume roughly equal to that of the earth. The atoms of the star are collapsed against each other, and the electrons are dislodged from their normal orbits. But electrons are not pushed into nuclei, and the quantum mechanical requirement that each electron have a certain amount of space around it prevents further collapse. The outer layers of the star's atmosphere become detached and float away as a large collection of gases called a planetary nebula. (The word "nebula" refers to a cloud of dust and gas and has several meanings in astronomy; a planetary nebula has nothing to do with planets and is derived from the demise of a single star of relatively small mass, while a diffuse nebula is a huge cloud of dust and gas from which many stars have formed.) Our sun will pass through a red giant stage and end its life as a white dwarf, around which will be a planetary nebula similar to the ones now visible through telescopes.

A very different fate awaits stars larger than about ten times the mass of our sun. Like any star, these stars begin life by fusing hydrogen into helium, and like stars of our sun's mass, they fuse helium into carbon when their hydrogen is exhausted and pass through a red giant stage. Unlike smaller stars, however, larger stars do not end their lives when all the helium is converted into carbon. When these larger stars have converted their helium into carbon, they again experience a gravitational collapse. Because of their greater mass, however, larger stars get hotter during this collapse than smaller stars do, and enough heat is generated to permit large stars to do something that smaller stars cannot—fuse carbon nuclei, forming still heavier elements, and use the energy so obtained to hold off further collapse. When the carbon is used up, heavier nuclei are fused, forming still heavier elements. This process continues in successive stages until iron is reached. The fusion of iron atoms requires, rather than furnishes, energy, and iron cannot be fused without energy input. The dying star is unable to furnish this energy, so there is no more fusion. Time has run out for the large star, and now it must shrink, but it does not shrink passively into a white dwarf like its smaller counterpart.

After the loss of mass characteristic of the red giant phase (a star may lose 80% of its mass in the this stage through stellar wind), these larger stars will finish that stage with more than 1.4 times the mass of the sun. Because 1.4 solar masses is the upper limit of a white dwarf, these stars will have too much mass to become white dwarves, and will therefore have a different fate. Their enormous gravity will overcome the quantum mechanical consideration that each electron must have space around it and drive the electrons into the nuclei, uniting them with protons to form neutrons. Atoms will lose their integrity, and the core becomes a mass of neutrons. These neutron stars are far denser than the already extremely dense white dwarfs and can contain most of their mass in a sphere some ten miles (sixteen kilometers) in diameter. New neutron stars rotate very rapidly and emit electromagnetic radiation continuously. As the star rotates, this continuous emission is evident to us as extremely regular pulses of radiation, very much as a lighthouse beacon, although continuous, appears as periodic flashes as it rotates. These neutron stars are called pulsars.

The second consequence of this gravitational collapse concerns the outer portions of the star. The enormous energy generated in the collapsed core drives the outer layers into space at very high velocity. The result is that the outer layers of gas explode as a supernova, although the energy powering the event comes largely from the core, which is left behind as a neutron star. Sometimes, we can see the supernova as an expanding cloud of gas, in which case the term "nebula" might again be applied. An example is the Crab nebula, the remnants of a supernova in the year 1054. A neutron star has been found in the center of this nebula, providing considerable experimental verification of our understanding of stellar evolution. Although also derived from the death of a single star, nebulae such as the Crab are different from planetary nebulae not only in having arisen from larger stars, but also by a different mechanism and much higher energies.

Supernovas can form another way. We have seen that any star that finishes its red giant stage with more than about 1.4 times the mass of our sun will eventually undergo a violent gravitational collapse with the release of vast amounts of energy. White dwarf stars with a mass just under 1.4 solar masses, if they are close to another star, may pull enough mass from the other star to exceed this limit and collapse just as the isolated large star does. Astronomers call this a type I supernova, while those arising from isolated large stars are called type II.

As the shell of a supernova flies into space, it carries with it many heavier elements made in the red giant stage. In addition, it is currently thought that great numbers of very high-energy neutrons are released during a supernova, and the accelerating atoms may capture these and undergo electron loss and proton gain, as described above, leading to the formation of additional heavy elements. This permits some very heavy elements to be made in the actual supernova event itself. Indeed, supernovas are the principal means by which some heavy elements are synthesized, and they are the only known source of elements heavier than bismuth. Although a small amount of lithium (atomic number three) was formed in the Big Bang, red giants and supernovas are essentially the only sources of elements heavier than helium.

Thus there are immensely more atoms of hydrogen and helium in the universe than heavier elements. The experimental verification of this is the third piece of compelling evidence that there really was a Big Bang (with the expansion of the universe and the presence of background radiation).

After the supernova, all of these elements become part of interstellar space and can be recycled into a new star through the mechanism of star formation, as described earlier. If that happens, the new star might start out with a small percentage of heavier elements, whereas the first-generation star started with only hydrogen and helium. More important, the heavier elements might become a planetary system for the new star. Indeed, our sun has one- or two-percent heavier elements, suggesting that it is a second- or third-generation star. The formation of our entire solar system depended on the life and death of the first stars and was probably made possible by a supernova. This must be so, since the universe as a whole contains 92% hydrogen, 8% helium, and only minute traces of heavier elements, while the earth contains a very different composition. Oxygen and silicon are the most abundant elements of the crust, and counting the earth's core, iron is probably the most abundant element in our world. The furniture in your house, the metals in your car, and many of the chemicals in your body, were once inside a large star that became a supernova.

Our world began as a supernova, followed by the re-forming of a new star and a solar system. Who we are began in an exploding star.

Now let us consider the evolution of stars with really large masses, so large that they will end their red giant phases with greater than about five solar masses (which means, taking into account the substantial loss of mass that occurs in the red giant phase, an initial mass much greater than our sun). To some extent, the evolution of these stars is similar to those only about ten times the mass of the sun. There are again successive stages of fusion, beginning with hydrogen into helium, and ending with the formation of iron. Again, fusion must cease with iron, and the core must collapse when its nuclear fuel runs out. But the fate of the core is different. Just as a core greater than 1.4 solar masses will collapse into pure neutrons, so a core with greater than about five solar masses (the necessary size has not been determined with complete certainty) can collapse even beyond the point of pure neutrons, into a state of such extreme density that it is difficult to imagine. Such an object is called a black hole and is more properly thought of as a region than as a discrete object. A black hole is a region of space of such great density that its gravitational field is strong enough to prevent any radiation from escaping from it in the usual manner, although Stephen Hawking (1942–) has demonstrated a type of radiation that can occur from the periphery of a black hole, involving an esoteric concept in physics called virtual particles. Any matter that gets too close to a black hole is drawn in and can never be recovered. Black holes are the only regions in our universe where the laws of physics as we know them do not hold. The verification in the last few years that these regions really do exist has been a triumph of astronomy.

If the core of a star ends its life as a black hole, would the outer layers be expelled as a supernova, or would the black hole engulf a supernova as it formed and make it disappear or prevent it from occurring? Some people believe this is possible, and that stars with really large masses may end their lives by simply disappearing without a trace into a black hole, with no supernova forming. Perhaps those stars just large enough to form a black hole may still release a supernova, while really large stars do not. That interesting question aside, both neutron stars and most black holes (there appears to be more than one way in which black holes can form) are the remains of the cores of massive stars. There is a direct connection between neutron stars, supernovas, and the metal in your car. This relationship may also involve black holes.

Before we leave the subject of black holes, mention should be made of quasars. Quasars are very distant objects, receding very rapidly and emitting a great deal of radiation at all wavelengths. There is substantial evidence that quasars are black holes at the center of galaxies, and that their great energy output is derived from compressed gases as they are pulled into the black hole.

In addition to the Crab nebula and its neutron star, another supernova was identified in 1987, and the subsequent study of it provided considerable indication that the above outline is substantially correct. As time goes on, we should be able to detect any residual from this supernova, unless a black hole was formed.

The age of the universe has proven difficult to ascertain. Hubble showed that the further away an object is, the faster it is receding from us. The speed of recession for a given distance from earth is called the Hubble constant. The higher the Hubble constant, the faster the universe is expanding, the less time it took to reach its present size, and the younger it is. A more slowly expanding universe (a smaller Hubble constant) would take longer to attain its current size, and would be older. (Although we must also take into account any changes in the Hubble constant over the lifetime of the universe.) The speed of recession of an object is readily obtained from the red shift of its spectrum. Determining the Hubble constant requires us to precisely measure the distance to a stellar object not in the immediate neighborhood of our galaxy (where local gravitational effects distort the overall expansion), and that is the rub. These distances are difficult to measure. Several approaches have been tried, all more or less relying on identifying objects of predictable intrinsic brightness and comparing that to their observed brightness. The uncertainties and disagreements about these distance measurements have led to some uncertainty about the age of the universe, but it appears to be between twelve and fifteen billion years old. Promising new ways of determining the distance to objects in the universe should help determine a more precise age in the near future.

Many theories, new ideas, and unexplained observations remind us that we remain on Newton's seashore, collecting seashells before an ocean of knowledge. New observations remind us that ours is a universe whose age, structure, and fate we do not know, and about most of whose matter we know nothing. Periods of great progress often spring from times of frustration and ignorance. If confirmed, new information such as the openness of the universe should not be thought of as subtracting from our conception of the universe, but as an opportunity to add to it. A major change in our thinking about the universe may be at hand. It is our task to approach these uncertainties with intelligent ignorance and an open mind.

Could there be more than one universe? The new theory of quantum cosmology—an attempt to unify relativity and quantum mechanics—suggests that there may be many universes within one giant multiverse. The multiverse has always been; it has no age. Within it, universes constantly form, each with its own Big Bang. Each universe evolves—perhaps eventually collapsing back into the tiny area of fantastic density from which it arose—independently of all others. While it may seem impossible, it can be shown mathematically that *universes can spring into existence from little or no matter.*

Current research in our model of the universe relies heavily not only on accelerators, but also on information gathered from telescopes. Many telescopes do not collect visible light, but rather gather information in portions of the electromagnetic spectrum that the eye cannot see, such as the x-ray, gamma ray, ultraviolet, infrared, and radio wavelengths. Several exciting new prospects in telescope design should prove very helpful. First, new technologies permit the construction of larger telescopes. Often, these telescopes consists of a number of smaller mirrors, the light from which is combined to create the equivalent of one large telescope. This arrangement requires sophisticated computer techniques to merge the images properly, but multiple smaller telescopes, working together, offer numerous advantages over a single large instrument. Second, there are more sophisticated ways to detect the light captured by telescopes. Instead of using film, images are formed by electronic means, which are more sensitive than photographic emulsion. (This is the use of the digital camera, discussed previously.) Third, in some situations, it is actually possible for a telescope to simultaneously observe multiple objects. Fourth, it is now possible to put telescopes in orbit, above the distortions of the earth's atmosphere. The most famous of these is the Hubble space telescope, a ninety-four inch (238 centimeter) telescope originally designed to operate in the visible and ultraviolet light regions. The 1997 addition of an infrared camera and a new type of spectrograph (an instrument which measures spectra) increased its range and versatility. Finally, progress is being made in compensating for the distortions of telescope images caused by the atmosphere. (This is called adaptive optics.)

So twentieth-century physics began with Planck, progressed through Einstein, the Rutherford and Bohr models of the atom, through quantum mechanics and the atomic bomb, and has now emerged with models of matter and the development of the universe. These models are incomplete, but their basic outlines are almost surely correct. They are a brilliant and exciting partial synthesis of a hundred years of human thought.

The Time Machine

Because telescopes collect light that was emitted at some time in the past, they tell us how things *were*, not how they *are*. They directly see the universe as it was. Particle accelerators indirectly see the past by simulating the conditions of the early universe. We have seen that today's particle accelerators can achieve energies comparable to those of the universe when it was 10^{-12} seconds old. In effect, these accelerators are time machines that can take us back to that early moment of the universe. But by 10^{-12} seconds, infinitesimal as this time period is, much of our universe had already taken the form we know today. To a great extent, we have arrived too late on the scene, rather like journeying back in time to prevent a murder, only to see the killer flee.

The superconducting supercollider, the most powerful accelerator ever conceived, would have taken us further back in time with its greater energies. What lessons we could have learned, we may never know, and the applications of this knowledge we may never guess. There is no more important part of who we are than exploration, and no greater tool for our survival than seeking knowledge. Our species and the quest for knowledge are inextricably linked and will survive or perish together. The superconducting supercollider was a time machine in the truest sense, and it may have launched us on the greatest journey of the imagination we have ever undergone. To my mind, its loss is both a tragedy in its own right and a symptom of a shortsighted society.

Superconductivity

In 1911, Heike Kamerlingh-Onnes (1853–1926), seeking to liquefy helium, incidentally found that mercury at very low temperatures conducted electricity with no resistance at all. This phenomenon became known as superconductivity, and an explanation of it was provided by John Bardeen (1908–1991, previously a contributor to transistor theory), Leon Cooper (1930–), and John Robert Schrieffer (1931–). Prior to 1986, superconductivity was only observed at extraordinarily low temperatures, close to absolute zero (minus 469 degrees Fahrenheit, or minus 273 degrees Centigrade; the lowest temperature matter can attain). This made it highly impractical to incorporate superconductivity into electronic components. If only we could have superconductivity at higher, more attainable temperatures.

In 1986, a team headed by Alex Muller (1927–) and Georg Bednorz (1950-) gave us just that when they found that certain materials would superconduct at temperatures of about minus 400 degrees Fahrenheit (minus 240 degrees Centigrade). While still extraordinarily cold, this temperature is much more easily attained. Further work has given us materials that superconduct at minus 197 degrees Fahrenheit (minus 109 degrees Centigrade), approaching temperatures that can reasonably be achieved in electronics.

These new materials are ceramics. (In art and sculpture, the word "ceramics" refers to materials derived from moistened clay, but in this context, it refers to nonorganic materials that are at least partially nonmetallic.) It remains to be seen whether the explanation provided by Bardeen, Cooper, and Schrieffer for conventional metals will prove to be true for these ceramics, or whether another explanation will have to be found. In any case, the applications of relatively high-temperature superconductivity to electronics are legion, as are applications in computer construction. Superconductivity will help greatly in the generation of electricity as well. Currently, the generation of electricity involves (as it has for a long time) the movement of a magnetic field relative to a conductor. A superconductor would have no resistance to the flow of electricity in it and would be much more efficient.

Research in superconductivity, as in many areas, requires a substantial amount of equipment and facilities. To contribute, people will need to be part of a very large team. While I am happy to see the large-scale cooperation required to answer many of today's pressing questions, I am concerned that the gifted individual, or the talented amateur, may not be heard as readily as in the past. There are two characteristics of many of our historical advancements: many have been serendipities, and many have been contributed by amateurs. We must preserve these two attributes in the science of the future.

Institutions, even those dedicated to research, can be confining. The present environment of grant proposals, publication pressure, and giant, single-purpose research projects is not always fertile ground for the renegade thoughts, daydreams, and serendipity upon which we so depend. Just as creative people are usually on the fringe of mainstream society, they are also on the periphery relative to those in established institutions and traditional research structure. The scientific research establishment is not exempt from the normal human tendency to ignore or suppress the unfamiliar. Progress has always come disproportionately from those who swim against the mainstream—of the macrosociety and of their profession. Now, those mainstreams are becoming more difficult to swim against.

It is to be fervently hoped that large scientific teams avoid the rigid hierarchical leadership structure that plagues many companies. This management structure stifles creativity, because only a small minority of workers—those at the top of the pyramid—have the opportunity to fully contribute to the organization. Such a hierarchy is bad enough in business, but it is catastrophic in research, where recognizing the value of all individuals is essential to success. Large research teams under the control of one or two people are deprived of the majority of their talent. History shouts that unconventional and unsanctioned thoughts from iconoclastic individuals have been the key to progress, and therefore that hierarchical investigative teams will achieve only a fraction of their potential productivity.

I am also concerned that these iconoclastic individuals may not be given enough time to mature and develop their ideas. The pathway to success today depends on achieving certain goals at specific times. We must pass examinations at particular times in college and thereafter, if we elect additional training. We are given a relatively short period of time in which to be productive after we assume a position, and that productivity has to be quickly recognizable to those who determine promotions. Creative people move at their own pace, which is often slower than society mandates.

The Blunted Miracle

The extent and impact of mental illness has always been denied by our society. Prior to the introduction of anti-psychotic medications, as many people were hospitalized for mental problems as for physical conditions. Not only do we know far less about mental illness, but we often do not recognize its presence. (It is my opinion that most criminals suffer from a mental illness we cannot recognize or diagnose.) Mental illness has been, and is still, pushed into the recesses of our thinking.

For most of our history, mental illness was regarded as a supernatural phenomenon, caused by demons and witches. One of the first to see differently was Edward Tyson (1651–1708), remembered as the founder of comparative anatomy and physical anthropology. Tyson championed moving the treatment of mental illness away from punishment and towards a more humanitarian approach. He also recognized the need for follow-up visits to the homes of patients after they were discharged.

The Enlightenment, with its focus on people and social improvement, brought a different attitude toward mental illness, and people began to view it as a disease needing treatment, rather than as a possession by supernatural forces. It was with Philippe Pinel (1745–1826) that contemporary psychiatry began. Pinel advocated humane treatment, diminished use of restraints, and more counseling. He worked to improve the abominable environment of mental institutions, and he undertook a series of objective studies that led to the first useful classification of mental disorders.

Jean Esquirol (1772–1840) furthered Pinel's advocacy of more humane treatment of mental patients. He also introduced the use of statistics in psychiatry and provided a better differentiation of the effects of mental illness from its causes. (That is, he recognized many strange behaviors as manifestation of an illness, rather than causative factors.)

Emil Kraepelin (1856–1927) combined anatomic studies (he stressed the need to perform autopsies on deceased mental patients) with experimentation and the study of case histories to classify mental disorders into three groups: manic and depressive disorders, paranoia, and dementia praecox (what we would now call schizophrenia). With his multifocal approach and nearly contemporary classification, Kraepelin made psychiatry into a science. He stands with Pinel and Freud as the giants of early psychiatry.

Wilhelm Griesinger (1817–1868) advocated that all mental illness is caused by dysfunction of the brain. His prescient remark was "Mental illnesses are brain diseases." But it would be another century before there was any medication for mental disorders, and the history of psychiatric drugs begins with yet another serendipity.

Shortly after the second World War, Henri Laborit, a neurosurgeon, sought to calm his patients before surgery. He guessed that since histamine was released during moments of anxiety, an antihistamine might have a calming effect. Laborit's focus on histamine was largely a lucky guess. There are many other substances released during stressful moments, and it was perhaps fortuitous that most of these were not known in the late 1940s. Laborit found that the antihistamine chlorpromazine did indeed relieve pre-operative anxiety in his patients. The manic phase of a manic-depressive disorder (an illness characterized by severe mood swings, varying from depression to great excitement) manifests symptoms somewhat similar to, but more severe than, ordinary anxiety. If chlorpromazine relieved anxiety in normal people facing stressful situations, could it work in these patients? The drug was tried and found to work. Could it be effective in other mental conditions? It was tried in patients with schizophrenia, a disorder characterized by delusions, hallucinations, dulled emotions, and deterioration of social interactions (Schizophrenia is sometimes confused with multiple personality disorder, but these are different conditions.) Again, chlorpromazine was found to be helpful.

The apparent effectiveness of chlorpromazine and other medications (termed anti-psychotics) in the treatment of schizophrenia led to the discharge of huge numbers of mental patients from hospitals into the community, where, with the assistance of outpatient care and counseling, they were to rejoin society. In many cases, anti-psychotic medications have been successful in restoring a patient to vitality and reuniting him with society. But for a second group of patients, results have been less encouraging. Shortly after the emptying of mental hospitals, homelessness exploded, and our streets filled with people clearly unable to fend for themselves. The partial effectiveness and great promise of anti-psychotic medications is clear. There is no doubt that even patients in the second group are better off with these drugs than without them. Whether these patients are well enough to be discharged from hospitals is a different question.

Not all homeless people are mentally ill. In fact, a third of America's homeless are families, generally headed by women, and not afflicted with mental illness. The causes of homelessness for these families strike at the heart of a capitalist economy and pose questions capitalist nations will have to answer if they are to survive. But many of the homeless single people are mental patients who would have been institutionalized in earlier times. For these people, anti-psychotics have proven effective enough to mislead us into believing they are truly effective.

To my mind, anti-psychotic medications are a giant step in the right direction and represent extraordinary promise, but their miracle has been blunted by the overestimation of their effectiveness, the premature discharge of patients based on this overestimation, and our failure to provide the ancillary social services these patients require. We are now forced, if we are up to it, to re-evaluate our treatment of the mentally ill. To my mind, we need more Pinels and Tysons to help us understand that dumping partially treated, still very ill patients onto our streets is little better than the mental asylums of yesteryear, and not as good as contemporary institutionalization. The current situation of hundreds of thousands of people aimlessly wandering the streets of a society to which they do not really belong will be recorded as a dark chapter in our long struggle to recognize and treat mental illness.

New Kinds of Life

In 1968, Werner Arber (1929–) learned that certain bacteria defend themselves against attack by viruses by producing an enzyme that cuts viral DNA, destroying the capacity of the virus to produce proteins or interfere with bacterial metabolic functions. No one could have known that this was the start of an extraordinary moment in our history.

In 1970, Hamilton Smith (1931–) and Daniel Nathans (1928–) isolated the first of these enzymes, by then called restriction enzymes. In 1973, Paul Berg (1926–) used restriction enzymes to open two circular fragments of DNA from two different species of virus. He then synthesized and added to the opened circles bases that would pull them together into one large circle of DNA. This was the first time that DNA from two distinct species were combined.

Berg's method was ingenious, but cumbersome and time consuming. Shortly after his work, Herbert Boyer (1936–) discovered a new restriction enzyme that cleaves in such a way that the resulting ends are already inclined to recombine, obviating the need for Berg's laborious process. With Boyer's enzyme, the ends of the cut DNA were already "sticky." If fragments of DNA from two different organisms could be subjected to this enzyme, and cut in such a way that their ends were immediately ready to recombine, might portions of DNA from the two species spontaneously join into one fragment? Stanley Cohen addressed this question with a bacterial plasmid, a portion of bacterial DNA that is completely independent of the chromosome and even replicates independently of it. Cohen exposed a bacterial plasmid and DNA from a toad to a restriction enzyme, which split both fragments of DNA. The resulting sticky ends allowed the ends of one of the fragments to stick to the ends of the other fragment, producing a single piece of DNA. The autonomous and self-replicating nature of the plasmid was unchanged, but now its replication also involved replication of the toad DNA. The ability to insert a piece of foreign DNA into a *self-replicating* DNA fragment created the possibility of making—literally manufacturing—portions of DNA that code for proteins of interest. This is the field of recombinant DNA, or genetic engineering.

Already, genetic engineering has allowed the insertion of the gene coding for human insulin into a plasmid, allowing sufficient quantities of this hormone to be made for medical purposes. Many other medically needed proteins and drugs have been or soon will be produced by recombinant techniques.

A second application for restriction enzymes is gene therapy. If a disease is known to be caused by a missing or defective gene, why not try to replace that gene? Inserting DNA into every cell of the body may seem an impossible task, but there are several promising avenues of approach. First, it is not necessarily true that the missing gene must be supplied to every cell. Every cell in the body contains a full complement of DNA, but only the portion relevant to that cell type is actually expressed in that cell. For example, muscle cells only use the portion of DNA that codes for proteins relevant to muscle function. Therefore, only those tissues and organs that would normally use the missing or defective gene need be supplied. In a disease of muscles, for example, only muscle tissue need be supplied with the appropriate gene. Second, nature has provided a very effective tool for entering cells and exchanging genetic material—viruses. Entering cells and inserting its nucleic acid into that of the host is what most viruses do for a living. If restriction enzymes can be used to modify the viral nucleic acid to carry the gene of interest, then deliberate infection of the patient with the virus may be highly beneficial. Success with gene therapy has been very limited so far, but the potential is as great as antibiotics or anesthesia.

A third application of restriction enzymes lies in the judicial system. Because each of us has a unique sequence of DNA base pairs, enzymes that cleave DNA result in unique fragments for every person, very much like the process of tearing single pages from different books results in different pages. This is the procedure of DNA fingerprinting, so named because the fragments of DNA formed are as specific for individuals as fingerprints. In addition to the determination of criminal guilt, DNA fingerprinting is of excellent value in paternity testing. Because the DNA of every individual is derived from two parents, knowing the DNA fingerprint of any two people involved in a mother-father-child question allows strong statements of probability to be made regarding the role of the third person.[6]

The last application of restriction enzymes carries the most potential and the greatest hazard. It gives us the opportunity of changing the genetic makeup of living creatures, as, for example, the genetic makeup of the bacteria is changed when the DNA in its plasmid receives the foreign DNA coding for insulin. In theory, genetic engineering means that the DNA of every organism can be modified, enabling the organism to perform functions it could not do before. Every animal and plant in the world can be modified to better serve man. Naturally, this carries serious ethical considerations as well as profound promise. Indeed, every person can be genetically changed to become stronger, smarter,

* See Notes starting on page 502.

taller, etc. This, too, carries danger and promise. Throughout history, promise has always arrived with danger, and our progress has always required that we harness the promise in a responsible manner, so as to minimize the danger. The frontiers of DNA will not be an exception.

Magic Bullets Revisited

Antibodies, originally postulated by Ehrlich, are proteins made by certain kinds of white blood cells to assist in fighting infection. They do this by binding to a specific portion of their target (called the antigen) and eliciting other components of the immune system in an orchestrated attack on the intruder. Antibodies exhibit strong specificity—each antibody will bind to only one specific portion of a molecule.

This specificity has long made antibodies a useful tool in biological research because it allows investigators rapid and reproducible access to a target area that may be very tiny. In effect, antibodies are the "homing pigeons" of biology and biological research.

The old method of raising antibodies was simply injecting an animal with the substance for which antibodies were sought, then removing part of the animal's serum. (The liquid part of blood that remains after the blood has clotted.) Antibodies could then be isolated from the serum, but since the serum also contained innumerable antibodies that were not of interest, the pertinent antibody had to be separated by a laborious process, and was usually in short supply.

In the 1970s, Georges Kohler (1946–) and Cesar Milstein (1927–) devised a clever and novel way to make large amounts of antibodies, called monoclonal antibodies. The concept exploited is that when normal cells are grown in culture outside of the body, they die after some period of time, but certain malignant cells can literally live forever in culture. Such cells are said to be transformed, or immortalized. Such malignant cells can make antibodies, and live and make antibodies forever in culture. But researchers have no control over which antibodies they make. Kohler and Milstein found a way to isolate and immortalize the lymphocytes that make the antibodies of interest even though they are not malignant, thus allowing large quantities of these antibodies to be quickly and easily made.[7]

The result of monoclonal antibody production is a large number of specific antibodies—a boon to researchers, because they can use these antibodies to

---

* See Notes starting on page 502.

gain access to molecules (or parts of molecules). Current work is focusing on attaching drugs to monoclonal antibodies so that these drugs can be delivered directly to the site of their intended action. Drugs delivered directly and exclusively to the pertinent site would not only be more potent, they would also be substantially free of side effects, which largely result from drug actions in tissues not affected by the disease process. The prototype example of such a situation would be an anticancer drug attached to a monoclonal antibody that will bind only to the portion of a cell responsible for the malignant change. This arrangement would be a monumental resurrection of Ehrlich's magic bullets.

The Plague of Our Time

In the early 1980s, it became clear that certain infections generally found only in patients who were immunocompromised were occurring with increasing frequency in patients who were either gay or abused intravenous drugs but were not thought to have a defect in their immune system. Within several short years, this observation developed into the characterization of a new disease entity: Acquired Immune Deficiency Syndrome—AIDS—now known to be caused by the Human Immunodeficiency Virus (HIV).

All viruses, including HIV, are incapable of replication by themselves. They must bind to the outside of the cell they target to gain entry to the cell's interior. Once inside, they use the machinery of the invaded cell to synthesize the components of new virus particles, which are then assembled into intact progeny.

HIV enters and destroys a type of white blood cell (called the T4 lymphocyte) critical to immunity against certain viruses, fungi, and protozoa. By destroying these lymphocytes, HIV compromises the immunity of a patient to organisms that are ubiquitous in the environment and generally held at bay without difficulty. HIV does not kill directly; it allows certain normally harmless organisms to gain an upper hand. (These are called opportunistic infections.)

HIV is unusual among viruses in that it is a retrovirus. The usual pathway in nature is for DNA to be transcribed into RNA, which is then translated into proteins. Most viruses have DNA as their nucleic acid, and therefore follow this pathway, using the enzymes of the host cell. Some viruses do not have DNA, but contain only RNA. When these viruses enter a cell, they either use the cell's enzymes to make more copies of RNA, thereby bypassing DNA, or they use a special enzyme of their own (called reverse transcriptase) to make DNA from RNA. This DNA then serves as the template for the production of more viral

RNA. Viruses that use reverse transcriptase to make DNA are called retroviruses, and it is to this unusual class that HIV belongs.

There are several approaches to treatment, all less than optimal. Azidothymidine (AZT, also called Zidovudine) inhibits the reverse transcriptase the virus needs to make DNA from RNA. Another drug, 3TC, has the same effect. These drugs target the early stages of viral replication, when the virus is still making components and has not yet assembled them into intact daughter virus particles. Because this assembly requires a protein called a protease, an additional therapeutic approach has been to inhibit the protease. Protease inhibitors may be used in combination with AZT and 3TC—a combination, when employed soon after infection, that has been more effective than anything heretofore tried. However, this combination therapy is expensive and cannot be tolerated by some patients. Moreover, resistant strains of HIV appear to be emerging in occasional cases.

Other avenues being examined include blocking the entry of the virus into cells. Treatment for AIDS, which is the full-blown disease state that occurs after HIV has fully established itself, is very difficult because viruses, unlike bacteria, generally integrate their nucleic acid into that of the host cell. This makes the virus an indistinct target, and its destruction often requires the destruction of the host cell.

A number of vaccines against HIV have been tried without success, and others are in trial now. Vaccines for HIV have proven more difficult than for other viruses for two reasons. First, HIV mutates (changes its nucleic acid, and thus the structure of its proteins) at a rapid rate. To be effective, a vaccine would have to be directed against a part of the virus that does not change with time.[8] The other reason is that the immune system may be ineffective in fighting HIV. AIDS patients have antibodies to the virus, but they do not seem to do much good. The reason for this is not known, but the virus appears to be able to "hide" in certain cells, protected from antibodies. Even a vaccine that successfully stimulated antibodies to HIV may not be as beneficial as one might think.

Prevention is our only effective weapon. HIV is principally transmitted through homosexual contact, heterosexual contact, and the sharing of infected needles among intravenous drug addicts. At this writing, the United States Congress has denied federal funding for needle-exchange programs, whereby addicts could swap a potentially infected needle for a new, sterile one. A majority of elected representatives thought that such an exchange program would encourage people to experiment with drugs, despite overwhelming evidence—

---

* See Notes starting on page 502.

and the clearly expressed opinion of scientists—that these exchange programs do not increase the number of addicts and are effective in limiting the spread of the virus. To my mind, this action is a perfect example of the damage that political leaders can do when they lack the basic scholarship necessary to approach societal problems in an intelligent manner.

At this time, many millions of people worldwide either have or will get this disease. Africa, where the virus appears to have originated, is particularly besieged. In Africa, we face the twin difficulties of widespread poverty and enormous numbers of people infected. The optimistic results obtained by therapy with protease inhibitors and inhibitors of reverse transcriptase will be difficult to achieve in Africa because of its rudimentary medical system.

I do not think the toll from AIDS will be as terrible as that of the Black Death in the fourteenth century, but I do think, as Petrarch wrote about the great plague, that future generations will find it difficult to believe that our civilization was crippled by a tiny virus. Because the lessons of history are forgotten, or never learned, I also believe that future generations will find it difficult to believe that it could happen to them. We, too, thought we were protected from microbial plagues.

AIDS is a worldwide threat because we lack basic knowledge: basic knowledge about viruses, basic knowledge about immunity, and basic knowledge about cells. There is no argument against research directed at a specific target, and certainly no argument against research that focuses on AIDS, but only by increasing our general knowledge base can we fully address AIDS, as well as any plagues yet to come. "Emergency" funding after a new disease appears is too little too late. A greater commitment to basic, broad-based research increases the likelihood that we will emerge truly victorious against every form of disease. To my mind, such research is best regarded as the responsibility of the government. Although Bell Laboratories (now greatly reduced in size and scope) is a notable historical exception, industry funded research will likely not be basic enough and will be directed to short-term monetary goals. It is unrealistic to expect any company to initiate the long-term projects, often taking decades, critical to our survival.

What We Know About Cancer

Cancer is the unrestrained replication of cells, often followed by the dissemination of some of these cells to distant sites, where they again replicate without restraint. (This dissemination to another site is called metastasis.) Cancer is second only to heart disease as a cause of death in the industrialized world.

When the germ theory of disease became understood, there was considerable thinking that cancer was an infectious disease. Some microorganisms had, in fact, been isolated from tumors. (We now know that they were secondarily infecting non-viable portions of tumors.) This led to attempts to make vaccines by injecting fragments of tumors into animals, after which serum was withdrawn and given to the patient.

The first cancer treatment to rise above worthlessness occurred in 1896, when it was realized that some breast cancer patients benefited from the removal of their ovaries, the principal site of synthesis of female hormones. This treatment was routinely used on premenopausal patients for fifty years (postmenopausal patients already had low levels of female hormones and did not benefit from the removal of the ovaries), but is now achieved with drugs blocking the effect of these hormones. By 1941, an equivalent effectiveness of castration was recognized in men with prostate cancer.

Hormonal manipulation was ineffective in most cancers. The answer had to lie in finding drugs that affect tumors without affecting their hosts. The model for the early days of this quest was Ehrlich's search for magic bullets against microorganisms. The origins of effective chemotherapeutic agents paradoxically lie in a most unexpected place—war, specifically the gas attacks of World War I. During World War II, Louis Goodman, Alfred Gilman, and David Karnofsky, working in the Allied division of biological warfare, studied the autopsy reports of victims of mustard gas attacks during the first World War. They noted that these autopsy reports consistently described destruction of bone marrow and lymphoid tissue such as lymph nodes. World War II confirmed these findings after a German attack on allied ships carrying mustard gas in Bari, Italy resulted in numerous fatalities. Stewart Alexander studied autopsies of these victims and again noticed the depletion of bone marrow and lymphoid tissue.

If mustard gas depleted marrow and lymphoid tissue, might it be of benefit in malignancies of those organs? During the second World War, Goodman, Gilman, and Karnofsky tried nitrogen mustard on mice into which tumors had been transplanted. Encouraged by positive results, they tried the toxic chemical on patients with lymphoma (cancer of lymphoid organs such as lymph nodes and spleen) and received beneficial results. The modern era of cancer chemotherapy is another example of the progress war can bring.

In the late 1940s, Sidney Farber found that increased levels of folic acid (a B vitamin) inhibited certain types of tumors in mice. Eager to try this in childhood leukemias, Farber found the opposite of what he had hoped; increased levels of folic acid made the disease worse. Farber then tried folic acid antagonists, which prevented the folic acid from participating in biochemical pathways, and achieved a remission.

By the 1950s, enough was understood of cell growth and division to begin the deliberate synthesis of new compounds for the express purpose of inhibiting tumors. Botanical sources were also productively exploited, and many of the agents in use today were discovered during this time. Some of these drugs have found utility in non-neoplastic disorders. The 1950s also saw the creation of large-scale clinical trials; so drugs could be evaluated alone, in combination with other drugs, or as adjuvants (used with surgery or radiation therapy). 1956 brought the first complete triumph in cancer treatment and a new era in medicine: the total cure of metastatic gestational choriocarcinoma, a rare type of cancer seen in pregnancy.

By the 1960s, the pharmacologic armamentarium of today was nearly complete, and much had been learned about using drugs in combination. Two new triumphs were achieved: the curing of most forms of Hodgkin's disease and childhood leukemia.

In the 1970s, there was a shift in our understanding of cancer. Cancer had been thought to originate in one area, then spread locally (for example, to a nearby lymph node), followed by distant dissemination. The idea behind the radical surgical procedures of the time was to remove all of the cancer, which may have spread locally, before distant spread had occurred. But it was becoming increasingly clear that such radical surgeries were not necessarily better. Why? Perhaps our understanding of cancer as initially being a local disease was incorrect. The idea arose that many cancers were systemic diseases *from the outset*, and that the initial manifestations were local. A nearby lymph node with metastatic cancer was no longer viewed as a potential "jumping off" point for distant metastases, to be removed as soon as possible, but a reflection of conditions that already made the disease generalized. This concept was responsible for the decline in radical surgical procedures, and changes in the way chemotherapeutic drugs were given.

The 1980s saw a new understanding of the genetics of cancer and the proteins that influence cancer cells. It became standard practice, for many types of cancers, to obtain additional information about the quantity of DNA in the tumor cells, and by what growth factors (proteins which facilitate the growth of certain types of tissues) they may be influenced. During this decade, we began to glimpse the true cause of cancer.

As long ago as 1911, Peyton Rous (1879–1970) showed that a virus can cause cancer in animals. It was subsequently shown that some viruses have genes that are not intrinsic to the virus, but instead derived from its previous host. Might the cancer-causing genes on the virus (called oncogenes) have come from an animal host? It was then learned that some oncogenes were actually quite similar to some genes normally present in the animal, suggesting that they may indeed have come to the virus from an animal host. Further work then focused on these genes in animals, and it was learned that in the normal animal, they are involved in the process of cell replication. Cells have to know when to divide and when to stop dividing, and a complex cascading sequence of events involving many proteins causes the cell to divide or to rest. A change in the DNA coding for any of the proteins in this cascade can cause unrestrained division, the essence of cancer. All of us carry many "oncogenes" in our DNA (some use the term "proto-oncogene" when referring to human or animal rather than viral nucleic acid), and we depend on them to tell cells when to divide and when to stop dividing. Oncogenes cause the production of proteins called oncoproteins. These oncoproteins, if functioning normally, are not necessarily cancer causing, and may actually be cancer preventing. In the latter case, it is when the DNA in oncogenes mutates or is rearranged so that the oncoproteins are different, and abnormally functioning, that cancer ensues. One of the genes that has moved to the forefront is called p53, which codes for a protein normally protective against cancer. Abnormalities of p53 lead to a defective protein and a predisposition for certain types of cancer.

Viruses themselves rarely cause cancer in people. (Exceptions include those malignancies associated with AIDS.) The link between viruses and cancer in people is indirect, and in many cancers, viruses are important only insofar as their service in illustrating that the cause of cancer lies in DNA. Much more common is some change in the DNA of the oncogenes that makes the proteins coded from this DNA abnormal. In fact, in those cases where viruses do cause cancer in people, they often do so by inserting their DNA in or next to the DNA of an oncogene, making it impossible for the oncogene to function properly. An increasing number of cancers are associated with specific abnormalities of DNA. As more examples are found associating a specific gene with a specific form of cancer, there will be more opportunities to identify these patients sooner by finding the pertinent DNA aberration, rather than waiting for the disease to become clinically evident.

For some forms of cancer, it appears that the fateful change in oncogene DNA must be accompanied by an environmental event, or series of events occurring over a long time, for malignancy to develop. An example of this is the association of cigarette smoking and lung cancer.

So it is, in one of the great detective stories of the century, that the search for the cause of cancer has come full circle, back to the DNA of the cell itself. New treatment modalities based on this knowledge will one day help defeat cancer. The current state of anti-cancer drugs depends on whether one sees the glass as half full or half empty. Although cancer treatment is much better than a decade ago—overall, 50% of patients diagnosed with cancer defeat it—much of the early optimism for the rapid development of drugs that will cure all forms of cancer has faded. I would characterize current anti-cancer therapy as primitive, which is actually substantially better than fifty years ago, when such therapy could only be described as barbaric. The difficulty with cancer treatment is somewhat similar to the difficulty in treating virally infected cells. Oncogenes are only a small part of the cell's DNA, and the changes to these genes are often subtle. The DNA and metabolic functions of a cancerous cell are still very much like that of a normal cell. It is consequently extremely difficult to develop drugs to kill cancerous cells without severely damaging their benign counterparts. As in the case of virally infected cells, killing cancerous cells can be thought of as looking for a needle that has gone inside the individual straws of hay in a haystack.

The Human Genome Project

The human body is composed of some 100 trillion cells, all of which have the same DNA within a given individual (except that the DNA of sperm and ova contains only half the normal amount). There is no difference in the DNA content of the cells of the skin, bone, brain, etc. All of these tissues contain genes that would appear to be unnecessary for that tissue. For example, all of the above tissues contain genes for eye color, skin color, and height. Different tissues express different portions of the genome, which is the total complement of DNA in the cell—one reason why so much of the genome is regulatory in nature. Regulatory DNA does not directly code for proteins, but is involved in determining whether or not those portions that do code for proteins are expressed or lie dormant. The genes for eye color are suppressed in bone DNA, but expressed in the DNA of the iris of the eye.

Each human cell has perhaps three billion (3,000,000,000 or 3×10^9) base pairs of DNA. The portion of DNA that is translated into proteins comprises perhaps 100,000 genes on our forty-six chromosomes. We have seen how the ultimate cause of cancer lies in our DNA. Many other diseases also are caused by defects in one or more genes. In fact, it may be that we grow old and die because we have genes whose specific function is to cause this to happen. Nature, after all, is more concerned with the welfare of a species than of individuals, and it may be advantageous to the species if individuals are regularly replaced. Knowing which chromosome is involved in a genetic defect and where on the chromosome the problem lies makes gene therapy conceivable, because we know which part of the genome to target.

In a few cases, the precise locations of responsible genes have been elucidated. However, for the most part, we do not know where, or on which chromosome, lies the genetic defect responsible for most diseases. Until we have this information, we cannot approach the cure to many diseases. A large, multicentered, and multifaceted project is now underway to identify the precise location of all of our genes, and to understand the complete sequence of base pairs in our DNA. This is called sequencing the genome. By analogy, our situation now is like opening a book to random pages and learning a few interesting facts here and there. Sequencing the genome is like reading the entire book, absorbing all of its contents, and having access to its index.

The genome is too big to sequence all at once. In fact, even a single chromosome is too large to sequence in its native state. Before actual DNA sequencing can be done, there must first be mapping, determining which chromosome certain landmark genes are on and where on that chromosome they are located. As an analogy, if you wanted to construct a map of a large city, you would start with a few major streets. Gene mapping is done largely by linkage studies— determining how often genes are inherited together. For example, if trait A is usually inherited along with trait B, they are probably on the same chromosome. If the traits are virtually always inherited together, they are most likely very close together on the same chromosome. Genes whose locations are known then serve as reference points.

Then each chromosome must be broken into many pieces with restriction enzymes. Once the DNA is fragmented, the sequence of each fragment can then be determined. But the fragments overlap one another, so the sequences of the fragments are not simply additive. Actually, sorting out the sequences of the fragments and assembling them into a sequence of the whole genome will require a great deal of high-powered computing, so the human genome project is a marriage of molecular biology and computing.

Ultimately, DNA is who we are. The cures to many of our diseases lie in our 100,000 genes. Everything we are, hope to be, or wish we were not, is locked away in those three billion base pairs. Therefore, we must know as much as possible about our DNA. Our newfound ability to sequence the genome is an opportunity unique in our history.

The Silent Earth?

DDT, short for dichlorodiphenyltrichloroethane, was discovered in 1874 by Othmar Ziedler. But it was not until 1939, when Paul Muller re-discovered it and proved its effectiveness as an insecticide, that DDT became part of our world. DDT was a nearly miraculous insecticide, which proved to be of enormous value in World War II and in public health.

By 1970, however, rain and the food chain had disseminated DDT to nearly every location on earth, and traces of it could be found in virtually every living creature. Four problems, all highly critical, were found with DDT. First, it had become universal in its distribution, despite application in only certain areas. Second, by killing insects, DDT removed the food source of animals that prey on them, resulting in diminished numbers of the predators that naturally restrained insect populations. The rapid reproductive rate of insects allowed them to rebound more quickly than their predators, resulting, in the long-term, in a paradoxical *increase* in the number of insects. Organisms low on the food chain generally have greater reproductive rates than do their predators, and can therefore recover from an insult more quickly. Third, insects developed appreciable resistance to DDT, a situation analogous to the development of antibiotic resistance by bacteria. Fourth, DDT was found in human tissues, confirming that toxins tend to work their way up the food chain to involve people, no matter how far we may be from the intended target. DDT, like anti-psychotic medications, had become a blunted miracle.

The general lesson was that nature has a built-in control mechanism for every aspect of our environment. We are likely to do more harm than good if we attempt to supersede natural control. We are an integral part of our environment, and we cannot escape the effects of damage to it.

Rachel Carson (1907–1964), a biologist and science writer, is remembered for works that stimulated thinking about the fragility of the environment, the best known of which is *Silent Spring* (1962), in which she discussed the dangers of DDT and other environmental toxins. The years since *Silent Spring* have confirmed Carson's fear of environmental pollution, and we now have a variety of pollutants jeopardizing our health and the health and safety of posterity. The combination of industrialization and an unprecedented population explosion gives us a terrifying capacity to damage the earth as never before, not only by generating unparalleled *quantities* of waste, but also by producing new *kinds* of waste, with which the earth is not equipped to deal.

Ozone is a rare form of molecular oxygen, consisting of three atoms of oxygen instead of the normal two. By itself, it is toxic, but in a paradoxical way, it is critical to life, because it screens out 99% of the ultraviolet light that would otherwise penetrate the atmosphere and cause skin damage. Ozone is concentrated in a band in the upper atmosphere. In 1985, Joseph Farman (1930–) discovered that a large region of the atmosphere over Antarctica was devoid of ozone. The culprit was shown by Sherwood Rowland and Mario Jose Molina to be chlorofluorocarbons, also called chlorinated fluorocarbons, which survive in the atmosphere for up to seventy-five years. Ozone destruction at the North Pole has also been documented, leaving no doubt that it is jeopardized worldwide. Attempts are in progress to decrease the emission of chlorofluorocarbons into the atmosphere, but old ways die hard.

Industry produces sulfur and nitrogen compounds, which undergo chemical reactions in the atmosphere to become sulfuric and nitric acid. These acids then precipitate as acid rain. Acid rain has its most profound effect on freshwater lakes and streams, where the increased acidity weakens and kills wildlife. Controlling acid rain requires shifting to fuels with lower sulfur content, such as hard coal (anthracite), which has less sulfur than soft coal (bituminous) but is less abundant and more expensive. Other approaches involve removing sulfur and nitrogen compounds from coal before it is burned and removing the harmful combustion products before the exhaust gases are released into the atmosphere. Alternative sources of energy (discussed momentarily) will help a great deal, if we can develop them in time.

Acid rain and chlorofluorocarbons are only two of the innumerable types of pollution. Our civilization produces a multiplicity of noxious materials that damage the delicate ecological balance and send many species to premature extinction. Thus far, some two million species have been identified, thousands of which are endangered by the world's industry and population. There are at least three to five million unidentified species at this time, perhaps tens of millions, so it appears likely that we will exterminate many species of life before we know of their presence. Each species is an irreplaceable monument, and its loss is the destruction of a museum not yet visited or a book not yet read. It is a sad irony that we share the world, in an unknowing way, temporarily, with unique and unknown species, most of which we will never know, and many of which we will destroy. The effects are most severe in the two places on earth where wildlife is at its most abundant and diverse: the rain forest of the land, and the coral reefs of the sea. Here, nature has concentrated its treasure-house of life, and here we must prevent the deleterious effects of our species on others.

Also in the rain forests and the coral reefs is the great potential of finding new drugs. We forget, in these days of chemistry and the preeminence of the laboratory, that many of our current pharmaceuticals are derived from plants, and many of the beneficial medications yet to be discovered will come from plants as well. The laboratory has not yet replaced nature as the sole source of effective drugs and is unlikely to do so in our lifetimes. The rain forests and the coral reefs are as great a source of potentially effective medicines as all of the world's laboratories, but this information passes from our memory very quickly.

Plants and animals are often an early indicator of environmental changes that will later affect humans. We are part of the ecological chain and cannot escape the destruction we have unleashed upon the world. Unless we harness our industrial waste, the silent spring may become the silent earth.

Respect for the environment requires an ability to think ahead, always our weakness. The immediate partial remedy is curbing the output of industrial waste products and holding business fully accountable for its damages. But beyond this, pollution has a deeper cause and will require a deeper solution. Every aspect of environmental destruction, from industrial pollution to the decimation of the rain forest, is made worse by overpopulation, and every aspect of it would be markedly improved with population control. Those who destroy the environment are sometimes greedy, but very often they are simply trying to exist. We will get further if we recognize that the problem of pollution is substantially a problem of overpopulation, and the prevention of a silent earth is primarily the prevention of unwanted pregnancies. As I hope to show in this work's final section, this can be done, but only with new thinking.

The Challenge of Energy

The term "energy crisis" was used in the 1970s, during the Middle Eastern petroleum embargo, with little comprehension of the complete, long-term problem. As our population passes the six billion mark, at the rate of almost one hundred million per year, our energy problem is not the result of an economic embargo, but rather of overpopulation and a lack of foresight. Only when these problems are addressed can there be any lasting resolution of the energy shortage first noticed in the 1970s. There are many potential fuel sources, each with its relative advantages and drawbacks.

The major sources of fuel in the industrialized world today are the fossil (also called hydrocarbon) fuels, which are organic (carbon containing) compounds derived from millions of years of evolution of life. There are three types of fossils fuels. Petroleum (crude oil) has only been a significant source of energy for some one hundred and thirty years. It is the raw material not just for gasoline, but also for a variety of other materials ranging from plastics to asphalt. Petroleum and its derivatives consist primarily of carbon and hydrogen, but burn with the release of a variety of impurities. Coal, which is predominantly carbon, is more abundant than petroleum and natural gas, but has sulfur and nitrogen impurities which, after combustion, form compounds which contribute to acid rain. Natural gas (which is primarily the simple hydrocarbon methane) is a fossil fuel that burns more cleanly than petroleum products or coal. But all fossil fuels, including natural gas, release carbon dioxide upon combustion. This carbon dioxide may be causing the temperature of the earth's atmosphere to increase in the process of global warming.

Most of the atmosphere derives little of its heat directly from sunlight because the wavelength of the sunlight is too short for atmospheric gases to absorb the energy. Rather, sunlight passes through the atmosphere and its energy is absorbed by the surface. The warmed surface then emits radiation of longer wavelength than sunlight, and the atmosphere can absorb heat from this longer wavelength radiation. Most of the atmosphere thus gets its heat from the earth's surface, not directly from the Sun, and as it does this, the effect is to keep within the earth's biosphere (the portion of the earth that sustains life) heat which would otherwise escape into space. This is called the greenhouse effect, because it is the mechanism by which greenhouses (and automobile interiors) heat up on sunny days. The greenhouse effect is not an intrinsically bad process, but rather a normal process on which we are dependent.

380

Carbon dioxide plays a leading role in the retention of heat. The issue of global warming involves the question of whether human activities accelerate this natural process to a significant extent, and upset a delicate balance. Humans can theoretically accelerate atmospheric heating by two mechanisms. One is the increased production of carbon dioxide. The other is the clearing of forests, which depletes the world of the trees which would normally absorb and metabolize carbon dioxide. In recent years, atmospheric carbon dioxide levels have been increasing, and the evidence is strong that we are slowly increasing the temperature of the biosphere. One price that we may be incurring in an increase in the amount of the earth's surface that is covered by desert. Desert land is increasing at the expense of grasslands, and it is probable that global warming is a cause.

There is some disagreement on the amount of available fossil fuels. But even if such stores are abundant, it is desirable to use energy sources which do not release carbon dioxide, and this means decreasing our dependence on fossil fuels. Power derived from water, wind, and the earth's interior (geothermal energy) has the potential of supplementing that from other sources, but it does not appear likely that these sources can be the mainstay of the future.

Nuclear fission, first used as a peacetime source of energy in 1956, produces energy in many parts of the world. Although it does not pollute in the same way as fossil fuels, fission is profoundly polluting in the form of radioactive waste. Since fission breaks large atoms into small atoms, its raw materials are such large and radioactive atoms as uranium and plutonium, which are dangerous and scarce. We are all aware of the difficulties of Three Mile Island and Chernobyl, the latter constituting a meltdown, where the radioactive materials gained full access to the environment, with catastrophic results. In addition, the threat of theft of raw materials, with subsequent nuclear terrorism, is very real. Tragically, a nuclear bomb is not hard to make, and little fissionable material is required.

Fusion is, in one sense, the opposite of fission. In fusion, small atoms combine to form larger atoms. The total mass of the atoms after the combination is less than that before the union; the difference is expressed as energy according to Einstein's equation $E=MC^2$. For most of the lives of stars, their fusion reactions use ordinary hydrogen, the nucleus of which is simply a proton. But man-made fusion reactions more often use deuterium, an isotope of hydrogen that has one neutron. Although deuterium is rare relative to ordinary hydrogen, there is still enough of it in the water of the oceans to last forever. Nuclear fusion, therefore, occupies a unique place in the challenge of energy, because the raw materials needed for it are present in essentially unlimited supply. The quantity of energy that can be released is numbingly vast. Depending on the precise mix of fusionable materials, fusion generates fewer hazardous waste products than fission, and fusion reactors will be less subject to meltdowns.

There are, however, two difficulties with fusion. First, fusion can only be achieved by subjecting hydrogen to conditions of extreme heat and pressure. With our present technology, more energy has to be put into creating the conditions for fusion than can be retrieved from the process. Ways are being sought to trigger the process without expending such great amounts of energy. The term "cold fusion" refers to the process, not yet achieved, wherein nuclear fusion is attained without a large energy input. Lasers are a leading candidate for triggering a small, controlled fusion reaction by heating and compressing a tiny pellet of hydrogen. In the meantime, slow progress is being made toward a self-sustaining fusion reaction that uses the energy it produces to create the conditions for continued fusion.

The second difficulty with fusion is that it is very difficult to control and cannot be safely carried out in ordinary fission reactors. However, much progress has been made in the construction of reactors that can confine the products of a fusion reaction. Opinions vary widely on the practicability of harnessing fusion. Let us hope the optimists prove correct, for the use of safe and controlled fusion reactions would solve much of our energy problems. However, even the successful harnessing of fusion would not bring an immediate end to our energy problems, because we must also diminish the use of gasoline in small engines such as automobiles, and it will be many more additional years before fusion can be used in such engines.

Batteries are limited as power sources in small engines, because they supply relatively little power and they run down, requiring either recharging or replacement. However, there is substantial research on new types of batteries of novel construction. One unusual type of battery is the fuel cell, in which external materials are added, becoming integral components of the chemical reactions. One of these external materials typically combines with the solution in one of the cells of the battery, resulting in a reaction that supplies electrons. These electrons then move through an external circuit and perform work, after which they return to the other cell of the battery. There, they react with another externally supplied material to yield a product that can again react with the first external material, generating more electrons and permitting the cycle to continue. Unlike batteries, fuel cells never run down, as long as the external materials are replenished. One of the most common fuel cells uses hydrogen and oxygen in a solution of potassium hydroxide, with hydrogen reacting with the solution to furnish electrons which, after completing their work, return to the cell and re-enter the solution by reacting with oxygen.

Chapter 34
Reflections of Ourselves

*We can see ourselves and our world in ways that
enrich our lives.*

THUS FAR IN THIS WORK, WE HAVE EXAMINED WHO WE ARE by what we have learned about the universe and how we have learned it. But much of who we are is not shown by what we have *learned* about the world, but by how we *contemplate* it, and ourselves. The arts are our vehicle of contemplation.

To my mind, art is anything that examines the human experience and makes that examination audible, visible, or tangible. The arts make possible self-discovery, and in a world where the expression of feelings between people is not often accepted, they become a way of conveying who we are to other people.

Art is an opportunity to put aside the frustrations of the past, the stresses of the present, and the uncertainties of the future, and step, if only for a moment, into a new world of awareness and tranquility. This chapter is a history of the arts, and therefore, a history of our search for expression.

In this chapter, we will examine the reflections of ourselves that have been created with the images, words, and sounds of the Western artistic tradition. This work now becomes what Daniel Boorstin refers to as a "view from the literate West." The major periods in the arts are described, leading up to their present form, but it should be remembered that the art, music, or literature of any time is an end unto itself, and does not achieve its significance as a stepping stone to any other period or style. Unlike science, the arts of one period do not replace or surpass those of another.

Images of Ourselves

*Painting is silent poetry
and poetry painting that speaks.*
— *Plutarch*

Our word art derives from *Ars*, Latin for skill. Used generally, art refers to all activities that examine the human experience. In this section, the word "art" is a specific reference to the visual arts: painting, sculpture, architecture, and related disciplines. These form the visual chronicle of who we are.

The visual arts are concerned chiefly with shape, color, light, and space. Because no reproduction can perfectly convey the subtleties and nuances of a work of art, such as fine details of texture and light, the full contribution that the visual arts make to our understanding of the world can only be realized when they are examined in person.

Visual arts are created for a variety of reasons, including religion, commemoration, expression, and aesthetic appeal. It is possible that the first visual arts had religious origins. The cave paintings alluded to in the first chapter may have been created to insure successful hunting. Contemporary with these paintings were stone carvings of female figures perhaps representing fertility or the gods who controlled fertility. We simply do not know the purpose of the first art, but it is remarkably expressive, vibrant, and sophisticated.

Egyptian art is commonly referred to as static, unchanging over the centuries, because it was functional and served to preserve the political and religious base of their society. However, this is often not the case, and much Egyptian art exudes expressivity as well as functionality. We must also remember that Egyptian art, even their hieroglyphic writing, was brilliantly colored. Such works as the *Golden Mask of Tutankhamun* and the *Bust of Nefertiti* are lovely and dynamic portraits, in which the loving care of the artist and the personality of the subject shine through the functionality of the work.

Architecture is a form of sculpture that encloses a space in a way rendering it usable for human activities. In Egypt, we find the first works of architecture to be substantially preserved. Egyptian architecture, such as the great pyramids of the Old Kingdom (early third millennium B.C.E.), is massive and permanent because it was intended to be the home of the Pharaoh, the central figure in the preservation of Egyptian culture, as he entered the afterlife. In addition to the pyramids, Egyptian temples are also great works of architecture.

Because Mesopotamia was a less stable region than Egypt, its artistic styles changed as cultures came and went, so the land between the rivers does not have the long, unbroken artistic tradition of the land of the Nile. Most surviving art of ancient Mesopotamia is in the form of cylinder seals, although a few statues survive. As we have seen, cylinder seals served a commercial as well artistic function.

Perhaps the first culture in which art became what we would call dynamic and emotional was the Minoan civilization of ancient Crete. Flourishing from about 2,000 B.C.E. to about 1,450 B.C.E., the Minoans created extraordinary miniature statues. They also left some of antiquity's finest frescoes. (Fresco painting is the application of water-soluble pigments to wet plaster; as the plaster and pigment dry, the pigment becomes an integral part of the plaster.)

Greek civilization achieved the climax of art in antiquity. After the fall of Mycenae, there was a relative dark age in Greece. By about 800 B.C.E., Greece had recovered sufficiently to enter the Archaic period. During this period the Greeks began to create the *Kouros*, a statue of the idealized young male nude, and the *Kore*, a statue of the clothed young woman.

No examples of Greek wall paintings survive, and we can only use surviving descriptions to speculate on this art. However, we do have examples of Greek painting on vases. In the late seventh century B.C.E., a method of painting pottery emerged known as the black figure technique, yielding black figures on a red background. This technique resulted in pottery that was more detailed and proportioned than any before and made possible the telling of entire stories on a single pot. By the mid-sixth century B.C.E., the red figure technique was introduced in Athens. This produced a red figure on a black background, and by 450 B.C.E., red figures had replaced black figures.

Greek temples rival Egyptian pyramids in grandeur, but in a different way. Not as massive or imposing, Greek temples were not monuments to eternity, but to people's ability to see perfection in form. The Greeks understood optical illusions such as a straight line appearing to sag in the middle and the parallel lines of the sides of a column appearing to move toward each other in the center. In the Parthenon, such illusions were compensated for, resulting in the appearance of perfection. Comparison of the Parthenon with the great pyramids leaves one with the feeling that these two cultures had very different outlooks on the world, but that they were equally triumphant in expressing these outlooks.

As we have seen, Roman achievements in science, with some exceptions, were often a recapitulation of Greek accomplishments. At one time, this view was also held for Roman art, but we now have a very different view of Roman visual arts, based on their several unique features.

The Greeks knew of the arch, but rarely employed it, whereas the Romans made it a common feature of their architecture. They also extended the principle of the arch into the vault, a series of intersecting arch shaped structures used to make a ceiling that is substantially self supporting. We have also seen that the Romans introduced concrete, wherein a hardening agent (cement) was mixed with water and stone or gravel, after which the hydrogen and oxygen in the water underwent chemical reactions, making them integral and permanent parts of the final structure. With concrete and the arch, the Romans could enclose larger volumes than had previously been possible, and therefore revolutionize the treatment of interior spaces. This is best seen in the Pantheon, the great Roman temple, the dome of which spans one hundred and forty-five feet (forty-four meters).

The giant of Roman architectural writing was Marcus Vitruvius Pollio (fl. first century B.C.E.). Vitruvius, as he is remembered, authored the sole surviving architectural treatise from antiquity. Called *De Architectura*, it consists of ten volumes, and exerted immense influence on Renaissance architects after the rediscovery of classical works.

Unlike Greece, some Roman wall paintings have survived. By blurring the images of distant objects, Roman painters were the first artists whose works have survived to achieve a degree of perspective. The Romans were interested less in the *Kouros*, the portrayal of an idealized fictitious person, than in the realistic depiction of living people. Roman portraiture gives us something new: authentic images of a particular subject's actual appearance, and Roman sculpture became a triumph of the individual.

After the fall of Rome, Italy was relatively silent in the arts, but the Western artistic tradition continued in Northern Europe and Byzantium. By the time of Justinian (c. 482–565 C.E.), a distinct Byzantine style was recognizable, an important medium for which was mosaic. A mosaic is an art form constructed from pieces of stone or pigmented glass embedded in plaster. Byzantine mosaicists, known throughout the Western and Middle Eastern world, were employed by Muslims in the decoration of some Mosques.

The architectural epitome of Byzantine art is the Hagia Sophia, a Christian Church built in the sixth century C.E. in Constantinople. The Hagia Sophia employed a novel way of placing a dome over a square—the pendentive. To understand this architectural innovation, consider the problem of building a dome over a square. The difficulty occurs at the corners, where the curved surface of the dome has to intersect the right angles of the square. One could simply construct the largest dome that would be completely contained within the square. This design avoids the corners, because the dome touches the square in the centers of the sides, but would be too small to be esthetically appealing. By building a dome larger than the square that touches the square only at the corners, with some of the dome hanging over the square, a higher dome can be achieved but is no longer contained within the square. Recognizing that the cross section of a dome is a circle, Byzantine engineers constructed a partial dome that touched the square only at its corners, omitting the top and the portion that would hang over the square. This resulted in four curved wedges and smoothed the corners into a round base, upon which a second, complete dome was built. The pendentive is thus a partial dome that provides a surface upon which to build a complete dome.

Employing the pendentive, the architects of the Hagia Sophia enclosed vast amounts of space without the pointed arch, which would not be effectively used until Gothic times of the twelfth century. Byzantine art also influenced artistic development in Western Europe and Russia.

Northern European architecture reverted to simpler forms and unvaulted construction. Early Christian painting in the West sought to religiously educate and convert the largely illiterate masses. It therefore relied heavily on symbolic imagery, much of which was calculated to inspire in its viewers the hope of salvation and the fear of eternal damnation. Significantly, the human figure was only very rarely portrayed in the West from 500–1000 C.E.

A major form of painting in this period was the illumination of manuscripts. In antiquity, books had been produced and illuminated by professionals, but during the Middle Ages, these tasks fell to the monasteries. Manuscript illumination began with simple illustration, the visual support of the text. Ornamental illumination, usually of religious books, followed, and was prevalent in England and Ireland by the year 700. The Frankish kingdom, roughly encompassing present-day France and Germany, was also a center for manuscript illumination during its attempt to revive the greatness of Rome. In the twelfth century, book production and illumination shifted from monasteries to workshops, and secular books were illuminated in large numbers.

The Romanesque style was so named because it was partially based on a revival of Roman ideas, especially the arch. The Romanesque period dates from about 1000 to 1150—a period corresponding to the beginning of economic stability in Western Europe. It arose from the influence of the Catholic Church on the local styles of Europe, a heritage of the barbarians. The Church had become a major landowner—the key to economic strength—and a great patron of the arts. The influence of Roman architecture and the Catholic Church transformed a variety of related regional styles into the first international artistic style of Europe. In addition, returning crusaders may have brought back ideas from the East that also contributed to this artistic movement.

This style is best seen in the Romanesque cathedral, a more elaborate structure than the simple rectangular church it replaced. Romanesque cathedrals were constructed with a long nave, which was intersected by a transept, giving the cathedral a cross shape. Small chapels were placed along the sides.

The use of an arch, in exchange for not overly stressing the center, creates an outward force that is not present in a post and lintel configuration. This outward force must be compensated for by building either very thick walls or an external buttress for the wall. For aesthetic reasons, the buttress was preferred. In Romanesque times, it took the form of a simple pier-shaped structure emanating from the exterior of the wall at a right angle.

The term "Gothic" denotes an artistic style that began in the mid-twelfth century and lasted, in some parts of Europe, into the sixteenth century. Renaissance "scholars" used the word "Gothic" in a derogatory manner, believing that style inferior to their own. As we shall see, many names for artistic movements and periods have a derogatory basis.

The beginning of the Gothic style can be more precisely dated than is usually possible for artistic movements. In 1140, the Abbey Church of Saint Denis in France was rebuilt. Suger, the Abbot of Saint Denis, used the Gothic arch, a pointed arch based on the ellipse rather than the circle. The Gothic arch was stronger than the common arch, permitting the great height characteristic of Gothic cathedrals. Again, external buttressing was used instead of thicker walls. But the very high, thin walls of the Gothic cathedral required higher external support than its Romanesque counterpart. Simple Romanesque buttresses raised to such a height would have required support, reducing their aesthetic appeal. So support came in the form of the flying buttress, a detached buttress connected to the wall by a portion of an arch that reaches up to the necessary height.

We have seen that vaults are a series of intersecting arch-shaped structures used to make a substantially self-supporting ceiling. Pointed arches led to pointed ribbed vaults. With the pointed arch, the pointed ribbed vault, and the flying buttress, internal walls could be sharply reduced in number, permitting wider interior spaces. Immense windows were set in exterior walls and filled with stained glass, creating an art form that is characteristic of this period (stained glass, made by mixing metal oxides into the molten glass during production, was first widely used in the West in the Romanesque period).

When people think of Gothic cathedrals, they often forget that their sides contain fine examples of sculpture. These sculptures represent a reintroduction of large-scale sculpture, largely absent from Western art for nearly a millennium. These sculptures and stained glass windows make Gothic cathedrals total works of art.

The great age of cathedral building lasted scarcely more than a hundred years, from the middle of the twelfth to the middle of the thirteenth centuries, but that brief time imparted more than a change in architectural styles. The great Gothic cathedrals of Saint Denis, Chartres, Notre Dame, Westminster Abbey, and other sites do not tower upward solely for the glory of God; they also serve to honor man. The Gothic cathedrals are a monument to something new in the human experience: humanism, the belief that people are a proper focus of humanity. During this century, the great cathedrals gave physical form to the new dualism of the Western mind: faith in God and exploration of the newly found power of the mind. Both the cathedrals and the ideas they represented were inconceivable two centuries before. Economic prosperity, coupled with the acquisition of and respect for new knowledge combined to refocus Western Europe.

Traditionally, the Gothic period is considered to be the stage of artistic development immediately before the Renaissance. As I have attempted to show in this work, the Renaissance was a gradual process, beginning about the year 1100 with increasing economic prosperity and contact with the Muslims, who had preserved and extended Greco-Roman learning. The Gothic period reflects the awakening of the human mind and the renewed desire to learn. The signature of man is written on the high walls of the Gothic cathedrals. The Renaissance had begun.

Arising from the general rebirth of intellectual development in Western Europe, much of what we call Renaissance art began in Florence about the year

1300. From this time forward, the names of individual artists become more prominent. Foremost among the artists of that time was Giotto di Bondone (c.1266-1337). In his paintings, Giotto portrayed religious themes in a human way. While God remained the focus of his work, he introduced drama, vitality, and emotion in a way that was new to the Western world, and which foreshadowed the Renaissance. In his frescoes at the Arena (also called Scrovegni) Chapel at Padua, Giotto created more natural renditions with lifelike faces and figures. Facial expressions disclose the feelings and thoughts of the subject, and light and shadow are used to give a degree of three dimensionality and to suggest movement. Bright, vivid colors (now somewhat faded) were employed to provide contrast and heighten emotional effect. The paintings in this little church were something new to Western art, and forever changed its techniques and goals. Upon seeing his works, one immediately knows that a frontier in the visual arts has been crossed. All subsequent Western artists, from the Renaissance to Picasso, have a profound debt to Giotto.

Giotto placed art on the verge of a new leap forward, but this would be interrupted by the great plague of the mid-fourteenth century. In the fifteenth century, this new approach was brought to the fruition that we call the Renaissance.

Renaissance art illustrates that great movements in the arts, like those in the sciences, are to some extent predictable. Just as the re-acquaintance with classical literature and knowledge began the West's ascent in science and technology, re-acquaintance with ancient cultures also ushered in a new age in the visual arts.

Filippo Brunelleschi (1377–1446) revived classical forms in architecture and based his designs on mathematics, proportion, and perspective. Perspective (the realistic rendering of three dimensionality on a two-dimensional surface) had been known to a limited extent in antiquity, and Giotto had achieved a degree of perspective by the judicious use of light and shadow. But it was largely Brunelleschi who more fully developed linear perspective—a mathematical and geometric method of rendering three dimensional images on a two dimensional surface, a key component of which is that lines which are perpendicular to the plane of the painting converge towards a single point in the distance (called the vanishing point). In 1418, he secured his place in history when he was commissioned to complete the dome of the Florence cathedral, which he did with a brilliant double-shelled design. Later, he would design the Church of San Lorenzo and the Pazzi chapel (the latter begun in 1441). These works, like most Renaissance buildings, were smaller than their Gothic counterparts, because they were constructed for man—a confident, prosperous man—as much as for God. Between 1415 and 1420, Brunelleschi created the first paintings with true perspective, although these have not survived.

What was the effect of artistic perspective on the larger civilization? Apart from contemporary applications in cartography and industrial design, perspective had abstract but important effects on Renaissance civilization. In fifteenth-century Florence, it provided an extension of human abilities, a more thorough, quantitative look at the world, and a way of seeing the world accurately for oneself. As we have seen, quantification and seeing for oneself were new hallmarks of Western civilization.

Masaccio (1401–1427), in a tragically brief career, was among the first to capitalize on the new technique of perspective in his frescoes for the Brancacci Chapel, such as *The Tribute Money* and *Saint Peter Healing With His Shadow*. The latter painting uses a contemporary setting to give increased relevance to the story. Donatello (1386–1466) re-introduced large-scale bronze sculptures. His *David* was the first freestanding, nude bronze cast since antiquity. Donatello also reintroduced the contrapposto position, wherein weight is born on one leg, permitting the rest of the body to be relaxed and natural. Leon Battista Alberti (1404–1472) brought the lessons of antiquity to architecture, largely by resurrecting the *De Architectura* of Vitruvius. Alberti wrote his own textbook of architecture, *De Re Aedificatoria* (*On Building*), and a mathematical treatment of perspective, *Della Pittura* (*On Painting*). Other artists of the Renaissance included Lorenzo Ghiberti (1381–1455), Fra Angelico (c. 1387–1455), Paolo Uccello (1397–1475), Filippo Lippi (c.1406–1469), Piero della Francesca (1420–1492), Andrea de Verrocchio (c.1434–1488), and Sandro Botticelli (1445–1510). Botticelli's *Birth of Venus* was an early study of the female nude.

These artists were inspired, as was the general intellectual rebirth, by ideas from antiquity. There was a scientific approach to the visual arts, as shown by the use of perspective. Artists studied anatomy texts, both ancient and contemporary, to facilitate the more realistic depiction of the human form. Renaissance artists and architects looked to ancient Greece not just for proportion and mathematical harmony, but also for humanism. Reflecting the increasing secularization of society, the primary concern of the visual arts shifted from religion to humanity.

New possibilities were opened by the introduction of oil pigments, whereby pigment is mixed with oil (usually linseed oil) and thinned with an organic fluid such as turpentine. No water is used, in contrast to fresco painting (where the pigment is dissolved in water) and tempera (where the pigment is mixed with egg yolk and thinned with water), which were the predominant media of the time. Oil painting permitted more depth of colors, a greater range in the depiction of light and dark, and subtler atmospheric effects, such as the misty background in the *Mona Lisa*. The new pigments also made possible chiaroscuro, the use of light to contrast areas of great illumination with areas of darkness. The painting of oil on canvas, which largely replaced fresco on plaster and tempera on wood, combined with perspective to make the artistic revolution of the Renaissance possible. One of the first to utilize oil pigments was Jan van Eyck (1380–1441), whose works, such as *Giovanni Arnolfini and His Bride*, give views of humanity that are not idealized, but reflect the practices and concerns of the day. He and his brother Hubert painted the *Ghent Altarpiece*.

Following van Eyck in northern Europe were Rogier van der Weyden (c. 1400–1464), best remembered for *Descent From the Cross*, Hieronymus Bosch (c.1450–1516), whose works include *The Garden of Earthly Delights*, and Hugo van der Goes (c. 1440–1482), whose masterpiece was the *Portinari Altarpiece*.

While the *ideas* of the Renaissance spread throughout Europe, the movement took different forms in northern and southern Europe. Events in the south (Italy) allow us to see that movements in the arts both shape and mirror the events and circumstances of the macrosociety. The artistic focus on humanism in Italy was made possible in part by increased secular patronage of the arts, best illustrated by Cosimo de' Medici the Elder (1389–1464) and his grandson Lorenzo (1449–1492). By the sixteenth century, increasing papal patronage drew many artists away from Florence to Rome, where many of the great works of the Italian High Renaissance can be found.

The great masters of the Italian High Renaissance were Leonardo da Vinci (1452–1519), Michelangelo Buonarroti (1475–1564), and Raffaello Sanzio (1483–1520, known to us as Raphael). Da Vinci received little formal education, but meticulously recorded his ideas and observations of nature in the notebooks that were his constant companions. Known for innovative thinking in many areas, he brought to his painting a superb understanding of anatomy and light. *Mona Lisa* is arguably the most famous single painting in the world. Ever an experimenter, da Vinci applied an oil and tempera mixture to plaster in *The Last Supper*. The fresco began to deteriorate within a few years of its completion and will be lost if a current restoration effort is not successful. Raphael followed da Vinci, and is best known for paintings commissioned for the Vatican Palace, the most famous of which is *School of Athens.*

Michelangelo was more influential than either of these two, and it was he, not da Vinci, who bent the course of history with his creativity. More than any other artist of history, Michelangelo was successful in all three disciplines of the visual arts—painting, sculpture, and architecture—and was an excellent poet. Sculpture was his true passion, and as a sculptor, he liberated his *David, Moses,* and *Pietà* from blocks of marble, and captured in marble the essence of who we are. As a painter, he left us the frescoes of the Sistine Chapel, which depict Biblical scenes ranging from the Creation to the drunkenness of Noah. Ironically, his rivals, headed by Donato Bramante (1444–1514), the principal architect of the Renaissance, persuaded the Pope to give Michelangelo the Sistine assignment, hoping to pull him away from sculpture, where he was without peer, toward fresco painting, in which he had no experience. Michelangelo transformed this treachery into the most famous set of paintings in history. Late in life, he returned to the Sistine Chapel to paint *The Last Judgment.* As an architect, he was one of a number of people to work on Saint Peter's Cathedral (designing the famous dome), and his designs have influenced architecture to the present day.

In contrast to Raphael, Michelangelo's works are permeated by constant struggle and the power of the human mind. His are not peaceful works, rather creations of power and restlessness, which seem to have driven their creator to release them from his mind. In his works, and in his unconquerable spirit, Michelangelo strikes a remarkable parallel with a composer born three centuries later. Indeed, if I were to pick the two most indomitable personalities of history, they would be Michelangelo and Beethoven. Both showed the power and the potential of the human mind, and therefore *who we can be,* as well as who we are.

Because Venice is in the northern part of Italy, it was influenced by Flanders (encompassing regions in contemporary Belgium and France) earlier than Florence or Rome. Since oil painting first became prevalent in Flanders, Venetian Renaissance painting showed a movement towards oil before the Italian cities of the south. Giovanni Bellini (1430–1516), in works such as *Saint Francis in Ecstasy,* was among the first Italian masters to fully understand and effectively employ oil painting. Other Venetian painters include Giorgione (1475–1510; famous for *The Tempest*), Antonio Corregio (c.1490–1534), and Paolo Veronese (1528–1588).

The greatest artist of the Venetian school was Titian (c.1487–1576). A student of Bellini, Titian was one of the first to bring the potential of oil painting to full bloom. After the brilliant colors and masterful use of light that characterize Titian's long career, there was no returning to tempera. His longevity, genius, and influence rivaled that of Michelangelo. Titian's portraits are more than a rendition of the subject's appearance; they show the emotions and strength of will beneath the features. Among his many masterpieces are *Bacchanalia at Andros*, *Venus of Urbino*, *Doge Andrea Gritti*, and *Rape of Europa.*

Northern European Renaissance art is on a smaller, less "grand" scale than that of Italy, accounting for the common misconception that only Italy produced great art during this period. But the art of the north reflected the humanistic spirit and questing mind just as much as that of the Italian High Renaissance. Lacking classical art and ruins to serve as a guide, Northern Europe turned to nature to express Renaissance ideas. Albrecht Dürer (1471–1528) was one of the finest observers of both nature and humanity in the history of Western art. In his engravings and paintings, Dürer demonstrated a masterful observation of nature and achieved precise reproduction of its details. Like Leonardo, he was a scholar in all fields. No one has surpassed his mastery of engravings and woodcuts. Two of his finest works are *Apocalypse*, a series of fourteen woodcuts, and *Melancholia*. Dürer's countryman, Matthias Grünewald (c. 1475–1528), is best known for his *Isenheim Altarpiece.*

Northern Renaissance artists depicted the local environment and daily lives of people more than Italian artists, best seen in the work of Pieter Bruegel (1528–1569; also spelled Brueghel). Bruegel was one of the first to explore genre painting, the depiction of secular scenes showing common people and everyday life, as exemplified in *Hunters in the Snow*. From this time forward, genre painting will alternate with painting stressing uncommon scenes, such as royalty, historical events, or religious activities.

1520, the year of Raphael's death and one year after the death of Leonardo, is often taken as the end of the High Renaissance in Italy. The period that followed, called Mannerism, is characterized by a desire to express more emotion and imagination than had been possible with the strictly rational style of the Renaissance. There is a theatrical effect wherein human figures are elongated and distorted. Lighting is often unnatural and appears otherworldly. The most famous Mannerist painter was El Greco (c.1541–1614), and his paintings, such as *The Burial of Count Orgaz*, clearly illustrate a compositional style different from the Renaissance. Some consider Tintoretto (1518–1594) to be a Mannerist also.

The period of Baroque art roughly corresponds to the seventeenth century.

To some extent, Baroque art developed as a reaction to Mannerism. Movements in the arts often develop from previous movements through a predictable building process similar to that observed in scientific development, but they sometimes result from an intentional movement away from the foundations of the past. In the case of the Baroque, it was desired to move away from the distorted figures of Mannerism and achieve a more realistic portraiture.

Baroque art took different forms in different parts of Europe. In the Protestant countries of the north, the principal sponsors of Baroque art were mercantilists, and the art addressed everyday life. In the Catholic countries of the south, in response to the Reformation, the Catholic Church fostered art that was colorful and dramatic, the purpose of which was to appeal to the masses and encourage people to remain loyal to the Church.

Annibale Carracci (1560–1609) and Michelangelo Caravaggio (1573–1610) were among the first artists whose works fall in the Baroque period. Carracci sought a revival of the classical style of the High Renaissance, while Caravaggio celebrated common people, using genre paintings to portray the drama of daily life. (In his religious works, he used ordinary people as models, even for holy figures.) By brilliantly using light to heighten dramatic effect, Caravaggio more fully developed the technique of chiaroscuro. His most striking and dramatic works include *The Calling of Saint Matthew* and the *Entombment of Christ*.

Peter Paul Rubens (1577–1640) is remembered for his depictions of female figures and his dazzling colors. His paintings are sensuous and of captivating majesty, as shown, for example, in the series of paintings he created for Marie de' Medici. Rubens's student, Anthony van Dyck (1599–1641), captured the essence of imperial power with sensitive portraits of royalty and aristocracy.

In southern Europe, Gianlorenzo Bernini (1598–1680) is the most remembered sculptor and architect of the Baroque. Some of his sculptures include *David* (where he shows the actual act of casting the stone) and *Ecstasy of Saint Teresa*. Diego Velázquez (1599–1660) painted *Las Meninas* (*The Maids of Honor*), one of the world's most famous paintings. In France, Nicolas Poussin (1594–1665) combined Baroque style with a considerable amount of classicism and rationality. Many of his works have classical ruins in the background. In the Protestant North, Franz Hals (1580–1666) was one of the supreme portrait artists of history. In his hands, the portrait conveys a scene of action with spontaneity and intricacy, virtually becoming a snapshot, as is well seen in *Laughing Cavalier*. Jan Vermeer (1632–1675) is known for his simple interior views of common life, such as *Young Woman With a Water Jug*. His *View of Delft* is considered by many to be his best painting.

The giant of this period was Rembrandt van Rijn (1606–1669). Like all great explorers, Rembrandt cannot simply be placed in a category. Not every artist wholly subscribes to the schools and trends of his time, and we will see other examples of artists whose contributions elevate them beyond rigid stylistic distinctions. It is well to think of the arts as progressing in movements, because creative artists, like scientists, tend to move as a group toward new realizations, but these movements are general trends, not all-encompassing classifications. Mistakes occur when assuming that an artist's (or a composer's or writer's) time limits him or her to a single style. Rembrandt's early work *was* Baroque, but his later work adopted a unique quality, defying classification in any particular period. These later works explore human emotions and personalities. The approximately three hundred paintings include such masterpieces as *The Night Watch* (more accurately referred to as *Captain Banning Cocq's Company*), *The Anatomy Lesson of Dr. Tulp*, *The Syndics of the Cloth Guild*, *The Return of the Prodigal Son*, and numerous self portraits. Some fourteen hundred sensitive and expressive drawings make Rembrandt arguably the master of this medium, while hundreds of superb etchings establish him as a graphic artist whose only rival is Dürer. Through dozens of self-portraits, he examines the effect of life on the human spirit—a visual autobiography that follows the artist throughout his lifetime. In them, we see the inner workings of his mind as he struggled through tragedies such as bankruptcy and the deaths of his wife and all but one of his children. No other works of art follow one person's journey through life as intimately as Rembrandt's self-portraits, except perhaps those of van Gogh. His art is a tender examination of humanity and a compassionate view of who we are.

The leading architect of the Baroque period was Christopher Wren (1632–1723). Wren began his architectural career at the age of twenty-nine, after achieving excellence in science and mathematics. A fire in London, which demolished many of the city's older buildings, afforded Wren the opportunity that is inherent in disaster. The Gothic cathedral of Saint Paul's was one of the casualties, and Wren's neoclassical design for its rebuilding is thought by many to be his masterpiece.

In the early eighteenth century, the Baroque was succeeded in France and Germany by the Rococo, a style of primarily decorative, light-hearted art that portrayed court life with gaiety, grace, delicacy, and attention to detail. Rococo art was not reflective of or painted for common people, but for the aristocracy. Exponents of this style include Antoine Watteau (1684–1721), Giambattista Tiepolo (1696–1770), and François Boucher (1703–1770). However, it would be wrong to think that these artists created only frivolous works. Many of their creations are masterpieces, such as Tiepolo's *Ceiling of the Great Stairs of the Episcopal Palace* at Würzburg and Watteau's *Embarkation for Cythera*.

Contemporary English artists included William Hogarth (1697–1764), Joshua Reynolds (1723–1792) and Thomas Gainsborough (1727-1788). Hogarth created a series of eight engravings called *The Rake's Progress*, centered around the rise and fall of an irresponsible person who actually represents all of us. Reynolds's greatest works were his portraits.

In 1748, the ruins of the Roman cities Pompeii and Herculaneum were discovered. These discoveries, as well as the writings of the archeologist and art historian Johann Winckelmann (1717–1768) led to the Neoclassical revival of the mid-eighteenth century, in which there was again a turning to the past for inspiration. In architecture, both European and American buildings reflected the renewed interest in styles of antiquity. (An example is Thomas Jefferson's Monticello.) In painting, the Neoclassical style was led by Jacques-Louis David (1748–1825) and Jean-Auguste-Dominique Ingres (1780–1867). David's *Oath of the Horatii* depicts three brothers who pledge their lives to the defense of Rome, encouraging the viewer to attain a similar level of devotion and courage.

Emerging from the Enlightenment and the rationalism of the scientific revolution, Romanticism retained a humanistic focus, but differed from the humanistic focus of the Enlightenment in concentrating on emotions and imagination rather than reason. In the Enlightenment, people were important because of their ability to be rational, and reason was considered our most important characteristic. In Romanticism, people were considered important because of their individuality and the many aspects of their personality. Romanticism discovered and examined new and previously unexplored aspects of humanity.

Art works in the Romantic school were often commentaries on social conditions of the time, frequently in a way critical of governments. Often drawing their subjects from events in history, Romantic works championed the power of perception and the role of emotions.

As is the case for all artistic movements, Romanticism did not suddenly spring fully formed, but rather evolved from the work of a number of artists over a period of time. Two of the first artists to suggest the new emphasis were Americans living in England. *Death of General Wolfe* by Benjamin West (1738–1820) and *Watson and the Shark* by John Singleton Copley (1738–1815) were both based on actual events, and they foreshadowed the desire to invoke an emotional response from the viewer.

The art of Francisco Goya (1746–1828) departed from the customs of his time and depicted irrationality and scenes of madness and cruelty. His *The Third of May, 1808*, based on an actual event he may have witnessed, is an arresting view of the cruelty of Napoleon's troops during their occupation of Spain. Like many other great artists, Goya is difficult to categorize. However, in his ability to elicit a powerful emotional response, he can be thought of as a true Romantic artist.

One of the first artists to fall fully into the Romantic period was Théodore Géricault (1791–1824). His masterpiece, *The Raft of the Medusa*, based on an actual event, is an unsettling look into the minds of desperate people who have escaped a shipwreck only to be abandoned by their supposed rescuers, and are attempting to survive on a raft. It is a landmark painting and perfectly illustrates Romanticism in its depiction of the range of emotions. Géricault also painted numerous portraits of people who had mental illness, masterfully probing their minds. Whereas Goya's paintings of madness focus on the *acts*, Gericault's renditions focus on the actual *faces* of the mentally ill, and in those faces, we can travel into the disturbed mind.

Romanticism was brought to full development by Eugène Delacroix (1798–1863), who was strongly influenced by Géricault. In works such as *Death of Sardanapalus* and *Women of Algiers*, Delacroix looks to non-Western sources for inspiration and creates animated, exotic scenes which clearly elicit a different response from us than that evoked by the Baroque or Neoclassical. *Liberty Leading the People*, painted to commemorate the 1830 revolution that forced Charles X to abdicate, celebrates the struggle of common people for civil rights.

The major German Romantic artist was Caspar David Friedrich (1774–1840), whose meticulously constructed landscapes and seascapes exhibit remarkable nuances in the use of light. His paintings, such as *Man and Woman Gazing at the Moon, Abbey under Oak Trees*, and *The Wanderer in the Mists* often have elements with symbolic meaning. Friedrich's ability to elicit an emotional response from the viewer is so complete that his work has a spiritual quality.

Depiction of nature was also an integral part of Romanticism, especially in England, where artists portrayed nature in different ways. John Constable (1776–

1837) was fascinated by nature scenes involving clouds. His paintings, such as *The Hay Wain*, are remarkable for their scientific and realistic landscapes. On the other hand, J.M.W. Turner (1775–1851) was captivated by the sea, as seen in works such as *The Fighting Temeraire*. His paintings depart from straight pictorial realism, communicating through color and emphasizing light and its effect on our perception. By employing color and light for their own sake, Turner foreshadowed Impressionism.

The depiction of nature was also central to American Romantic painting, called the Hudson River School. American romantic artists, such as Thomas Cole (1801–1848) and Frederick Edwin Church (1826–1900), captured the untamed American wilderness in a way that presents its beauty and drama to the viewer.

A major artistic movement of the second half of the nineteenth century was Realism, which was centered in France and flourished from the years 1840 to 1870. Realism attempted to portray people, their surroundings, and their circumstances precisely as they appear in life. The rise of Realism was concurrent with the rise of photography. It was initially thought that photography would severely limit painting, as the camera would take over functions previously reserved for the canvas. However, the passage of time showed the opposite to be true; photography had a liberating experience on painting. Freed from mundane portraiture, painters could now concentrate on the creation of images beyond the scope of the camera and not readily observable in daily life.

In France, the major realistic artists were Honoré Daumier (1808–1879), Jean-François Millet (1814–1875), and Gustave Courbet (1819–1877). Although Daumier was known as a political caricaturist, he was also a master at depicting social inequality and unrest. Millet and Courbet captured the toils and travails of people doing the best they could in difficult situations. Millet's *Sower* and Courbet's *Stonebreakers* (destroyed 1945) are among the best known paintings of the Realist school. Courbet expressed the hopes of realists when he wrote:

> To record the manners, ideas, and aspect of the age as I myself have seen them . . . that has been my aim.

In the latter part of the nineteenth century, France gave us another artistic innovation: Impressionism. The use and consideration of light has always been of paramount importance to artists, and there were a number of artists whose approach to a scene and whose treatment of light influenced the Impressionists. One such artist was Édouard Manet (1832–1883). Manet began as a realist, but he did not follow the tendency to describe a scene just as it might be seen. Rather, he asserted that painting should have the capacity to appeal to the eye. In opposition to the established academic school, he used colors to outline and give the suggestion of form, and his visible brush strokes drew attention to the actual canvas. Some of Manet's work expressed traditional themes in a contemporary context, contradicting social and artistic conventions of the time, as we see in *Olympia*, where Manet placed a Parisian prostitute in a pose immortalized by Titian. In *Bar at the Folies-Bergère*, a view of a Parisian barmaid and her environment, we see a spontaneous view of ordinary life, just as we do in Impressionism. Manet influenced the Impressionists but never exhibited his work with them. While it would be wrong to think of Manet as a true Impressionist, his influence in the development of that movement cannot be denied.

Impressionist painters felt stifled by the conventions of the day, and specifically by the French Royal Academy, an organization founded in the seventeenth century and consisting of established artists. Because recognition by the Academy was important for artists, it exerted enormous influence on artistic styles. This learned body of accomplished people was not exempt from the human frailty of preferring the known to the unknown, and it inadvertently stultified the creativity of young artists. The influence of experts and the inertia of authority can be as stifling as the intolerance of the public. We cannot provide an optimal environment for innovative minds to flourish until we have protected them from the repression their mentors and peers might impose upon them.

Impressionists focused on light and color, and their paintings used these elements to create a scene and evoke an emotional response. Many Impressionists painted outdoors, breaking from the traditional practice of sketching outdoors and then returning to the studio for the actual painting. The recent commercial availability of pigments in tubes gave the Impressionists the portability needed to paint outdoors. The Impressionists attempted to take into account what was known of light and visual perception. As an example, because the eye generally focuses on only a portion of the image it views, Impressionist paintings may show only part of a scene in focus.

Traditionally, artists mixed colors on a palette, where a precise shade could be obtained before the paint was applied to the canvas. By contrast, Impressionists often mixed the paint on the canvas, willing to accept a hue that was not completely foreseeable in exchange for spontaneity and expression. Impressionists often used short, quick brush strokes and juxtaposed complementary colors (for example, red and green, yellow and violet, blue and orange) to achieve dramatic effects. In contrast to the Realists, Impressionists were not interested in the precise details of form and sacrificed these details for fleeting patches of light and color. The portrayal of scenes from daily life has led to the common view of Impressionists paintings as depicting a "slice of life."

Less commonly remembered as a factor in the development of Impressionism was the contribution of Japanese art. Japan was opened to trade by the American commodore Matthew Perry in 1854, and Japanese prints became available in Europe in the 1860s. Among the features of Japanese art to catch the eye of the Impressionists were aerial perspective, where the viewer appears to be looking down on a scene, and cropping, where an element of the scene is sharply and unexpectedly cut off.

Impressionism is associated with Claude Monet (1840–1926) more than anyone else. Indeed, a critic's derogatory comments about one of Monet's paintings gave the movement its name. Monet was fascinated by water and by the reflection of light on its changing surface, and many of his paintings, including the famous *Water Lilies* series, are water scenes. Other founders of Impressionism include Auguste Renoir (1841–1919), Camille Pissarro (1830–1903), and Alfred Sisley (1839–1899). Americans responding to the Impressionists included Mary Cassett (1845–1926) and James McNeill Whistler (1834–1903).

Few artists have continued to grow and develop throughout life as much as Monet. In his later years, he was completely blind in one eye, and had only 10% vision in the other. A series of cataract operations partially restored his sight, but he remained unable to discern colors properly, and was forced to rely on the labels on the tubes of paint, or on another person to place the paint on the palette in a consistent location. He retired to Giverny and devoted himself to painting his garden, and it was here that his handicap became his strength. His poor vision prevented him from realistic depiction and forced him to concentrate on form. In lovely paintings, many executed when he was past eighty, Monet gave free rein to his imagination, followed his conscience, and anticipated abstract expressionism. He spoke of the need to trust one's own judgment when he said "I've always worked better in solitude . . . following my own impressions."

The developments in art that followed Impressionism form the foundation of modern art. Post-Impressionists (also called Neo-Impressionists) continued the Impressionists' practice of de-emphasizing literal portrayal and retained some of the Impressionistic use of color, although they treated light somewhat differently. Edgar Degas (1834–1917) was an Impressionist in many ways, but his depictions of motion, as in his portraits of dancers, and his aversion to painting outdoors mark a transition to Post-Impressionism. Paul Gauguin (1848–1903), Georges Seurat (1859–1891), and Henri de Toulouse-Lautrec (1864–1901) were other

Post-Impressionists. Seurat is known for his technique of pointillism, the application of color in small dots. The eye merges these dots into an image, as it does in *Sunday Afternoon on the Island of La Grande Jatte.* As painting prefaced the camera, so pointillism prefaced the digital image, which is composed of minute dots that are blended by the eye.

The two giants of the Post-Impressionism period, Paul Cézanne (1839–1906) and Vincent van Gogh (1853–1890), both exerted a direct and commanding influence on twentieth-century painting. Cézanne, like other pioneers, worked largely outside the mainstream of his time, and primarily for his own satisfaction rather than for commercial success. Once an Impressionist, Cézanne left the movement to make a great leap in painting; he thought of objects as geometric forms common in nature, such as the cylinder, cone, and sphere, and rendered his subject in those terms. This simplified conception of objects would become the essence of Cubism. Some of his paintings showed his subject from more than one viewpoint, as if the observer or object were moving. Cézanne was not an abstract artist (pure abstraction did not occur in Western art until the twentieth century), but he was an important transition figure in the pathway to abstraction. He foreshadowed the spirit of twentieth century art when he said "painting does not mean copying the object, but producing colored sensations." Picasso called him "my one and only master."

Van Gogh was one of the most influential painters in the Western tradition, despite his troubled personal life. He suffered from sporadic mental illness, which would take his life at age thirty-seven. (One of his most famous paintings, *Starry Night*, was painted while he was in a mental institution.) Van Gogh's work evokes an emotional response not from its subject, but from its colors and composition. In seeking to convey how he *felt* about the subject, rather than the subject itself, van Gogh would be the direct precursor of twentieth-century Expressionism, even though his mature style lasted less than three years.

Edvard Munch (1863–1944) was also important in the rise of Expressionism. Troubled by neuroses and anxiety, he portrayed the anguish of life in paintings that engender an uneasy emotional response. Few paintings are more appropriately autobiographical than *The Scream.*

Auguste Rodin (1840–1917), perhaps the greatest sculptor since Bernini, is one of those rare creators whose work bridged two periods. As the last major Romantic artist, Rodin created characters whose emotions leap off the surface and make contact with our minds. But Rodin went beyond the representation of feelings and sought to portray the inner mind of his subjects. This search caused him to distort anatomy in some of his works. The broken and uneven surfaces in his work helped to open new frontiers beyond the purely representational and strongly influenced sculpture of the twentieth century.

Twentieth-century thinking in all of the arts is characterized by an unwillingness to trust the senses to divulge the true state of reality, a reluctance to rely on traditional methods and forms, and a belief that the unconscious is the key to understanding the mind. Twentieth-century painting, arising from Post-Impressionism, is often said to consist of "isms", movements which end in the letters i-s-m: Expressionism, Fauvism, Cubism, Futurism, Dadaism, Surrealism, Minimalism, and Abstract Expressionism, among others.

We begin by addressing two common and often misunderstood terms: "abstract art" and "Expressionism." There is no movement called abstract art. "Abstract art" is a general and informal term used for any art that is non-representational—that is, which does not produce a realistic image of the subject. "Abstract art" may portray a real object in way that renders it only partially recognizable, or it may portray no actual object at all, and be an emotional expression based only on color and form. Examples of art portraying common objects in a way that still leaves them recognizable include works from many twentieth-century movements; therefore, many of the movements we are about to discuss are examples of "abstract art." Purely abstract art—bearing no similarity to any object—is the hallmark of the movement called Abstract Expressionism. Non-representational art is neither a Western nor a twentieth-century invention. For example, African art has long avoided strict realism, and African artists influenced Picasso.

Although the term "Expressionism" may refer to a movement started by a small group of maverick German artists in the early years of the twentieth century, it more commonly refers to all works in which reality is distorted so that the artist can appeal to our emotions and communicate something about his state of mind. The work appeals to our emotions through color and form rather than the actual subject of the painting. It is a direct expression of an idea, a thought, or a feeling, not an object. In this larger sense, Expressionism is not so much a distinct movement as a general trend that is an outgrowth of the work of artists like van Gogh, Gauguin, and Munch. All art that is not rigorously representational is expressionist to some extent, and virtually all movements in twentieth-century art are somewhat expressionist. Although not generally denoting a distinct movement, the term "Expressionism" is a legitimate term used by art historians, whereas the unqualified term "abstract art" is not used.

Fauvism was an example of expressionism employing striking, non-realistic colors and distorted perspective to invoke a response. The name derives from *fauve*, French for wild beast. The leader of Fauvism was Henri Matisse (1869–1954), who subsequently departed from the movement to create a style based on the extensive use of curves.

Cubism (so named because the geometrical construction reminded an unsympathetic critic of a painting composed of little cubes) was an outgrowth of the work of Cézanne, extended by two superlative artists: Georges Braque (1882–1963) and Pablo Picasso (1881–1973). Many regard Picasso's *Les Demoiselles D'Avignon* (1907) as the first cubist painting and one of the most influential works of art in the twentieth century. Between 1907 and 1914, Braque and Picasso worked so closely together that their works are nearly indistinguishable. The two artists broke off their collaboration at the start of World War I. Although others briefly carried on with Cubism, the movement quickly lost its coherence. As Kenneth Clark reminds us, great movements in art can only last a few years, because creative people are supreme individualists who can work together only for brief periods of time.

Cubism treats space in a geometric way, as pioneered by Cézanne, and departs from the usual single-viewpoint treatment of perspective to portray an object from multiple viewpoints, or multiple points in time. Cubism is a rendition of what is *known*, not what is *seen*. It is therefore an *exploration*, not a *reproduction*, of the object. Cubism reflects a general characteristic of twentieth-century progress by accepting what the mind perceives more than what the senses perceive. Picasso described Cubism and other non-representational art with the statement "I paint things as I think them, not as I see them." Cubism appears to be non-representational and to distort objects, but examined from another viewpoint, it actually attempts to portray the object more completely. Is portraying all you know in a more complete way a distortion if the portrait is unconventional in its appearance? Or is the distortion our usual, single-reference-point view of an object? One's answer to this question depends on one's viewpoint, and this is why Cubism has been likened to relativity; both provide an alternative view of the world that can only be appreciated with an open mind.

Cubism is an example of art that is "abstract" in the sense that it offers images that do not have an exact counterpart in the real world. But it is not completely abstract because there is an identifiable subject. A cubist view of a table does not look like a table we see in our daily lives, but it is still recognizable as a table.

Picasso created great works both before and after his cubist period. Like all great creators, his art changed as he changed. To my mind, there is no better visual expression of emotion than Picasso's *Guernica*. In 1937, during the Spanish Civil War, Franco's Nationalist forces invited Nazi Germany to participate in the war against Spanish Republicans. Hitler accepted the invitation, and sent bombers to destroy the Spanish town of Guernica. In a massive canvas, Picasso documented the destruction in a moving and compelling manner. The shock, the pain, and the cruelty are captured on canvas in a way that leaves no doubt that Picasso is rightly regarded as the premier artist of the twentieth century. Displayed for many years in the Museum of Modern Art in New York, *Guernica* has now been returned to Spain.

Futurism was a movement based on the hope that technology would make the world better. Futurist works did not directly depict technological advancements, but rather portrayed objects and people as machines, often in scenes involving motion. Marcel Duchamp (1887–1968) combined concepts of cubism with the depiction of a person as a machine descending a flight of stairs to create a famous parody on futurism called *Nude Descending a Staircase No. 2.*

Dadaism grew out of a protest movement at the end of the first World War. It created some outlandish works, such as *Mona Lisa* with a moustache. These were not works of humor. Rather, they were satirical works ridiculing society and reflecting disgust with it. The Dadaists, in keeping with their protest, gave themselves a nonsense name (Dada means hobbyhorse in French and has no meaning in German). Marcel Duchamp was a leading contributor to many styles of art, including Dadaism.

Surrealism was influenced by Freud, whose *The Interpretation of Dreams* was published in 1900. Surrealist artists portrayed scenes from hallucinations, the unconscious, and other unlikely sources. Surrealist artists include Giorgio de Chirico (1888–1978), Joan Miro (1893–1983) and Salvador Dali (1904–1989).

Minimalism is a movement in art that focuses on primary colors and simple forms, such as parallel and perpendicular lines. These are the paintings with only a dot or a line, and have been the subject of much undeserved public ridicule ("I could have done that"). What Minimalism really does is attempt to remove unnecessary layers which obscure a central point. It is valuable because it is a reduction that provides a new way of seeing. Piet Mondrian (1872–1944), after passing through Impressionism and Cubism, created simplified paintings very similar to contemporary Minimalism.

As we have seen before, not all artists of a particular time are necessarily associated with identifiable movements. Max Beckmann (1894–1950) was such an artist. His works fall into the loose category of Expressionism, but not into the specific movements discussed above. A medical corpsman in World War I, where he was deeply impacted by the suffering that he witnessed, his pessimistic view of society was strengthened by the rise of Fascism in his native Germany. After the Nazis removed Beckmann from his art professorship, he painted the triptych (three-paneled painting) *Departure*, a sensitive expression of despair and hope. When Beckmann emigrated to The Netherlands in 1937, *Departure* could be removed from Germany only by telling Nazi border guards that the painting depicted scenes from a Shakespeare play. For a time, Picasso's *Guernica* and Beckmann's *Departure* hung on opposite walls of one room at the Museum of Modern Art in New York, a spectacular juxtaposition of two of the greatest protest paintings in history.

Abstract expressionism follows from Expressionism, but removes any hint of a realistic subject. Whereas the Expressionist painting may have a vaguely recognizable subject, the abstract expressionist work has none at all. To my mind, there is no purpose in attempting to discern what a work of abstraction really "is." It "is" nothing. Its value lies in the response it elicits.

In the years after World War II, New York City became the leading center of art, largely because of the great numbers of European artists who fled fascism, and it was here that abstract expressionism developed. Wassily Kandinsky (1866–1944) turned to non-representational paintings in the first decade of the twentieth century to avoid the distraction of the familiar. He returned to this idea thirty years later and is generally credited with creating the first paintings with no definable subject. Famous abstract expressionist artists include Jackson Pollock (1912–1956) and Willem de Kooning (1904–1997). In the late 1940s, Pollock began to remove his canvas from its easel and place it on the floor. He then poured, dripped, or even threw paint on it *spontaneously and without forethought*, allowing him to achieve a greater expression by being free of both a subject and established customs of composition. Abstract expressionism has remained a major movement in art since the late 1940s.

Pop Art was a movement, popular in the 1960s, which critiqued the banalities of popular culture. Examples include the *Campbells Soup Cans* by Andy Warhol (1930–1987), and the comic strip art of Roy Lichtenstein (1923–1997).

Much of the sculpture of the twentieth century has been non-representational. The twentieth century has also seen the creation of sculpture from the assemblage of a variety of new materials. Sculptures containing glass, ceramics, and sheet metal now supplement the traditional techniques of modeling in clay, bronze casting, and direct cutting of stone. New ways are indeed slow to gain acceptance. Constantin Brancusi (1876–1957) was told that his sculpture *Bird in Space* could not enter the United States as a tax-free work of art and would be taxed, as was the case for any pile of raw metal. Isamu Noguchi (1904–1988), a former student of Brancusi, was one of the foremost abstract and experimental sculptors of the twentieth century. In works such as *Kouros*, and his many outdoor projects, Noguchi used sculpture to open the mind to new three-dimensional possibilities. Jacques Lipchitz (1891–1973) was arguably the foremost cubist sculptor. Later, he departed from Cubism to create more representational work of great sensitivity.

Alexander Calder (1898–1976) created moving abstract sculptures that were suspended in air. These are now called mobiles.

The skyscraper is the hallmark of twentieth-century commercial architecture. As space in urban areas became more limited, and the need for tall buildings developed, it quickly became clear that simple masonry design would not be sufficient because the stone and concrete at the bottom would not support the weight of a very tall building. The impracticality of tall masonry buildings was illustrated by 1891, when the sixteen-story Monadnock building in Chicago (still the world's tallest masonry structure) required walls fourteen feet (four meters) thick at the base.

As so often happens in history, change results from several stimuli acting simultaneously. One of these was the introduction of large amounts of high-grade steel, mostly from the Bessemer and open hearth processes. A second stimulus was the advent of practical elevators, allowing tall buildings to be used to their potential. In 1853, Elisha Otis (1811–1861) developed an elevator in which, should the supporting rope sever, locking clamps would automatically spring out and prevent decent. By 1900, counterweights were used, decreasing the amount of power needed to lift the elevator. The third stimulus for skyscraper production was once again catastrophe, in the form of the great Chicago fire of 1871, which provided the incentive to employ the new technology in architecture. The contemporary skyscraper is additional evidence that tumult is fertile ground for change and innovation.

The cage configuration was the initial answer to the inability of masonry to support great weight. In this design, walls supported themselves, but a steel skeleton supported the floors. From this developed the true skyscraper, wherein a metal frame supports both the floors and the walls, and the walls generally do not serve a load-bearing purpose. The first metal frame skyscraper was the Home Insurance Building, designed by William Jenney (1832–1907) and built in 1883. The Rand McNally Building, completed in Chicago in 1890, was the first all steel-frame skyscraper. The design of skyscrapers, wherein the steel frame carries the weight, freed the walls from structural responsibility and permitted them to be constructed for aesthetic reasons, in a manner analogous to the way that the pointed arch and flying buttress permitted lighter, more artistic walls in Gothic cathedrals.

Even the most fortuitous set of circumstances cannot lead to innovation unless recognized and capitalized on by people with vision and foresight. One such person was Louis Sullivan (1856–1924). At one time the younger associate of Jenney, Sullivan opposed the classical revival prevalent in the nineteenth

407

century and believed that the exterior surface of a building should reflect and support its function. Although he did not design the first skyscraper, his work was instrumental in its evolution.

Sullivan's most gifted student was Frank Lloyd Wright (1869–1959), whose nontraditional designs blend in with nature to relax the eye and mind. Some of his most important work was the design of private homes. To my mind, there is no better example of a building constructed in harmony with nature than Wright's *Falling Water* in Pennsylvania, a private home now open to the public. As one approaches the house, the walkway is cut around trees, announcing an intention to integrate with rather than dominate nature. The stone ledge on which the house is built forms some of the walls, and concrete balconies cantilever over a waterfall, making the falls a part of the house.

I.M. Pei (1917–), following Wright's innovative designs, has designed numerous world-famous buildings and additions, such as the East Building of the National Gallery of Art in Washington, D.C., and the Pyramid at the entrance of the Louvre. These designs, and smaller buildings, such as the Everson art museum in Syracuse, New York, show again that architecture is in every sense a type of sculpture.

Art of the twentieth century, often called modern art, is frequently confusing and frustrating to people, a reaction perhaps based on the natural human tendency to avoid the new in favor of the familiar. But just as progress in all areas requires that this natural tendency be set aside in order to explore, so the viewer of modern art must also be willing to set aside the comfort of the familiar. To explore, by definition, is to leave the familiar and the comfortable. All works of art require the participation of the viewer as well as the creator, and those viewers who allow themselves to become explorers will be able to use modern art to examine the human experience.

A Musical Form of Language

In the end, the poem is not the thing we see;
it is, rather, a light by which we may see —
and what we see is life.

— Robert Penn Warren

Our word poetry comes from the Greek word *poiein*, meaning to make. Poetry is difficult to define, and even great poets have struggled to define their medium. For our purposes, it is a form of imaginative writing, characterized by the use of words for their sound and rhythm as much as for their literal meaning, to create an image or to convey a thought or feeling. Poetry is concentrated and intense; indeed, no other art form conveys as much intensity in so brief a time.

Poetry generally does not translate well from one language to another, as its construction is heavily dependent on nuances of sound and rhythm unique to each language. It is therefore difficult for us to become fully acquainted with poetry written in another language.

Broadly speaking, poems are divided into three categories. The first category, narrative poems, tell a story. Epics are long narrative poems, generally chronicling the life of a single, heroic figure or a group of people over a protracted time period. Examples include the *Iliad* and *Odyssey* of Homer. Metrical Romances are narrative poems portraying a romantic tale, usually combined with adventure and heroism. Ballads are narrative poems that generally portray a single episode, often with musical accompaniment. Narrative poetry was important in the development of the Western novel.

Dramatic poetry is the use of poetic techniques in plays. Until comparatively recently, most plays were written in verse. Dramatic poetry is illustrated by most of the writing of Shakespeare.

Lyric poems were originally written to be sung to the accompaniment of a lyre (hence the name). With the passage of time, however, lyric poems were not necessarily written for musical accompaniment, and the term has come to signify a poem characterized by emphasis on emotion. Usually written in the first person, the lyric poem is a direct communication of the poet's feelings, and is the most intense expression of emotion in literature. There are numerous forms of lyric poetry. The hymn is a praise, either to God or a person. The ode is a celebration of a person or occasion. The elegy is a lyric poem that contemplates death, or a loss. The eclogue is a lyric poem celebrating rustic life. A sonnet is a lyric poem of fourteen lines. The first established form of a sonnet was the Italian sonnet, as exemplified by those of Petrarch. The English sonnet, as exemplified by those of Shakespeare, developed from the Italian sonnet in Renaissance England and uses a different rhyme pattern.

There are four elements to a poem that concern us. Rhythm refers to the regular recurrence of similar patterns of sounds, or features such as accents, and is analogous to rhythm in music. Some form of rhythm is found in all poetry, and it is more essential than rhyme. Not all poems rhyme, but all have rhythm. Indeed, the rhythmic use of words defines poetry and distinguishes it as, in effect, a musical form of language.

Closely related to rhythm is meter, which defines the rhythm of the poem. Most poems in English are based on a combination of the number of syllables and the number of accents per line. Most poems can be broken down into subunits of two or three syllables, with a characteristic pattern of accents. As an example, a unit of two syllables with the first unaccented and the second accented is the rhythmic subunit called an iamb. Meter refers to the type of rhythmic subunit, and the number of these subunits per line. Five iambic units to a line (ten syllables, accented on syllables two, four, six, eight, and ten) forms the meter of iambic pentameter. Iambic tetrameter is a meter composed of four such pairs of unaccented-accented syllables to a line. When Shakespeare closes his eighteenth sonnet with:

So long lives this, and this gives life to thee

he uses iambic pentameter, as there are five syllable pairs, with the second of the pair accented. When Robert Frost writes in *Stopping by Woods on a Snowy Evening*:

Whose woods these are I think I know
His house is in the village though

he employs iambic tetrameter, and gives his poem a rhythm based on this meter.

Historically, the constraints placed on the poet by requiring such compositional restrictions were viewed as integral to the art form, and the ability to express ideas in this manner was considered the essence of poetry. As we shall see, more recent poets have not always adhered to traditional compositional forms.

Interlocking sounds is a means to link words at the ends of lines (or less often, within a line). The most common mechanism for interlocking sounds is the rhyme, but it is by no means essential in poetry. Also used are alliteration, whereby the initial sound of successive words is the same (Peter Piper picked a peck) and assonance, whereby successive words use similar vowel sounds.

Form refers to the grouping of lines into the completed poem. Form encompasses collections of lines called stanzas. For example, the English sonnet has three four-line stanzas followed by one doublet.

Many people have difficulty appreciating poetry because they do not approach a poem in a systematic manner and do not know what to look for in reading a poem. To my mind, an effective approach is to first read the poem for its literal meaning and look up any unfamiliar words. Then identify the meter of the poem, so that subsequent readings will reflect the proper rhythm. The symbolism of the poem should then be examined. There are many types of symbolism in poetry. Some symbols are direct and obvious, simple statements that one thing is another or is like another. Other symbols are subtler. Some symbols refer only to a particular object in the poem, while in other cases, the entire subject of the poem is a symbol. Be alert for direct and indirect symbols, both restricted and global. Why did the poet choose these symbols? It might then be helpful to study the verbs of the poem. Are these the expected verbs for the subjects? If unusual actions are attributed to people or objects, ask yourself why. A similar study of the adjectives of the poem may also be beneficial. If unusual adjectives are applied to people or objects, think of what they might convey.

As the visual arts should be seen in their original form, so poetry is meant to be heard or to be read aloud. The full impact of its rhythm cannot be appreciated when read silently, but the audible rendition of poetry connects the listener to this uniquely passionate art form.

The oldest form of literature and the precursor to other forms, poetry was common in antiquity. Homer's *Iliad* and *Odyssey*, which were probably put into verse before writing came to ancient Greece, are still read today, as are some of the works of the eighth-century-B.C.E. poet Hesiod. Sappho (fl. c. 600 B.C.E.) is noted for love poetry. (The early Christian Church considered her work blasphemous and destroyed much of it; only about seven hundred lines—fragments of greatness—remain.) Pindar (c.518–438 B.C.E.), a great lyric poet, wrote of his art:

> *No sculptor I, to fashion images that shall stand idly on one pedestal for eye. No, go thou forth from Aegina, sweet song of mine, on every freighted ship, on each light bark.*

The dramatic tragedies of Aeschylus, Euripides, and Sophocles, which we shall shortly encounter, are additional examples of poetry from ancient Greece.

Lucius Livius Andronicus (c. 284–204 B.C.E.) was captured by the Romans during their early military campaigns in southern Italy. His knowledge of Greek permitted him to translate the *Odyssey* into Latin. In addition to composing the

411

first plays in Latin, he was also an epic poet, earning the title of the father of Roman literature. His younger contemporary, Ennius (c. 239– 169 B.C.E.), is often spoken of as the father of Roman poetry. Lucretius (c. 99–55 B.C.E.) was a scientist as well as a poet. He believed in the existence of gods, but doubted that they concerned themselves with the affairs of people. He therefore encouraged people not to fear the gods, and not to believe in an afterlife. Among his works is *De Rerum Natura* (*On the Nature of Things*), which bequeathed to us much of what we know about the thinking of Democritus and Epicurus. Virgil (70–19 B.C.E.; also spelled Vergil), wrote the *Aeneid,* a blend of history and myth that portrays the full gamut of the actions and emotions of humanity. Virgil also created the *Eclogues,* a set of ten poems written between 45 and 35 B.C.E. and the *Georgics,* a poem ostensibly written for the purpose of teaching farming, but actually a celebration of the land and nature. Horace (65–8 B.C.E.) is best remembered for his odes. Sextus Propertius (c.55–16 BC) is noted for his love poetry. Ovid (43 B.C.E.–17 C.E.) composed *Metamorphosis,* stories of mythology.

In the Middle Ages, a number of epic poems were written in vernacular languages. Examples include *Beowulf,* in Old English, dating from about 700 C.E., and the *Song of Roland,* in Old French, dating to about 1100 C.E. There were also lyric poems in vernacular languages during the Middle Ages.

Toward the end of the medieval period, bridging into the Renaissance, are the vernacular works of Dante Alighieri (1265–1321), Petrarch (Francesco Petrarca, 1304–1374), Giovanni Boccaccio (1313–1375), and Geoffrey Chaucer (c.1340–1400). People whose lives bridge two epochs are always interesting. Dante wrote in Tuscan, an early form of Italian, establishing it as the literary language of Italy and of the Italian Renaissance. His masterpiece, the *Divine Comedy,* a tour of Heaven, Hell, and Purgatory, is one of the seminal poetic works of our history. Dante simply called his work *Comedy* (the word "comedy" in Dante's time did not imply humor, but referred to a story with a more-or-less happy ending). "Divine" was added after his death. The Roman poet Virgil, representing reason, is Dante's guide through Hell and Purgatory. But for his tour of Heaven, Dante needed a guide that represented human attributes beyond reason. He had long loved a woman named Beatrice, and let her—representing faith and love—guide him through paradise.

Petrarch was a poet and historian who influenced many other writers, including Boccaccio and Chaucer. Like Dante, Petrarch loved a woman and immortalized her in his writing. He is best remembered for love sonnets to a woman he called Laura. Boccaccio was an authority on the life of Dante, and wrote his biography. Like Dante and Petrarch, he may have been inspired by the love of a woman. He writes of a woman named Fiammetta, who may have been based on a real person. Petrarch and Boccaccio met in 1350, and subsequently traveled together looking for lost manuscripts from the past. (Petrarch would in fact find letters from Cicero that had been thought lost, and he was instrumental in the revival of classical literature.) Chaucer, a civil servant and amateur writer, was the first great English language poet. Boccaccio's *The Decameron* and Chaucer's *Canterbury Tales* were important in the development of the novel, and we will revisit them later.

These four writers are considered to have foreshadowed the Renaissance of Italian literature, but whether they were harbingers of the Renaissance or participants therein depends on when one considers the Renaissance to have begun. So much of what we think of as the Western European Renaissance was already underway during the period of 1100–1400 that we should avoid the traditional dating of this period to the fifteenth century. When the re-awakening we call the Renaissance is more properly understood as occurring in the early twelfth century, these poets emerge as the first great poets of the Renaissance, rather than the last of the Middle Ages.

Vernacular poetry flowered in the Renaissance. Poetry of this time reflected the general Renaissance belief that contemporary man could equal the greatness of the past. As in other areas of human endeavor, there was a rebirth of the idea that people had power, creativity, and intrinsic value. Renaissance poetry reflects the belief, which we have encountered in other areas, that the affairs of people ought to be the focus of art and science.

In Italy, Ludovico Ariosto (1474–1533) composed the influential narrative poem *Orlando Furioso*, as well as numerous works for the Italian stage. In France, a group of seven poets, headed by Pierre de Ronsard (1524–1585), called themselves the *Pléiade*. They championed the use of the French vernacular and developed guidelines for the composition of poems.

But it was in England that Renaissance poetry reached its greatest bloom. Edmund Spenser (1552–1599) and Philip Sidney (1554–1586) advanced the form and structure of English poetry. Christopher Marlowe (1564–1593) was one of the first English poets to adapt blank verse (unrhymed iambic pentameter) from Italian sources. Perhaps his most famous poem is *The Passionate Shepard to His Love*, which contains the line "Come live with me and be my love."

Marlowe's death caused a profound void in English letters and left the full

413

development of blank verse to the person whom we stipulate as the greatest poet of our civilization, William Shakespeare (1564–1616). There has long been a debate as to whether Shakespeare was the true author of the works that bear his name, and many feel that these masterpieces are the work of another person. To my mind, the case for an alternative authorship is strongest for Edward de Vere (1550–1604). The interested reader is referred to *The Mysterious William Shakespeare*, by Charlton Ogburn, for a more complete discussion of this evidence. In addition to developing blank verse in his tragic plays, Shakespeare (or de Vere) was a master of many meters. Poems such as *Venus and Adonis, The Rape of Lucrece,* and *The Phoenix and Turtle* are monuments to human creativity. His one hundred and fifty-four sonnets each summarize, in their scant fourteen lines, the essence of who we are.

After the explosion of poetic genius during the Renaissance, the dramatic tradition was strong in France, while England produced poets such as John Donne (1571–1631), John Dryden (1631–1700), and John Milton (1608–1674). Milton, blind from middle age, is considered by many as the finest English language poet next to Shakespeare and is best known for *Paradise Lost* and *Paradise Regained.*

Alexander Pope (1688–1744) was crippled by a childhood illness and suffered from headaches all of his life. This made him disagreeable in personality, but did not affect his poetic creativity. Among his many masterpieces are *The Rape of the Lock* and *Essay on Man.* Pope's use of the heroic couplet (a rhyming iambic pentameter couplet) made this form dominant during his time. Because his works often focus on man or nature, some regard him as a prelude to Romanticism in poetry.

Samuel Johnson (1709–1784) wrote numerous poems and prose works, but is most remembered for his *Dictionary of the English Language* and for *The Lives of the English Poets.* Johnson is important for another reason. He was the focal point of English literature in his lifetime, and the nidus for a number of important literary groups. It is curious how, in all fields, certain people are able to organize and inspire entire movements with their personalities as much as with their creative talents. His biography, *The Life of Johnson*, by James Boswell (1740–1795), is one of the foremost biographies in English. Boswell knew Johnson for many years, and his biography gives us not just Johnson's *life*, but also his *mind*. Among the many quotations from Johnson that Boswell gives us, one seems to capture the essence of the man, and the essence of our potential:

It is wonderful what a difference learning makes upon people, even in the common intercourse of life, which does not appear to be much connected to it. The desire for knowledge is the natural feeling of mankind, and every human being whose mind is not debauched would be willing to give all that he has to get knowledge.

The next major development in poetry was the rise of literary Romanticism. Literary Romanticism began in the late eighteenth century, at about the same time as Romanticism in art and music. It came about gradually, and no one person or time is responsible for its beginning. In Germany, Gotthold Lessing (1729–1781), a playwright, critic, and essayist, exerted profound influence on the literature of that country. Like Johnson, he was more important for his influence than for his creations. By insisting that Germany separate itself from French influence and develop its own literary style (he advocated using Shakespeare as a model), he helped make possible the Sturm und Drang (Storm and Stress) movement, which was a reaction against the rationalism of the Enlightenment and a move toward the expression of emotion in all literary forms.

Sturm und Drang was in large part the beginning of Romanticism. The Sturm und Drang movement championed individual freedom, and was led by Johann Wolfgang von Goethe (1749–1832) and Friedrich Schiller (1759–1805). Goethe was a student of man and nature, a poet and scientist uniquely suited to bring out this new aspect of ourselves, and it is therefore fitting that he should be a principal figure of Romanticism.

Literary Romanticism, like that in art and music, examined the emotional as well as the rational aspects of people, and focused on individuals rather than collective humanity. As part of the emphasis on non-rational aspects of life, Romantic writers often focused on nature, and we find the twin themes of nature and emotion throughout Romantic literature, often in the examination of the events of daily life. Romantic writers did not focus on heroes, royalty, or God, but on the dreams and sadnesses of common people. The human mind is explored by describing a natural event or object.

In poetry, there was an increase in lyric poems, as they facilitated the communication of emotion. William Blake (1757–1827), who made his living as an engraver, published most of his poetry himself. Works like Blake's *Songs of Innocence* and *Songs of Experience* are harbingers of the English Romantic style, but poetic Romanticism in the English language was substantially inaugurated by one book, called *Lyrical Ballads*, published in 1798 by William Wordsworth

(1770–1850) and Samuel Coleridge (1772–1834). Dealing with common events and individuals who had not often received consideration from poets, this single collection of poems sent English language poetry down a different path, one characterized by greater emotional content, very much as the Eroica symphony six years later would send music down the pathway of greater emotional expressivity. The poems in *Lyrical Ballads* often have variable numbers of syllables in each line, and variable placement of the accents. This change in meter allows for greater expression of spontaneity, but violated the compositional standards of the time. In his *Preface* to the second edition of *Lyrical Ballads*, Wordsworth foresaw the uneasiness that people often have when confronted with something different:

> Readers . . . if they persist in reading this book to its conclusion, will perhaps frequently have to struggle with feelings of strangeness and awkwardness . . . but . . . they should ask themselves if it contains a natural delineation of human passions, human characters, and human incidents . . .

In his poetry, Wordsworth conveyed a love of both humanity and nature. No other Romantic poet so clearly personifies these dual themes, which were the bedrock of Romanticism. Revolted by the cruelty of man, he turned to nature to find solace and peace, and much of his poetry was the result of thoughts he collected during long walks. Perhaps no other writer, not even Dickens, was so deeply affected by the cruelty and inequality of his environment. Among Wordsworth's many great poems are *Tintern Abbey* and *The Prelude*.

Coleridge devised what is often called the conversational poem, which was intended to be autobiographical and introspective. It is an intimate blank verse conversation with an unseen listener. Coleridge's most remembered works are *The Rime of the Ancient Mariner* (the first poem of *Lyrical Ballads*) and *Kubla Khan*. Coleridge and Wordsworth were the only Romantic poets to work together, temporarily setting aside their very different personalities to forge a common bond in verse.

Following the lead of *Lyrical Ballads*, the nineteenth century became a cornucopia of extraordinary poetic emotional expression. Joining Wordsworth and Coleridge in England was the so-called second generation of Romantic poets: George Gordon Byron (1788–1824), Percy Bysshe Shelley (1792–1822), and John Keats (1795–1821). Shelley's *Adonais* was a tribute to Keats, written after the latter died from tuberculosis. The following year, Shelley himself died in a boating accident. The great poems he wrote in his last two years leave no doubt that, had he lived, there would have been many more. Shelley's *A Defense of Poetry* is a moving tribute to the power and worth of poetry, in which Shelley reminds us:

> Poets . . . colour all that they combine with the evanescent hues of this ethereal world; a word, or a trait in the representation of a scene or a passion, will touch the enchanted chord, and reanimate, in those who have ever experienced these emotions, the sleeping, the cold, the buried images of the past. Poetry thus makes immortal all that is best and most beautiful in the world; it arrests the vanishing apparitions which haunt . . . life, and . . . in language or in form sends them forth among mankind, bearing sweet news of kindred joy . . . Poetry redeems from decay the visitations of the divinity in man . . .

Byron and Keats also died in or before their prime. Indeed, the cumulative lifespans of Byron, Shelley, and Keats were only ninety-two years. Alfred Tennyson (1809–1892), Robert Browning (1812–1889), and Elizabeth Barrett Browning (1806–1861) are usually considered to be in the first generation of Post-Romantic poets. Tennyson wrote the popular *Charge of the Light Brigade*, as well as *In Memoriam* (commemorating his beloved friend Arthur Hallam), *Maud*, and *Idylls of the King*, a collection of poems written between 1859 and 1885 dealing with King Arthur. He succeeded Wordsworth as the poet laureate of England upon the latter's death.

In the United States, a partial list of great nineteenth-century poets includes William Cullen Bryant (1794–1878), Henry Wadsworth Longfellow (1807–1882), John Greenleaf Whittier (1807–1892), Edgar Allan Poe (1809–1849), James Russell Lowell (1819–1891), and Emily Dickinson (1830–1886).

Ralph Waldo Emerson (1803–1882) and Henry David Thoreau (1817–1862) were American poets better remembered for their essays. Emerson was the author of *Self Reliance*, a brilliant plea for individualism. How different might our history have been if the ideas espoused in *Self Reliance* had been part of our heritage, and how different our future would be if we valued the individual as Emerson pleaded. Some excerpts regarding the worth of the individual:

> If you can love me for what I am, we shall be the happier. If you cannot, I will still seek to deserve that you should.
>
> Your own gift you can present every moment with the cumulative force of a whole life's cultivation; but of the adopted talent of another, you have only an extemporaneous half possession.

In every work of genius, we recognize our own rejected thoughts.

Nothing can bring you peace but yourself. Nothing can bring you peace but the triumph of principles.

Trust thyself: every heart vibrates to that iron string.

In addressing the tendency for recognized masters and established ideas to suppress new thinking:

. . . the classification is idolized, passes for an end and not for a speedily exhaustible means, so that the walls of the system blend to their eye in the remote horizon with the walls of the universe; the luminaries of Heaven seem to them hung on the arch their master built.

Thoreau was the author of *Walden* and *Civil Disobedience*. The former is better known, but it was the latter that laid a foundation for nonviolent resistance, and as we shall see, inspired Gandhi. In *Civil Disobedience*, Thoreau argues that we should value our conscience over the laws of the state, championing the greatness of the individual mind very much as Emerson had done. From *Civil Disobedience*:

A wise man will not leave the right to the mercy of chance, nor wish it to prevail through the power of the majority.

The best thing a man can do for his culture when he is rich is to endeavor to carry out those schemes which he entertained when he was poor.

There will never be a really free and enlightened state until the state comes to recognize the individual as a higher and independent power, from which all its own power and authority are derived, and treats him accordingly.

After a youth spent as a teacher and journalist, Walt Whitman (1819–1892) issued the first of many editions of *Leaves of Grass*, one of the great works in American literature, in 1855. His frank use of anatomic terms in *Leaves of Grass* left him unable to find a publisher, and he published the work at his own expense. The best known poem in this first edition is *Song of Myself*. In 1866, he published two of his best known poems, *When Lilacs Last in the Dooryard Bloom'd* and *O Captain! My Captain!*, which commemorated the death of Lincoln.

Whitman's poems were based on the American nation and its people, but their true subject is the strength of the human spirit and the worth of the ordinary individual. He broke with prevailing styles and subjects and wrote poetry centered on the everyday experiences of common people, including sexuality.

New subjects demanded new poetic forms, and Whitman departed from traditional meter and form in favor of a natural flow of words. He was one of the first to make use of free verse, a rhymed or unrhymed verse that does not employ a strict meter but maintains a rhythm, as does all poetry. Free verse is sometimes confused with the much older blank verse, which is unrhymed, but very metrical (iambic pentameter). Because of his subject matter and his use of free verse, many thought Whitman's poems an affront to poetry, but he is now remembered as one of the poetic world's great champions of the worth of the individual, and the greatness of democracy and freedom.

Other poets of this time included Alessandro Manzoni (1785–1873), Aleksandr Pushkin (1799–1837), and Victor Hugo (1802–1885), all three of whom were also novelists.

William Butler Yeats (1865–1939) is often spoken of as the greatest English language poet of the twentieth century. Intimately involved in the struggle for Irish independence, Yeats served in the Irish senate shortly after its formation. *Easter, 1916* commemorates the British execution of Irish nationalists who had occupied a post office building. Other poetic masterpieces of Yeats include *Prayer For My Daughter, The Second Coming, Meditations in Time of Civil War, For Anne Gregory,* and *Among School Children.* Unlike many great poets, Yeats did much of his best work late in life.

Ezra Pound (1885–1972) gave fuller meaning to imagist poetry, wherein a poetic image of a passing scene or fleeting moment is created. Pound's greater contribution to poetry, however, lay in his association with others. As a confidant and friend to Yeats, Eliot, Joyce, and Hemingway, Pound exerted enormous vicarious influence.

As a young man, T.S. Eliot (1888–1965) went to England to study, and made his permanent residence there, becoming a British citizen in 1927. For a time, he earned his living as a teacher and a bank clerk. Eliot pioneered new rhythms and forms, and was largely responsible for moving poetry beyond Romanticism's exploration of feelings into the exploration of the mind. In reading his works, we do not feel that we know the poet personally, as we might after reading a poem of Wordsworth or Coleridge, but that we have searched ourselves. This change in focus would be a hallmark of twentieth-century literary forms of all types. Eliot's most famous poem is *The Waste Land,* published in 1922, and extensively edited by Ezra Pound. *The Waste Land* is a difficult poem, with multiple layers of meaning and juxtapositions of thought that seem strange.

It has been interpreted by some as an indictment of contemporary society, but others prefer to regard it as an expression of private feelings that do not necessarily convey contempt for modern humanity. Other great poems by Eliot include *The Love Song of J. Alfred Prufrock* and *Four Quartets*. The latter was Eliot's last great work, and his personal favorite.

Other English language poets of the late nineteenth and early twentieth centuries include Rudyard Kipling (1865–1936), A.E. Housman (1859–1935), Robert Frost (1874–1963), E.E. Cummings (1894–1962), W. H. Auden (1907–1973), and Dylan Thomas (1914–1953). Kipling, born in India and educated in England, was also a master of the short story. Housman left Oxford without a degree, but unwavering self-study of Latin and the classics made him a highly regarded classical scholar and professor. Frost, in poems such as *Stopping By Woods On a Snowy Evening*, *The Road Not Taken*, and *Mending Wall*, spoke a gentle poetic voice for many millions. Cummings was highly experimental and innovative, and is famous for his nonconformity of punctuation, capitalization, and syntax. Auden is often regarded as the greatest poet of his generation, while Thomas was one of a number of twentieth-century poets to skillfully use free verse.

In France, Charles Péguy (1873–1914), before his death in the first World War, not only published many great poems of his own, but founded a publication called *Cahiers de la Quinzaine* (*Fortnightly Journals*), active from 1900 to 1914, which published the work of many important writers. In Italy, Giosuè Carducci (1835–1907) and Gabriele D'Annunzio (1863–1938) have given us lasting poetry.

Other great poets of the late nineteenth and early twentieth centuries are identified predominantly with the symbolist movement, which opposed objective description and used symbols to express ideas and emotions. By using symbols, the symbolist movement had the effect of placing the imagination foremost in poetry. While multiple people contributed to the origin of symbolist poetry, including Edgar Allan Poe, the single most important person in its development was Charles Baudelaire (1821–1867). Other important nineteenth-century French symbolist poets include Stéphane Mallarmé (1842–1898), Paul Verlaine (1844–1896), and Arthur Rimbaud (1854–1891). Twentieth-century examples of this form of poetry have been composed by Paul Claudel (1868–1955) and Paul Valery (1871–1945) in French; Stefan George (1868–1933), Hugo von Hofmannsthal (1874–1929), and Rainer Maria Rilke (1875–1926) in German; and Aleksandr Blok (1880–1921) in Russian.

By stressing the imagination, symbolism led to surrealism (beyond realism), the extreme use of imagination to portray images of madness, hallucinations, and unconsciousness. Guillaume Apollonaire (1880–1918) was a symbolist poet who inspired surrealism. The predominant surrealist poet was André Breton (1896–1966). To facilitate the capture of fleeting thoughts from the unconscious, Breton encouraged rapid writing, concluding the work before any of it was pondered or proofread.

Surrealism was a desire to turn away from all traditional means of communication and all conventions. As in Modern art, the turning away from a previous heritage is difficult for many to appreciate, but the possibilities opened by a new way of seeing and communicating are immense. Surrealistic poetry has much in common with contemporary trends in drama and novels, as well as in art and music. Indeed, the attempt to view the world in a startlingly different manner is a hallmark of twentieth-century intellectual activity in every area of the human experience.

Two Art Forms Come Together

As the visual arts should be seen in the original form, and poetry is meant to be heard, so drama is meant to be seen in performance. Reading a play cannot capture the intricacies that a performance makes available to the viewer. Drama is a combination of two art forms: writing and performance. The reader can capture only the first of these.

Although the Egyptians performed some of their religious rituals as drama, our concept of drama emerged in Greece. The origins of theater lie in ritual and religion, at the annual festivals celebrating Dionysus, the god of wine and fertility. Greek plays were written in verse and presented at these festivals. Initially, everyone present actively participated in the celebration, but with time, some became observers. Then an individual stood out from the rest of the participants and performed as a response to them. The actor was born. The first actors were priests of Dionysus and alternated with the chorus during the performance. Tradition holds that Thespis, a shadowy figure in the sixth century B.C.E., was the first to use an actor; hence our word Thespian. Thespis is also said to have introduced masks, but no surviving works are attributed to him. Drama became an integral part of Greek cultural life, and, in 534 B.C.E., annual playwrighting contests began at the Dionysus festivals.

Aeschylus (525–456 B.C.E.) introduced a second actor and was the first

421

playwright from whom entire plays survive. Among his great plays are *Prometheus Bound*, and the trilogy *Oresteia* (consisting of the plays *Agamemnon*, *Libation Bearers*, and *Eumenides*). Sophocles (496–406 B.C.E.) added a third actor and employed more intricate plots. *Electra*, *Oedipus*, and *Antigone* are among his masterpieces. Euripides (c. 484–406 B.C.E.) depicted people in a less idealized manner, making theater more relevant to daily life. Nineteen of his plays survive, more than the combined total for Aeschylus and Sophocles. His most famous is *Medea*, an examination of the conflict between love and the desire for revenge. All three of these ancient playwrights examined people and explored the defects of humanity. Their characters are constantly unable to overcome the deficiencies common to all of us.

Aristophanes (c. 448–380 B.C.E.) and Menander (c. 342–292 B.C.E.) wrote insightful comedic drama. The former wrote *Lysistrata*, where women withheld sex from their husbands until peace was restored.

Livius Andronicus, the first major Roman poet, was also the first principal Roman playwright. The Romans did not equal their Greek predecessors in drama, but the comedies of Plautus (fl. 200 B.C.E.) and Terence (c. 185–159 B.C.E.) are among the best of classical literature.

Although Greek and Roman drama survived, and the latter was performed in the late Middle Ages, medieval drama is only partially connected to ancient theater, and is better thought of as a new art form that largely originated independently of previous theater. To a great extent, medieval drama arose from the early Christian Church, where elaborations of liturgical text allowed priests to assume the roles of Biblical characters in church services. Further development permitted secular elements to drift in, at first as an accompaniment to the religious text, and later as independent productions.

As in other areas, Renaissance drama was fueled by an interest in classical writers. The desire to imitate them led to the composition of original works as confidence grew. Renaissance theater began in Italy, where the attempt to imitate classicism led to the composition of neoclassical plays in Latin. As in other areas of endeavor, the vernacular language prevailed, and by the early sixteenth century, plays were being performed in Italian. Early Italian Renaissance playwrights were Pietro Aretino (1492–1556) and Niccolò Machiavelli (1469–1527). Machiavelli was also a political and military theorist, and is better remembered for his book *The Prince*, a manual for how to obtain and keep political power. *The Prince* has given Machiavelli an undeserved reputation as a ruthless man. We must remember that all works are reflective of their times. The opinions for which people of the past are remembered are opinions they may not have held under different circumstances, and which any of us may have subscribed to in similar circumstances. In the case of Machiavelli, he lived in a divided Italy, and much of *The Prince* reflected his desire to see his homeland united. *The Prince* is simply an insightful treatise of political and military events of history by a man who wished to make the results of his study available to the leaders of his country, and who is today misunderstood and unjustly maligned. Parts of *The Prince* are applicable today:

> There is nothing more difficult to handle, more doubtful of success, and more dangerous to carry through than changes…The innovator makes enemies of all those who prosper under the old order, and only lukewarm support is forthcoming from those who would prosper under the new.

After 1550, a form of theater called commedia dell'arte arose in Italy. Lasting into the eighteenth century, the commedia dell'arte consisted of traveling professional companies whose performances were intended for the public, as opposed to the court. Their performances, largely improvised, offered a newness and vitality not present in the more established and structured drama of the time. As so often happens, newness and vitality are more important than even the finest representation of form and structure. The commedia dell'arte influenced, among others, Molière and Shakespeare.

The founder of Spanish drama was Lope de Vega (1562–1635). A prodigious playwright, he composed some eight hundred plays, of which about one-half have survived. His work shows well-developed characters and poetic beauty mixed with an affirmation of traditional virtues, such as Catholicism and loyalty to the king and state. Pedro Calderón de la Barca (1600–1681), the successor to de Vega, known in his time primarily for his comedies, was instrumental in the development of Spanish opera. His plots and characters are more complex than those of de Vega.

But it was in England, during Elizabethan times, that Renaissance drama changed the literary world. Early English playwrights included John Heywood (c. 1497–1550), Nicholas Udall (1505–1556), John Lyly (c. 1554–1606), Robert Greene (c. 1558–1592), and Thomas Kyd (1558–1594).

Christopher Marlowe (1564–1593) can reasonably be regarded as England's first great playwright. Skillfully using blank verse, Marlowe created such plays as *Tamburlaine the Great* and *Doctor Faustus*. Like Shakespeare, Marlowe was clearly well read, and his works reflect and depend on this.

William Shakespeare, possibly a pseudonym of Edward de Vere (1550–1604), was the behemoth of literature and used his giant fund of knowledge and experience to give us thirty-eight plays, comprising tragedies, comedies, and histories. Each is a synopsis of and triumph for the human experience. The real marks of a person's greatness are his influence on others and his ability to appeal to many people over a long time. By those criteria, Shakespeare, whoever he may have been, deserves his reputation as the greatest dramatist of history.

Ben Jonson (1572–1637) was second only to Shakespeare as a playwright in this period. His *Volpone* and *The Alchemist* are still performed. Jonson was also the principal English writer of the Masque, a theatrical form common in Europe in the late sixteenth and early seventeenth centuries, using masked dancers and stressing allegory and symbolism. (An allegory is a literary work, prose or poetry, where one object or concept stands for another to which it has no direct connection. The allegory, unlike the novel, seeks not to contemplate, but to teach by analogy. Symbolism involves a similar idea, except that there is a direct connection between the symbol and the object or concept for which it stands. For example, the cross is a symbol for Christianity.)

English drama reached a low point in 1642, when the Puritans came to power and closed the theaters in London. After the Restoration (1660), theaters reopened, but the plays of Shakespeare fell partially out of favor, and attention was focused on the collaborative efforts of Francis Beaumont (1584–1616) and John Fletcher (1579–1625). Toward the end of the seventeenth century and into the eighteenth, the plays of John Dryden (1631–1700) became very popular.

The seventeenth century was a golden age of French drama. Pierre Corneille (1606–1684) and Jean Racine (1639–1699) created tragedies of the first magnitude, while Jean Baptiste Poquelin (1622–1673; known to us by his pseudonym of Molière, which he took to avoid embarrassment to his family) was the foremost comic actor and writer of comedic drama in his day.

The Sturm und Drang movement of the late eighteenth century would revolutionize the theater as it did poetry, leading into the Romantic period of drama, which was well underway by the nineteenth century. Dramatic Romanticism de-emphasized literal realism (sometimes called verisimilitude) and rationality of play construction, preferring to focus on people and their emotions. Love of nature and the championing of freedom also figure heavily in many plays of this time. This new emphasis is parallel to and reflective of similar new thinking in music, poetry, novels, and art. Intellectual ideas in the air at a given time tend to become incorporated into all of the arts. The great play to arise from Sturm und Drang was Goethe's *Faust*, based on a longstanding tale, in which the main character comes to understand that true happiness comes from being of service to others.

Melodrama, theater that employs strongly emotional situations and love themes, arose as a consequence of Romanticism's emphasis on emotion and its de-emphasis of realism, and was important in conveying the new importance of emotional expression. Today, melodrama has an undeserved negative image because of the perception that its plots are simplistic and wildly improbable. Such dramas are often pejoratively called "tearjerkers", but this perception misjudges the contribution that melodrama made to the theater. While character development was not strong in melodrama, it was a serious and important form of drama in the nineteenth century. Melodrama remains part of contemporary drama (soap operas are an example).

Romanticism in drama required novel staging techniques to bring the new ideas to fruition. Foremost among these were new ways of lighting. Oil lamps began to replace candles in the latter part of the eighteenth century. Gaslight, obtained by the combustion of coal gas, was introduced in Covent Garden in 1815. Limelight, obtained by heating a ball of lime (calcium oxide or calcium hydroxide) was first used in 1830. These new methods offered not just an increase in intensity of lighting, but also greater possibilities of control and shading. Moreover, gaslight and limelight, unlike oil lamps, could be focused on a single point: the spotlight was born. By the end of the nineteenth century, electric lighting was part of theatrical staging.

Beyond improvements in staging, Romanticism required a fuller expression of emotions on stage and a portrayal of aspects of the character not previously conveyed by the performer. A new approach to acting was needed to meet these demands, and it came from Konstantin Alexeyev (1865–1938). Known by the name Stanislavski, which he felt compelled to take to avoid embarrassing his family, Alexeyev elaborated a system of acting wherein the actor must examine every aspect of his character. He must understand his character's background, life experiences, and come to know him to the smallest detail. To grasp his character's emotional expressions, the actor must draw on his own emotional reactions in situations similar to those his character encounters. By interweaving his knowledge of the character with his educated inference of how the individual would react to a situation, the actor is able to give the audience the totality of his character. Alexeyev's contribution to acting was the mechanism

425

that made dramatic Romanticism possible. This approach is still very widely used, and in its fully developed form, has grown into the method school of acting.

Because of the increased complexity of plots, the intricacies of staging, and the more complete portrayal of characters, productions required the coordination of a non-actor who oversaw the performance. By the end of the nineteenth century, the director became preeminent.

Important playwrights of the nineteenth century (both in and out of the Romantic movement proper) include Heinrich von Kleist (1777–1811), Anton Chekhov (1860–1904), and Oscar Wilde (1854–1900). Wilde created witty and farcical comedic plays presenting alternative moralities that would have been shocking in the earlier part of the nineteenth century. Plays such as *The Importance of Being Earnest* present social criticism in a form that is easy for the audience to take.

To my mind, the most important and influential playwright of the nineteenth century was Henrik Ibsen (1828–1906). Early in his career, Ibsen wrote dramatic verse, such as *Peer Gynt* and *Brand*. Later, he switched to prose and wrote plays focusing on specific problems faced by ordinary people. These plays dealt realistically with the social and psychological pressures that individuals experience. For this reason, he was a major figure in literary naturalism, a movement from the mid-nineteenth century that examined the cause and effect of social problems. In naturalist drama, people were depicted in difficult circumstances, and people of lower social groups were often the major characters. Performers no longer interacted with or gave any thought to the audience. The audience was no longer privy to the innermost thoughts of the characters, but was rather like a mouse in the corner, watching the actors as if they were overhearing conversations not intended for them. What unfolded before the audience was a study of how the characters got into their present condition, and what the consequences of that condition were. Naturalism also played a major role in the development of the novel.

In plays such as *A Doll's House, Ghosts*, and *Hedda Gabler*, Ibsen gives us well-developed characters, whose inner mind we glimpse, wrestling with the conflict between social norms and how they see themselves. Ibsen believed that drama should be society's conscience, and he was perhaps the first great playwright to portray women as the equals of men. His influence on the world's stages is profound.

Twentieth-century dramatists have followed Ibsen in examining the formation of thoughts and feelings, and have shown us the human mind at work as it forms its perceptions and emotions. George Bernard Shaw (1856–1950) was influenced by Ibsen, with whom he shared the belief that drama should be the conscience of the world. The plays of Maxim Gorky (1868–1936) spoke for workers and the common people. Eugene O'Neill (1888–1953) is usually regarded as America's first great playwright. In plays such as *The Iceman Cometh*, *Long Days Journey Into Night*, and *A Moon For the Misbegotten*, O'Neill adopted a pessimistic outlook because he felt that faith alone was no longer adequate to relieve the anxiety of civilization, and he saw no substitute. Thornton Wilder (1897–1975) wrote *The Skin of Our Teeth*, *The Matchmaker* (from which the musical *Hello Dolly* was adapted), and *Our Town*. The latter, an examination of a small town in New Hampshire over a long period of time, reminds us that life is short; we should cherish and take advantage of every moment. Thomas Lanier Williams (1911–1983; known as Tennessee Williams) has been a popular playwright throughout the twentieth century. Among his plays are *The Glass Menagerie* and *A Streetcar Named Desire*.

Arthur Miller (1915–) has written a number of insightful and probing plays. To my mind, there is no better play, in any language, from any time, than Miller's *Death of a Salesman*. In this play, the viewer reaches new understandings of many of the difficult aspects of life. Relationships with parents, relationships with children, relationships with spouses, dreams and hopes, mortality, and coping with aspects of life that do not work out, are all dealt with in a penetrating manner, allowing *Death of a Salesman* to approach poetry in the intensity and concentration of its emotional expression. Among Miller's many other masterpieces, *The Crucible* (1953) uses the setting of the Salem witchcraft trials to explore the McCarthyism sweeping the United States at the time.

Before we leave drama, two approaches to theater, new to the twentieth century, should be discussed. Bertolt Brecht (1898–1956) sought to remind audiences that theater is not reality by employing staging deliberately intended to indicate to the audience that they were spectators (for example, making no attempt to conceal set props or stage hands). This is sometimes called epic theater. Brecht felt that traditional theater, by permitting the audience to identify with characters and become absorbed in the play, did not permit the viewer to form an impartial opinion on the issues raised by the performance. The intent of epic theater was to allow the audience to make objective judgements that would not be possible with complete assimilation into the play. Perhaps the best-known example of Brecht's epic theater is *The Threepenny Opera*, a satire of capitalism.

Theater of the absurd places less emphasis on a coherent, sequential plot, and no emphasis on traditional character development. Plays in this genre take place in no specific time or location, and the dialogue is not meaningful in the usual, literal sense. The idea of theater of the absurd is to force the viewer to ponder deeper questions of human existence by denying him any possibility of focusing on more superficial aspects. Samuel Beckett (1906–1989) was a master of theater of the absurd, as shown by his most famous play, *Waiting For Godot*. Read or viewed literally, *Waiting For Godot* is nonsense. Viewed with a broader perspective, it is an insightful and imaginative commentary on the human condition. Theater of the absurd brings drama full circle from the days of verisimilitude, where plays were judged by the accuracy with which they portrayed the literal details of the world.

Movies, that curious blend of science and art, are a mass-produced, two-dimensional form of theater, and now command the widest and largest audience of any art form. As photography did not end painting, so movies have not ended theater.

Reflections in Prose

The novel is a more recent literary form than poetry or drama and can be defined as a fictional prose narrative of substantial length. Recalling that the essential characteristics of poetry are rhythm and (except for free verse) meter, the word "prose" implies a relatively nonrhythmical and unmetered style of writing. This is, however, not an absolute differentiation; some prose achieves a fluidity of style that can reasonably be taken as an intrinsic rhythm.

Whereas poetry should be heard or read aloud, and drama should be seen in performance, the novel can render its gifts when read silently alone. Because the novel tends to translate more easily than other literary forms (especially poetry), we can maximally enjoy and benefit from novels written anywhere at any time. Moreover, novelists from all over the world, through translation, can communicate with and influence each other quite readily in their medium.

Fictional prose narratives were written in ancient times, but very little ancient literature is considered a true novel in the contemporary sense. In the second century B.C.E., the Greek Aristides composed *Milesiaka*, a series of stories about the town in which he was raised; and other prose narratives were written in Roman times. The first universally accepted novel was *The Tale of the Genji*, written about 1000 C.E. by the Japanese noblewoman Murasaki Shikibu.

These works are not demonstrable precursors to the novel in the West. Rather, the Western novel has multifactorial origins. Its deepest origins lie in poetry, particularly narrative poetry, and in Romance narratives. Romance narratives, popular in the Middle Ages, were prose or verse tales dealing with stories of adventure and heroism. The name derives from their composition in vernacular or romance languages, not from a literally romantic content. Also important in the development of the novel was the fabliaux, a short poem developed in France in the twelfth century. The fabliaux told a story, often centered on human frailties.

Building on the traditions of narrative prose, narrative poetry, Romance narratives, and fabliau, a number of works in the late Middle Ages (or early in the Renaissance) were important in the development of the Western novel. The *Decameron,* by Giovanni Boccaccio, is the story of ten people who flee the great plague of the 1340s to a country villa. While there, to pass the time, each person tells one story a day for ten days (the title means ten days' work). The *Decameron* is in both prose and verse, and makes use of fabliaux.

Influenced by Boccaccio, Geoffrey Chaucer (c. 1340–1400) was the first great, recorded author to write in English (what is now called middle English). Born just before the black death, his works portray England during its aftermath. His most remembered work is *The Canterbury Tales*, the story of a group of people on a religious pilgrimage. En route, they tell stories to each other to ease the journey. Not only are the tales themselves masterpieces, but so also is the interlocking narrative. *The Canterbury Tales* are unfinished: only twenty-four tales, of a planned one hundred and twenty, were found among Chaucer's works. Like the *Decameron*, *The Canterbury Tales* is in both prose and verse, and employs fabliaux.

The legendary King Arthur, if he existed at all, was probably a sixth-century Celtic leader who defended England against Saxon invaders. Romantic tales of King Arthur had long existed in French and English, and were adapted into *Morte D'Arthur* in the fifteenth century by Thomas Malory. Published by William Caxton, *Morte D'Arthur* is a story of love, loyalty, sexual betrayal, and the unraveling of human relationships.

From this background, the works of two seminal writers would give us the novel in its contemporary form. François Rabelais (c.1493–1553), showing the restlessness common in innovative minds, left his monastery to become a physician. Remembered as a Renaissance humanist writer, Rabelais wrote *Pantagruel* (1532), a satirical story of a giant. Two years later, he wrote a sequel called *Gargantua.*

Miguel de Cervantes Saavedra (1547–1616), drawing on the picaresque narrative—an art form originating in sixteenth-century Spain and consisting of a sequence of stories involving and connected by a central character—created the first Western work to be universally accepted as a novel in contemporary form: *Don Quixote,* a study of the conflict between the ideal and the real world.

John Bunyan (1628–1688), a devout Puritan, spent twelve years in jail for preaching without a license. (He could have been released sooner, but he would not agree to change his behavior.) *Pilgrim's Progress,* written in 1678, is an allegorical tale of a person's journey in search of salvation, and is not generally accepted as a true novel. However, *Pilgrim's Progress* not only gives a view of life in seventeenth-century England, it was also very influential on subsequent English prose. Its significance in our story is the same as if it were a true novel.

Jonathan Swift (1667–1745) is remembered for works of sharp and biting satire. His was not an optimistic outlook, and his works often convey frustration and despair. The most famous of these is *Gulliver's Travels,* published anonymously in 1726. More than a clever children's story, *Gulliver's Travels* uses an adventure story to satirize human follies—another layer of complexity that can only be appreciated by the mature reader—and is an early and effective use of the novel to examine ourselves. The main character, Lemuel Gulliver, speaks to contemporary readers when he says, speaking of people who misuse their ability to reason, "They use their reason to magnify, yet excuse their vices." After concluding four fantastic journeys, Gulliver tells us "In the end, I concluded that history is not at all what it seems."

The first major English novelist was Daniel Defoe (c. 1660–1731). Trained as a minister, Defoe decided instead on a career in business and journalism. Although he wrote a variety of works as a young man, including a number of excellent political essays, it was not until late middle age that he wrote the novels for which he is remembered. Defoe was among the first novelists to employ plots centered around events resembling those in ordinary life. He was also among the first to present characters who were simultaneously struggling with the world and with themselves. Defoe's novels, although emphasizing what would *happen* next, also exhibit the beginnings of character development. In *Robinson Crusoe* (1719), patterned after the actual experiences of a shipwrecked sailor, Defoe wrote in the first person (i.e., as if he were one of the characters).

In *Moll Flanders*, he gives us a meticulous portrayal of a woman struggling against difficult circumstances and wrestling with conflicting inner feelings.

Samuel Richardson (1689–1761), in *Pamela*, allowed the plot to unfold as a series of letters, written by a maid named Pamela Andrews to her parents (this is called the epistolary format). In contrast to Defoe, Richardson focused not on plot, but on character. The reader is less concerned with the sequence of events and more concerned with learning about Pamela. Richardson continued this format in *Clarissa*, but in this novel he presented letters from many characters, giving multiple, often conflicting viewpoints.

Henry Fielding (1707–1754) advanced the composition of the novel by expanding the epistolary technique into a third-person narrative and by permitting the characters and the plot to develop simultaneously. He is best remembered for *Tom Jones*. Other eighteenth-century novelists include Tobias Smollet (1721–1771) and Laurence Sterne (1713–1768).

The eighteenth century was the time of the Enlightenment, that great period in our history when we realized (or perhaps, re-realized) that people could make themselves and civilization better through scholarly activities and the support of liberty. The writings of Voltaire, Jean Jacques Rousseau, and Denis Diderot were pivotal in reaching this understanding, and their work impacted the development of the novel by helping to change the focus of society.

Jean Jacques Rousseau (1712–1778), whom we have already met as an advocate of less-regimented education, was important in the development of the next stage of the novel—Romanticism. In prose works such as *La Nouvelle Héloïse* and *Confessions*, Rousseau emphasized intense emotional expression, personal experience, and exploration of conflicts. Rousseau's *Confessions* was an autobiography of a different type. Departing from the usual format of recounting the author's accomplishments in chronological order, *Confessions* instead shows Rousseau's inner thoughts and feelings. Therefore, Rousseau had great influence on literature, specifically the novel, just as he did on philosophy, politics, and psychology. This central figure of the Enlightenment thus became a major contributor to Romanticism.

The Sturm und Drang movement, so important in the development of Romanticism in poetry and drama, was no less influential in the history of the novel. In 1774, the German Shakespeare, Goethe, published *The Sorrows of Young Werther*—an epistolary novel concerned with the conflict between the inner life of ambitions and dreams and the constraints of the world. Its hero suffered the frustrations of external forces before succumbing to suicide. By championing emotion and the fulfillment of the individual, *Werther* was instrumental in ushering in the Romantic period in novels.

As in poetry and drama, the Romantic period reached a peak in novels in the first half of the nineteenth century. As in other areas of literature, novels of this period are distinguished by their focus on the thoughts and emotions of their characters, thus presenting the reader with a more detailed description of the human condition.

Walter Scott (1771–1832), the most popular English novelist of his time, is thought of as the founder of the historical novel—a blend of fiction and history. The historical novel made history understandable and appealing to many who would not otherwise have had contact with it. *Ivanhoe*, a study of loyalties, prejudices, conflicts, and love, remains a widely read work today.

One of the most influential novelists of this period was Jane Austen (1775–1817). Austen, as much as any other English writer, inaugurated Romanticism in the English novel. In novels such as *Sense and Sensibility* and *Pride and Prejudice*, Austen focused on a small number of families in a country village. She was thus one of the first to portray the larger world by examining the smaller world of a few individuals. Hers are not passionate works, where emotions take center stage, but they do show a side of humanity beyond the purely rational, and in the background, depict emotional aspects of life.

The Brontë sisters occupy a special place in English letters. Charlotte (1816–1855), Emily (1818–1848), and Anne (1820–1849) all published initially under male pseudonyms (as Currer, Ellis, and Acton Bell). In 1847, Charlotte Brontë published the substantially autobiographical *Jane Eyre*, the story of a woman who overcomes multiple adversities, while her sister Emily published *Wuthering Heights*, a superbly crafted story within a story that is one of the most celebrated novels in English literature. *Wuthering Heights* gives a skillful and intricate portrayal of its main character, Heathcliff, and offers one of the first suggestions in literature that people abused as children often become abusive adults.

Charles Dickens (1812–1870) wrote many of his novels in serial form for magazines, which had become a major literary forum of the day. He was often required to work on multiple novels at the same time, and usually worked against a deadline. These were very different working conditions from those facing most novelists of his day. While they hardly seem enviable, they may have given his work a spontaneity that might otherwise be lacking.

Dickens was perhaps the first great novelist to fully see the negative effects of the Industrial Revolution and the urbanization of society. Especially apparent in his later works, he was struck by industry's dehumanization and exploitation of its workers, particularly its use of children. Dicken's novels, enormously popular in the nineteenth century, were instrumental in the passage of legislation giving children some protection against industrial exploitation.

His writing was successful because he juxtaposed social commentary with sentiment. His works rarely take us into the inner workings of his characters' minds, but they do explore the relationship between a character and his environment. *David Copperfield* and *Great Expectations* are both recollections of adults who were orphaned as children. The hero of *Great Expectations* comes upon an unexpected endowment, then loses awareness of his background and priorities. Only after his hopes are frustrated does he reacquire acceptance of his roots. The opening and closing lines of *A Tale of Two Cities* are among the most famous passages in literature.

Mary Ann Evans (1819–1880; known by her pseudonym of George Eliot) was influenced by and extended the ideas of Austen. *Silas Marner*, the story of a man embittered by being falsely accused of a crime who is transformed when he adopts a little girl, is a study of the harmful consequences of anger and bitterness. In reading *Silas Marner*, we see that acceptance of the past and feeling love in the present are the keys to happiness, and can transform us. Two of her other masterworks are *Adam Bede* and *Middlemarch*. Evans explored the thought process and examined the connection between thought and action: in her work is the beginning of a psychological examination of characters. She points to the essence of who we are as she closes *Middlemarch*:

> . . . for the growing good of the world is partly dependent on unhistoric acts, and that things are not so ill with you and me as they might have been, is partly owing to the number who lived faithfully a hidden life, and rest in unvisited tombs.

William Makepeace Thackeray (1811–1863) is most remembered for *Vanity Fair*, a satirical view of early nineteenth century society, but he also wrote a number of other fine novels, such as *The History of Henry Esmond*. The novels of Anthony Trollope (1815–1882) often deal with the effects of power on individuals.

Nineteenth-century France gave us a number of great novelists. Marie Henri Beyle (1783–1842; writing under the pseudonym Stendhal), in *The Red and the Black* and *Charterhouse of Parma*, gives penetrating analyses of characters and the struggles that engulf them. Victor Hugo (1802–1885) is remembered for such novels as *The Hunchback of Notre Dame* and *Les Miserables*. Alexandre Dumas (1802–1870) wrote historical novels such as *The Three Musketeers* and *The Count of Monte Cristo*, while his illegitimate son of the same name (1824–1895) used his novels and plays to examine the difficulties of real life. Honoré de Balzac (1799–1850) began his career as a journalist and wrote nearly a hundred novels, whose plots are loosely connected. Most of these novels are part of a continuous giant creation called *La Comédie Humaine* (*The Human Comedy*). Collectively, Balzac's novels are a comprehensive view of nineteenth-century society, and he regarded himself as "secretary to the nineteenth century."

Balzac was one of the first novelists of the realist school. Realism was a movement in literature, primarily affecting the novel, that began in the mid nineteenth century, contemporary with realism in art. Realists, feeling that Romanticism presented an idealized view of humanity, strove to portray the actual world as it exists, using details observable in daily life.

If the purpose of art is to expand life, perhaps no one did that better than Aurore Dupin (1804–1876; occasionally called by her married name of Dudevant, and more often called by her pseudonym of George Sand). Like Evans, she was born in a time when women writers often had to take masculine pseudonyms to receive recognition. In her work, as in her personal life, she stood for individualism and the right of all people to follow their conscience and desires without the hindrance of social conventions. Dupin's writing (which included seventy novels, twenty-four plays, and voluminous other works) deals with "choice at odds with necessity," as she herself wrote, and her work was among the first to show that the conventions prescribed by society, by oppressing women and those without political power, detract from the quality of all of our lives. Her work, and her life, are testament to the constraints and possibilities of our lives.

To my mind, the giant of nineteenth-century French novelists, and the epitome of realism, was Gustave Flaubert (1821–1880). The son and brother of successful doctors, Flaubert was widely regarded as the family imbecile, particularly after failing law examinations in 1843. A perfectionist, Flaubert published only five novels, including *Madame Bovary*. Regarded as the principal French realist novel, *Madame Bovary* is the story (like so many great works of literature) of a person who sought more meaning in her life than societal conventions would allow.

Flaubert, like other explorers, believed in the undiscovered potential of his craft, and felt there were new worlds that the novel had not yet conquered. Using ordinary settings and subjects in his novels, he was a pioneer in the rendering of psychological profiles of his characters. This would become the hall-mark of the twentieth-century novel.

Nineteenth-century Russia produced an abundance of great novelists. Aleksandr Pushkin (1799–1837) was the progenitor in this long line, and his *Eugene Onegin*, a novel in verse, was the first great Russian novel. Following Pushkin, and influenced by him, were Nikolai Gogol (1809–1852), Mikhail Lermontov (1814–1841), and Ivan Turgenev (1818–1883). Turgenev, the first Russian author to be widely read outside of his country, is remembered for *Fathers and Sons*, which reminds us of the constancy of family love, although the contemporary family often has a different form from Turgenev's time.

Few have taken us into the mind and the thought process as well as Fyodor Dostoyevsky (1821–1881). *Crime and Punishment* follows a young man before and after he kills two people. We follow him in his struggle to determine whether or not he should commit the crime, and after, we follow his anguish over the act and his ambivalent feelings about being caught. *The Brothers Karamazov* portrays three brothers and shows the struggles each goes through after their father is murdered.

Lev Tolstoy (1828–1910; also written Leo) showed the power and restlessness of a searching mind in both his novels and his personal philosophy. *War and Peace* portrays four aristocratic families from 1805 to 1812, offering two levels of analysis—the lives of the individuals, and a larger view of the common human experience as played out by his characters. Tolstoy believed the efforts of many people and random chance determined history more than the inherent superiority of individuals. He felt that human destiny was "the ferment of the people", and by showing us this ferment, his work captures the essence of the human spirit. Although fictionalized, *War and Peace* is a more accurate account of early nineteenth-century Russia than can be found in history books. It shows the daily lives and conflicts of people; it does not matter whether or not those specific people actually existed. *War and Peace* examines virtually every aspect of the human experience, public and private, and makes that examination available to its readers. How comforting it is when Tolstoy uses one of his main characters to tell us "We imagine that as soon as we are torn out of our habitual path, all is over. But it is only the beginning of something new and good."

In *Anna Karenina*, we again witness a conflict between the expectations a woman has for herself and the mandates of society. *Anna Karenina* does not give the panoramic view of society that characterizes *War and Peace*, but we come to know Anna very well. Tolstoy's later novels are not as well known, but they are masterpieces in foreshadowing twentieth-century techniques.

Interested in the welfare of serfs and peasants, Tolstoy started a school to champion more progressive teaching methods. Spiritually unsettled in his later years, he found refuge in three principles from the New Testament: universal love, a simple life, and absence of hostility to evil. As we shall see, Tolstoy's philosophy influenced Gandhi.

In the nineteenth century, the United States began to contribute important novels. James Fenimore Cooper (1789–1851) had an early grasp of the perils of America's technological and social progress, at a time when others saw nothing but unbridled opportunities. Cooper was particularly concerned about the plight of native Americans. Nathaniel Hawthorne (1806–1864) studied the conflict between sensual desires and religious conscience. *The Scarlet Letter* examines this conflict, addresses the self-destructiveness of the desire for vengeance, attacks intolerance, points out that we all make mistakes, and asks us to be forgiving to each other. Herman Melville (1819–1891) was a master of allegorical writing, of which *Moby Dick* is a prime example. Beyond the literal story of a ship seeking a whale, *Moby Dick* is an examination of the self-destructiveness of fanaticism and the desire for vengeance.

Samuel Langhorne Clemens (1835–1910; remembered as Mark Twain), by writing in the American vernacular, helped establish an American version of literary English and influenced a number of American writers. His novels, considered by some critics of his time to be superficial, frivolous, and even vulgar, were well received by the public (but even the public valued him as a humorist and entertainer, and did not grasp the true significance of his work). Twain's novels, although usually read for enjoyment, contain important social commentary. For example, *The Prince and the Pauper* tells us that mindless rituals and superficial appearances can prevent a person from being happy. Almost every American has read *Tom Sawyer*, but Twain's masterpiece is considered to be its sequel, *The Adventures of Huckleberry Finn*, considered the first true American realist novel. Like Dickens, Twain succeeded by mixing commentary with sentiment. His later works show a pessimistic view, undoubtedly partially a reflection of the deaths of his wife and two of his children, as well financial difficulties that Twain experienced later in life.

Movements in the arts derive from many sources. They may be a reflection of political and social change. They may flow naturally from previous artistic movements. They may arise as a negative reaction to previous thinking in the arts. Or they may be inspired by developments in science. An example of the latter was literary naturalism. Impressed by the ability of science to elucidate cause and effect relationships, naturalism intensely examined the causes and effects of social problems. Often considered synonymous with realism, naturalism is more properly thought of as a specific form of realism involving a deliberate attempt to document and examine every social problem. Whereas Romanticism pioneered the exploration of the non-rational side of humanity and realism strove to depict all aspects of people—good and bad, naturalism *went looking* for the darker side of our society and then asked, "How did this happen?" Naturalism adopted a fatalistic attitude toward human affairs, believing that much of the human condition was under the control of natural laws and beyond free will.

We have seen that Henrik Ibsen's naturalist approach revolutionized theater. Émile Zola (1840–1902) was the leading naturalist novelist. Inspired by developments in science, Zola attempted to apply the scientific method to analyze the human condition. From 1871 to 1893, Zola developed this approach in twenty novels chronicling one family and examining the circumstances governing their choices. These novels have independent names, but are collectively called *Les Rougon-Macquart*.

Thomas Hardy (1840–1928), a novelist and poet, participated in the naturalist movement and portrayed humanity as substantially under the control of external circumstances. In novels such as *Far From the Madding Crowd*, *Tess of the D'Urbervilles*, and *The Return of the Native*, Hardy depicts the frustrations and defeats of people who struggle against passions and situations they cannot govern. He strove to portray "the worthy encompassed by the inevitable." Hardy was among the first to offer psychological profiles of his characters, and also pioneered the use of symbolism and allegory in novels. Disillusioned with novels after the poor reception of *Jude the Obscure*, he continued to write poetry and wrote over a thousand poems. His poems, not as well known to the public, are valued by scholars as much as his novels.

One of the first American naturalist novelists was Stephen Crane (1871–1900). In *Maggie, a Girl of the Streets*, Crane examined life in the tenements of New York City. In *A Red Badge of Courage*, he offers a psychological profile of a soldier in the American Civil War.

The latter part of the nineteenth century brought an uneasy feeling that the world was not as ordered and straightforward as had been thought. A narrow but reassuring view of the world, based on religion, sexual conservatism, and strict codes of conduct, was gradually replaced by a broader, more daring, but less comforting view. This view gave rise to the twentieth-century thinking that the true state of reality is not apparent to the senses, and that the unconscious is the key to understanding the mind. The literary movement of the first few decades of the twentieth century is called Modernism (a term also used for movements in music and art during this time period) and sought a new view through the unconscious.

No one demonstrated this new view better than the great nineteenth-century novelist Henry James (1843–1916), the first American novelist to have worldwide influence, and the first American writer to leave the United States for Europe. Influenced by Evans, he elaborated on her tendency to probe the psychology of characters; his novels were not so much a reflection of reality in the strict sense as they were examinations of the mind. James used the term "stream of consciousness" (actually first used by his brother, the psychologist William James) to refer to the portrayal of the thoughts (even half-formed and illogical thoughts), memories, feelings, perceptions, and misperceptions of his characters. Like Flaubert, James focused on the indirect examination of characters' minds through their conversations and observations. Events and places are simply background to the focus of the novel, which is the workings of the mind. By examining the nuances and subtleties of the mind, he was a chronicler of our inner selves.

Much of James's work deals with loneliness, and people who feel displaced or without a sense of belonging. This is perhaps because of his own experience as an American emigrant to Europe, and perhaps because loneliness exposes the human mind and makes it more amenable to analysis. In *The Portrait of a Lady*, we see the development of a young woman through thought processes rather than events. James thought the best moment in *The Portrait of a Lady* was a period of reflection by the main character when she pondered her husband, their relationship, and their future, in a scene without action.

Comparisons of Defoe, Dickens, and James allow us to summarize the development of the novel to this point. These three were equally brilliant novelists. Defoe emphasized the sequence of *events*. Dickens went beyond events and developed the thoughts and emotions of his characters, but the focus of his work was the realistic depiction of the world. For James, the focus *was* the character, and his or her psychological constitution.

For the most part, the twentieth-century novel has de-emphasized the description of the external world and explored the structure and origin of individual thought processes. This exploration has often been from multiple viewpoints, reflecting Modernism's belief that there is no one correct way to examine the world. Symbolism has entered into the novel, as it has into poetry. D.H.Lawrence (1885–1930) focused intensely on his characters' sexual feelings. Virginia Woolf (1882–1941) often employed multiple first-person perspectives and further developed the stream of consciousness technique. She expressed succinctly much of essence of art and science when she wrote:

> It is in our idleness, in our dreams, that the submerged truth sometimes comes to the top.

The novelist to most fully develop stream of consciousness writing (also called interior monologue) was James Joyce (1882–1941). As the nineteenth-century novel examined the larger world by focusing on the smaller world of a few people, stream of consciousness writing examined individual people by focusing on their thoughts and perceptions. In *Portrait of the Artist as a Young Man* (1916), *Ulysses* (1922), and *Finnegan's Wake* (1939), the reader faces a stream of memories, feelings, and thoughts of a character *as they occur*, not in retrospect. This allows the author to present the full extent of his character's mind, including the effect of external forces and experiences of the past. Joyce's stream of consciousness writing is a dissection of a mind. It is the realistic portrayal, not of the world, but of the mind. *Portrait of the Artist as a Young Man* is autobiographical, but not in the usual narrative manner. *Ulysses,* published in the same year as Eliot's poem *The Waste Land*, is a study of the lives of two Dubliners on one day—June 16, 1904.

Not all twentieth-century novelists have used stream of consciousness, but twentieth-century writers of all types of literature have accepted that much of who we are results from thoughts and memories not readily apparent in our daily lives. To expose the reader to these, they may use language that has a less obvious immediate meaning, so the reader is required to approach the work in a non-traditional way.

Like modern art, theater of the absurd, surrealistic poetry, and the uncertainties of contemporary physics, stream of consciousness writing is often difficult and disquieting for people. This difficulty, combined with the rise of films and novels written purely for entertainment, has resulted in diminished popularity of the serious novel relative to a century ago, when readers would wait at the dock for the next installment of Dicken's novels. But stream of consciousness writing is irreplaceable because it provides a unique way of reflecting on the human experience and examining who we are.

Other important American novelist of the twentieth century include Sinclair Lewis (1885–1951), Pearl Buck (1892–1973), and Saul Bellow (1915–). F. Scott Fitzgerald (1896–1940) examined the pitfalls of reaching for material success and social status. In *The Great Gatsby*, Fitzgerald illustrates the corruption of materialism, the sorrow caused by striving for false goals, and the effects of self-delusion.

The novels of William Faulkner (1897–1962) generally take place in one fictitious county in Mississippi, and often employ stream of consciousness surrealistic techniques and discontinuous narrative (which disrupts the perception of cause and effect). His later work expresses his disappointment, as a southerner, that the southern part of the United States had not progressed more rapidly and was still clinging to old ways and racial prejudice.

Ernest Hemingway (1899–1961) was instrumental in developing a distinctive American prose style. Hemingway usually depicted heroism with actions, not thoughts, and his male characters often have stereotypical masculinity. In *A Farewell to Arms*, he shows the effect of a World War on a single individual. *For Whom the Bell Tolls* shows us Hemingway's belief that we must always seek to control our own destiny. *The Old Man and the Sea* is considered by many to be Hemingway's finest work. It is an intimate study of the struggle of an old fisherman to land a giant fish, only to lose it to sharks. Although defeated in one sense, the old man achieves a spiritual victory as he accepts and deals with fate in isolation.

John Steinbeck (1902–1968) wrote with compassion about those who are less fortunate, particularly migrant farm workers, in such novels as *Of Mice and Men* and *The Grapes of Wrath*. In writing about disadvantaged people, Steinbeck showed that those with more means are often insensitive and cruel. His work invites us to re-examine the plight of other people, and at the same time, to re-examine ourselves.

Important French novelists of the twentieth century include Marcel Proust (1871–1922), whose massive *Remembrance of Things Past* is an autobiographical flow of memories. Albert Camus (1913–1960) focused on questions on existence, as did Samuel Beckett (1906–1989). As he did in his theater of the absurd, Beckett disrupts the common meaning of words and the usual sequence of events to force the reader to ponder human existence.

In Germany, Thomas Mann (1875–1955) became the most universally regarded German novelist since Goethe. In novels such as *The Magic Mountain*, Mann recognizes, and invites us to recognize, the hidden problems beneath apparently successful contemporary culture.

The novels and short stories of Franz Kafka (1883–1924) examine lonely and unhappy people trapped by the circumstances of their lives. His works received little recognition in his lifetime but are now recognized as insightful examinations of the deleterious effects of civilization on the positive intrinsic aspects of human nature.

Boris Pasternak (1890–1960) was primarily a poet, until condemnation of his works by the communist party forced him away from original work and towards translation. After the death of Stalin, he began his masterpiece, *Doctor Zhivago*. Like Pasternak himself, the novel's main character initially embraced the Russian Revolution, only to see political reality set in. The novel was banned from publication in the Soviet Union, and Pasternak was not allowed to accept the Nobel Prize.

Battles with the Communist Party, the curse of intellectual progress in the former Soviet Union, were also the fate of Aleksandr Solzhenitsyn (1918–). Imprisoned for anti-Stalin remarks, Solzhenitsyn would, upon freedom, write such masterpieces as *One Day in the Life of Ivan Denisovich, First Circle, Cancer Ward,* and *August, 1914*. But his greatest work, to my mind, came from the memories of his incarceration. *Gulag Archipelago* is a terrifying account of life in Stalinist labor camps. The word "Gulag" refers to the prison camps, placed throughout the country in a manner reminiscent of an archipelago of islands. Like the composer Shostakovich, Solzhenitsyn fought a running battle with Soviet oppressiveness, striking a profound blow for humanity with his eventual victory. This is literature, and art, at its finest.

The Sounds of History

What Passion Cannot Music Raise and Quell!
— John Dryden, *A Song For St. Cecilia's Day*

Music, When Soft Voices Die, Vibrates in the Memory.
— Percy Bysshe Shelley, *Music, When Soft Voices Die*

From artifacts, and from ancient man's depiction of musical instruments in art, it is clear that music has been a part of our heritage for many millennia, going far back into the Stone Age. We shall never know how music came to be, but it possibly began for religious purposes. Music was an important part of the ancient civilizations discussed in the first chapters of this work, and indeed, our word music comes from the Greek *Mousike*, meaning art of the Muse. (In Greek

441

mythology, there were nine muses, daughters of Zeus, each presiding over an area of art, literature, or science.) Pythagoras, to whom we owe the idea that nature is expressed in numbers, discovered the mathematical ratio of tones that is still used today. For example, vibrations at twice a given frequency, obtained by cutting the length of the vibrating string in half, are an octave higher.

Because there was minimal musical notation in antiquity, very early music had little influence on that of more recent times. Therefore, music does not have the long, unbroken tradition of art or literature. Music up to and including Roman times was important in transmitting the *idea* of music, but for our purposes, music of today can be said to begin with the early Christian Church. In the first centuries after Jesus, in a practice borrowed from the Eastern Church and Jewish services, it was customary in Western European services to chant the scriptures. Several schools of chant developed, but the foremost was that established and supported by Pope Gregory I (r. 590–604). Known as Gregorian chants, they are also called plainchant or plainsong. These vocalizations of Roman Catholic liturgical texts are the direct predecessor to all of the music of the Western world. They were monophonic (having only one melody) and unaccompanied. (The Church discouraged the use of instruments, either alone or as an accompaniment, fearing that they would dilute the sung word of God.) Gregorian chants are usually thought of as having no rhythm or beat, although surviving manuscripts are not completely clear on this point. Early chants, as far as we can tell, had only a single tone, and even later chants, because of their narrow pitch range, often sound monotonous to contemporary listeners. Although a smattering of musical notation was performed in antiquity, the earliest surviving manuscripts date from the eighth century. The musical signs in these manuscripts, called neumes, are the root of contemporary musical notation.

From the sixth to the ninth centuries, Gregorian chants underwent two important modifications. First came the multitone chant, called Concentus, which replaced the single tone chant. Of the several types of Concentus, the most elaborate used different tones for *each syllable* of text. Then came tropes, additions of new music or text to the chant. Progress in all areas is essentially the elaboration of an existing idea. In all probability, tropes came about for two reasons: the additional text conferred a degree of continuity and made the text easier to remember; and the composer desired to place his personal stamp and creativity into the work.

The advances of Concentus and troping still involved only one melody. In the ninth century, the Gregorian chant took the first steps toward a third advance—polyphony, the simultaneous rendition of more than one melody (polyphony and counterpoint are essentially synonymous terms). Polyphony began as a musical style called organum, which was the addition of a second voice, singing the same text at the same time, a fourth or fifth (i.e., a portion of an octave) above the primary voice. With time, the second voice became more independent and moved at varying intervals and with a different tempo from the primary voice. Polyphony became a distinguishing characteristic of Western music, and even today, is more pronounced in Western music than in that of other cultures. This developed at about the same time as the Gothic cathedrals and was an audible expression of the new confidence, desire to explore, and humanism so well expressed visually by those great structures.

More complex music required a more complex notation. The neumes of the early Middle Ages had no time value and no exact pitch. Guido d'Arezzo (d. c. 1050) devised a staff notation—wherein the line of the staff on which the note was written indicated its pitch—the forerunner to contemporary musical notation.

Music from the middle of the twelfth century to the beginning of the fourteenth is often called Ars Antiqua. The leading center of European music during the twelfth century was the singing school of the Church of Notre Dame, led by Leonin (fl. c. 1160–1190) and Perotin (fl. c. 1190–1225). During this time, secular music became respectable (although its relatively fully developed form indicates that it must have flourished even under the Church's earlier prohibitions). In the courts, Troubadours and Minnesingers were poets and musicians who composed songs in vernacular languages (the latter were the forerunner of the German Meistersinger). Although some of their music was religious, most was secular. Among the populace, secular music was expostulated by the Jongleurs and Minstrels.

The notation of music at this time began to include a means of indicating rhythm. The motet, a song that originated in the thirteenth century from the troping of Gregorian chants, became the most important form of medieval polyphony. It was generally based on a sacred Latin text and was written for three voice parts.

The region of present-day France continued its hegemony in early music with the introduction of Ars Nova (the New Art) in the fourteenth century. Expounded by Philippe de Vitry (c. 1291–1361) and Guillaume de Machaut (c. 1300–1377), the Ars Nova was an elaboration of compositional ideas begun in the Ars Antiqua period. Machaut's *Notre Dame Mass* is regarded by many as the finest religious music of the fourteenth century.

The period in music from about 1400 to 1600 is referred to as Renaissance music. As we have seen, in this period, the rise of universities and the formation of large commercial centers with an affluent middle class facilitated economic prosperity. There was also a diminished influence of the Church, and an emphasis on humanism and secular activities.

Like so many movements in the arts, the Renaissance period was a reaction against preceding thinking—in this case, the complexities of the Ars Nova period. In the early fifteenth century, composers placed more emphasis on harmony, which is the blending of notes sounded together at one moment in time (as opposed to melody, which refers to a pleasing sequential flow of tones over a period of time).

Secular music became more accepted and more common in the Renaissance, and rivaled sacred music in popularity. As secular music rose, so did the fortunes of instrumental music. Long shunned or valued only as an accompaniment to the voice, music for instruments and those who performed it achieved more recognition. The advancement of any profession begins with the elevation of the status of its practitioners, and so it was with instrumental music. Particularly popular were pieces written for the lute (a plucked string instrument with pegs to allow for tuning), the harpsichord (a keyboard instrument in which depressing the key produces sound by plucking strings with a quill), and the clavichord (a keyboard instrument in which depressing the key produces sound by striking the strings with a small portion of metal).

The chief musical form of the period was imitative counterpoint, where successive voices were added, each imitating the original melody. Each new voice came in with the same melody, but at a different time (think of *Row, Row, Row Your Boat* or *Frère Jacques*). Because the cleverness of the composition lay with blending these voices, imitative counterpoint placed emphasis on harmony and vertical structure (tones sounded at the same time), as opposed to the horizontal structure (tones sounded sequentially) of medieval melodies. Imitative counterpoint became the universal compositional standard of the period and was routinely used in all forms of composition.

The motet and the Mass, a vocal religious work derived from the Ordinary of the Catholic Mass (those portions of the Mass that are not changed from day to day), were the principal musical forms. The motet adopted new forms and was often based on four or five voice parts, usually in vernacular languages. The secular counterpart to the motet was the madrigal, a short vocal composition usually based on an amorous poem in a vernacular language.

John Dunstable (c.1370–1453), Guillaume Dufay (1400–1474), and Johannes Ockeghem (c. 1410–1497) were prominent in the early Renaissance period, while Josquin des Prez (c.1440–1521) was the leading composer during the mid-Rennaissance. Giovanni Palestrina (c.1525–1594) was preeminent in the late Renaissance. Except for the Englishman Dunstable, present-day France and Belgium furnished the musical leadership in the Renaissance, and music scholars speak of the Franco-Flemish School (also called Burgundian School) during this time.

Few people realize how vibrant and alive early music is, especially when performed on instruments of the period. Although some early music may sound better on contemporary instruments, its unique effect is often lost when it is not performed on the instruments for which it was written. Music is an auditory time capsule, an opportunity to step back in time and experience the sounds of history.

Developments in one field always impact on other areas, and we cannot leave the Renaissance without mentioning a non-musical development which enormously impacted the history of music—the advent of printing, making the reproduction and dissemination of musical manuscripts much easier.

The Baroque period, from about 1600 to 1750, is the first period of music with which people are generally familiar. During this time, the superior construction of instruments allowed instrumental music to eclipse vocal music for the first time. There was emphasis on the interweaving of voice and instrument parts in an equal fashion, and on the contrasts of instruments, volumes, and tempo. The octave was divided into twelve equal tones, a system that remains in use today. (The name of this method of division—equal temperance—furnished the title for Bach's *The Well Tempered Clavier*.) The crowning achievement of the Baroque period was the introduction of the system of tonality, which would dominate Western music until the twentieth century. Prior to Baroque times, there were no scales, chords, or other familiar rules of harmony in the contemporary sense. Composers used a set of guidelines called modes. With the tonal system, a composition is built from structures based on a single note of the twelve in the octave. It deals with scales and systems of chords that are ultimately related to one key note (the "key" of the composition). When we say a piece is "in C", it means that of the twelve notes in the octave, harmonic structures based on "C" form the backbone of the piece.

Tonality created a more complex harmony and was often combined with modulation, the changing from one fundamental tone, or key, to another. With the new tonal system, there was renewed concern with harmony and the vertical structure of a piece, and many of the rules of harmony that we know today came into being. Polyphony, the simultaneous occurrence of more than one melody, remained important, but many pieces were constructed with one central melody, and harmonic accompaniment based on the tonal system.

Several new musical forms appeared in the Baroque. The imitative polyphony characteristic of Renaissance music was replaced by the basso continuo, a style of writing in which the composer wrote out the melody and bass lines in full, but allowed the performer some discretion in the portion between these lines.

Music and drama have always been combined, even in antiquity, but the Baroque is the period of the first true operas, written in Florence at the end of the sixteenth century by a group of composers known as the Camerata. In seeking a perceived classic ideal, the Camerata championed the monody—the solo voice with instrumental accompaniment. More complete integration of drama and music was obtained by the recitative, the use of spoken words with musical accompaniment. The recitative, in effect, is half speech and half song, and was the cornerstone of early opera. Operas were originally written for the aristocracy, but by the late seventeenth century, they were composed for the masses— one of the first forms of music to be written for the general public. Only in the nineteenth century, over a century after the routine public performances of opera, would instrumental music follow opera into public concert halls.

Claudio Monteverdi (1567–1643) brought opera to a fuller form in the early seventeenth century by successfully making a transition from polyphony to monody. His opera *Orfeo* (1607), while not the first opera, is the first music of this form to be widely recognized. Early opera deliberately emphasized the text, and therefore, gave priority to the recitative, thus imparting a sound that is unfamiliar to most contemporary listeners.

Other forms also developed in the Baroque period. The Oratorio is a musical story, performed without staging, whose text often comes from the *Bible*. The most famous Oratorio is Handel's *Messiah*. The Cantata, a narrative work for chorus, orchestra, and soloists, was written to be performed as part of a church service. Among the most widely performed cantatas are the two-hundred-plus written by Bach. The sonata, a composition written in a particular form for one or two instruments, was developed during this time, although it was not fully formed until the classical period. Music written for an ensemble consisting of members of the violin family and a harpsichord became common.

Baroque interest in contrasts led to a compositional form featuring two or more instruments contrasted with a larger ensemble. Called concerto grosso, this form is virtually unique to the Baroque. The most famous examples of concerti grossi are Bach's Brandenburg concertos (although not all of these are strictly in the style of a concerto grosso). The Baroque period also saw the first concertos for solo instruments. Vivaldi was a master of the solo concerto, and a set of his violin concertos called *The Four Seasons* remains very popular today.

In the Baroque, music was divided into measures, with a note in each measure accented, as is done today. Musical notation achieved its contemporary form. Trumpets and horns were added to the orchestra, and there were technical advances in instrument design and construction. The common stringed instruments of today began as medieval fiddles, succeeded by the viol stringed family, which had sloping shoulders and a flat back. By the latter portion of the seventeenth century, the instruments of the violin family (violin, viola, and cello) became standardized in their form and had largely replace their counterparts in the viol family. (Many contemporary double basses are in the violin family, but many retain the shape of the viol family.)

The great advantage of keyboard instruments is that they can easily create multiple tones simultaneously. The organ, wherein the depression of a key allowed moving air to gain access to a hollow tube, assumed its present form about 1500, although it had been known much earlier. The clavichord, originating in about the fourteenth century, created a tone when the key struck a metal blade, which then struck the string. The blade remained in contact with the string as long as the key was depressed, but there was no separate dampening mechanism. To a limited extent, greater force applied to the key resulted in greater volume. By the sixteenth century, the clavichord was largely replaced by the harpsichord, wherein the striking of a key resulted in the *plucking* of a string. Immediately upon release of the key, dampers stopped the string from vibrating. The harpsichord offered a different tone from the clavichord and quickly became popular in Baroque times; but unlike the clavichord, gradations of volume were not possible by varying the force with which the key was struck.

In the early 1700s, Bartolomeo Christofori (1655–1731) successfully combined characteristics of the clavichord and the harpsichord into the pianoforte. To do this, he solved several problems, more mechanical than musical. From the clavichord, he borrowed the hammer, but made it of wood rather than metal. His mechanism allowed the hammer to strike the string, but unlike the clavichord's hammer, it fell back immediately, even if the key was still depressed. Like the harpsichord, there was a separate dampening mechanism that engaged

447

only when the key was released. These qualities gave the piano characteristics of both a stringed and a percussion instrument. The name pianoforte—meaning soft-loud—derived from the ability to vary the volume by the force applied to the key, although this feature was not new, having been present to a small extent in the clavichord. It took time for the piano, as it came to be known, to catch on, and it was not widely written for prior to 1750. Although the piano was invented in the Baroque period, it would be left to composers of the classical period to bring it into history.

The Baroque period saw the principal music center shift from present-day France to contemporary Italy. Indeed, it is because of the pre-eminence of Italian musicians at this time that contemporary music terminology is Italian.

Antonio Vivaldi (1678–1741) was a teacher of music at a church-supported orphanage for girls. Vivaldi's students were lucky, but so was he, as his students provided him with an orchestra at his regular disposal. In addition to Monteverdi and Vivaldi, some of the composers of the Baroque include Jean Baptiste Lully (1633–1687), Arcangelo Corelli (1653–1713), Henry Purcell (1659–1695), Alessandro Scarlatti (1660–1725), Georg Philipp Telemann (1681–1767), and Jean Philippe Rameau (1683–1764). Corelli was the first great violin virtuoso of record. Alessandro Scarlatti advanced operatic and vocal composition.

1685 saw the birth of three giants of the late Baroque, but fate would carry each to different destinies. Domenico Scarlatti (1685–1757), through his performances and compositions, principally the harpsichord sonatas, developed much of the early repertoire of keyboard instruments and formulated much of our contemporary keyboard technique. Johann Sebastian Bach (1685–1750) spent all of his professional life at a boys' school and in the musical service of the Church. He came from a musical family that must be regarded as history's greatest concentration of familial musical talent. Indeed, although Bach was the premier organist of his day, when used for a composer, the name "Bach" evoked the image of his son Carl Philip Emmanuel (1714–1788). Bach used some of the new tonal techniques but retained many of the older polyphonic techniques. Coming at the end of the Baroque period, Bach was a brilliant synthesizer of styles rather than an innovator. Perhaps no other composer has given us such an excellent snapshot of the musical forms of his time. George Frideric Handel (1685–1759) traveled widely and wrote music in a variety of forms, including operas, oratorios, and secular music.

The classical period of music derives its name from the perception held at the time that its forms and harmonic structures were close to the classical ideal of perfection. It began about 1750, although, like all transitions, it was a gradual process that defies specific dates. In common usage, the term "classical" is generally used to refer to reflective, intellectual music of all periods. Thus, classical music is distinguished from the classical period. The early years of the classical period are sometimes called pre-classical or Rococo, although the latter term is somewhat out of favor now. François Couperin (1668–1733) and Carl Philip Emanuel Bach (1714–1788) exemplify this time.

Whereas Baroque music often followed a program or a story, music of the classical period was generally written for its own sake. Homophonic techniques, which focused on a single melody accompanied by harmonic structures, were given priority over polyphonic techniques, which focused on multiple melodies. The forms of the sonata and the concerto were more fully developed. The fully developed sonata stressed the presentation of a theme (which music scholars call exposition), followed by its development and restatement (recapitulation). The sonata was to this period what the motet was to the sixteenth century: a universal form. Although the full, contemporary form of the orchestra had not yet developed, the four sections we know today—strings, woodwinds, brass, and percussion—had taken shape and the orchestra became a standardized ensemble. This standardization, with the application of the sonata form to a composition for the entire orchestra, resulted in the symphony (which is a sonata for orchestra).

The three great developers of the sonata form in this period were Franz Joseph Haydn (1732–1809), Wolfgang Amadeus Mozart (1756–1791), and the young Ludwig van Beethoven (1770–1827). Although Haydn is often underappreciated by the public, music scholars recognize him as the pioneer of the classical period. More than anyone else, he matured the sonata form, both for chamber and orchestral music. His finest works were his last twelve symphonies, written late in life during two visits to London. To my mind, because of his longevity, his influence on others (the death of Mozart caused Haydn to become a teacher of Beethoven), and his development of forms fundamental to the subsequent history of Western music, Haydn is the most influential composer whose career was entirely contained within the classical period. He was more influential and more important than his younger contemporary Mozart. Only Beethoven is his equal in terms of influence among Western composers of the last several centuries. Haydn's creativity was remarkably intact throughout his long life, in part because of his willingness to learn from his younger contemporaries and former students—Mozart and Beethoven.

Mozart composed, in his short thirty-five years, some of the best known and most revered works in music history. Mozart promoted the growth of opera with such works as *Don Giovanni, The Magic Flute, Cosi Fan Tutte*, and *The Marriage of Figaro*. In his last symphonies, numbers thirty-five to forty-one, one can hear, with only a little imagination, the foreshadowing of the Romantic period. Like Haydn, Mozart wrote extensively for the piano, and his concertos are some of the finest works in that form.

We have seen that people whose lives bridge two epochs are interesting. Beethoven was the quintessential such person. His life bridged two periods in music, the latter of which was largely his own creation. As a young composer, he sat beside Haydn and Mozart in the classical period. As a maturer creator, he expanded every part of the process of making music. He enlarged and elaborated the sonata form. He wrote for an orchestra of greater size, took full advantage of technical advances in instrument design (although more were yet to come), and brought the trombone into symphonic music. The results were giant works that allow us to see the human mind at work.

Born into a family scarred by his father's alcoholism, Beethoven moved to Vienna as a young man. Still in his twenties, he made the horrifying discovery that he was going deaf. By his early thirties, it was clear that the hearing loss was progressive and permanent. He considered suicide, but the strength of his spirit prevailed. In a letter to his brothers, he wrote:

> It seemed to me impossible to leave the world until I had brought forth
> all that I felt was within me.

He went on to hear in his mind the greatest music ever conceived by humanity. That great music began with one composition—his third symphony, which carries the appellation *Eroica*. Written in 1803 and 1804, the *Eroica* combined new and daring tonal forms, foreshadowing the perfection of instrumental blending that was to be Beethoven's hallmark. Although Beethoven would go beyond the *Eroica*, he never took so great a single step. From this symphony would develop many of the styles and forms of the Romantic period, which was in large part the single-handed creation of the deaf musician.

If his deafness took no toll on his creativity, it did extract a price from the person. It is true that he did not have harmonious relations with the rest of humanity, but deafness—the catastrophe which separated his body from his soul—deprived him of so much joy that we cannot expect normal interactions. Beethoven's isolation and irritability were a predictable consequence of his deafness, and not reflective of the man we might have known. As a young man, before his tragedy, he was described as amiable and soft-spoken. He wrote to his brothers:

> My misfortune pains me doubly, inasmuch as it leads to my being mis-judged.

He personified the characteristics of genius: he was consumed by his passion, defiantly non-conformist, able to look at his field in a totally new manner, and he was unhappy. If I were to pick two people whose indomitable spirit and uncompromising individualism symbolize human courage, genius, and forti-tude, I would choose Beethoven and Michelangelo. I take heart that Beethoven did not believe man to be unworthy. Rather, he felt humanity, beneath its diffi-culties, had value, worthiness, and potential. It is not clear that our world is getting better, but it is not getting worse, and it has been our triumph that the hope for a better world has not diminished. As much as anyone else, Beethoven personifies that hope.

Commencing in the aftermath of the *Eroica* symphony, the Romantic period encompasses most of the nineteenth century and the early years of the twenti-eth. The Romantic period includes many of the best-known examples of the sonata and the symphony. The emphasis of this time was on emotion, which became more important to composers than form. Music became an intense expression of the composer's personal emotions, and was written to elicit an emotional, rather than intellectual, response from the listener.

During the Romantic period, one cannot so quickly point to universal forms, such as the motet and sonata in earlier times. Nationalism became a powerful trend in music. Political events (such as the formation of Germany and Italy into their present form) led to a desire for national styles in music; and Roman-ticism, with its great emphasis on emotional expression, was an excellent me-dium to popularize the music of regions and arouse nationalistic fervor.

The Romantic period was a time of individualism in compositions, and it is therefore fitting that it started with the supreme individual—Beethoven. More than any other Western composer, Beethoven was comfortable with all musical forms. His nine symphonies, thirty-two piano sonatas, and seven concertos brought those genres to their greatest heights. His chamber music, his favorite works, is unsurpassed. With Beethoven, chamber music reached the peak of intimacy and sublimeness for which it is noted. A small number of instruments playing together without a leader can achieve a privacy, tenderness, and closeness that eludes a larger ensemble. Larger works, such as symphonies, concertos, and operas, can be thought of as lectures—a power from above—while chamber music is a conversation, an intimate exchange of ideas.

Beethoven had patrons, but substantially supported himself through the sale of his compositions, in contrast to the patronage on which Baroque and classical composers depended. In this respect too, he was a harbinger of the future, as nineteenth- and twentieth-century composers depended less on patronage than their predecessors, and performed their works in public halls rather than churches or courts. Like theater, music began in the Church and moved to the court. Beethoven was one of the first to bring it directly to the public.

In the nineteenth century, orchestras became larger, and their greater size, combined with the increasing complexity of music, meant a larger role for the conductor, as similar complexities gave a larger role to the director in theatrical productions at about the same time. Brass and percussion instruments were more prominently featured. The piccolo, clarinet, trombone, and contrabassoon, already employed in other settings, came into the orchestra. A host of new types of compositions were written for the larger and more versatile piano, including the ballad, etude, caprice, fantasy, impromptu, and prelude.

Brass instruments were significantly improved by the addition of valves. The laws of physics are such that brass instruments can play consecutive notes at higher pitches, but not at lower pitches. There were, therefore, unfortunate and noticeable gaps in these instruments in lower registers. The eighteenth-century discovery that some of these lower notes could be obtained by placing the performer's hand in the bell of the instrument somewhat ameliorated the problem, but a lasting solution was not obtained until the early nineteenth century, when valves were added.

In composition, tonality continued to be used, but the desire for emotional expressiveness led to greater use of modulation, which is the changing from one key to another. This practice de-emphasized the permanent importance of one key note. There was also an increasing use of chromatic scales, which traverse the octave in twelve equal steps. This is in contrast to the traditional scales, called diatonic, which traverse the octave in seven steps, not all of them equal. Romantic harmonic structures and compositional methods resulted in sudden changes in tempo and volume, creating sounds thought dissonant at the time, but which now form the backbone of the classical music repertoire. As we shall see, the compositional methods of the Romantic period pointed the way toward the twentieth century revolutions in music.

Franz Schubert (1797–1828) was Beethoven's younger contemporary, but it is unclear if the two ever met. Like the great master, Schubert was proficient in all forms and all styles of music, and was a superb creator of melodies. He was a master of the new form of art songs (called *lieder* in German), which were independent songs usually written to piano accompaniment. In over six hundred lieder, Schubert explored every aspect of humanity. Never have we lost so much so early as in the death of Schubert at age thirty-one. Haydn and Beethoven would not have nearly the recognition they do if they had died so young. Even Mozart, who died at age thirty-five, would not have been able to complete his last symphonies, his Requiem, or *The Magic Flute* if he had died four years earlier. On Schubert's tombstone is inscribed:

> Music has here buried a rich treasure but still fairer hopes.

In the late nineteenth century, many composers sought material in the folk songs of their country in an attempt to create music that reflected a general desire for a national identity. Richard Wagner (1813–1883), the protagonist of German opera, advocated the Gesamtkunstwerk (total art work), and composed operas of extraordinary drama, often based on German mythology. Wagner's frequent use of modulation strengthened the idea that one note need not be dominant in compositional technique—an idea exploited in twentieth-century atonality. His intensely nationalistic style and his antisemitism made him Hitler's favorite composer.

Johannes Brahms (1833–1897), a decent and humble man, was a Romantic composer, but also used the best of classical styles in his compositions, creating a compositional form often opposed to that of Wagner. He wrote for every media except opera. Among his many great works are the *German Requiem*, four symphonies, four concertos, as well as piano and chamber works that are second only to Beethoven's.

Petr (or Pyotr) Tchaikovsky (1840–1893) mixed Russian folk tunes into his work and is the best remembered of the Russian composers. His most famous works are his last three symphonies, the first of his three piano concertos, his violin concerto, *Overture 1812*, and his ballets. His chamber music is treasured by those who follow the music of small groups.

Tchaikovsky was thought to have died during a cholera outbreak. However, reexamination of the circumstances of his death provides an alternative explanation. Tchaikovsky was homosexual, and was trained as a lawyer before he totally dedicated himself to music. The thinking of many scholars now is that Tchaikovsky's former law school classmates, enraged at an alleged sexual advance made by the composer toward a man, and at the disgrace he was felt to have brought upon society and their profession, pressured him into committing suicide.

French and Italian schools of opera flourished alongside the German school led by Wagner. Charles Gounod (1818–1893) and Georges Bizet (1838–1875) represented the French operatic school. In Italy, the operas of Gioacchino Rossini (1792–1868), Vincenzo Bellini (1801–1835), and Gaetano Donizetti (1797–1848) are among the world's most beloved. Giuseppe Verdi (1813–1901) is perhaps the most revered opera composer in the world. His *Rigoletto*, *Aida*, *La Traviata*, and *Il Trovatore* are among the most popular operas on the world's stages. Late in life, he composed *Otello* and *Falstaff*. Giacomo Puccini (1858–1924) continued Italian operatic tradition into the twentieth century.

A partial list of some other composers of the Romantic period, many writing in a nationalistic style, includes Hector Berlioz (1803–1869), Felix Mendelssohn (1809–1847), Robert Schumann (1810–1856), Frederic Chopin (1810–1849), Franz Liszt (1811–1886), Camille Saint-Saens (1835–1921), Modest Moussorgsky (1839–1881), Antonin Dvorak (1841–1904), Nikolai Rimsky-Korsakov (1844–1908), and Edvard Grieg (1843–1907).

Claude Debussy (1862–1918) was well acquainted with literature and art, and his music was influenced by other art forms. Debussy broke with the conventional compositional techniques of his time. Instead of using traditional diatonic scales, which consist of both whole and half tones, his harmonic structures are based on whole-tone scales, and his music was built around patterns of sound rather than traditional harmonic structure. Moreover, a less clearly defined rhythm gives his compositions a flowing quality reminiscent of an Impressionist painting, and his music evokes feelings and moods very much as Impressionism in art did. For these reasons, he is sometimes called an Impressionist composer. Maurice Ravel (1875–1937) is also thought by many to be an Impressionist composer. Impressionist music can be thought of as a French nationalism in music.

The music of Gustav Mahler (1860–1911), Richard Strauss (1864–1949), Sergei Rachmaninoff (1873–1943), and Jean Sibelius (1865–1957) is a bridge to modern times. As a young composer, Mahler admired Wagner. As a mature creator, in *Das Lied von der Erde* (*The Song of The Earth*) and his massive symphonies, Mahler found novel expressions of harmonies and foreshadowed the twentieth century. In a letter, he wrote that "oneself is . . . merely an instrument through which the universe plays."

Twentieth-century "classical" (using the broader meaning of the term) music has placed a premium on individuality. Some, but not all, examples have emphasized sounds and their properties, rather than traditional harmony and melody. This emphasis, and the techniques that have grown from it, gives some modern music a certain dissonance in the minds of many who are not experienced with it. But much twentieth-century music is based on the same harmonic techniques as nineteenth-century, and nationalism continued to flourish in such composers as Bela Bartok (1881–1945), Zoltan Kodaly (1882–1967), Leos Janacek (1854–1928), and Manuel de Falla (1876–1946). Bartok is the most highly regarded, and is best known for his *Concerto For Orchestra* and his string quartets.

The principal innovation of the early part of the century was atonality. Introduced by Arnold Schoenberg (1874–1951), atonality is the abandonment of the principle of tonality, present since Baroque times. In atonality, the composition is not built primarily on structures derived from one key note. Atonality was not as radical a departure from existing forms as might initially be thought. In the nineteenth century, the increasing use of modulation (the changing of the key) weakened the dominance of any one key note. Likewise, the increased use of chromaticism (scales based on twelve equal divisions of the octave) led to a greater equality of all of the tones. The major method of achieving atonality was Schoenberg's twelve-tone system, wherein the twelve tones of the octave are lined up in any order of the composer's choosing. Throughout the composition, the composer follows this order. Any given tone is not used until all eleven other tones have been used. Schoenberg was followed in the twelve-tone technique by his students Alban Berg (1885–1935) and Anton von Webern (1883–1945). While the use of a strict order of tones may appear limiting and restrictive, and the departure from traditional harmony may sound dissonant, atonality has one distinct advantage: no one tone is more important than any other, and therefore, a new range of compositional possibilities is opened. The twelve-tone technique gave rise to serialism, wherein the concept of a strict order was applied to qualities other than tone. (For example, from a set of volume levels, a given volume level is not employed until all other levels in the set have been used.) Exponents of serialism include Olivier Messiaen (1908–1994) and Pierre Boulez (1925–), although not all of their work is serial. Indeed, one of Messiaen's best known works is the *Quartet For the End of Time*, a nonserial work written for clarinet, violin, cello, and piano—the only instruments available while he was interned in a German prison camp in 1940.

So we see that the terms atonality, twelve tone, and serialism, although often used synonymously, have slightly different meanings. As expressionist artists seek a response from pure color elements, so twelve-tone and serialist composers seek a response from pure sound elements, and composers using these techniques are sometimes called expressionist composers.

Opposing atonality for much of the twentieth century was Neoclassicism, the other major musical style of recent times. Neoclassicism is a comprehensive approach to composition involving more than harmony. A modified form of tonality is combined with some musical forms of the past (not just from the classical period). A number of twentieth-century composers drew on classical techniques, but Igor Stravinsky (1888–1971) is often regarded as the foremost exponent of the Neoclassical style.

In his extraordinary experimental period from 1910 to 1920, Stravinsky found new ways to put sounds together, very much as Picasso and Braque, at about the same time, found new ways to put images together, and Einstein found new ways to envision the universe. Stravinsky's three great ballet scores—*The Firebird, Petrushka,* and *The Rite of Spring* (also called *Le Sacre du Printemps*)—are exquisite musical expressions of the movement of the human body and date from this time. With his compositions from the 1920s and his influence on other composers, he became the leading Neoclassical composer.

Sergei Prokofiev (1891–1953), whose first symphony is called the classical symphony, and Paul Hindemith (1895–1961) were also Neoclassical composers. Benjamin Britten (1911–1976) used some neoclassical techniques. Indeed, Neoclassicism became the dominant compositional style of the century, with most composers primarily using some form of this technique.

It bears noting, however, that at one time or another, most twentieth-century composers had some experience in both atonal and neoclassical techniques. Schoenberg, the exponent of atonality, wrote some lovely tonal pieces, and even Stravinsky, ever the explorer, investigated atonality late in his life. As we have seen with visual artists, creative people are difficult to place into a single movement or style.

Charles Ives (1875–1954), William Grant Still (1895–1978), George Gershwin (1898–1937), Aaron Copland (1900–1990), and Leonard Bernstein (1918–1990) are significant American composers, and represent an American nationalism in music. Like many twentieth-century composers, they blended a variety of styles, such as traditional "classical", jazz, and (especially for Still) African-American spirituals.

Ives was a remarkable person who worked completely outside the mainstream of music. Independent of other musicians, he experimented with many of the central ideas of twentieth-century music. He deliberately remained an amateur so he would not have to compromise his ideas to suit employers, publishers, or the public. From one viewpoint, Ives was one of those extraordinary and rare people who flies to the heights of his craft despite the burden of being isolated from the achievements of his contemporaries and the ideas of his time. From another viewpoint, it was precisely *because* Ives isolated himself from the mainstream that he could reach his potential without pressure to conform to an established convention. As is so often the case with those who work alone, his handicap was also his strength.

The music of Dmitri Shostakovich (1906–1975) was an auditory chronicle of life in the Stalinist Soviet Union, and it is nothing short of a miracle that the composer was able to create his work amidst the terror of Stalin's concentration camps. In constant danger of imprisonment and death, he sometimes slept in the hall of his apartment building, so that if the secret police came to take him away, they would not wake his wife and children. The music of Shostakovich outlasted, and in a very real way, ultimately defeated the tyranny of Joseph Stalin.

Other interesting experiments in twentieth-century music include polytonality (the simultaneous basing of a composition on more than one central tone), and microtonality (the division of the octave into more than twelve tones). The intersection of technology and music insures that today's electronic and computer-generated music will be tomorrow's sounds of history.

The twentieth century has seen more diversity in music than any other era. In fact, twentieth-century music has diversified more than any other art form in any time. Modern times have seen a bewildering array of musical types and forms, ranging from the continuation and extension of traditional forms to the popular music that is more familiar to most people. New forms of music have permitted a greater number of people to appreciate this art. This diversity has partly resulted from mass communication and world travel, which expose people to a variety of styles, and partly from the advent of recording. Recording technology has been to music what the printing press was to literature—the opportunity to disseminate.

To my mind, much of this diversification is directly traceable to the influence of African music. The key element in African music is rhythm. Melody is de-emphasized, and harmonic structures are simpler. This musical tradition was brought to the United States, surprisingly intact, by slaves. Torn from their homeland, separated from their families, transported in unimaginable horror, driven to early deaths by forced labor, and coping with cultural devastation, African-Americans have miraculously managed to hold on to their musical heritage. Their triumphant journey in musical expression is a tribute to human resilience.

Shut out of the traditional music establishment, this untapped talent created new art forms. The work songs of the slaves are the direct predecessors to the blues, a contemporary musical lament. Ragtime resulted from the African-American influence on a European musical form called the march. In ragtime, accents are in unexpected places (this is called a syncopated beat), suggesting a ragged rhythm, which furnished its name.

Jazz arose in large part from the blending of blues and ragtime in early twentieth-century United States. Jazz is easier to characterize than to define. Its principal attributes are syncopation and collective improvisation, wherein a group of musicians extemporize individually and as a group. Jazz was popularized by African-Americans, first in New Orleans, then in Chicago. Among the giants of early jazz were Fletcher Henderson (1897–1952), Louis Armstrong (1900–1971), Edward "Duke" Ellington (1899–1974), and Count Basie (1904–1984).

By the 1930s, white musicians had learned jazz and performed it as a softer form in big bands, such as those of Glenn Miller (1904–1944), Jimmy Dorsey (1904–1957), Tommy Dorsey (1905–1956), and Benny Goodman (1909–1986). It was the big band form of jazz that white Americans regarded as respectable, associating "colored" jazz with gambling and prostitution.

Country and western is a traditional American folk music resulting from a union of rural music from southeastern United States with cowboy music from the western part of the country. Dating from the 1920s and 1930s, country and western has been influenced by the blues. Bluegrass is a form of country and western characterized by more complex rhythms.

Perhaps the most unlikely and extraordinary blending of musical styles resulted in rock music, beginning in the 1950s. Among the contributing styles are the blues and country and western. In the 1960s, it was heavily infused with a British influence (the Beatles, the Rolling Stones, etc.). The association of rock music with a specific age group—youth—is unusual among art forms.

The latest new form of music is rap, which arose in large part in prison populations in the United States. In the diversification of twentieth century music, we see again that the blending of cultures permits maximal innovation.

One final personal note as we close our survey of the arts. Twentieth-century music, like Modern Art, surrealist poetry, Theater of the Absurd, and stream of consciousness novels, is an attempt to transcend the limitations that are so much a part of our traditional thinking. As such, it often takes the listener into acoustic experiences that are initially strange and unwelcome. Instead of being rejected as foreign, contemporary music should be welcomed as an invitation to explore new avenues and horizons. Exploration of all types brings the discomfort of the unfamiliar, but the effort is always worth it.

We have seen that contemporary creative artists of all types, in the process of finding new ways to explore and reflect on who we are, have found it necessary to increase the distance between themselves and the larger society. Some of this is unavoidable; creative people have always functioned outside the mainstream, and their presence on the periphery is necessary to perceive a problem or situation in a new way.

The spectator, listener, or reader of the contemporary arts must realize that progress in all areas depends on new ways of seeing; and new ways, by definition, may appear alien and uncomfortable. If we are to take the voyage of self-discovery, an invitation issued in the prologue of this work, we must be open to new ideas and novel viewpoints. We must reserve judgement, and then render it on the basis of the ability of the work to make us think differently, not on our immediate reaction.

We are all prisoners of our time, and therefore, of our time's way of seeing. Any work of art is an opportunity to view the world through someone else's eyes, to step into another mind or another time and magnify our experience of the world. To slip the bonds of the present, we must view all reflections on our time as opportunities to transcend it.

Chapter 35
Profiles of Humanity

People of daring who espouse new ideas bring out the best in humanity. We can all be such people.

NOW THAT WE HAVE EXAMINED THE HISTORY OF IDEAS, let us examine the greatest idea of all: we are all equal. Considering its simplicity, it is tragic that this idea has to be learned and taught. There are no greater heros in history than those who bring us this message, and there is no greater advancement for our species than the mastery of this concept. Equality is the simplest and greatest idea to ever emerge from the human mind.

The many struggles for equality raise the question of whose liberation is at stake. The race, sex, national origin, religion, and sexual orientation of people who struggle for equality are the same as yours or mine—they are humanity. We are all Hindu and Muslim, male and female, black and white, gay and straight, Russian, Chinese, and Native American. We are all rich and poor, courageous and cowardly, brilliant and obtuse; we are all homeless as long as any of us is homeless.

We are people first, and people of a particular type second. Setting any segment of the population aside as distinct, different, and inferior deprives us of the creativity and unique heritage that segment might have given us. We will never know the great scientific discoveries, the great works of literature, the operas that we have lost because we have not allowed each of us to partake of the full range of the human experience. There are holes in our history and in our lives where creativity, friendship, simple acts of kindness, and tender moments might have been. To discriminate against a person or treat them as if they were different from others, is to deny them a right basic to each of us—the right to be who we are. Accepting the equality of all allows each of us to benefit from the insight and knowledge of all of us.

We are all unique, with a unique contribution to make. In shared uniqueness, we are truly equal. The winds of change are blowing subtly, but persistently, for equality. Never before, not even in the Renaissance or the Enlightenment, has equality been so championed and so near. The slow, inexorable changes in how we see each other make this an exciting time in which to live.

Nowhere is there a better example of an idea coming to fruition from the input and sacrifice of innumerable people than in our struggle for equality. From innumerable individuals, four profiles are presented to illustrate that prejudice and the struggle for equality are part of who we are.

Profound Simplicity

Let freedom reign. The sun never set
on so glorious a human achievement.

— Nelson Mandela

Great ideas can never be precisely dated, and a number of people believed in the equality of women during and after the Enlightenment. In 1792, Mary Wollstonecraft (1759–1797; the mother of Mary Wollstonecraft Shelley, the author of *Frankenstein*) published *A Vindication of the Rights of Women*. The nineteenth century saw movements in many countries for women's suffrage, but only one country would enfranchise women in that century (New Zealand, 1893).

Elizabeth Cady (1815–1902) became active in the temperance (abolition of alcoholic beverages) and anti-slavery movements early in her life. Through the abolitionist movement, she met and married Henry Stanton, taking his last name. In 1848, she and Lucretia Coffin Mott (1793–1880) organized the Seneca Falls Convention, the first large-scale effort for women's suffrage in the United States. One hundred delegates (including thirty-two men) listed sixteen forms of discrimination, one of which was the denial of the right to vote. For that convention, Elizabeth Stanton wrote *A Declaration of Sentiments*, in which she simply said "men and women are created equal." Like all great ideas, we are retrospectively struck by its profound simplicity.

In 1851, Stanton began a long collaboration with Susan B. Anthony (1820–1906). Anthony was born into a Quaker family in Massachusetts, but moved to upstate New York as a child. Unhappy with her position as a teacher in a girls school, she became a manager of the family farm, where she met and was influenced by guests of her abolitionist father. (One such guest was the ex-slave

Frederick Douglass.) Anthony realized that she, too, could join reform movements. (Like Stanton, she supported both temperance and abolition). However, she soon made the unsettling discovery that as a woman, she was a victim of the same discriminatory practices from which she was attempting to liberate others.

In 1869, when the fifteenth amendment to the United States (enfranchising African-American men) was proposed, Stanton and Anthony refused to support it because women were not included. They formed the National Woman Suffrage Association, which focused its attention on a federal constitutional amendment for women's suffrage. Another group supported the fifteenth amendment, believing that the enfranchising of African-American men would lead to universal suffrage. This group formed the American Woman Suffrage Association, and concentrated on the state level. In 1890, the two groups merged into the National American Woman Suffrage Association. In the same year, Wyoming, which as a territory had permitted women's suffrage as early as 1869, became a state, and thus the first state in which women could vote.

In 1872, Anthony attempted to vote in the presidential election—a violation of the law. While awaiting trial (she would be convicted and assessed a fine of $100, which she refused to pay), she began a series of lectures that made her a leading spokesperson for women's suffrage. Stanton and Anthony made an exceptional combination. Anthony acknowledged that her older contemporary was the founder of the women's rights movement in the United States. It is fair to conclude, however, that the two women share equal credit for the achievement of women's suffrage, although neither would live to see it. (Suffrage for American women over the age of twenty-one came as the nineteenth amendment to the constitution, which was not ratified until August, 1920.) Stanton often furnished the ideas, and Anthony's organizational ability and speaking prowess aroused public consciousness. It was not uncommon for Stanton to write speeches that Anthony would deliver.

The influence of both women extended beyond America. In 1888, Stanton was a founder of the International Council of Women; and later in life, Anthony spoke in Europe. With Matilda Gage (1826–1898), they co-authored *The History of Women's Suffrage* (four volumes, 1881–1902).

In Great Britain, parallel efforts were spearheaded by Emmeline Pankhurst (1858–1928) and her daughters Christabel (1880–1958) and Sylvia (1882–1960). In 1918, British women over the age of thirty received the right to vote, but younger women were not enfranchised until 1928.

Alice Paul (1885–1977) was expelled from the National American Woman Suffrage Association because she was perceived as being excessively militant. She then formed the National Woman's Party, which adopted protest marches and hunger strikes to gain suffrage. Today, Paul's strategies hardly qualify as militant, and in fact, are examples of the nonviolent approach we will see in our next profile. Interviewed late in life, Paul, who lived to see so much more than either Stanton or Anthony, decried the fact that women were all too often excluded from positions of power. "We still have no power," she said, testifying that the right to vote is not the end of the struggle for equality.

The pace of progress is indeed slow, and profound simplicity does not always carry the day. In 1972, The Equal Rights Amendment was proposed to the United States Constitution. One of the shorter amendments, it simply said:

Equality of rights under the law shall not be denied or abridged by the United States, or by any state, on account of sex.

The amendment was passed by Congress, but received ratification by only thirty-five of the required thirty-eight states. The arguments against it were varied and often cleverly disguised misogynistic opinions, quite frequently from women. A letter from Voltaire to Rousseau in the eighteenth century quite adequately sums it up: "No one has ever used so much intelligence to persuade us to be stupid." Profoundly simple statements of equality do not need to be dissected to ferret out hidden evils and weaknesses. It is on these simple truths that our future depends. What would we say to Stanton and Anthony? What will we say to posterity?

Satyagraha

Mohandas Gandhi (1867–1948) was born into a Hindu home, but his mother was a follower of Jainism, a religion that stressed nonviolence and vegetarianism. Starting with these two religions, Gandhi would incorporate, over the course of his life, aspects of every major religion, becoming a person of all faiths and the quintessential spiritual human being.

He initially desired a career in medicine, but a family tradition of civil service caused him to choose a legal career, and in 1888 he went to England to become a lawyer. In England, he became fully acquainted with the *Bhagavad Gita*, a poem from the Hindu epic *Mahabharata* that would comfort him throughout his life. Two admonishments in the *Bhagavad Gita* made a particularly powerful and lasting impression on him—the concepts of nonpossession and equability (remaining calm and free of anger, even in the presence of adversaries). Returning to India in 1891, Gandhi found employment as a lawyer more difficult than he had imagined, so in 1893 he took a position with an Indian company in South Africa, where he would live for the next twenty years.

In South Africa, he felt the full brunt of racism. His first conspicuous political action was in 1894 when he organized opposition to a bill in the South African province of Natal that would deprive Indians of the right to vote. The bill passed anyway, but Gandhi found his calling. In the Boer war of 1899–1902 (in which the British defeated residents of South Africa descended from other European nations, particularly the Netherlands), Gandhi's belief in nonviolence prohibited him from a taking a combative role, but he organized an ambulance corps and directed a Red Cross unit.

1906 was perhaps the year in which Gandhi's political agenda matured. In that year, the South African government passed a law requiring the registration of Indian citizens. Under Gandhi, Indians defied the ordinance, but did so in a manner that was to become the historic hallmark of nonviolent protest. Gandhi's defiance had three characteristics that would make a mark in history:

1. Noncooperation with the authorities, and disobedience of the law

2. Complete nonviolence, not even verbal violence

3. The acceptance of all penalties and suffering associated with this position

Gandhi called this approach Satyagraha, Sanskrit for "steadfastness in truth."

Gandhi was the principal architect of the nonviolent protest movement, but he was influenced by others. Having developed a knowledge of and respect for all religions, he was influenced by Jesus, who is remembered as having taught a nonviolent response to violence. The writings of Henry David Thoreau (1817–1862), particularly his *Civil Disobedience*, were an important influence on Gandhi. He also corresponded with and was deeply influenced by the Russian writer Lev Tolstoy (1828–1910), whose fearless attacks of social injustice in czarist Russia were coupled with pleas for the absence of personal animosity toward adversaries. In 1910, Gandhi founded a cooperative living arrangement for Indians in South Africa, and in tribute to the Russian writer, named it the Tolstoy colony.

Over the next seven years, Gandhi elicited vast sacrifices from the Indian people of South Africa, including loss of jobs, imprisonment, and occasional deaths. In 1913, pressure from the international community forced the South African authorities to compromise with Gandhi regarding Indian registration. Gandhi had become, in the words of Jeanette Eaton, a fighter without a sword.

Gandhi left for India in 1914, the mature Indian man of peace having actually been fully formed in England and South Africa. He supported Britain in World War I, but after the war, became an advocate of Indian independence, using the same strategy of Satyagraha that he had crafted in South Africa. Gandhi spearheaded a boycott of British goods, and of all businesses and institutions that dealt with or abetted the British. Thousands of Indians unhesitatingly accepted prison, thus rendering it ineffective as a punitive measure. So complete was the Indian people's reverence for Gandhi that he was called Mahatma, meaning "the great soul." In 1918, Gilbert Murray characterized the British Empire's foe as "a dangerous and uncomfortable enemy, because his body, which you can always conquer, gives you so little purchase on his soul."

In 1919, the British Parliament passed the Rowlett Acts, giving British authorities in India increased authority to deal aggressively with the nationalist movement. The clash of British intransigence and Satyagraha resulted in the massacre of four hundred Indian civilians at Amritstar, after which Indian resolve only deepened. In 1922, Gandhi was convicted of sedition and spent two years in prison. When he emerged in 1924, he found that the movement had splintered into competing groups. Especially painful was the bitterness that had developed between the Muslims and Hindus. Often fueled by the British, the chasm would not heal in Gandhi's lifetime and would be his greatest defeat.

By the late 1920s, he was active again. In 1930, Gandhi called on Indians to refuse to pay taxes to Britain. Particularly oppressive was a tax on salt, which fell disproportionately on the poor. Indians marched to the ocean, and obtained salt from the evaporation of seawater. Gandhi was imprisoned but soon released, because the British realized that they could control his body, but not the influence of his mind.

Jailed again in the early 1930s for civil disobedience, he fasted for better treatment of the Untouchables, India's lowest socio-economic class. Gandhi maintained that the poor treatment of the Untouchables was partly a result of the Indian caste system, which he deplored, and partly a result of British policy, which permitted them to be a separately considered segment of the population. As his death in British hands would surely have ignited a revolution and precipitated war, he received cooperation from the British, and the Untouchables were benefited.

From the mid-1930s, he concentrated on education, especially in rural areas. He wanted India to be economically independent so that it would be able to boycott British goods. At the same time, believing in a simple lifestyle and nonpossession, he opposed heavy industry. The solution, he felt, was hand spinning and weaving—simple industries that Indians could do at home, and which would give them a product that was marketable worldwide.

World War II taxed the nonviolent beliefs of Gandhi, as it did for one of his admirers, Albert Einstein. After much soul searching, Gandhi and the Indian National Congress—the principal organization in the fight for Indian independence—declared that they would not support the British effort unless India was given total independence. Britain refused, and Gandhi was jailed in 1942. By his release in 1944, Indian independence was essentially inevitable, and Britain agreed to it, provided that the Hindus and Muslims resolved their conflicts. The victory of the Labour party in Britain in 1945 removed the last obstacle, and initiated discussions between the Indian National Congress (primarily controlled by Hindus), the Muslim league, and the British government. India became free on June 3, 1947, but only after partition of the subcontinent into India and Pakistan. There would be Indian independence, but not Indian unity. Gandhi's moment of victory was simultaneously his moment of defeat.

Gandhi accepted this division, however, and attempted to reconcile the two groups. When his efforts failed, he fasted. His fasting stopped rioting in Calcutta, and resulted in a truce in Delhi. All of his life, he was criticized by militants of all sides: repressive British, Indian militants, fanatic Hindus and Muslims. It is the fate of people of peace and wisdom to be constantly criticized by extremists. One such misguided militant, who misinterpreted Gandhi's tolerance of Islam as anti-Hindu sentiment, shot and killed Gandhi early in 1948.

It was Gandhi's genius that he could forge coalitions between divergent groups. By simplicity, gentleness, and strength of convictions, he brought out the commonality in all people. He was a spiritual leader, not a politician, but he understood that spiritual peace should be expressed in the freedom and self-determination of people. Gandhi's influence extends beyond Indian independence and the dignity of the Indian people. He helped collapse colonialism, and he brought dignity to all people of the world. He proved that the human will is supremely powerful, and that the improvements in our civilization are made possible by it. It is no wonder that Einstein, the master capturer of the human spirit, said of him: "generations to come, it may be, will scarce believe that such a one as this ever in flesh and blood walked upon this earth." Many have followed the teachings of the Mahatma, one of the most important of whom is our next profile of humanity.

Free at Last

Martin Luther King, Jr. (1929–1968) hailed from a long tradition of Baptist ministers; his father, grandfather, and great grandfather were all of that profession. (For many years, the Seminary was the only place African-Americans could get an education, and the Church was the only place they could gather without harassment.) King entered college at the age of fifteen and graduated at age nineteen. After considering both medicine and law, he elected to follow the family tradition and enter seminary training. In 1951, he graduated first in his class from divinity school, and went on to earn a doctorate in 1955. During his seminary years, he became acquainted with Gandhi and his philosophy of nonviolence. No one who bends the course of human history is influenced by only one person, but there is a direct line of influence from Tolstoy to Gandhi to Martin Luther King, Jr.

In 1953, he married Coretta Scott, with whom he would have four children. After completing his doctoral degree, he took a position as minister at Dexter Avenue Baptist Church in Montgomery, Alabama. During his first year in that capacity, fate began to deal to King the hand that would change his life and so many others. In December, 1955, an African-American woman named Rosa Parks (1913–) refused to surrender her seat on a Montgomery public bus to a white rider. After she was arrested, African-Americans organized a boycott of the Montgomery public bus system, and King became the leader of this effort. Inspired by Gandhi, and adopting his tactics, King guided this boycott to success. After 381 days, Montgomery buses were desegregated by order of the U.S. Supreme Court.

King then fully realized the potential of the nonviolent approach, and organized the Southern Christian Leadership Conference, the organization through which his efforts would be conveyed throughout his life. Advocating the nonviolent approach, King said:

> If you will protest courageously, and yet with dignity and Christian love, when the history books are written in future generations, historians will have to pause and say 'There lived a great people—a black people— who injected new meaning into the veins of civilization.'

He began a speaking tour, which made him a household personality through-out the United States. He also traveled to India and met with Prime Minister Nehru. In 1960, he moved to his hometown of Atlanta and became co-pastor (with his father) of Ebenezer Baptist Church. Later that year, he and others were arrested for protesting the segregation at a diner in an Atlanta department store. Charges against all of the protestors were dropped, but in a vindictive move, King was charged with violating probation for a minor traffic offense and sentenced to prison (a national outcry ensued and led to his freedom).

In 1963, the American Gandhi and his followers demonstrated in Birming-ham, Alabama for equitable hiring practices and desegregated restaurants. In the days before the demonstrations, anticipating that violence would be used against them, King told his followers "in my judgement, some of the people sitting here today will not come back alive from this campaign." He was right. The full force of ignorance and racism was unleashed upon the marchers. Dogs and fire hoses were freely used and King was imprisoned. After the firehoses were turned on, Birmingham police chief Bull Connor said "look at them niggers run."

While King was imprisoned in Birmingham, the local newspaper published two letters concerning the protest march. One was from African-Americans supportive of the march, while the other was critical of King and his followers, suggesting that they should have postponed their protest and praising the po-lice for restoring order. The source of the second letter was surprising; it came from eight white clergymen. King had the brilliant idea of answering his clergy-men colleagues in the form of an open letter. Using a pen smuggled in by his attorneys, and writing partly on toilet paper, King composed his letter from Birmingham jail. Some excerpts are presented below:

> Injustice anywhere is a threat to justice everywhere. We are caught in an inescapable network of mutuality, tied in a single garment of destiny.

> [The purpose of civil disobedience is] to create such a crisis and foster such a tension that a community which has constantly refused to negotiate is forced to confront the issue. It seeks so to dramatize the issue that it can no longer be ignored.

> Just as Socrates felt that it was necessary to create a tension in the mind so that individuals could rise from the bondage of myths and half truths to the unfettered realm of creative analysis and objective appraisal, so we must see the need for nonviolent gadflies to create the kind of tension in

society that will help men rise from the dark depths of prejudice and racism to the majestic heights of understanding and brotherhood.

Freedom is never voluntarily given by the oppressor; it must be demanded by the oppressed.

The nations of Asia and Africa are moving with jetlike speed toward gaining political independence, but we still creep at horse and buggy pace toward gaining a cup of coffee at a lunch counter.

Specifically addressing the point that the time was not right for protest, he wrote:

When you see the vast majority of your twenty million Negro brothers smothering in an airtight cage of poverty in the midst of an affluent society; when you suddenly find your tongue twisted and your speech stammering as you seek to explain to your six year old daughter why she can't go to the public amusement park…when you have to concoct an answer for a five year old son who is asking 'Daddy, why do white people treat colored people so mean?'; when you take a cross country drive and find it necessary to sleep night after night in the uncomfortable corners of your automobile because no motel will accept you…when you are forever fighting a degenerating sense of 'nobodiness'—then you will understand why we find it difficult to wait.

After noting some disappointment with the lack of support of white moderates and the Christian Church, King wrote:

If the inexpressible cruelties of slavery could not stop us, the opposition we now face will surely fail.

He closed with:

Let us all hope that the dark clouds of racial prejudice will soon pass away, and the deep fog of misunderstanding will be lifted from our fear-drenched communities, and in some not too distant tomorrow the radiant stars of love and brotherhood will shine over our great nation with all their scintillating beauty.

The letter was smuggled out of the jail, page by page, and typed at a local motel. It became the foremost explanation of the nonviolent approach to protest, and a famous example of the freedom of the will in the face of the incarceration of the body. The eight clergymen never responded. As Stephen Oates writes, the letter from Birmingham jail was unanswerable.

After Birmingham, King was a prime organizer of the famous march on Washington. On August 28, 1963, two hundred thousand people gathered around the Lincoln Memorial, unaware that they were about to hear one of the most powerful and moving speeches of our civilization. Excerpts, including the entire final portion, are reprinted below:

> Five score years ago, a great American, in whose symbolic shadow we stand, signed the Emancipation Proclamation. This momentous decree came as a great beacon light of hope to millions of Negro slaves who had been seared in the flames of withering injustice. But one hundred years later, we must face the tragic fact that the Negro is still not free. One hundred years later, the life of the Negro is still sadly crippled by the manacles of segregation and the chains of discrimination. One hundred years later, the Negro lives on a lonely island of poverty in the midst of a vast ocean of material prosperity. One hundred years later, the Negro is still languishing in the corners of American society and finds himself an exile in his own land.

> . . . *Now* is the time to rise from the dark and desolate valley of segregation to the sunlit path of racial justice. *Now* is the time to open the doors of opportunity to all of God's children. *Now* is the time to lift our nation from the quicksand of racial injustice to the solid rock of brotherhood.

> . . . In the process of gaining our rightful place, we must not be guilty of wrongful deeds . . . Again and again, we must rise to the majestic heights of meeting physical force with soul force.

> . . . I say to you today, my friends, that in spite of the difficulties and frustrations of the moment, I still have a dream. It is a dream deeply rooted in the American dream. I have a dream that one day this nation will rise up and live out the true meaning of its creed: 'We hold these truths to be self evident—that all men are created equal.' I have a dream that one day on the red hills of Georgia, the sons of former slave owners will be able to sit down together at the table of brotherhood. I have a dream that one day, even the state of Mississippi, a desert state sweltering with the heat of injustice and oppression, will be transformed into

an oasis of freedom and justice. I have a dream that my four little children will one day live in a nation where they will not be judged by the color of their skin, but by the content of their character.

I have a dream today. I have a dream that one day the state of Alabama, whose governor's lips are presently dripping with the words of interposition and nullification, will be transformed into a situation where little black boys and black girls will be able to join hands with little white boys and white girls and walk together as sisters and brothers.

I have a dream today. I have a dream that one day every valley shall be exalted, every hill and mountain shall be made low, the rough places will be made plains, and the crooked places will be made straight, and the glory of the Lord shall be revealed, and all flesh shall see it together.

This is our hope. This is the faith I shall return to the South with. With this faith, we will be able to hew out of the mountain of despair a stone of hope. With this faith, we will be able to transform the dangling discords of our nation into a beautiful symphony of brotherhood. With this faith, we will be able to work together, pray together, struggle together, go to jail together, stand up for freedom together, knowing that we will be free one day.

This will be the day when all of God's children will be able to sing with new meaning 'My country 'tis of thee, sweet land of liberty, of thee I sing. Land where my fathers died, land of the Pilgrim's pride, from every mountaintop, let freedom ring.' And if America is to be a great nation, this must be true. So let freedom ring from the prodigious hilltops of New Hampshire. Let freedom ring from the mighty mountains of New York. Let freedom ring from the heightening Alleghenies of Pennsylvania. But not only that; let freedom ring from Stone Mountain of Georgia. Let freedom ring from Lookout Mountain of Tennessee. Let freedom ring from every hill and molehill of Mississippi. From every mountaintop, let freedom ring.

When we let freedom ring, when we let it ring from every village and every hamlet, from every state and every city, we will be able to speed up that day when all of God's children, black men and white men, Jews and Gentiles, Protestants and Catholics, will be able to join hands and sing in the words of the old Negro spiritual, 'Free at last! Free at last! Thank God almighty, we are free at last!'

This speech defines who we are, and who we can be. It is a beacon from the past, a voice of wisdom for the present and the future. For generations to come, people of every type and from every place will be able to turn to these words and see a snapshot of our time and theirs. Like the admonition to the white man of the Duwamish Indian chief Sealth, these words are a record of our prejudice, and a pathway to justice and gentleness.

1964 brought two major triumphs for King. Congress passed the 1964 Civil Rights Act, and King was the recipient of the Nobel Peace Prize. Excerpts from his Nobel acceptance speech:

> I refuse to accept the idea that man is mere flotsam and jetsam in the river of life which surrounds him. I refuse to accept the view that mankind is so tragically bound to the starless midnight of racism and war that the bright daylight of peace and brotherhood can never become a reality. I believe that even amid today's mortar bursts and whining bullets, there is still hope for a brighter tomorrow.
>
> Yet when the years have rolled past and the blazing light of truth is focused on this marvelous age in which we live, men and women will know, and children will be taught that we have a finer land, a better people, a more noble civilization because these humble children of God were willing to suffer for righteousness' sake.

But frustration and setbacks became apparent in 1965. King organized three marches from Selma, Alabama to Montgomery in support of a federal voting rights law. The first of these was beaten back by state police. King led the second march himself, but voluntarily turned it back in the face of opposition. But a third march was successful, a courageous triumph which led to the passage of a national voting rights act that year by congress. King then ran into the same problem that had bedeviled Gandhi; impatience and increasing frustration led to militancy, which manifested as rioting in major cities. King opposed this approach, but realized that there was more to freedom than laws could grant, and that the more subtle aspects of racism were less amenable to his approach.

King saw that this militancy was driven by a frustration made worse by poverty. During a tour of northern cities, he saw the relationship of poverty to racism. He therefore identified poverty as the ultimate enemy and broadened his agenda to encompass poor people generally. To that end, he also opposed the Vietnam War, because it diverted money needed for social programs.

King accepted with grace and played with brilliance the hand that fate dealt him. On April 3, 1968, he answered one final call of destiny. He went to Memphis, Tennessee, to support striking sanitation workers. In that city, he delivered his last address, ending with the tragically prophetic words:

> We've got some difficult days ahead. But it really doesn't matter with me now. Because I've been to the mountaintop. Like anybody, I would like to live a long life. Longevity has its place. But I'm not concerned about that now . . . And I've looked over and I've seen the Promised Land. And I may not get there with you. But I want you to know tonight that we as a people will get to the Promised Land.

The next day he was shot and killed while standing on the balcony of his motel room. One person was tried and convicted, but questions of conspiracy persist. The skills of peace are more complex and subtle than those of war, but its champions have a more lasting legacy. The loss of this irreplaceable giant created a wound that can never heal.

Profit and Loss

Mikhail Gorbachev (1931–) was raised in Stalinist Russia, became a lawyer, and worked his way up through the ranks of the Soviet Communist Party. Three years after the death of the Soviet Union's long time leader, Leonid Brezhnev (1906–1982), Gorbachev became the General Secretary of the Soviet Communist Party, making him the most powerful person in the country.

Gorbachev realized that the Soviet Union could not solve its problems unless it had normal interactions with other countries, and he began the normalization of international relations. In addition, he set in motion two reforms, both of which had consequences beyond his or the world's imagination and would make him, as Gail Sheehy has written, the man who changed the world.

The first was Perestroika, an economic restructuring. Although permitting some privatization of business and reducing the power of the Communist Party, Perestroika was intended only to reform communism, not replace it. The second reform was called by the Russian word Glasnost, which refers to openness, candor, or the ability to criticize. Some maintain that the specter of American military power forced these changes in the Soviet Union. To my mind, it was the internal, specifically economic, conditions of the Soviet Union, in conjunction with the enlightened thinking of Gorbachev, rather than the American position, which led to these reforms.

Beginning in 1989, changes came in the communist world at a dizzying speed, as decades of frustration exploded into events of momentous importance. In that year, elections were held for positions in the Soviet Parliament. This was considered safe by the communist establishment, since all the candidates were from the communist party and many were unopposed. But the results were shocking to the old guard; many conservatives were defeated, and a number of liberals were elected. The people had made it clear they were not as enthralled with communism as their leaders had supposed.

The freedom of speech that Gorbachev had permitted spread to the communist countries of Eastern Europe. 1989 was a year of freedom, beginning in Poland. In 1980, a Polish electrician named Lech Walesa (1943–) organized Solidarity, a trade union for workers. The following year, Solidarity was banned and Walesa was imprisoned. Solidarity survived underground, however, and international pressure forced Polish authorities to legalize it in January, 1989. A few months later, the first free election in post-war Poland gave Solidarity, and freedom, a victory. Walesa was elected president in 1990.

Encouraged by events in Poland, people of courage throughout Eastern Europe renewed their struggle for freedom. Hungary replaced its communist monopoly with a multiparty system. In Czechoslovakia (which subsequently peacefully divided into the Czech Republic and Slovakia), dissident playwright Vaclav Havel (1936–) became president. East Germans, bitterly resentful of the Berlin Wall, which prevented their crossing into the West, demonstrated for safe passage and basic freedoms. At this juncture, Gorbachev made a crucial decision; he refused to commit Soviet troops to suppress the demonstrations, permitting the voice of the people to be heard. Before the end of 1989, this unstoppable voice brought down the Berlin Wall, simultaneously toppled hard-line communist governments in many Eastern European countries, and demanded freedoms previously unknown to that part of the world. Perestroika and Glasnost had progressed far beyond their original intent, and had accelerated into newfound freedoms for tens of millions of people.

Then came the first of two consequences that Gorbachev did not foresee, or want. The Union of Soviet Socialist Republics was a confederation of fifteen states, of which Russia was the largest. Many of the others had been forcibly annexed during Stalinist times. These states, feeling a sense of ethnic pride and cultural difference from the other states, voiced the desire to be independent. Gorbachev strongly opposed, *but did not crush*, these separatist movements, thus permitting their ultimate success, with the consequent breakup of the Soviet Union, which officially dissolved on December 24, 1991.

The second unforeseen consequence of Perestroika and Glasnost was the tragedy of Yugoslavia. During the early 1990s, four of the six states of Yugoslavia (Bosnia and Hercegovina, Croatia, Macedonia, and Slovenia) declared independence, leaving the other two (Serbia and Montenegro) to reform as the Federal Republic of Yugoslavia. Within the state of Bosnia and Hercegovina (usually just called Bosnia), generations of ethnic and religious differences (people of the Serbian majority are Orthodox Christian, while people of Croatian descent are Roman Catholic, and there is also a sizable Islamic population) exploded into a bloody civil war. People of Serbian origin launched a military campaign to achieve control of the state, to forcibly relocate people of non-Serbian origin, and to suppress other ethnic groups, especially Muslims. At this writing, a tenuous peace hangs in the air of Bosnia after three years of civil war and tens of thousands of deaths.

Mikhail Gorbachev had no idea that extending a measure of freedom to people would cause this behavior. As the partition of the Indian subcontinent into India and Pakistan was a defeat for Gandhi, the Bosnian civil war and Yugoslavian ethnic cleansing were defeats for Gorbachev. Most wars are reflections of the general human characteristic to desire the familiar and to be hostile toward that we do not understand. Unless we can learn from Bosnia and Yugoslavia, one of the prices of freedom from totalitarianism may be ethnic clashes. We cannot expect major changes in our social structure to be free of trauma. We accept that even good developments may have short-term tragic consequences. We rejoice in the liberation of people and nations, but it is difficult, in any view of history, to ascribe loss of life simply as short-term consequences. Time equates the profit and loss in all human events.

As we must not make the mistake of believing that Nazi Germany suffered from a unique pathology, so we must not believe that Serbs are inherently crueler than other peoples. As with all tragedies of history, the pathology lies with all of humanity, and so does the solution.

Chapter 36
Root Causes and Underlying Reasons

The ability to think long-term will decide our fate.

Quality from Equality

As a young man, Edwards Deming (1900–1993) studied physics, but in the 1930s, an interest in statistics led him to investigate sampling techniques for the United States Census. He subsequently developed statistical methods of quality control for industry. During World War II, his methods were used to advantage by the American industrial war machine. However, after the war, the United States found itself without competitors in the world market. Deming's methods of quality control were no longer thought necessary, and their long-term benefit was not understood by business leaders. American business began its fifty-year love affair with quarterly profits and stock prices. Deming valiantly attempted to get Americans to understand that their success would not continue unless long-term plans for continuous quality improvement were made. No one listened.

In 1947, Douglas MacArthur invited Deming to Japan to plan a census, using some of the same statistical techniques he had used in the United States a decade earlier. While in Japan, Deming developed a deep compassion for the Japanese people and wanted to help them out of poverty. He realized that the quality of Japanese goods must improve for them to develop the world markets they so desperately needed. We have seen that tumult is fertile ground for new ideas, while stability is often the prison of the mind. So it was that Japan, devastated from the war, was much more receptive to Deming's managerial ideas. By this time, his statistical quality control had developed into an entire *system* of management and production. The outgrowth of this is today called total quality management (TQM), and in its contemporary form, it has the following characteristics:

1. A traditional hierarchical management structure, where a small number of managers give instructions to workers, stifles the creativity of most of the workforce because only the small minority of workers at the top have the opportunity to be heard, or to inject innovation into the organization. Anyone and everyone can contribute to making a product or the service better. Therefore, there must be substantial equality of all people involved in all steps of the production process. Management styles that champion equality promote teamwork and allow the talents and abilities of all to contribute. Workplaces have vast, untapped resources of dedicated and valuable talent in their workers. This is particularly true since problems are always best solved by those closest to them.

   Hierarchical management structures are a reflection of the competitive spirit integral to our culture. We are taught from an early age to compete, to *win*, to make someone else *lose*. The manifestation of this in the workplace is to *dominate*, to make someone else—a business subordinate—*submit*. Deming showed that this win-lose situation need not apply. With a cooperative spirit, everyone can win. Respect for all people at all parts of the process pays dividends.

2. Most problems have their roots many stages before the apparent cause. Problems can be truly solved only by addressing their underlying, root cause. As an example, consider a ship that often veers off course. Whose fault is this? The captain? He gives orders to the navigator. There is little probability that he ordered the ship to veer off course. The navigator? He steers the ship in accordance with established protocols and procedures. There is little likelihood that he derives pleasure from pursuing a deviant course. The builders of the ship? Possibly. But it is more likely that the underlying reason for the problem is that the ship has a faulty design. No amount of berating or punishment of the captain, navigator, or builders will be of any value if the design is at fault. Since defects derive from deeper causes, a single inspection of products at the end of a production line is unlikely to be beneficial. Rather, there should be many inspections during production, one at each stage of the process.

3. Individuals are rarely the cause of problems. To the contrary, most people take pride in their work and sincerely want to do the best job they can. Workers are not lackadaisical, needing to be *forced* into doing a good job. On the contrary, workers should be *allowed* to do quality work by being respected, trusted, and empowered. Only 15% of the time is the problem due to poor performance by an individual. The other 85% of the time, the problem lies in a faulty system.

4. Fix the problem, not the blame. Criticizing individuals is an ineffective, childish technique. Finding out why they behaved as they did leads to lasting improvements.

5. Employee evaluations are not good, because they are aimed at the wrong target—individuals. The effort spent in evaluating workers is much better spent asking them for their opinion on how to improve the system. Not only do evaluations fail to address process improvement, they also reinforce the traditional hierarchy and breed conflict and competition within the organization.

6. Invest in the education and training of your people. Nowhere is the concept of a small sacrifice now for a big gain later more evident. As Adam Smith showed that people were more important than land, so Deming showed that people are more important than machines. At this writing, layoffs are sweeping American businesses because they lead to short-term increases in profits and stock prices. In the long run, they devastate the company because they literally destroy its infrastructure. Nowhere is the inability of people to learn from history more apparent than in American business.

7. Quality improvement never ends. Like life itself, it is a journey, not a destination.

Deming's total quality management looks at business from a new perspective. It has proven itself wherever and whenever it has been given a fair chance. We are still in the Industrial Revolution, and our treatment of workers is proof that there are still aspects of the Revolution that we must correct. Total quality management is a major part of the continued development of the Industrial Revolution, because it gives us the opportunity to liberate workers. To my mind, TQM is the emancipation proclamation of industry and ranks with continued exploitation of computers and a greater concern for the environment as the three greatest frontiers at this point in the Industrial Revolution. TQM reflects an incipient movement in business to champion each of us as equal individuals.

For industry to be maximally productive, it must recognize the value of individual workers in the workplace, just as the value of individuals has been amply proven in the development of great ideas. But to be effective, TQM requires two attributes from managers that they have historically not possessed. Only when those in charge make these two leaps of understanding can TQM deliver its massive full potential.

First, managers must think long-term. Total quality management does not raise the profits or the stock price of the next quarter. After an implementation period that is lengthy and entails the natural discomfort of change, TQM raises the *long-term* profits, as well as the productivity and the quality of life of the organization and the people affiliated with it. Managers manage for the next quarter. Total quality managers manage for the next twenty years.

Second, those who are in charge of organizations must delegate responsibility *and authority* to others. The world is full of people who profess to support TQM, but who will not give up the authority necessary to let it work. TQM cannot and will not flourish in a traditional hierarchical management structure. Throughout the world, business organizations of all types achieve a fraction of their capability because those in charge insist that they know best and that they alone are capable of decision making. Meanwhile, millions of more talented subordinates languish in frustration because their abilities are not wanted, and may even be perceived as a threat by those above them in the corporate hierarchy.

To my mind, the largest single factor preventing those at the top of our unfortunate hierarchical management structure from delegating responsibility and authority is thinking that is based on military and athletic experiences. Throughout the corporate world, businesses are often run as if they were military units or sports teams about to take the field. These analogies are outmoded in the new technological world before us. "Leadership" is a buzzword in business now. But true leaders understand that the best leadership is an egalitarian attitude that permits everyone to contribute his or her best. For us to meet the terrible challenges of the twenty-first century, we must set aside the antiquated analogies of war and sports, and bring on a new attitude of egalitarian teamwork. Respect for individuals, and for the value of their ideas, must be given priority over the obsolete military chain of command now prevalent in business. A chain of command management structure impedes innovation because there is a great probability that good ideas will be diluted or dismissed before they get a fair hearing. History teaches us that we are more alike than we realize, and we need a management structure that recognizes this.

The business world is society in microcosm. The same misconception that only a very small number of "geniuses" can understand or contribute to scientific developments causes those in business to believe that only a few can make decisions that benefit the organization. Just as the bruised egos of conservative people in power have been a major stumbling block to progress in scientific advancement, those who control our business and industry are often threatened by employees who have innovative ideas. The loss to the business world, like that to the larger world, is incalculable. We are fortunate to have in our civilization, in our personal lives, and in our workplaces, a diversity of opinions and experiences, and we must achieve a structure that permits us to take advantage of this. I plead again for us to understand that human history has not been fueled by a small number of qualitatively superior minds, but rather by the collective effort and insight of all of us. So, too, in the workplace.

The Total Quality Management of Society

In this work's final section, some of our most difficult problems are discussed, and I will propose a new perspective, with daring and controversial solutions. As we enter the twenty-first century, we must all ask "whither humanity?" On one hand, in the last century, we have fought two World Wars of unprecedented violence. Even without them, the twentieth century has been brutal and cruel. The nuclear weapons we possess afford the unparalleled opportunity to destroy millennia of progress. An even greater problem, to my mind, is overpopulation. The world now sustains four times as many people as at the beginning of the twentieth century, and overpopulation is a root cause of or an aggravating factor in virtually every difficulty before us.

On the other hand, the successful conclusion of World War II and the peaceful end of the Cold War substantially corrected two catastrophes of our time. It is also encouraging to realize that technology gives us tools we never imagined. As the ability to dream and to foresee success is crucial to an individual's prosperity, so they are central to the continuation of our civilization. Technology gives us a mechanism with which to dream.

What follows is a personal view of what we need to do. The ability to think long-term seems invariably to be lost in civilizations as they grow old and die. As a tenth lesson of history, I submit that the only hope we have to solve our problems and create the world we all want is to think long-term, and to recognize that our problems have deep-seated social causes that will demand daring innovations and patience to resolve. Whether we are liberal or conservative, Democrat or Republican, our necessity is to address the root cause of our problems. Making the world better is like playing chess—the final victory goes to those who think long-term. Our civilization will succeed or fail based on how farsighted we are.

To my mind, overpopulation is the single largest root cause of most of our society's problems. At the turn of the twentieth century, the world's population stood at some one and a half billion people, virtually an ideal level. It has only been in the last one hundred years that population has spiraled from a complete nonissue to the world's most pressing problem. The problem of overpopulation is a prototype example of the opportunity to apply Deming's total quality management to the world as a whole. What I mean by this is that we should stop blaming individuals for what we perceive to be irresponsible behavior and develop a world system that makes it easier to avoid unwanted reproduction. Indigent people with large families may appear to us to be irresponsible, but they have not chosen this lifestyle, just as the factory worker generally does not choose to make a defective product. People are pushed into these decisions because of the circumstances of their lives, and we cannot expect different behavior until we provide different alternatives. Around the world, there are, to my mind, three principal considerations in addressing overpopulation. First, there is a lack of available, affordable birth control. Indigent people from every nation want and will use birth control if it is available. We now have the ability, unique in our history, to permit effective birth control for all who desire it. Indeed, there are newer birth control methods, based on the same scientific principle as the birth control pill, that are effective for prolonged time periods. Studies so far suggest that these methods are safe, effective, and do not cause permanent infertility. Effective birth control is now within our grasp, but it must be coupled with courage and a willingness to act. The chilling question faces us: has effective birth control arrived too late in our history?

The second consideration in addressing overpopulation is the lack of education. Without education, people become trapped in their lives and are unable to see an alternative way of living. Wise decisions require a sense of control over one's life and a belief that there are alternatives. These are not possible without education.

Third, throughout the world, women are still considered second-class citizens, whose only purpose is to have children. At one time, it was required that women have as many babies as possible, because so few survived into adulthood. Falling infant mortality rates free women from this burden, but only if we adapt to changing times. Elevation of the status of women will provide all of us with the understanding that there is an alternative to constant reproduction.

In the United States, the tragic triad of poverty, drugs, and crime rips at the fabric of the nation. A lack of accessible and effective family planning for individuals who are not in a position to have a family is an underlying cause of poverty, in turn a major cause of drug addiction and crime. The industrialized world has not escaped the problem of overpopulation, but it is subtler in its expression. As increasing crime cuts into the quality of our lives, there are shouts of more and longer prison sentences. That is a decision for the short term, not a total quality management decision. There are individuals who are a menace to society and must be segregated, but the application of Deming's principles to crime teaches us that prevention is the only lasting pathway to success. No plan to reduce crime based on punitive actions will give us the long-term effectiveness of a plan targeted at the prevention of crime's major causes—poverty and drug addiction. Overwhelmingly, most violent crime is caused by people from disadvantaged backgrounds, who often believe that their lives are so miserable that they have nothing to lose by committing a crime. Locked in a sense of hopelessness and helplessness, these people are unable to experience the two characteristics fundamental to normal behavior—a sense of belonging and the opportunity to dream. Unable to form normal bonds with society as a whole, they either form abnormal bonds with a small group of people whose lives have been equally disrupted (gangs) or they commit crimes as a way to obtain self-esteem or gain acceptance in their circle. For them, imprisonment ceases to be a deterrent, and drugs and violence become a viable alternative in their lives.

For people in crowded conditions, with no job skills, poverty and its sequelae are virtually guaranteed. People do not choose these sequelae any more than they chose the social conditions of their lives that make these sequelae inevitable. These people cannot "just say no" to drugs and crime any more than an asthmatic can "just say no" to wheezing. What people are told has a small effect on their behavior, but what they perceive in their environment has a very large effect on how they behave. Downtrodden people are not able to see alternatives. Beware the knife blade of those who believe the problems of our lives are affairs of black and white.

Recently imposed time limits on how long welfare recipients can receive benefits are predicated on the assumption that there are sufficient resources in the community to enable recipients to obtain and keep a job. In fact, this is often not the case. Mandated time limits may be effective in removing some people from welfare roles, but the passage of time will reveal a second group of recipients who are not able, even upon threat of loss of benefits, to enter the workforce. We must realize that poverty is not a voluntary way of life for anyone. The stereotype of a lazy welfare recipient who would rather receive a handout than work is a myth. People will leave welfare roles not when mandated limits expire, but when there is a program in place that gives them the means to leave.

Besides the difficulties of family planning, other causes of poverty need to be understood. Most indigent people lack job skills. Moreover, many have small children and are handicapped by a lack of accessible and affordable child care. Because many poor people do not have automobiles, getting to a job is a challenge. Finally, many of our disadvantaged citizens, especially women, have been subjected to physical and mental abuse to a degree that impedes their full participation in life.

An anti-poverty program, therefore, cannot be effective unless it simultaneously and continuously provides six key ingredients: family planning, job training, jobs, child care, transportation, and a basic quality of life with minimized risk of further abuse. Again, we cannot expect different behavior until we provide different alternatives; we cannot demand accountability until we provide the means by which to be accountable. The first two lessons of history are that people who are deprived of basic needs will behave irrationally and cruelly, and that our ability to cope with life and find success is in large measure dependent on our early environment. I believe the problem of poverty and its sequelae illustrates those two lessons. I submit as history's eleventh lesson that individual people, for the most part, are less to blame for actions that appear irresponsible and reprehensible than we may think. Although it may not be apparent to us, people do the best they can, where they are, with what they have. The problem is generally the conditions of their lives, past and present, and the blame often lies with all of us.

We have seen how progress is impeded when circumstances are assumed to be as they appear at first glance, such as the flat earth doctrine, the earth-centered universe, spontaneous generation, etc. It is our challenge to understand that we must go beyond our initial impressions, in the social arena as well as in the scientific arena. Social problems can be effectively addressed only when attention is given to the underlying causes that prevent people from behaving in a rational manner. Many people, especially those in policy-making positions, do not realize how difficult it is to become a fully developed human being, capable of obtaining, appreciating, and exercising options, *because for them it was not difficult to become such a person.*

The problem is not that we are "coddling" criminals, it is that we are breeding them. The problem is not that we are too lenient with long-term welfare recipients, it is that we have not provided a way for them to change the circumstances of their lives. We do not grasp this because we do not understand mental illness and societal pressure as well as we understand physical illness.

Those who speak for harsher treatment of criminals fail to realize that certainty of punishment is more important than severity of punishment, and prevention of the relevant social conditions is more important than either. Almost five hundred years ago, Thomas More (1478–1535), writing in *Utopia*, gives us our answer:

> Great and horrible punishments are provided for thieves, whereas much rather provision should have been made to provide some means whereby they might get their living so that no man should be driven to this extreme necessity. Doubtless, unless you find a remedy for these enormities, you shall in vain pride yourself in executing upon felons because this justice has more the appearance than the actuality of justice. For you suffer your youth to be wantonly and viciously brought up and infected even from a tender age, little by little, with vice, then in God's name to be punished...On this point I pray you: what other thing do you do but make thieves and then punish them?

It is true that attempts to rehabilitate violent criminals have been disappointing, and this goal is probably not fully achievable at this point in our history. This has turned people toward punitive measures and away from what should have been the focus all along—prevention. Social problems are like viral illnesses—much easier to prevent than to cure. We should concentrate our efforts on the three reasons why people become violent in situations outside of war: they are or have been impoverished, they have a mental illness, or something terrible has happened to them.

If implemented, the widespread use of contraception has the potential to revolutionize our treatment of poverty, crime, and environmental pollution, because this is the first measure with the capability to effectively target the root cause of so much of our present and future misery—overpopulation. Science can help us in another regard as well. There is likely a synergistic effect between social conditions and disordered brain function that leads to criminal tendencies. For most violent offenders, both may be necessary to lead to criminal behavior. Eventually, if we make the necessary commitment to research the biochemistry and physiology of the brain, the biological basis of aggression can be identified and corrected. The implementation of such a plan will tax society's patience to the limit, but choice do we have? Over a million Americans are incarcerated, and the number is sharply growing. An additional four million Americans are on parole or probation. There are thus in excess of five million Americans significantly at odds with our society, triple the number of just fifteen years ago. These five million people constitute almost three percent of the adult population, and nearly half of these people have been in serious legal trouble at least three times before. Current punitive methods, which do not target the underlying social and biological causes, are clearly not working. More of the same is like doubling the dose of an ineffective drug—there is no benefit, and toxicity becomes acute.

It is difficult for us to understand that these problems are not amenable to the use of force, because normal, rational people *are* deterred by force and punishment. We all draw on our own experiences in forming decisions, and it is only natural to assume that the people whose behavior we wish to modify will be amenable to the same negative incentives that we are.

The ultimate solution involves a process most of us do not understand and a commitment we are unwilling to make. As Abraham Lincoln said "we must think anew and act anew." We must begin to develop long-term solutions aimed at the causes of criminal behavior, or we will shortly become a police state. We will not overcome the many faces of poverty until our leaders understand that early years of deprivation forever destroy the ability of many people to cope with the basic situations of life or to behave rationally. We must accept the fact that the ultimate solutions to our major problems will not come in our lifetimes, and begin to lay the groundwork that will benefit posterity.

So it is that the application of total quality management to societal problems can work. But the same condition applies as in industry; the results will not be evident for a number of years. Breaking the cycle of unwanted pregnancies, poverty and its sequelae, and more unwanted pregnancies will take several generations. Understanding the biology of aggressive behavior will take several more generations. No politician will win reelection because of the successful implementation of this plan. Indeed, if the populace remains impatient and short-sighted, it is likely that a number of politicians will lose their offices if they support such a plan. It is precisely when people become angry or frightened that they lose the ability to think long-term. And yet, it is in these times that reason and patience are most needed. The ability to plan ahead is the hallmark of our species, but it remains our most difficult task.

I submit as history's twelfth lesson that political leaders must understand the true origins of social problems before they can legislate genuine solutions. We need political leaders who are willing to become scholars, and who recognize that the solutions to social problems are not as simple as might first appear. Politicians must transcend their constituents, exceed their knowledge, and understand how social problems come to be.

Politics is the only profession that does not require its practitioners to develop a specialized body of knowledge that exceeds the knowledge base of the general public. All other professions hold their practitioners accountable for knowledge and behavior exceeding that of the general public in their area of expertise. Imagine an airline pilot who flew through a storm to save time because "the passengers were in a hurry," or a surgeon who did not sterilize his instruments because "the patient said he didn't care." We demand of all professionals that they acquire and use specialized training and knowledge, even if this use violates our immediate desires, because we understand that the greater good comes from their possessing and using expertise we do not have. But politicians routinely make decisions based on woefully inadequate knowledge because they are not required to understand the pathogenesis of social problems any better than their constituents. There is much in Plato's *The Republic* that is not applicable to today's world, but there is one concept that is decisively applicable—leaders must be scholars. They must be trained to understand all aspects of the issues facing them. Scholarship must replace "leadership" as a politician's most important attribute.

Civilization has always depended on many more people than is generally realized, and ours will be much the poorer if it depends on a minority. But the situation now is that very many of us are not able to contribute to society because they have not had the necessary opportunities, and we must address the causes of this. Such an effort will not be easy, but we have always been at our best, and proudest of who we are, when we try to make ourselves better.

Epilogue
A Letter to the Future

As those who have come before me have shared much with me, and imparted much to me, I would like to share my thoughts with those who will follow me.

It must strike you as odd—a history book written before so much of what you know as history occurred. Writing this book has given me a sense of who I am, and it has filled me with the hopes I have for you.

I hope you believe in people, whatever your religious beliefs, and I hope you understand that people are the common thread bridging all religions and all cultures. I hope you believe in the power of the mind and the comprehensibility of the universe, whether or not you believe in God. I hope your curiosity will push you to explore all things, and to treasure knowledge not for what it can do, but for what it is.

I hope you will be partners in humanity in a way that we were not. And I hope you will be kind to our planet and to our companion creatures. I hope you will express your feelings and your fears. No success can change the incompleteness of a life lived without a heart. And no failure can dim the fire of a life that embraces the range of human hope and love.

I hope you will come together as equals, valuing the uniqueness and equality of every faith and belief. From diversity and differences come unity and strength. I hope you will believe in the inherent, everlasting, and absolute respect for living creatures, human and otherwise.

Whatever you may think you are not, you are. A differing religion, an opposing opinion, another race or sex. You are all of these, and if you understand this, you will be magnified by the collective wisdom of all of humanity.

It is the tragedy of the past and the present that people focus on differences, not similarities. I hope you will understand that the commonality of the human experience binds us all to similar lives and a shared destiny. Therefore, we owe kindness, generosity, and grace to each other. The world is full of quiet heroes, and each of the billions of people with whom you share your planet has a story to tell. Listen to them.

487

I hope you will address your problems with farsighted thinking, not with shortsighted reactions. People who can see the present and look ahead with a mind and a heart have a way of shaping the future and improving the world.

Do not be afraid of change, the unknown, or unforeseen circumstances, even if they come to you as trauma. Such changes provide a chance for growth. From the difficulties of today come the opportunities of tomorrow. I hope you will dare to explore the unknown, and I hope you will be willing to fail. When you are confused, return to first principles: respect for all people, reverence for learning, a willingness to dare, kindness to all creatures. Following these principles and valuing them in others will bring you home from any storm. I hope you will particularly seek these qualities in your lovers and spouses; those with whom we form the strongest bonds should be the most firmly anchored.

I have tried to reflect the infinite varieties of human experience for people in my time, and I hope that you will continue to enjoy these varieties. From simple kindness to our standard model of matter to a Beethoven quartet to the terrible inequalities of our society. This is who we are. And it is who you are.

I hope that you see the full flowering of human kindness and intelligence that I have seen so many flashes of. I wish you happiness in a better world. But do not be certain that you are better than we are. No era in history has absorbed its lessons or avoided its mistakes. You will not be the first. We live very much as you do. The challenges and the pleasures of life, in any era, lie in the mind. Like you, we are imprisoned by our fears and liberated by our hopes. Our imaginings are as powerful as your technology, and therefore, we sail into the stars just as you do.

We have suffered from the ignorance of our ancestors, but we primarily suffer from our own ignorance. Likewise, you have suffered from our mistakes, but your world can always be better if you will make it so. When you wish the world were different, be satisfied with small victories and slow progress. The pace of change should not frustrate you. The joy of love and the exhilaration of discovery remain available to you amidst the collective failure of society to understand. In truth, neither our lives nor yours would be much different if we lived in another time.

Individually and collectively, we are a work in progress. Like any work in progress, we should not be judged as we are developing. We are neither "good" nor "bad", but some of both as we continue to mature. Please do not be too harsh in your judgement of us. We did the best we could. Like you, we are trying to discover who we are.

Appendix
The Lessons of History:
A Personal View

As stated in the prologue of this work, I believe the real lessons of history are not in the flow of political and military events, but in how we think. If only we could learn the true lessons of history as well as we have accumulated knowledge. I offer these twelve lessons as what I have learned in preparing this work.

1. People deprived of basic needs are very likely to behave cruelly and irrationally, and the target of that behavior will be those perceived as more fortunate. People who are angry or frightened do not think clearly, but look for a quick and simple solution, abdicating reason in the process. This is why it is so essential that we provide a reasonable standard of living for all people and enough prosperity to prevent our crueler sides from becoming manifest.

2. If our early environment nurtures us, teaches us, and gives us the self-esteem to believe we can control our destiny, we will do well. If that environment is hostile, fragmented, unsupportive, and affords minimal opportunities, we will do poorly.

3. Human nature and the human experience do not fundamentally change from one era in history to another. Technology and knowledge advance; political situations change; and many aspects of our civilization improve through our intellectual efforts, but who we are is constant. Ultimately, we do not live very different lives from people in any other time or place.

4. Single individuals matter, and when their worth is placed ahead of that of tradition, religion, conformity, and rituals, there will be enormous progress. Today, our very numbers make us feel prosaic and ordinary. When we are confused or feel small, it is best to return to first principles. The first principle of our lives should be that we are all unique individuals, worthy of self and societal esteem.

489

5. Power inevitably comes to be concentrated in the hands of a few. We thus sit within a pyramid structure. This has had two great consequences. First, it is a tragedy for most of humanity, who do not have the opportunity to control their fate. Second, it means that we have been deprived of the full contribution of most people.

6. The belief in God, the holding of any religion, or the acceptance of the divinity of any person is not by itself dangerous to our civilization. These beliefs can be among the best of our thought. What are dangerous are the opinions that too often follow those beliefs: that this way of thinking is the only correct way; that the use of rational thinking to understand the world, or to better our lot, conflicts with the will of the Creator; or that any religion has a nobler origin, a superior history, or a greater destiny than other religions. If ever there is a lesson to be learned from history, it is in the commonalities and similar origins of religions.

7. Great ideas have indistinct beginnings and result from the contributions of many people. We tend to remember only the last step of an achievement, not understanding the full development of the idea. It is therefore little wonder that we have concluded that our civilization has been made by a small number of people. Any great idea, design, or invention, if carefully enough examined, will be found to be the work of many people, some remembered, most forgotten.

   The stuff of genius is not the instant flash of brilliance by a person of superhuman abilities, but a slow methodical synthesis based on simple assumptions, the ideas of many, and the courage to think anew without the prejudice of prevailing dogma. It is in this process—and in the respect for all individuals that make this process possible—that our hope lies.

   Progress arises not because of a few inherently superior people, but rather because all of us, being closer in ability than we realize, work together in a strange and uneven sort of way to make possible the prominent last step. When we think of progress as being made by a few geniuses, we rob ourselves of the credit we deserve. It is the triumph of our history that we have been able to improve our lot, and every one of us deserves credit for that achievement.

8. Amateurs have contributed enormously to our progress, and we must create and maintain conditions that will permit them to continue to contribute. The best of our thought appears in the living room of the amateur as

much as in the laboratory of the professional. As progress has been made possible by the value of the individual, we must make it possible for all individuals to contribute as much as they are able.

9. The pursuit of knowledge always leads to practical applications undreamed of at the time of the endeavor. Knowledge for its own sake has given us our civilization, and it has made us who we are. It must be encouraged at all times and at any cost. Our species and the quest for knowledge are inextricably linked and will survive or perish together.

10. The only hope we have to solve our problems and create the world we all want is to think long-term, and to recognize that our problems have deep-seated social causes that will demand daring innovations and patience to resolve. Whether we are liberal or conservative, Democrat or Republican, our necessity is to address the root cause of our problems. Making the world better is like playing chess—the final victory goes to those who think long-term. Our civilization will succeed or fail based on how far-sighted we are.

11. Individual people, for the most part, are less to blame for actions which appear irresponsible and reprehensible than we may think. Although it may not be apparent to us, people do the best they can, where they are, with what they have. The problem is generally the conditions of their lives, past and present, and the blame often lies with all of us. Societal problems can only be effectively addressed when attention is given to the underlying causes preventing people from behaving in a rational manner. Many people, especially those in policy-making positions, do not realize how difficult it is to become a fully developed human being, capable of obtaining, appreciating, and exercising options, *because for them it was not difficult to become such a person.*

12. Political leaders must understand the true origins of social problems before they can legislate genuine solutions. We need political leaders who are willing to become scholars, and who recognize that the solutions to social problems are not as simple as might first appear. Politicians must transcend their constituents, exceed their knowledge, and understand how social problems come to be. Scholarship must replace "leadership" as a politician's most important attribute.

Bibliography

LISTED BELOW ARE SOME OF THE REFERENCES USED in the preparation of this work. In addition to these books, there is much to be said for a good encyclopedia. While the *Encyclopaedia Britannica* remains the gold standard of reference works, we are fortunate to have many other encyclopedias to provide a different viewpoint. Many of these are available on CD-ROM or through a number of online services. I encourage the interested reader to investigate these encyclopedias as well, because multiple viewpoints often provide more insight than a single source, even a revered one.

Some of the works listed below are older, and are contemporary with the advancements described in this work. Although history is a growing and developing discipline, we must remember that the best sources for the past are often the works of the past.

While books form the mainstay of this work, I am also indebted to many magazine articles and television programs. It is comforting to know that the joy of knowledge can also be found in the television set and at the newsstand.

Finally, I have a debt of gratitude to the very many people who have taught me. Some were formal teachers in institutions, while many others were friends, acquaintances, or strangers kind enough to share part of their life with me. From these sources, as well as from my own thoughts, I have assembled this statement of who I am.

Ackerknecht, Erwin H. *A Short History of Medicine*. The Johns Hopkins University Press, Baltimore and London. Revised Edition, 1982.

Anderson, Clifford N. *The Fertile Crescent: Travels in the Footsteps of Ancient Science*. Sylvester Press, Fort Lauderdale, Florida. Second Edition, 1972.

Armstrong, Karen. *A History of God*. Ballantine Books, New York. 1993.

Asimov, Isaac. *The History of Physics*. Walker and Company, New York. 1966.

Asimov, Isaac, and Frank White. *The March of the Millennia*. Walker and Company, New York. 1991.

Bibliography

Baltimore, David. *The Brain of a Cell.* In: Science 84, Volume 5, Number 9, pages 149–151. The American Association for the Advancement of Science, Washington, D.C. 1984.

Bardeen, John. *To a Solid State.* In: Science 84, Volume 5, Number 9, pages 143–145. The American Association for the Advancement of Science, Washington, D.C. 1984.

Bliss, Michael. *The Discovery of Insulin.* The University of Chicago Press. 1982.

Boorstin, Daniel J. *The Discoverers.* Vintage Books (Division of Random House), New York. 1983.

Boorstin, Daniel J. *The Creators.* Random House, New York. 1992.

Boorstin, Daniel J. *The Seekers.* Random House, New York, 1998.

Bromberg, Joan. *The Laser in America, 1950–1970.* MIT press, Cambridge. 1991.

Bronowski, Jacob. *The Ascent of Man.* Little, Brown, and Company, Boston and Toronto. 1973.

Brown, John Russell (ed.). *The Oxford Illustrated History of Theatre.* Oxford University Press, Oxford and New York. 1995.

Brown, William L. *Hybrid Vim and Vigor.* In: Science 84, Volume 5, Number 9, pages 77–78. The American Association for the Advancement of Science, Washington, D.C. 1984.

Burenhult, Goran, Peter Rowley-Conwy, Wulf Schiefenhovel, David Hurst Thomas, and J. Peter White (eds.). *Old World Civilizations* (Volume 3 in the series *The Illustrated History of Mankind* by the American Museum of Natural History). Weldon Owen Pty, Limited, Australia and Bra Bocker AB, Sweden. 1994.

Burenhult, Goran, Peter Rowley-Conwy, Wulf Schiefenhovel, David Hurst Thomas, and J. Peter White (eds.). *New World and Pacific Civilizations* (Volume 4 in the series *The Illustrated History of Mankind* by the American Museum of Natural History). Weldon Owen Pty, Limited, Australia and Bra Bocker AB, Sweden. 1994. Burke, James. *Connections.* Little, Brown, and Company, Boston and Toronto. 1978.

Burke, James. *The Day the Universe Changed.* Little, Brown, and Company, Boston, Toronto, and London. 1985.

Butler, Chris. *Ancient Egypt*. Available on the internet at www.uni.uiuc.edu/ departments/social_studies/history/hyper_flow/eg_flood.html. 1997.

Cahill, Thomas. *How the Irish Saved Civilization*. Doubleday, New York, London, Sydney, Toronto, Auckland. 1995.

Caird, Rod (in collaboration with Robert Foley). *Ape Man*. MacMillan, New York. 1994.

Campbell-Kelly, Martin, and William Aspray. *Computers: A History of the Information Machine*. Basic Books, New York. 1996.

Cartwright, Frederick F. (In collaboration with Michael D. Biddiss). *Disease and History*. Dorset Press, New York. 1972.

Chase, Carl Trueblood. *A History of Experimental Physics*. D. Van Nostrand Company, Inc., New York. 1932.

Clark, Kenneth. *Civilization*. Harper and Row, New York, San Francisco, London, Evanston. 1969.

Close, Frank, Michael Marten, and Christine Sutton. *The Particle Explosion*. Oxford University Press, New York, Tokyo, Melbourne. 1986.

Coe, Michael D. *Breaking the Maya Code*. Thames and Hudson, New York. 1992.

Cole, Bruce, and Adelpheid Gealt. *Art of the Western World: From Ancient Greece to Post-Modernism*. Summit Books, New York, London, Toronto, Sidney, Tokyo. 1989.

Collon, Dominique. *Near Eastern Seals*. British Museum Publications, London. 1990.

Cotterell, Arthur (ed.). *The Penguin Encyclopedia of Ancient Civilizations*. Rainbird Publishing Group, Ltd. and Penguin Books, London, New York, Auckland, Middlesex, Ringwood, Australia. 1980.

Cowan, C. Wesley, and Patty Jo Watson (eds.). *The Origins of Agriculture*. Smithsonian Institution Press, Washington and London. 1992.

Crossan, John Dominic. *Jesus: A Revolutionary Biography*. HarperCollins, New York. 1989.

Dale, Henry, and Rodney Dale. *The Industrial Revolution*. The British Library, London. 1992.

Bibliography

Davidson, Marshall B. *A History of Art: From 25,000 B.C. to the Present.* Random House, New York. 1984.

Diakonoff, I.M. (ed.). *Early Antiquity.* The University of Chicago Press, Chicago. 1991. Translated by Alexander Kirjanov.

Dickinson, Mary B. (ed.). *Wonders of the Ancient World: National Geographic Atlas of Archaeology.* National Geographic Society, Washington, D.C. 1994.

Dixon, Bernard. *Of Different Bloods.* In: Science 84, Volume 5, Number 9, pages 65–67. The American Association for the Advancement of Science, Washington, D.C. 1984.

Djerassi, Carl. *The Making of the Pill.* In: Science 84, Volume 5, Number 9, pages 127–129. The American Association for the Advancement of Science, Washington, D.C. 1984.

Durant, Will and Ariel. *The Lessons of History.* MJF Books, New York. 1968.

Eaton, Jeanette. *Fighter Without a Sword.* William Morrow and Company, New York. 1950.

Erwin, Douglas H. *The Mother of Mass Extinctions.* In: Scientific American, Volume 275, Number 1 (July, 1996), pages 72–78. Scientific American, Inc., New York. 1996.

Ferris, Timothy. *Einstein's Wonderful Year.* In: Science 84, Volume 5, Number 9, pages 61–63. The American Association for the Advancement of Science, Washington, D.C. 1984.

Finger, Stanley. *Origins of Neuroscience.* Oxford University Press, Oxford and New York. 1994.

Fink, Donald G. *The Tube.* In: Science 84, Volume 5, Number 9, pages 121–123. The American Association for the Advancement of Science, Washington, D.C. 1984.

Fischer, Louis. *The Life of Mahatma Gandhi.* Harper and Row, New York, Evanston, and London. 1950.

Flowers, Charles. *A Science Odyssey: 100 Years of Discovery.* William Morrow and Co., New York. 1998.

Friedel, Robert. *The Plastics Man.* In: Science 84, Volume 5, Number 9, pages 49–51. The American Association for the Advancement of Science, Washington, D.C. 1984.

Gardner, Helen. *Art Through the Ages.* Seventh Edition, revised by Horst de La Croix and Richard G. Tansey. Harcourt Brace Jovanovich, Inc., New York, San Diego, Chicago, San Francisco, Atlanta, London, Sidney, Toronto. 1980.

Gattuso, John (ed.). *Native America.* APA Publications (HK) Ltd. 1992.

Gerrish, Howard H., and William E. Dugger. *Electricity and Electronics.* The Goodheart-Wilcox Company, Inc., South Holland, Illinois. 1989.

Golob, Richard, and Eric Brus (eds.). *The Almanac of Science and Technology.* Harcourt Brace Jovanovich, Boston, New York, San Diego. 1990.

Grout, Donald Jay, and Claude V. Palisca. *A History of Western Music.* W. W. Norton and Company, Inc., New York. Fifth Edition, 1996.

Hacking, Ian. *Trial By Number.* In: Science 84, Volume 5, Number 9, pages 69–70. The American Association for the Advancement of Science, Washington, D.C. 1984.

Hart, Michael H. *The 100: A Ranking of the Most Influential Persons in History.* Citadel Press (Trademark of Carol Communications, Inc.), New York, Toronto, Secaucus, New Jersey. 1992.

Hazen, Robert M., and James Trefil. *Science Matters.* Bantam Doubleday Dell Publishing Group, Inc., New York. 1991.

Heiser, Charles B. Jr. *Seed to Civilization: The Story of Food.* W.H. Freeman and Company, San Francisco. 1981.

Hellemans, Alexander, and Bryan Bunch. *The Timetables of Science.* Simon and Shuster, Inc., New York, London, Toronto, Sydney, Tokyo, Singapore. 1988.

Hellemans, Alexander, and Bryan Bunch. *The Timetables of Technology.* Simon and Shuster, Inc., New York, London, Toronto, Sydney, Tokyo, Singapore. 1988.

Hickok, Robert. *Exploring Music.* Brown and Benchmark, Madison, Dubuque, Indianapolis, Melbourne, and Oxford. Fifth Edition, 1993.

Hindley, Geoffrey (ed.). *The Larousse Encyclopedia of Music.* Barnes and Noble, New York. 1994.

Hitler, Adolf. *Mein Kampf.* Houghton Mifflin, Boston. 1971. Translated by Ralph Manheim.

Bibliography

Hughes, Thomas P. *The Inventive Continuum*. In: Science 84, Volume 5, Number 9, pages 83–86. The American Association for the Advancement of Science, Washington, D.C. 1984.

Ingpen, Robert, and Philip Wilkinson. *Encyclopedia of Events that Changed the World*. Viking Penguin, a division of Penguin Books, New York, London, Toronto, Auckland, Janson, H.W. Middlesex, Ringwood, Australia. 1991.

Ingpen, Robert, and Philip Wilkinson. *Encyclopedia of Ideas that Changed the World*. Viking Penguin, a division of Penguin Books, New York, London, Toronto, Auckland, Middlesex, Ringwood, Australia. 1991.

Jakab, Peter L. *Visions of a Flying Machine: The Wright Brothers and the Process of Invention*. Smithsonian Institution Press, Washington and London. 1990.

Jean, Georges. *Writing: The Story of Alphabets and Scripts*. Gallimard. 1987. (English translation by Jenny Oates and published by Thames and Hudson, Ltd. 1992.)

Johanson, Donald, and Lenora Johanson (with Blake Edgar). *Ancestors*. Villard books, New York. 1994.

Jones, Roger S. *Physics For the Rest of Us*. Contemporary Books, Chicago. 1992.

Kardinal, Carl G. *Cancer Chemotherapy: Historical Aspects and Future Considerations*. In: Postgraduate Medicine, Volume 77, Number 6, Pages 165–174. McGraw Hill Health Care Publications Group, Minneapolis. 1985.

Kardinal, Carl G., and John W. Yarbro. *A Conceptual History of Cancer*. In: Seminars in Oncology, Volume 6, Number 4, pages 396–408. W. B. Saunders Co., Philadelphia. 1979.

Laidler, Keith J. *To Light Such a Candle*. Oxford University Press, Oxford and New York. 1998.

Leicester, Henry M. *The Historical Background of Chemistry*. John Wiley and Sons, Inc. New York. 1956.

Lemonick, Michael D. *The Light at the Edge of the Universe*. Princeton University Press, Princeton, New Jersey. 1993.

Lightman, Alan P. *To Cleave an Atom*. In: Science 84, Volume 5, Number 9, pages 103–108. The American Association for the Advancement of Science, Washington, D.C. 1984.

Lyons, Albert S., and R. Joseph Petrucelli II. *Medicine: An Illustrated History*. Harry N. Abrams, Inc., New York. 1978.

Magoun, F. Alexander, and Eric Hodgins. *A History of Aircraft*. Whittlesey House, a division of McGraw Hill Book Company, Inc. 1931, reprinted 1972.

Marshack, Alexander. *The Roots of Civilization*. Moyer Bell Ltd., Mount Kisco, New York. Second Edition, 1991.

McCorduck, Pamela. *The Conquering Machine*. In: Science 84, Volume 5, Number 9, pages 131–138. The American Association for the Advancement of Science, Washington, D.C. 1984.

McLeish, John. *The Story of Numbers*. Fawcett Columbine, New York. 1991.

Meadows, Jack. *The Great Scientists*. Oxford University Press, Oxford and New York. 1992.

Miller, Hugh, Paul Taylor, and Edgar Williams. *Introduction to Music*. HarperCollins, New York. Third Edition, 1991.

Moores, Eldridge. *The Story of earth*. In: earth, Volume 5, Number 6 (December, 1996), pages 30–33. Kalmbach Publishing Co., Waukesha, Wisconsin. 1996.

Neal, Valerie, Cathleen S. Lewis, and Frank Winter. *Spaceflight*. Ligature, Inc., Boston and MacMillan, New York. 1995.

Oates, Stephen B. *Let the Trumpet Sound: The Life of Martin Luther King, Jr.* Harper and Row, New York. 1982.

Ogburn, Charlton. *The Mysterious William Shakespeare*. EPM Publications, Inc., McLean, Virginia. Second Edition, 1990.

Penrose, Roger. *The Emperor's New Mind*. Penguin Books, New York, London, Toronto, Auckland, Middlesex, Ringwood, Australia. 1989.

Perry, Marvin, Myrna Chase, James Jacob, Margaret Jacob, and Theodore Von Laue. *Western Civilization: Ideas, Politics, and Society*. Houghton Mifflin, Boston and Toronto. 1996.

Reade, Julian. *Mesopotamia*. British Museum Press, London. 1991.

Bibliography

Reich, Leonard. *From Edison's Wastebasket*. In: Science 84, Volume 5, Number 9, pages 73–75. The American Association for the Advancement of Science, Washington, D.C. 1984.

Ries, Julien. *The Origins of Religion*. Editoriale Jaca Book spa, Milan, 1993. Translated by Kate Singleton and published in English by William B. Eerdmans Publishing Company, Grand Rapids, Michigan in 1994.

Roberts, J.M. *A Concise History of the World*. Oxford University Press, New York. 1995.

Robinson, Andrew. *The Story of Writing: Alphabets, Hieroglyphs, and Pictograms*. Thames and Hudson, London and New York. 1995.

Rogers, Pat (ed.). *The Oxford Illustrated History of English Literature*. Oxford University Press, Oxford and New York. 1987.

Saggs, H.W.F. *Civilization Before Greece and Rome*. Yale University Press, New Haven and London. 1989.

Sandage, Allan. *Inventing the Beginning*. In: Science 84, Volume 5, Number 9, pages 111–113. The American Association for the Advancement of Science, Washington, D.C. 1984.

Sanders, Andrew. *The Short Oxford History of English Literature*. Clarendon Press, Oxford. 1994.

Schwartz, George, and Philip W. Bishop (eds.). *Moments of Discovery: The Origins of Science*. Basic Books, New York. 1958.

Schick, Kathy D., and Nicholas Toth. *Making Silent Stones Speak*. Simon and Shuster, New York, London, Toronto, Sydney, Tokyo, Singapore. 1993.

Senner, Wayne M. (ed.). *The Origins of Writing*. The University of Nebraska Press, Lincoln and London. 1989.

Shirer, William L. *The Rise and Fall of the Third Reich*. Fawcett Crest, New York. 1960.

Silberman, Neil Asher. *Searching for Jesus: The Politics of First Century Judea*. In: Archaeology Magazine, Volume 47, Number 6, pages 30–40. Archaeological Institute of America, New York. 1994.

Singer, Charles. *A History of Scientific Ideas*. Oxford University Press and Dorset Press, New York. 1959.

Smith, Bruce D. *The Emergence of Agriculture*. Scientific American Library, New York. 1995.

Smith, Huston. *The World's Religions*. HarperCollins, New York. Second Edition, 1991.

Smoot, George, and Keay Davidson. *Wrinkles in Time*. Avon Books, New York. 1993.

Snyder, Solomon H. *Medicated Minds*. In: Science 84, Volume 5, Number 9, pages 141–142. The American Association for the Advancement of Science, Washington, D.C. 1984.

Story, Alfred T. *The Story of Photography*. George Newnes, Limited. London. 1898.

Starr, Chester G. *A History of the Ancient World*. Oxford University Press. Fourth Edition, 1991.

Szarkowski, John. *Photography Until Now*. The Museum of Modern Art, New York. 1989.

Tarnas, Richard. *The Passion of the Western Mind*. Ballantine Books, New York. 1991.

Taylor, John W. R., and Kenneth Munson. *History of Aviation*. New English Library, London. 1972.

Taylor, F. Sherwood. *A Short History of Science and Scientific Thought*. W.W. Norton and Company, New York and London. 1949.

Thomas, Lewis. *Medicine's Second Revolution*. In: Science 84, Volume 5, Number 9, pages 93–95. The American Association for the Advancement of Science, Washington, D.C. 1984.

Thuan, Trinh Xuan. *The Secret Melody*. Oxford University Press, Oxford and New York. 1995. Translated by Storm Dunlop.

Tobias, Phillip V. *The Child From Taung*. In: Science 84, Volume 5, Number 9, pages 99–100. The American Association for the Advancement of Science, Washington, D.C. 1984.

Townes, Charles H. *Harnessing Light*. In: Science 84, Volume 5, Number 9, pages 153–155. The American Association for the Advancement of Science, Washington, D.C. 1984.

Bibliography

Trefil, James. *From Atoms to Quarks*. Bantam Doubleday Dell Publishing Group, Inc., New York. Second Edition, 1994.

Van Doren, Charles. *A History of Knowledge*. Ballantine, Books, New York. 1991.

Wernick, Robert. *A Woman Writ Large In Our History and Hearts*. In: Smithsonian Magazine, Volume 27, Number 9 (December, 1996), pages 122–136. Washington, D.C. 1996.

Williams, Trevor I. *Science: A History of Discovery in the Twentieth Century*. Oxford University Press, Oxford and New York. 1990.

Wills, Camfield, and Deirdre Wills. *History of Photography*. Hamlyn Publishing Group Limited, London, New York, Sydney, Toronto. 1980.

Wold, Milo, and Edmund Cykler. *An Introduction to Music and Art in the Western World*. William C. Brown Company, Dubuque, Iowa. 1967.

Wood, Michael. *Legacy: A Search for the Origins of Civilization*. Network Books (Division of BBC Enterprises). 1992.

Woodwell, George M. *Broken Eggshells*. In: Science 84, Volume 5, Number 9, pages 115–117. The American Association for the Advancement of Science, Washington, D.C. 1984.

Notes

1. There are other distinguishing characteristics as well. A sophisticated vocal ability is characteristic of humans, but it is unclear how much of this is a result of anatomic changes in the vocal apparatus and how much is secondary to the evolution of the brain. A prehensile thumb and stereoscopic vision have been important to humans, but are also found in other primates. The ability to use tools is almost (but not completely) unique to humans, but appears to follow in large part from increased brain size and a prehensile thumb. A longer life span than other primates appears to be genetically possible, but was not consistently achieved by people until relatively modern times, and was not a factor in our development until quite recently.

Comparisons of humans and other primates have been rewarding. Indeed, Jane Goodall (1934–) has shown that chimpanzees live in groups characterized by considerable organization, communication, and the capacity for violence. Her observations of chimpanzees have provided insight on how we may have come to use tools, and suggest that much of who we are was established even before we evolved as a species.

2. The Babylonians, for example, grasped some, but not all of the features of a zero. As another example, the Chinese, early in their history, left an empty space to hold place, which is different from an explicit symbol because the latter allows zero to be a true number and to be included in all arithmetic operations. Zero, as we now understand it, has the following characteristics:
   1) There is an explicit symbol for it.
   2) It is a number like any other, and can therefore participate in the full range of operations.
   3) It is a complete place-value holder, such that its presence anywhere in the number, even at the end, always has significance.

The first Old World number system known to have incorporated a zero as we now understand it occurred in India or Indo-China in the ninth century C.E., but the Indians may have had full knowledge of zero much before this time. It appears that the Maya probably had a full understanding of zero before any Old World civilization.

Notes

3. The Julian calendar overestimated the actual year by eleven minutes and fourteen seconds, so that by the year 1582, the accumulated error amounted to ten days. This discrepancy meant that religious days could not be properly observed. Therefore, Pope Gregory XIII, in that year, dropped ten days from the calendar. To prevent the problem from recurring, the leap year was removed from years that were not divisible by 400 (for example, the year 2000 will be a normal leap year, but the year 2100, although divisible by four, will not be a leap year). This is the Gregorian Calendar still used.

4. Today, we know that plant cells are surrounded by a thick wall, giving them the appearance that Hooke observed. Inside the wall is a thinner cell membrane. Animal cells have only the cell membrane. If Hooke had examined animal cells instead of plant cells, he would not have been as impressed with their resemblance to architectural cells, and we might be using a different term for the basic unit of life.

5. For mathematically inclined readers, Napier constructed his logarithm table by realizing that if the logarithms of two numbers are known, the square root of the product of the two numbers has a logarithm that is given by the arithmetic mean of the known logarithms. As an example, consider that $10^1=10$ and $10^2=100$. The square root of 10 x 100 is the square root of 1000, which is 31.62. The arithmetic mean of the logarithms (1 and 2) is 1.5. Therefore, the logarithm to the base 10 of 31.62 is 1.5, which is to say that $10^{1.5} = 31.62$. A tedious chore was then made much easier by realizing that once a logarithm for a number had been calculated, adding one to this logarithm gave the logarithm for ten times this number, adding two gave the logarithm for one hundred times the number, etc. In the above example, the logarithm for 316.2 is 2.5 and the logarithm for 3162 is 3.5.

6. In this technique, a person's DNA is cleaved by restriction enzymes and the resulting fragments are placed on a gelatinous medium (called a gel) and subjected to an electric current. Because the fragments of DNA are charged, they will migrate in the gel when exposed to this current. Fragments of different sizes and properties settle in different places in the gel. Because the base pairs of each person's DNA are unique, the restriction enzyme generates a unique set of fragments for each person, and therefore, each person's fragments form a unique migration pattern in the gel, very much as the pattern of bands in a supermarket UPC uniquely identifies a product. The problem then becomes one of detecting the location of these fragments in the gel. To do this, small pieces of DNA—which are not from the patient, and which will seek out and bind to certain common sequences of DNA found in all people—are then applied to the gel (these small pieces are called probes). These probes have been attached to a radioactive substance, and after they bind to their target fragments, wherever in the gel they may be, the gel is exposed to a photographic emulsion. The subatomic particles emitted by the radioactive atoms in the probe expose the emulsion, allowing the

presence and position of the fragments of the DNA to be determined. It is the position of DNA fragments in the gel, as determined by the binding of the radioactive probe, that makes a particular person's pattern unique.

7. As in the traditional approach, Kohler and Milstein began by inoculating an animal with the substance of interest. Then, instead of isolating antibodies, they withdrew and isolated lymphocytes. Then there is a series of steps to isolate and immortalize the particular lymphocytes that make the relevant antibodies. The process of monoclonal antibody production begins by modifying malignant, transformed lymphocytes so that they no longer possess the capacity to grow forever in culture unless their DNA is fused with that from nonmalignant lymphocytes obtained from the inoculated animal. Now the only lymphocytes that can grow indefinitely in culture will be a genetic combination of the malignant and nonmalignant cells. These hybrid cells live indefinitely in culture, and produce large numbers of antibodies, but each cell produces a different antibody (the antibody made by a particular combination of malignant and nonmalignant lymphocytes is the antibody that was made by the nonmalignant cell prior to its fusion with the malignant lymphocyte). Only one or a small number of these hybrid cells make an antibody of interest, and this cell or cells must be isolated, after which they serve as a permanent factory of the pertinent antibody.

8. It may be that one reason why HIV mutates so rapidly is that it is passed quickly from one host to another. Each host is a new environment, and new environments facilitate changes in nucleic acid because whenever the environment changes, some organisms with a slightly different nucleic acid composition are at a relative reproductive advantage. Changing environments do not cause changes in nucleic acid, but they reward and perpetuate some of those changes. This follows from Darwinian evolution and is true of all life forms.

It may be that HIV arose as a threat because the rapid sexual transmission that has recently taken place in Africa—where it is thought to have originated—made it virulent, and it is possible that rapid spread from one person to another is the principal cause of HIV's continuing rapid mutation rate.

INDEX

Index

Index

Index

Index